FOURTH EDITION

PLAYS
FOR THE
THEATRE

AN
ANTHOLOGY
OF WORLD DRAMA

Edited by

Oscar G. Brockett

Plays for the Theatre

An Anthology
of World Drama

Plays for the Theatre
An Anthology of World Drama

Fourth Edition

Edited by **Oscar G. Brockett**
(earlier editions co-edited by Lenyth Brockett)

Holt, Rinehart and Winston
New York   Chicago   San Francisco   Philadelphia
Montreal   Toronto   London   Sydney
Tokyo   Mexico City   Rio de Janeiro   Madrid

The editors of *Plays for the Theatre* are grateful to the following publishers, playwrights, and translators for permission to reprint the plays in this volume:

The Oedipus Rex of Sophocles, translated by Dudley Fitts and Robert Fitzgerald, copyright 1949 by Harcourt Brace Jovanovich, Inc., and reprinted with their permission. CAUTION: All rights, including professional, amateur, motion picture, recitation, lecturing, public reading, radio broadcasting, and television are strictly reserved. Inquiries on all rights should be addressed to Harcourt Brace Jovanovich, Inc., 757 Third Avenue, New York, New York 10017.

The Menaechmi by Plautus, reprinted by permission of the publishers from *The Menaechmi of Plautus,* translated into English prose and verse by Richard W. Hyde and Edward C. Weist, Cambridge, Mass.: Harvard University Press, copyright © 1930 by the President and Fellows of Harvard College; © 1958 by Richard W. Hyde and Edward C. Weist.

The Second Shepherds' Play, reprinted from *An Anthology of English Drama Before Shakespeare* by permission of the editor, Robert B. Heilman.

Tartuffe by Molière, from *The Misanthrope and Other Plays,* translated by John Wood (Penguin Classics, 1959). Copyright © 1959 by John Wood. Reprinted by permission of Penguin Books Ltd.

The Wild Duck by Henrik Ibsen, reprinted with minor adaptations with the permission of Charles Scribner's Sons from Volume VIII, *The Collected Works of Henrik Ibsen,* translated by William Archer. Copyright 1907 by Charles Scribner's Sons; copyright renewed 1935 by Frank Archer.

"The Hairy Ape" by Eugene O'Neill, from *The Plays of Eugene O'Neill,* Vol. I. Copyright © 1922 and renewed 1950 by Eugene O'Neill. Reprinted by permission of Random House, Inc.

Mother Courage and Her Children by Bertolt Brecht, from *Collected Plays,* Vol. 5. Translated by Ralph Manheim. Copyright 1940 by Arvid Englind Teaterforlag, a.b., renewed June 1967 by Stefan S. Brecht. Copyright 1949 Suhrkamp Verlag, Frankfurt am Main. Reprinted by permission of Random House, Inc.

Death of a Salesman, by Arthur Miller. Copyright 1949, © renewed 1977 by Arthur Miller. Reprinted by permission of The Viking Press. This play in its printed form is designed for the reading public only. All dramatic rights in it are fully protected by copyright, and no public or private performance—professional or amateur—may be given without the written permission of the author and the payment of royalty. As the courts have also ruled that the public reading of a play constitutes a public performance, no such reading may be given except under the conditions stated above. Communication should be addressed to the author's representative, International Creative Management, Inc., 40 W. 57th St., New York, N.Y. 10019

Happy Days by Samuel Beckett. Reprinted by permission of Grove Press, Inc. Copyright 1961 by Grove Press, Inc.

(*continued on p. vi*)

Library of Congress Cataloging in Publication Data
Main entry under title:

Plays for the theatre.

1. Drama—Collections.   2. Brockett, Oscar Gross, 1923–
PN6112.P57   1984   808.82   93-18684
ISBN 0-03-063697-3

CBS COLLEGE PUBLISHING
Holt, Rinehart and Winston
The Dryden Press
Saunders College Publishing

**For
Francesca**

Contents

Introduction

Selecting the plays for an anthology of world drama is a task accompanied by both anguish and risk—anguish at the realization of how many excellent plays must be left out, and risk because it is always uncertain whether plays traditionally regarded as masterpieces will still speak to the contemporary reader. Any selection is arbitrary to a degree, but we have chosen plays that have stood the test of long performance in the theatre or, in the case of recent dramas, those that seem to have the likelihood of doing so. We have also selected plays that are representative of various periods, countries, and genres. Obviously, the impression of world drama gained by knowing only some of its masterpieces is incomplete. Nevertheless, a useful if limited view of past drama can be obtained by reading some outstanding examples, much as one might get acquainted with a new terrain by noting its highest mountain peaks. This collection, then, offers a rough map of Western drama as revealed by significant plays ranging from the classic to the contemporary.

Oedipus Rex [c. 430 B.C.]   The world's oldest surviving dramas are the tragedies that were presented during the fifth century B.C. at the religious and civic festivals held in Athens to honor the god Dionysus. *Oedipus Rex* is considered by many critics to be the greatest of these works, and in modern times it has been one of the most frequently produced Greek plays. Aristotle, in his celebrated discussion of tragedy (written in the fourth century B.C.) refers to it often as an ideal example of the tragic form.

The most striking feature of Greek tragedy is the alternation of dramatic episodes (or scenes) with choral passages. Little is known for certain about the Greek tragic chorus, but in Sophocles' day it probably included fifteen performers who sang (or recited) and danced the choral passages to flute accompaniment. The Chorus (in *Oedipus Rex* composed of Elders from the City of Thebes) acts as a group, gives advice to the leading characters, expresses the community's point of view (and sometimes the playwright's), and functions as an "ideal spectator." Other typical features of Greek tragedy are the small number of individualized characters, the restriction of the action to a single place, the tightly unified plot, the serious and philosophic tone, and the poetic language.

The action of *Oedipus Rex* is extremely concentrated, for a complete reversal of the hero's position takes place in a single day. The story follows Oedipus, King of Thebes, as he attempts to discover the murderer of Laius, the former king, after an oracle has declared that the plague now destroying the people will not be lifted until the guilty one is cast out. Oedipus' search gradually uncovers terrible truths about the past and his own origins. The initial suspicion that Oedipus himself may be the slayer of Laius is a moment of high dramatic tension; it is followed by other electrifying moments (such as Jocasta's recognition that she is both Oedipus' wife and his mother) and the ultimate outcome: blindness, exile, and anguish for the once mighty king.

Sophocles is particularly admired for his skillful management of extensive plot materials: he accomplishes the gradual unveiling of mystery after mystery and a steady increase in dramatic tension, with the utmost economy of means. Although, like many great plays, *Oedipus Rex* is open to many interpretations, most critics have agreed that its central concern is the uncertainty of fate and man's helplessness in the face of destiny.

The Menaechmi [c. 184 B.C.]   Of the few Roman plays that survive, the majority are comedies. Indeed, rollicking farces (exemplified by Plautus' *The Menaechmi*) designed solely for entertainment are a peculiarly Roman contribution to the development of drama. The subject matter of surviving Roman comedies is drawn from everyday domestic life and features intrigues that turn on mistaken identity, misunderstood motives, and deliberate deception. The characters are familiar, if sometimes exaggerated types: the old man obsessed with his money or children, the young man who rebels against parental authority, the clever slave, the parasite who lives by flattery and trickery, the courtesan or mistress, the shrewish wife, the unscrupulous slave dealer, and the cowardly soldier. Latin comedy has no chorus, but the action is sometimes interrupted by songs. Thus, it often resembles modern musical comedy.

Plautus opens *The Manaechmi* with a prologue designed to put the audience at ease and to set forth humorously all the information needed to understand what is to come. The opening scenes introduce the characters and situation, the comical possibilities of which are then fully exploited as the twins are in turn mistaken for each other. Plautus' inventiveness is everywhere evident, but especially in the reunion, for its potential sentimentality is subverted by good-natured cynicism when Menaechmus I offers all his property for sale—including his wife.

Although wholly different in tone, Latin comedy shares with Greek tragedy many structural conventions: a story is taken up near the climactic moment; action and time are restricted in scope; and there is no intermingling of serious and comic elements. In the Renaissance, when dramatists turned to antiquity for guidance, it was the Latin writers, above all, from whom they learned. Thus Roman comedy is important not only in its own right but also for its influence on later practices.

The Second Shepherds' Play [1425–1450 A.D.]   After Rome was overrun by invaders in the sixth century A.D., public performances financed by the state ceased, and thereafter for approximately four hundred years theatrical activity in Western Europe was at best sporadic. Then drama was revived by the Catholic Church, although in a form radically different from that seen in Greece or Rome. Beginning in the tenth century, short playlets dramatizing Biblical events were performed in Latin in connection with church services. Around 1200, plays began to be presented out of doors, and eventually they were elaborated into lengthy series, or cycles, of plays dramatizing events ranging from the Creation to the Last Judgment. Productions of cycles were usually financed by trade guilds or religious societies; written in the vernacular language, they often required several days to perform in their entirety. *The Second Shepherds' Play* is the thirteenth segment (out of a total of thirty-two) from the cycle performed at Wakefield, England. Thus it is only one part of a much larger whole.

The major portion of *The Second Shepherds' Play* is an elaboration of a single sentence in the New Testament (Luke 2:8): "And there were in the same country shepherds abiding in the field, keeping watch over their flock by night." This hint has been transformed into a short play rich in contemporary medieval detail and farcical humor. The anonymous author opens his story with a scene in which each of three shepherds complains of his hardships; thus, characters and situation are introduced in a leisurely fashion. Forward movement of the action does not begin until Mak appears, but thereafter it progresses swiftly as Mak steals a sheep, takes it home, and attempts to pass it off as a newborn baby when the suspicious shepherds arrive looking for the missing animal; the ruse is discovered and Mak is punished. Then, in a manner not unusual in medieval literature, the tone of the play alters suddenly, an angel appears to announce the birth of Christ, and the shepherds go to Bethlehem to worship him. The Biblical text thus is the basis for a short, entertaining farce that has been linked to a wholly serious and devotional playlet celebrating the birth of Christ. The mingling of such diverse elements and the rapid shift in tone and locale, typical of medieval practice, clearly distinguishes the drama of this age from that of the classical era.

Hamlet [c. 1600]   For many reasons, but primarily because of religious controversies, the production of medieval cycles was forbidden or abandoned in the sixteenth century. This separation of drama from the church stimulated the development of a wholly secular theatre. The first country to produce a drama of lasting excellence was England during the years between 1580 and 1640. Indeed, the plays of William Shakespeare, which date from this period, often are said to be the finest every written.

The plays of the English Renaissance were still sufficiently close to their medieval predecessors to retain many practices from the earlier era: a sprawling, often episodic plot; scenes set in many times and places; and intermingled comic and serious elements. Before the end of the sixteenth century, however, renewed interest in classical drama had modified and refined medieval practices considerably to create more complex conceptions of dramatic form and characterization. A synthesis of medieval and classical inheritances can be noted in Shakespeare's works, which are both numerous and varied in dramatic type. Shakespeare's genius is probably seen at its best, however, in the tragedies, of which *Hamlet* is an outstanding example.

Like *Oedipus Rex*, *Hamlet* has as its protagonist a man who is charged with punishing the murderer of a king. But Shakespeare uses a much broader canvas than Sophocles does and includes within his drama more facets of his story, more characters, and a wider sweep of time and place. *Hamlet* is rich in implications, of which the most important is the pervasiveness of betrayal—brother of brother, wife of husband, parent of child, friend of friend—which almost overpowers Hamlet as he learns that his father has been murdered by his uncle, that his mother has been unfaithful to his father, that his mother has accepted his uncle's usurpation of the throne that is rightfully his, and that his supposed friends have become his uncle's spies. A second set of implications is related to the opposing demands made on Hamlet—that he right the injustices occasioned by his father's death (seemingly requiring him to murder his uncle) and that he adhere to Christian teachings (under which that murder would be a deadly sin). Another group of implications concerns the nature of kingship and the need to rule oneself before attempting to rule others. This motif is seen especially in the conduct of Claudius and is suggested through the contrast between Claudius and his dead brother and with Hamlet and Fortinbras (who is left to return order to the state). Shakespeare's dramatic poetry is generally conceded to be the finest in the English language. The basic medium is blank verse, which allows the flexibility of ordinary speech while elevating it through imagery and rhythm.

Because of its compelling story, powerful characters, and great poetry, *Hamlet* is one of the world's finest achievements in drama. Although it embodies many ideas typical of its time, it transcends the limitations of a particular era. It continues to move spectators in the theatre as it has since its first presentation around 1600.

Tartuffe [1669] While English drama retained many medieval traditions, continental dramatists were more inclined to follow Greek and Roman practices. This conscious imitation of the classics led to a set of literary standards summed up in the term *neoclassicism*; these included the unities of time, place, and action; strict distinction between tragedy and comedy, with no intermingling of serious and comic elements; the use of universalized character types; and the demand that drama teach moral lessons. Most of the plays written in compliance with these rules now seem lifeless, but the tragedies of Racine and the comedies of Molière, written in France during the seventeenth century, reached a peak of artistry in the neoclassical mode. Molière is one of the most skillful and inventive comic dramatists of all times, and *Tartuffe* is one of his best plays. Here, within the restricted frame of one room, one day, and one main story, using a limited number of characters and little physical action, Molière has created an excellent comedy of character in the neoclassic style.

The plot of *Tartuffe* can be divided into five stages: the demonstration of Tartuffe's complete hold over Orgon, the unmasking of Tartuffe, Tartuffe's attempted revenge, the foiling of Tartuffe's plan, and the happy resolution. Each scene of the play, with the possible exception of the young lovers' quarrel, contributes to the main action and hence to the play's unity. The scene in which Orgon hides under the table while Tartuffe attempts to seduce Elmire, Orgon's wife, is one of the most amusing in all comic drama. Molière has been criticized for delaying Tartuffe's appearance until the third act, but he makes skillful use of this delay by having other characters discuss Tartuffe at length, thereby establishing clearly his hypocrisy and Orgon's gullibility in trusting him. The final resolution, in which Tartuffe is suddenly discovered to be a notorious criminal, has also been criticized as overly contrived, but it is emotionally satisfying since it punishes Tartuffe and reestablishes the norm. *Tartuffe* was first presented in its five-act form in 1669 and has since remained in the repertory almost continuously. It is still performed more often than any other play by Molière.

The School for Scandal [1777] In England the neoclassic rules (which dominated the French drama until the early nineteenth century) were recognized but not followed slavishly. In Richard Brinsley Sheridan's *The School for Scandal* the unity of time prescribed by neoclassic theory is retained, but unity of place is broadly interpreted to include four different though neighboring houses, and the single plot is replaced by several related intrigues. Thus the play may be called an English response to continental critical precepts. It is also related to other important developments, particularly the comedies of manners written by English dramatists of the late seventeenth century. Like these earlier playwrights, Sheridan satirizes upper-class social foibles with wit and urbanity.

The main action is set against the background of a "school for scandal" in which a circle of malicious men and women, over their teacups, destroy reputations. Attending this circle, the impressionable young Lady Teazle tries to ape their sophisticated manners. The shallowness of this group allows hypocrites to flourish, since the group cannot distinguish between fashionable behavior and true character. Sheridan places much of the blame for this state of affairs on the then-current vogue for sentimentalism, epitomized by the comic villain, Joseph Surface, who is admired because he sprinkles his conversation with moral maxims. On the other hand, Charles, his brother, is widely condemned merely because his speech and behavior are natural for a young man of his age and situation. Sheridan is thus concerned with the distinction between true virtue and pious words, but he treats this contrast comically. But if Sheridan satirizes sentimentality, he has not succeeded in freeing his own play from it. His admirable characters are themselves inclined to moralize or fall into "sentiments," and the play as a whole illustrates the lesson typical of sentimental comedy; true virtue will be rewarded—and with a sizable fortune. Sheridan is free of the worst excesses of sentimentality, however, and his moralizing is lightened by amusing dialogue and an air of high spirits.

Sheridan's skill in play construction is especially evident in the way he integrates the subplot and the main plot. At the beginning of the play, the Sir Peter-Lady Teazle story has little connection with the Joseph-Maria-Charles story. As the play progresses, however, the two stories move closer and closer together, and in the "screen scene" (one of the most skillfully contrived in the history of drama) the revelation of Joseph's relationship to Lady Teazle leads to the resolution of both the subplot and the main plot.

The School for Scandal has been called the greatest comedy of manners written in the English language. Its story, its urbane and polished dialogue, and its comic inventiveness have made it popular with each succeeding generation.

The Wild Duck [1884] During the nineteenth century a revolt against the ideals of Romanticism and sentimentality gave rise to a new literary mode, Realism. Many influences contributed to the realistic outlook, among them deepening interest in the emerging sciences of sociology and psychology and emphasis on environment as a determinant of human behavior. The result was a drama based on contemporary events closely observed and carefully rendered through lifelike dialogue and detailed settings. Henrik Ibsen's plays epitomize the new trend so well that he is often called the founder of modern Realism. *The Wild Duck* illustrates many of the techniques Ibsen used; it reproduces the speech and actions of ordinary people of the middle and lower classes in a fully detailed environment that plays an essential part in the story. In his dialogue Ibsen abandoned the older devices of the aside and soliloquy; instead, his characters reveal themselves as they would in real life, through indirection rather than explicit statement.

In *The Wild Duck*, the idealistic Gregers Werle returns home after an absence of fifteen years, decides that the lives of all his acquaintances are based on lies, and determines to make them face the truth. His efforts lead to catastrophe: in forcing some unwelcome truths on his former schoolmate, Hjalmar Ekdal, he sets in train a series of events that end with a child's suicide. Opposed to Gregers in this tug of war between truth and illusion is Dr. Relling, who believes that people need a "saving lie" in order to endure life. Hjalmar illustrates this principle, for he enjoys a lazy, happy and self-centered life under the illusion that he will someday discover a great invention. Because of Ibsen's ironic treatment of Hjalmar, the play has many passages of genuine humor that relieve the generally somber tone.

Ibsen's themes are related to the central motif of the wild duck, which seems to symbolize various stages in human experience: the unfettered freedom of youth, the wounds of experiences, the effort to escape, and the necessity of going on living, though wounded and in an environment of illusions (symbolized by the Ekdals' attic). An engrossing play because of its tightly woven story, believable characters, and skillful balance of the serious and the satiric, *The Wild Duck* is significant from a historical viewpoint both as one of the works that helped to establish a new realistic drama and as a forerunner of Symbolist drama which was to become important in the next decade.

"The Hairy Ape" [1921]   Of the several revolts against Realism in the late nineteenth and early twentieth centuries, the earliest was Symbolism. Rejecting the Realists' belief that truth is discovered by close observation of the environment, the Symbolists held that external appearances were merely the mask of inner spiritual realities that could only be communicated through the use of symbols. Although the appeal of this drama was limited, it foreshadowed other antirealistic movements, including Expressionism, which emerged in Germany around 1912 and which spread to other countries after 1918. The Expressionists proclaimed the supreme importance of the human spirit, which they believed was being crushed or distorted by materialism and industrialization; like the Symbolists, they regarded appearance as the mask of significant inner truths. Therefore, to comprehend Expressionist drama the reader must be prepared to look behind its deliberate distortions for deeper significance.

"The Hairy Ape" shows the influence of Expressionism on American drama. The unity of the play derives from a central theme: man's frustrated search for identity in a hostile environment. In the first scene, Yank is confident that he and his fellow stokers are the only ones who "belong" because it is they who make the ship go (and, by extension, the factories and machines of modern, industrialized society). But when the shipowner's pampered, anemic daughter (who represents the power of money and influence) calls Yank a "filthy beast" (a "hairy ape"), his confidence is shattered. Seeking to reestablish his identity, he first visits Fifth Avenue, the home territory of the rich and powerful, where he proclaims his superiority by physically attacking the men only to have his very existence go unacknowledged. Thrown into jail, he decides that the answer lies in destroying

the steel and machinery over which he originally thought he had power. In jail he learns that the IWW opposes the owners of factories and ships and, when he is released, he offers to blow up the IWW's enemies. Rejected there too, Yank decides that the answer may lie with the apes at the zoo. When he releases a gorilla, it crushes him, and he dies still without a sense of belonging.

Yank is symbolic of modern man in an industrialized society—cut off from a past when human beings had an integral relationship with the natural environment and now little better than cogs in the industrial machine—he feels alienated from his world and lacks all sense of belonging. As Yank says to the gorilla, "I ain't got no past to tink in, nor nothin' dat's comin', on'y what's now—and dat don't belong."

"The Hairy Ape" is representative of the outlook and techniques of Expressionism. The episodic structure and distorted visual elements are typical of the movement, as is the longing for fulfillment, which suggests a need to change society so that the individual can find a coherent, satisfying relationship between himself and his world.

Mother Courage and Her Children [1937]

The Expressionists' idealistic dream of transforming mankind foundered in disillusionment during the 1920s. Some writers came to believe that society could be improved only by adopting a program of concrete political action, and in the theatre they sought to focus attention on the great difference between human needs and existing conditions. Attempts to use the theatre as a weapon of social action took several forms, but the most significant and fruitful from an aesthetic viewpoint was Epic Theatre, exemplified in the plays of Bertolt Brecht. Brecht used many of the devices of Expressionist drama, such as episodic structure, unity derived from theme or thesis, and nonillusionistic visual elements. But Brecht, unlike the Expressionists, did not suggest that external appearance is untruthful or insignificant; rather, he wished to provoke audiences to reflect on the immediate world and its injustices, and he believed that he could do so most effectively if his audience remained fully conscious that it was in a theatre. Rejecting the theatre of illusion on the basis that it merely lulls the spectator's critical faculties, Brecht devised several techniques (such as inserted songs, projected captions, and presentational acting) to interrupt the empathetic response and intensify the spectator's awareness of social, economic, and political injustices. It was his hope that the spectator would become aware of the need to work for change outside the theatre.

Mother Courage and Her Children seeks to establish a causal relationship between war and capitalism—to suggest that war is merely an exaggeration of the business methods used in private enterprise. In the beginning, Mother Courage welcomes the war as an opportunity to better her lot. She loves her children and tries to protect them, but the war makes her stifle her human reactions for the sake of her business, and eventually all of the children are killed. As Brecht commented: "War, which is a continuation of business by other means, makes the human virtues fatal even to their possessors." Most audiences have seen in Mother Courage a woman of indomitable strength—a tragic survivor of the evils of war. But Brecht wanted them to see Mother Courage's "crimes, her participation, her desire to share in the profits of the war business," and to recognize that her tragedy results from her belief that she can reap the monetary benefits of war without paying the human consequences. About his ultimate goal, Brecht wrote that he wished to make the proletariat see that it "can do away with war by doing away with capitalism."

Mother Courage and Her Children alternates dialogue and song. The songs serve to break up and comment on the action and to forward Brecht's aim of making the audience reflect on what it has seen. Scenery plays only a small role. Time and place are established by lengthy captions projected onto a screen at the beginning of each scene.

Although the audience may reject Brecht's solution for ending war, it surely must acknowledge the play's power to make us see the price that human beings pay for war.

Death of a Salesman [1949]   Symbolism, Expressionism, Epic Theatre, and other antirealistic styles by no means replaced Realism in the modern theatre, but they unquestionably altered it. Realistic plays written since World War II are radically different in tone and technique from the works of Ibsen and earlier Realists. In general outlook, they differ from earlier drama principally by portraying human personality as more complex, and by being less optimistic about the likelihood of improving society. At the same time, dramatic techniques have been taken over from nonrealistic drama.

Many of these results are seen to good effect in Arthur Miller's *Death of a Salesman*. The play's structure, with its fluid handling of time and place to follow the shifting thoughts of the protagonist, is so unlike the drama of Ibsen that on first acquaintance it may seem an entirely different style. Yet, like Ibsen, Miller evokes a specific social milieu, carefully observed and rendered, and creates a highly individualized protagonist, the vivid and memorable Willy Loman.

Death of a Salesman develops a primary conflict in the American consciousness: its tendency to measure success in wholly material terms even though it upholds love and family cohesiveness as major values. As a result, the play suggests, Americans often unconsciously mingle these goals in such a way that love and approval are withheld from those who have not succeeded materially. Miller has embodied this conflict in Willy Loman's obsessive desire to succeed and his confusion of success with the right to be loved. Miller has used two characters to represent the poles between which Willy is pulled. Uncle Ben, Willy's brother, epitomizes material success, while Linda, Willy's wife, represents love given without question or conditions.

It is interesting to compare Miller's play with works from earlier periods. Both *Death of a Salesman* and *Oedipus Rex* involve a search into the past to find the roots of present evils. The scenes in *Oedipus Rex*, however, all take place in the present, and the past is revealed only through narration. *Death of a Salesman*, on the other hand, uses "flashbacks" to transport the audience backward in time to witness various scenes. The play shares with *Mother Courage and Her Children* a concern for the destructiveness of materialistic values.

In *Death of a Salesman* Miller has combined believable characters and a plausible environment with technical devices taken over from nonrealistic styles. When first produced, the play seemed startlingly novel because of this mixture of elements, but subsequent developments have served to define it more clearly as modified Realism. After more than a quarter century it is still one of the most effective and moving of all American plays.

Happy Days [1961]   In the 1950s a new style, now usually called Absurdism, emerged. *Absurdism* is a term coined by the critic Martin Esslin to describe the work of Samuel Beckett, Eugene Ionesco, and several other dramatists. Esslin concludes that Absurdism grew out of a "sense that the certitudes and unshakable basic assumptions of former ages have been swept away, that they have been . . . discredited as cheap and somewhat childish illusions." Or, as Ionesco put it, "cut off from his religious, metaphysical, and transcendental roots, man is lost; all his actions become senseless, absurd and useless." Most Absurdist plays, rather than telling a story, explore this condition, in which the characters are depicted as seeking to insulate themselves against the void with meaningless activities or abortive attempts at communication.

Happy Days embodies most of the tenets of Absurdism. It has virtually abandoned action. The first act shows a middle-aged woman trapped up to her waist in a mound of earth. She does not struggle against her physical entrapment but fills her days with a routine built around objects which she keeps in a shopping bag; she speaks often to her husband, who for the most part remains unseen behind the mound and who responds only rarely. In the second act, she is buried up to her neck and can only move her eyes and mouth; at first she is not even sure that her husband is still alive, but eventually he crawls up the mound into her view. Despite her situation, the woman remains determinedly cheerful; she speaks often of her blessings and the small things that will make this "another happy day." She never questions why she is in this situation, nor does she wonder at her isolation. She apparently accepts her lot as something no more to be questioned than human existence itself.

As in others of his plays. in *Happy Days* Beckett uses visual imagery to sum up his vision of the human situation. Here, as in other plays, he shows human beings trapped in a symbolic wasteland, cut off from all but the most minimal contact, passing time as best they can while waiting doggedly or hoping desperately for something that will give meaning to the moment or to life itself. Occasionally they reveal flashes of anxiety, but they quickly divert themselves with games, memories, and speculations.

The form, structure, and mood of *Happy Days* cannot be separated from its meaning. Beckett has said that his plays formulate as clearly as he can what he is trying to convey. In them, there is little progression and there is no resolution in the usual sense. The plays end much as they started; they explore a state of being rather than show a developing action.

A Raisin in the Sun [1959]   A fruitful development of the late 1950s, and particularly of the 1960s, was the emergence of plays written by blacks and other minority playwrights. One of the best examples of this drama is *A Raisin in the Sun* by Lorraine Hansberry, the first play by a black woman to appear on Broadway and to be the winner of both the New York Drama Critics Circle and Best Play of the Year Awards.

In many respects it is a traditional play: it focuses on a family and its dreams, and in structure it is a play of impeccable craftsmanship. It concerns the Younger family: the tenacious Lena, or Mama; Beneatha, her daughter, who wants to become a doctor; Walter, Lena's son, a chauffeur; his wife Ruth, a cleaning woman; and Travis, the young son of Walter and Ruth. Poor but proud, they dream of bettering their position in a world where they have been held back because they are black. When they receive the insurance on Mama's recently deceased husband, their dreams seem within reach, but circumstances thwart them. Nevertheless, all come to a better understanding of themselves and, as the play ends, they courageously move into an all-white neighborhood, determined to continue their struggle.

Despite its traditional form, the play introduces almost every theme that has since been developed by black playwrights. The opposition of the white community to the intrusion of the Youngers explores the problem of integration. The contrast between the opportunistic Walter and the idealistic Beneatha dramatizes the difference between materialism and altruism. The issue of the blacks' loss of their heritage is developed through one of Beneatha's suitors, a Nigerian student who arouses the girl's interest in her African "roots." The theme of growth and maturity is touchingly shown by Mama's nurturing of a spindly plant in a tenement window. The final moment, when she takes the plant with her to their new home, implies that the family will not "dry up like a raisin in the sun," but will survive and flourish. In a play of universal appeal, Hansberry makes clear the injustice American society has done to blacks.

Streamers [1976]   The 1960s was a time of near-frenetic experimentation with dramatic and theatrical techniques, but the 1970s saw a partial return to more realistic modes and a renewed interest in storytelling and complex characterization. *Streamers*, by David Rabe, is an outstanding example of this new drama. The third of Rabe's plays to use the Vietnam war as background, *Streamers* takes place just before the conflict escalated into a major war. It concerns an American myth: army life as the essence of masculinity. The effects of this myth are explored through a story that emphasizes two explosive and controversial elements, homosexuality and violence.

In Rabe's play, the myth is shown from several angles. Two young soldiers, Billy and Roger, seek to live up to it, while another, Richie, scorns it. But the myth is most completely embodied in two middle-aged sergeants who served as parachutists in World War II and Korea. The situation is relatively stable until the arrival of Carlyle, a recent black draftee, whose dislike of the army acts as a catalyst. The outsiders, Carlyle and Richie, are drawn together and propose a sexual liaison; Billy tries to interfere; and both he and one of the sergeants are killed by Carlyle.

The title of the play is taken from a song sung by the sergeants, a prayer for a parachute to open. It is sung twice, the first time as an indication of what it means to be "a real man," the second, following the deaths, as a lamentation for all wasted lives. *Streamers* is not a defense of homosexuality nor an anti-war play; rather, it is about the human need for love and understanding in conflict with a myth that makes violence the ultimate test of manhood. In the compassionate treatment of complex characters caught in a situation over which they lose control, Rabe has created a play with true tragic dimensions.

Detailed analyses of the plays in this volume, accompanied by descriptions of contemporary conditions and other pertinent historical information, may be found in Oscar G. Brockett's *The Essential Theatre*, 3d edition (Holt, Rinehart and Winston, 1984). In addition, a number of these plays are discussed in Oscar G. Brockett's *The Theatre: An Introduction*, 4th edition (Holt, Rinehart and Winston, 1979) and *Historical Edition: The Theatre* (1979).

Sophocles

Oedipus Rex

English Version by Dudley Fitts and Robert Fitzgerald

PERSONS REPRESENTED

OEDIPUS
A PRIEST
CREON
TEIRESIAS
IOCASTE [JOCASTA]
MESSENGER
SHEPHERD OF LAÏOS
SECOND MESSENGER
CHORUS OF THEBAN ELDERS

THE SCENE——*Before the palace of* OEDIPUS, *King of Thebes. A central door and two lateral doors open onto a platform which runs the length of the façade. On the platform, right and left, are altars; and three steps lead down into the "orchestra," or chorus-ground. At the beginning of the action these steps are crowded by suppliants who have brought branches and chaplets of olive leaves and who lie in various attitudes of despair.* OEDIPUS *enters.*

PROLOGUE

OEDIPUS: My children, generations of the living
In the line of Kadmos, nursed at his ancient hearth:
Why have you strewn yourselves before these altars
In supplication, with your boughs and garlands?
The breath of incense rises from the city
With a sound of prayer and lamentation.
                                    Children,
I would not have you speak through messengers,
And therefore I have come myself to hear you—
I, Oedipus, who bear the famous name.
        [*To a* PRIEST.]
You, there, since you are eldest in the company,
Speak for them all, tell me what preys upon you,

1

Whether you come in dread, or crave some blessing:
Tell me, and never doubt that I will help you
In every way I can; I should be heartless
Were I not moved to find you suppliant here.

PRIEST: Great Oedipus, O powerful King of Thebes!
You see how all the ages of our people
Cling to your altar steps: here are boys
Who can barely stand alone, and here are priests
By weight of age, as I am a priest of God,
And young men chosen from those yet unmarried;
As for the others, all that multitude,
They wait with olive chaplets in the squares,
At the two shrines of Pallas, and where Apollo
Speaks in the glowing embers.
                              Your own eyes
Must tell you: Thebes is tossed on a murdering sea
And can not lift her head from the death surge.
A rust consumes the buds and fruits of the earth;
The herds are sick; children die unborn,
And labor is vain. The god of plague and pyre
Raids like detestable lightning through the city,
And all the house of Kadmos is laid waste,
All emptied, and all darkened; Death alone
Battens upon the misery of Thebes.

You are not one of the immortal gods, we know;
Yet we have come to you to make our prayer
As to the man surest in mortal ways
And wisest in the ways of God. You saved us
From the Sphinx, that flinty singer, and the tribute
We paid to her so long; yet you were never
Better informed than we, nor could we teach you:
It was some god breathed in you to set us free.

Therefore, O mighty King, we turn to you:
Find us our safety, find us a remedy,
Whether by counsel of the gods or men.
A king of wisdom tested in the past
Can act in a time of troubles, and act well.
Noblest of men, restore
Life to your city! Think how all men call you
Liberator for your triumph long ago;
Ah, when your years of kingship are remembered,
Let them not say *We rose, but later fell*—
Keep the State from going down in the storm!
Once, years ago, with happy augury,

You brought us fortune; be the same again!
No man questions your power to rule the land:
But rule over men, not over a dead city!
Ships are only hulls, citadels are nothing,
When no life moves in the empty passageways.

OEDIPUS: Poor children! You may be sure I know
All that you longed for in your coming here.
I know that you are deathly sick; and yet,
Sick as you are, not one is as sick as I.
Each of you suffers in himself alone
His anguish, not another's; but my spirit
Groans for the city, for myself, for you.

I was not sleeping, you are not waking me.
No, I have been in tears for a long while
And in my restless thought walked many ways.
In all my search, I found one helpful course,
And that I have taken: I have sent Creon,
Son of Menoikeus, brother of the Queen,
To Delphi, Apollo's place of revelation,
To learn there, if he can,
What act or pledge of mine may save the city.
I have counted the days, and now, this very day,
I am troubled, for he has overstayed his time.
What is he doing? He has been gone too long.
Yet whenever he comes back, I should do ill
To scant whatever duty God reveals.

PRIEST: It is a timely promise. At this instant
They tell me Creon is here.

OEDIPUS: O Lord Apollo!
May his news be fair as his face is radiant!

PRIEST: It could not be otherwise: he is crowned with bay,
The chaplet is thick with berries.

OEDIPUS: We shall soon know;
He is near enough to hear us now.
    [*Enter* CREON.]
                  O Prince:
Brother: son of Menoikeus:
What answer do you bring us from the god?

CREON: A strong one. I can tell you, great afflictions
Will turn out well, if they are taken well.

OEDIPUS: What was the oracle? These vague words
Leave me still hanging between hope and fear.

CREON: Is it your pleasure to hear me with all these
Gathered around us? I am prepared to speak,
But should we not go in?

OEDIPUS: Let them all hear it.
   It is for them I suffer, more than for myself.
CREON: Then I will tell you what I heard at Delphi.

   In plain words
   The god commands us to expel from the land of Thebes
   An old defilement we are sheltering.
   It is a deathly thing, beyond cure;
   We must not let it feed upon us longer.
OEDIPUS: What defilement? How shall we rid ourselves of it?
CREON: By exile or death, blood for blood. It was
   Murder that brought the plague-wind on the city.
OEDIPUS: Murder of whom? Surely the god has named him?
CREON: My lord: long ago Laïos was our king,
   Before you came to govern us.
OEDIPUS: I know;
   I learned of him from others; I never saw him.
CREON: He was murdered; and Apollo commands us now
   To take revenge upon whoever killed him.
OEDIPUS: Upon whom? Where are they? Where shall we find a clue
   To solve that crime, after so many years?
CREON: Here in this land, he said.

                      If we make enquiry,
   We may touch things that otherwise escape us.
OEDIPUS: Tell me: Was Laïos murdered in his house,
   Or in the fields, or in some foreign country?
CREON: He said he planned to make a pilgrimage.
   He did not come home again.
OEDIPUS: And was there no one,
   No witness, no companion, to tell what happened?
CREON: They were all killed but one, and he got away
   So frightened that he could remember one thing only.
OEDIPUS: What was that one thing? One may be the key
   To everything, if we resolve to use it.
CREON: He said that a band of highwaymen attacked them,
   Outnumbered them, and overwhelmed the King.
OEDIPUS: Strange, that a highwayman should be so daring—
   Unless some faction here bribed him to do it.
CREON: We thought of that. But after Laïos' death
   New troubles arose and we had no avenger.
OEDIPUS: What troubles could prevent your hunting down the killers?
CREON: The riddling Sphinx's song
   Made us deaf to all mysteries but her own.
OEDIPUS: Then once more I must bring what is dark to light.
   It is most fitting that Apollo shows,
   As you do, this compunction for the dead.
   You shall see how I stand by you, as I should,

To avenge the city and the city's god,
And not as though it were for some distant friend,
But for my own sake, to be rid of evil.
Whoever killed King Laïos might—who knows?—
Decide at any moment to kill me as well.
By avenging the murdered king I protect myself.

Come, then, my children: leave the altar steps,
Lift up your olive boughs!
                                   One of you go
And summon the people of Kadmos to gather here.
I will do all that I can; you may tell them that.
        [*Exit a* PAGE.]
So, with the help of God,
We shall be saved—or else indeed we are lost.
PRIEST: Let us rise, children. It was for this we came,
        And now the King has promised it himself.
        Phoibos has sent us an oracle; may he descend
        Himself to save us and drive out the plague.
            [*Exeunt* OEDIPUS *and* CREON *into the palace by the central door. The*
            PRIEST *and the* SUPPLIANTS *disperse R and L. After a short pause the*
            CHORUS *enters the orchestra.*]

PARODOS

CHORUS: What is God singing in his profound   [STROPHE 1]
        Delphi of gold and shadow?
        What oracle for Thebes, the sunwhipped city?

        Fear unjoints me, the roots of my heart tremble.

        Now I remember, O Healer, your power, and wonder:
        Will you send doom like a sudden cloud. or weave it
        Like nightfall of the past?

        Speak, speak to us, issue of holy sound:
        Dearest to our expectancy: be tender!

        Let me pray to Athenê, the immortal daughter of Zeus,   [ANTISTROPHE 1]
        And to Artemis her sister
        Who keeps her famous throne in the market ring,
        And to Apollo, bowman at the far butts of heaven—

        O gods, descend! Like three streams leap against
        The fires of our grief, the fires of darkness;
        Be swift to bring us rest!

As in the old time from the brilliant house
Of air you stepped to save us, come again!

Now our afflictions have no end,   [STROPHE 2]
Now all our stricken host lies down
And no man fights off death with his mind;

The noble plowland bears no grain,
And groaning mothers can not bear—

See, how our lives like birds take wing,
Like sparks that fly when a fire soars,
To the shore of the god of evening.

The plague burns on, it is pitiless,   [ANTISTROPHE 2]
Though pallid children laden with death
Lie unwept in the stony ways,

And old gray women by every path
Flock to the strand about the altars

There to strike their breasts and cry
Worship of Phoibos in wailing prayers:
Be kind, God's golden child!

There are no swords in this attack by fire,   [STROPHE 3]
No shields, but we are ringed with cries.
Send the besieger plunging from our homes
Into the vast sea-room of the Atlantic
Or into the waves that foam eastward of Thrace—

For the day ravages what the night spares—

Destroy our enemy, lord of the thunder!
Let him be riven by lightning from heaven!

Phoibos Apollo, stretch the sun's bowstring,   [ANTISTROPHE 3]
That golden cord, until it sing for us,
Flashing arrows in heaven!
                              Artemis, Huntress,
Race with flaring lights upon our mountains!

O scarlet god, O golden-banded brow,
O Theban Bacchos in a storm of Maenads,
     [*Enter* OEDIPUS, C.]
Whirl upon Death, that all the Undying hate!
Come with blinding torches, come in joy!

SCENE I

OEDIPUS: Is this your prayer? It may be answered. Come,
　　Listen to me, act as the crisis demands,
　　And you shall have relief from all these evils.

　　Until now I was a stranger to this tale,
　　As I had been a stranger to the crime.
　　Could I track down the murderer without a clue?
　　But now, friends,
　　As one who became a citizen after the murder,
　　I make this proclamation to all Thebans:
　　If any man knows by whose hand Laïos, son of Labdakos,
　　Met his death, I direct that man to tell me everything,
　　No matter what he fears for having so long withheld it.
　　Let it stand as promised that no further trouble
　　Will come to him, but he may leave the land in safety.

　　Moreover: If anyone knows the murderer to be foreign,
　　Let him not keep silent: he shall have his reward from me.
　　However, if he does conceal it; if any man
　　Fearing for his friend or for himself disobeys this edict,
　　Hear what I propose to do:

　　I solemnly forbid the people of this country,
　　Where power and throne are mine, ever to receive that man
　　Or speak to him, no matter who he is, or let him
　　Join in sacrifice, lustration, or in prayer.
　　I decree that he be driven from every house,
　　Being, as he is, corruption itself to us: the Delphic
　　Voice of Zeus has pronounced this revelation.
　　Thus I associate myself with the oracle
　　And take the side of the murdered king.

　　As for the criminal, I pray to God—
　　Whether it be a lurking thief, or one of a number—
　　I pray that that man's life be consumed in evil and wretchedness.
　　And as for me, this curse applies no less
　　If it should turn out that the culprit is my guest here,
　　Sharing my hearth.
　　　　　　　　　　You have heard the penalty.
　　I lay it on you now to attend to this
　　For my sake, for Apollo's, for the sick
　　Sterile city that heaven has abandoned.
　　Suppose the oracle had given you no command:
　　Should this defilement go uncleansed for ever?

You should have found the murderer: your king,
A noble king, had been destroyed!
                                        Now I,
Having the power that he held before me,
Having his bed, begetting children there
Upon his wife, as he would have, had he lived—
Their son would have been my children's brother,
If Laïos had had luck in fatherhood!
(But surely ill luck rushed upon his reign)—
I say I take the son's part, just as though
I were his son, to press the fight for him
And see it won! I'll find the hand that brought
Death to Labdakos' and Polydoros' child,
Heir of Kadmos' and Agenor's line.
And as for those who fail me,
Many the gods deny them the fruit of the earth,
Fruit of the womb, and may they rot utterly!
Let them be wretched as we are wretched, and worse!

For you, for loyal Thebans, and for all
Who find my actions right, I pray the favor
Of justice, and of all the immortal gods.
CHORAGOS: Since I am under oath, my lord, I swear
    I did not do the murder, I can not name
    The murderer. Might not the oracle
    That has ordained the search tell where to find him?
OEDIPUS: An honest question. But no man in the world
    Can make the gods do more than the gods will.
CHORAGOS: There is one last expedient—
OEDIPUS: Tell me what it is.
    Though it seem slight, you must not hold it back.
CHORAGOS: A lord clairvoyant to the lord Apollo,
    As we all know, is the skilled Teiresias.
    One might learn much about this from him, Oedipus.
OEDIPUS: I am not wasting time:
    Creon spoke of this, and I have sent for him—
    Twice, in fact; it is strange that he is not here.
CHORAGOS: The other matter—that old report—seems useless.
OEDIPUS: Tell me. I am interested in all reports.
CHORAGOS: The King was said to have been killed by highwaymen.
OEDIPUS: I know. But we have no witnesses to that.
CHORAGOS: If the killer can feel a particle of dread,
    Your curse will bring him out of hiding!
OEDIPUS: No.
    The man who dared that act will fear no curse.
        [*Enter the blind seer* TEIRESIAS, *led by a* PAGE.]

CHORAGOS: But there is one man who may detect the criminal.
    This is Teiresias, this is the holy prophet
    In whom, alone of all men, truth was born.
OEDIPUS: Teiresias: seer: student of mysteries,
    Of all that's taught and all that no man tells,
    Secrets of Heaven and secrets of the earth:
    Blind though you are, you know the city lies
    Sick with plague; and from this plague, my lord,
    We find that you alone can guard or save us.

    Possibly you did not hear the messengers?
    Apollo, when we sent to him,
    Sent us back word that this great pestilence
    Would lift, but only if we established clearly
    The identity of those who murdered Laïos.
    They must be killed or exiled.
                      Can you use
    Birdflight or any art of divination
    To purify yourself, and Thebes, and me
    From this contagion? We are in your hands.
    There is no fairer duty
    Than that of helping others in distress.
TEIRESIAS: How dreadful knowledge of the truth can be
    When there's no help in truth! I knew this well,
    But made myself forget. I should not have come.
OEDIPUS: What is troubling you? Why are your eyes so cold?
TEIRESIAS: Let me go home. Bear your own fate, and I'll
    Bear mine. It is better so: trust what I say.
OEDIPUS: What you say is ungracious and unhelpful
    To your native country. Do not refuse to speak.
TEIRESIAS: When it comes to speech, your own is neither temperate
    Nor opportune. I wish to be more prudent.
OEDIPUS: In God's name, we all beg you—
TEIRESIAS: You are all ignorant.
    No; I will never tell you what I know.
    Now it is my misery; then, it would be yours.
OEDIPUS: What! You do know something, and will not tell us?
    You would betray us all and wreck the State?
TEIRESIAS: I do not intend to torture myself, or you.
    Why persist in asking? You will not persuade me.
OEDIPUS: What a wicked old man you are! You'd try a stone's
    Patience! Out with it! Have you no feeling at all?
TEIRESIAS: You call me unfeeling. If you could only see
    The nature of your own feelings . . .
OEDIPUS: Why,
    Who would not feel as I do? Who could endure
    Your arrogance toward the city?

TEIRESIAS: What does it matter!
  Whether I speak or not, it is bound to come.
OEDIPUS: Then, if "it" is bound to come, you are bound to tell me.
TEIRESIAS: No, I will not go on. Rage as you please.
OEDIPUS: Rage? Why not!
                           And I'll tell you what I think:
  You planned it, you had it done, you all but
  Killed him with your own hands: if you had eyes,
  I'd say the crime was yours, and yours alone.
TEIRESIAS: So? I charge you, then,
  Abide by the proclamation you have made:
  From this day forth
  Never speak again to these men or to me;
  You yourself are the pollution of this country.
OEDIPUS: You dare say that! Can you possibly think you have
  Some way of going free, after such insolence?
TEIRESIAS: I have gone free. It is the truth sustains me.
OEDIPUS: Who taught you shamelessness? It was not your craft.
TEIRESIAS: You did. You made me speak. I did not want to.
OEDIPUS: Speak what? Let me hear it again more clearly.
TEIRESIAS: Was it not clear before? Are you tempting me?
OEDIPUS: I did not understand it. Say it again.
TEIRESIAS: I say that you are the murderer whom you seek.
OEDIPUS: Now twice you have spat out infamy. You'll pay for it!
TEIRESIAS: Would you care for more? Do you wish to be really angry?
OEDIPUS: Say what you will. Whatever you say is worthless.
TEIRESIAS: I say you live in hideous shame with those
  Most dear to you. You can not see the evil.
OEDIPUS: It seems you can go on mouthing like this for ever.
TEIRESIAS: I can, if there is power in truth.
OEDIPUS: There is:
  But not for you, not for you,
  You sightless, witless, senseless, mad old man!
TEIRESIAS: You are the madman. There is no one here
  Who will not curse you soon, as you curse me.
OEDIPUS: You child of endless night! You can not hurt me
  Or any other man who sees the sun.
TEIRESIAS: True: it is not from me your fate will come.
  That lies within Apollo's competence.
  As it is his concern.
OEDIPUS: Tell me.
  Are you speaking for Creon, or for yourself?
TEIRESIAS: Creon is no threat. You weave your own doom.
OEDIPUS: Wealth, power, craft of statesmanship!
  Kingly position, everywhere admired!
  What savage envy is stored up against these,
  If Creon, whom I trusted, Creon my friend,

For this great office which the city once
Put in my hands unsought—if for this power
Creon desires in secret to destroy me!

He has bought this decrepit fortune-teller, this
Collector of dirty pennies, this prophet fraud—
Why, he is no more clairvoyant than I am!

                                    Tell us.
Has your mystic mummery ever approached the truth?
When that hellcat the Sphinx was performing here,
What help were you to these people?
Her magic was not for the first man who came along:
It demanded a real exorcist. Your birds—
What good were they? or the gods, for the matter of that?
But I came by,
Oedipus, the simple man, who knows nothing—
I thought it out for myself, no birds helped me!
And this is the man you think you can destroy,
That you may be close to Creon when he's king!
Well, you and your friend Creon, it seems to me,
Will suffer most. If you were not an old man,
You would have paid already for your plot.

CHORAGOS: We can not see that his words or yours
Have been spoken except in anger, Oedipus,
And of anger we have no need. How can God's will
Be accomplished best? That is what most concerns us.

TEIRESIAS: You are a king. But where argument's concerned
I am your man, as much a king as you.
I am not your servant, but Apollo's.
I have no need of Creon to speak for me.

Listen to me. You mock my blindness, do you?
But I say that you, with both your eyes, are blind:
You can not see the wretchedness of your life,
Nor in whose house you live, no, nor with whom.
Who are your father and mother? Can you tell me?
You do not even know the blind wrongs
That you have done them, on earth and in the world below.
But the double lash of your parents' curse will whip you
Out of this land some day, with only night
Upon your precious eyes.
Your cries then—where will they not be heard?
What fastness of Kithairon will not echo them?
And that bridal-descant of yours—you'll know it then,
The song they sang when you came here to Thebes
And found your misguided berthing.

All this, and more, that you can not guess at now,
Will bring you to yourself among your children.

Be angry, then. Curse Creon. Curse my words.
I tell you, no man that walks upon the earth
Shall be rooted out more horribly than you.
OEDIPUS: Am I to bear this from him?—Damnation
Take you! Out of this place! Out of my sight!
TEIRESIAS: I would not have come at all if you had not asked me.
OEDIPUS: Could I have told that you'd talk nonsense, that
You'd come here to make a fool of yourself, and of me?
TEIRESIAS: A fool? Your parents thought me sane enough.
OEDIPUS: My parents again!—Wait: who were my parents?
TEIRESIAS: This day will give you a father, and break your heart.
OEDIPUS: Your infantile riddles! Your damned abracadabra!
TEIRESIAS: You were a great man once at solving riddles.
OEDIPUS: Mock me with that if you like; you will find it true.
TEIRESIAS: It was true enough. It brought about your ruin.
OEDIPUS: But if it saved this town?
TEIRESIAS: [*to the* PAGE] Boy, give me your hand.
OEDIPUS: Yes, boy; lead him away.
                                —While you are here
We can do nothing. Go; leave us in peace.
TEIRESIAS: I will go when I have said what I have to say.
How can you hurt me? And I tell you again:
The man you have been looking for all this time,
The damned man, the murderer of Laïos,
That man is in Thebes. To your mind he is foreign-born,
But it will soon be shown that he is a Theban,
A revelation that will fail to please.
                                A blind man,
Who has his eyes now; a penniless man, who is rich now;
And he will go tapping the strange earth with his staff
To the children with whom he lives now he will be
Brother and father—the very same; to her
Who bore him, son and husband—the very same
Who came to his father's bed, wet with his father's blood.

Enough. Go think that over.
If later you find error in what I have said,
You may say that I have no skill in prophecy.
            [*Exit* TEIRESIAS, *led by his* PAGE. OEDIPUS *goes into the palace.*]

ODE I

CHORUS: The Delphic stone of prophecies   [STROPHE 1]
        Remembers ancient regicide
        And a still bloody hand.

That killer's hour of flight has come.
He must be stronger than riderless
Coursers of untiring wind,
For the son of Zeus armed with his father's thunder
Leaps in lightning after him;
And the Furies follow him, the sad Furies.

Holy Parnassos' peak of snow   [ANTISTROPHE 1]
Flashes and blinds that secret man,
That all shall hunt him down:
Though he may roam the forest shade
Like a bull wild from pasture
To rage through glooms of stone.
Doom comes down on him; flight will not avail him;
For the world's heart calls him desolate,
And the immortal Furies follow, for ever follow.

But now a wilder thing is heard   [STROPHE 2]
From the old man skilled at hearing Fate in the wingbeat of a bird.
Bewildered as a blown bird, my soul hovers and can not find
Foothold in this debate, or any reason or rest of mind.
But no man ever brought—none can bring
Proof of strife between Thebes' royal house,
Labdakos' line, and the son of Polybos;
And never until now has any man brought word
Of Laïos' dark death staining Oedipus the King.

Divine Zeus and Apollo hold   [ANTISTROPHE 2]
Perfect intelligence alone of all tales ever told;
And well though this diviner works, he works in his own night;
No man can judge that rough unknown or trust in second sight,
For wisdom changes hands among the wise.
Shall I believe my great lord criminal
At a raging word that a blind old man let fall?
I saw him, when the carrion woman faced him of old,
Prove his heroic mind! These evil words are lies.

SCENE II

CREON: Men of Thebes:
   I am told that heavy accusations
   Have been brought against me by King Oedipus.

   I am not the kind of man to bear this tamely.

   If in these present difficulties
   He holds me accountable for any harm to him
   Through anything I have said or done—why, then,

I do not value life in this dishonor.
It is not as though this rumor touched upon
Some private indiscretion. The matter is grave.
The fact is that I am being called disloyal
To the State, to my fellow citizens, to my friends.
CHORAGOS: He may have spoken in anger, not from his mind.
CREON: But did you not hear him say I was the one
Who seduced the old prophet into lying?
CHORAGOS: The thing was said; I do not know how seriously.
CREON: But you were watching him! Were his eyes steady?
Did he look like a man in his right mind?
CHORAGOS: I do not know.
I can not judge the behavior of great men.
But here is the King himself.
       [enter OEDIPUS.]
OEDIPUS: So you dared come back.
Why? How brazen of you to come to my house,
You murderer!
                    Do you think I do not know
That you plotted to kill me, plotted to steal my throne?
Tell me, in God's name: am I coward, a fool,
That you should dream you could accomplish this?
A fool who could not see your slippery game?
A coward, not to fight back when I saw it?
You are the fool, Creon, are you not? hoping
Without support or friends to get a throne?
Thrones may be won or bought: you could do neither.
CREON: Now listen to me. You have talked; let me talk, too.
You can not judge unless you know the facts.
OEDIPUS: You speak well: there is one fact; but I find it hard
To learn from the deadliest enemy I have.
CREON: That above all I must dispute with you.
OEDIPUS: That above all I will not hear you deny.
CREON: If you think there is anything good in being stubborn
Against all reason, then I say you are wrong.
OEDIPUS: If you think a man can sin against his own kind
And not be punished for it, I say you are mad.
CREON: I agree. But tell me: what have I done to you?
OEDIPUS: You advised me to send for that wizard, did you not?
CREON: I did. I should do it again.
OEDIPUS: Very well. Now tell me:
How long has it been since Laïos—
CREON: What of Laïos?
OEDIPUS: Since he vanished in that onset by the road?
CREON: It was long ago, a long time.
OEDIPUS: And this prophet,
Was he practicing here then?
CREON: He was; and with honor, as now.

OEDIPUS: Did he speak of me at that time?
CREON: He never did;
   At least, not when I was present.
OEDIPUS: But . . . the enquiry?
   I suppose you held one?
CREON: We did, but we learned nothing.
OEDIPUS: Why did the prophet not speak against me then?
CREON: I do not know; and I am the kind of man
   Who holds his tongue when he has no facts to go on.
OEDIPUS: There's one fact that you know, and you could tell it.
CREON: What fact is that? If I know it, you shall have it.
OEDIPUS: If he were not involved with you, he could not say
   That it was I who murdered Laïos.
CREON: If he says that, you are the one that knows it!—
   But now it is my turn to question you.
OEDIPUS: Put your questions. I am no murderer.
CREON: First, then: You married my sister?
OEDIPUS: I married your sister.
CREON: And you rule the kingdom equally with her?
OEDIPUS: Everything that she wants she has from me.
CREON: And I am the third, equal to both of you?
OEDIPUS: That is why I call you a bad friend.
CREON: No. Reason it out, as I have done.
   Think of this first: Would any sane man prefer
   Power, with all a king's anxieties,
   To that same power and the grace of sleep?
   Certainly not I.
   I have never longed for the king's power—only his rights.
   Would any wise man differ from me in this?
   As matters stand, I have my way in everything
   With your consent, and no responsibilities.
   If I were king, I should be a slave to policy.

   How could I desire a scepter more
   Than what is now mine—untroubled influence?
   No, I have not gone mad; I need no honors,
   Except those with the perquisites I have now.
   I am welcome everywhere; every man salutes me,
   And those who want your favor seek my ear,
   Since I know how to manage what they ask.
   Should I exchange this ease for that anxiety?
   Besides, no sober mind is treasonable.
   I hate anarchy
   And never would deal with any man who likes it.

   Test what I have said. Go to the priestess
   At Delphi, ask if I quoted her correctly.
   And as for this other thing: if I am found

Guilty of treason with Teiresias,
Then sentence me to death! You have my word
It is a sentence I should cast my vote for—
But not without evidence!
                              You do wrong
When you take good men for bad, bad men for good.
A true friend thrown aside—why, life itself
Is not more precious!
                              In time you will know this well:
For time, and time alone, will show the just man,
Though scoundrels are discovered in a day.

CHORAGOS: This is well said, and a prudent man would ponder it.
    Judgments too quickly formed are dangerous.

OEDIPUS: But is he not quick in his duplicity?
    And shall I not be quick to parry him?
    Would you have me stand still, hold my peace, and let
    This man win everything, through my inaction?

CREON: And you want—what is it, then? To banish me?

OEDIPUS: No, not exile. It is your death I want,
    So that all the world may see what treason means.

CREON: You will persist, then? You will not believe me?

OEDIPUS: How can I believe you?

CREON: Then you are a fool.

OEDIPUS: To save myself?

CREON: In justice, think of me.

OEDIPUS: You are evil incarnate.

CREON: But suppose that you are wrong?

OEDIPUS: Still I must rule.

CREON: But not if you rule badly.

OEDIPUS: O city, city!

CREON: It is my city, too!

CHORAGOS: Now, my lords, be still. I see the Queen,
    Iocastê, coming from her palace chambers;
    And it is time she came, for the sake of you both.
    This dreadful quarrel can be resolved through her.
        [*enter* IOCASTE.]

IOCASTE: Poor foolish men, what wicked din is this?
    With Thebes sick to death, is it not shameful
    That you should rake some private quarrel up?
        [*to* OEDIPUS:]
    Come into the house.

        —And you, Creon, go now:
    Let us have no more of this tumult over nothing.

CREON: Nothing? No, sister: what your husband plans for me
    Is one of two great evils: exile or death.

OEDIPUS: He is right.
                    Why, woman I have caught him squarely
    Plotting against my life.
CREON: No! Let me die
    Accurst if ever I have wished you harm!
IOCASTE: Ah, believe it, Oedipus!
    In the name of the gods, respect this oath of his
    For my sake, for the sake of these people here!

[STROPHE 1]

CHORAGOS: Open your mind to her, my lord. Be ruled by her, I beg you!
OEDIPUS: What would you have me do?
CHORAGOS: Respect Creon's word. He has never spoken like a fool,
    And now he has sworn an oath.
OEDIPUS: You know what you ask?
CHORAGOS: I do.
OEDIPUS: Speak on, then.
CHORAGOS: A friend so sworn should not be baited so,
    In blind malice, and without final proof.
OEDIPUS: You are aware, I hope, that what you say
    Means death for me, or exile at the least.
CHORAGOS: No, I swear by Helios, first in Heaven!   [STROPHE 2]
        May I die friendless and accurst,
    The worst of deaths, if ever I meant that!
            It is the withering fields
                That hurt my sick heart:
            Must we bear all these ills,
                And now your bad blood as well?
OEDIPUS: Then let him go. And let me die, if I must,
    Or be driven by him in shame from the land of Thebes.
    It is your unhappiness, and not his talk,
    That touches me.
                As for him—
    Wherever he goes, hatred will follow him.
CREON: Ugly in yielding, as you were ugly in rage!
    Natures like yours chiefly torment themselves.
OEDIPUS: Can you not go? Can you not leave me?
CREON: I can.
    You do not know me; but the city knows me,
    And in its eyes, I am just, if not in yours.
        [*Exit* CREON.]

[ANTISTROPHE 1]

CHORAGOS: Lady Iocastê, did you not ask the King to go to his chambers?
IOCASTE: First tell me what has happened.
CHORAGOS: There was suspicion without evidence; yet it rankled
    As even false charges will.
IOCASTE: On both sides?
CHORAGOS: On both.

IOCASTE: But what was said?
CHORAGOS: Oh let it rest, let it be done with!
 Have we not suffered enough?
OEDIPUS: You see to what your decency has brought you:
 You have made difficulties where my heart saw none.
CHORAGOS: Oedipus, it is not once only I have told you— [ANTISTROPHE 2]
  You must know I should count myself unwise
  To the point of madness, should I now forsake you—
   You, under whose hand,
    In the storm of another time,
   Our dear land sailed out free.
   But now stand fast at the helm!
IOCASTE: In God's name, Oedipus, inform your wife as well:
 Why are you so set in this hard anger?
OEDIPUS: I will tell you, for none of these men deserves
 My confidence as you do. It is Creon's work,
 His treachery, his plotting against me.
IOCASTE: Go on, if you can make this clear to me.
OEDIPUS: He charges me with the murder of Laïos.
IOCASTE: Has he some knowledge? Or does he speak from hearsay?
OEDIPUS: He would not commit himself to such a charge,
 But he has brought in that damnable soothsayer
 To tell his story.
IOCASTE: Set your mind at rest.
 If it is a question of soothsayers, I tell you
 That you will find no man whose craft gives knowledge
 Of the unknowable.

     Here is my proof:

 An oracle was reported to Laïos once
 (I will not say from Phoibos himself, but from
 His appointed ministers, at any rate)
 That his doom would be death at the hands of his own son—
 His son, born of his flesh and of mine!

 Now, you remember the story: Laïos was killed
 By marauding strangers where three highways meet.
 But his child had not been three days in this world
 Before the King had pierced the baby's ankles
 And left him to die on a lonely mountainside.

 Thus, Apollo never caused that child
 To kill his father, and it was not Laïos' fate
 To die at the hands of his son, as he had feared.
 This is what prophets and prophecies are worth!
 Have no dread of them.
     It is God himself
 Who can show us what he wills, in his own way.

OEDIPUS: How strange a shadowy memory crossed my mind,
   Just now while you were speaking; it chilled my heart.
IOCASTE: What do you mean? What memory do you speak of?
OEDIPUS: If I understand you, Laïos was killed
   At a place where three roads meet.
IOCASTE: So it was said;
   We have no later story.
OEDIPUS: Where did it happen?
IOCASTE: Phokis, it is called: at a place where the Theban Way
   Divides into the roads toward Delphi and Daulia.
OEDIPUS: When?
IOCASTE: We had the news not long before you came
   And proved the right to your succession here.
OEDIPUS: Ah, what net has God been weaving for me?
IOCASTE: Oedipus! Why does this trouble you?
OEDIPUS: Do not ask me yet.
   First, tell me how Laïos looked, and tell me
   How old he was.
IOCASTE: He was tall, his hair just touched
   With white; his form was not unlike your own.
OEDIPUS: I think that I myself may be accurst
   By my own ignorant edict.
IOCASTE: You speak strangely.
   It makes me tremble to look at you, my King.
OEDIPUS: I am not sure that the blind man can not see.
   But I should know better if you were to tell me—
IOCASTE: Anything—though I dread to hear you ask it.
OEDIPUS: Was the King lightly escorted, or did he ride
   With a large company, as a ruler should?
IOCASTE: There were five men with him in all: one was a herald,
   And a single chariot, which he was driving.
OEDIPUS: Alas, that makes it plain enough!
                                        But who—
   Who told you how it happened?
IOCASTE: A household servant,
   The only one to escape.
OEPIDUS: And is he still
   A servant of ours?
IOCASTE: No; for when he came back at last
   And found you enthroned in the place of the dead king,
   He came to me, touched my hand with his, and begged
   That I would send him away to the frontier district
   Where only the shepherds go—
   As far away from the city as I could send him.
   I granted his prayer; for although the man was a slave,
   He had earned more than this favor at my hands.
OEDIPUS: Can he be called back quickly?

IOCASTE: Easily.
    But why?
OEDIPUS: I have taken too much upon myself
    Without enquiry; therefore I wish to consult him.
IOCASTE: Then he shall come.
                        But am I not one also
    To whom you might confide these fears of yours?
OEDIPUS: That is your right; it will not be denied you,
    Now least of all; for I have reached a pitch
    Of wild foreboding. Is there anyone
    To whom I should sooner speak?

    Polybos of Corinth is my father.
    My mother is a Dorian: Meropê.
    I grew up chief among the men of Corinth
    Until a strange thing happened—
    Not worth my passion, it may be, but strange.

    At a feast, a drunken man maundering in his cups
    Cries out that I am not my father's son!

    I contained myself that night, though I felt anger
    And a sinking heart. The next day I visited
    My father and mother, and questioned them. They stormed,
    Calling it all the slanderous rant of a fool;
    And this relieved me. Yet the suspicion
    Remained always aching in my mind;
    I knew there was talk; I could not rest;
    And finally, saying nothing to my parents,
    I went to the shrine at Delphi.
    The god dismissed my question without reply;
    He spoke of other things.
                        Some were clear,
    Full of wretchedness, dreadful, unbearable:
    As, that I should lie with my own mother, breed
    Children from whom all men would turn their eyes;
    And that I should be my father's murderer.

    I heard all this, and fled. And from that day
    Corinth to me was only in the stars
    Descending in that quarter of the sky,
    As I wandered farther and farther on my way
    To a land where I should never see the evil
    Sung by the oracle. And I came to this country
    Where, so you say, King Laïos was killed.

    I will tell you all that happened there, my lady.

There were three highways
Coming together at a place I passed;
And there a herald came towards me, and a chariot
Drawn by horses, with a man such as you describe
Seated in it. The groom leading the horses
Forced me off the road at his lord's command;
But as this charioteer lurched over towards me
I struck him in my rage. The old man saw me
And brought his double goad down upon my head
As I came abreast.

　　　　　　　He was paid back, and more!
Swinging my club in this right hand I knocked him
Out of his car, and he rolled on the ground.

　　　　　　　　　　　　　　　　　I killed him.

I killed them all.
Now if that stranger and Laïos were—kin,
Where is a man more miserable than I?
More hated by the gods? Citizen and alien alike
Must never shelter me or speak to me—
I must be shunned by all.

　　　　　　　　　And I myself
Pronounced this malediction upon myself!

Think of it: I have touched you with these hands,
These hands that killed your husband. What defilement!

Am I all evil, then? It must be so,
Since I must flee from Thebes, yet never again
See my own countrymen, my own country,
For fear of joining my mother in marriage
And killing Polybos, my father.

　　　　　　　　　　　Ah,
If I was created so, born to this fate,
Who could deny the savagery of God?

O holy majesty of heavenly powers!
May I never see that day! Never!
Rather let me vanish from the race of men
Than know the abomination destined me!
CHORAGOS: We too, my lord, have felt dismay at this.
　　　　But there is hope: you have yet to hear the shepherd.
OEDIPUS: Indeed, I fear no other hope is left me.
IOCASTE: What do you hope from him when he comes?
OEDIPUS: 　　　　　　　　　　　　　　　　This much:
　　　　If his account of the murder tallies with yours,
　　　　Then I am cleared.

IOCASTE: What was it that I said
        Of such importance?
OEDIPUS: Why, "marauders," you said,
        Killed the King, according to this man's story.
        If he maintains that still, if there were several,
        Clearly the guilt is not mine: I was alone.
        But if he says one man, singlehanded, did it,
        Then the evidence all points to me.
IOCASTE: You may be sure that he said there were several;
        And can he call back that story now? He cán not.
        The whole city heard it as plainly as I.
        But suppose he alters some detail of it:
        He can not ever show that Laïos' death
        Fulfilled the oracle: for Apollo said
        My child was doomed to kill him; and my child—
        Poor baby!—it was my child that died first.

        No. From now on, where oracles are concerned,
        I would not waste a second thought on any.
OEDIPUS: You may be right.
                              But come: let someone go
        For the shepherd at once. This matter must be settled.
IOCASTE: I will send for him.
        I would not wish to cross you in anything,
        And surely not in this.—Let us go in.
        [*Exeunt into the palace.*]

ODE II

CHORUS: Let me be reverent in the ways of right,   [STROPHE 1]
        Lowly the paths I journey on;
        Let all my words and actions keep
        The laws of the pure universe
        From highest Heaven handed down.
        For Heaven is their bright nurse,
        Those generations of the realms of light;
        Ah, never of mortal kind were they begot,
        Nor are they slaves of memory, lost in sleep;
        Their Father is greater than Time, and ages not.

        The tyrant is a child of Pride   [ANTISTROPHE 1]
        Who drinks from his great sickening cup
        Recklessness and vanity,
        Until from his high crest headlong
        He plummets to the dust of hope.
        That strong man is not strong.
        But let no fair ambition be denied;

May God protect the wrestler for the State
In government, in comely policy,
Who will fear God, and on His ordinance wait.

Haughtiness and the high hand of disdain   [STROPHE 2]
Tempt and outrage God's holy law;
And any mortal who dares hold
No immortal Power in awe
Will be caught up in a net of pain:
The price for which his levity is sold.
Let each man take due earnings, then,
And keep his hands from holy things,
And from blasphemy stand apart—
Else the crackling blast of heaven
Blows on his head, and on his desperate heart;
Though fools will honor impious men,
In their cities no tragic poet sings.

Shall we lose faith in Delphi's obscurities,   [ANTISTROPHE 2]
We who have heard the world's core
Discredited, and the sacred wood
Of Zeus at Elis praised no more?
The deeds and the strange prophecies
Must make a pattern yet to be understood.
Zeus, if indeed you are lord of all,
Throned in light over night and day,
Mirror this in your endless mind:
Our masters call the oracle
Words on the wind, and the Delphic vision blind!
Their hearts no longer know Apollo,
And reverence for the gods has died away.

SCENE III

[*Enter* IOCASTE.]
IOCASTE: Princes of Thebes, it has occurred to me
   To visit the altars of the gods, bearing
   These branches as a suppliant, and this incense.
   Our King is not himself: his noble soul
   Is overwrought with fantasies of dread,
   Else he would consider
   The new prophecies in the light of the old.
   He will listen to any voice that speaks disaster,
   And my advice goes for nothing.
      [*She approaches the altar, R.*]
                        To you, then, Apollo,
   Lycean lord, since you are nearest, I turn in prayer.

Receive these offerings, and grant us deliverance
From defilement. Our hearts are heavy with fear
When we see our leader distracted, as helpless sailors
Are terrified by the confusion of their helmsman.
> [*Enter* MESSENGER.]

MESSENGER: Friends, no doubt you can direct me:
Where shall I find the house of Oedipus,
Or, better still, where is the King himself?

CHORAGOS: It is this very place, stranger; he is inside.
This is his wife and mother of his children.

MESSENGER: I wish her happiness in a happy house,
Blest in all the fulfillment of her marriage.

IOCASTE: I wish as much for you: your courtesy
Deserves a like good fortune. But now, tell me:
Why have you come? What have you to say to us?

MESSENGER: Good news, my lady, for your house and your husband.

IOCASTE: What news? Who sent you here?

MESSENGER: I am from Corinth.
The news I bring ought to mean joy for you,
Though it may be you will find some grief in it.

IOCASTE: What is it? How can it touch us in both ways?

MESSENGER: The word is that the people of the Isthmus
Intend to call Oedipus to be their king.

IOCASTE: But old King Polybos—is he not reigning still?

MESSENGER: No. Death holds him in his sepulchre.

IOCASTE: What are you saying? Polybos is dead?

MESSENGER: If I am not telling the truth, may I die myself.

IOCASTE: [*to a* MAIDSERVANT:] Go in, go quickly; tell this to your master.

O riddlers of God's will, where are you now!
This was the man whom Oedipus, long ago,
Feared so, fled so, in dread of destroying him—
But it was another fate by which he died.
> [*Enter* OEDIPUS, *C.*]

OEDIPUS: Dearest Iocastê, why have you sent for me?

IOCASTE: Listen to what this man says, and then tell me
What has become of the solemn prophecies.

OEDIPUS: Who is this man? What is his news for me?

IOCASTE: He has come from Corinth to announce your father's death!

OEDIPUS: Is it true, stranger? Tell me in your own words.

MESSENGER: I can not say it more clearly: the King is dead.

OEDIPUS: Was it by treason? Or by an attack of illness?

MESSENGER: A little thing brings old men to their rest.

OEDIPUS: It was sickness, then?

MESSENGER: Yes, and his many years.

OEDIPUS: Ah!
Why should a man respect the Pythian hearth, or
Give heed to the birds that jangle above his head?

They prophesied that I should kill Polybos,
Kill my own father; but he is dead and buried,
And I am here—I never touched him, never,
Unless he died of grief for my departure,
And thus, in a sense, through me. No. Polybos
Has packed the oracles off with him underground.
They are empty words.

IOCASTE: Had I not told you so?

OEDIPUS: You had; it was my faint heart that betrayed me.

IOCASTE: From now on never think of those things again.

OEDIPUS: And yet—must I not fear my mother's bed?

IOCASTE: Why should anyone in this world be afraid,
Since Fate rules us and nothing can be foreseen?
A man should live only for the present day.

Have no more fear of sleeping with your mother:
How many men, in dreams, have lain with their mothers!
No reasonable man is troubled by such things.

OEDIPUS: That is true; only—
If only my mother were not still alive!
But she is alive. I can not help my dread.

IOCASTE: Yet this news of your father's death is wonderful.

OEDIPUS: Wonderful. But I fear the living woman.

MESSENGER: Tell me, who is this woman that you fear?

OEDIPUS: It is Meropê, man; the wife of King Polybos.

MESSENGER: Meropê? Why should you be afraid of her?

OEDIPUS: An oracle of the gods, a dreadful saying.

MESSENGER: Can you tell me about it or are you sworn to silence?

OEDIPUS: I can tell you, and I will.
Apollo said through his prophet that I was the man
Who should marry his own mother, shed his father's blood
With his own hands. And so, for all these years
I have kept clear of Corinth, and no harm has come—
Though it would have been sweet to see my parents again.

MESSENGER: And is this the fear that drove you out of Corinth?

OEDIPUS: Would you have me kill my father?

MESSENGER: As for that
You must be reassured by the news I gave you.

OEDIPUS: If you could reassure me, I would reward you.

MESSENGER: I had that in mind, I will confess: I thought
I could count on you when you returned to Corinth.

OEDIPUS: No: I will never go near my parents again.

MESSENGER: Ah, son, you still do not know what you are doing—

OEDIPUS: What do you mean? In the name of God tell me!

MESSENGER: —If these are your reasons for not going home.

OEDIPUS: I tell you, I fear the oracle may come true.

MESSENGER: And guilt may come upon you through your parents?

OEDIPUS: That is the dread that is always in my heart.

MESSENGER: Can you not see that all your fears are groundless?

OEDIPUS: How can you say that? They are my parents, surely?

MESSENGER: Polybos was not your father.

OEDIPUS: Not my father?

MESSENGER: No more your father than the man speaking to you.

OEDIPUS: But you are nothing to me!

MESSENGER: Neither was he.

OEDIPUS: Then why did he call me son?

MESSENGER: I will tell you:
    Long ago he had you from my hands, as a gift.

OEDIPUS: Then how could he love me so, if I was not his?

MESSENGER: He had no children, and his heart turned to you.

OEDIPUS: What of you? Did you buy me? Did you find me by chance?

MESSENGER: I came upon you in the crooked pass of Kithairon.

OEDIPUS: And what were you doing there?

MESSENGER: Tending my flocks.

OEDIPUS: A wandering shepherd?

MESSENGER: But your savior, son, that day.

OEDIPUS: 'rom what did you save me?

MESSENG'.R: Your ankles should tell you that.

OEDIPUS Ah, stranger, why do you speak of that childhood pain?

MESSEN ER: I cut the bonds that tied your ankles together.

OEDIPL.s: I have had the mark as long as I can remember.

MESSENGER: That was why you were given the name you bear.

OEDIPUS: God! Was it my father or my mother who did it?
    Tell me!

MESSENGER: I do not know. The man who gave you to me
    Can tell you better than I.

OEDIPUS: It was not you that found me, but another?

MESSENGER: It was another shepherd gave you to me.

OEDIPUS: Who was he? Can you tell me who he was?

MESSENGER: I think he was said to be one of Laïos' people.

OEDIPUS: You mean the Laïos who was king here years ago?

MESSENGER: Yes; King Laïos; and the man was one of his herdsmen.

OEDIPUS: Is he still alive? Can I see him?

MESSENGER: These men here
    Know best about such things.

OEDIPUS: Does anyone here
    Know this shepherd that he is talking about?
    Have you seen him in the fields, or in the town?
    If you have, tell me. It is time things were made plain.

CHORAGOS: I think the man he means is that same shepherd
    You have already asked to see. Iocastê perhaps
    Could tell you something.

OEDIPUS: Do you know anything
    About him, Lady? Is he the man we have summoned?
    Is that the man this shepherd means?

IOCASTE: Why think of him?
     Forget this herdsman. Forget it all.
     This talk is a waste of time.
OEDIPUS: How can you say that,
IOCASTE: For God's love, let us have no more questioning!
     Is your life nothing to you?
     My own is pain enough for me to bear.
OEDIPUS: You need not worry. Suppose my mother a slave,
     And born of slaves: no baseness can touch you.
IOCASTE: Listen to me, I beg you: do not do this thing!
OEDIPUS: I will not listen; the truth must be made known.
IOCASTE: Everything that I say is for your own good!
OEDIPUS: My own good
     Snaps my patience, then; I want none of it.
IOCASTE: You are fatally wrong! May you never learn who you are!
OEDIPUS: Go, one of you, and bring the shepherd here.
     Let us leave this woman to brag of her royal name.
IOCASTE: Ah, miserable!
     That is the only word I have for you now.
     That is the only word I can ever have.
        [*Exit into the palace.*]
CHORAGOS: Why has she left us, Oedipus? Why has she gone
     In such a passion of sorrow? I fear this silence:
     Something dreadful may come of it.
OEDIPUS: Let it come!
     However base my birth, I must know about it.
     The Queen, like a woman, is perhaps ashamed
     To think of my low origin. But I
     Am a child of Luck; I can not be dishonored.
     Luck is my mother; the passing months, my brothers,
     Have seen me rich and poor.
                     If this is so,
     How could I wish that I were someone else?
     How could I not be glad to know my birth?

ODE III

CHORUS: If ever the coming time were known   [STROPHE]
     To my heart's pondering,
     Kithairon, now by Heaven I see the torches
     At the festival of the next full moon,
     And see the dance, and hear the choir sing
     A grace to your gentle shade:
     Mountain where Oedipus was found,
     O mountain guard of a noble race!
     May the god who heals us lend his aid,

And let that glory come to pass
For our king's cradling-ground.

Of the nymphs that flower beyond the years,   [ANTISTROPHE]
Who bore you, royal child,
To Pan of the hills or the timberline Apollo,
Cold in delight where the upland clears,
Or Hermês for whom Kyllenê's heights are piled?
Or flushed as evening cloud,
Great Dionysos, roamer of mountains,
He—was it he who found you there,
And caught you up in his own proud
Arms from the sweet god-ravisher
Who laughed by the Muses' fountains?

SCENE IV

OEDIPUS: Sirs: though I do not know the man,
　　I think I see him coming, this shepherd we want:
　　He is old, like our friend here, and the men
　　Bringing him seem to be servants of my house.
　　But you can tell, if you have ever seen him.
　　　　[*Enter* SHEPHERD *escorted by servants.*]
CHORAGOS: I know him, he was Laïos' man. You can trust him.
OEDIPUS: Tell me first, you from Corinth: is this the shepherd
　　We were discussing?
MESSENGER:　　　　　　　This is the very man.
OEDIPUS: [*to* SHEPHERD] Come here. No, look at me. You must answer
　　Everything I ask.—You belonged to Laïos?
SHEPHERD: Yes: born his slave, brought up in his house.
OEDIPUS: Tell me: what kind of work did you do for him?
SHEPHERD: I was a shepherd of his, most of my life.
OEDIPUS: Where mainly did you go for pasturage?
SHEPHERD: Sometimes Kithairon, sometimes the hills near-by.
OEDIPUS: Do you remember ever seeing this man out there?
SHEPHERD: What would he be doing there? This man?
OEDIPUS: This man standing here. Have you ever seen him before?
SHEPHERD: No. At least, not to my recollection.
MESSENGER: And that is not strange, my lord. But I'll refresh
　　His memory: he must remember when we two
　　Spent three whole seasons together, March to September,
　　On Kithairon or thereabouts. He had two flocks;
　　I had one. Each autumn I'd drive mine home
　　And he would go back with his to Laïos' sheepfold.—
　　Is this not true, just as I have described it?
SHEPHERD: True, yes; but it was all so long ago.
MESSENGER: Well, then: do you remember, back in those days,
　　That you gave me a baby boy to bring up as my own?

SHEPHERD: What if I did? What are you trying to say?
MESSENGER: King Oedipus was once that little child.
SHEPHERD: Damn you, hold your tongue!
OEDIPUS: No more of that!
    It is your tongue needs watching, not this man's.
SHEPHERD: My King, my Master, what is it I have done wrong?
OEDIPUS: You have not answered his question about the boy.
SHEPHERD: He does not know . . . He is only making trouble . . .
OEDIPUS: Come, speak plainly, or it will go hard with you.
SHEPHERD: In God's name, do not torture an old man!
OEDIPUS: Come here, one of you; bind his arms behind him.
SHEPHERD: Unhappy king! What more do you wish to learn?
OEDIPUS: Did you give this man the child he speaks of?
SHEPHERD: I did.
    And I would to God I had died that very day.
OEDIPUS: You will die now unless you speak the truth.
SHEPHERD: Yet if I speak the truth, I am worse than dead.
OEDIPUS: Very well; since you insist upon delaying—
SHEPHERD: No! I have told you already that I gave him the boy.
OEDIPUS: Where did you get him? From your house? From somewhere else?
SHEPHERD: Not from mine, no. A man gave him to me.
OEDIPUS: Is that man here? Do you know whose slave he was?
SHEPHERD: For God's love, my King, do not ask me any more!
OEDIPUS: You are a dead man if I have to ask you again.
SHEPHERD: Then . . . Then the child was from the palace of Laïos.
OEDIPUS: A slave child? or a child of his own line?
SHEPHERD: Ah, I am on the brink of dreadful speech!
OEDIPUS: And I of dreadful hearing. Yet I must hear.
SHEPHERD: If you must be told, then . . .
                    They said it was Laïos' child;
    But it is your wife who can tell you about that.
OEDIPUS: My wife!—Did she give it to you?
SHEPHERD: My lord, she did.
OEDIPUS: Do you know why?
SHEPHERD: I was told to get rid of it.
OEDIPUS: An unspeakable mother!
SHEPHERD: There had been prophecies . . .
OEDIPUS: Tell me.
SHEPHERD: It was said that the boy would kill his own father.
OEDIPUS: Then why did you give him over to this old man?
SHEPHERD: I pitied the baby, my King,
    And I thought that this man would take him far away
    To his own country.
                 He saved him—but for what a fate!
    For if you are what this man says you are,
    No man living is more wretched than Oedipus.

OEDIPUS: Ah God!
  It was true!
           All the prophecies!
                      —Now,
  O Light, may I look on you for the last time!
  I, Oedipus,
  Oedipus, damned in his birth, in his marriage damned,
  Damned in the blood he shed with his own hand!
       [*He rushes into the palace.*]

ODE IV

CHORUS: Alas for the seed of men.   [STROPHE 1]

   What measure shall I give these generations
   That breathe on the void and are void
   And exist and do not exist?

   Who bears more weight of joy
   Than mass of sunlight shifting in images,
   Or who shall make his thought stay on
   That down time drifts away?

   Your splendor is all fallen.

   O naked brow of wrath and tears,
   O change of Oedipus!
   I who saw your days call no man blest—
   Your great days like ghósts góne.

   That mind was a strong bow.   [ANTISTROPHE 1]

   Deep, how deep you drew it then, hard archer,
   At a dim fearful range,
   And brought dear glory down!

   You overcame the stranger—
   The virgin with her hooking lion claws—
   And though death sang, stood like a tower
   To make pale Thebes take heart.

   Fortress against our sorrow!

   True king, giver of laws,
   Majestic Oedipus!
   No prince in Thebes had ever such renown,
   No prince won such grace of power.

And now of all men ever known
Most pitiful is this man's story:
His fortunes are most changed, his state
Fallen to a low slave's
Ground under bitter fate.

O Oedipus, most royal one!
The great door that expelled you to the light
Gave at night—ah, gave night to your glory:
As to the father, to the fathering son.

All understood too late.

How could that queen whom Laïos won,
The garden that he harrowed at his height,
Be silent when that act was done?

But all eyes fail before time's eye,
All actions come to justice there.
Though never willed, though far down the deep past,
Your bed, your dread sirings,
Are brought to book at last.
Child by Laïos doomed to die,
Then doomed to lose that fortunate little death,
Would God you never took breath in this air
That with my wailing lips I take to cry:

For I weep the world's outcast.

I was blind, and now I can tell why:
Asleep, for you had given ease of breath
To Thebes, while the false years went by.

ÉXODOS

[*Enter, from the palace,* SECOND MESSENGER.]
SECOND MESSENGER: Elders of Thebes, most honored in this land,
   What horrors are yours to see and hear, what weight
   Of sorrow to be endured, if, true to your birth,
   You venerate the line of Labdakos!
   I think neither Istros nor Phasis, those great rivers,
   Could purify this place of the corruption
   It shelters now, or soon must bring to light—
   Evil not done unconsciously, but willed.

   The greatest griefs are those we cause ourselves.
CHORAGOS: Surely, friend, we have grief enough already;
   What new sorrow do you mean?

SECOND MESSENGER: The Queen is dead.
CHORAGOS: Iocastê? Dead? But at whose hand?
SECOND MESSENGER: Her own.
    The full horror of what happened you can not know,
    For you did not see it; but I, who did, will tell you
    As clearly as I can how she met her death.

    When she had left us,
    In passionate silence, passing through the court,
    She ran to her apartment in the house,
    Her hair clutched by the fingers of both hands.
    She closed the doors behind her; then, by that bed
    Where long ago the fatal son was conceived—
    That son who should bring about his father's death—
    We hear her call upon Laïos, dead so many years,
    And heard her wail for the double fruit of her marriage,
    A husband by her husband, children by her child.

    Exactly how she died I do not know:
    For Oedipus burst in moaning and would not let us
    Keep vigil to the end: it was by him
    As he stormed about the room that our eyes were caught.
    From one to another of us he went, begging a sword,
    Cursing the wife who was not his wife, the mother
    Whose womb had carried his own children and himself.
    I do not know: it was none of us aided him,
    But surely one of the gods was in control!
    For with a dreadful cry
    He hurled his weight, as though wrenched out of himself,
    At the twin doors: the bolts gave, and he rushed in.
    And there we saw her hanging, her body swaying
    From the cruel cord she had noosed about her neck.
    A great sob broke from him, heartbreaking to hear,
    As he loosed the rope and lowered her to the ground.

    I would blot out from my mind what happened next!
    For the King ripped from her gown the golden brooches ˏ
    That were her ornament, and raised them, and plunged them down
    Straight into his own eyeballs, crying, "No more,
    No more shall you look on the misery about me,
    The horrors of my own doing! Too long you have known
    The faces of those whom I should never have seen,
    Too long been blind to those for whom I was searching!
    From this hour, go in darkness!;" And as he spoke,
    He struck at his eyes—not once, but many times;
    And the blood spattered his beard,
    Bursting from his ruined sockets like red hail.

So from the unhappiness of two this evil has sprung,
A curse on the man and woman alike. The old
Happiness of the house of Labdakos
Was happiness enough: where is it today?
It is all wailing and ruin, disgrace, death—all
The misery of mankind that has a name—
And it is wholly and for ever theirs.

CHORAGOS: Is he in agony still? Is there no rest for him?

SECOND MESSENGER: He is calling for someone to lead him to the gates
So that all the children of Kadmos may look upon
His father's murderer, his mother's—no,
I can not say it!
                            And then he will leave Thebes,
Self-exiled, in order that the curse
Which he himself pronounced may depart from the house.
He is weak, and there is none to lead him,
So terrible is his suffering.
                            But you will see:
Look, the doors are opening; in a moment
You will see a thing that would crush a heart of stone.

[*The central door is opened;* OEDIPUS, *blinded, is led in.*]

CHORAGOS: Dreadful indeed for men to see.
    Never have my own eyes
    Looked on a sight so full of fear.

    Oedipus!
    What madness came upon you, what daemon
    Leaped on your life with heavier
    Punishment than a mortal man can bear?
    No: I can not even
    Look at you, poor ruined one.
    And I would speak, question, ponder,
    If I were able. No.
    You make me shudder.

OEDIPUS: God.   God.
    Is there a sorrow greater?
    Where shall I find harbor in this world?
    My voice is hurled far on a dark wind.
    What has God done to me?

CHORAGOS: Too terrible to think of, or to see.

OEDIPUS: O cloud of night,   [STROPHE 1]
    Never to be turned away: night coming on,
    I can not tell how: night like a shroud!

    My fair winds brought me here.
                            O God. Again
    The pain of the spikes where I had sight,

    The flooding pain
    Of memory, never to be gouged out.
CHORAGOS: This is not strange.
    You suffer it all twice over, remorse in pain,
    Pain in remorse.
OEDIPUS: Ah dear friend   [ANTISTROPHE 1]
    Are you faithful even yet, you alone?
    Are you still standing near me, will you stay here,
    Patient, to care for the blind?
                      The blind man!
    Yet even blind I know who it is attends me,
    By the voice's tone—
    Though my new darkness hide the comforter.
CHORAGOS: Oh fearful act!
    What god was it drove you to rake black
    Night across your eyes?
OEDIPUS: Apollo. Apollo. Dear   [STROPHE 2]
    Children, the god was Apollo.
    He brought my sick, sick fate upon me.
    But the blinding hand was my own!
    How could I bear to see
    When all my sight was horror everywhere?
CHORAGOS: Everywhere; that is true.
OEDIPUS: And now what is left?
    Images? Love? A greeting even,
    Sweet to the senses? Is there anything?
    Ah, no, friends: lead me away.
    Lead me away from Thebes.
                      Lead the great wreck
    And hell of Oedipus, whom the gods hate.
CHORAGOS: Your fate is clear, you are not blind to that.
    Would God you had never found it out!
OEDIPUS: Death take the man who unbound   [ANTISTROPHE 2]
    My feet on that hillside
    And delivered me from death to life! What life?
    If only I had died,
    This weight of monstrous doom
    Could not have dragged me and my darlings down.
CHORAGOS: I would have wished the same.
OEDIPUS: Oh never to have come here
    With my father's blood upon me! Never
    To have been the man they call his mother's husband!
    Oh accurst! Oh child of evil,
    To have entered that wretched bed—
                      the selfsame one!
    More primal than sin itself, this fell to me.

CHORAGOS: I do not know how I can answer you.
   You were better dead than alive and blind.
OEDIPUS: Do not counsel me any more. This punishment
   That I have laid upon myself is just.
   If I had eyes,
   I do not know how I could bear the sight
   Of my father, when I came to the house of Death,
   Or my mother: for I have sinned against them both
   So vilely that I could not make my peace
   By strangling my own life.
                              Or do you think my children,
   Born as they were born, would be sweet to my eyes?
   Ah never, never! Nor this town with its high walls,
   Nor the holy images of the gods.
                              For I,
   Thrice miserable!—Oedipus, noblest of all the line
   Of Kadmos, have condemned myself to enjoy
   These things no more, by my own malediction
   Expelling that man whom the gods declared
   To be a defilement in the house of Laïos.
   After exposing the rankness of my own guilt,
   How could I look men frankly in the eyes?
   No, I swear it,
   If I could have stifled my hearing at its source,
   I would have done it and made all this body
   A tight cell of misery, blank to light and sound:
   So I should have been safe in a dark agony
   Beyond all recollection.
                              Ah Kithairon!
   Why did you shelter me? When I was cast upon you,
   Why did I not die? Then I should never
   Have shown the world my execrable birth.

   Ah Polybos! Corinth, city that I believed
   The ancient seat of my ancestors: how fair
   I seemed, your child! And all the while this evil
   Was cancerous within me!
                              For I am sick
   In my daily life, sick in my origin.

   O three roads, dark ravine, woodland and way
   Where three roads met: you, drinking my father's blood,
   My own blood, spilled by my own hand: can you remember
   The unspeakable things I did there, and the things
   I went on from there to do?
                              O marriage, marriage!
   The act that engendered me, and again the act

Performed by the son in the same bed—
                              Ah, the net
Of incest, mingling fathers, brothers, sons,
With brides, wives, mothers: the last evil
That can be known by men: no tongue can say
How evil!
                No. For the love of God, conceal me
Somewhere far from Thebes; or kill me; or hurl me
Into the sea, away from men's eyes for ever.

Come, lead me. You need not fear to touch me.
Of all men, I alone can bear this guilt.
    [*Enter* CREON.]
CHORAGOS: We are not the ones to decide; but Creon here
    May fitly judge of what you ask. He only
    Is left to protect the city in your place.
OEDIPUS: Alas, how can I speak to him? What right have I
    To beg his courtesy whom I have deeply wronged?
CREON: I have not come to mock you, Oedipus,
    Or to reproach you, either.

    [*To* ATTENDANTS:]—You, standing there:
If you have lost all respect for man's dignity,
At least respect the flame of Lord Helios:
Do not allow this pollution to show itself
Openly here, an affront to the earth
And Heaven's rain and the light of day. No, take him
Into the house as quickly as you can.
For it is proper
That only the close kindred see his grief.
OEDIPUS: I pray you in God's name, since your courtesy
    Ignores my dark expectation, visiting
    With mercy this man of all men most execrable:
    Give me what I ask—for your good, not for mine.
CREON: And what is it that you would have me do?
OEDIPUS: Drive me out of this country as quickly as may be
    To a place where no human voice can ever greet me.
CREON: I should have done that before now—only,
    God's will had not been wholly revealed to me.
OEDIPUS: But his command is plain: the parricide
    Must be destroyed. I am that evil man.
CREON: That is the sense of it, yes; but as things are,
    We had best discover clearly what is to be done.
OEDIPUS: You would learn more about a man like me?
CREON: You are ready now to listen to the god.
OEDIPUS: I will listen. But it is to you
    That I must turn for help. I beg you, hear me.

The woman in there—
Give her whatever funeral you think proper:
She is your sister.
                —But let me go, Creon!
Let me purge my father's Thebes of the pollution
Of my living here, and go out to the wild hills,
To Kithairon, that has won such fame with me,
The tomb my mother and father appointed for me,
And let me die there, as they willed I should.
And yet I know
Death will not ever come to me through sickness
Or in any natural way: I have been preserved
For some unthinkable fate. But let that be.

As for my sons, you need not care for them.
They are men, they will find some way to live.
But my poor daughters, who have shared my table,
Who never before have been parted from their father—
Take care of them. Creon; do this for me.
And will you let me touch them with my hands
A last time, and let us weep together?
Be kind, my lord,
Great prince, be kind!
                      Could I but touch them,
They would be mine again, as when I had my eyes.
    [*Enter* ANTIGONE *and* ISMENE, *attended.*]
Ah, God!
Is it my dearest children I hear weeping?
Has Creon pitied me and sent my daughters?

CREON: Yes, Oedipus: I knew that they were dear to you
    In the old days, and know you must love them still.

OEDIPUS: May God bless you for this—and be a friendlier
    Guardian to you than he has been to me!

Children, where are you?
Come quickly to my hands: they are your brother's—
Hands that have brought your father's once clear eyes
To this way of seeing—
                Ah dearest ones,
I had neither sight nor knowledge then, your father
By the woman who was the source of his own life!
And I weep for you—having no strength to see you—,
I weep for you when I think of the bitterness
That men will visit upon you all your lives.
What homes, what festivals can you attend
Without being forced to depart again in tears?
And when you come to marriageable age,

Where is the man, my daughters, who would dare
Risk the bane that lies on all my children?
Is there any evil wanting? Your father killed
His father; sowed the womb of her who bore him;
Engendered you at the fount of his own existence!
That is what they will say of you.

                                        Then, whom
Can you ever marry? There are no bridegrooms for you,
And your lives must wither away in sterile dreaming.

O Creon, son of Menoikeus!
You are the only father my daughters have,
Since we, their parents, are both of us gone for ever.
They are your own blood: you will not let them
Fall into beggary and loneliness;
You will keep them from the miseries that are mine!
Take pity on them; see, they are only children,
Friendless except for you. Promise me this,
Great Prince, and give me your hand in token of it.
        [CREON *clasps his right hand.*]
Children:
I could say much, if you could understand me,
But as it is, I have only this prayer for you:
Live where you can, be as happy as you can—
Happier, please God, than God has made your father!
CREON: Enough. You have wept enough. Now go within.
OEDIPUS: I must; but it is hard.
CREON: Time eases all things.
OEDIPUS: But you must promise—
CREON: Say what you desire.
OEDIPUS: Send me from Thebes!
CREON: God grant that I may!
OEDIPUS: But since God hates me . . .
CREON: No, he will grant your wish
OEDIPUS: You promise?
CREON: I can not speak beyond my knowledge.
OEDIPUS: Then lead me in.
CREON: Come now, and leave your children.
OEDIPUS: No! Do not take them from me!
CREON: Think no longer
That you are in command here, but rather think
How, when you were, you served your own destruction.
        [*Exeunt into the house all but the* CHORUS; *the* CHORAGOS
        chants directly to the audience:]
CHORAGOS: Men of Thebes: look upon Oedipus.

This is the king who solved the famous riddle
And towered up, most powerful of men.
No mortal eyes but looked on him with envy,
Yet in the end ruin swept over him.

Let every man in mankind's frailty
Consider his last day; and let none
Presume on his good fortune until he find
Life, at his death, a memory without pain.

Plautus

The Menaechmi

Translated by Richard W. Hyde
and Edward C. Weist

DRAMATIS PERSONAE

PROLOGUS
PENICULUS (SPONGE), *a parasite*
MENAECHMUS I, *of Epidamnus*
EROTIUM, *a courtesan*
CULINDRUS, *cook of Erotium*
MENAECHMUS II (SOSICLES), *of Syracuse*
MESSENIO, *slave of Menaechmus II*
MAID *of Erotium*
WIFE *of Menaechmus I*
FATHER-IN-LAW *of Menaechmus I*
DOCTOR
sailors; DECIO *and other slaves*

SCENE——*Epidamnus: a street, on which stand the houses of* MENAECHMUS I
   (L.) *and* EROTIUM (R.).

PROLOGUE

PROLOGUS: Now first and above all, spectators, I'm bringing a few
      Of the best of good wishes to me—and then also to you;
      I'm bringing you Plautus—by mouth, of course, not in his person,
      And therefore I pray you receive him with kindliest ears.
      To the argument gird up your minds, as I babble my verse on,
      And I shall explain it—in briefest of terms, have no fears.
         Now, once an old merchant was living in Syracuse city,
      And he by some chance had a couple of twin sons,—yes, two of 'em—
      And they looked so alike that the nurse couldn't tell (more's the pity)
      Which one she gave suck to; no more could their mother, in lieu of whom
      The nurse was called in, no, not even their mother who'd borne 'em.
         Much later, the boys being now about seven years old,
      Their father filled up a big ship with a lot of his goods

And, putting one twin in safe-keeping with them in the hold,
Betook himself off to Tarentum to market, to turn 'em
To cash; and the other twin, having been naughty in moods,
Stayed home with his mother. Tarentum was holding some games
When they got there, and people were flocking to town, as they ever
Will do for the games; and the little boy strayed, as one never
Should do, from his father among all the crowds, and got lost.
He was found by a rich Epidamnian merchant (whose fame's
The worse for the story) who grabbed him and took him off home.
The father, however, by such a deep blow so star-crossed,
(That is, after the boy disappeared) was dejected at heart,
And only a little while later he died of despair.
Syracuse at last heard the bad news that the father was dead
And that some one had picked up the twin who had gone off to roam;
So the grandfather changed the remaining twin's name then and there,
Since the other had been so beloved (*he* could tell 'em apart);
The other one's name he bestowed on the twin safe at home,
And called him Menaechmus, the same as the one I have said.
And lest you get muddled, as I am, I'm free to confess,
I'll tell you both twins are the same in their name. What a mess!

But now on the poet's rude feet I must seek Epidamnus,
To speed on my tale, or the *Transcript* critic will be slammin' us
For being so dull. The old merchant I told you about
Had no children whatever, unless you may count all his money.
He adopted the stolen young twin, so that neither made out
Much worse on the deal, for the man got a son, and the youth
At length got a wife and a dowry, and (this strikes me funny)
Came into the property after the old wretch's death.
For, wandering into the country—to tell you the truth—
Where torrents of rain had been falling, not far from the town, the
Epidamnian stepped in a freshet, and thought himself still able
To cross as of old. None the less, as he got out of breath,
The current caught quickly the kidnapper's feet, and pulled down the
Epidamnian—down to the place where they act his third syllable.
So from him the young man inherits a whale of a fortune,
And there is the house where the rich kidnapped twin is now dwelling.

The other twin, living in Syracuse—pray don't importune,
For I've not forgotten it—comes with his slave now today
To seek out his twin brother here, as you've just heard me telling.
This town's Epidamnus in the present play,
In other plays the city's changed straightway;
So with the families in these two houses,
Where now Menaechmus dwells and now he souses.
The next incumbent may be beggar, thief,
Procurer, doctor, thug, or Indian chief.

ACT I

[*Enter* PENICULUS, L. *He looks at houses, and finally notices audience.*]

PENICULUS: My nickname's Sponge [Peniculus], because when I eat I wipe the table clean.

Men who bind prisoners with chains and put shackles on runaway slaves are very foolish, if you ask me. You see, if you add insult to injury, a poor fellow is going to want all the more to escape and go wrong. They'll get out of their chains somehow, you can be sure,—file away a link, or knock out a nail with a stone.—That way's ridiculous.

If you really want to keep hold on somebody so he won't get away, you want to tie him with food and drink; first hitch his beak to a full dinner-pail. Give him all he wants to eat and drink every day, and he'll never try to run away, not even if he's committed murder; you'll keep him all right if you bind him this way. The bonds of food and drink are very elastic, you know; the farther you stretch them, the tighter they hold you. [*crosses towards house of* MENAECHMUS I]

I'm just going over to see my friend Menaechmus, with whom I've been serving a long term: I'm going to let him bind me. He does more than feed a man, you see; he reforms you and builds you up; there isn't a better doctor alive. Just to show you what kind of man he is—he gives wonderful feasts, regular Thanksgiving dinners: he builds such skyscrapers of dishes that you have to stand on your couch to get anything off the top. But I haven't been there for quite a few days; I've been confined at home with my dear ones (I don't eat or buy anything but what is dear). But my army of dear ones is deserting, and I must go see him. [*Approaches door. Enter* MENAECHMUS I, *projected from doorway; the impulse evidently comes from his wife. He wears cloak under his pallium.*] But the door is opening. There's Menaechmus—he's coming out. [*Withdraws U. C.*]

MENAECHMUS I: [SONG]

> If you were not
>   Stubborn, bad,
> Stupid, and a
>   Little mad,
> What your husband hates, you'd see
> And behave accordingly.
> Mind your manners—do you hear—
> Or home you go to "father dear."—
> When I say I'm going out,
> You're on hand to ask about
> Where I'm going,
>   What to do,
> What's my business,
>   What's for you.
> I can't get out anywhere,

But you want me to declare
All I've done and all I do,
Customs officer—that's you!
I've handled you with too much care;
Listen what I'm going to do:
Food I give you,
    Maids, indeed,
Gold and dresses—
    All you need;
Now you'll keep your spying eyes
Off your husband, if you're wise.

And besides that, so you won't have your watching for nothing, I'm going to invite a courtesan out to dinner somewhere, to spite you. [*Looks back into house.*]

PENICULUS: [*aside*] The man pretends he's cursing his wife, but he's really cursing me. It's me that he hurts by dining out, not his wife.

MENAECHMUS I: Can you beat it? I've finally scolded my wife away from the door. [*to audience*] Where are you philandering husbands? Why don't you come up and congratulate me, and reward me for my brave fight? [*shows cloak*] I've just stolen this cloak from my wife inside, and I'm going to take it to my mistress. This is a fine way to cheat my clever watchdog. It's

An excellent job,
An honest job,
A gentleman's job,
A workmanlike job.

I stole it from that shrew at my expense, and it's going to be a total loss. [*indicating house of* EROTIUM] But I got the spoils from the enemy without losing a man.

PENICULUS: [*accosting him*] Here, sir, is any of that haul for me?

MENAECHMUS I: [*retreating left and covering his head with his cloak*] The game's up. I've fallen into a trap.

PENICULUS: O no, sir, into a body guard, rather; don't be afraid.

MENAECHMUS I: Who are you?

PENICULUS: It's me.

MENAECHMUS I: [*grasping his hand*] O, my period of light-heartedness, my psychological moment, good morning!

PENICULUS: Good morning.

MENAECHMUS I: What are you up to?

PENICULUS: Why, holding my friend-in-need by the hand.

MENAECHMUS I: You couldn't have met me at a better time.

PENICULUS: That's my way: I am an expert in fitting occasions.

MENAECHMUS I: Want to see a rich treat?

PENICULUS: What cook cooked it? I'll know if the pan slipped when I see the leavings.

MENAECHMUS I: Say, did you ever see the painting in the temple where the eagle steals Ganymede, or Venus Adonis?

PENICULUS: Plenty of times. But what's that got to do with me?

MENAECHMUS I: [*revealing cloak*] Well, look at me. Do I look like that picture?

PENICULUS: What's that rig?

MENAECHMUS I: Say that I'm a gallant soul.

PENICULUS: When do we eat?

MENAECHMUS I: Say what I tell you.

PENICULUS: [*listlessly*] All right; gallant soul.

MENAECHMUS I: Won't you add anything of your own?

PENICULUS: [*with a sigh*] Well, gay dog.

MENAECHMUS I: Go on, go on.

PENICULUS: I will not go on until I know what I'm going to get. You've had a squabble with your wife and so I've got to be careful.

MENAECHMUS I: Suppose we find a place where we can have a funeral without my wife's knowing it—and then burn up the day?

PENICULUS: [*enthusiastically*] Wonderful, but go on—how soon can I light the pyre? The day's already dead up to the waist.

MENAECHMUS I: You'll wait, if you're going to contradict me.

PENICULUS: Knock my eye out, Menaechmus, if I say anything you don't tell me to.

MENAECHMUS I: Move over here away from the door. [*Pulls* PENICULUS R., *and twirls him around.*]

PENICULUS: Yes.

MENAECHMUS I: [*cautiously*] Come farther away. [*Twirling him around again.*]

PENICULUS: All right.

MENAECHMUS I: Come boldly away from the lion's den. [*Twirling him a third time.*]

PENICULUS: See here, I have an idea you'd make a good charioteer.

MENAECHMUS I: Why?

PENICULUS: Because you're always looking around to see that your wife is not following you.

MENAECHMUS I: But what do you say—

PENICULUS: What do I say? Any thing you want, sir.

MENAECHMUS I: Can you make a good guess from the odor of something if you smell it?

PENICULUS: Why, if you got the board of augurs,—

MENAECHMUS I: [*interrupting*] Come on, smell this cloak I've got. [*holds up the hem of the cloak*] What does it smell of? [PENICULUS *sniffs and draws back*] Why do you hang back?

PENICULUS: You ought to smell the top of a woman's dress, because the smell here is unforgettable.

MENAECHMUS I: Then smell here, Peniculus. [*Holding up another part.*] How dainty you are!

PENICULUS: [*smelling cautiously*] It smells.

MENAECHMUS I: Of what? What does it smell of?

PENICULUS: [*triumphantly*] A theft, a courtesan, and luncheon! And you—

MENAECHMUS I: You've said it. Now I'm going to take this to the courtesan Erotium here, and I'll have lunch prepared for us three.

PENICULUS: Great!

MENAECHMUS I: And after that we'll drink till tomorrow's morning star.

PENICULUS: You've said a mouthful! Shall I knock now?

MENAECHMUS I: Yes. [PENICULUS *crosses, and standing with his back to* EROTIUM's *door, raises one leg to knock*] But wait a minute.

PENICULUS: You've held up the drinking a mile.

MENAECHMUS I: Knock gently.

PENICULUS: I think you're afraid the door is made of Samian ware.

[*Enter* EROTIUM *from her house. Music.*]

MENAECHMUS I: [*dragging* PENICULUS *to* C.] Wait, wait, please. She's coming out herself. See how the sun is blinded beside her body's splendor.

EROTIUM: Menaechmus, sweetheart, good morning.

PENICULUS: [*interrupting*] What about me?

EROTIUM: [*pushing* PENICULUS *away*] You don't count.

PENICULUS: That's what usually happens to the reserves in a regiment.

MENAECHMUS I: I'd like you to get ready for him and me today—a battle.

EROTIUM: So it shall be.

PENICULUS: [*pushing in*] Yes, and we'll drink in this battle, and the better fighter will be found by the bottle. You're at the head of the regiment, and you'll decide which of us shall spend the night with you.

MENAECHMUS I: [*pulling* PENICULUS *away from* EROTIUM] My heart's delight, how I hate my wife when I see you!

EROTIUM: [*spying the cloak*] Incidentally you can't keep from wearing her clothes. What's this? [*Examining the edge of the cloak.*]

MENAECHMUS I: Clothes for you from my wife, rosebud.

EROTIUM: You're an easy winner over every one of my other lovers. [*Crossing to her door and posing before it.*]

PENICULUS: [*aside*] The courtesan is flattering him now that she sees what he's stolen. [*looking towards* EROTIUM.] If you really loved him, you should have bitten his nose off with your kisses.

MENAECHMUS I: Take this, Peniculus. I want to make the offering I have vowed.

PENICULUS: Yes, [*holding* MENAECHMUS' *pallium*] but please, dance with that cloak on.

MENAECHMUS I: I dance? You must be mad.

PENICULUS: Either I or you. If you won't dance, take that thing off.

MENAECHMUS I: [*removing cloak*] I ran a great risk getting this.

PENICULUS: Yes, I think you ran a greater risk than Hercules when he stole the girdle of Hippolyta.

MENAECHMUS I: [*beckoning to* EROTIUM] Take this. [*He hands her the cloak.*] You are the only person who really understands me.

EROTIUM: That's the spirit that should inspire honest lovers.

PENICULUS: [*aside*] At least the ones that are on their way to the poorhouse.

MENAECHMUS I: [*taking cloak and holding it up*] I paid four minae for that last year for my wife. [*He teases* EROTIUM *by drawing away the cloak as she reaches for it, but finally hands it to her.*]

PENICULUS: [*aside*] Four minae gone up in smoke, as I foot up the account.

MENAECHMUS I: Do you know what I want you to do?

EROTIUM: Name it; I'll do anything you want.

MENAECHMUS I: Have a luncheon prepared for us at your house—

PENICULUS: [*Pushing him aside*; MENAECHMUS I *listens approvingly*.] And
dainties bought at the market:

> The son of a glandule of pork,
> > Or the son of a fattened ham,
> Or the jowl of a hog—
> > Some food of that sort,
> Which set on the table,
> Will tickle my palate
> And give me the gorge of a kite.

And hurry up.

EROTIUM: Very good.

MENAECHMUS I: We'll go on to the forum but we'll be back soon. We'll pass
the time when the lunch is being cooked in drinking.

EROTIUM: Come when you will. [*crossing to her door*] Things will be ready.

MENAECHMUS I: Hurry now. [*to* PENICULUS] You follow me.

PENICULUS: By Hercules, I'll watch over you and follow you, and I wouldn't
take the wealth of heaven if I had to lose you. [*Exeunt* MENAECHMUS
and PENICULUS *at his heels, L.*]

EROTIUM [*calling inside*]: Call out my cook Culindrus in there at once. [*Enter
CULINDRUS.*] Take a basket [*Exit* CULINDRUS, *who returns immediately with
a market basket*] and some money. [*giving him coins*] There's three
nummi.

CULINDRUS: Yes.

EROTIUM: Go and get some provisions, enough for three people—not too little,
and not too much.

CULINDRUS: What sort of men will they be?

EROTIUM: I and Menaechmus and his parasite.

CULINDRUS: There's ten already, because a parasite easily does the work of eight
men.

EROTIUM: I've told you the guests. You take care of the rest.

CULINDRUS: Yes indeed. [*running off, L.*] Everything's cooked. Tell them dinner
is served.

EROTIUM: Hurry back. [*Exit into her house.*]

CULINDRUS: I'm back already. [*Exit, L.*]

ACT II

[*Enter* MENAECHMUS II, R., *and his slave* MESSENIO *carrying a bag,
followed at a distance by sailors with baggage. Sailors cross to extreme
L., where they deposit baggage and loll.*]

MENAECHMUS II: I think, Messenio, that there is no greater joy for sea travellers
than sighting the distant land while still far out at sea.

MESSENIO: Frankly, it's a greater pleasure if it is your native land you're coming
to. But, pray, why is it that we have now come to Epidamnus? Are we to
be like the ocean, and go round all the islands?

MENAECHMUS II: [*sadly*] We are searching for my twin brother.

MESSENIO: Is there never to be an end to this search? This is the sixth year that we have spent on it: we have knocked about Histria, Spain, Massilia, Illyria, the whole Adriatic, all the Italian coast—every place that the sea touches; if you had been hunting a needle you'd have found it long ago, if there had been one. We're trying to find a dead man among the living; for if he were alive, we should have found him long ago.

MENAECHMUS II: Then, if you please, I am looking for some one who says he knows my brother is dead. Assured of this, I shall seek no further. But otherwise I shall never give up the search as long as I live; I know how dear he is to my heart.

MESSENIO: You might as well try to find a knot in a bulrush. Let's leave this place and go home.—Or are we, perhaps, going to write a book of travels?

MENAECHMUS II: [*angrily*] You had better stop making these witty remarks, unless you want to get into trouble. Don't provoke me; I am not carrying on this affair to suit you.

MESSENIO: [*aside*] Hey, now! That remark puts me in my place; he couldn't have put it more neatly and completely! But just the same I can't help talking. [*aloud*] Harkee, Menaechmus: when I look into the purse, it seems as though we were lightly clad for a summer journey! By heaven, if you don't go back home now, you'll be searching for that blessed brother of yours without a penny to bless *yourself* with. For Epidamnus is full of rakes and tremendous drinkers; a tremendous lot of swindlers and spongers live here, and their courtesans are called the most seductive in the whole world. That's why the place is called Epidamnus: scarcely anybody can come here without getting damned.

MENAECHMUS II: I'll be on my guard against that; just hand the purse over to me.

MESSENIO: What do you want with it?

MENAECHMUS II: I am worried about you, from what you have said.

MESSENIO: And why?

MENAECHMUS II: I am afraid you might get me damned in Epidamnus. You are very fond of the ladies, Messenio, and I am an irascible man of the most unmanageable disposition; with the money in my possession I shall be able to protect you doubly, both from any mishap and also from my anger.

MESSENIO: [*hands him purse*] Take it and keep it; I'm agreeable. [*Enter* CULINDRUS, *the cook, L., with his market basket of provisions.*]

CULINDRUS: [*to audience*] I have done a good job of marketing—just what I like myself! I'll set a fine lunch before the company.—Glory, there I see Menaechmus. Woe to my back! Here are the guests walking about at the door before I am back with the provisions. I'll go and speak to him. [*to* MENAECHMUS II] Good day, Menaechmus.

MENAECHMUS II: The lord love you, whoever you are. [*to* MESSENIO] This fellow seems to know my name. Do you know who he is?

MESSENIO: Not I, by heaven.

CULINDRUS: Where are the other guests?

MENAECHMUS II: What guests?

CULINDRUS: Why, your parasite.

MENAECHMUS II: My parasite? [*to* MESSENIO] Why, the man is mad.

MESSENIO: [*to* MENAECHMUS II] Didn't I tell you this place was full of swin
dlers?

MENAECHMUS II: What parasite of mine are you looking for, young man?

CULINDRUS: 'Sponge.'

MESSENIO: Nonsense, I have the sponge safe in the bag.

CULINDRUS: [*paying no attention to him*] You come too early for lunch
Menaechmus; I've just got back from the marketing.

MENAECHMUS II: [*gently*] Young man, tell me: what is the price of pigs i
this town—unblemished ones, for sacrifice?

CULINDRUS: [*puzzled*] A drachma each.

MENAECHMUS II: Well, I'll give you a drachma; [*holds it out, but takes i
back*] go get yourself purified of your insanity at my expense. For really
you must be perfectly mad, to be bothering a perfect stranger like me,—
whoever you are.

CULINDRUS: I am Culindrus. Don't you know my name?

MENAECHMUS II: The devil take you, whether your name is Cylinder or Col
lander; I don't know you and I don't want to.

CULINDRUS: Your name is Menaechmus, I am sure of that much.

MENAECHMUS II: Now you're talking sense, since you call me by my righ
name. But where have you known me?

CULINDRUS: Where have I known *you*, who keep my mistress Erotium as you
lady?

MENAECHMUS II: By heaven, I keep no such person, and I don't know you
either.

CULINDRUS: You don't know me, who have so often filled your cup for yo
here, when you have been drinking?

MESSENIO: O miserable me, not to have anything to break this fellow's hea
with!

MENAECHMUS II: You used to be cup-bearer for me, who have never befor
today been in Epidamnus or even seen it?

CULINDRUS: You deny it?

MENAECHMUS II: By heaven, I most certainly do deny it.

CULINDRUS: Don't you live in that house over there?

MENAECHMUS II: May the devil fly away with those that do!

CULINDRUS: [*aside*] Why, then, this man is mad too, calling the devil on hi
own head. [*aloud*] Harkee, Menaechmus.

MENAECHMUS II: Well, what do you want?

CULINDRUS: If you should ask me, I should advise you to take that drachm
you promised me a minute ago and get a pig for yourself, because you ar
most certainly mad if you bedevil yourself this way.

MENAECHMUS II: Gad, what a chatterer this man is; he makes me tired.

CULINDRUS: [*to audience*] He often jokes with me like this. How droll he is
so long as his wife is not about! [*to* MENAECHMUS II, *showing his baske
of provisions*] What do you say to that?

MENAECHMUS II: What do you want now, you good for nothing?

CULINDRUS: Is what you see here enough provision for the three of you, or should I go buy some more for yourself, the parasite, and the lady?

MENAECHMUS II: What ladies, what parasites are you talking about?

MESSENIO: What's the matter with you? Why are you badgering the gentleman?

CULINDRUS: [to MESSENIO] What business is it of yours? I never saw you before. I am just having a talk with this gentleman, whom I know.

MENAECHMUS II: By the lord, you're no sane man, I'm sure of that.

CULINDRUS: These things shall be cooked, I promise you, and without delay. [crossing to EROTIUM's door] Don't go too far from the house! Do you wish anything more?

MENAECHMUS II: Yes. I wish you to go utterly and completely to the devil!

CULINDRUS: It would be better if you were to go—inside and take your place at table while I [grandly] am exposing these morsels to the violence of Vulcan! I'll go in and tell Erotium that you are out here, so that she can bring you in instead of your having to cool your heels outside. [Exit into house.]

MENAECHMUS II: Has he gone away? He has. Oh, Messenio, I see that your warning was far from being false.

MESSENIO: Yes, but watch out; I am sure that a courtesan lives here, just as that madman said who just went away.

MENAECHMUS II: All the same, I wonder how he knew my name.

MESSENIO: Nothing strange in that; it's just a way these courtesans have. They send their serving-boys and serving-girls down to the harbor; if a foreign ship comes in, they ask where it comes from and what the owner's name is, and then they immediately glue themselves to him. If he is taken in by them, he is sent home a ruined man. [grandly] Now in the harbor there [pointing to EROTIUM's house] rides a pirate craft, of which we must be wary.

MENAECHMUS II: By heaven, that is good advice.

MESSENIO: I'll soon know how good it is, if you'll only take it.

MENAECHMUS II: Be quiet a minute; I heard the door creak. Let's see who comes out.

MESSENIO: I'll set this bag down, then. [to sailors] Keep a sharp eye on those bundles, you toilers of the sea!

[Enter EROTIUM from her house.]

EROTIUM: [SONG]—[to slaves within]
　　Go in, and do not close the door,
　　　　I want it left just so.
　　See what there is to do inside
　　　　And do it all—now go.
The couches must be spread, and perfumes burned:
Neatness entices lovers, I have learned.
Splendor to lovers' loss, to our gain is turned. [coming forward and looking about her]
But where is the man they said was before my door? [catching sight of MENAECHMUS II] Ah, there he is: he's been of use before,

Yet is, as he deserves, my governor.
I'll go and speak to him myself.—My dear,
I am amazed to see you standing here;
Less wide your door than mine when you appear.
    Now all you ordered is prepared,
        The doors are opened wide,
    Your lunch is cooked, and when you like,
        Come take your place inside.

MENAECHMUS II: [*to* MESSENIO] Whom is this woman talking to?

ROTIUM: [*surprised*] Why, to whom but yourself?

MENAECHMUS II: What have you had to do with me, now or ever? Why d
you speak to me?

EROTIUM: Because, in truth, it is the will of Love that I should exalt you c
all others, and not beyond your desert, for it is you alone who make n
flourish, by your kindness.

MENAECHMUS II: [*aside to* MESSENIO] Surely this woman is either insane c
drunk, Messenio, to address an unknown man like me so familiarly.

MESSENIO: Didn't I tell you that was the way here? Why, these are just fallin
leaves compared to what will happen if we stay here a couple of day
more: then it will be trees falling on you. All the courtesans here are ju:
wheedlers of money. But let me speak to her a bit. [*to* EROTIUM, *who
looking into her house*] Harkee, my lady, I'm speaking to you.

EROTIUM: What is it?

MESSENIO: [*escaping her advances*] Where have you known this gentlema
before?

EROTIUM: In the same place where he has known me for this long time, i
Epidamnus.

MESSENIO: [*sarcastically*] In Epidamnus! A man who before this day has neve
set foot in the place?

EROTIUM: Ha, ha, you are joking.—Menaechmus, why don't you be a dear an
come in? It will be nicer for you there.

MENAECHMUS II: [*aside to* MESSENIO] Great Scott, the woman has called me b
my own name! I'd like very much to know the meaning of it all.

MESSENIO: She has got scent of that purse you have there.

MENAECHMUS II: That's a sound warning. Here, take it [*gives him purse*]; I'
soon find out which she loves better, me or my purse.

EROTIUM: [*attempting to draw* MENAECHMUS II *into her house*] Let us go in
side to lunch.

MENAECHMUS II: You are very kind, but [*backing away*] no, thank you.

EROTIUM: But then why did you tell me just a little while ago to prepare
lunch for you?

MENAECHMUS II: *I* told you to prepare a lunch?

EROTIUM: Why of course, for you and your parasite.

MENAECHMUS II: Plague take it, what parasite? [*to* MESSENIO] Certainly thi
woman is not quite sane.

EROTIUM: 'Sponge.'

MENAECHMUS II: What is this sponge you all keep talking about? The kind you rub your shoes with?

EROTIUM: The one who came here with you a little while ago when you brought me the cloak you had stolen from your wife.

MENAECHMUS II: What? I gave you a cloak that I had stolen from my wife? Are you in your right senses? [to MESSENIO] Why, this woman dreams standing up, like a horse.

EROTIUM: Why do you enjoy making fun of me and denying what you have done?

MENAECHMUS II: Tell me what I have done, that I deny.

EROTIUM: That you gave me your wife's cloak today.

MENAECHMUS II: [angrily] I still deny it. I haven't a wife, never had one, and I have never in my life set foot in this place before. I had breakfast on board my ship, and from there I came by here and met you.

EROTIUM: Alack, I am a lost woman! What ship?

MENAECHUM II: [grandiloquently] A wooden one is she, often bruised and often busted, often smitten with sledge; like the furrier's furniture,—peg is paired with peg.

EROTIUM: Oh, my love, stop this joking and come inside with me at once.

MENAECHMUS II: [beginning to weaken] But, madam, you are looking for some other man, not me.

EROTIUM: Don't I know you,—Menaechmus, son of Moschus, who was born in Sicily, the story goes, at Syracuse where King Agathocles reigned, and after him Pintia, and then Liparo, who at his death left the kingdom to Hiero, who now is king?

MENAECHUM II: What you say is quite true.

MESSENIO: By heaven, the woman isn't from there herself, is she, to know you so well?

MENAECHMUS II: [capitulating] I don't think I can refuse. [Moves toward EROTIUM's house.]

MESSENIO: [seizing his arm] You are a lost man if you cross that threshold.

MENAECHMUS II: Be quiet. The affair goes well. I shall assent to anything she says, so long as it means entertainment. [confidentially to EROTIUM] I have been contradicting you for a purpose: I was afraid that this fellow might tell my wife about the cloak and the breakfast. Now, whenever you please, let us go indoors.

EROTIUM: Are you going to wait for the parasite any longer?

MENAECHMUS II: Certainly not. I don't care a straw about him, and if he comes, I don't want to have him let in.

EROTIUM: Goodness, that's quite agreeable to me.—But do you know what I should like to have you do for me?

MENAECHMUS II: Command me.

EROTIUM: I wish you would take that cloak you gave me just now to the embroiderer's to be repaired, and get them to add some new trimming that I want.

MENAECHMUS II: [scenting booty] By heaven, that's a good idea. It shall be so disguised that my wife wouldn't recognise it if she saw you wearing it in the street.

EROTIUM: You can take it with you presently, when you go.

MENAECHMUS II: Yes, certainly.

EROTIUM: Let us go inside.

MENAECHMUS II: I'll follow you; I just want to speak to this fellow. [*Exit* EROTIUM *into the house.* MENAECHMUS II *crosses* MESSENIO *to bag, R.*] Hi there, Messenio, come here.

MESSENIO: What for?

MENAECHMUS II: Pick up that bag.

MESSENIO: What for?

MENAECHMUS II: Never mind what for. [*shamefacedly*] I know what you are going to call me.

MESSENIO: So much the worse.

MENAECHMUS II: Hold your accursed tongue, you knave. I have the booty practically in my hands, such a siegework I have begun! You go as quickly as you can and take these porters immediately to an inn; then do you be sure to come back for me before sundown. [*Crosses to* EROTIUM's *door.*]

MESSENIO: Master, you don't know what these courtesans are!

MENAECHMUS II: Be quiet, I tell you, and go. It is my loss, not yours, if I do anything foolish. This woman is silly and inexperienced; and as far as I can judge, there is plunder for us here. [*Exit into* EROTIUM's *house.*]

MESSENIO: I am lost! Are you going? He is surely lost too. The pirate craft is leading the yacht straight to destruction. But I'm a fool to expect to rule my master. He brought me to obey, not to give him orders. [*to sailors*] You, follow me, so that I can come back in time to meet my master, as he ordered. [*Exeunt.*]

[*Enter* PENICULUS, *exasperated.*]

PENICULUS: More than thirty years old I am, but in all that time I have never done anything more mischievous or evil than I did to-day when, miserable me, I pushed into the middle of the assembly. While I stood there gaping, Menaechmus sneaked off from me and went away to see his lady friend, I suppose, and didn't want to take me.—May the devil take the men who invented the scurvy practice of holding assemblies to take up the time of busy men! Wouldn't it be better, now, to pick on unengaged people for that, and if they didn't appear when the roll was called, let *them* pay the fine on the spot? There are plenty of men who eat only once a day, who have nothing to do, who are never invited out to dine or give a dinner themselves; that's the sort of people who should have the job of sitting in the assembly and the law courts. If things were run that way, I shouldn't have missed my breakfast to-day; on my life, he was willing enough to give it to me.—I'll just go anyhow. I may still get some scraps, and the hope whets my appetite. [*Door opens, revealing* MENAECHMUS II *very drunk, with a garland on his head and wearing the cloak.*] But what's this? Menaechmus coming out of the house with a garland on? The dinner's over; I've just come in time to fetch him away, egad! I'll see what he's about, and then I'll go speak to him. [*Withdraws.*]

MENAECHMUS II: [*to* EROTIUM *within*] It will be so changed that you won't recognize it.

PENICULUS: [*to audience*] He is taking the mantle to an embroiderer's; the breakfast's eaten, the wine drunk, and the parasite shut outside. By heaven, I'll revenge myself handsomely for this trick, or my name's not Peniculus. Just watch how you'll catch it!

MENAECHMUS II: [*not seeing* PENICULUS] Ye gods! to whom did you ever in one day give more blessings, beyond all expectation? I've wined and dined with a courtesan, I've got me this [*indicating the cloak*], and she'll never have it again.

PENICULUS: [*aside*] From my hiding place I can't hear what he says. Now that he is full of dinner he is talking about me and my share.

MENAECHMUS II: [*still not noticing* PENICULUS] She says I stole this cloak from my wife and gave it to her. As soon as I saw she was mistaken, I began to assent, as though there had been something between us; whatever she said, I said too. Why waste words?—I have never had a better time at less expense.

PENICULUS: I'll go up to him. I'm just aching for a row.

MENAECHMUS II: Who is this coming towards me?

PENICULUS: [*violently*] What's that you say, you fellow lighter than a feather, you villain, you knave, you disgrace of humanity, you trickster, you cheap clown? What have I done to deserve ill of you? Sneak away from me in the forum a while ago and celebrate the funeral of the breakfast in my absence, would you? How did you dare do that, when I was entitled to it just as much as you were?

MENAECHMUS II: I beg you, young man, what have you to do with me, that you should ignorantly berate a stranger this way? Do you want to get a whipping for your insolence?

PENICULUS: Ha! you've given me that already.

MENAECHMUS II: Answer me, young man. What is your name?

PENICULUS: Are you mocking me too, pretending not to know my name?

MENAECHMUS II: As far as I can tell, I have never either seen or known you before this day. But, whoever you are, if you behave decently, we may get on together.

PENICULUS: You don't know me?

MENAECHMUS II: If I did, I should not deny it.

PENICULUS: Menaechmus, wake up! [*shakes him*]

MENAECHMUS II: By heaven, I *am* awake, I should think.

PENICULUS: Don't you know your own parasite?

MENAECHMUS II: I see that your head isn't sound, young man.

PENICULUS: Answer me: Did you not filch that cloak today from your wife and give it to Erotium?

MENAECHMUS II: Good Lord, I haven't any wife, I didn't give any mantle to Erotium, and I never stole it!

PENICULUS: Are *you* sane? [*aside*] This affair is done for. [*to* MENAECHMUS] Didn't I see you come out of that house with a woman's cloak on?

MENAECHMUS II:[*angry*] Plague take you! Do you think that everybody is an effeminate rogue simply because you are one? You declare that I had on a woman's cloak?

PENICULUS: I certainly do.

MENAECHMUS II: Go to the devil where you belong, or get yourself purified, you utter madman.

PENICULUS: [*furious*] By heaven, no one shall persuade me not to tell this whole affair, just as it happened, to your wife at once. All your abuse will fall back on your own head. I'll make you pay for hogging that breakfast. [*Exit into house of* MENAECHMUS I.]

MENAECHMUS II: What sort of a business is this? Is everybody going to make fun of me this way as soon as I meet them?—But I heard the door creak. [*Enter a servant-girl from house of* EROTIUM, *with a bracelet in her hand.*]

MAID: Menaechmus, Erotium says she would love to have you take this bracelet along to the goldsmith's and have an ounce of gold added and have it done over.

MENAECHMUS II: I promise to take care of this and anything else she wants attended to, anything at all. [*Takes it.*]

MAID: Do you know what bracelet this is?

MENAECHMUS II: Only that it's a gold one.

MAID: It is the one which you said you once stole from your wife's cupboard on the sly.

MENAECHMUS II: By all that's holy, I never did!

MAID: Don't you remember, pray? Give it back if you don't. [*Reaches for it.*]

MENAECHMUS II: [*keeping it out of reach*] Wait a moment. I do indeed remember it. [*lamely*] Why, it's the — one I gave her.

MAID: The very same.

MENAECHMUS II: Where are the armlets I gave her along with it?

MAID: You never gave her any.

MENAECHMUS II: I certainly did, along with the bracelet.

MAID: I'll say you will look after it?

MENAECHMUS I: Do. It shall be taken care of. I'll see that it's brought back — as soon as the cloak.

MAID: [*coaxingly*] Menaechmus, I'd love to have you give me some earrings. Have them made to weigh two drachmas each! Then I'd be glad to see you when you come here.

MENAECHMUS II: Certainly! Give me the gold, and I'll pay for working.

MAID: Oh, please, *you* give the gold. I'll repay you later.

MENAECHMUS II: No, you give it. Later I'll repay you double!

MAID: I haven't any.

MENAECHMUS II: [*no longer interested*] Well, when you get some, you can give it to me then.

MAID: [*turning to go*] Is there anything else, please? [*Exit.*]

MENAECHMUS II: Say I will take good care to sell these things for what they will bring! Has she gone inside? [*examines door to make sure*] Yes; the door is shut. The gods certainly aid me, prosper me, and love me. But why do I linger when now is the time and the chance to escape from these courtesan liars? Hasten, Menaechmus! Right foot forward, march! [*starts reeling off stage*] I'll take off this garland and throw it away over to the left [*throws it beyond house of* MENAECHMUS I], and then if they follow me they'll think I went that way. I'm off to find my slave, if I can, to tell himself about the blessings that the gods are sending me.

    [*Exit, R.*]

ACT III

    [*Enter* WIFE *from house of* MENAECHMUS I, *followed by* PENICULUS.]

WIFE: [*coming C.*] How can I put up with married life when my husband sneaks out of the house with anything he can lay his hands on and carries it off to his mistress?

PENICULUS: Keep quiet a minute. You'll catch him in the act — I'll warrant you that. Come here a minute. He was wearing a wreath, he was reeling drunk, he was taking the cloak he stole from you today to the dyers'. [*seeing wreath*] But look, here's the wreath he had on. Now am I a liar? See, this is the way he went, if you want to hunt him down. [*Looking off L. Enter* MENAECHMUS I, L.] For heaven's sake, there's the fellow himself coming back. What a piece of luck! But he hasn't got the cloak with him.

WIFE: What'll I do to him?

PENICULUS: The same as usual — treat him rough.

WIFE: All right.

PENICULUS: Let's step aside and catch him from ambush. [*Drawing her back between houses. Pantomine during* MENAECHMUS I's *song: they listen in vain for something that will betray him.* WIFE *gives up in disgust, and exit haughtily.* PENICULUS *sits dejected.* WIFE *returns in time to hear* MENAECHMUS I *tell of stealing of cloak.*]

MENAECHMUS I: [SONG]

It's very silly fashion and an awful nuisance, too,
That all of us obey, especially the titled few.
We want a lot of hangers-on — who may be good or bad:
Reputation doesn't matter when there's money to be had.
You may be poor and honest — as a fool you're sent away;
But if you're rich and wicked, you're a worthy protégé.
The lawless man, who when he's trusted with a thing, will swear
He never saw it — that's the man for whom we patrons care —
The contentious man, the trickster, who by means of perjury
Or bribes supports a life of law-suits, greed, and luxury.
But the patron has no holiday when law-days are decreed;
He must defend the guilty man and see that he is freed.
In just this way was I detained today by some poor sinner,
And now I've missed my mistress, to say nothing of the dinner.
I spoke before the aediles to allay their just suspicions,
And proposed a set of intricate and tortuous conditions,
Which, if we could have proved them, would have surely won the case.
But then this brainless fellow brought a bondsman to the place!

I'm sure I never saw a man more clearly caught than he:
Three witnesses were there, who swore to all his deviltry.
May heaven destroy the man who's made a ruin so complete
Of all my day — and me, who in the law-courts set my feet!
As soon as it was possible, I came directly here.
I've ordered lunch; I know she's waiting for me; yet I fear —
> She's mad at me now;
>> But the cloak ought to move her,
>> That I stole from my wife,
>> And took to my lover.

PENICULUS: [*aside to wife*] What do you say to that?

WIFE: I'm blessed with a bad marriage and a bad husband.

PENICULUS: Can you hear what he's saying all right?

WIFE: I should say I could.

MENAECHMUS I: Now the best thing for me to do is to go in here, [*starting towards* EROTIUM's *door*] where I can have a good time.

PENICULUS: [*Suddenly blocking his way;* WIFE *steps forward on other side.*] Wait a minute; there's a bad time coming first.

MENAECHMUS I: [*to audience*] Who's this? What do I see? My wife and my parasite standing together in front of my house? She doesn't seem to be in good humor; I don't like it. I'll go up and speak to her, though. [*approaching* WIFE] Tell me, my dear, what's wrong with you?

PENICULUS: Soft soap!

MENAECHMUS I: [*pushing* PENICULUS *away*] Stop making a nuisance of yourself. Am I talking to you? [*He goes to* WIFE *and attempts to fondle her.*]

WIFE: [*resisting*] Take away your arm; cut out your pawing!

PENICULUS: Keep at him, madam!

MENAECHMUS I: Why are you so disagreeable to me?

WIFE: You ought to know.

PENICULUS: He does, the villain, but he's making out he doesn't.

MENAECHMUS I: Has one of the slaves been cutting up? Have the maids or menservants answered you back? Tell me; they'll be punished.

WIFE: Nonsense!

MENAECHMUS I: You must be angry with one of the servants.

WIFE: Nonsense!

MENAECHMUS I: Well, are you angry with me?

WIFE: Now that is not nonsense.

MENAECHMUS I: What the deuce! I haven't done anything.

WIFE: There you are — back where you started. Nonsense!

MENAECHMUS I: What is the trouble, wife?

WIFE: A fine question to ask me!

MENAECHMUS I: Do you want me to ask *him*, then? What's the trouble?

WIFE: [*emphatically*] A cloak.

MENAECHMUS I: [*taken aback*] A cloak? What about a cloak?

PENICULUS: What are you trembling for?

MENAECHMUS I: I'm not trembling —

PENICULUS: Except for one thing: the cloak's no joke. You won't sneak away from me again and eat dinner! [*to* WIFE] Go at the fellow!

MENAECHMUS I: Will you shut up?

PENICULUS: No, by George, I will not shut up. [*tattling to* WIFE] He's shaking his head at me to keep me from talking.

MENAECHMUS I: I am not, or winking either.

PENICULUS: That beats all: he says he's not doing a thing when you can see he's doing it.

MENAECHMUS I: [*loudly invoking*] By Jupiter and all the gods — is that enough for you, my dear? — I swear I did not shake my head at him.

PENICULUS: She'll believe that of you; get back to business.

MENAECHMUS I: What business?

PENICULUS: Oh, the dyers', I suppose. Come on now, give the cloak back.

MENAECHMUS I: What cloak are you talking about?

PENICULUS: I give up, if he can't remember his own affairs.

WIFE: So you thought you could get away with all this underhand business and me not know it, did you? You'll pay interest on what you stole, I'm sure of that. Take that! [*Slapping him down.*]

PENICULUS: [*echoing the triumph*] Take that! Now will you go and eat dinner behind my back? Now will you come out drunk and make fun of me in front of the house with a garland on your head?

MENAECHMUS I: I haven't had dinner or set foot in that house to-day.

PFNICULUS: Do you mean to say that?

MENAECHMUS I: I guess I do!

PENICULUS: This fellow takes the cake! Didn't I see you standing here in front of the door just now, wearing a garland, and you said I was crazy and you didn't know me, and you insisted you were a foreigner?

MENAECHMUS I: Listen here, since I left you, this is the first time I've been home.

PENICULUS: Oh, I know you. You thought I didn't have any way of getting even with you. Now I've told everything to your wife.

MENAECHMUS I: What did you tell her?

PENICULUS: I don't know; ask her.

MENAECHMUS I: [*crossing to* WIFE] What is it, my dear? What stories has he been telling you? What is it? Why don't you say something? Why don't you tell me what it is?

WIFE: As if you didn't know! Oh dear, I am an unlucky woman!

MENAECHMUS I: Why unlucky? Explain yourself.

WIFE: What a thing for you to ask me!

MENAECHMUS I: Well, I wouldn't ask you if I knew, would I?

PENICULUS: What a man! Look how he makes believe. You can't hide it; she knows all about it. I told her everything.

MENAECHMUS I: What is it?

WIFE: Well, if you aren't ashamed and won't own up yourself, listen to me and keep your ears open. A cloak has been stolen from me out of the house.

MENAECHMUS I: A cloak stolen from me?

PENICULUS: See how the fellow is trying to catch you. It was stolen from her, not from you. If it had been stolen from you, it would be safe now.

MENAECHMUS I: [*pushing* PENICULUS *aside*] I'm not doing business with you. [*to* WIFE] What is it you're saying, madam?

WIFE: A cloak has disappeared from the house, I tell you.

MENAECHMUS I: Who stole it?

WIFE: I suppose the man that took it knows that.

MENAECHMUS I: Who is this man?

WIFE: A certain Menaechmus.

MENAECHMUS I: A rotten thing to do! But what Menaechmus do you mean? [*searching the stage*]

WIFE: You, I say!

MENAECHMUS I: Me?

WIFE: Yes, you, you!

MENAECHMUS I: Who accuses me?

WIFE: I do.

PENICULUS: I do, too; and you took the cloak over here to your mistress Erotium's.

MENAECHMUS I: What? I gave it to her?

WIFE: Yes, you — you [*like an owl*], I say!

PENICULUS: Do you want me to go and get an owl to say, "You, you!" to you? [*mocking her*] You see, we're tired of saying it.

MENAECHMUS I: By Jupiter and all the gods — is that enough for you, my dear? — I swear I didn't give —

PENICULUS: And we swear we're telling nothing but the truth.

MENAECHMUS I: But I didn't give it to her; I only lent it.

WIFE: Maybe you did, but I don't ever lend your dress-suit or your top-coat to anybody. [*By degrees she drives* MENAECHMUS I *and incidentally* PENICULUS, *R.*] It's the wife's business to lend her clothes, and the husband's to lend his. Now go and bring that cloak back home.

MENAECHMUS I: I'll see it's brought home.

WIFE: Well, you'd better, because you won't get into my house again unless you bring that cloak with you. [*marching to her door*] I'm going home.

PENICULUS: [*following* WIFE] What's to become of me after taking so much trouble for you?

WIFE: The trouble will be repaid when something is stolen from your house. [*Exit into house.*]

PENICULUS: That'll never be, because I haven't got anything at home to lose. Curse the husband and the wife, too! I'll go down to town; I can see I'm through with this family. [*Exit, L.*]

MENAECHMUS I: [*runs to door, peeks in, then turns laughing to audience*] My wife thinks she's punished me by shutting me out — as if I didn't have a better place where they'll let me in. If you don't like me, you've got to put up with me; Erotium here likes me. She won't shut me out from her: she'll shut me in *with* her. Well, I'll go and ask her to give me back the cloak I gave her this morning. I'll buy her a better one. [*knocking at* EROTIUM's *door*] Here, where's the doorman? Open up, and call Erotium out, somebody.

[*Enter* EROTIUM *from her house.*]

EROTIUM: Who wants me?

MENAECHMUS I: A greater enemy to himself than to your tender years.

EROTIUM: Menaechmus, my love, why do you stand out there? Come in.

MENAECHMUS I: By and by. Do you know why I've come to see you?

EROTIUM: Of course: to enjoy yourself with me.

MENAECHMUS I: No, it's that cloak I gave you a little while ago: give it back to me, that's a dear. My wife has found out about the whole thing. I'll buy you any cloak you want, worth twice as much.

EROTIUM: Why, I just gave it to you to take to the dyer's, and the bracelet, too, to take to the jeweler's to be done over.

MENAECHMUS I: You gave me the cloak and the bracelet? How could you, when I've just got back and seen you for the first time since I gave it to you and went to town?

EROTIUM: Oh, I get your idea. You're trying to cheat me out of what I let you take.

MENAECHMUS I: No, no, I don't want the cloak to cheat you; I tell you, my wife's found out about it.

EROTIUM: [*with mounting fury*] No, no, I didn't go out of my way to ask you to give it to me in the first place. You brought it to me yourself, and you gave it to me for a present. Now you want it back. All right. Have it. Take the old thing. Wear it yourself, or let your wife wear it, or lock it up in your trunk if you want to. After this you won't set foot inside this house again, you trifler with the affections of an innocent woman. [*changing her mood momentarily*] Unless you bring me money, you haven't got a chance. Go and find some other poor girl you can deceive. [*Exit into her house, slamming door.*]

MENAECHMUS I: By George, her temper's up! [*rushing to her door*] Here, woman, stop, say! Come back! Won't you wait? Won't you please come back for my sake? She's gone and closed the door. Now I'm the shut-outenest of men! They don't believe me at home or at my mistress's. I'll have to go and see what my friends advise me to do. [*Exit, L.*]

ACT IV

[*Enter* MENAECHMUS SOSICLES, *R.*]

MENAECHMUS II: That was a foolish thing I did a while ago when I handed over my purse and money to Messenio. He has got himself into a chop-house somewhere, I suppose.

[*Enter* WIFE, *from her house.*]

WIFE: I'll watch and see how soon my husband will get home. Ah ha, there he is. I'm saved! He is bringing back the cloak

MENAECHMUS II: [*to himself*] I wonder where Messenio can be rambling now.

WIFE: I'll go up to the fellow and welcome him as he deserves. [*to* MENAECHMUS II] You scoundrel, aren't you ashamed to come into my sight with that garment?

MENAECHMUS II: [*surprised*] What's this? What is troubling you, madam?

WIFE: You shameless wretch, do you dare say a single word to me? Do you dare to speak?

MENAECHMUS II: Pray, what have I done, that I shouldn't dare to speak to you?

WIFE: You ask me? Oh, the shameless impudence of the man!

MENAECHMUS II: [*mockingly*] I suppose you know, madam, why it was that the Greeks used to call Hecuba a bitch?

WIFE: No. I do *not*.

MENAECHMUS II: Because Hecuba used to act just the way you do now: she used to heap abuse on everybody that she saw. That's how she got to be called a bitch, and she deserved it, too.

WIFE: It's impossible to put up with such outrages. I'd rather be husbandless all my life than stand for such outrages!

MENAECHMUS II: Is it any of *my* business whether you can put up with the state of marriage or whether you are going to leave your husband? Or is it the custom here to babble to perfect strangers?

WIFE: Babble, you say? I swear I'll remain married not an instant longer — to put up with your ways!

MENAECHMUS II: For all of me, by heaven, you can be a widow as long as Jove sits on his throne.

WIFE: For that, by goodness, I'll call my father and tell him about your outrages. [*calls within the house to* SLAVE, *who comes at once*] Here, Decio, go find my father, and ask him to come with you to me. [SLAVE *runs off L.*] Tell him it's absolutely necessary. [*to* MENAECHMUS II] I'll tell him of all your outrages!

MENAECHMUS II: Are you mad? What outrages? [*mocking her*]

WIFE: You steal cloaks and money from your wife and take them to your mistress. Is that straight enough?

MENAECHMUS II: [*applauding*] Bravo, woman! You certainly are a bad one, and a bold one, too! Do you dare say that I stole this when I got it from another woman, who wanted me to have it repaired?

WIFE: A few minutes ago you didn't deny stealing it; and are you going to hold it now before my very eyes? Aren't you ashamed?

MENAECHMUS II: I beg of you, woman, tell me, if you can, what potion I can drink that will make me able to put up with your bad humor. I don't know whom you take me for. As for you, I don't know you any more than I know the man in the moon.

WIFE: You may make fun of me, but you won't be able to make fun of my father. He's coming now. [*pointing off L., where* FATHER *appears hobbling towards them*] Back there. Do you know *him*?

MENAECHMUS II: [*facetiously*] Yes, I knew him when I knew Methuselah. I met him the same day I met you.

WIFE: You deny that you know me? that you know my father?

MENAECHMUS II: Yes, and your grandfather too, if you want to lug *him* in. [*Stalks to extreme R.*]

WIFE: By heaven, that's the way you always are about everything.

[*Enter* FATHER.]

FATHER: [SONG]

    I'm getting along just as fast as my age will permit and this business requires.

But if some of you say that that's easy for me — very briefly I'll show that
    you're liars:
My body's a burden, my nimbleness gone, and of strength I've a notable
    lack,
I am quite overgrown with my years — oh, confounded old age is a curse
    on the back!
Why, if I were to tell all the terrible evils that age, when it comes, brings
    along,
I'm certain as certain can be that past suitable limits I'd lengthen this
    song.

However my mind is a little disturbed at this thing, for it seems a bit
    queer
That my daughter should suddenly send to my house with directions for
    me to come here.
And how the affair is related to me, she has not let me know up to now;
But I'm a good guesser, and feel pretty sure that her husband and she've
    had a row.
That's what usually happens when men are enslaved by their wives and
    must come when they call;
And then it's the wives who are mostly to blame, while the husbands
    aren't guilty at all.

And yet there are bounds, which we all must observe, to the things that a
    wife can endure,
And a woman won't call in her father unless the offense of her husband is
    sure.
But I think very soon the suspense will be over, and then I'll know what
    is the matter—
But look, there's my daughter in front of the door, and her husband; he's
    not looking at her.
        It's just as I suspected.

I'll speak to her.
WIFE: I'll go meet him [*meeting him C.*] I hope you are well, father.
FATHER: I hope you are well. Do I find you well? Are you well, that you sum-
moned me? Why are you sad? Why does he [*pointing with staff*] stand
apart from you, in anger? You have been quarreling about something. Tell
me which of you is at fault, and be brief about it; no rigmarole.
WIFE: I am guilty of nothing on my part; I'll ease you on this point first, father.
But I can't live here, and I can't stand it another minute. Take me away.
FATHER: Why, what's the matter?
WIFE: I'm made fun of, father.
FATHER: By whom?
WIFE: By *him*, to whom you gave me: my husband.
FATHER: [*to audience*] Look at that now! A squabble! [*to* WIFE] How many

times have I told you to see to it that neither of you come to me with your complaints?

WIFE: [*tearfully*] But father, how could I help it? I think you could understand—unless you don't want to.

FATHER: How many times have I told you to humor your husband? Pay no attention to what he does, or where he goes, or what he is about.

WIFE: Why, he has been making love to a courtesan who lives right next door.

FATHER: That's sensible enough. And I'll warrant he'll make love to her all the more, with you spying on him this way.

WIFE: And he drinks there, too.

FATHER: Well, will he drink any the less on your account, here or anywhere else that he chooses? Devil take it, why will you be so foolish? You might as well expect to forbid him to accept dinner invitations or to entertain guests at his own house. Do you want husbands to be slaves? You might as well expect to give him a stint of work, and have him sit among the slave-girls and card wool.

WIFE: [*resentfully*] Apparently I had you come here to defend my husband's case, father, not mine! You're *my* attorney, but you plead *his* case.

FATHER: If he has been delinquent in any way, I'll be even more severe with him than I was with you. But since he keeps you well supplied with gold trinkets and clothes and gives you servants and provisions as he should it is better for you, girl, to take a sane view of things.

WIFE: But he steals my gold and my cloaks from the cupboard. He robs me and takes my trinkets to courtesans on the sly.

FATHER: He does wrong if he does; you do wrong if he doesn't: that's accusing an innocent man.

WIFE: But he has the cloak right now, father, and the bracelet that he took to the woman. He is bringing them back now because I have found out about it.

FATHER: I'll find out from him just what has happened. I'll go speak to him. [*goes over to* MENAECHMUS II *and taps him with staff*] Menaechmus, for my enlightenment tells me what you are quarreling about. Why are you sad? Why does she stand apart from you, in anger?

MENAECHMUS II: Whoever you are, whatever your name is, old man, I call as my witnesses great Jupiter and the gods—

FATHER: Why? Wherefore? And for what?

MENAECHMUS II: That I have neither wronged this woman, who accuses me of stealing this cloak from her house—

WIFE: Perjury, eh?

MENAECHMUS II: If I have ever set my foot inside the house in which she lives, may I be the most accursedly accursed!

FATHER: Are you in your right mind, to make such a wish? Do you deny that you have ever set foot in the house you live in, you utter madman?

MENAECHMUS II: Old man, do you say I live in that house?

FATHER: Do you deny it?

MENAECHMUS II: I' faith, I do deny it.

FATHER: No; you deny not "in faith" but in joke—unless, of course, you have moved out overnight. [*motions* WIFE *to* C.]—Come here, please, daughter. What do you say? You haven't moved from the house, have you?

WIFE: Why should we, or where should we move *to*, I ask you?

FATHER: By heaven, I don't know.

WIFE: It's clear that he is making fun of you. Don't you get that?

FATHER: Menaechmus, you have joked long enough; now attend to business.

MENAECHMUS II: I ask you, what business have I with you? Or who are you? Are you sane? And this woman, who has been plaguing me this way and that—is she sane? [*tears his hair in exasperation*]

WIFE: [*to* FATHER, *frightened*] Do you see the color of his eyes? See how a green color is coming over his temples and forehead! How his eyes shine!

MENAECHMUS II: [*to audience*] Alack, they say I'm crazy, whereas it is they who are really that way themselves. What could be better for me, since they say I am mad, than to pretend to be insane, to scare them off? [*begins to jump about madly*]

WIFE: How he stretches and gapes! What shall I do, father?

FATHER: Come over here, my child, as far as you can from him. [*Retreating L.*]

MENAECHMUS II: [*pretending madness*] Ho, Bacchus! Ho, Bromius! Where in this forest do you bid me to the hunt? I hear, but cannot leave this place, so closely am I guarded by that rabid bitch upon my left. And behind there is that bald goat, who often in his time has ruined innocent citizens by his false testimony.

FATHER: Curse you!

MENAECHMUS II: Lo, Apollo from his oracle bids me to burn out the eyes of that woman with flaming torches. [*Charges at* WIFE, *then immediately retreats*]

WIFE: I am lost, father! He threatens to burn out my eyes.

FATHER: [*to* WIFE, *aside*] Hist, daughter!

WIFE: What? What shall we do?

FATHER: Suppose I summon the slaves? I'll go bring some people to take this man away and chain him up indoors before he makes any more disturbance.

MENAECHMUS II: [*aside*] I'm stuck; if I don't hit upon a scheme, they'll take me into the house with them. [*aloud*] Apollo, you forbid me to spare her face with my fists unless she leaves my sight and goes utterly to the devil? [*advances threateningly*] I'll do your bidding, Apollo!

FATHER: Run home as fast as you can, before he thumps you.

WIFE: I am running. Watch him father; don't let him get away! Oh! am I not a miserable woman to have to listen to such things! [*Exit into her house.*]

MENAECHMUS II: [*aside*] I got rid of her rather well. [*aloud, threatening* FATHER] Now, Apollo, as for this most filthy wretch, this bearded tremulous Tithonus, who is called the son of Cygnus, you bid me break his limbs and bones and joints with that staff which he holds?

FATHER: [*retreats, shaking his staff*] You'll get a beating if you touch me or come any closer.

MENAECHMUS II: I'll do your bidding! I'll take a double-edged axe and chop the flesh of this old man to mince meat, down to the very bones!

FATHER: [*aside*] Well then, I must beware and take care of myself. Really, I am afraid, from the way he threatens, that he may do me harm. [MENAECHMUS *retreats C.*]

MENAECHMUS II: You give me many commands, Apollo! Now you bid me take my fierce untamed yoked horses and mount my chariot, to crush this old stinking toothless lion. Now I've mounted! [*business*] Now I hold the reins! Now the goad is in my hand! Forward, my steeds, make loud the clatter of your hooves! And in swift flight make undiminished the fleetness of your feet [*Gallops about the stage.*]

FATHER: Do you threaten me with yoked horses?

MENAECHMUS II: Lo, Apollo, again you bid me make a charge at him, this fellow who stands here, and slay him. [*rushes forward, then suddenly stops*] But who is this, who drags me from my chariot by the hair? He alters your commands, even the commands of Apollo! [*pretends to fall senseless to the ground*]

FATHER: [*advances cautiously*] Alas, by heaven, it is a severe disease! O gods, by your faith. what sudden changes do ye work! Take this madman—how strong he was a little while before. This disease has smitten him all of a sudden. I'll go get a doctor as quick as I can. [*Exit, L.*]

MENAECHMUS II: [*getting up*] Lord! These idiots who compel me, a sane man, to act like a madman! Have they got out of my sight now, I wonder? Why don't I go straight back to the ship while the going is good? [*as he starts to go, R., to audience*] I beg of all of you, if the old man comes back don't tell him what street I've taken. [*Exit, R.*]

ACT V

[*Enter* FATHER.]

FATHER: I've waited on the doctor's leisure until my limbs ache from sitting and my eyes from looking! I had a hard time persuading him to leave his patients. He says he set the broken leg of Aesculapius and the arm of Apollo, so that now I wonder whether I should say I am bringing a doctor or a joiner! [*glancing off L.*] Here he comes. Hurry up that ant's pace, will you!

[*Enter* DOCTOR.]

DOCTOR: What did you say was his disease? Tell me about it. sir. Has he a demoniacal affliction, or hallucinations? Explain. Is he lethargic, or has he a dropsical propensity?

FATHER: That's why I'm bringing you here; I want you to tell me just that and make him sound again.

DOCTOR: Ah, that is quite simple. He shall be sound as a nut, upon my honor.

FATHER: I want him cared for very carefully.

DOCTOR: I shall contrive a cure that will last a century; that is how carefully I shall care for him for you.

FATHER: There's the man himself.

DOCTOR: Let us observe what he does. [*They withdraw C.*]

[*Enter* MENAECHMUS I.]

MENAECHMUS I: [*to audience, while* DOCTOR *observes*] Good Lord, this has certainly been a perverse and adverse day for me! I thought I was acting on the sly, but that parasite has let everything out. He has filled me with fear and covered me with disgrace; he's my Ulysses. stirring up trouble for his master! As sure as I'm alive, I'll rid him of his life! But I'm a fool to call it *his*. It's mine; it was my food and money that gave him life. Well then, I'll take the breath out of him!—The courtesan acted true to form, in the regular courtesan way: because I asked for the cloak so that I could take it back to my wife, she said she had given it to me! [*sighs*] By heaven, I certainly lead a miserable life!

FATHER: Do you hear what he says?

DOCTOR: He says that he is miserable.

FATHER: I wish you'd go up to him.

DOCTOR: [*going up to* MENAECHMUS I] How do you do, Menaechmus. Please, why do you leave your arm uncovered? Do you not know how injurious that is to your present indisposition?

MENAECHMUS I: Go hang yourself!

FATHER: [*to* DOCTOR] Do you notice anything?

DOCTOR: Notice anything! This case cannot be cured with an acre of hellebore! But, Menaechmus,—

MENAECHMUS I: Well?

DOCTOR: Answer me this question: is it white or red wine that you drink?

MENAECHMUS I: And what is it to you? Go to the devil!

DOCTOR: Ah, the first symptoms of insanity.

MENAECHMUS I: Why not ask whether the bread I eat is crimson or purple or orange-colored? or whether I eat scaly birds and feathered fish?

FATHER: Dear me! Do you hear how he raves? Why don't you give him some kind of a potion before complete madness sets in?

DOCTOR: One moment. I wish to continue my diagnosis.

FATHER: You're killing me with your talk!

DOCTOR: [*to* MENAECHMUS I] Tell me this: do you ever notice a hardening of your eyes?

MENAECHMUS I: What! Do you take me for a lobster, you good-for-nothing?

DOCTOR: Tell me, are you subject to rumbling of the bowels—as far as you know?

MENAECHMUS I: When I've a full stomach, no. But when I go hungry, then there is a rumbling.

DOCTOR: [*to* FATHER] Dear me, that is no madman's answer! [*to* MENAECHMUS I] Do you sleep soundly at night? Do you go to sleep readily on retiring?

MENAECHMUS I: Yes, if I have paid my bills. [*angrily*] Jupiter and all the gods destroy you, you confounded busybody!

DOCTOR: The madness begins again. [*to* FATHER] You hear what he says; be on your guard.

FATHER: On the contrary, he talks like a perfect Nestor now, compared to what he was a while ago. Why, a few minutes ago he called his wife a rabid bitch.

MENAECHMUS I: I said *what?*

FATHER: You were raving, I say.

MENAECHMUS I: I raving?

FATHER: Yes, you. You threatened to trample me to death with a four-horse chariot. I myself saw you do it. I myself accuse you of it.

MENAECHMUS I: [*to* FATHER, *furiously, pushing* DOCTOR *aside*] Yes, and I know that you stole the sacred chaplet from the statue of Jupiter, and that you were clapped into jail for it; also that after you got out of prison you were strung up and flogged; also that you killed your father and sold your mother! Isn't that a sane man's retort? One flock of abuse deserves another.

FATHER: For God's sake, doctor, I beg of you; hurry! Whatever you are going to do, do it! Can't you see the man is raving?

DOCTOR: [*aside to* FATHER] It would be best if he were to be conveyed to my house.

FATHER: You think so?

DOCTOR: By all means. I shall be able to care for him there according to my own prescriptions.

FATHER: Just as you say.

DOCTOR: [*rubbing his hands, to* MENAECHMUS I] I shall set you to drinking hellebore for some twenty days!

MENAECHMUS I: [*savagely*] Yes, and I'll string you up and jab you with oxgoads for *thirty* days!

DOCTOR: [*aside to* FATHER] Go, fetch men to take him to my house.

FATHER: How many do we need?

DOCTOR: As I judge the extent of his madness, four; no less.

FATHER: They shall be here directly. [*starts to go*] Guard him, doctor!

DOCTOR: No, no! I shall go to my house and make the necessary preparations. Have the slaves bring him to me.

FATHER: I'll have him there immediately.

DOCTOR: Good. I leave you [*Exit L.*]

FATHER: [*calling after him*] Good-bye. [*Exit R. to get slaves.*]

MENAECHMUS I: [*watching them off*] Father-in-law gone; doctor gone; I'm alone. Great Jupiter! what makes all these people say that I'm insane? Since I was born I've never had a day's illness. I'm not mad; I don't brawl or pick fights in court. I'm sane, and I realize that others are, too. I recognize people, talk to them. These people who say falsely that I'm mad, perhaps they're mad themselves.—What shall I do? I want to go home, but my wife won't have it. Nobody will let me in here [*looking at* EROTIUM'S *house*] either. What cursed luck! I'll be standing here forever! Well perhaps they'll let me into my house by evening. [*Withdraws U. C. to wait, where he sits and dozes.*]

[*Enter* MESSENIO L.; *does not observe* MENAECHMUS]

MESSENIO: [SONG]

> It's a proof of an excellent slave,
> If, his master's belongings to save,
>   He'll use as much care
>   When his master's not there
> As when master is watching the slave.

For his back and his shins he must fear,
The demands of his stomach not hear,
    And the punishment know
    Of the slothful and slow—
This servant whose conscience is clear.

There are beatings, and chains, and the mills,
Hunger, weariness, terrible chills—
    The reward of the lazy;
    But since I'm not crazy,
I'm good, and avoid all these ills.

I'm good at taking a tongue-lashing but a whip-lashing I don't like, and I very much prefer to eat the meal to turning the mill. Therefore I follow my master's orders properly and gravely. My principle is to consider my back; it's worth my while. Let others behave the way they think best suits them; I'll be what I should. If that's my rule, if I keep out of trouble so I can serve my master at all times, I've little to fear. The day's near when my master will reward me for my good services. I've left the baggage and the slaves at the inn, as he ordered, and now I've come to meet him. I'll knock on the door to let him know I'm here, and to get him safely out of this place of ruin. But I'm afraid that I'll be too late and get there after the battle is over. [*Goes to* EROTIUM'S *door, but seeing slaves approach, withdraws to extreme R. to watch.*]

[*Enter* FATHER *with a corporal's guard of four burly slaves.*]

FATHER: By all the gods and men I bid you take wise heed to my orders past and present. Pick up that man [*pointing to* MENAECHMUS] and fetch him to the doctor's at once, unless you care nothing for your shanks and sides. A straw for his threats, do you hear? Why do you stand there? Why do you hesitate? He should have been shoulder-high and hustled off already. I go to the doctor's; I'll be waiting there when you come. [*Exit L.*]

[*Slaves advance towards* MENAECHMUS I.]

MENAECHMUS I: [*awakening and seeing himself surrounded*] I'm lost! What is this? Why do these men run at me? What do you want? What are you after? Why do you surround me? [*They raise him on their shoulders.*] Where are you taking me? Where are you carrying me? Murder! Help! Good folk of Epidamnus, help! Let me go!

MESSENIO: [*coming forward*] By the immortal gods, what's this I see? A gang of thugs carrying off my master bodily!

MENAECHMUS I: [*shouting*] Doesn's anybody dare to help me?

MESSENIO: [*dramatically*] I do, master. I dare most daringly! [*to audience, singing*]:
    Oh! what an outrageous crime I see!
    Epidamnians, this man was free,
    My master, when he came today:
    And now they're carrying him away,
    While you're at peace, by light of day!

[*cuffs one of the slaves*] Let go of him, you.

MENAECHMUS I: I implore you, whoever you are, help me: protect me from this outrage.

MESSENIO: [*acting the faithful slave*] Yes, yes, I'll help and defend and stand by you. I'll never let you be murdered. Sooner myself than you! [*general scuffle, in time with music*] Gouge the eye out of that fellow who has you by the shoulder. I'll plow these faces for the sowing of my fists! You shall smart to-day for trying to carry him off! Let go!

MENAECHMUS I: I've got him by the eye!

MESSENIO: Good; make us see the socket! You villains! You robbers! You bandits!

SLAVES: Murder! Stop, for God's sake!

MESSENIO: Let go then! [*They drop* MENAECHMUS I.]

MENAECHMUS I: [*to slaves*] Lay hands on me, will you? [*to* MESSENIO] Give 'em your fists!

MESSENIO: [*to slaves*] Go on, get out! Get out of here, devil take you! There's one for you [*gives a final kick to last slave*]; take it as a prize for being the last to go! [*Exeunt slaves; to* MENAECHMUS I:] I measured those faces pretty well, all right, and just to my taste. I came to your help in the nick of time then, master!

MENAECHMUS I: May the gods bless you forever, young man, whoever you may be: If it hadn't been for you, I should never have seen the sun set this day!

MESSENIO: Well then, by George, if you did the right thing you'd set me free.

MENAECHMUS I: *I* set you free?

MESSENIO: To be sure, master; because I saved your life.

MENAECHMUS I: What's this? There's some mistake, young man.

MESSENIO: [*worried*] What do you mean?

MENAECHMUS I: By father Jupiter I swear that I am not your master.

MESSENIO: What!

MENAECHMUS I: That's the truth. No slave of mine ever served me as you have.

MESSENIO: Well then, if you say I'm not your slave, let me go free.

MENAECHMUS I: By heaven, as far as I am concerned you can be free to go wherever you please.

MESSENIO: [*eagerly*] Those are really your orders?

MENAECHMUS I: Why yes, if I have any power over you.

MESSENIO: Hail, my patron! How happy I am that you have freed me!

MENAECHMUS I: [*dryly*] I can believe it!

MESSENIO: But, my patron, please do not command me any less now than when I was your slave. I shall live with you and go with you when you go back home.

MENAECHMUS I: [*aside*] I guess not!

MESSENIO: Wait for me. I'm off to the inn to bring the baggage and the money. The journey-money is safely sealed up in your bag. I'll have it here directly.

MENAECHMUS I: [*much interested*] Do, by all means.

MESSENIO: I'll give it back to you all safe, just as you gave it to me. Wait for me here. [*Exit L.*]

MENAECHMUS I: [*alone*] There certainly have been strange things happening to me today, and in strange ways! People denying that I am I, and that fellow whom I just freed, who said he was my slave! He says he will bring me a purse with money in it. If he does, I'll tell him he is free to go away wherever he wishes, so that when he comes to his senses he won't try to get the money back.—My father-in-law and the doctor said I was insane. Heaven only knows what it all means! It seems just like a dream.—Now I'll go in here to the courtesan, even though she is angry with me, and see if I can't get her to give me back the cloak, so I can take it home. [*Exit into the house of* EROTIUM.]

> MENAECHMUS II *enters L. looking about stage for* MESSENIO. *Exit L., but returns immediately with him.*]

MENAECHMUS II: [*angrily*] You brazen rascal, do you dare tell me that you have been with me to-day since the time I ordered you to meet me here?

MESSENIO: [*angrily. thinking that his master is trying to cheat him*] Why, I rescued you just a few minutes ago when four men were carrying you off bodily, before this very house. You were yelling for help to all of heaven and earth when I ran up and rescued you with my fists, in spite of them. Therefore, because I had saved your life, you set me free. When I said I was going to get the money and the luggage, you ran ahead to meet me, so you could deny what you had done!

MENAECHMUS II: I set you free?

MESSENIO: Yes.

MENAECHMUS II: [*emphatically*] I'd turn slave myself sooner than free you, and that's that!

> [*Enter* MENAECHMUS I *from the house of* EROTIUM.]

MENAECHMUS I: [*shouting into the house*] Swear by your eyes if you want to, but you can't make out that I took away the cloak and the armlet, you wantons!

MESSENIO: [*crossing towards* MENAECHMUS I] Immortal gods! what do I see!

MENAECHMUS II: What do you see?

MESSENIO: Your mirror.

MENAECHMUS II: What do you mean?

MESSENIO: He's your very image, as like you as can be.

MENAECHMUS II: [*comparing himself with the stranger*] Well! He's certainly not unlike me, now that I look at myself.

MENAECHMUS I: [*seeing* MESSENIO] The young man who saved me! Hail, whoever you are.

MESSENIO: Saving your presence, sir, tell me your name, for heaven's sake!

MENAECHMUS I: Well, by Apollo, you have not deserved so of me that I should object to your question. Menaechmus is my name.

MENAECHMUS II: [*surprised*] No, by Apollo, it's *mine*!

MENAECHMUS I: I'm a Sicilian, from Syracuse.

MENAECHMUS II: That's just where I came from!

MENAECHMUS I: What's that you say?

MENAECHMUS II: The truth.

MESSENIO: [*standing between them, indicating* MENAECHMUS I] This is the man I know, of course; *this* is my master. I'm *his* slave, though I thought

I was that fellow's. I thought he was you, and made a nuisance of myself to him. [*to* MENAECHMUS II] I beg your pardon, sir, if I said anything indiscreet to you.

MENAECHMUS II: [*angrily, to* MESSENIO] Why you're raving! Don't you remember coming off the ship with me today?

MESSENIO: [*hurriedly changing sides*] Yes, yes, you're quite right. You are my master. [*to* MENAECHMUS I] You can hunt for another slave. [*to* MENAECHMUS II] Good-day to you. [*to* MENAECHMUS I] Good-bye to you. I say that this man is Menaechmus.

MENAECHMUS I: Well, I say *I* am.

MENAECHMUS II: What's this nonsense! *You* Menaechmus?

MENAECHMUS I: Yes; Menaechmus, Son of Moschus.

MENAECHMUS II: *My* father's son?

MENAECHMUS I: No indeed, young man, not yours. [*dryly*] I've no wish to appropriate your father and tear him away from you.

MESSENIO: [*steps forward to audience*] Immortal gods! Fulfil this unhoped-for hope of mine! For unless my mind is playing me tricks, these two are the twin brothers! They both recall the same father and country. I'll speak to my master. [*aloud*] Menaechmus!

MENAECHMUS I *and* II: [*together*] What is it?

MESSENIO: I don't want both of you; just my master. Which of you came here in the ship with me?

MENAECHMUS I: Not I.

MENAECHMUS II: I did.

MESSENIO: [*aside to* MENAECHMUS II] This man is either a sycophant or your own twin brother. I've never seen anyone who looked so like you; water is not more like water, or milk like milk, than he is like you and you like him. Also, he says his father and his country are the same as yours. We'd better go up to him and investigate.

MENAECHMUS II: By heaven, that's good advice, and I'm grateful. Keep on helping me, for goodness' sake. If you prove he is my brother, you shall be free.

MESSENIO: I hope so.

MENAECHMUS II: And I hope so too.

MESSENIO: [*between them again; he assumes the dignity of a cross-questioner*] Let's see now. [*to* MENAECHMUS I] Menaechmus is your name, I believe you said?

MENAECHMUS I: Indeed it is.

MESSENIO: This man's name is Menaechmus, too. You are a Sicilian, from Syracuse. That's where he comes from. Moschus was your father, you said. His father, too. Now, both of you can help me, and yourselves as well.

MENAECHMUS |: You deserve to receive from me anything you ask. I'm your humble servant, as though you had bought me with money.

MESSENIO: [*dramatically*] I hope that I'll find you two to be twin brothers, born on the same day to the same mother and father.

MENAECHMUS I: This is a strange tale. I wish you could make your hope come true.

MESSENIO: I can. Come now, each of you, answer me some questions.

MENAECHMUS: Ask whenever you wish. I'll answer. I'll keep back nothing that I know.

MESSINO: [*interrogating each in turn*] Is your name Menaechmus?

MENAECHMUS I: It is.

MESSENIO: And it is yours too?

MENAECHMUS II: It is.

MESSENIO: Moschus, you say, was your father?

MENAECHMUS I: He was.

MENAECHMUS II: And mine too.

MESSENIO: Are you from Syracuse?

MENAECHMUS I: Yes.

MESSENIO: And you?

MENAECHMUS II: Yes, of course.

MESSENIO: So far the evidence agrees without a flaw. Give me your attention further. [*to* MENAECHMUS I] Tell me, what is the earliest thing that you remember in your native land?

MENAECHMUS I: I can remember going away with my father to the market at Tarentum. Then, in the crowd I strayed off from him, and after that I was carried off.

MENAECHMUS II: God save us!

MESSENIO: [*to* MENAECHMUS II] What are you shouting about? Won't you be still? [*to* MENAECHMUS I] How old were you when your father took you away from home?

MENAECHMUS I: I was seven at the time, for I was just beginning to lose my teeth. And from that time I never saw my father again.

MESSENIO: So. How many sons were there in the family at that time?

MENAECHMUS I: Two, if I am not mistaken.

MESSENIO: Which was the elder, you or your brother?

MENAECHMUS I: We were both the same age.

MESSENIO: How can that be so?

MENAECHMUS I: We were twins.

MENAECHMUS II: [*breaking in*] Thank Heaven!

MESSENIO: [*with finality*] If you interrupt again, I'll be still.

MENAECHMUS II: [*contritely*] No, I'll be still.

MESSENIO: Tell me, did you both have the same name?

MENAECHMUS I: Of course not. My name was Menaechmus, as it is now. My brother was called Sosicles.

MENAECHMUS II: That's enough proof. I can't keep from embracing him. My own twin brother, come to my arms! I am Sosicles. [*crosses and tries to embrace* MENAECHMUS I]

MENAECHMUS I: [*doubting*] Then how did your name become Menaechmus?

MENAECHMUS II: After we heard that you had been carried away and father was dead, grandfather changed my name and gave me yours.

MENAECHMUS I: [*still doubting*] I believe it happened just as you say. But answer me this.

MENAECHMUS II: What?

MENAECHMUS I: What was our mother's name?

MENAECHMUS II: Teuximarcha.

MENAECHMUS I: Everything fits together.—Let me embrace you, brother, unexpected sight after so many years. [*They embrace warmly.*]

MENAECHMUS II: And you, too, for whom till now I have been searching with so many trials and troubles, and at whose discovery I now rejoice.

MESSENIO: And this was why the courtesan here called you by his name: she mistook you for him, I suppose, when she invited you to lunch.

MENAECHMUS I: Why, of course. I ordered luncheon here (my wife didn't know) and gave her a cloak that I'd stolen from home.

MENAECHMUS II: Do you mean the cloak I have in my hand, brother?

MENAECHMUS I: How did you get it?

MENAECHMUS II: The courtesan who took me in to lunch here said I'd given it to her. I dined well, wined well, and had a glorious time with her. She gave me this cloak and jewelry.

MENAECHMUS I: I'm certainly glad if you've had any fun because of me. I think she thought you were I when she invited you in.

MESSENIO: [*hopefully*] Is there anything to prevent me from being free, as you promised?

MENAECHMUS I: A very good and fair request, brother. Grant it, for my sake.

MENAECHMUS II: Have your freedom. [MESSENIO *cuts a caper.*]

MENAECHMUS I: Congratulations on your freedom, Messenio.

MESSENIO: There ought to be a formal ceremony, so I'll be free forever.

MENAECHMUS II: Since we've had so much good fortune, brother, let's both return to our native land. [*They start R.*]

MENAECHMUS I: I'll do as you wish, brother, and I'll have an auction and sell all my property. But meanwhile, let's go in.

MENAECHMUS II: Very well.

[*They cross towards* MENAECHMUS' *house.*]

MESSENIO: [*to* MENAESCHMUS I] Will you do me a favor?

MENAECHMUS I: What is it?

MESSENIO: Give me the job of auctioneer.

MENAECHMUS I: Certainly.

MESSENIO: Do you want the auction cried at once?

MENAECHMUS I: Yes, for a week from today.

[*Exeunt* MENAECHMUS I *and* II *into house of* MENAECHMUS I]

MESSENIO: EXTRAORDINARY AUC—TION
                          WEEK—FROM TODAY
                    MENAECHMUS SELLS HIS PROPERTY
                          CASH AND NO DELAY
                    ALL MUST GO—HOUSE AND LOT
                       SLAVES AND FURNITURE
                    WIFE GOES TOO IF ANY ONE
                       TAKES A FANCY TO HER

[*aside*] I scarcely think he'll make a million out of the whole auction. [*to audience*] Now, spectators, fare you well, and lustily applaud us all. [*Exit, R.*]

The Wakefield Cycle

The Second Shepherds' Play[1]

[Anonymous] Editing and notes by
Robert B. Heilman

CHARACTERS

FIRST SHEPHERD	GILL, *his wife*
SECOND SHEPHERD	ANGEL
THIRD SHEPHERD	JESUS
MAK	MARY

[*Enter the* FIRST SHEPHERD.]
FIRST SHEPHERD: Lord! What these weathers are cold, and I am ill wrapped.
My hands nearly numb, so long have I napped.
My legs they fold, my fingers are chapped;
It is not as I would, for I am all lapped
    In sorrow 5
In storms and tempest,
Now in the east, now in the west,
Woe is him has never rest
    Midday nor morrow!

But we poor shepherds that walk on the moor, 10
In faith, we are near-hands out of the door;
No wonder, as it stands, if we be poor,
For the tilth of our lands lies fallow as the floor,
    As ye ken.
We are so hamyd, 15
For-taxed and ramyd[2],
We are made hand-tamed
    By these gentlery-men.
Thus they rob us of our rest. Our Lady them curse!
These men that are lord-fast, they make the plough tarry. 20
That, men say, is for the best; we find it contrary.
Thus are husbandmen oppressed, in point to miscarry,
    In life.

[1] C. 1425–1450.
[2] Crippled, taxed to death, ruined.

Thus hold they us under;
Thus they bring us in blunder.   25
It were great wonder
    If ever should we thrive.

For may he get a painted sleeve, or a brooch, now-a-days,
Woe to him that him grieves, or one word gainsays!
Dare no man him reprove, what mastery he has.   30
And yet may no man believe one word that he says,
    No letter.
He can make purveyance[3],
With boast and arrogance;
And all is through maintenance   35
    Of men that are greater.

There shall come a swain as proud as a peacock,
He must borrow my wagon, my plough also,
That I am full fain to grant ere he go.
Thus live we in pain, anger, and woe   40
    By night and day.
He must have if he longéd;
If I should forgang[4] it,
I were better be hanged
    Than once say him nay.   45

It does me good, as I walk thus by mine own,
Of this world for to talk in manner of moan.
To my sheep will I stalk and hearken anon;
There abide on a ridge, or sit on a stone,
    Full soon.   50
For I trow, pardie,
True men if they be,
We get more company
    Ere it be noon. [*Moves aside.*]

    [*Enter the* SECOND SHEPHERD.]
SECOND SHEPHERD: Ben'c'te[5] and Dominus! What may this bemean?   55
Why, fares this world thus, oft have we not seen?
Lord, these weathers are spiteful, and the winds full keen,
And the frosts so hideous, they water my eyes,
    No lie.
Now in dry, now in wet,   60
Now in snow, now in sleet,
When my shoes freeze to my feet,
    It is not all easy.

[3] Provision.
[4] Do without.
[5] Benedicite.

But as far as I ken, or yet as I go,
We poor wedded men endure much woe;   65
We have sorrow then and then, it falls oft so.
Silly Capel, our hen, both to and fro
    She cackles;
But begin she to croak,
To groan or to cluck,   70
Woe is him, is our cock,
    For he is in the shackles.

These men that are wed have not all their will.
When they are full hard bestead, they sigh full still.
God knows they are led full hard and full ill;   75
In bower nor in bed they say naught theretill,
    This tide.
My part have I found,
I know my lesson.
Woe is him that is bound,   80
    For he must abide.

But now late in our lives—a marvel to me,
That I think my heart rives such wonders to see,
What that destiny drives, it should so be—
Some men will have two wives, and some men three   85
    In store.
Some are woe that has any;
But so far ken I,
Woe is him that has many,
    For he feels sore.   90

But, young men, of wooing, for God that you bought,
Be well ware of wedding, and think in your thought,
"Had I known" is a thing it serves of naught.
Mickle still mourning has wedding home brought,
    And griefs,   95
With many a sharp shower;
For thou may catch in an hour
What shall seem full sour
    As long as thou lives.

For, as ever read I epistle[6], I have one to my fere[7],   100
As sharp as a thistle, as rough as a briar;
She is browed like a bristle, with a sour-laden cheer;
Had she once wet her whistle, she could sing full clear
    Her paternoster.

[6] In the Bible.
[7] Mate.

She is as great as a whale;   105
She has a gallon of gall;
By him that died for us all[8],
    I would I had run till I had lost her!

FIRST SHEPHERD: God, look over the row! Full deafly ye stand.
SECOND SHEPHERD: Yea, the devil in thy maw—so tarrying!   110
    Sawest thou anywhere Daw?
FIRST SHEPHERD: Yea, on a lea-land
    Heard I him blow. He comes here at hand,
        Not far.
    Stand still.
SECOND SHEPHERD: Why?
FIRST SHEPHERD: For he comes, hope I.   115
SECOND SHEPHERD: He will make us both a lie
    Unless we beware.
      [*Enter* THIRD SHEPHERD, *a boy.*]
THIRD SHEPHERD: Christ's cross me speed, and Saint Nicholas!
    Thereof had I need; it is worse than it was.
    Whoso could, take heed and let the world pass;   120
    It is ever in dread and brittle as glass,
        And slides.
    This world fared never so,
    With marvels more and moe,
    Now in weal, now in woe,   125
        And all things writhes.

Was never since Noah's flood such floods seen,
Winds and rains so rude, and storms so keen;
Some stammered, some stood in doubt, as I ween.
Now God turn all to good! I say as I mean,   130
    For ponder.
These floods so they drown,
Both in fields and in town,
And bear all down,
    And that is a wonder.   135

We that walk in the nights our cattle to keep,
We see sudden sights when other men sleep.
Yet methinks my heart lightens; I see shrews[9] peep.
Ye are two tall wights! I will give my sheep
    A turn.   140
But full ill have I meant;
As I walk on this land,
I may lightly repent,

[8] Note the many anachronisms in the play.
[9] Rogues.

My toes if I spurn.
[*To the other two.*]
Ah, sir, God you save, and master mine!   145
A drink fain would I have, and somewhat to dine.
ST SHEPHERD: Christ's curse, my knave, thou art an evil hind!
OND SHEPHERD: What! the boy likes to rave! Abide until syne[10]
       We have made it.
Ill thrift on thy pate!   150
Though the fellow came late,
Yet is he in state
       To dine—if he had it.

RD SHEPHERD: Such servants as I, that sweats and swinks[11],
Eat our bread full dry. and that me forthinks[12].   155
We are oft wet and weary when master men winks;
Yet come full late both dinners and drinks.
       But neatly
Both our dame and our sire,
When we have run in the mire,   160
They can nip at our hire,
       And pay us full lately.

But hear my truth, master, for the fare that ye make:
I shall do, hereafter, work as I take[13];
I shall do a little, sir, and between times play,   165
For yet lay my supper never on my stomach
       In fields.
Whereto should I threap[14]?
With my staff can I leap;
And men say "Light cheap   170
       Badly for-yields[15]."

ST SHEPHERD: Thou were an ill lad, to ride a-wooing
With a man that had but little of spending.
OND SHEPHERD: Peace, boy! I bade; no more jangling,
Or I shall make thee a-feared, by the Heaven's King,   175
       With thy gawds[16].
Where are our sheep, boy? We scorn.
RD SHEPHERD: Sir, this same day at morn
I them left in the corn,
       When they rang lauds[17].   180

---

10 After.   11 Labors.
12 I regret.   13 As I am paid.
14 Talk back.   15 An easy bargain badly pays back.
16 Tricks.   17 Early church service.

They have pasture good; they cannot go wrong.
FIRST SHEPHERD: That is right. By the rood, these nights are long!
   Yet I would, ere we go, one gave us a song.
SECOND SHEPHERD: So I thought as I stood, for mirth us among.
THIRD SHEPHERD: I grant.   1
FIRST SHEPHERD: Let me sing the tenory.
SECOND SHEPHERD: And I the treble so high.
THIRD SHEPHERD: Then the mean falls to me.
     Let see how ye chant.
     [*Enter* MAK. *with a cloak thrown over his smock.*]
MAK: Now, Lord, for thy names seven, that made both moon and stars,   1
   Well more than I can name; thy will, Lord, of me tharns[18].
   I am all uneven; that moves oft my brains.
   Now would God I were in heaven, for there weep no bairns
     So still.
FIRST SHEPHERD: Who is that pipes so poor?   1
MAK: Would God ye knew how I fare!
   Lo, a man that walks on the moor,
     And has not all his will!

SECOND SHEPHERD: Mak, where hast thou gone? Tell us tidings.
THIRD SHEPHERD: Is he come? Then everyone take heed to his things.   2
     [*Takes the cloak from* MAK.]
MAK: What! Ich be[19] a yeoman, I tell you, of the king;
   The self and the same, sent from a great lording,
     And such.
   Fie on you! Go hence,
   Out of my presence!   2
   I must have reverence.
     Why, who be ich?

FIRST SHEPHERD: Why make ye it so quaint? Mak, ye do wrong.
SECOND SHEPHERD: But Mak, list ye saint[20]? I trow for that you long.
THIRD SHEPHERD: I trow the shrew can paint! The devil might him hang!   2
MAK: Ich shall make complaint, and give you all a whang
     At a word,
   And tell even how ye doth.
FIRST SHEPHERD: But, Mak, is that truth?
   Now take out that southern tooth,   2
     And set in a turd.

SECOND SHEPHERD: Mak, the devil in your eye! A stroke would I lend you.
THIRD SHEPHERD: Mak, know ye not me? By God, I could 'tend to you.
MAK: God, look you all three! Methought I had seen you.
   Ye are a fair company.

---

18 Finds me wanting.
19 Mak affects southern accent.
20 Do you like to show off?

ʀsт sнернеrd: Can ye now mean you?[21]   220
ᴄond sнернеrd: Rascal, jape!
> Thus late as thou goes,
> What will men suppose?
> And thou hast an ill noise[22]
> > Of stealing of sheep.   225

ᴀк: And I am true as steel, all men wot,
> But a sickness I feel that holds me full hot;
> My belly fares not well, it is out of state.
ɪʀd sнернеrd: Seldom lies the devil dead by the gate.
ᴀк: Therefore   230
> Full sore am I and ill;
> If I stand stone still,
> I eat not a needle
> > This month and more.

ʀsт sнернеrd: How fares thy wife? By my hood, how fares she?   235
ᴀк: Lies weltering, by the rood, by the fire, lo!
> And a house full of brood. She drinks well, too;
> Ill speed other good that she will do!
> > But so,
> Eats as fast as she can;   240
> And every year that comes to man
> She brings forth a lakan[23],
> > And some years two.

> Although I were more gracious and richer by far,
> I were eaten out of house and of harbor.   245
> Yet she is a foul dowse[24] if ye come near;
> There is none that trows nor knows a worse
> > Than ken I.
> Now will ye see what I proffer—
> To give all in my coffer   250
> Tomorrow at next to offer
> > Her head-mass penny.[25]
ᴄond sнернеrd: I wot so for-wakéd[26] is none in this shire.
> I would sleep, if I takéd less to my hire.
ɪʀd sнернеrd: I am cold and naked, and would have a fire.   255
ʀsт sнернеrd: I am weary, for-rakéd[27], and run in the mire.
> Stay awake, thou!
ᴄond sнернеrd: Nay, I will lie down by,
> For I must sleep, truly.
ɪʀd sнернеrd: As good a man's son was I   260
> > As any of you.

---

[21] Identify yourself.   [22] Bad reputation.
[23] Plaything; i. e., child.   [24] Whore.
[25] He will gladly pay for her requiem mass.
[26] Worn out with watching.   [27] Worn out with walking.

But, Mak, come hither! Between shalt thou lie down.
MAK: Then might I stop you, certain, of that ye would rown[28].
    No dread.
From my top to my toe,
Manus tuas commendo,
Pontio Pilato,
    Christ's cross me speed! [*Then he rises, the shepherds being aslee*
    and says:]
Now were time for a man that lacks what he would
To stalk privily then unto a fold,
And nimbly to work then, and be not too bold,
For he might pay for the bargain, if it were told,
    At the ending.
Now were time for to begin,
But he needs good counsel
That fain would fare well,
    And has but little spending.

But about you a circle as round as a moon,
Till I have done that I will, till that it be noon,
That ye lie stone still till that I have done,
And I shall say thereto of good words a few.
    On height
Over your heads my hand I lift:
Out go your eyes, foredo your sight!
But yet I must make better shift
    If it be right.

Lord, how they sleep hard! That may ye all hear.
I never was a shepherd, but now will I learn.
If the flock be scared, yet shall I nip near.
How! Draw hitherward! Now mends our cheer
    From sorrow.
A fat sheep, I dare say;
A good fleece, dare I lay!
Pay back when I may,
    But this will I borrow.
    [MAK *crosses the stage to his house.*]
How, Gill, art thou in? Get us some light.
WIFE: Who makes such din this time of the night?
I am set for to spin; I hope[29] not I might
Rise a penny to win. I curse them on height.
    So fares
A housewife that has been
To be rushed thus between;
Here may no work be seen,
    Because of such chores.

[28] Whisper.
[29] Expect.

ᴀᴋ: Good wife, open the hek[30]! Seest thou not what I bring? 305
ɪғᴇ: I may let thee draw the snek[31]. Ah, come in, my sweeting!
ᴀᴋ: Yea, thou dost not reck of my long standing.
ɪғᴇ: By thy naked neck art thou like for to hang.
ᴀᴋ: Go way:
  I am worthy of my meat, 310
  For in a pinch can I get
  More than they that swink and sweat
    All the long day.

  Thus it fell to my lot, Gill, I had such grace.
ɪғᴇ: It were a foul blot to be hanged for the case. 315
ᴀᴋ: I have escaped, Gillot, often as hard a place.
ɪғᴇ: But so long goes the pot to the water, men say,
    At last
  Comes it home broken.
ᴀᴋ: Well know I the token, 320
  But let it never be spoken;
    But come and help fast.

  I would he were slain; I like well to eat.
  This twelvemonth was I not so fain of one sheep's meat.
ɪғᴇ: Should they come ere he be slain, and hear the sheep bleat— 325
ᴀᴋ: Then might I be ta'en! That were a cold sweat!
    Go bar
  The gate door.
ɪғᴇ: Yes, Mak,
  For if they come at thy back—
ᴀᴋ: Then might I pay for all the pack! 330
    The devil of them warn.

ɪғᴇ: A good trick have I spied, since thou ken none.
  Here shall we him hide till they be gone—
  In my cradle abide. Let me alone,
  And I shall lie beside in childbed, and groan. 335
ᴀᴋ: Thou hast said:
  And I shall say thou was light
  Of a male child this night.
ɪғᴇ: Now well is the day bright,
    That ever was I bred. 340

  This is a good disguise and a far cast;
  Yet a woman's advice helps at the last!
  I wot never who spies. Again go thou fast.
ᴀᴋ: Unless I come ere they rise, there blows a cold blast!
    I will go sleep. 345
    [ᴍᴀᴋ *returns to the shepherds and resumes his place.*]

[30] Hatch.
[31] Latch.

    Yet sleeps all this company;
    And I shall go stalk privily,
    As it never had been I
        That carried their sheep.

FIRST SHEPHERD: *Resurrex a mortruis!* Take hold of my hand.   35
    Judas carnas dominus! I may not well stand;
    My foot sleeps, by Jesus; and I walter fastand[32].
    I thought that we laid us full near England.
SECOND SHEPHERD: Ah, yea!
    Lord, but I have slept well.   35
    As fresh as an eel,
    As light I me feel
        As leaf on a tree.

THIRD SHEPHERD: Ben'c'te be herein! So my body shakes,
    My heart is out of skin, what so it quakes.   36
    Who makes all this din? So my brows blacks[33]
    To the door will I win. Hark, fellows, wake!
      We were four:
    See ye aught of Mak now?
FIRST SHEPHERD: We were up ere thou.   36
SECOND SHEPHERD: Man, I give God a vow,

    Yet went he nowhere.
THIRD SHEPHERD: Methought he was lapped in a wolf's skin.
FIRST SHEPHERD: So are many wrapped now—namely, within.
THIRD SHEPHERD: When we had long napped, methought with a gin[34]   37
    A fat sheep he trapped; but he made no din.
SECOND SHEPHERD: Be still!
    Thy dream makes thee mad;
    It is but phantom, by the rood.
FIRST SHEPHERD: Now God turn all to good,   37
      If it be his will!

SECOND SHEPHERD: Rise, Mak! For shame! Thou liest right long.
MAK: Now Christ's holy name be us among!
    What is this? By Saint James, I may not well gang!
    I think I be the same. Ah! my neck has lain wrong   38
      Enough.
      [*They help* MAK *up.*]
    Mickle thank! Since yester even,
    Now, by Saint Stephen,
    I was flayed with a dream
        That my heart of slough[35].   38

[32] Roll about famishing; cf. *wallow, welter.*
[33] Head aches (?).   [34] Trick.
[35] Slew my heart.

I thought Gill began to croak and travail full sad,
Well nigh at the first cock, of a young lad
For to mend our flock. Then be I never glad;
I have tow on my rock[36] more than ever I had.
    Ah, my head!   390
A house full of young tharnes[37]!
The devil knock out their brains!
Woe is him has many bairns,
    And thereto little bread!

I must go home, by your leave, to Gill, as I thought.   395
I pray you look in my sleeve that I steal naught;
I am loath you to grieve or from you take aught.
HIRD SHEPHERD: Go forth; ill might thou live! Now would I we sought,
    This morn.
That we had all our store.   400
IRST SHEPHERD: But I will go before;
    Let us meet.
ECOND SHEPHERD: Where?
HIRD SHEPHERD: At the crooked thorn.
    [MAK *crosses to his cottage.*]
ΚAK: Undo this door! Who is here? How long shall I stand?
ʹIFE: Who makes such a stir? Now walk in the wenyand![38]   405
ΚAK: Ah, Gill, what cheer? It is I, Mak, your husband.
ʹIFE: Then may we see here the devil in a band,
    Sir Guile.
Lo, he comes with a lote[39]
As he were holden in the throat.   410
I may not sit at my note[40]
    A hand-long while.

ΚAK: Will ye hear what to-do she makes to get her a gloze[41]?
She does naught but plays, and wiggles her toes.
ʹIFE: Why, who wanders? Who wakes? Who comes? Who goes?   415
Who brews? Who bakes? What makes me thus do?
    And then,
It is ruth to behold,
Now in hot, now in cold,
Full woeful is the household   420
    That wants a woman.

But what end has thou made with the shepherds, Mak?
ΚAK: The last word that they said, when I turned my back,
They would look that they had their sheep, all the pack.

---

[36] Distaff.   [37] Bellies.
[38] Waning (of the moon) — supposedly unlucky.
[39] Noise, i. e., as if he were being hanged.   [40] Work.
[41] Lie, excuse.

I expect they will not be well paid when they their sheep lack,   4.
    Perdie.
But how so the game goes,
To me they will suppose,
And make a foul noise,
    And cry out upon me.   4

But thou must do as thou hight[42].
WIFE: I accord me theretill;
    I shall swaddle him right in my cradle.
    If it were a greater plight, yet could I help till.
    I will lie down straight. Come, cover me.
MAK: I will.
WIFE: Behind!   4:
    Come Coll and his maroo[43],
    They will nip us full narrow.
MAK: But I may cry "Out, harrow!"
    The sheep if they find.

WIFE: Hearken aye when they call; they will come anon.   44
    Come and make ready all, and sing by thine own;
    Sing lullaby thou shall, for I must groan
    And cry out by the wall on Mary and John,
    For sore.
    Sing lullaby fast   44
    When thou hears at the last;
    Unless I play a false cast,
        Trust me no more!
    [*The* SHEPHERDS *meet at the crooked hawthorne.*]
THIRD SHEPHERD: Ah, Coll, good morn! Why sleep thou not?
FIRST SHEPHERD: Alas, that ever was I born! We have a foul blot.   45
    A fat wether have we lorn.
THIRD SHEPHERD: Marry, God forbid!
SECOND SHEPHERD: Who should do us that scorn? That were a foul spot.
FIRST SHEPHERD: Some shrew.
    I have sought with my dogs
    All Horbury Shrogs,
    And of fifteen hogs[44]   45
        Found I but one ewe.

THIRD SHEPHERD: Now trust me if ye will; by Saint Thomas of Kent,
    Either Mak or Gill was at that assent.
FIRST SHEPHERD: Peace, man, be still! I saw when he went.   46
    Thou slanders him ill. Thou ought to repent,
        Good speed.

[42] Promised.
[43] Mate.
[44] Year-old sheep.

ECOND SHEPHERD: Now as ever might I thrive,
    If I should even here die,
    I would say it were he   465
        That did that same deed.
HIRD SHEPHERD: Go we thither, I rede, and run on our feet.
    I shall never eat bread the truth till I wit.
IRST SHEPHERD: Nor drink, in my heed, with him I meet.
ECOND SHEPHERD: I will rest in no stead till that I him greet,   470
      My brother!
    One thing I will plight:
    Till I see him in sight
    Shall I never sleep one night
      Where I do another.   475
    [*At* MAK's *house they hear* GILL *groan and* MAK *sing a lullaby.*]
HIRD SHEPHERD: Will ye hear how they hack? Our sir likes to croon.
IRST SHEPHERD: Heard I never one crack so clear out of tune!
    Call on him.
ECOND SHEPHERD: Mak! Undo your door soon.
MAK: Who is it that spake as it were noon
      On loft?   480
    Who is that, I say?
HIRD SHEPHERD: Good fellows, were it day—
MAK: As far as ye may,
      Good, speak soft,

    Over a sick woman's head that is at malaise;   485
    I had liefer be dead e'er she had any dis-ease.
WIFE: Go to another place! I may not well wheeze.
    Each foot that ye tread goes through my nose,
      So high!
IRST SHEPHERD: Tell us, Mak, if ye may,   490
    How fare ye, I say?
MAK: But are ye in this town today?
      How fare ye, I say?
    Ye have run in the mire, and are wet yet
    I shall make you a fire if ye will sit.   495
    .A nurse would I hire, think ye on it.
    Well paid is my hire; my dream—this is it,
      In season.
    I have bairns, if ye knew,
    Well more than enow.   500
    But we must drink as we brew,
      And that is but reason.

    I would have ye dine ere ye go. Methinks that ye sweat.
ECOND SHEPHERD: Nay, neither mends our mood, drink nor meat.
MAK: Why, sir, ails you aught but good?

THIRD SHEPHERD: Yea, our sheep that we get   50
   Are stolen as they go. Our loss is great.
MAK: Sirs, drink!
   Had I been there,
   Some should have paid full sore.
FIRST SHEPHERD: Marry, some men think that ye were;
     And that makes us think.   51

SECOND SHEPHERD: Mak, some men trows that it should be ye.
THIRD SHEPHERD: Either ye or your spouse, so say we.
MAK: Now, if ye have suspicion of Gill or me,
   Come and rip our house, and then ye may see   51
     Who had her.
   If I any sheep got,
   Any cow or stott[45],
   And Gill, my wife, rose not
     Since here she laid her,   52
   As I am true and leal, to God here I pray
   That this be the first meal that I shall eat this day.
FIRST SHEPHERD: Mak, as have I weal, advise thee, I say:
   He learned timely to steal that could not say nay.
WIFE: I swelt[46]!   52
   Out, thieves, from my house!
   Ye come to rob us, for the nonce.
MAK: Hear ye not how she groans?
     Your hearts should melt.

WIFE: Out, thieves, from my bairn! Approach him not there!   53
MAK: Knew ye what she had borne, your hearts would be sore.
   Ye do wrong, I you warn, that thus come before
   To a woman that has farne[47]. But I say no more.
WIFE: Ah, my middle!
   I pray to God so mild,   53
   If ever I you beguiled,
   That I eat this child
     That lies in this cradle.

MAK: Peace, woman, for God's pain, and cry not so!
   Thou hurts thy brain, and makes me full of woe.   54
SECOND SHEPHERD: I think our sheep be slain. What find ye two?
THIRD SHEPHERD: All work we in vain; as well may we go.
     But, hatters[48],
   I can find no flesh,
   Hard nor nesh[49],   54
   Salt nor fresh,
     But two empty platters.

[45] Young steer.   [46] Faint.
[47] Fared; i. e., had a child.   [48] Confound it.
[49] Soft.

Live cattle but this, tame nor wild,
None, as have I bliss, so loud as he smelled.
IFE: No, so God me bless, and give me joy of my child! 550
RST SHEPHERD: We have marked amiss; I hold us beguiled.
COND SHEPHERD: Sir, done.
    Sir, Our Lady him save!
    Is your child a knave[50]?
AK: Any lord might him have, 555
      This child as his son.

When he wakens he skips, that joy is to see.
HIRD SHEPHERD: In good time to his hips, and in glee.
    Who were his godfathers, so soon ready?
AK: So fair fall their lips!
RST SHEPHERD: Hark now, a lie! 560
AK: So God them thank,
    Parkin and Gibbon Waller, I say,
    And gentle John Horn, in good faith,
    He made all the garray[51]
      With his great shank. 565

COND SHEPHERD: Mak, friends will we be, for we are all one.
AK: We! Now I hold for me, for amends get I none.
    Farewell, all three! All glad were ye gone! [*Shepherds go out.*]
HIRD SHEPHERD: Fair words may there be, but love there is none
      This year. 570
RST SHEPHERD: Gave ye the child anything?
COND SHEPHERD: I trow, not one farthing!
HIRD SHEPHERD: Fast back will I fling;
    Abide ye me here.
    [SHEPHERDS *re-enter.*]
    Mak, take it to no grief, if I come to thy bairn. 575
AK: Nay, thou does me great reproof; and foul has thou fared.
HIRD SHEPHERD: The child will it not grieve, that little daystar.
    Mak, with your leave, let me give your bairn
    But sixpence.
AK: Nay, go 'way; he sleeps. 580
HIRD SHEPHERD: Methinks he peeps.
AK: When he wakens he weeps;
    I pray you, go hence!

HIRD SHEPHERD: Give me leave him to kiss, and lift up the clout.
    What the devil is this? He has a long snout! 585
RST SHEPHERD: He is marked amiss. We wait ill about.
ECOND SHEPHERD: "Ill spun weft," ywis, "aye comes foul out."

---

[50] Boy.
[51] Commotion.

Aye, so!
He is like to our sheep!
THIRD SHEPHERD: How, Gib, may I peep?   59
FIRST SHEPHERD: I trow, nature will creep
    Where it may not go!

SECOND SHEPHERD: This was a quaint gawd[52] and a far cast!
It was a high fraud!
THIRD SHEPHERD: Yea, sirs, was't.
Let's burn this bawd, and bind her fast.   59
Ah, false scold, hang at the last,
    So shall thou.
Will ye see how they swaddle
His four feet in the middle?
Saw I never in a cradle   60
    A hornéd lad ere now.

MAK: Peace, bid I! What! Let be your fare!
I am he that him begot, and yon woman him bare.
FIRST SHEPHERD: After what devil shall he be hatt[53]? "Mak"?
Lo, God, Mak's heir!
SECOND SHEPHERD: Let be all that. Now God give him care, I say.   60
WIFE: A pretty child is he
As sits on a woman's knee;
A dilly-downe, perdie,
    To make a man laugh.   61

THIRD SHEPHERD: I know him by the ear-mark; that is a good token.
MAK: I tell you, sirs, hark! His nose was broken;
Later told me a clerk that he was forespoken[54].
FIRST SHEPHERD: This is a false work; I would fain be wroken[55].
    Get a weapon.   61
WIFE: He was taken by an elf,
    I saw it myself;
When the clock struck twelve
    Was he misshapen.

SECOND SHEPHERD: Ye two are well gifted, same in a stead.
THIRD SHEPHERD: Since they maintain their theft, let's do them to death.   62
MAK: If I trespass eft, gird off my head!
    With you will I be left.
FIRST SHEPHERD: Sirs, take my lead:

[52] Trick.   [53] Named.
[54] Enchanted.   [55] Avenged.

For this trespass
We will neither curse nor fight, 625
Quarrel nor chide,
But have done as tight[56],
    And cast him in canvas.
    [*They toss him and go back to the fields.*]
IRST SHEPHERD: Lord, what! I am sore in point for to burst.
In faith, I may no more; therefore will I rest. 630
ECOND SHEPHERD: As a sheep of seven score he weighed in my fist.
For to sleep anywhere methinks that I list.
HIRD SHEPHERD: Now I pray you,
Lie down on this green.
IRST SHEPHERD: On these thieves yet I mind. 635
HIRD SHEPHERD: Whereto should ye strain
    So, I say you? [*They sleep.*]
    [*An* ANGEL *sings "Gloria in excelsis"; then let him say:*]
NGEL: Rise, herd-men kind! For now is he born
That shall take from the fiend what Adam had lorn:
That devil to sheynd[57] this night is he born; 640
God is made your friend now at this morn.
    He behests
At Bethlehem go see,
Where lies the Free
In a crib full poorly 645
    Between two beasts.

IRST SHEPHERD: This was a wise voice that ever yet I heard.
It is a marvel to name, thus to be scared.
ECOND SHEPHERD: Of God's son of heaven he spake upward
All the wood in a levin[58] methought that he made 650
    To appear.
HIRD SHEPHERD: He spake of a bairn
In Bethlehem, I you warn.
IRST SHEPHERD: That betokens yon star;
    Let us seek him there. 655

ECOND SHEPHERD: Say, what was his song? Heard ye not how he cracked it,
    Three briefs to a long?
HIRD SHEPHERD: Yea, marry, he hacked it;
Was no crotchet wrong, nor nothing that lacked it.
IRST SHEPHERD: For to sing us among, right as he knacked it, I can. 660
ECOND SHEPHERD: Let's see how ye croon.
    Can ye bark at the moon?
HIRD SHEPHERD: Hold your tongues, have done!
IRST SHEPHERD: Hark after, then!

[56] Quickly.
[57] Destroy.
[58] Lightning.

SECOND SHEPHERD: To Bethlehem he bade that we should gang;   66
    I am full afeared that we tarry too long.
THIRD SHEPHERD: Be merry and not sad; o mirth is our song;
    Everlasting glad our reward may we fang[59]
        Without noise.
FIRST SHEPHERD: Therefore thither hie we,   67
    If we be wet and weary,
    To that child and that lady.
        We have it not to lose.
SECOND SHEPHERD: We find by the prophecy—let be your din—
    Of David and Isaiah and more than I mind,   67
    They prophesied by clergy that in a virgin
    Should he light and lie, to slacken our sin
        And slake it,
    Our Race from woe.
    For Isaiah said so: 68
    "*Ecce virgo*
        Concipiet" a child that is naked.

THIRD SHEPHERD: Full glad may we be, and abide that day
    That lovely to see, that all mights may.
    Lord, well were me, for once and for aye,   68
    Might I kneel on my knee some word for to say
        To that child.
    But the angel said,
    In a crib was he laid;
    He was poorly arrayed,   69
        Both humble and mild.

FIRST SHEPHERD: Patriarchs that have been, and prophets before,
    They desired to have seen this child that is born.
    They are gone full clean; that have they lorn.
    We shall see him, I ween, ere it be morn,   69
        To token.
    When I see him and feel,
    Then know I full well
    It is true as steel
        That prophets have spoken: 70

    To so poor as we are that he would appear,
    First find, and declare by his messenger.
SECOND SHEPHERD: Go we now, let us fare; the place is us near.
THIRD SHEPHERD: I am ready, prepared; go we together
        To that bright.   70
    Lord, if thy will be—
    We are simple all three—

[59] Take.

Grant us some kind of glee
    To comfort thy wight.
    [*They enter the stable.*]

FIRST SHEPHERD: Hail, comely and clean! Hail, young child!
    Hail, maker, as I mean, from a maiden so mild!   711
    Thou has cursed, I ween, the devil so wild;
    The false guiler of teen[60], now goes he beguiled.
        Lo, he merry is!
    Lo, he laughs, my sweeting!   715
    A welfare meeting
    I have holden my heting[61].
        Have a bob of cherries!

SECOND SHEPHERD: Hail, sovereign Savior, for thou hast us sought!
    Hail! noble child and flower, that all things has wrought!
    Hail, full of favor, that made all of naught!   721
    Hail! I kneel and I cower. A bird have I brought
        To my bairn.
    Hail, little tiny mop!
    Of our creed thou art crop.   725
    I would drink of thy cup,
        Little day-star.

THIRD SHEPHERD: Hail, darling dear, full of godhead!
    I pray thee be near when that I have need.
    Hail! Sweet is thy cheer! My heart would bleed   730
    To see thee sit here in so poor weed,
        With no pennies.
    Hail! Put forth thy dall[62]
    I bring thee but a ball:
    Have and play thee withal,   735
        And go to the tennis.

MARY: The Father of Heaven, God omnipotent,
    That set all in seven days, his Son has sent.
    My name could he neven[63] and descend ere he went.
    I conceived him full even, through might as he meant;   740
        And now he is born.
    Keep ye you from woe!
    I shall pray him so.
    Tell it forth as ye go,
        And mind on this morn.   745

FIRST SHEPHERD: Farewell, lady, so fair to behold,
    With thy child on thy knee!

---

[60] Contriver of evil.   [61] Held to my promise.
[62] Hand.   [63] Call.

SECOND SHEPHERD: But he lies full cold.
    Lord, well is me. Now we go, thou behold.
THIRD SHEPHERD: Forsooth, already it seems to be told
    Full oft.   75
FIRST SHEPHERD: What grace we have found!
SECOND SHEPHERD: Come forth; now are we won!
THIRD SHEPHERD: To sing are we bound:
    Let take aloft!

                EXPLICIT PAGINA PASTORUM

William Shakespeare

Hamlet, Prince of Denmark

CLAUDIUS, *King of Denmark*
HAMLET, *son to the former and nephew to the present King*
POLONIUS, *Lord Chamberlain*
HORATIO, *friend to Hamlet*
LAERTES, *son to Polonius*
VOLTEMAND
CORNELIUS
ROSENCRANTZ   } *courtiers*
GUILDENSTERN
OSRIC
A GENTLEMAN
A PRIEST
MARCELLUS   } *officers*
BERNARDO
FRANCISCO, *a soldier*
REYNALDO, *servant to Polonius*
PLAYERS
TWO CLOWNS, *grave-diggers*
FORTINBRAS, *Prince of Norway*
A NORWEGIAN CAPTAIN
ENGLISH AMBASSADORS
GERTRUDE, *Queen of Denmark, and mother of Hamlet*
OPHELIA, *daughter to Polonius*
GHOST *of Hamlet's father*
LORDS, LADIES, OFFICERS, SOLDIERS, SAILORS, MESSENGERS, AND
  ATTENDANTS

SCENE——*Denmark.*

ACT I

SCENE I——*Elsinore. The guard-platform of the Castle.*

[FRANCISCO *at his post. Enter to him* BERNARDO.]
BERNARDO: Who's there?
FRANCISCO: Nay, answer me. Stand and unfold yourself.

BERNARDO: Long live the King!

FRANCISCO: Bernardo?

BERNARDO: He.

FRANCISCO: You come most carefully upon your hour.

BERNARDO: 'Tis now struck twelve; get thee to bed, Francisco.

FRANCISCO: For this relief much thanks. 'Tis bitter cold,
    And I am sick at heart.

BERNARDO: Have you had quiet guard?

FRANCISCO: Not a mouse stirring.

BERNARDO: Well; good night.
    If you do meet Horatio and Marcellus,
    The rivals of my watch, bid them make haste.

        [*Enter* HORATIO *and* MARCELLUS.]

FRANCISCO: I think I hear them. Stand, ho! Who is there?

HORATIO: Friends to this ground.

MARCELLUS: And liegemen to the Dane.

FRANCISCO: Give you good night.

MARCELLUS: O, farewell, honest soldier!
    Who hath reliev'd you?

FRANCISCO: Bernardo hath my place.
    Give you good night.   [*Exit.*]

MARCELLUS: Holla, Bernardo!

BERNARDO: Say—
    What, is Horatio there?

HORATIO: A piece of him.

BERNARDO: Welcome, Horatio; welcome, good Marcellus.

HORATIO: What, has this thing appear'd again to-night?

BERNARDO: I have seen nothing.

MARCELLUS: Horatio says 'tis but our fantasy,
    And will not let belief take hold of him
    Touching this dreaded sight, twice seen of us;
    Therefore I have entreated him along
    With us to watch the minutes of this night,
    That, if again this apparition come,
    He may approve our eyes and speak to it.

HORATIO: Tush, tush, 'twill not appear.

BERNARDO: Sit down awhile,
    And let us once again assail your ears,
    That are so fortified against our story,
    What we have two nights seen.

HORATIO: Well, sit we down,
    And let us hear Bernardo speak of this.

BERNARDO: Last night of all,

When yond same star that's westward from the pole
Had made his course t' illume that part of heaven
Where now it burns, Marcellus and myself,
The bell then beating one—
    [*Enter* GHOST.]
MARCELLUS: Peace, break thee off; look where it comes again.
BERNARDO: In the same figure, like the King that's dead.
MARCELLUS: Thou art a scholar; speak to it, Horatio.
BERNARDO: Looks 'a not like the King? Mark it, Horatio.
HORATIO: Most like. It harrows me with fear and wonder.
BERNARDO.: It would be spoke to.
MARCELLUS: Question it, Horatio.
HORATIO: What art thou that usurp'st this time of night
    Together with that fair and warlike form
    In which the majesty of buried Denmark
    Did sometimes march? By heaven I charge thee, speak!
MARCELLUS: It is offended.
BERNARDO: See, it stalks away.
HORATIO: Stay! speak, speak! I charge thee, speak!
    [*Exit* GHOST.]
MARCELLUS: 'Tis gone, and will not answer.
BERNARDO: How now, Horatio! You tremble and look pale.
    Is not this something more than fantasy?
    What think you on't?
HORATIO: Before my God, I might not this believe
    Without the sensible and true avouch
    Of mine own eyes.
MARCELLUS: Is it not like the King?
HORATIO: As thou art to thyself:
    Such was the very armour he had on
    When he the ambitious Norway combated;
    So frown'd he once when, in an angry parle,
    He smote the sledded Polacks on the ice.
    'Tis strange.
MARCELLUS: Thus twice before, and jump at this dead hour,
    With martial stalk hath he gone by our watch.
HORATIO: In what particular thought to work I know not;
    But, in the gross and scope of mine opinion,
    This bodes some strange eruption to our state.
MARCELLUS: Good now, sit down, and tell me, he that knows,
    Why this same strict and most observant watch
    So nightly toils the subject of the land;
    And why such daily cast of brazen cannon,

And foreign mart for implements of war;
Why such impress of shipwrights, whose sore task
Does not divide the Sunday from the week;
What might be toward, that this sweaty haste
Doth make the night joint-labourer with the day:
Who is't that can inform me?

HORATIO: That can I;
At least, the whisper goes so. Our last King,
Whose image even but now appear'd to us,
Was, as you know, by Fortinbras of Norway,
Thereto prick'd on by a most emulate pride,
Dar'd to the combat; in which our valiant Hamlet—
For so this side of our known world esteem'd him—
Did slay this Fortinbras; who, by a seal'd compact,
Well ratified by law and heraldry,
Did forfeit, with his life, all those his lands
Which he stood seiz'd of, to the conqueror;
Against the which a moiety competent
Was gaged by our King; which had return'd
To the inheritance of Fortinbras,
Had he been vanquisher; as, by the same comart
And carriage of the article design'd,
His fell to Hamlet. Now, sir, young Fortinbras,
Of unimproved mettle hot and full,
Hath in the skirts of Norway, here and there,
Shark'd up a list of lawless resolutes,
For food and diet, to some enterprise
That hath a stomach in't; which is no other,
As it doth well appear unto our state,
But to recover of us, by strong hand
And terms compulsatory, those foresaid lands
So by his father lost; and this, I take it,
Is the main motive of our preparations,
The source of this our watch, and the chief head
Of this post-haste and romage in the land.

BERNARDO: I think it be no other but e'en so.
Well may it sort, that this portentous figure
Comes armed through our watch; so like the King
That was and is the question of these wars.

HORATIO: A mote it is to trouble the mind's eye.
In the most high and palmy state of Rome,
A little ere the mightiest Julius fell,
The graves stood tenantless, and the sheeted dead

Did squeak and gibber in the Roman streets;
As, stars with trains of fire, and dews of blood,
Disasters in the sun; and the moist star
Upon whose influence Neptune's empire stands
Was sick almost to doomsday with eclipse;
And even the like precurse of fear'd events,
As harbingers preceding still the fates
And prologue to the omen coming on,
Have heaven and earth together demonstrated
Unto our climatures and countrymen.
  [*Re-enter* GHOST.]
But, soft, behold! Lo, where it comes again!
I'll cross it, though it blast me. Stay, illusion.
  [GHOST *spreads its arms*.]
If thou hast any sound or use of voice,
Speak to me.
If there be any good thing to be done,
That may to thee do ease and grace to me,
Speak to me.
If thou art privy to thy country's fate,
Which happily foreknowing may avoid,
O, speak!
Or if thou hast uphoarded in thy life
Extorted treasure in the womb of earth,
For which, they say, you spirits oft walk in death,
  [*The cock crows*.]
Speak of it. Stay, and speak. Stop it, Marcellus.
MARCELLUS: Shall I strike at it with my partisan?
HORATIO: Do, if it will not stand.
BERNARDO: 'Tis here!
HORATIO: 'Tis here!
MARCELLUS: 'Tis gone!   [*Exit* GHOST.]
  We do it wrong, being so majestical,
  To offer it the show of violence;
  For it is, as the air, invulnerable,
  And our vain blows malicious mockery.
BERNARDO: It was about to speak, when the cock crew.
HORATIO: And then it started like a guilty thing
  Upon a fearful summons. I have heard
  The cock, that is the trumpet to the morn,
  Doth with his lofty and shrill-sounding throat
  Awake the god of day; and at his warning,
  Whether in sea or fire, in earth or air,

Th' extravagant and erring spirit hies
To his confine; and of the truth herein
This present object made probation.
MARCELLUS: It faded on the crowing of the cock.
Some say that ever 'gainst that season comes
Wherein our Saviour's birth is celebrated,
This bird of dawning singeth all night long;
And then, they say, no spirit dare stir abroad,
The nights are wholesome, then no planets strike,
No fairy takes, nor witch hath power to charm,
So hallowed and so gracious is that time.
HORATIO: So have I heard, and do in part believe it.
But look, the morn, in russet mantle clad,
Walks o'er the dew of yon high eastward hill.
Break we our watch up; and, by my advice,
Let us impart what we have seen to-night
Unto young Hamlet; for, upon my life,
This spirit, dumb to us, will speak to him.
Do you consent we shall acquaint him with it,
As needful in our loves, fitting our duty?
MARCELLUS: Let's do't, I pray; and I this morning know
Where we shall find him most convenient.   [*Exeunt.*]

SCENE II———*Elsinore. The Castle.*

[*Flourish. Enter* CLAUDIUS KING OF DENMARK, GERTRUDE THE QUEEN, *and*
COUNCILLORS, *including* POLONIUS, *his son* LAERTES, VOLTEMAND,
CORNELIUS, *and* HAMLET.]
KING: Though yet of Hamlet our dear brother's death
The memory be green; and that it us befitted
To bear our hearts in grief, and our whole kingdom
To be contracted in one brow of woe;
Yet so far hath discretion fought with nature
That we with wisest sorrow think on him,
Together with remembrance of ourselves.
Therefore our sometime sister, now our queen,
Th' imperial jointress to this warlike state,
Have we, as 'twere with a defeated joy,
With an auspicious and a dropping eye,
With mirth in funeral, and with dirge in marriage,
In equal scale weighing delight and dole,
Taken to wife; nor have we herein barr'd
Your better wisdoms, which have freely gone
With this affair along. For all, our thanks.

Now follows that you know: young Fortinbras,
Holding a weak supposal of our worth,
Or thinking by our late dear brother's death
Our state to be disjoint and out of frame,
Co-leagued with this dream of his advantage—
He hath not fail'd to pester us with message
Importing the surrender of those lands
Lost by his father, with all bands of law,
To our most valiant brother. So much for him.
Now for ourself, and for this time of meeting,
Thus much the business is: we have here writ
To Norway, uncle of young Fortinbras—
Who, impotent and bed-rid, scarcely hears
Of this his nephew's purpose—to suppress
His further gait herein, in that the levies,
The lists, and full proportions, are all made
Out of his subject; and we here dispatch
You, good Cornelius, and you, Voltemand,
For bearers of this greeting to old Norway;
Giving to you no further personal power
To business with the King more than the scope
Of these dilated articles allow.
Farewell; and let your haste commend your duty.

CORNELIUS: }
VOLTEMAND: } In that and all things will we show our duty.

KING: We doubt it nothing; heartily farewell.
      [*Exeunt* VOLTEMAND *and* CORNELIUS.]
And now, Laertes, what's the news with you?
You told us of some suit; what is't, Laertes?
You cannot speak of reason to the Dane
And lose your voice. What wouldst thou beg, Laertes,
That shall not be my offer, not thy asking?
The head is not more native to the heart,
The hand more instrumental to the mouth,
Than is the throne of Denmark to thy father.
What wouldst thou have, Laertes?

LAERTES: My dread lord,
Your leave and favour to return to France;
From whence though willingly I came to Denmark
To show my duty in your coronation,
Yet now, I must confess, that duty done,
My thoughts and wishes bend again toward France,
And bow them to your gracious leave and pardon.

KING: Have you your father's leave? What says Polonius?

POLONIUS: 'A hath, my lord, wrung from me my slow leave
    By laboursome petition; and at last
    Upon his will I seal'd my hard consent.
    I do beseech you, give him leave to go.
KING: Take thy fair hour, Laertes; time be thine,
    And thy best graces spend it at thy will!
    But now, my cousin Hamlet, and my son—
HAMLET: [*Aside*] A little more than kin, and less than kind.
KING: How is it that the clouds still hang on you?
HAMLET: Not so, my lord; I am too much in the sun.
QUEEN: Good Hamlet, cast thy nighted colour off,
    And let thine eye look like a friend on Denmark.
    Do not for ever with thy vailed lids
    Seek for thy noble father in the dust.
    Thou know'st 'tis common—all that lives must die,
    Passing through nature to eternity.
HAMLET: Ay, madam, it is common.
QUEEN: If it be,
    Why seems it so particular with thee?
HAMLET: Seems, madam! Nay, it is; I know not seems.
    'Tis not alone my inky cloak, good mother,
    Nor customary suits of solemn black,
    Nor windy suspiration of forc'd breath,
    No, nor the fruitful river in the eye,
    Nor the dejected haviour of the visage,
    Together with all forms, moods, shapes of grief,
    That can denote me truly. These, indeed, seem;
    For they are actions that a man might play;
    But I have that within which passes show—
    These but the trappings and the suits of woe.
KING: 'Tis sweet and commendable in your nature, Hamlet,
    To give these mourning duties to your father;
    But you must know your father lost a father;
    That father lost, lost his; and the survivor bound,
    In filial obligation, for some term
    To do obsequious sorrow. But to persever
    In obstinate condolement is a course
    Of impious stubbornness; 'tis unmanly grief;
    It shows a will most incorrect to heaven,
    A heart unfortified, a mind impatient,
    An understanding simple and unschool'd;
    For what we know must be, and is as common
    As any the most vulgar thing to sense,

Why should we in our peevish opposition
Take it to heart? Fie! 'tis a fault to heaven,
A fault against the dead, a fault to nature,
To reason most absurd; whose common theme
Is death of fathers, and who still hath cried,
From the first corse till he that died to-day,
'This must be so.' We pray you throw to earth
This unprevailing woe, and think of us
As of a father; for let the world take note
You are the most immediate to our throne;
And with no less nobility of love
Than that which dearest father bears his son
Do I impart toward you. For your intent
In going back to school in Wittenberg,
It is most retrograde to our desire;
And we beseech you bend you to remain
Here, in the cheer and comfort of our eye,
Our chiefest courtier, cousin, and our son.

QUEEN: Let not thy mother lose her prayers, Hamlet:
I pray thee stay with us; go not to Wittenberg.

HAMLET: I shall in all my best obey you, madam.

KING: Why, 'tis a loving and a fair reply.
Be as ourself in Denmark. Madam, come;
This gentle and unforc'd accord of Hamlet
Sits smiling to my heart; in grace whereof,
No jocund health that Denmark drinks to-day
But the great cannon to the clouds shall tell,
And the King's rouse the heaven shall bruit again,
Re-speaking earthly thunder. Come away.
[*Flourish. Exeunt all but* HAMLET.]

HAMLET: O, that this too too solid flesh would melt,
Thaw, and resolve itself into a dew!
Or that the Everlasting had not fix'd
His canon 'gainst self-slaughter! O God! God!
How weary, stale, flat, and unprofitable,
Seem to me all the uses of this world!
Fie on't! Ah, fie! 'tis an unweeded garden,
That grows to seed; things rank and gross in nature
Possess it merely. That it should come to this!
But two months dead! Nay, not so much, not two.
So excellent a king that was to this
Hyperion to a satyr; so loving to my mother,
That he might not beteem the winds of heaven

Visit her face too roughly. Heaven and earth!
Must I remember? Why, she would hang on him
As if increase of appetite had grown
By what it fed on; and yet, within a month—
Let me not think on't. Frailty, thy name is woman!—
A little month, or ere those shoes were old
With which she followed my poor father's body,
Like Niobe, all tears—why she, even she—
O God! a beast that wants discourse of reason
Would have mourn'd longer—married with my uncle,
My father's brother; but no more like my father
Than I to Hercules. Within a month,
Ere yet the salt of most unrighteous tears
Had left the flushing in her galled eyes,
She married. O, most wicked speed, to post
With such dexterity to incestuous sheets!
It is not, nor it cannot come to good.
But break, my heart, for I must hold my tongue.
    [*Enter* HORATIO, MARCELLUS, *and* BERNARDO.]
HORATIO: Hail to your lordship!
HAMLET: I am glad to see you well.
    Horatio—or I do forget myself.
HORATIO: The same, my lord, and your poor servant ever.
HAMLET: Sir, my good friend. I'll change that name with you.
    And what make you from Wittenberg, Horatio?
    Marcellus?
MARCELLUS: My good lord!
HAMLET: I am very glad to see you. [*to* BERNARDO] Good even, sir.—
    But what, in faith, make you from Wittenberg?
HORATIO: A truant disposition, good my lord.
HAMLET: I would not hear your enemy say so;
    Nor shall you do my ear that violence,
    To make it truster of your own report
    Against yourself. I know you are no truant.
    But what is your affair in Elsinore?
    We'll teach you to drink deep ere you depart.
HORATIO: My lord, I came to see your father's funeral.
HAMLET: I prithee do not mock me, fellow-student;
    I think it was to see my mother's wedding.
HORATIO: Indeed, my lord, it followed hard upon.
HAMLET: Thrift, thrift, Horatio! The funeral bak'd-meats
    Did coldly furnish forth the marriage tables.
    Would I had met my dearest foe in heaven

Or ever I had seen that day, Horatio!
My father—methinks I see my father.

HORATIO: Where, my lord?

HAMLET: In my mind's eye, Horatio.

HORATIO: I saw him once; 'a was a goodly king.

HAMLET: 'A was a man, take him for all in all,
I shall not look upon his like again.

HORATIO: My lord, I think I saw him yesternight.

HAMLET: Saw who?

HORATIO: My lord, the King your father.

HAMLET: The King my father!

HORATIO: Season your admiration for a while
With an attent ear, till I may deliver,
Upon the witness of these gentlemen,
This marvel to you.

HAMLET: For God's love, let me hear.

HORATIO: Two nights together had these gentlemen,
Marcellus and Bernardo, on their watch,
In the dead waste and middle of the night,
Been thus encount'red. A figure like your father,
Armed at point exactly, cap-a-pe,
Appears before them, and with solemn march
Goes slow and stately by them; thrice he walk'd
By their oppress'd and fear-surprised eyes,
Within his truncheon's length; whilst they, distill'd
Almost to jelly with the act of fear,
Stand dumb and speak not to him. This to me
In dreadful secrecy impart they did;
And I with them the third night kept the watch;
Where, as they had delivered, both in time,
Form of the thing, each word made true and good,
The apparition comes. I knew your father;
These hands are not more like.

HAMLET: But where was this?

MARCELLUS: My lord, upon the platform where we watch.

HAMLET: Did you not speak to it?

HORATIO: My lord, I did;
But answer made it none; yet once methought
It lifted up it head and did address
Itself to motion, like as it would speak;
But even then the morning cock crew loud,
And at the sound it shrunk in haste away
And vanish'd from our sight.

HAMLET: 'Tis very strange.

HORATIO: As I do live, my honour'd lord, 'tis true;
  And we did think it writ down in our duty
  To let you know of it.

HAMLET: Indeed, indeed, sirs, but this troubles me.
  Hold you the watch to-night?

ALL: We do, my lord.

HAMLET: Arm'd, say you?

ALL: Arm'd, my lord.

HAMLET: From top to toe?

ALL: My lord, from head to foot.

HAMLET: Then saw you not his face?

HORATIO: O yes, my lord; he wore his beaver up.

HAMLET: What, look'd he frowningly?

HORATIO: A countenance more in sorrow than in anger.

HAMLET: Pale or red?

HORATIO: Nay, very pale.

HAMLET: And fix'd his eyes upon you?

HORATIO: Most constantly.

HAMLET: I would I had been there.

HORATIO: It would have much amaz'd you.

HAMLET: Very like, very like. Stay'd it long?

HORATIO: While one with moderate haste might tell a hundred.

BOTH: Longer, longer.

HORATIO: Not when I saw't.

HAMLET: His beard was grizzl'd—no?

HORATIO: It was, as I have seen it in his life,
  A sable silver'd.

HAMLET: I will watch to-night;
  Perchance 'twill walk again.

HORATIO: I warr'nt it will.

HAMLET: If it assume my noble father's person,
  I'll speak to it, though hell itself should gape
  And bid me hold my peace. I pray you all,
  If you have hitherto conceal'd this sight,
  Let it be tenable in your silence still;
  And whatsoever else shall hap to-night,
  Give it an understanding, but no tongue;
  I will requite your loves. So, fare you well—
  Upon the platform, 'twixt eleven and twelve,
  I'll visit you.

ALL: Our duty to your honour.

HAMLET: Your loves, as mine to you; farewell.

  [*Exeunt all but* HAMLET.]

My father's spirit in arms! All is not well.
I doubt some foul play. Would the night were come!
Till then sit still, my soul. Foul deeds will rise,
Though all the earth o'erwhelm them, to men's eyes.   [*Exit.*]

SCENE III————*Elsinore. The house of* POLONIUS.

[*Enter* LAERTES *and* OPHELIA *his sister.*]

LAERTES: My necessaries are embark'd. Farewell.
    And, sister, as the winds give benefit
    And convoy is assistant, do not sleep,
    But let me hear from you.
OPHELIA.: Do you doubt that?
LAERTES: For Hamlet, and the trifling of his favour,
    Hold it a fashion and a toy in blood,
    A violet in the youth of primy nature,
    Forward not permanent, sweet not lasting,
    The perfume and suppliance of a minute;
    No more.
OPHELIA: No more but so?
LAERTES: Think it no more;
    For nature crescent does not grow alone
    In thews and bulk, but as this temple waxes,
    The inward service of the mind and soul
    Grows wide withal. Perhaps he loves you now,
    And now no soil nor cautel doth besmirch
    The virtue of his will; but you must fear,
    His greatness weigh'd, his will is not his own;
    For he himself is subject to his birth:
    He may not, as unvalued persons do,
    Carve for himself; for on his choice depends
    The sanity and health of this whole state;
    And therefore must his choice be circumscrib'd
    Unto the voice and yielding of that body
    Whereof he is the head. Then if he says he loves you,
    It fits your wisdom so far to believe it
    As he in his particular act and place
    May give his saying deed; which is no further
    Than the main voice of Denmark goes withal.
    Then weigh what loss your honour may sustain,
    If with too credent ear you list his songs,
    Or lose your heart, or your chaste treasure open
    To his unmast'red importunity.
    Fear it, Ophelia, fear it, my dear sister;

And keep you in the rear of your affection,
Out of the shot and danger of desire.
The chariest maid is prodigal enough
If she unmask her beauty to the moon.
Virtue itself scapes not calumnious strokes;
The canker galls the infants of the spring
Too oft before their buttons be disclos'd;
And in the morn and liquid dew of youth
Contagious blastments are most imminent.
Be wary, then; best safety lies in fear:
Youth to itself rebels, though none else near.

OPHELIA: I shall the effect of this good lesson keep
As watchman to my heart. But, good my brother,
Do not, as some ungracious pastors do,
Show me the steep and thorny way to heaven,
Whiles, like a puff'd and reckless libertine,
Himself the primrose path of dalliance treads
And recks not his own rede.

LAERTES: O, fear me not!
    [*Enter* POLONIUS.]
I stay too long. But here my father comes.
A double blessing is a double grace;
Occasion smiles upon a second leave.

POLONIUS: Yet here, Laertes! Aboard, aboard, for shame!
The wind sits in the shoulder of your sail,
And you are stay'd for. There—my blessing with thee!
And these few precepts in thy memory
Look thou character. Give thy thoughts no tongue,
Nor any unproportion'd thought his act.
Be thou familiar, but by no means vulgar.
Those friends thou hast, and their adoption tried,
Grapple them to thy soul with hoops of steel;
But do not dull thy palm with entertainment
Of each new-hatch'd, unfledg'd comrade. Beware
Of entrance to a quarrel; but, being in,
Bear't that th' opposed may beware of thee.
Give every man thy ear, but few thy voice;
Take each man's censure, but reserve thy judgment.
Costly thy habit as thy purse can buy,
But not express'd in fancy; rich, not gaudy;
For the apparel oft proclaims the man;
And they in France of the best rank and station
Are of a most select and generous choice in that.

Neither a borrower nor a lender be;
For loan oft loses both itself and friend,
And borrowing dulls the edge of husbandry.
This above all—to thine own self be true,
And it must follow, as the night the day,
Thou canst not then be false to any man.
Farewell; my blessing season this in thee!

LAERTES: Most humbly do I take my leave, my lord.

POLONIUS: The time invites you; go, your servants tend.

LAERTES: Farewell, Ophelia; and remember well
What I have said to you.

OPHELIA: 'Tis in my memory lock'd,
And you yourself shall keep the key of it.

LAERTES: Farewell. [*Exit.*]

POLONIUS: What is't, Ophelia, he hath said to you?

OPHELIA: So please you, something touching the Lord Hamlet.

POLONIUS: Marry, well bethought!
'Tis told me he hath very oft of late
Given private time to you; and you yourself
Have of your audience been most free and bounteous.
If it be so—as so 'tis put on me,
And that in way of caution—I must tell you
You do not understand yourself so clearly
As it behoves my daughter and your honour.
What is between you? Give me up the truth.

OPHELIA: He hath, my lord, of late made many tenders
Of his affection to me.

POLONIUS: Affection! Pooh! You speak like a green girl,
Unsifted in such perilous circumstance.
Do you believe his tenders, as you call them?

OPHELIA: I do not know, my lord, what I should think.

POLONIUS: Marry, I will teach you: think yourself a baby
That you have ta'en these tenders for true pay
Which are not sterling. Tender yourself more dearly;
Or—not to crack the wind of the poor phrase,
Running it thus—you'll tender me a fool.

OPHELIA: My lord, he hath importun'd me with love
In honourable fashion.

POLONIUS: Ay, fashion you may call it; go to, go to.

OPHELIA: And hath given countenance to his speech, my lord,
With almost all the holy vows of heaven.

POLONIUS: Ay, springes to catch woodcocks! I do know,
When the blood burns, how prodigal the soul

Lends the tongue vows. These blazes, daughter,
Giving more light than heat—extinct in both,
Even in their promise, as it is a-making—
You must not take for fire. From this time
Be something scanter of your maiden presence;
Set your entreatments at a higher rate
Than a command to parle. For Lord Hamlet,
Believe so much in him, that he is young,
And with a larger tether may he walk
Than may be given you. In few, Ophelia,
Do not believe his vows; for they are brokers,
Not of that dye which their investments show,
But mere implorators of unholy suits,
Breathing like sanctified and pious bonds,
The better to beguile. This is for all—
I would not, in plain terms, from this time forth
Have you so slander any moment leisure
As to give words or talk with the Lord Hamlet.
Look to't, I charge you. Come your ways.
OPHELIA: I shall obey, my lord.   [Exeunt.]

SCENE IV——Elsinore. The guard-platform of the Castle.

[Enter HAMLET, HORATIO, and MARCELLUS.]
HAMLET: The air bites shrewdly; it is very cold.
HORATIO: It is a nipping and an eager air.
HAMLET: What hour now?
HORATIO: I think it lacks of twelve.
MARCELLUS: No, it is struck.
HORATIO: Indeed? I heard it not. It then draws near the season
     Wherein the spirit held his wont to walk.
         [A flourish of trumpets, and two pieces go off.]
     What does this mean, my lord?
HAMLET: The King doth wake to-night and takes his rouse,
     Keeps wassail, and the swagg'ring up-spring reels,
     And, as he drains his draughts of Rhenish down,
     The kettle-drum and trumpet thus bray out
     The triumph of his pledge.
HORATIO: Is it a custom?
HAMLET: Ay, marry, is't;
     But to my mind, though I am native here
     And to the manner born, it is a custom
     More honour'd in the breach than the observance.

This heavy-headed revel east and west
Makes us traduc'd and tax'd of other nations;
They clepe us drunkards, and with swinish phrase
Soil our addition; and, indeed, it takes
From our achievements, though perform'd at height,
The pith and marrow of our attribute.
So, oft it chances in particular men
That, for some vicious mole of nature in them,
As in their birth, wherein they are not guilty,
Since nature cannot choose his origin;
By the o'ergrowth of some complexion,
Oft breaking down the pales and forts of reason;
Or by some habit that too much o'er-leavens
The form of plausive manners—that these men,
Carrying, I say, the stamp of one defect,
Being nature's livery or fortune's star,
His virtues else, be they as pure as grace,
As infinite as man may undergo,
Shall in the general censure take corruption
From that particular fault. The dram of eale
Doth all the noble substance of a doubt
To his own scandal.
    [*Enter* GHOST.]
HORATIO: Look, my lord, it comes.
HAMLET: Angels and ministers of grace defend us!
Be thou a spirit of health or goblin damn'd,
Bring with thee airs from heaven or blasts from hell,
Be thy intents wicked or charitable,
Thou com'st in such a questionable shape
That I will speak to thee. I'll call thee Hamlet,
King, father, royal Dane. O, answer me!
Let me not burst in ignorance, but tell
Why thy canoniz'd bones, hearsed in death,
Have burst their cerements; why the sepulchre
Wherein we saw thee quietly enurn'd
Have op'd his ponderous and marble jaws
To cast thee up again. What may this mean
That thou, dead corse, again in complete steel
Revisits thus the glimpses of the moon,
Making night hideous, and we fools of nature
So horridly to shake our disposition
With thoughts beyond the reaches of our souls?
Say, why is this? wherefore? What should we do?

[GHOST *beckons* HAMLET.]

HORATIO: It beckons you to go away with it,
As if it some impartment did desire
To you alone.

MARCELLUS: Look with what courteous action
It waves you to a more removed ground.
But do not go with it.

HORATIO: No, by no means.

HAMLET: It will not speak; then I will follow it.

HORATIO: Do not, my lord.

HAMLET: Why, what should be the fear?
I do not set my life at a pin's fee;
And for my soul, what can it do to that,
Being a thing immortal as itself?
It waves me forth again; I'll follow it.

HORATIO: What if it tempt you toward the flood, my lord,
Or to the dreadful summit of the cliff
That beetles o'er his base into the sea,
And there assume some other horrible form,
Which might deprive your sovereignty of reason
And draw you into madness? Think of it:
The very place puts toys of desperation,
Without more motive, into every brain
That looks so many fathoms to the sea
And hears it roar beneath.

HAMLET: It waves me still.
Go on; I'll follow thee.

MARCELLUS: You shall not go, my lord.

HAMLET: Hold off your hands.

HORATIO: Be rul'd; you shall not go.

HAMLET: My fate cries out,
And makes each petty arture in this body
As hardy as the Nemean lion's nerve.   [GHOST *beckons*.]
Still am I call'd. Unhand me, gentlemen.
By heaven, I'll make a ghost of him that lets me.
I say, away! Go on; I'll follow thee.

[*Exeunt* GHOST *and* HAMLET.]

HORATIO: He waxes desperate with imagination.

MARCELLUS: Let's follow; 'tis not fit thus to obey him.

HORATIO: Have after. To what issue will this come?

MARCELLUS: Something is rotten in the state of Denmark.

HORATIO: Heaven will direct it.

MARCELLUS: Nay, let's follow him.   [*Exeunt*.]

SCENE V———*Elsinore. The battlements of the Castle.*

[*Enter* GHOST *and* HAMLET.]

HAMLET: Whither wilt thou lead me? Speak. I'll go no further.

GHOST: Mark me.

HAMLET: I will.

GHOST: My hour is almost come,
    When I to sulph'rous and tormenting flames
    Must render up myself.

HAMLET: Alas, poor ghost!

GHOST: Pity me not, but lend thy serious hearing
    To what I shall unfold.

HAMLET: Speak; I am bound to hear.

GHOST: So art thou to revenge, when thou shalt hear.

HAMLET: What?

GHOST: I am thy father's spirit,
    Doom'd for a certain term to walk the night,
    And for the day confin'd to fast in fires,
    Till the foul crimes done in my days of nature
    Are burnt and purg'd away. But that I am forbid
    To tell the secrets of my prison-house,
    I could a tale unfold whose lightest word
    Would harrow up thy soul, freeze thy young blood,
    Make thy two eyes, like stars, start from their spheres,
    Thy knotted and combined locks to part,
    And each particular hair to stand an end,
    Like quills upon the fretful porpentine.
    But this eternal blazon must not be
    To ears of flesh and blood. List, list, O, list!
    If thou didst ever thy dear father love—

HAMLET: O God!

GHOST: Revenge his foul and most unnatural murder.

HAMLET: Murder!

GHOST: Murder most foul, as in the best it is;
    But this most foul, strange, and unnatural.

HAMLET: Haste me to know't, that I, with wings as swift
    As meditation or the thoughts of love,
    May sweep to my revenge.

GHOST: I find thee apt;
    And duller shouldst thou be than the fat weed
    That roots itself in ease on Lethe wharf,
    Wouldst thou not stir in this. Now, Hamlet, hear:
    'Tis given out that, sleeping in my orchard,

A serpent stung me; so the whole ear of Denmark
Is by a forged process of my death
Rankly abus'd; but know, thou noble youth,
The serpent that did sting thy father's life
Now wears his crown.

HAMLET: O my prophetic soul!
My uncle!

GHOST: Ay, that incestuous, that adulterate beast,
With witchcraft of his wits, with traitorous gifts—
O wicked wit and gifts that have the power
So to seduce!—won to his shameful lust
The will of my most seeming virtuous queen.
O Hamlet, what a falling off was there,
From me, whose love was of that dignity
That it went hand in hand even with the vow
I made to her in marriage; and to decline
Upon a wretch whose natural gifts were poor
To those of mine!
But virtue, as it never will be moved,
Though lewdness court it in a shape of heaven,
So lust, though to a radiant angel link'd,
Will sate itself in a celestial bed
And prey on garbage.
But soft! methinks I scent the morning air.
Brief let me be. Sleeping within my orchard,
My custom always of the afternoon,
Upon my secure hour thy uncle stole,
With juice of cursed hebona in a vial,
And in the porches of my ears did pour
The leperous distilment; whose effect
Holds such an enmity with blood of man
That swift as quicksilver it courses through
The natural gates and alleys of the body;
And with a sudden vigour it doth posset
And curd, like eager droppings into milk,
The thin and wholesome blood. So did it mine;
And a most instant tetter bark'd about,
Most lazar-like, with vile and loathsome crust,
All my smooth body.
Thus was I, sleeping, by a brother's hand
Of life, of crown, of queen, at once dispatch'd;
Cut off even in the blossoms of my sin,
Unhous'led, disappointed, unanel'd;

No reck'ning made, but sent to my account
With all my imperfections on my head.
O, horrible! O, horrible! most horrible!
If thou hast nature in thee, bear it not;
Let not the royal bed of Denmark be
A couch for luxury and damned incest.
But, howsomever thou pursuest this act,
Taint not thy mind, nor let thy soul contrive
Against thy mother aught; leave her to heaven,
And to those thorns that in her bosom lodge
To prick and sting her. Fare thee well at once.
The glowworm shows the matin to be near,
And gins to pale his uneffectual fire.
Adieu, adieu, adieu! Remember me.   [*Exit.*]

HAMLET: O all you host of heaven! O earth! What else?
And shall I couple hell? O, fie! Hold, hold, my heart;
And you, my sinews, grow not instant old,
But bear me stiffly up. Remember thee!
Ay, thou poor ghost, whiles memory holds a seat
In this distracted globe. Remember thee!
Yea, from the table of my memory
I'll wipe away all trivial fond records,
All saws of books, all forms, all pressures past,
That youth and observation copied there,
And thy commandment all alone shall live
Within the book and volume of my brain,
Unmix'd with baser matter. Yes, by heaven!
O most pernicious woman!
O villain, villain, smiling, damned villain!
My tables—meet it is I set it down
That one may smile, and smile, and be a villain;
At least I am sure it may be so in Denmark. [*writing*]
So, uncle, there you are. Now to my word:
It is 'Adieu, adieu! Remember me.'
I have sworn't.

HORATIO: [*within*] My lord, my lord!

          [*Enter* HORATIO *and* MARCELLUS.]

MARCELLUS: Lord Hamlet!

HORATIO: Heavens secure him!

HAMLET: So be it!

MARCELLUS: Illo, ho, ho, my lord!

HAMLET: Hillo, ho, ho, boy! Come, bird, come.

MARCELLUS: How is't, my noble lord?

HORATIO: What news, my lord?

HAMLET: O, wonderful!

HORATIO: Good my lord, tell it.

HAMLET: No; you will reveal it.

HORATIO: Not I, my lord, by heaven!

MARCELLUS: Nor I, my lord.

HAMLET: How say you, then; would heart of man once think it?
    But you'll be secret?

BOTH: Ay, by heaven, my lord!

HAMLET: There's never a villain dwelling in all Denmark
    But he's an arrant knave.

HORATIO: There needs no ghost, my lord, come from the grave
    To tell us this.

HAMLET: Why, right; you are in the right;
    And so, without more circumstance at all,
    I hold it fit that we shake hands and part;
    You, as your business and desire shall point you—
    For every man hath business and desire,
    Such as it is; and for my own poor part,
    Look you, I will go pray.

HORATIO: These are but wild and whirling words, my lord.

HAMLET: I am sorry they offend you, heartily;
    Yes, faith, heartily.

HORATIO: There's no offence, my lord.

HAMLET: Yes, by Saint Patrick, but there is, Horatio,
    And much offence too. Touching this vision here—
    It is an honest ghost, that let me tell you.
    For your desire to know what is between us,
    O'ermaster't as you may. And now, good friends,
    As you are friends, scholars, and soldiers,
    Give me one poor request.

HORATIO: What is't, my lord? We will.

HAMLET: Never make known what you have seen to-night.

BOTH: My lord, we will not.

HAMLET: Nay, but swear't.

HORATIO: In faith,
    My lord, not I.

MARCELLUS: Nor I, my lord, in faith.

HAMLET: Upon my sword.

MARCELLUS: We have sworn, my lord, already.

HAMLET: Indeed, upon my sword, indeed.

GHOST: [*cries under the stage*] Swear.

HAMLET: Ha, ha, boy! say'st thou so? Art thou there, true-penny?
Come on. You hear this fellow in the cellarage:
Consent to swear.
HORATIO: Propose the oath, my lord.
HAMLET: Never to speak of this that you have seen,
Swear by my sword.
GHOST: [*beneath*] Swear.
HAMLET: Hic et ubique? Then we'll shift our ground.
Come hither, gentlemen,
And lay your hands again upon my sword.
Swear by my sword
Never to speak of this that you have heard.
GHOST: [*beneath*] Swear, by his sword.
HAMLET: Well said, old mole! Canst work i' th' earth so fast?
A worthy pioneer! Once more remove, good friends.
HORATIO: O day and night, but this is wondrous strange!
HAMLET: And therefore as a stranger give it welcome.
There are more things in heaven and earth, Horatio,
Than are dreamt of in your philosophy.
But come.
Here, as before, never, so help you mercy,
How strange or odd some'er I bear myself—
As I perchance hereafter shall think meet
To put an antic disposition on—
That you, at such times, seeing me, never shall,
With arms encumb'red thus, or this head-shake,
Or by pronouncing of some doubtful phrase,
As 'Well, well, we know' or 'We could, an if we would'
Or 'If we list to speak' or 'There be, an if they might'
Or such ambiguous giving out, to note
That you know aught of me—this do swear,
So grace and mercy at your most need help you.
GHOST: [*beneath*] Swear.
HAMLET: Rest, rest, perturbed spirit! So, gentlemen,
With all my love I do commend me to you;
And what so poor a man as Hamlet is
May do t'express his love and friending to you,
God willing, shall not lack. Let us go in together;
And still your fingers on your lips, I pray.
The time is out of joint. O cursed spite,
That ever I was born to set it right!
Nay, come, let's go together.   [*Exeunt.*]

ACT II

SCENE I———*Elsinore. The house of* POLONIUS.

[*Enter* POLONIUS *and* REYNALDO.]

POLONIUS: Give him this money and these notes, Reynaldo.

REYNALDO: I will, my lord.

POLONIUS: You shall do marvellous wisely, good Reynaldo,
 Before you visit him, to make inquire
 Of his behaviour.

REYNALDO: My lord, I did intend it.

POLONIUS: Marry, well said; very well said. Look you, sir,
 Enquire me first what Danskers are in Paris;
 And how, and who, what means, and where they keep,
 What company, at what expense; and finding
 By this encompassment and drift of question
 That they do know my son, come you more nearer
 Than your particular demands will touch it.
 Take you, as 'twere, some distant knowledge of him;
 As thus: 'I know his father and his friends,
 And in part him.' Do you mark this, Reynaldo?

REYNALDO: Ay, very well, my lord.

POLONIUS: 'And in part him—but' you may say 'not well;
 But if't be he I mean, he's very wild;
 Addicted so and so'; and there put on him
 What forgeries you please; marry, none so rank
 As may dishonour him; take heed of that;
 But, sir, such wanton, wild, and usual slips
 As are companions noted and most known
 To youth and liberty.

REYNALDO: As gaming, my lord.

POLONIUS: Ay, or drinking, fencing, swearing, quarrelling.
 Drabbing—you may go so far.

REYNALDO: My lord, that would dishonour him.

POLONIUS: Faith, no; as you may season it in the charge.
 You must not put another scandal on him,
 That he is open to incontinency;
 That's not my meaning. But breathe his faults so quaintly
 That they may seem the taints of liberty;
 The flash and outbreak of a fiery mind,
 A savageness in unreclaimed blood,
 Of general assault.

REYNALDO: But, my good lord—

POLONIUS: Wherefore should you do this?
REYNALDO: Ay, my lord,
    I would know that.
POLONIUS: Marry, sir, here's my drift,
    And I believe it is a fetch of warrant:
    You laying these slight sullies on my son,
    As 'twere a thing a little soil'd wi' th' working,
    Mark you,
    Your party in converse, him you would sound,
    Having ever seen in the prenominate crimes
    The youth you breathe of guilty, be assur'd
    He closes with you in this consequence—
    'Good sir' or so, or 'friend' or 'gentleman'
    According to the phrase or the addition
    Of man and country.
REYNALDO: Very good, my lord.
POLONIUS: And then, sir, does 'a this—'a does—What was I
    about to say? By the mass, I was about to say something;
    where did I leave?
REYNALDO: At 'closes in the consequence,' at 'friend or so'
    and 'gentleman.'
POLONIUS: At 'closes in the consequence'—ay, marry,
    He closes thus: 'I know the gentleman;
    I saw him yesterday, or t'other day,
    Or then, or then; with such, or such; and, as you say,
    There was 'a gaming; there o'ertook in's rouse;
    There falling out at tennis'; or perchance
    'I saw him enter such a house of sale,'
    Videlicet, a brothel, or so forth. See you now
    Your bait of falsehood take this carp of truth;
    And thus do we of wisdom and of reach,
    With windlasses and with assays of bias,
    By indirections find directions out;
    So, by my former lecture and advice,
    Shall you my son. You have me, have you not?
REYNALDO: My lord, I have.
POLONIUS: God buy ye; fare ye well.
REYNALDO: Good my lord!
POLONIUS: Observe his inclination in yourself.
REYNALDO: I shall, my lord.
POLONIUS: And let him ply his music.
REYNALDO: Well, my lord.
POLONIUS: Farewell!   [*Exit* REYNALDO.]

[*Enter* OPHELIA.]

    How now, Ophelia! What's the matter?

OPHELIA: O my lord, my lord, I have been so affrighted!

POLONIUS: With what, i' th' name of God?

OPHELIA: My lord, as I was sewing in my closet,
    Lord Hamlet, with his doublet all unbrac'd,
    No hat upon his head, his stockings fouled,
    Ungart'red and down-gyved to his ankle;
    Pale as his shirt, his knees knocking each other,
    And with a look so piteous in purport
    As if he had been loosed out of hell
    To speak of horrors—he comes before me.

POLONIUS: Mad for thy love?

OPHELIA: My lord, I do not know,
    But truly I do fear it.

POLONIUS: What said he?

OPHELIA: He took me by the wrist, and held me hard;
    Then goes he to the length of all his arm,
    And, with his other hand thus o'er his brow,
    He falls to such a perusal of my face
    As 'a would draw it. Long stay'd he so.
    At last, a little shaking of mine arm,
    And thrice his head thus waving up and down,
    He rais'd a sigh so piteous and profound
    As it did seem to shatter all his bulk
    And end his being. That done, he lets me go,
    And, with his head over his shoulder turn'd,
    He seem'd to find his way without his eyes;
    For out adoors he went without their helps
    And to the last bended their light on me.

POLONIUS: Come, go with me. I will go seek the King.
    This is the very ecstasy of love,
    Whose violent property fordoes itself,
    And leads the will to desperate undertakings
    As oft as any passion under heaven
    That does afflict our natures. I am sorry—
    What, have you given him any hard words of late?

OPHELIA: No, my good lord; but, as you did command,
    I did repel his letters, and denied
    His access to me.

POLONIUS: That hath made him mad.
    I am sorry that with better heed and judgment
    I had not quoted him. I fear'd he did but trifle,

And meant to wreck thee; but beshrew my jealousy!
By heaven, it is as proper to our age
To cast beyond ourselves in our opinions
As it is common for the younger sort
To lack discretion. Come, go we to the King.
This must be known; which, being kept close, might move
More grief to hide than hate to utter love.
Come.   [*Exeunt.*]

SCENE II———*Elsinore. The Castle.*

[*Flourish. Enter* KING, QUEEN, ROSENCRANTZ, GUILDENSTERN, *and atten-dants.*]

KING: Welcome, dear Rosencrantz and Guildenstern!
Moreover that we much did long to see you,
The need we have to use you did provoke
Our hasty sending. Something have you heard
Of Hamlet's transformation; so I call it,
Sith nor th' exterior nor the inward man
Resembles that it was. What it should be,
More than his father's death, that thus hath put him
So much from th' understanding of himself,
I cannot deem of. I entreat you both
That, being of so young days brought up with him,
And sith so neighboured to his youth and haviour,
That you vouchsafe your rest here in our court
Some little time; so by your companies
To draw him on to pleasures, and to gather,
So much as from occasion you may glean,
Whether aught to us unknown afflicts him thus
That, open'd, lies within our remedy.

QUEEN: Good gentlemen, he hath much talk'd of you;
And sure I am two men there is not living
To whom he more adheres. If it will please you
To show us so much gentry and good will
As to expend your time with us awhile
For the supply and profit of our hope,
Your visitation shall receive such thanks
As fits a king's remembrance.

ROSENCRANTZ: Both your Majesties
Might, by the sovereign power you have of us,
Put your dread pleasures more into command
Than to entreaty.

GUILDENSTERN: But we both obey,
  And here give up ourselves, in the full bent,
  To lay our service freely at your feet,
  To be commanded.
KING: Thanks, Rosencrantz and gentle Guildenstern.
QUEEN: Thanks, Guildenstern and gentle Rosencrantz.
  And I beseech you instantly to visit
  My too much changed son. Go, some of you,
  And bring these gentlemen where Hamlet is.
GUILDENSTERN: Heavens make our presence and our practices
  Pleasant and helpful to him!
QUEEN: Aye amen! [*Exeunt* ROSENCRANTZ, GUILDENSTERN, *and some
  attendants.*]
      [*Enter* POLONIUS.]
POLONIUS: Th' ambassadors from Norway, my good lord,
  Are joyfully return'd.
KING: Thou still hast been the father of good news.
POLONIUS: Have I, my lord? I assure you, my good liege,
  I hold my duty, as I hold my soul,
  Both to my God and to my gracious King;
  And I do think—or else this brain of mine
  Hunts not the trail of policy so sure
  As it hath us'd to do—that I have found
  The very cause of Hamlet's lunacy.
KING: O, speak of that; that do I long to hear.
POLONIUS: Give first admittance to th' ambassadors;
  My news shall be the fruit to that great feast.
KING: Thyself do grace to them, and bring them in.
      [*Exit* POLONIUS.]
  He tells me, my dear Gertrude, he hath found
  The head and source of all your son's distemper.
QUEEN: I doubt it is no other but the main,
  His father's death and our o'erhasty marriage.
KING: Well, we shall sift him.
      [*Re-enter* POLONIUS, *with* VOLTEMAND *and* CORNELIUS.]
  Welcome, my good friends!
  Say, Voltemand. what from our brother Norway?
VOLTEMAND: Most fair return of greetings and desires.
  Upon our first, he sent out to suppress
  His nephew's levies; which to him appear'd
  To be a preparation 'gainst the Polack;
  But, better look'd into, he truly found
  It was against your Highness. Whereat griev'd,

That so his sickness, age, and impotence,
Was falsely borne in hand, sends out arrests
On Fortinbras; which he, in brief, obeys;
Receives rebuke from Norway; and, in fine,
Makes vow before his uncle never more
To give th' assay of arms against your Majesty.
Whereon old Norway, overcome with joy,
Gives him threescore thousand crowns in annual fee,
And his commission to employ those soldiers,
So levied as before, against the Polack;
With an entreaty, herein further shown, [*gives a paper*]
That it might please you to give quiet pass
Through your dominions for this enterprise,
On such regards of safety and allowance
As therein are set down.

KING: It likes us well;
And at our more considered time we'll read,
Answer, and think upon this business.
Meantime we thank you for your well-took labour.
Go to your rest; at night we'll feast together.
Most welcome home!   [*Exeunt* AMBASSADORS *and attendants.*]

POLONIUS: This business is well ended.
My liege, and madam, to expostulate
What majesty should be, what duty is,
Why day is day, night night, and time is time,
Were nothing, but to waste night, day, and time.
Therefore, since brevity is the soul of wit,
And tediousness the limbs and outward flourishes,
I will be brief. Your noble son is mad.
Mad call I it; for, to define true madness,
What is't but to be nothing else but mad?
But let that go.

QUEEN: More matter with less art.

POLONIUS: Madam, I swear I use no art at all.
That he's mad, 'tis true: 'tis true 'tis pity;
And pity 'tis 'tis true. A foolish figure!
But farewell it, for I will use no art.
Mad let us grant him, then; and now remains
That we find out the cause of this effect;
Or rather say the cause of this defect,
For this effect defective comes by cause.
Thus it remains, and the remainder thus.
Perpend.

I have a daughter—have while she is mine—
Who in her duty and obedience, mark,
Hath given me this. Now gather, and surmise. [*reads*]
'To the celestial, and my soul's idol, the most beautified Ophelia.' That's an
ill phrase, a vile phrase; 'beautified' is a vile phrase. But you shall hear. Thus:
[*reads*]
'In her excellent white bosom, these, &c.'

QUEEN: Came this from Hamlet to her?

POLONIUS: Good madam, stay awhile; I will be faithful. [*reads*]

> 'Doubt thou the stars are fire;
> Doubt that the sun doth move;
> Doubt truth to be a liar;
> But never doubt I love.

'O dear Ophelia, I am ill at these numbers. I have not art to reckon my
groans; but that I love thee best, O most best, believe it. Adieu.

> 'Thine evermore, most dear lady, whilst
>   this machine is to him,
>   HAMLET.'

This, in obedience, hath my daughter shown me;
And more above, hath his solicitings,
As they fell out by time, by means, and place,
All given to mine ear.

KING: But how hath she
Receiv'd his love?

POLONIUS: What do you think of me?

KING: As of a man faithful and honourable.

POLONIUS: I would fain prove so. But what might you think,
When I had seen this hot love on the wing,
As I perceiv'd it, I must tell you that,
Before my daughter told me—what might you,
Or my dear Majesty your Queen here, think,
If I had play'd the desk or table-book;
Or given my heart a winking, mute and dumb;
Or look'd upon this love with idle sight—
What might you think? No, I went round to work,
And my young mistress thus I did bespeak:
'Lord Hamlet is a prince out of thy star;
This must not be.' And then I prescripts gave her,
That she should lock herself from his resort,
Admit no messengers, receive no tokens.
Which done, she took the fruits of my advice;
And he repelled, a short tale to make,
Fell into a sadness, then into a fast,

Thence to a watch, thence into a weakness,
Thence to a lightness, and, by this declension,
Into the madness wherein now he raves
And all we mourn for.

KING: Do you think 'tis this?

QUEEN: It may be, very like.

POLONIUS: Hath there been such a time—I would fain know that—
That I have positively said ' 'Tis so,'
When it prov'd otherwise?

KING: Not that I know.

POLONIUS: Take this from this, if this be otherwise.
If circumstances lead me, I will find
Where truth is hid, though it were hid indeed
Within the centre.

KING: How may we try it further?

POLONIUS: You may know sometimes he walks four hours together,
Here in the lobby.

QUEEN: So he does, indeed.

POLONIUS: At such a time I'll loose my daughter to him.
Be you and I behind an arras then;
Mark the encounter: if he love her not,
And be not from his reason fall'n thereon,
Let me be no assistant for a state,
But keep a farm and carters.

KING: We will try it.
       [*Enter* HAMLET, *reading on a book*.]

QUEEN: But look where sadly the poor wretch comes reading.

POLONIUS: Away, I do beseech you, both away:
I'll board him presently. O, give me leave.
       [*Exeunt* KING *and* QUEEN.]
How does my good Lord Hamlet?

HAMLET: Well, God-a-mercy.

POLONIUS: Do you know me, my lord?

HAMLET: Excellent well; you are a fishmonger.

POLONIUS: Not I, my lord.

HAMLET: Then I would you were so honest a man.

POLONIUS: Honest, my lord!

HAMLET: Ay, sir; to be honest, as this world goes, is to be one man pick'd out of ten
thousand.

POLONIUS: That's very true, my lord.

HAMLET: For if the sun breed maggots in a dead dog, being a good kissing carrion—
Have you a daughter?

POLONIUS: I have, my lord.

HAMLET: Let her not walk i' th' sun. Conception is a blessing. But as your daughter may conceive—friend, look to't.

POLONIUS: How say you by that? [*aside*] Still harping on my daughter. Yet he knew me not at first; 'a said I was a fishmonger. 'A is far gone, far gone. And truly in my youth I suff'red much extremity for love. Very near this. I'll speak to him again.—What do you read, my lord?

HAMLET: Words, words, words.

POLONIUS: What is the matter, my lord?

HAMLET: Between who?

POLONIUS: I mean, the matter that you read, my lord.

HAMLET: Slanders, sir; for the satirical rogue says here that old men have grey beards; that their faces are wrinkled; their eyes purging thick amber and plum-tree gum; and that they have a plentiful lack of wit, together with most weak hams—all which, sir, though I most powerfully and potently believe, yet I hold it not honesty to have it thus set down; for you yourself, sir, shall grow old as I am, if, like a crab, you could go backward.

POLONIUS: [*aside*] Though this be madness, yet there is method in't.—Will you walk out of the air, my lord?

HAMLET: Into my grave?

POLONIUS: Indeed, that's out of the air. [*aside*] How pregnant sometimes his replies are! a happiness that often madness hits on, which reason and sanity could not so prosperously be delivered of. I will leave him, and suddenly contrive the means of meeting between him and my daughter.—My lord. I will take my leave of you.

HAMLET: You cannot, sir, take from me anything that I will more willingly part withal—except my life, except my life, except my life.

[*Enter* ROSENCRANTZ *and* GUILDENSTERN.]

POLONIUS: Fare you well, my lord.

HAMLET: These tedious old fools!

POLONIUS: You go to seek the Lord Hamlet; there he is.

ROSENCRANTZ: [*to* POLONIUS] God save you, sir!

[*Exit* POLONIUS.]

GUILDENSTERN: My honour'd lord!

ROSENCRANTZ: My most dear lord!

HAMLET: My excellent good friends! How dost thou, Guildenstern? Ah, Rosencrantz! Good lads, how do you both?

ROSENCRANTZ: As the indifferent children of the earth.

GUILDENSTERN: Happy in that we are not over-happy;
On fortune's cap we are not the very button.

HAMLET: Nor the soles of her shoe?

ROSENCRANTZ: Neither, my lord.

HAMLET: Then you live about her waist, or in the middle of her favours?

GUILDENSTERN: Faith, her privates we.

HAMLET: In the secret parts of Fortune? O, most true; she is a strumpet. What news?

ROSENCRANTZ: None, my lord, but that the world's grown honest.

HAMLET: Then is doomsday near. But your news is not true. Let me question more in particular. What have you, my good friends, deserved at the hands of Fortune, that she sends you to prison hither?

GUILDENSTERN: Prison, my lord!

HAMLET: Denmark's a prison.

ROSENCRANTZ: Then is the world one.

HAMLET: A goodly one; in which there are many confines, wards, and dungeons, Denmark being one o' th' worst.

ROSENCRANTZ: We think not so, my lord.

HAMLET: Why, then, 'tis none to you; for there is nothing either good or bad, but thinking makes it so. To me it is a prison.

ROSENCRANTZ: Why, then your ambition makes it one; 'tis too narrow for your mind.

HAMLET: O God, I could be bounded in a nutshell and count myself a king of infinite space, were it not that I have bad dreams.

GUILDENSTERN: Which dreams indeed are ambition; for the very substance of the ambitious is merely the shadow of a dream.

HAMLET: A dream itself is but a shadow.

ROSENCRANTZ: Truly, and I hold ambition of so airy and light a quality that it is but a shadow's shadow.

HAMLET: Then are our beggars bodies, and our monarchs and oustretch'd heroes the beggars' shadows. Shall we to th' court? for, by my fay, I cannot reason.

BOTH: We'll wait upon you.

HAMLET: No such matter. I will not sort you with the rest of my servants; for, to speak to you like an honest man, I am most dreadfully attended. But, in the beaten way of friendship, what make you at Elsinore?

ROSENCRANTZ: To visit you, my lord; no other occasion.

HAMLET: Beggar that I am, I am even poor in thanks; but I thank you; and sure, dear friends, my thanks are too dear a half-penny. Were you not sent for? Is it your own inclining? Is it a free visitation? Come, come, deal justly with me. Come, come; nay, speak.

GUILDENSTERN: What should we say, my lord?

HAMLET: Why any thing. But to th' purpose: you were sent for; and there is a kind of confession in your looks, which your modesties have not craft enough to colour; I know the good King and Queen have sent for you.

ROSENCRANTZ: To what end, my lord?

HAMLET: That you must teach me. But let me conjure you by the rights of our fellowship, by the consonancy of our youth, by the obligation of our ever-preserved love, and by what more dear a better proposer can charge you withal, be even and direct with me, whether you were sent for or no?

ROSENCRANTZ: [*aside to* GUILDENSTERN] What say you?

HAMLET: [*aside*] Nay, then, I have an eye of you.—If you love me, hold not off.

GUILDENSTERN: My lord, we were sent for.

HAMLET: I will tell you why; so shall my anticipation prevent your discovery, and your secrecy to the King and Queen moult no feather. I have of late—but wherefore I know not—lost all my mirth, forgone all custom of exercises; and indeed it goes so heavily with my disposition that this goodly frame, the earth, seems to me a sterile promontory; this most excellent canopy the air, look you, this brave o'er-hanging firmament, this majestical roof fretted with golden fire—why, it appeareth no other thing to me than a foul and pestilent congregation of vapours. What a piece of work is a man! How noble in reason! how infinite in faculties! in form and moving, how express and admirable! in action, how like an angel! in apprehension, how like a god! the beauty of the world! the paragon of animals! And yet, to me, what is this quintessence of dust? Man delights not me—no, nor woman neither, though by your smiling you seem to say so.

ROSENCRANTZ: My lord, there was no such stuff in my thoughts.

HAMLET: Why did ye laugh, then, when I said 'Man delights not me'?

ROSENCRANTZ: To think, my lord, if you delight not in man, what lenten entertainment the players shall receive from you. We coted them on the way; and hither are they coming to offer you service.

HAMLET: He that plays the king shall be welcome—his Majesty shall have tribute on me; the adventurous knight shall use his foil and target; the lover shall not sigh gratis; the humorous man shall end his part in peace; the clown shall make those laugh whose lungs are tickle a' th' sere; and the lady shall say her mind freely, or the blank verse shall halt for't. What players are they?

ROSENCRANTZ: Even those you were wont to take such delight in—the tragedians of the city.

HAMLET: How chances it they travel? Their residence, both in reputation and profit, was better both ways.

ROSENCRANTZ: I think their inhibition comes by the means of the late innovation.

HAMLET: Do they hold the same estimation they did when I was in the city? Are they so followed?

ROSENCRANTZ: No, indeed, are they not.

HAMLET: How comes it? Do they grow rusty?

ROSENCRANTZ: Nay, their endeavour keeps in the wonted pace; but there is, sir, an eyrie of children, little eyases that cry out on the top of question, and are most tyrannically clapp'd for't. These are now the fashion, and so berattle the common stages—so they call them—that many wearing rapiers are afraid of goose quills and dare scarce come thither.

HAMLET: What, are they children? Who maintains 'em? How are they escoted? Will they pursue the quality no longer than they can sing? Will they not say afterwards, if they should grow themselves to common players—as it is most like, if their means are no better—their writers do them wrong to make them exclaim against their own succession?

ROSENCRANTZ: Faith, there has been much to-do on both sides; and the nation holds it no sin to tarre them to controversy. There was for a while no money bid for argument, unless the poet and the player went to cuffs in the question.

HAMLET: Is't possible?

GUILDENSTERN: O, there has been much throwing about of brains.

HAMLET: Do the boys carry it away?

ROSENCRANTZ: Ay, that they do, my lord—Hercules and his load too.

HAMLET: It is not very strange; for my uncle is King of Denmark, and those that would make mows at him while my father lived give twenty, forty, fifty, a hundred ducats apiece for his picture in little. 'Sblood, there is something in this more than natural, if philosophy could find it out.

[A *flourish*.]

GUILDENSTERN: There are the players.

HAMLET: Gentlemen, you are welcome to Elsinore. Your hands, come then; th' appurtenance of welcome is fashion and ceremony. Let me comply with you in this garb; lest my extent to the players, which, I tell you, must show fairly outwards, should more appear like entertainments than yours. You are welcome. But my uncle-father and aunt-mother are deceived.

GUILDENSTERN: In what, my dear lord?

HAMLET: I am but mad north-north-west; when the wind is southerly I know a hawk from a handsaw.

[*Re-enter* POLONIUS.]

POLONIUS: Well be with you, gentlemen!

HAMLET: Hark you, Guildenstern, and you too—at each ear a hearer: that great baby you see there is not yet out of his swaddling clouts.

ROSENCRANTZ. Happily he is the second time come to them; for they say an old man is twice a child.

HAMLET: I will prophesy he comes to tell me of the players; mark it. You say right, sir: a Monday morning; 'twas then indeed.

POLONIUS: My lord, I have news to tell you.

HAMLET: My lord, I have news to tell you. When Roscius was an actor in Rome—

POLONIUS: The actors are come hither, my lord.

HAMLET: Buzz, buzz!

POLONIUS: Upon my honour—

HAMLET: Then came each actor on his ass—

POLONIUS: The best actors in the world, either for tragedy, comedy, history, pastoral, pastoral-comical, historical-pastoral, tragical-historical, tragical-comical-historical-pastoral, scene individable, or poem unlimited. Seneca cannot be too heavy nor Plautus too light. For the law of writ and the liberty, these are the only men.

HAMLET: O Jephthah, judge of Israel, what a treasure hadst thou!

POLONIUS: What a treasure had he, my lord?

HAMLET: Why—

> 'One fair daughter, and no more,
> The which he loved passing well.'

POLONIUS: [*aside*] Still on my daughter.

HAMLET: Am I not i' th' right, old Jephthah?

POLONIUS: If you call me Jephthah, my lord, I have a daughter that I love passing well.

HAMLET: Nay, that follows not.

POLONIUS: What follows then, my lord?

HAMLET: Why—

> 'As by lot, God wot'

and then, you know,

> 'It came to pass, as most like it was.'

The first row of the pious chanson will show you more; for look where my abridgement comes.

> [*Enter the* PLAYERS.]

You are welcome, masters; welcome, all.—I am glad to see thee well.— Welcome, good friends.—O, my old friend! Why thy face is valanc'd since I saw thee last; com'st thou to beard me in Denmark?—What, my young lady and mistress! By'r lady, your ladyship is nearer to heaven than when I saw you last by the altitude of a chopine. Pray God, your voice, like a piece of uncurrent gold, be not crack'd within the ring.—Masters, you are all welcome. We'll e'en to't like French falconers, fly at anything we see. We'll have a speech straight. Come, give us a taste of your quality; come, a passionate speech.

FIRST PLAYER: What speech, my good lord?

HAMLET: I heard thee speak me a speech once, but it was never acted; or, if it was, not above once; for the play, I remember, pleas'd not the million; 'twas caviary to the general. But it was—as I received it, and others whose judgments in such matters cried in the top of mine—an excellent play, well digested in the scenes, set down with as much modesty as cunning. I remember one said there were no sallets in the lines to make the matter savoury, nor no matter in the phrase that might indict the author of affectation; but call'd it an honest method, as wholesome as sweet, and by very much more handsome than fine. One speech in it I chiefly lov'd; 'twas Aeneas' tale to Dido; and thereabout of it especially where he speaks of Priam's slaughter. If it live in your memory, begin at this line—let me see:

> 'The rugged Pyrrhus, like th' Hyrcanian beast,'

'Tis not so; it begins with Pyrrhus.

> 'The rugged Pyrrhus, he whose sable arms,
> Black as his purpose, did the night resemble

When he lay couched in the ominous horse,
Hath now this dread and black complexion smear'd
With heraldry more dismal; head to foot
Now is he total gules, horridly trick'd
With blood of fathers, mothers, daughters, sons,
Bak'd and impasted with the parching streets,
That lend a tyrannous and damned light
To their lord's murder. Roasted in wrath and fire,
And thus o'er-sized with coagulate gore,
With eyes like carbuncles, the hellish Pyrrhus
Old grandsire Priam seeks.'
  So proceed you.
POLONIUS: Fore God, my lord, well spoken, with good accent and good discretion.
FIRST PLAYER: 'Anon he finds him
Striking too short at Greeks; his antique sword,
Rebellious to his arm, lies where it falls,
Repugnant to command. Unequal match'd,
Pyrrhus at Priam drives, in rage strikes wide;
But with the whiff and wind of his fell sword
Th' unnerved father falls. Then senseless Ilium,
Seeming to feel this blow, with flaming top
Stoops to his base, and with a hideous crash
Takes prisoner Pyrrhus' ear. For, lo! his sword,
Which was declining on the milky head
Of reverend Priam, seem'd i' th' air to stick.
So, as a painted tyrant, Pyrrhus stood
And, like a neutral to his will and matter,
Did nothing.
But as we often see, against some storm,
A silence in the heavens, the rack stand still,
The bold winds speechless, and the orb below
As hush as death, anon the dreadful thunder
Doth rend the region; so, after Pyrrhus' pause,
A roused vengeance sets him new a-work;
And never did the Cyclops' hammers fall
On Mars's armour, forg'd for proof eterne,
With less remorse than Pyrrhus' bleeding sword
Now falls on Priam.
Out, out, thou strumpet, Fortune! All you gods,
In general synod, take away her power;
Break all the spokes and fellies from her wheel,
And bowl the round nave down the hill of heaven,
As low as to the fiends.'
POLONIUS: This is too long.

HAMLET: It shall to the barber's, with your beard. Prithee say on. He's for a jig, or a
  tale of bawdry, or he sleeps. Say on; come to Hecuba.

FIRST PLAYER: 'But who, ah, who had seen the mobled queen—'

HAMLET: 'The mobled queen'?

POLONIUS: That's good; 'mobled queen' is good.

FIRST PLAYER: 'Run barefoot up and down, threat'ning the flames
  With bisson rheum; a clout upon that head
  Where late the diadem stood, and for a robe,
  About her lank and all o'er teemed loins,
  A blanket, in the alarm of fear caught up—
  Who this had seen, with tongue in venom steep'd,
  'Gainst Fortune's state would treason have pronounc'd.
  But if the gods themselves did see her then,
  When she saw Pyrrhus make malicious sport
  In mincing with his sword her husband's limbs,
  The instant burst of clamour that she made—
  Unless things mortal move them not at all—
  Would have made milch the burning eyes of heaven,
  And passion in the gods.'

POLONIUS: Look whe'er he has not turn'd his colour, and has tears in 's eyes.
  Prithee no more.

HAMLET: 'Tis well; I'll have thee speak out the rest of this soon.—Good my lord,
  will you see the players well bestowed? Do you hear: let them be well used;
  for they are the abstract and brief chronicles of the time; after your death you
  were better have a bad epitaph than their ill report while you live.

POLONIUS: My lord, I will use them according to their desert.

HAMLET: God's bodykins, man, much better. Use every man after his desert, and
  who shall scape whipping? Use them after your own honour and dignity: the
  less they deserve, the more merit is in your bounty. Take them in.

POLONIUS: Come, sirs.

HAMLET: Follow him, friends. We'll hear a play to-morrow. Dost thou hear me,
  old friend; can you play 'The Murder of Gonzago'?

FIRST PLAYER: Ay, my lord.

HAMLET: We'll ha't to-morrow night. You could, for a need, study a speech of
  some dozen or sixteen lines which I would set down and insert in't, could
  you not?

FIRST PLAYER: Ay, my lord.

HAMLET: Very well. Follow that lord; and look you mock him not. [*Exeunt*
  POLONIUS *and* PLAYERS.] My good friends, I'll leave you till night. You are
  welcome to Elsinore.

ROSENCRANTZ: Good my lord!

     [*Exeunt* ROSENCRANTZ *and* GUILDENSTERN.]

HAMLET: Ay, so God buy to you! Now I am alone.

O, what a rogue and peasant slave am I!
Is it not monstrous that this player here,
But in a fiction, in a dream of passion,
Could force his soul so to his own conceit
That from her working all his visage wann'd;
Tears in his eyes, distraction in's aspect,
A broken voice, and his whole function suiting
With forms to his conceit? And all for nothing!
For Hecuba!
What's Hecuba to him or he to Hecuba,
That he should weep for her? What would he do,
Had he the motive and the cue for passion
That I have? He would drown the stage with tears,
And cleave the general ear with horrid speech;
Make mad the guilty, and appal the free,
Confound the ignorant, and amaze indeed
The very faculties of eyes and ears.
Yet I,
A dull and muddy-mettl'd rascal, peak,
Like John-a-dreams, unpregnant of my cause,
And can say nothing; no, not for a king
Upon whose property and most dear life
A damn'd defeat was made. Am I a coward?
Who calls me villain, breaks my pate across,
Plucks off my beard and blows it in my face,
Tweaks me by the nose, gives me the lie i' th' throat
As deep as to the lungs? Who does me this?
Ha!
'Swounds, I should take it; for it cannot be
But I am pigeon-liver'd and lack gall
To make oppression bitter, or ere this
I should 'a fatted all the region kites
With this slave's offal. Bloody, bawdy villain!
Remorseless, treacherous, lecherous, kindless villain!
O, vengeance!
Why, what an ass am I! This is most brave,
That I, the son of a dear father murder'd,
Prompted to my revenge by heaven and hell,
Must, like a whore, unpack my heart with words,
And fall a-cursing like a very drab,
A scullion! Fie upon't! foh!
About, my brains. Hum—I have heard
That guilty creatures, sitting at a play,

Have by the very cunning of the scene
Been struck so to the soul that presently
They have proclaim'd their malefactions;
For murder, though it have no tongue, will speak
With most miraculous organ. I'll have these players
Play something like the murder of my father
Before mine uncle. I'll observe his looks;
I'll tent him to the quick. If 'a do blench,
I know my course. The spirit that I have seen
May be a devil; and the devil hath power
T' assume a pleasing shape; yea and perhaps
Out of my weakness and my melancholy,
As he is very potent with such spirits,
Abuses me to damn me. I'll have grounds
More relative than this. The play's the thing
Wherein I'll catch the conscience of the King.   [*Exit.*]

ACT III

SCENE I———*Elsinore. The Castle.*

[*Enter* KING, QUEEN, POLONIUS, OPHELIA, ROSENCRANTZ, *and* GUILDENSTERN.]

KING: And can you by no drift of conference
  Get from him why he puts on this confusion,
  Grating so harshly all his days of quiet
  With turbulent and dangerous lunacy?
ROSENCRANTZ: He does confess he feels himself distracted,
  But from what cause 'a will by no means speak.
GUILDENSTERN: Nor do we find him forward to be sounded;
  But, with a crafty madness, keeps aloof
  When we would bring him on to some confession
  Of his true state.
QUEEN: Did he receive you well?
ROSENCRANTZ: Most like a gentleman.
GUILDENSTERN: But with much forcing of his disposition.
ROSENCRANTZ: Niggard of question; but of our demands
  Most free in his reply.
QUEEN: Did you assay him
  To any pastime?
ROSENCRANTZ: Madam, it so fell out that certain players
  We o'er-raught on the way. Of these we told him;
  And there did seem in him a kind of joy
  To hear of it. They are here about the court,

And, as I think, they have already order
This night to play before him.
POLONIUS: 'Tis most true;
And he beseech'd me to entreat your Majesties
To hear and see the matter.
KING: With all my heart; and it doth much content me
To hear him so inclin'd.
Good gentlemen, give him a further edge,
And drive his purpose into these delights.
ROSENCRANTZ: We shall, my lord.
        [*Exeunt* ROSENCRANTZ *and* GUILDENSTERN.]
KING: Sweet Gertrude, leave us too;
For we have closely sent for Hamlet hither,
That he, as 'twere by accident, may here
Affront Ophelia.
Her father and myself—lawful espials—
Will so bestow ourselves that, seeing unseen,
We may of their encounter frankly judge,
And gather by him, as he is behav'd,
If't be th' affliction of his love or no
That thus he suffers for.
QUEEN: I shall obey you;
And for your part, Ophelia, I do wish
That your good beauties be the happy cause
Of Hamlet's wildness; so shall I hope your virtues
Will bring him to his wonted way again,
To both your honours.
OPHELIA: Madam, I wish it may.   [*Exit* QUEEN.]
POLONIUS: Ophelia, walk you here.—Gracious, so please you,
We will bestow ourselves.—Read on this book;
That show of such an exercise may colour
Your loneliness.—We are oft to blame in this:
'Tis too much prov'd, that with devotion's visage
And pious action we do sugar o'er
The devil himself.
KING: [*aside*] O, 'tis too true!
How smart a lash that speech doth give my conscience!
The harlot's cheek, beautied with plast'ring art,
Is not more ugly to the thing that helps it
Than is my deed to my most painted word.
O heavy burden!
POLONIUS: I hear him coming; let's withdraw, my lord.
        [*Exeunt* KING *and* POLONIUS.]

[*Enter* HAMLET.]

HAMLET: To be, or not to be—that is the question;
    Whether 'tis nobler in the mind to suffer
    The slings and arrows of outrageous fortune,
    Or to take arms against a sea of troubles,
    And by opposing end them? To die, to sleep—
    No more; and by a sleep to say we end
    The heart-ache and the thousand natural shocks
    That flesh is heir to. 'Tis a consummation
    Devoutly to be wish'd. To die, to sleep;
    To sleep, perchance to dream. Ay, there's the rub;
    For in that sleep of death what dreams may come,
    When we have shuffled off this mortal coil,
    Must give us pause. There's the respect
    That makes calamity of so long life;
    For who would bear the whips and scorns of time,
    Th' oppressor's wrong, the proud man's contumely,
    The pangs of despis'd love, the law's delay,
    The insolence of office, and the spurns
    That patient merit of th' unworthy takes,
    When he himself might his quietus make
    With a bare bodkin? Who would these fardels bear,
    To grunt and sweat under a weary life,
    But that the dread of something after death—
    The undiscover'd country, from whose bourn
    No traveller returns—puzzles the will,
    And makes us rather bear those ills we have
    Than fly to others that we know not of?
    Thus conscience does make cowards of us all;
    And thus the native hue of resolution
    Is sicklied o'er with the pale cast of thought,
    And enterprises of great pitch and moment,
    With this regard, their currents turn awry
    And lose the name of action.—Soft you now!
    The fair Ophelia.—Nymph, in thy orisons
    Be all my sins rememb'red.

OPHELIA: Good my lord,
    How does your honour for this many a day?

HAMLET: I humbly thank you; well, well, well.

OPHELIA: My lord, I have remembrances of yours
    That I have longed long to re-deliver.
    I pray you now receive them.

HAMLET: No, not I;

I never gave you aught.

OPHELIA: My honour'd lord, you know right well you did,
And with them words of so sweet breath compos'd
As made the things more rich; their perfume lost,
Take these again; for to the noble mind
Rich gifts wax poor when givers prove unkind.
There, my lord.

HAMLET: Ha, ha! Are you honest?

OPHELIA: My lord?

HAMLET: Are you fair?

OPHELIA: What means your lordship?

HAMLET: That if you be honest and fair, your honesty should admit no discourse to your beauty.

OPHELIA: Could beauty, my lord, have better commerce than with honesty?

HAMLET: Ay, truly; for the power of beauty will sooner transform honesty from what it is to a bawd than the force of honesty can translate beauty into his likeness. This was sometime a paradox, but now the time gives it proof. I did love you once.

OPHELIA: Indeed, my lord, you made me believe so.

HAMLET: You should not have believ'd me; for virtue cannot so inoculate our old stock but we shall relish of it. I loved you not.

OPHELIA: I was the more deceived.

HAMLET: Get thee to a nunnery. Why wouldst thou be a breeder of sinners? I am myself indifferent honest, but yet I could accuse me of such things that it were better my mother had not borne me: I am very proud, revengeful, ambitious; with more offences at my beck than I have thoughts to put them in, imagination to give them shape, or time to act them in. What should such fellows as I do crawling between earth and heaven? We are arrant knaves, all; believe none of us. Go thy ways to a nunnery. Where's your father?

OPHELIA: At home, my lord.

HAMLET: Let the doors be shut upon him, that he may play the fool nowhere but in's own house. Farewell.

OPHELIA: O, help him, you sweet heavens!

HAMLET: If thou dost marry, I'll give thee this plague for thy dowry: be thou as chaste as ice, as pure as snow, thou shalt not escape calumny. Get thee to a nunnery, go, farewell. Or, if thou wilt needs marry, marry a fool; for wise men know well enough what monsters you make of them. To a nunnery go; and quickly too. Farewell.

OPHELIA: O heavenly powers, restore him!

HAMLET: I have heard of your paintings too, well enough; God hath given you one face, and you make yourselves another. You jig and amble, and you lisp, and nickname God's creatures, and make your wantonness your ignorance.

Go to, I'll no more on't; it hath made me mad. I say we will have no moe
marriage: those that are married already, all but one, shall live; the rest shall
keep as they are. To a nunnery, go.
    [*Exit.*]
OPHELIA: O, what a noble mind is here o'erthrown!
        The courtier's, soldier's, scholar's, eye, tongue, sword;
        Th' expectancy and rose of the fair state,
        The glass of fashion and the mould of form,
        Th' observ'd of all observers—quite, quite down!
        And I, of ladies most deject and wretched,
        That suck'd the honey of his music vows,
        Now see that noble and most sovereign reason,
        Like sweet bells jangled, out of time and harsh;
        That unmatch'd form and feature of blown youth
        Blasted with ecstasy. O, woe is me
        T' have seen what I have seen, see what I see!
            [*Re-enter* KING *and* POLONIUS.]
KING: Love! His affections do not that way tend;
        Nor what he spake, though it lack'd form a little,
        Was not like madness. There's something in his soul
        O'er which his melancholy sits on brood;
        And I do doubt the hatch and the disclose
        Will be some danger; which to prevent
        I have in quick determination
        Thus set it down: he shall with speed to England
        For the demand of our neglected tribute.
        Haply the seas and countries different,
        With variable objects, shall expel
        This something-settled matter in his heart
        Whereon his brains still beating puts him thus
        From fashion of himself. What think you on't?
POLONIUS: It shall do well. But yet do I believe
        The origin and commencement of his grief
        Sprung from neglected love. How now, Ophelia!
        You need not tell us what Lord Hamlet said;
        We heard it all. My lord, do as you please;
        But if you hold it fit, after the play
        Let his queen mother all alone entreat him
        To show his grief. Let her be round with him;
        And I'll be placed, so please you, in the ear
        Of all their conference. If she find him not,
        To England send him; or confine him where
        Your wisdom best shall think.

KING: It shall be so:

Madness in great ones must not unwatch'd go. *[Exeunt.]*

SCENE II———*Elsinore. The Castle.*

[*Enter* HAMLET *and three of the* PLAYERS.]

HAMLET: Speak the speech, I pray you, as I pronounc'd it to you, trippingly on the tongue; but if you mouth it, as many of our players do, I had as lief the town-crier spoke my lines. Nor do not saw the air too much with your hand, thus, but use all gently; for in the very torrent, tempest, and, as I may say, whirlwind of your passion, you must acquire and beget a temperance that may give it smoothness. O, it offends me to the soul to hear a robustious periwig-pated fellow tear a passion to tatters, to very rags, to split the ears of the groundlings, who, for the most part, are capable of nothing but inexplicable dumb shows and noise. I would have such a fellow whipp'd for o'erdoing Termagant; it out-herods Herod. Pray you avoid it.

FIRST PLAYER: I warrant your honour.

HAMLET: Be not too tame neither, but let your own discretion be your tutor. Suit the action to the word, the word to the action; with this special observance, that you o'erstep not the modesty of nature; for anything so o'erdone is from the purpose of playing, whose end, both at the first and now, was and is to hold, as 'twere, the mirror up to nature; to show virtue her own feature, scorn her own image, and the very age and body of the time his form and pressure. Now, this overdone or come tardy off, though it makes the unskilful laugh, cannot but make the judicious grieve; the censure of the which one must, in your allowance, o'erweigh a whole theatre of others. O, there be players that I have seen play—and heard others praise, and that highly—not to speak it profanely, that, neither having th' accent of Christians, nor the gait of Christian, pagan, nor man, have so strutted and bellowed that I have thought some of Nature's journeymen had made men, and not made them well, they imitated humanity so abominably.

FIRST PLAYER: I hope we have reform'd that indifferently with us, sir.

HAMLET: O, reform it altogether. And let those that play your clowns speak no more than is set down for them; for there be of them that will themselves laugh, to set on some quantity of barren spectators to laugh too, though in the meantime some necessary question of the play be then to be considered. That's villainous, and shows a most pitiful ambition in the fool that uses it. Go, make you ready.

[*Exeunt* PLAYERS.]

[*Enter* POLONIUS, ROSENCRANTZ, *and* GUILDENSTERN.]

How now, my lord! Will the King hear this piece of work?

POLONIUS: And the Queen too, and that presently.

HAMLET: Bid the players make haste.   [*Exit* POLONIUS.]
    Will you two help to hasten them?
ROSENCRANTZ: Ay, my lord.   [*Exeunt they two.*]
HAMLET: What, ho, Horatio!
    [*Enter* HORATIO.]
HORATIO: Here, sweet lord, at your service.
HAMLET: Horatio, thou art e'en as just a man
    As e'er my conversation cop'd withal.
HORATIO: O my dear lord!
HAMLET: Nay, do not think I flatter;
    For what advancement may I hope from thee,
    That no revenue hast but thy good spirits
    To feed and clothe thee? Why should the poor be flatter'd?
    No, let the candied tongue lick absurd pomp,
    And crook the pregnant hinges of the knee
    Where thrift may follow fawning. Dost thou hear?
    Since my dear soul was mistress of her choice
    And could of men distinguish her election,
    Sh'hath seal'd thee for herself; for thou hast been
    As one, in suff'ring all, that suffers nothing;
    A man that Fortune's buffets and rewards
    Hast ta'en with equal thanks; and blest are those
    Whose blood and judgment are so well comeddled
    That they are not a pipe for Fortune's finger
    To sound what stop she please. Give me that man
    That is not passion's slave, and I will wear him
    In my heart's core, ay, in my heart of heart,
    As I do thee. Something too much of this.
    There is a play to-night before the King;
    One scene of it comes near the circumstance
    Which I have told thee of my father's death.
    I prithee, when thou seest that act afoot,
    Even with the very comment of thy soul
    Observe my uncle. If his occulted guilt
    Do not itself unkennel in one speech,
    It is a damned ghost that we have seen,
    And my imaginations are as foul
    As Vulcan's stithy. Give him heedful note;
    For I mine eyes will rivet to his face;
    And, after, we will both our judgments join
    In censure of his seeming.
HORATIO: Well, my lord.
    If 'a steal aught the whilst this play is playing,

And scape detecting, I will pay the theft.

[*Enter trumpets and kettledrums. Danish march. Sound a flourish. Enter* KING, QUEEN, POLONIUS, OPHELIA, ROSENCRANTZ, GUILDENSTERN, *and other* LORDS *attendant, with the guard carrying torches.*]

HAMLET: They are coming to the play; I must be idle.
Get you a place.

KING: How fares our cousin Hamlet?

HAMLET: Excellent, i' faith; of the chameleon's dish. I eat the air promise-cramm'd; you cannot feed capons so.

KING: I have nothing with this answer, Hamlet; these words are not mine.

HAMLET: No, nor mine now. [*to* POLONIUS] My lord, you play'd once in th' university, you say?

POLONIUS: That did I, my lord, and was accounted a good actor.

HAMLET: What did you enact?

POLONIUS.: I did enact Julius Caesar; I was kill'd i' th' Capitol; Brutus kill'd me.

HAMLET: It was a brute part of him to kill so capital a calf there. Be the players ready?

ROSENCRANTZ: Ay, my lord; they stay upon your patience.

QUEEN: Come hither, my dear Hamlet, sit by me.

HAMLET: No, good mother; here's metal more attractive.

POLONIUS: [*to the* KING] O, ho! do you mark that?

HAMLET: Lady, shall I lie in your lap? [*lying down at* OPHELIA'S *feet*]

OPHELIA: No, my lord.

HAMLET: I mean, my head upon your lap?

OPHELIA: Ay, my lord.

HAMLET: Do you think I meant country matters?

OPHELIA: I think nothing, my lord.

HAMLET: That's a fair thought to lie between maids' legs.

OPHELIA: What is, my lord?

HAMLET: Nothing.

OPHELIA: You are merry, my lord.

HAMLET: Who, I?

OPHELIA: Ay, my lord.

HAMLET: O God, your only jig-maker! What should a man do but be merry? For look you how cheerfully my mother looks, and my father died within's two hours.

OPHELIA: Nay, 'tis twice two months, my lord.

HAMLET: So long? Nay then, let the devil wear black, for I'll have a suit of sables. O heavens! die two months ago, and not forgotten yet? Then there's hope a great man's memory may outlive his life half a year; but, by'r lady, 'a must build churches, then; or else shall 'a suffer not thinking on, with the hobby-horse, whose epitaph is 'For O, for O, the hobby-horse is forgot!'

[*The trumpet sounds. Hautboys play. The Dumb Show enters.*]

[Enter a KING *and a* QUEEN, *very lovingly; the* QUEEN *embracing him and he her. She kneels, and makes a show of protestation unto him. He takes her up, and declines his head upon her neck. He lies him down upon a bank of flowers; she, seeing him asleep, leaves him. Anon comes in a* FELLOW, *takes off his crown, kisses it, pours poison in the sleeper's ears, and leaves him. The* QUEEN *returns; finds the* KING *dead, and makes passionate action. The* POISONER, *with some two or three* MUTES, *comes in again, seeming to condole with her. The dead body is carried away. The* POISONER *woos the* QUEEN *with gifts: she seems harsh awhile, but in the end accepts his love. Exeunt.]*

OPHELIA: What means this, my lord?

HAMLET: Marry, this is miching mallecho; it means mischief.

OPHELIA: Belike this show imports the argument of the play.

[*Enter* PROLOGUE.]

HAMLET: We shall know by this fellow: the players cannot keep counsel; they'll tell all.

OPHELIA: Will 'a tell us what this show meant?

HAMLET: Ay, or any show that you will show him. Be not you asham'd to show, he'll not shame to tell you what it means.

OPHELIA: You are naught, you are naught. I'll mark the play.

PROLOGUE: *For us, and for our tragedy,*
    Here stooping to your clemency,
    We beg your hearing patiently.
[*Exit.*]

HAMLET: Is this a prologue, or the posy of a ring?

OPHELIA: 'Tis brief, my lord.

HAMLET: As woman's love.

[*Enter the* PLAYER KING *and* QUEEN.]

PLAYER KING: *Full thirty times hath Phoebus' cart gone round*
Neptune's salt wash and Tellus' orbed ground,
And thirty dozen moons with borrowed sheen
About the world have times twelve thirties been,
Since love our hearts and Hymen did our hands
Unite comutual in most sacred bands.

PLAYER QUEEN: *So many journeys may the sun and moon*
Make us again count o'er ere love be done!
But, woe is me, you are so sick of late,
So far from cheer and from your former state,
That I distrust you. Yet, though I distrust,
Discomfort you, my lord, it nothing must;
For women fear too much even as they love,
And women's fear and love hold quantity,
In neither aught, or in extremity.

Now, what my love is, proof hath made you know;
And as my love is siz'd, my fear is so.
Where love is great, the littlest doubts are fear;
Where little fears grow great, great love grows there.

PLAYER KING: Faith, I must leave thee, love, and shortly too:
My operant powers their functions leave to do;
And thou shalt live in this fair world behind,
Honour'd, belov'd; and haply one as kind
For husband shalt thou—

PLAYER QUEEN: O, confound the rest!
Such love must needs be treason in my breast.
In second husband let me be accurst!
None wed the second but who kill'd the first.

HAMLET: That's wormwood, wormwood.

PLAYER QUEEN: The instances that second marriage move
Are base respects of thrift, but none of love.
A second time I kill my husband dead,
When second husband kisses me in bed.

PLAYER KING: I do believe you think what now you speak;
But what we do determine oft we break.
Purpose is but the slave to memory,
Of violent birth, but poor validity;
Which now, the fruit unripe, sticks on the tree;
But fall unshaken when they mellow be.
Most necessary 'tis that we forget
To pay ourselves what to ourselves is debt.
What to ourselves in passion we propose,
The passion ending, doth the purpose lose.
The violence of either grief or joy
Their own enactures with themselves destroy.
Where joy most revels grief doth most lament;
Grief joys, joy grieves, on slender accident.
This world is not for aye; nor 'tis not strange
That even our loves should with our fortunes change;
For 'tis a question left us yet to prove,
Whether love lead fortune or else fortune love.
The great man down, you mark his favourite flies;
The poor advanc'd makes friends of enemies.
And hitherto doth love on fortune tend;
For who not needs shall never lack a friend,
And who in want a hollow friend doth try,
Directly seasons him his enemy.
But, orderly to end where I begun,

Our wills and fates do so contrary run
That our devices still are overthrown;
Our thoughts are ours, their ends none of our own.
So think thou wilt no second husband wed;
But die thy thoughts when thy first lord is dead.

PLAYER QUEEN: *Nor earth to me give food, nor heaven light,*
Sport and repose lock from me day and night,
To desperation turn my trust and hope,
An anchor's cheer in prison be my scope,
Each opposite that blanks the face of joy
Meet what I would have well, and it destroy,
Both here and hence pursue me lasting strife,
If, once a widow, ever I be wife!

HAMLET: If she should break it now!

PLAYER KING: *'Tis deeply sworn. Sweet, leave me here awhile;*
My spirits grow dull, and fain I would beguile
The tedious day with sleep.   [*Sleeps.*]

PLAYER QUEEN: *Sleep rock thy brain,*
And never come mischance between us twain!

HAMLET: Madam, how like you this play?

QUEEN: The lady doth protest too much, methinks.

HAMLET: O, but she'll keep her word.

KING: Have you heard the argument? Is there no offence in't?

HAMLET: No, no; they do but jest, poison in jest; no offence i' th' world.

KING: What do you call the play?

HAMLET: 'The Mouse-trap.' Marry, how? Tropically. This play is the image of a
murder done in Vienna: Gonzago is the duke's name; his wife, Baptista. You
shall see anon. 'Tis a knavish piece of work; but what of that? Your Majesty,
and we that have free souls, it touches us not. Let the galled jade wince, our
withers are unwrung.

　　　　[*Enter* LUCIANUS.]

This is one Lucianus, nephew to the King.

OPHELIA: You are as good as a chorus, my lord.

HAMLET: I could interpret between you and your love, if I could see the puppets
dallying.

OPHELIA: You are keen, my lord, you are keen.

HAMLET: It would cost you a groaning to take off mine edge.

OPHELIA: Still better, and worse.

HAMLET: So you mis-take your husbands. —Begin, murderer; pox, leave thy
damnable faces and begin. Come; the croaking raven doth bellow for
revenge.

LUCIANUS: *Thoughts black, hands apt, drugs fit, and time agreeing;*
Confederate season, else no creature seeing;

> *Thou mixture rank, of midnight weeds collected,*
> *With Hecat's ban thrice blasted, thrice infected.*
> *Thy natural magic and dire property*
> *On wholesome life usurps immediately.*
> > [*Pours the poison in his ears.*]

HAMLET: 'A poisons him i' th' garden for his estate. His name's Gonzago. The story is extant, and written in very choice Italian. You shall see anon how the murderer gets the love of Gonzago's wife.

OPHELIA: The King rises.

HAMLET: What, frighted with false fire!

QUEEN: How fares my lord?

POLONIUS: Give o'er the play.

KING: Give me some light. Away!

POLONIUS: Lights, lights, lights!
> [*Exeunt all but* HAMLET *and* HORATIO.]

HAMLET: Why, let the strucken deer go weep,
> The hart ungalled play;
> > For some must watch, while some must sleep;
> > > Thus runs the world away.

Would not this, sir, and a forest of feathers—if the rest of my fortunes turn Turk with me—with two Provincial roses on my raz'd shoes, get me a fellowship in a cry of players, sir?

HORATIO: Half a share.

HAMLET: A whole one, I.

> For thou dost know, O Damon dear,
> > This realm dismantled was
> Of Jove himself; and now reigns here
> > A very, very—peacock.

HORATIO: You might have rhym'd.

HAMLET: O good Horatio, I'll take the ghost's word for a thousand pound. Didst perceive?

HORATIO: Very well, my lord.

HAMLET: Upon the talk of the poisoning.

HORATIO: I did very well note him.

HAMLET: Ah, ha! Come, some music. Come, the recorders.

> For if the King like not the comedy,
> Why, then, belike he likes it not, perdy.

Come, some music.
> [*Re-enter* ROSENCRANTZ *and* GUILDENSTERN.]

GUILDENSTERN: Good my lord, vouchsafe me a word with you.

HAMLET: Sir, a whole history.

GUILDENSTERN: The King, sir—

HAMLET: Ay, sir, what of him?

GUILDENSTERN: Is, in his retirement, marvellous distemp'red.

HAMLET: With drink, sir?

GUILDENSTERN: No, my lord, rather with choler.

HAMLET: Your wisdom should show itself more richer to signify this to his doctor; for for me to put him to his purgation would perhaps plunge him into far more choler.

GUILDENSTERN: Good my lord, put your discourse into some frame, and start not so wildly from my affair.

HAMLET: I am tame, sir. Pronounce.

GUILDENSTERN: The Queen, your mother, in most great affliction of spirit, hath sent me to you.

HAMLET: You are welcome.

GUILDENSTERN: Nay, good my lord, this courtesy is not of the right breed. If it shall please you to make me a wholesome answer, I will do your mother's commandment; if not, your pardon and my return shall be the end of my business.

HAMLET: Sir, I cannot.

ROSENCRANTZ: What, my lord?

HAMLET: Make you a wholesome answer; my wit's diseas'd. But, sir, such answer as I can make, you shall command: or rather, as you say, my mother. Therefore no more, but to the matter: my mother, you say—

ROSENCRANTZ: Then thus she says: your behaviour hath struck her into amazement and admiration.

HAMLET: O wonderful son, that can so stonish a mother! But is there no sequel at the heels of this mother's admiration? Impart.

ROSENCRANTZ: She desires to speak with you in her closet ere you go to bed.

HAMLET: We shall obey, were she ten times our mother. Have you any further trade with us?

ROSENCRANTZ: My lord, you once did love me.

HAMLET: And do still, by these pickers and stealers.

ROSENCRANTZ: Good my lord, what is your cause of distemper? You do surely bar the door upon your own liberty, if you deny your griefs to your friend.

HAMLET: Sir, I lack advancement.

ROSENCRANTZ: How can that be, when you have the voice of the King himself for your succession in Denmark?

HAMLET: Ay, sir, but 'While the grass grows'—the proverb is something musty.
    [Re-enter the PLAYERS, with recorders.]
    O, the recorders! Let me see one. To withdraw with you—why do you go about to recover the wind of me, as if you would drive me into a toil?

GUILDENSTERN: O my lord, if my duty be too bold, my love is too unmannerly.

HAMLET: I do not well understand that. Will you play upon this pipe?

GUILDENSTERN: My lord, I cannot.

HAMLET: I pray you.

GUILDENSTERN: Believe me, I cannot.

HAMLET: I do beseech you.

GUILDENSTERN: I know no touch of it, my lord.

HAMLET: It is as easy as lying: govern these ventages with your fingers and thumb, give it breath with your mouth, and it will discourse most eloquent music. Look you, these are the stops.

GUILDENSTERN: But these cannot I command to any utterance of harmony; I have not the skill.

HAMLET: Why, look you now, how unworthy a thing you make of me! You would play upon me; you would seem to know my stops; you would pluck out the heart of my mystery; you would sound me from my lowest note to the top of my compass; and there is much music, excellent voice, in this little organ, yet cannot you make it speak. 'Sblood, do you think I am easier to be play'd on than a pipe? Call me what instrument you will, though you can fret me, yet you cannot play upon me.
    [*Re-enter* POLONIUS.]
God bless you, sir!

POLONIUS: My lord, the Queen would speak with you, and presently.

HAMLET: Do you see yonder cloud that's almost in shape of a camel?

POLONIUS: By th' mass, and 'tis like a camel indeed.

HAMLET: Methinks it is like a weasel.

POLONIUS: It is back'd like a weasel.

HAMLET: Or like a whale?

POLONIUS: Very like a whale.

HAMLET: Then I will come to my mother by and by. [*aside*] They fool me to the top of my bent.—I will come by and by.

POLONIUS: I will say so.   [*Exit* POLONIUS.]

HAMLET: 'By and by' is easily said. Leave me, friends.
    [*Exeunt all but* HAMLET.]
'Tis now the very witching time of night,
When churchyards yawn, and hell itself breathes out
Contagion to this world. Now could I drink hot blood,
And do such bitter business as the day
Would quake to look on. Soft! now to my mother.
O heart, lose not thy nature; let not ever
The soul of Nero enter this firm bosom.
Let me be cruel, not unnatural:
I will speak daggers to her, but use none.
My tongue and soul in this be hypocrites—

How in my words somever she be shent,
To give them seals never, my soul, consent!   [*Exit.*]

SCENE III———*Elsinore. The Castle.*

[*Enter* KING, ROSENCRANTZ, *and* GUILDENSTERN.]

KING: I like him not; nor stands it safe with us
    To let his madness range. Therefore prepare you;
    I your commission will forthwith dispatch,
    And he to England shall along with you.
    The terms of our estate may not endure
    Hazard so near's as doth hourly grow
    Out of his brows.
GUILDENSTERN: We will ourselves provide.
    Most holy and religious fear it is
    To keep those many many bodies safe
    That live and feed upon your Majesty.
ROSENCRANTZ: The single and peculiar life is bound
    With all the strength and armour of the mind
    To keep itself from noyance; but much more
    That spirit upon whose weal depends and rests
    The lives of many. The cease of majesty
    Dies not alone, but like a gulf doth draw
    What's near it with it. It is a massy wheel,
    Fix'd on the summit of the highest mount,
    To whose huge spokes ten thousand lesser things
    Are mortis'd and adjoin'd; which when it falls,
    Each small annexment, petty consequence,
    Attends the boist'rous ruin. Never alone
    Did the king sigh, but with a general groan.
KING: Arm you, I pray you, to this speedy voyage;
    For we will fetters put about this fear,
    Which now goes too free-footed.
ROSENCRANTZ: We will haste us.
    [*Exeunt* ROSENCRANTZ *and* GUILDENSTERN.]
    [*Enter* POLONIUS.]
POLONIUS: My lord, he's going to his mother's closet.
    Behind the arras I'll convey myself
    To hear the process. I'll warrant she'll tax him home;
    And, as you said, and wisely was it said,
    'Tis meet that some more audience than a mother,
    Since nature makes them partial, should o'erhear
    The speech, of vantage. Fare you well, my liege.

I'll call upon you ere you go to bed,
And tell you what I know.
KING: Thanks, dear my lord.   [*Exit* POLONIUS.]
    O, my offence is rank, it smells to heaven;
It hath the primal eldest curse upon't—
A brother's murder! Pray can I not,
Though inclination be as sharp as will.
My stronger guilt defeats my strong intent,
And, like a man to double business bound,
I stand in pause where I shall first begin,
And both neglect. What if this cursed hand
Were thicker than itself with brother's blood,
Is there not rain enough in the sweet heavens
To wash it white as snow? Whereto serves mercy
But to confront the visage of offence?
And what's in prayer but this twofold force,
To be forestalled ere we come to fall,
Or pardon'd being down? Then I'll look up;
My fault is past. But, O, what form of prayer
Can serve my turn? 'Forgive me my foul murder'!
That cannot be; since I am still possess'd
Of those effects for which I did the murder—
My crown, mine own ambition, and my queen.
May one be pardon'd and retain th' offence?
In the corrupted currents of this world
Offence's gilded hand may shove by justice;
And oft 'tis seen the wicked prize itself
Buys out the law. But 'tis not so above:
There is no shuffling; there the action lies
In his true nature; and we ourselves compell'd,
Even to the teeth and forehead of our faults,
To give in evidence. What then? What rests?
Try what repentance can. What can it not?
Yet what can it when one can not repent?
O wretched state! O bosom black as death!
O limed soul, that, struggling to be free,
Art more engag'd! Help, angels. Make assay:
Bow, stubborn knees; and, heart, with strings of steel,
Be soft as sinews of the new-born babe.
All may be well.   [*He kneels.*]
    [*Enter* HAMLET.]
HAMLET: Now might I do it pat, now 'a is a-praying;
And now I'll do't—and so 'a goes to heaven,

And so am I reveng'd. That would be scann'd:
A villain kills my father; and for that,
I, his sole son, do this same villain send
To heaven.
Why, this is hire and salary, not revenge.
'A took my father grossly, full of bread,
With all his crimes broad blown, as flush as May;
And how his audit stands who knows save heaven?
But in our circumstance and course of thought
'Tis heavy with him; and am I then reveng'd
To take him in the purging of his soul,
When he is fit and season'd for his passage?
No.
Up, sword, and know thou a more horrid hent.
When he is drunk asleep, or in his rage;
Or in th' incestuous pleasure of his bed;
At game, a-swearing, or about some act
That has no relish of salvation in't—
Then trip him, that his heels may kick at heaven,
And that his soul may be as damn'd and black
As hell, whereto it goes. My mother stays.
This physic but prolongs thy sickly days.   [*Exit.*]
KING: [*rising*] My words fly up, my thoughts remain below.
Words without thoughts never to heaven go.   [*Exit.*]

SCENE IV———*The* QUEEN's *closet.*

[*Enter* QUEEN *and* POLONIUS.]
POLONIUS: 'A will come straight. Look you lay home to him;
Tell him his pranks have been too broad to bear with,
And that your Grace hath screen'd and stood between
Much heat and him. I'll silence me even here.
Pray you be round with him.
HAMLET: [*within*] Mother, mother, mother!
QUEEN: I'll warrant you. Fear me not.
Withdraw, I hear him coming.
[POLONIUS *goes behind the arras.*]
[*Enter* HAMLET.]
HAMLET: Now, mother, what's the matter?
QUEEN: Hamlet, thou hast thy father much offended.
HAMLET: Mother, you have my father much offended.
QUEEN: Come, come, you answer with an idle tongue.
HAMLET: Go, go, you question with a wicked tongue.

QUEEN: Why, how now, Hamlet!

HAMLET: What's the matter now?

QUEEN: Have you forgot me?

HAMLET: No, by the rood, not so:
  You are the Queen, your husband's brother's wife;
  And—would it were not so!—you are my mother.

QUEEN: Nay then, I'll set those to you that can speak.

HAMLET: Come, come, and sit you down; you shall not budge.
  You go not till I set you up a glass
  Where you may see the inmost part of you.

QUEEN: What wilt thou do? Thou wilt not murder me?
  Help, help, ho!

POLONIUS: [*behind*] What, ho! help, help, help!

HAMLET: [*draws*] How now! a rat?
  Dead, for a ducat, dead!
    [*kills* POLONIUS *with a pass through the arras*]

POLONIUS: [*behind*] O, I am slain!

QUEEN: O me, what hast thou done?

HAMLET: Nay, I know not:
  Is it the King?

QUEEN: O, what a rash and bloody deed is this!

HAMLET: A bloody deed!—almost as bad, good mother,
  As kill a king and marry with his brother.

QUEEN: As kill a king!

HAMLET: Ay, lady, it was my word. [*parting the arras*]
  Thou wretched, rash, intruding fool, farewell!
  I took thee for thy better. Take thy fortune;
  Thou find'st to be too busy is some danger.
  Leave wringing of your hands. Peace; sit you down,
  And let me wring your heart; for so I shall,
  If it be made of penetrable stuff;
  If damned custom have not braz'd it so
  That it be proof and bulwark against sense.

QUEEN: What have I done that thou dar'st wag thy tongue
  In noise so rude against me?

HAMLET: Such an act
  That blurs the grace and blush of modesty;
  Calls virtue hypocrite; takes off the rose
  From the fair forehead of an innocent love,
  And sets a blister there; makes marriage-vows
  As false as dicers' oaths. O, such a deed
  As from the body of contraction plucks
  The very soul, and sweet religion makes

A rhapsody of words. Heaven's face does glow
O'er this solidity and compound mass
With heated visage, as against the doom—
Is thought-sick at the act.

QUEEN: Ay me, what act,
That roars so loud and thunders in the index?

HAMLET: Look here upon this picture and on this,
The counterfeit presentment of two brothers.
See what a grace was seated on this brow;
Hyperion's curls; the front of Jove himself;
An eye like Mars, to threaten and command;
A station like the herald Mercury
New lighted on a heaven-kissing hill—
A combination and a form indeed
Where every god did seem to set his seal,
To give the world assurance of a man.
This was your husband. Look you now what follows:
Here is your husband, like a mildew'd ear
Blasting his wholesome brother. Have you eyes?
Could you on this fair mountain leave to feed,
And batten on this moor? Ha! have you eyes?
You cannot call it love; for at your age
The heyday in the blood is tame, it's humble,
And waits upon the judgment; and what judgment
Would step from this to this? Sense, sure, you have,
Else could you not have motion; but sure that sense
Is apoplex'd; for madness would not err,
Nor sense to ecstasy was ne'er so thrall'd
But it reserv'd some quantity of choice
To serve in such a difference. What devil was't
That thus hath cozen'd you at hoodman-blind?
Eyes without feeling, feeling without sight,
Ears without hands or eyes, smelling sans all,
Or but a sickly part of one true sense
Could not so mope. O shame! where is thy blush?
Rebellious hell,
If thou canst mutine in a matron's bones,
To flaming youth let virtue be as wax
And melt in her own fire; proclaim no shame
When the compulsive ardour gives the charge,
Since frost itself as actively doth burn,
And reason panders will.

QUEEN: O Hamlet, speak no more!

Thou turn'st my eyes into my very soul;
And there I see such black and grained spots
As will not leave their tinct.

HAMLET: Nay, but to live
In the rank sweat of an enseamed bed,
Stew'd in corruption, honeying and making love
Over the nasty sty!

QUEEN: O, speak to me no more!
These words like daggers enter in my ears;
No more, sweet Hamlet.

HAMLET: A murderer and a villain!
A slave that is not twentieth part the tithe
Of your precedent lord; a vice of kings;
A cutpurse of the empire and the rule,
That from a shelf the precious diadem stole
And put it in his pocket!

QUEEN: No more!

[*Enter* GHOST.]

HAMLET: A king of shreds and patches—
Save me, and hover o'er me with your wings,
You heavenly guards! What would your gracious figure?

QUEEN: Alas, he's mad!

HAMLET: Do you not come your tardy son to chide,
That, laps'd in time and passion, lets go by
Th' important acting of your dread command?
O, say!

GHOST: Do not forget; this visitation
Is but to whet thy almost blunted purpose.
But look, amazement on thy mother sits.
O, step between her and her fighting soul!
Conceit in weakest bodies strongest works.
Speak to her, Hamlet.

HAMLET: How is it with you, lady?

QUEEN: Alas, how is't with you,
That you do bend your eye on vacancy,
And with th' incorporal air do hold discourse?
Forth at your eyes your spirits wildly peep;
And, as the sleeping soldiers in th' alarm,
Your bedded hairs like life in excrements
Start up and stand an end. O gentle son,
Upon the heat and flame of thy distemper
Sprinkle cool patience! Whereon do you look?

HAMLET: On him, on him! Look you how pale he glares.

His form and cause conjoin'd, preaching to stones,
Would make them capable.—Do not look upon me,
Lest with this piteous action you convert
My stern effects; then what I have to do
Will want true colour—tears perchance for blood.

QUEEN: To whom do you speak this?

HAMLET: Do you see nothing there?

QUEEN: Nothing at all; yet all that is I see.

HAMLET: Nor did you nothing hear?

QUEEN: No, nothing but ourselves.

HAMLET: Why, look you there. Look how it steals away.
My father, in his habit as he liv'd!
Look where he goes even now out at the portal.
        [*Exit* GHOST.]

QUEEN: This is the very coinage of your brain.
This bodiless creation ectasy
Is very cunning in.

HAMLET: Ecstasy!
My pulse as yours doth temperately keep time.
And makes as healthful music. It is not madness
That I have utt'red. Bring me to the test,
And I the matter will re-word which madness
Would gambol from. Mother, for love of grace,
Lay not that flattering unction to your soul,
That not your trespass but my madness speaks:
It will but skin and film the ulcerous place,
Whiles rank corruption, mining all within,
Infects unseen. Confess yourself to heaven;
Repent what's past; avoid what is to come;
And do not spread the compost on the weeds,
To make them ranker. Forgive me this my virtue;
For in the fatness of these pursy times
Virtue itself of vice must pardon beg,
Yea, curb and woo for leave to do him good.

QUEEN: O Hamlet, thou hast cleft my heart in twain.

HAMLET: O, throw away the worser part of it,
And live the purer with the other half.
Good night—but go not to my uncle's bed;
Assume a virtue, if you have it not.
That monster custom, who all sense doth eat,
Of habits devil, is angel yet in this,
That to the use of actions fair and good
He likewise gives a frock or livery

That aptly is put on. Refrain to-night;
And that shall lend a kind of easiness
To the next abstinence; the next more easy;
For use almost can change the stamp of nature,
And either curb the devil, or throw him out,
With wondrous potency. Once more, good night;
And when you are desirous to be blest,
I'll blessing beg of you. For this same lord
I do repent; but Heaven hath pleas'd it so,
To punish me with this, and this with me,
That I must be their scourge and minister.
I will bestow him, and will answer well
The death I gave him. So, again, good night.
I must be cruel only to be kind;
Thus bad begins and worse remains behind.
One word more, good lady.

QUEEN: What shall I do?

HAMLET: Not this, by no means, that I bid you do:
Let the bloat King tempt you again to bed;
Pinch wanton on your cheek; call you his mouse;
And let him, for a pair of reechy kisses,
Or paddling in your neck with his damn'd fingers,
Make you to ravel all this matter out,
That I essentially am not in madness,
But mad in craft. 'Twere good you let him know;
For who that's but a queen, fair, sober, wise,
Would from a paddock, from a bat, a gib,
Such dear concernings hide? Who would do so?
No, in despite of sense and secrecy,
Unpeg the basket on the house's top,
Let the birds fly, and, like the famous ape,
To try conclusions, in the basket creep
And break your own neck down.

QUEEN: Be thou assur'd, if words be made of breath
And breath of life, I have no life to breathe
What thou hast said to me.

HAMLET: I must to England; you know that?

QUEEN: Alack,
I had forgot. 'Tis so concluded on.

HAMLET: There's letters seal'd; and my two school-fellows,
Whom I will trust as I will adders fang'd—
They bear the mandate; they must sweep my way
And marshal me to knavery. Let it work;

For 'tis the sport to have the engineer
Hoist with his own petar; and't shall go hard
But I will delve one yard below their mines
And blow them at the moon. O, 'tis most sweet
When in one line two crafts directly meet.
This man shall set me packing.
I'll lug the guts into the neighbour room.
Mother, good night. Indeed, this counsellor
Is now most still, most secret, and most grave,
Who was in life a foolish prating knave.
Come, sir, to draw toward an end with you.
Good night, mother.

[*Exeunt severally*; HAMLET *tugging in* POLONIUS.]

ACT IV

SCENE I———*Elsinore. The Castle.*

[*Enter* KING, QUEEN, ROSENCRANTZ, *and* GUILDENSTERN.]

KING: There's matter in these sighs, these profound heaves,
You must translate; 'tis fit we understand them.
Where is your son?

QUEEN: Bestow this place on us a little while.

[*Exeunt* ROSENCRANTZ *and* GUILDENSTERN.]
Ah, mine own lord, what have I seen to-night!

KING: What, Gertrude? How does Hamlet?

QUEEN: Mad as the sea and wind, when both contend
Which is the mightier. In his lawless fit,
Behind the arras hearing something stir,
Whips out his rapier, cries 'A rat, a rat!'
And in this brainish apprehension kills
The unseen good old man.

KING: O heavy deed!
It had been so with us had we been there.
His liberty is full of threats to all—
To you yourself, to us, to every one.
Alas, how shall this bloody deed be answer'd?
It will be laid to us, whose providence
Should have kept short, restrain'd, and out of haunt,
This mad young man. But so much was our love,
We would not understand what was most fit;
But, like the owner of a foul disease,
To keep it from divulging, let it feed
Even on the pith of life. Where is he gone?

QUEEN: To draw apart the body he hath kill'd;
O'er whom his very madness, like some ore
Among a mineral of metals base,
Shows itself pure: 'a weeps for what is done.
KING: O Gertrude, come away!
The sun no sooner shall the mountains touch
But we will ship him hence; and this vile deed
We must with all our majesty and skill
Both countenance and excuse. Ho Guildenstern!
[*Re-enter* ROSENCRANTZ *and* GUILDENSTERN.]
Friends, both go join you with some further aid:
Hamlet in madness hath Polonius slain,
And from his mother's closet hath he dragg'd him;
Go seek him out; speak fair, and bring the body
Into the chapel. I pray you haste in this.
[*Exeunt* ROSENCRANTZ *and* GUILDENSTERN.]
Come, Gertrude, we'll call up our wisest friends
And let them know both what we mean to do
And what's untimely done; so haply slander—
Whose whisper o'er the world's diameter,
As level as the cannon to his blank,
Transports his pois'ned shot—may miss our name,
And hit the woundless air. O, come away!
My soul is full of discord and dismay.   [*Exeunt.*]

SCENE II———*Elsinore. The Castle.*

[*Enter* HAMLET.]
HAMLET: Safely stow'd.
GENTLEMEN: [*within*] Hamlet! Lord Hamlet!
HAMLET: But soft! What noise? Who calls on Hamlet? O, here they come!
[*Enter* ROSENCRANTZ *and* GUILDENSTERN.]
ROSENCRANTZ: What have you done, my lord, with the dead body?
HAMLET: Compounded it with dust, whereto 'tis kin.
ROSENCRANTZ: Tell us where 'tis, that we may take it thence And bear it to the chapel.
HAMLET: Do not believe it.
ROSENCRANTZ: Believe what?
HAMLET: That I can keep your counsel, and not mine own. Besides, to be demanded of a sponge—what replication should be made by the son of a king?
ROSENCRANTZ: Take you me for a sponge, my lord?
HAMLET: Ay, sir; that soaks up the King's countenance, his rewards, his

authorities. But such officers do the King best service in the end: he keeps
them, like an ape an apple in the corner of his jaw; first mouth'd to be last
swallowed; when he needs what you have glean'd, it is but squeezing you
and, sponge, you shall be dry again.

ROSENCRANTZ: I understand you not, my lord.

HAMLET: I am glad of it; a knavish speech sleeps in a foolish ear.

ROSENCRANTZ: My lord, you must tell us where the body is, and go with us to the
King.

HAMLET: The body is with the King, but the King is not with the body. The King is
a thing—

GUILDENSTERN: A thing, my lord!

HAMLET: Of nothing. Bring me to him. Hide fox, and all after.   [*Exeunt.*]

SCENE III———*Elsinore. The Castle.*

[*Enter* KING, *attended.*]

KING: I have sent to seek him, and to find the body.
How dangerous is it that this man goes loose!
Yet must not we put the strong law on him:
He's lov'd of the distracted multitude,
Who like not in their judgment but their eyes;
And where 'tis so, th' offender's scourge is weigh'd,
But never the offence. To bear all smooth and even,
This sudden sending him away must seem
Deliberate pause. Diseases desperate grown
By desperate appliance are reliev'd,
Or not at all.

[*Enter* ROSENCRANTZ.]
How now! what hath befall'n?

ROSENCRANTZ: Where the dead body is bestow'd, my lord,
We cannot get from him.

KING: But where is he?

ROSENCRANTZ: Without, my lord; guarded, to know your pleasure.

KING: Bring him before us.

ROSENCRANTZ: Ho, Guildenstern! bring in the lord.

[*Enter* HAMLET *and* GUILDENSTERN.]

KING: Now, Hamlet, where's Polonius?

HAMLET: At supper.

KING: At supper! Where?

HAMLET: Not where he eats, but where 'a is eaten; a certain convocation of politic
worms are e'en at him. Your worm is your only emperor for diet: we fat all
creatures else to fat us, and we fat ourselves for maggots; your fat king and
your lean beggar is but variable service—two dishes, but to one table. That's
the end.

KING: Alas, alas!

HAMLET: A man may fish with the worm that hath eat of a king, and eat of the fish that hath fed of that worm.

KING: What dost thou mean by this?

HAMLET: Nothing but to show you how a king may go a progress through the guts of a beggar.

KING: Where is Polonius?

HAMLET: In heaven; send thither to see; if your messenger find him not there, seek him i' th' other place yourself. But if, indeed, you find him not within this month, you shall nose him as you go up the stairs into the lobby.

KING: [*to attendants*] Go seek him there.

HAMLET: 'A will stay till you come. [*Exeunt attendants.*]

KING: Hamlet, this deed, for thine especial safety—
Which we do tender, as we dearly grieve
For that which thou hast done—must send thee hence
With fiery quickness. Therefore prepare thyself;
The bark is ready, and the wind at help,
Th' associates tend, and everything is bent
For England.

HAMLET: For England!

KING: Ay, Hamlet.

HAMLET: Good!

KING: So is it, if thou knew'st our purposes.

HAMLET: I see a cherub that sees them. But, come; for England! Farewell, dear mother.

KING: Thy loving father, Hamlet.

HAMLET: My mother: father and mother is man and wife; man and wife is one flesh; and so, my mother. Come, for England. [*Exit.*]

KING: Follow him at foot; tempt him with speed aboard;
Delay it not; I'll have him hence to-night.
Away! for everything is seal'd and done
That else leans on th' affair. Pray you make haste.
[*Exeunt all but the* KING.]
And, England, if my love thou hold'st at aught—
As my great power thereof may give thee sense,
Since yet thy cicatrice looks raw and red
After the Danish sword, and thy free awe
Pays homage to us—thou mayst not coldly set
Our sovereign process; which imports at full,
By letters congruing to that effect,
The present death of Hamlet. Do it, England:
For like the hectic in my blood he rages,
And thou must cure me. Till I know 'tis done,
Howe'er my haps, my joys were ne'er begun. [*Exit.*]

SCENE IV——*A plain in Denmark.*

[*Enter* FORTINBRAS *with his army over the stage.*]

FORTINBRAS: Go, Captain, from me greet the Danish king.
  Tell him that by his license Fortinbras
  Craves the conveyance of a promis'd march
  Over his kingdom. You know the rendezvous.
  If that his Majesty would aught with us,
  We shall express our duty in his eye;
  And let him know so.
CAPTAIN: I will do't, my lord.
FORTINBRAS: Go softly on.   [*Exeunt all but the* CAPTAIN.]

[*Enter* HAMLET, ROSENCRANTZ, GUILDENSTERN, *and others.*]

HAMLET: Good sir, whose powers are these?
CAPTAIN: They are of Norway, sir.
HAMLET: How purpos'd, sir, I pray you?
CAPTAIN: Against some part of Poland.
HAMLET: Who commands them, sir?
CAPTAIN: The nephew to old Norway, Fortinbras.
HAMLET: Goes it against the main of Poland, sir,
  Or for some frontier?
CAPTAIN: Truly to speak, and with no addition,
  We go to gain a little patch of ground
  That hath in it no profit but the name.
  To pay five ducats, five, I would not farm it;
  Nor will it yield to Norway or the Pole
  A ranker rate should it be sold in fee.
HAMLET: Why, then the Polack never will defend it.
CAPTAIN: Yes, it is already garrison'd.
HAMLET: Two thousand souls and twenty thousand ducats
  Will not debate the question of this straw.
  This is th' imposthume of much wealth and peace,
  That inward breaks, and shows no cause without
  Why the man dies. I humbly thank you, sir.
CAPTAIN: God buy you, sir.   [*Exit.*]
ROSENCRANTZ: Will't please you go, my lord?
HAMLET: I'll be with you straight. Go a little before.

[*Exeunt all but* HAMLET.]

  How all occasions do inform against me,
  And spur my dull revenge! What is a man,
  If his chief good and market of his time
  Be but to sleep and feed? A beast, no more!
  Sure he that made us with such large discourse,
  Looking before and after, gave us not

That capability and godlike reason
To fust in us unus'd. Now, whether it be
Bestial oblivion, or some craven scruple
Of thinking too precisely on th' event—
A thought which, quarter'd, hath but one part wisdom
And ever three parts coward—I do not know
Why yet I live to say 'This thing's to do,'
Sith I have cause, and will, and strength, and means,
To do't. Examples gross as earth exhort me:
Witness this army, of such mass and charge,
Led by a delicate and tender prince,
Whose spirit, with divine ambition puff'd,
Makes mouths at the invisible event,
Exposing what is mortal and unsure
To all that fortune, death, and danger dare,
Even for an egg-shell. Rightly to be great
Is not to stir without great argument,
But greatly to find quarrel in a straw,
When honour's at the stake. How stand I, then,
That have a father kill'd, a mother stain'd,
Excitements of my reason and my blood,
And let all sleep, while to my shame I see
The imminent death of twenty thousand men
That, for a fantasy and trick of fame,
Go to their graves like beds, fight for a plot
Whereon the numbers cannot try the cause,
Which is not tomb enough and continent
To hide the slain? O, from this time forth,
My thoughts be bloody, or be nothing worth!   [*Exit.*]

SCENE V———*Elsinore. The Castle.*

[*Enter* QUEEN, HORATIO, *and a* GENTLEMAN.]
QUEEN: I will not speak with her.
GENTLEMAN: She is importunate, indeed distract.
    Her mood will needs be pitied.
QUEEN: What would she have?
GENTLEMAN: She speaks much of her father; says she hears
    There's tricks i' th' world, and hems, and beats her heart;
    Spurns enviously at straws; speaks things in doubt,
    That carry but half sense. Her speech is nothing,
    Yet the unshaped use of it doth move
    The hearers to collection; they yawn at it,

And botch the words up fit to their own thoughts;
Which, as her winks and nods and gestures yield them,
Indeed would make one think there might be thought,
Though nothing sure, yet much unhappily.
HORATIO: 'Twere good she were spoken with; for she may strew
Dangerous conjectures in ill-breeding minds.
QUEEN: Let her come in.   [*Exit* GENTLEMAN.]
[*aside*] To my sick soul, as sin's true nature is,
Each toy seems prologue to some great amiss.
So full of artless jealousy is guilt,
It spills itself in fearing to be spilt.
     [*Enter* OPHELIA *distracted.*]
OPHELIA: Where is the beauteous Majesty of Denmark?
QUEEN: How now, Ophelia!
OPHELIA: [*sings*]

> How should I your true love know
>   From another one?
> By his cockle hat and staff,
>   And his sandal shoon.

QUEEN: Alas, sweet lady, what imports this song?
OPHELIA: Say you? Nay, pray you, mark.   [*sings*]

> He is dead and gone, lady,
>   He is dead and gone;
> At his head a grass-green turf,
>   At his heels a stone.

  O, ho!
QUEEN: Nay, but, Ophelia—
OPHELIA: Pray you, mark.   [*sings*]

> White his shroud as the mountain snow—

    [*Enter* KING.]
QUEEN: Alas, look here, my lord.
OPHELIA: Larded with sweet flowers;

> Which bewept to the grave did not go
>   With true-love showers.

KING: How do you, pretty lady?
OPHELIA: Well, God dild you! They say the owl was a baker's daughter. Lord, we
   know what we are, but know not what we may be. God be at your table!
KING: Conceit upon her father.
OPHELIA: Pray let's have no words of this; but when they ask you what it means, say
   you this: [*sings*]

> To-morrow is Saint Valentine's day,
>   All in the morning betime,
> And I a maid at your window,
>   To be your Valentine.

> Then up he rose, and donn'd his clothes,
>> And dupp'd the chamber-door;
> Let in the maid, that out a maid
>> Never departed more.

KING: Pretty Ophelia!

OPHELIA: Indeed, la, without an oath, I'll make an end on't.   [*sings*]

> By Gis and by Saint Charity,
>> Alack, and fie for shame!
> Young men will do't, if they come to't;
>> By Cock, they are to blame.
> Quoth she 'Before you tumbled me,
>> You promis'd me to wed.'

  He answers:

> 'So would I 'a done, by yonder sun,
>> An thou hadst not come to my bed.'

KING: How long hath she been thus?

OPHELIA: I hope all will be well. We must be patient; but I cannot choose but weep to think they would lay him i' th' cold ground. My brother shall know of it; and so I thank you for your good counsel. Come, my coach! Good night, ladies; good night, sweet ladies, good night, good night.
   [*Exit.*]

KING: Follow her close; give her good watch, I pray you.
   [*Exeunt* HORATIO *and* GENTLEMAN.]
O, this is the poison of deep grief; it springs
All from her father's death. And now behold—
O Gertrude, Gertrude!
When sorrows come, they come not single spies,
But in battalions! First, her father slain;
Next, your son gone, and he most violent author
Of his own just remove; the people muddied,
Thick and unwholesome in their thoughts and whispers
For good Polonius' death; and we have done but greenly
In hugger-mugger to inter him; poor Ophelia
Divided from herself and her fair judgment,
Without the which we are pictures, or mere beasts;
Last, and as much containing as all these,
Her brother is in secret come from France;
Feeds on his wonder, keeps himself in clouds,
And wants not buzzers to infect his ear
With pestilent speeches of his father's death;
Wherein necessity, of matter beggar'd,
Will nothing stick our person to arraign
In ear and ear. O my dear Gertrude, this,
Like to a murd'ring piece, in many places

Gives me superfluous death.   [*A noise within.*]
QUEEN: Alack, what noise is this?
KING: Attend!
      [*Enter a* GENTLEMAN.]
Where are my Switzers? Let them guard the door.
What is the matter?
GENTLEMAN: Save yourself, my lord:
    The ocean, overpeering of his list,
    Eats not the flats with more impetuous haste
    Than young Laertes, in a riotous head,
    O'erbears your officers. The rabble call him lord;
    And, as the world were now but to begin,
    Antiquity forgot, custom not known,
    The ratifiers and props of every word,
    They cry 'Choose we; Laertes shall be king.'
    Caps, hands, and tongues, applaud it to the clouds,
    'Laertes shall be king, Laertes king.'
QUEEN: How cheerfully on the false trail they cry!
    [*Noise within.*]
    O, this is counter, you false Danish dogs!
KING: The doors are broke.
    [*Enter* LAERTES, *with others, in arms.*]
LAERTES: Where is this king?—Sirs, stand you all without.
ALL: No, let's come in.
LAERTES: I pray you give me leave.
ALL: We will, we will.
    [*Exeunt.*]
LAERTES: I thank you. Keep the door.—O thou vile king,
    Give me my father!
QUEEN: Calmly, good Laertes.
LAERTES: That drop of blood that's calm proclaims me bastard;
    Cries cuckold to my father; brands the harlot
    Even here, between the chaste unsmirched brow
    Of my true mother.
KING: What is the cause, Laertes,
    That thy rebellion looks so giant-like?
    Let him go, Gertrude; do not fear our person:
    There's such divinity doth hedge a king
    That treason can but peep to what it would,
    Acts little of his will. Tell me, Laertes,
    Why thou art thus incens'd. Let him go, Gertrude.
    Speak, man.
LAERTES: Where is my father?

KING: Dead.
QUEEN: But not by him.
KING: Let him demand his fill.
LAERTES: How came he dead? I'll not be juggled with.
    To hell, allegience! Vows, to the blackest devil!
    Conscience and grace, to the profoundest pit!
    I dare damnation. To this point I stand,
    That both the worlds I give to negligence,
    Let come what comes; only I'll be reveng'd
    Most thoroughly for my father.
KING: Who shall stay you?
LAERTES: My will, not all the world's.
    And for my means, I'll husband them so well
    They shall go far with little.
KING: Good Laertes,
    If you desire to know the certainty
    Of your dear father, is't writ in your revenge
    That, swoopstake, you will draw both friend and foe,
    Winner and loser?
LAERTES: None but his enemies.
KING: Will you know them, then?
LAERTES: To his good friends thus wide I'll ope my arms
    And, like the kind life-rend'ring pelican,
    Repast them with my blood.
KING: Why, now you speak
    Like a good child and a true gentleman.
    That I am guiltless of your father's death,
    And am most sensibly in grief for it,
    It shall as level to your judgment 'pear
    As day does to your eye.

                        [A *noise within:* 'Let her come in.']

LAERTES: How now! What noise is that?
    [*Re-enter* OPHELIA.]
    O, heat dry up my brains! tears seven times salt
    Burn out the sense and virtue of mine eye!
    By heaven, thy madness shall be paid with weight
    Till our scale turn the beam. O rose of May!
    Dear maid, kind sister, sweet Ophelia!
    O heavens! is't possible a young maid's wits
    Should be as mortal as an old man's life?
    Nature is fine in love; and where 'tis fine
    It sends some precious instance of itself
    After the thing it loves.

OPHELIA: [*sings*]

>They bore him barefac'd on the bier;
>Hey non nonny, nonny, hey nonny;
>And in his grave rain'd many a tear—

Fare you well, my dove!

LAERTES: Hadst thou thy wits, and didst persuade revenge,
It could not move thus.

OPHELIA: You must sing 'A-down, a-down,' an you call him a-down-a. O, how the wheel becomes it! It is the false steward, that stole his master's daughter.

LAERTES: This nothing's more than matter.

OPHELIA: There's rosemary, that's for remembrance; pray you, love, remember. And there is pansies, that's for thoughts.

LAERTES: A document in madness—thoughts and remembrance fitted.

OPHELIA: There's fennel for you, and columbines. There's rue for you; and here's some for me. We may call it herb of grace a Sundays. O, you must wear your rue with a difference. There's a daisy. I would give you some violets, but they wither'd all when my father died. They say 'a made a good end.

[*sings*] For bonny sweet Robin is all my joy.

LAERTES: Thought and affliction, passion, hell itself,
She turns to favour and to prettiness.

OPHELIA: [*sings*]

>And will 'a not come again?
>And will 'a not come again?
> No, no, he is dead,
> Go to thy death-bed,
>He never will come again.
>
>His beard was as white as snow,
>All flaxen was his poll;
> He is gone, he is gone,
> And we cast away moan:
>God-a-mercy on his soul!

And of all Christian souls, I pray God. God buy you.
    [*Exit.*]

LAERTES: Do you see this, O God?

KING: Laertes, I must commune with your grief,
Or you deny me right. Go but apart,
Make choice of whom your wisest friends you will,
And they shall hear and judge 'twixt you and me.
If by direct or by collateral hand
They find us touch'd, we will our kingdom give,
Our crown, our life, and all that we call ours,
To you in satisfaction; but if not,
Be you content to lend your patience to us,

And we shall jointly labour with your soul
  To give it due content.
LAERTES: Let this be so.
  His means of death, his obscure funeral—
  No trophy, sword, nor hatchment, o'er his bones,
  No noble rite nor formal ostentation—
  Cry to be heard, as 'twere from heaven to earth,
  That I must call't in question.
KING: So you shall;
  And where th' offence is, let the great axe fall.
  I pray you go with me.   [*Exeunt.*]

SCENE VI——*Elsinore. The Castle.*

[*Enter* HORATIO *with an* ATTENDANT.]
HORATIO: What are they that would speak with me?
ATTENDANT: Sea-faring men, sir; they say they have letters for you.
HORATIO: Let them come in.   [*Exit* ATTENDANT.]
  I do not know from what part of the world
  I should be greeted, if not from Lord Hamlet.
    [*Enter sailors.*]
SAILOR: God bless you, sir.
HORATIO: Let Him bless thee too.
SAILOR: 'A shall, sir, an't please Him. There's a letter for you, sir; it came from th'
  ambassador that was bound for England—if your name be Horatio, as I am
  let to know it is.
HORATIO: [*reads*] 'Horatio, when thou shalt have overlook'd this, give these fellows
  some means to the King: they have letters for him. Ere we were two days old
  at sea, a pirate of very warlike appointment gave us chase. Finding ourselves
  too slow of sail, we put on a compelled valour; and in the grapple I boarded
  them. On the instant they got clear of our ship; so I alone became their
  prisoner. They have dealt with me like thieves of mercy; but they knew what
  they did; I am to do a good turn for them. Let the King have the letters I have
  sent; and repair thou to me with as much speed as thou wouldest fly death. I
  have words to speak in thine ear will make thee dumb; yet are they much too
  light for the bore of the matter. These good fellows will bring thee where I
  am. Rosencrantz and Guildenstern hold their course for England; of them I
  have much to tell thee. Farewell.
                      'He that thou knowest thine, HAMLET.'
  Come, I will give you way for these your letters,
  And do't the speedier that you may direct me
  To him from whom you brought them.   [*Exeunt.*]

SCENE VII——Elsinore. The Castle.

[*Enter* KING *and* LAERTES.]

KING: Now must your conscience my acquittance seal,
    And you must put me in your heart for friend,
    Sith you have heard, and with a knowing ear,
    That he which hath your noble father slain
    Pursu'd my life.
LAERTES: It well appears. But tell me
    Why you proceeded not against these feats,
    So crimeful and so capital in nature,
    As by your safety, wisdom, all things else,
    You mainly were stirr'd up.
KING: O, for two special reasons,
    Which may to you, perhaps, seem much unsinew'd,
    But yet to me th' are strong. The Queen his mother
    Lives almost by his looks; and for myself,
    My virtue or my plague, be it either which—
    She is so conjunctive to my life and soul
    That, as the star moves not but in his sphere,
    I could not but by her. The other motive,
    Why to a public count I might not go,
    Is the great love the general gender bear him;
    Who, dipping all his faults in their affection,
    Work like the spring that turneth wood to stone,
    Convert his gyves to graces; so that my arrows,
    Too slightly timber'd for so loud a wind,
    Would have reverted to my bow again,
    But not where I have aim'd them.
LAERTES: And so have I a noble father lost;
    A sister driven into desp'rate terms,
    Whose worth, if praises may go back again,
    Stood challenger on mount of all the age
    For her perfections. But my revenge will come.
KING: Break not your sleeps for that. You must not think
    That we are made of stuff so flat and dull
    That we can let our beard be shook with danger,
    And think it pastime. You shortly shall hear more.
    I lov'd your father, and we love our self;
    And that, I hope, will teach you to imagine—
        [*Enter a* MESSENGER *with letters.*]
    How now! What news?
MESSENGER: Letters, my lord, from Hamlet:
    These to your Majesty; this to the Queen.

KING: From Hamlet! Who brought them?
MESSENGER: Sailors, my lord, they say; I saw them not.
    They were given me by Claudio; he receiv'd them
    Of him that brought them.
KING: Laertes, you shall hear them.
    Leave us.   [*Exit* MESSENGER.]
    [*reads*] 'High and Mighty. You shall know I am set naked on your kingdom.
    To-morrow shall I beg leave to see your kingly eyes; when I shall, first asking
    your pardon thereunto, recount the occasion of my sudden and more
    strange return.
                HAMLET.'
    What should this mean? Are all the rest come back?
    Or is it some abuse, and no such thing?
LAERTES: Know you the hand?
KING: 'Tis Hamlet's character. 'Naked'!
    And in a postscript here, he says 'alone.'
    Can you devise me?
LAERTES: I am lost in it, my lord. But let him come;
    It warms the very sickness in my heart
    That I shall live and tell him to his teeth
    'Thus didest thou.'
KING: If it be so, Laertes—
    As how should it be so, how otherwise?—
    Will you be rul'd by me?
LAERTES: Ay, my lord;
    So you will not o'errule me to a peace.
KING: To thine own peace. If he be now return'd,
    As checking at his voyage, and that he means
    No more to undertake it, I will work him
    To an exploit now ripe in my device,
    Under the which he shall not choose but fall;
    And for his death, no wind of blame shall breathe;
    But even his mother shall uncharge the practice
    And call it accident.
LAERTES: My lord, I will be rul'd
    The rather, if you could devise it so
    That I might be the organ.
KING: It falls right.
    You have been talk'd of since your travel much,
    And that in Hamlet's hearing, for a quality
    Wherein they say you shine. Your sum of parts
    Did not together pluck such envy from him
    As did that one; and that, in my regard,
    of the unworthiest siege.

LAERTES: What part is that, my lord?

KING: A very riband in the cap of youth,
Yet needful too; for youth no less becomes
The light and careless livery that it wears
Than settled age his sables and his weeds,
Importing health and graveness. Two months since
Here was a gentleman of Normandy—
I have seen myself, and serv'd against, the French,
And they can well on horseback; but this gallant
Had witchcraft in't; he grew into his seat,
And to such wondrous doing brought his horse,
As had he been incorps'd and demi-natur'd
With the brave beast. So far he topp'd my thought,
That I, in forgery of shapes and tricks,
Come short of what he did.

LAERTES: A Norman was't?

KING: A Norman.

LAERTES: Upon my life, Lamord.

KING: The very same.

LAERTES: I know him well. He is the brooch indeed
And gem of all the nation.

KING: He made confession of you;
And gave you such a masterly report
For art and exercise in your defence,
And for your rapier most especial,
That he cried out 'twould be a sight indeed
If one could match you. The scrimers of their nation
He swore had neither motion, guard, nor eye,
If you oppos'd them. Sir, this report of his
Did Hamlet so envenom with his envy
That he could nothing do but wish and beg
Your sudden coming o'er, to play with you.
Now out of this—

LAERTES: What out of this, my lord?

KING: Laertes, was your father dear to you?
Or are you like the painting of a sorrow,
A face without a heart?

LAERTES: Why ask you this?

KING: Not that I think you did not love your father;
But that I know love is begun by time,
And that I see, in passages of proof,
Time qualifies the spark and fire of it.
There lives within the very flame of love

SECOND CLOWN: Marry, now I can tell.

FIRST CLOWN: To 't.

SECOND CLOWN: Mass, I cannot tell.

[*Enter* HAMLET *and* HORATIO, *afar off.*]

FIRST CLOWN: Cudgel thy brains no more about it, for your dull ass will not mend his pace with beating; and when you are ask'd this question next, say 'a grave-maker': the houses he makes lasts till doomsday. Go, get thee to Yaughan; fetch me a stoup of liquor.   [*Exit* SECOND CLOWN.]

[*digs and sings*] In youth, when I did love, did love,
　　　　Methought it was very sweet,
　　　To contract-o-the time for-a my behove,
　　　O, methought there-a-was nothing-a meet.

HAMLET: Has this fellow no feeling of his business, that 'a sings in grave-making?

HORATIO: Custom hath made it in him a property of easiness.

HAMLET: 'Tis e'en so; the hand of little employment hath the daintier sense.

FIRST CLOWN: [*sings*]
　　　　But age, with his stealing steps,
　　　　　Hath clawed me in his clutch,
　　　　And hath shipped me intil the land,
　　　　　As if I had never been such.

[*throws up a skull*]

HAMLET: That skull had a tongue in it, and could sing once. How the knave jowls it to the ground, as if 'twere Cain's jawbone, that did the first murder! This might be the pate of a politician, which this ass now o'erreaches; one that would circumvent God, might it not?

HORATIO: It might, my lord.

HAMLET: Or of a courtier; which could say 'Good morrow, sweet lord! How dost thou, sweet lord?' This might be my Lord Such-a-one, that prais'd my Lord Such-a-one's horse, when 'a meant to beg it—might it not?

HORATIO: Ay, my lord.

HAMLET: Why, e'en so; and now my Lady Worm's, chapless, and knock'd about the mazard with a sexton's spade. Here's fine revolution, an we had the trick to see't. Did these bones cost no more the breeding, but to play at loggats with them? Mine ache to think on't.

CLOWN: [*sings*]
　　　　A pickaxe, and a spade, a spade,

[*throws up another skull*]

HAMLET: There's another. Why may not that be the skull of a lawyer? Where be his quiddities now, his quillets, his cases, his tenures, and his tricks? Why does he suffer this rude knave

A kind of wick or snuff that will abate it;
And nothing is at a like goodness still;
For goodness, growing to a pleurisy,
Dies in his own too much. That we would do,
We should do when we would; for this 'would' changes,
And hath abatements and delays as many
As there are tongues, are hands, are accidents;
And then this 'should' is like a spendthrift's sigh
That hurts by easing. But to the quick of th' ulcer:
Hamlet comes back; what would you undertake
To show yourself in deed your father's son
More than in words?

LAERTES: To cut his throat i' th' church.

KING: No place, indeed, should murder sanctuarize;
Revenge should have no bounds. But, good Laertes,
Will you do this? Keep close within your chamber.
Hamlet return'd shall know you are come home.
We'll put on those shall praise your excellence,
And set a double varnish on the fame
The Frenchman gave you; bring you, in fine, together,
And wager on your heads. He, being remiss,
Most generous, and free from all contriving,
Will not peruse the foils; so that with ease
Or with a little shuffling, you may choose
A sword unbated, and, in a pass of practice,
Requite him for your father.

LAERTES:　　　　　　　　　I will do't;
And for that purpose I'll anoint my sword.
I bought an unction of a mountebank,
So mortal that but dip a knife in it,
Where it draws blood no cataplasm so rare,
Collected from all simples that have virtue
Under the moon, can save the thing from death
That is but scratch'd withal. I'll touch my point
With this contagion, that, if I gall him slightly,
It may be death.

KING:　　　　　　　　Let's further think of this;
Weigh what convenience both of time and means
May fit us to our shape. If this should fail,
And that our drift look through our bad performance,
'Twere better not assay'd, therefore this project
Should have a back or second, that might hold
If this did blast in proof. Soft! let me see.

We'll make a solemn wager on your cunnings—
I ha't.
When in your motion you are hot and dry—
As make your bouts more violent to that end—
And that he calls for drink, I'll have preferr'd him
A chalice for the nonce; whereon but sipping,
If he by chance escape your venom'd stuck,
Our purpose may hold there. But stay; what noise?
      [Enter QUEEN.*]*
QUEEN: One woe doth tread upon another's heel,
  So fast they follow. Your sister's drown'd, Laertes.
LAERTES: Drown'd? O, where?
QUEEN: There is a willow grows aslant the brook
  That shows his hoar leaves in the glassy stream;
  Therewith fantastic garlands did she make
  Of crowflowers, nettles, daisies, and long purples
  That liberal shepherds give a grosser name,
  But our cold maids do dead men's fingers call them.
  There, on the pendent boughs her coronet weeds
  Clamb'ring to hang, an envious sliver broke;
  When down her weedy trophies and herself
  Fell in the weeping brook. Her clothes spread wide
  And, mermaid-like, awhile they bore her up;
  Which time she chanted snatches of old lauds,
  As one incapable of her own distress,
  Or like a creature native and indued
  Unto that element; but long it could not be
  Till that her garments, heavy with their drink,
  Pull'd the poor wretch from her melodious lay
  To muddy death.
LAERTES: Alas, then she is drown'd!
QUEEN: Drown'd, drown'd.
LAERTES: Too much of water hast thou, poor Ophelia,
  And therefore I forbid my tears; but yet
  It is our trick; nature her custom holds,
  Let shame say what it will. When these are gone,
  The woman will be out. Adieu, my lord.
  I have a speech o' fire that fain would blaze
  But that this folly douts it.   *[Exit.]*
KING: Let's follow, Gertrude.
  How much I had to do to calm his rage!
  Now fear I this will give it start again;
  Therefore let's follow.   *[Exeunt.]*

ACT V

SCENE I——*Elsinore. A churchyard.*

[Enter two CLOWNS *with spades and picks.]*

FIRST CLOWN: Is she to be buried in Christian burial when she
  own salvation?
SECOND CLOWN: I tell thee she is; therefore make her grave stra
  hath sat on her, and finds it Christian burial.
FIRST CLOWN: How can that be, unless she drown'd herself in
SECOND CLOWN: Why, 'tis found so.
FIRST CLOWN: It must be 'se offendendo'; it cannot be else. For
  I drown myself wittingly, it argues an act; and an act hath
  is to act, to do, to perform; argal, she drown'd herself
SECOND CLOWN: Nay, but hear you, Goodman Delver.
FIRST CLOWN: Give me leave. Here lies the water; good. Here s
  If the man go to this water and drown himself, it is,
  goes—mark you that; but if the water come to him
  drowns not himself. Argal, he that is not guilty of his o
  his own life.
SECOND CLOWN: But is this law?
FIRST CLOWN: Ay, marry, is't; crowner's quest law.
SECOND CLOWN: Will you ha' the truth an't? If this had not
  she should have been buried out a Christian burial
FIRST CLOWN: Why, there thou say'st; and the more pity tha
  count'nance in this world to drown or hang themselv
  Christen. Come, my spade. There is no ancient g
  ditchers, and grave-makers; they hold up Adam's
ND CLOWN: Was he a gentleman?
CLOWN: 'A was the first that ever bore arms.
CLOWN: Why, he had none.
WN: What, art a heathen? How dost thou unde
ture says Adam digg'd. Could he dig witho
n to thee. If thou answerest me not to the
: Go to.
hat is he that builds stronger than ei
he carpenter?
e gallows-maker; for that frame ou
y wit well; in good faith the gallow
l to those that do ill. Now thou
the church; argal, the gallow

stronger than a mason,
t, and unyoke.

shovel, and will not tell him of his action of battery? Hum! This fellow might be in's time a great buyer of land, with his statutes, his recognizances, his fines, his double vouchers, his recoveries. Is this the fine of his fines, and the recovery of his recoveries, to have his fine pate full of fine dirt? Will his vouchers vouch him no more of his purchases, and double ones too, than the length and breadth of a pair of indentures? The very conveyances of his lands will scarcely lie in this box; and must th' inheritor himself have no more, ha?

HORATIO: Not a jot more, my lord.

HAMLET: Is not parchment made of sheep-skins?

HORATIO: Ay, my lord, and of calves' skins too.

HAMLET: They are sheep and calves which seek out assurance in that. I will speak to this fellow. Whose grave's this, sirrah?

FIRST CLOWN: Mine, sir. [*sings*]

        O, a pit of clay for to be made
        For such a guest is meet.

HAMLET: I think it be thine indeed, for thou liest in't.

FIRST CLOWN: You lie out on't, sir, and therefore 'tis not yours. For my part, I do not lie in't, yet it is mine.

HAMLET: Thou dost lie in't, to be in't and say it is thine; 'tis for the dead, not for the quick; therefore thou liest.

FIRST CLOWN: 'Tis a quick lie, sir; 'twill away again from me to you.

HAMLET: What man dost thou dig it for?

FIRST CLOWN: For no man, sir.

HAMLET: What woman, then?

FIRST CLOWN: For none neither.

HAMLET: Who is to be buried in't?

FIRST CLOWN: One that was a woman, sir; but, rest her soul, she's dead.

HAMLET: How absolute the knave is! We must speak by the card, or equivocation will undo us. By the Lord, Horatio, this three years I have took note of it: the age is grown so picked that the toe of the peasant comes so near the heel of the courtier, he galls his kibe. How long hast thou been a grave-maker?

FIRST CLOWN: Of all the days i' th' year, I came to't that day that our last King Hamlet overcame Fortinbras.

HAMLET: How long is that since?

FIRST CLOWN: Cannot you tell that? Every fool can tell that: it was that very day that young Hamlet was born—he that is mad, and sent into England.

HAMLET: Ay, marry, why was he sent into England?

FIRST CLOWN: Why, because 'a was mad: 'a shall recover his wits there; or, if 'a do not, 'tis no great matter there.

HAMLET: Why?

FIRST CLOWN: 'Twill not be seen in him there: there the men are as mad as he.

HAMLET: How came he mad?

FIRST CLOWN: Very strangely, they say.

HAMLET: How strangely?

FIRST CLOWN: Faith, e'en with losing his wits.

HAMLET: Upon what ground?

FIRST CLOWN: Why, here in Denmark. I have been sexton here, man and boy, thirty years.

HAMLET: How long will a man lie i' th' earth ere he rot?

FIRST CLOWN: Faith, if 'a be not rotten before 'a die—as we have many pocky corses now-a-days that will scarce hold the laying in—'a will last you some eight year or nine year. A tanner will last you nine year.

HAMLET: Why he more than another?

FIRST CLOWN: Why, sir, his hide is so tann'd with his trade that 'a will keep out water a great while; and your water is a sore decayer of your whoreson dead body. Here's a skull now; this skull has lien you i' th' earth three and twenty years.

HAMLET: Whose was it?

FIRST CLOWN: A whoreson mad fellow's it was. Whose do you think it was?

HAMLET: Nay, I know not.

FIRST CLOWN: A pestilence on him for a mad rogue! 'A poured a flagon of Rhenish on my head once. This same skull, sir, was, sir, Yorick's skull, the King's jester.

HAMLET: This?

FIRST CLOWN: E'en that.

HAMLET: Let me see. [*takes the skull*] Alas, poor Yorick! I knew him, Horatio: a fellow of infinite jest, of most excellent fancy; he hath borne me on his back a thousand times. And now how abhorred in my imagination it is! My gorge rises at it. Here hung those lips that I have kiss'd I know not how oft. Where be your gibes now, your gambols, your songs, your flashes of merriment that were wont to set the table on a roar? Not one now to mock your own grinning—quite chap-fall'n? Now get you to my lady's chamber, and tell her, let her paint an inch thick, to this favour she must come; make her laugh at that. Prithee, Horatio, tell me one thing.

HORATIO: What's that, my lord?

HAMLET: Dost thou think Alexander look'd a this fashion i' th' earth?

HORATIO: E'en so.

HAMLET: And smelt so? Pah!   [*throws down the skull*]

HORATIO: E'en so, my lord.

HAMLET: To what base uses we may return, Horatio! Why may not imagination trace the noble dust of Alexander till 'a find it stopping a bung-hole?

HORATIO: 'Twere to consider too curiously to consider so.

HAMLET: No, faith, not a jot; but to follow him thither with modesty enough, and likelihood to lead it, as thus: Alexander died, Alexander was buried, Alexander returneth to dust; the dust is earth; of earth we make loam; and why of that loam whereto he was converted might they not stop a beer-barrel?

   Imperious Caesar, dead and turn'd to clay,
   Might stop a hole to keep the wind away.
   O, that that earth which kept the world in awe
   Should patch a wall t' expel the winter's flaw!

But soft! but soft! awhile. Here comes the King.

[*Enter the* KING, QUEEN, LAERTES, *in funeral procession after the coffin,*
with PRIEST *and* LORDS *attendant.*]

The Queen, the courtiers. Who is this they follow?
And with such maimed rites? This doth betoken
The corse they follow did with desperate hand
Fordo it own life. 'Twas of some estate.
Couch we awhile and mark.   [*retiring with* HORATIO]

LAERTES: What ceremony else?
HAMLET: That is Laertes, a very noble youth. Mark.
LAERTES: What ceremony else?
PRIEST: Her obsequies have been so far enlarg'd
 As we have warrantise. Her death was doubtful;
 And, but that great command o'ersways the order,
 She should in ground unsanctified have lodg'd
 Till the last trumpet; for charitable prayers,
 Shards, flints, and pebbles, should be thrown on her;
 Yet here she is allow'd her virgin crants,
 Her maiden strewments, and the bringing home
 Of bell and burial.
LAERTES: Must there no more be done?
PRIEST: No more be done.
 We should profane the service of the dead
 To sing sage requiem and such rest to her
 As to peace-parted souls.
LAERTES: Lay her i' th' earth;
 And from her fair and unpolluted flesh
 May violets spring! I tell thee, churlish priest,
 A minist'ring angel shall my sister be
 When thou liest howling.
HAMLET: What, the fair Ophelia!
QUEEN: Sweets to the sweet; farewell! [*scattering flowers*]
 I hop'd thou shouldst have been my Hamlet's wife;
 I thought thy bride-bed to have deck'd, sweet maid,
 And not have strew'd thy grave.
LAERTES: O, treble woe
 Fall ten times treble on that cursed head
 Whose wicked deed thy most ingenious sense

Depriv'd thee of! Hold off the earth awhile,
Till I have caught her once more in mine arms.
    [*leaps into the grave*]
Now pile your dust upon the quick and dead,
Till of this flat a mountain you have made
T' o'er-top old Pelion or the skyish head
Of blue Olympus.
HAMLET: [*advancing*] What is he whose grief
    Bears such an emphasis, whose phrase of sorrow
    Conjures the wand'ring stars, and makes them stand
    Like wonder-wounded hearers? This is I,
    Hamlet the Dane.   [*leaps into the grave*]
LAERTES: The devil take thy soul! [*grappling with him*]
HAMLET: Thou pray'st not well.
    I prithee take thy fingers from my throat;
    For, though I am not splenitive and rash,
    Yet have I in me something dangerous,
    Which let thy wiseness fear. Hold off thy hand.
KING: Pluck them asunder.
QUEEN: Hamlet! Hamlet!
ALL: Gentlemen!
HORATIO: Good my lord, be quiet.
    [*The attendants part them, and they come out of the grave.*]
HAMLET: Why, I will fight with him upon this theme
    Until my eyelids will no longer wag.
QUEEN: O my son, what theme?
HAMLET: I lov'd Ophelia: forty thousand brothers
    Could not, with all their quantity of love
    Make up my sum. What wilt thou do for her?
KING: O, he is mad, Laertes.
QUEEN: For love of God, forbear him.
HAMLET: 'Swounds, show me what th'owt do:
    Woo't weep, woo't fight, woo't fast, woo't tear thyself,
    Woo't drink up eisel, eat a crocodile?
    I'll do't. Dost come here to whine?
    To outface me with leaping in her grave?
    Be buried quick with her, and so will I;
    And, if thou prate of mountains, let them throw
    Millions of acres on us, till our ground,
    Singeing his pate against the burning zone,
    Make Ossa like a wart! Nay, an thou'lt mouth,
    I'll rant as well as thou.

QUEEN: This is mere madness;
     And thus awhile the fit will work on him;
     Anon, as patient as the female dove
     When that her golden couplets are disclos'd
     His silence will sit drooping.
HAMLET: Hear you, sir:
     What is the reason that you use me thus?
     I lov'd you ever. But it is no matter.
     Let Hercules himself do what he may,
     The cat will mew, and dog will have his day.   [*Exit.*]
KING: I pray thee, good Horatio, wait upon him.
          [*Exit* HORATIO.]
     [*to* LAERTES] Strengthen your patience in our last night's speech;
     We'll put the matter to the present push.—
     Good Gertrude, set some watch over your son.—
     This grave shall have a living monument.
     An hour of quiet shortly shall we see;
     Till then in patience our proceeding be.   [*Exeunt.*]

          SCENE II——*Elsinore. The Castle.*

     [*Enter* HAMLET *and* HORATIO.]
HAMLET: So much for this, sir; now shall you see the other. You do remember all
     the circumstance?
HORATIO: Remember it, my lord!
HAMLET: Sir, in my heart there was a kind of fighting
     That would not let me sleep. Methought I lay
     Worse than the mutines in the bilboes. Rashly,
     And prais'd be rashness for it—let us know,
     Our indiscretion sometime serves us well,
     When our deep plots do pall; and that should learn us
     There's a divinity that shapes our ends,
     Rough-hew them how we will.
HORATIO: That is most certain.
HAMLET: Up from my cabin,
     My sea-gown scarf'd about me, in the dark
     Grop'd I to find out them; had my desire;
     Finger'd their packet, and in fine withdrew
     To mine own room again, making so bold,
     My fears forgetting manners, to unseal
     Their grand commission; where I found, Horatio,
     Ah, royal knavery! an exact command,

Larded with many several sorts of reasons,
Importing Denmark's health and England's too,
With, ho! such bugs and goblins in my life—
That, on the supervise, no leisure bated,
No, not to stay the grinding of the axe,
My head should be struck off.
HORATIO: Is't possible?
HAMLET: Here's the commission; read it at more leisure.
But wilt thou hear now how I did proceed?
HORATIO: I beseech you.
HAMLET: Being thus benetted round with villainies—
Ere I could make a prologue to my brains,
They had begun the play—I sat me down;
Devis'd a new commission; wrote it fair.
I once did hold it, as our statists do,
A baseness to write fair, and labour'd much
How to forget that learning; but sir, now
It did me yeoman's service. Wilt thou know
Th' effect of what I wrote?
HORATIO: Ay, good my lord.
HAMLET: An earnest conjuration from the King,
As England was his faithful tributary,
As love between them like the palm might flourish,
As peace should still her wheaten garland wear
And stand a comma 'tween their amities,
And many such like as-es of great charge,
That, on the view and knowing of these contents,
Without debatement further more or less,
He should those bearers put to sudden death,
Not shriving-time allow'd.
HORATIO: How was this seal'd?
HAMLET: Why, even in that was heaven ordinant.
I had my father's signet in my purse,
Which was the model of that Danish seal;
Folded the writ up in the form of th' other;
Subscrib'd it, gave't th' impression, plac'd it safely,
The changeling never known. Now, the next day
Was our sea-fight; and what to this was sequent
Thou knowest already.
HORATIO: So Guildenstern and Rosencrantz go to't.
HAMLET: Why, man, they did make love to this employment;
They are not near my conscience; their defeat
Does by their own insinuation grow:

'Tis dangerous when the baser nature comes
Between the pass and fell incensed points
Of mighty opposites.

HORATIO: Why, what a king is this!

HAMLET: Does it not, think thee, stand me now upon—
He that hath kill'd my king and whor'd my mother;
Popp'd in between th' election and my hopes;
Thrown out his angle for my proper life,
And with such coz'nage—is't not perfect conscience
To quit him with this arm? And is't not to be damn'd
To let this canker of our nature come
In further evil?

HORATIO: It must be shortly known to him from England
What is the issue of the business there.

HAMLET: It will be short; the interim is mine.
And a man's life's no more than to say 'one.'
But I am very sorry, good Horatio,
That to Laertes I forgot myself;
For by the image of my cause I see
The portraiture of his. I'll court his favours.
But sure the bravery of his grief did put me
Into a tow'ring passion.

HORATIO: Peace; who comes here?

[*Enter young* OSRIC.]

OSRIC: Your lordship is right welcome back to Denmark.

HAMLET: I humbly thank you, sir. [*aside to* HORATIO] Dost know this water-fly?

HORATIO: [*aside to* HAMLET] No, my good lord.

HAMLET: [*aside to* HORATIO] Thy state is the more gracious; for 'tis a vice to know
him. He hath much land, and fertile. Let a beast be lord of beasts, and his
crib shall stand at the king's mess. 'Tis a chough; but, as I say, spacious in the
possession of dirt.

OSRIC: Sweet lord, if your lordship were at leisure, I should impart a thing to you
from his Majesty.

HAMLET: I will receive it, sir, with all diligence of spirit. Put your bonnet to his
right use; 'tis for the head.

OSRIC: I thank your lordship; it is very hot.

HAMLET: No, believe me, 'tis very cold; the wind is northerly.

OSRIC: It is indifferent cold, my lord, indeed.

HAMLET: But yet methinks it is very sultry and hot for my complexion.

OSRIC: Exceedingly, my lord; it is very sultry, as 'twere—I cannot tell how. But,
my lord, his Majesty bade me signify to you that 'a has laid a great wager on
your head. Sir, this is the matter—

HAMLET: I beseech you, remember.

[HAMLET *moves him to put on his hat*.]

OSRIC: Nay, good my lord; for my ease, in good faith. Sir, here is newly come to court Laertes; believe me, an absolute gentleman, full of most excellent differences, of very soft society and great showing. Indeed, to speak feelingly of him, he is the card or calendar of gentry, for you shall find in him the continent of what part a gentleman would see.

HAMLET: Sir, his definement suffers no perdition in you; though, I know, to divide him inventorially would dozy th' arithmetic of memory, and yet but yaw neither in respect of his quick sail. But, in the verity of extolment, I take him to be a soul of great article, and his infusion of such dearth and rareness, as to make true diction of him, his semblable is his mirror, and who else would trace him, his umbrage, nothing more.

OSRIC: Your lordship speaks most infallibly of him.

HAMLET: The concernancy, sir? Why do we wrap the gentleman in our more rawer breath?

OSRIC: Sir?

HORATIO: [*aside to* HAMLET] Is't not possible to understand in another tongue? You will to't, sir, really.

HAMLET: What imports the nomination of this gentleman?

OSRIC: Of Laertes?

HORATIO: [*aside*] His purse is empty already; all's golden words are spent.

HAMLET: Of him, sir.

OSRIC: I know you are not ignorant—

HAMLET: I would you did, sir; yet, in faith, if you did, it would not much approve me. Well, sir.

OSRIC: You are not ignorant of what excellence Laertes is—

HAMLET: I dare not confess that, lest I should compare with him in excellence; but to know a man well were to know himself.

OSRIC: I mean, sir, for his weapon; but in the imputation laid on him by them, in his meed he's unfellowed.

HAMLET: What's his weapon?

OSRIC: Rapier and dagger.

HAMLET: That's two of his weapons—but well.

OSRIC: The King, sir, hath wager'd with him six Barbary horses; against the which he has impon'd, as I take it, six French rapiers and poniards, with their assigns, as girdle, hangers, and so—three of the carriages, in faith, are very dear to fancy, very responsive to the hilts, most delicate carriages, and of very liberal conceit.

HAMLET: What call you the carriages?

HORATIO: [*aside to* HAMLET] I knew you must be edified by the margent ere you had done.

OSRIC: The carriages, sir, are the hangers.

HAMLET: The phrase would be more germane to the matter if we could carry a cannon by our sides. I would it might be hangers till then. But on: six

Barbary horses against six French swords, their assigns, and three liberal conceited carriages; that's the French bet against the Danish. Why is this all impon'd, as you call it?

OSRIC: The King, sir, hath laid, sir, that in a dozen passes between yourself and him he shall not exceed you three hits; he hath laid on twelve for nine, and it would come to immediate trial if your lordship would vouchsafe the answer.

HAMLET: How if I answer no?

OSRIC: I mean, my lord, the opposition of your person in trial.

HAMLET: Sir, I will walk here in the hall. If it please his Majesty, it is the breathing time of day with me; let the foils be brought, the gentleman willing, and the King hold his purpose, I will win for him an I can; if not, I will gain nothing but my shame and the odd hits.

OSRIC: Shall I redeliver you e'en so?

HAMLET: To this effect, sir, after what flourish your nature will.

OSRIC: I commend my duty to your lordship.

HAMLET: Yours, yours. [*Exit* OSRIC.] He does well to commend it himself; there are no tongues else for's turn.

HORATIO: This lapwing runs away with the shell on his head.

HAMLET: 'A did comply, sir, with his dug before 'a suck'd it. Thus has he, and many more of the same bevy, that I know the drossy age dotes on, only got the tune of the time and outward habit of encounter—a kind of yesty collection, which carries them through and through the most fann'd and winnowed opinions; and do but blow them to their trial, the bubbles are out.

[*Enter a* LORD.]

LORD: My lord, his Majesty commended him to you by young Osric, who brings back to him that you attend him in the hall. He sends to know if your pleasure hold to play with Laertes, or that you will take longer time.

HAMLET: I am constant to my purposes; they follow the king's pleasure: if his fitness speaks, mine is ready now—or whensoever, provided I be so able as now.

LORD: The King and Queen and all are coming down.

HAMLET: In happy time.

LORD: The Queen desires you to use some gentle entertainment to Laertes before you fall to play.

HAMLET: She well instructs me.   [*Exit* LORD.]

HORATIO: You will lose this wager, my lord.

HAMLET: I do not think so; since he went into France I have been in continual practice. I shall win at the odds. But thou wouldst not think how ill all's here about my heart; but it is no matter.

HORATIO: Nay, good my lord—

HAMLET: It is but foolery; but it is such a kind of gaingiving as would perhaps trouble a woman.

HORATIO: If your mind dislike anything, obey it. I will forestall their repair hither, and say you are not fit.

HAMLET: Not a whit, we defy augury: there is a special providence in the fall of a sparrow. If it be now, 'tis not to come; if it be not to come, it will be now; if it be not now, yet it will come—the readiness is all. Since no man owes of aught he leaves, what is't to leave betimes? Let be.

      [*A table prepared. Trumpets, drums, and officers with cushions, foils and daggers. Enter* KING, QUEEN, LAERTES, *and all the state.*]

KING: Come, Hamlet, come, and take this hand from me.

      [*The* KING *puts* LAERTES'S *hand into* HAMLET'S.]

HAMLET: Give me your pardon, sir. I have done you wrong;
    But pardon't, as you are a gentleman.
    This presence knows,
    And you must needs have heard how I am punish'd
    With a sore distraction. What I have done
    That might your nature, honour, and exception,
    Roughly awake, I here proclaim was madness.
    Was 't Hamlet wrong'd Laertes? Never Hamlet.
    If Hamlet from himself be ta'en away,
    And when he's not himself does wrong Laertes,
    Then Hamlet does it not, Hamlet denies it.
    Who does it, then? His madness. If 't be so,
    Hamlet is of the faction that is wrong'd;
    His madness is poor Hamlet's enemy.
    Sir, in this audience,
    Let my disclaiming from a purpos'd evil
    Free me so far in your most generous thoughts
    That I have shot my arrow o'er the house
    And hurt my brother.

LAERTES: I am satisfied in nature,
    Whose motive in this case should stir me most
    To my revenge; but in my terms of honour
    I stand aloof, and will no reconcilement
    Till by some elder masters of known honour
    I have a voice and precedent of peace
    To keep my name ungor'd—but till that time
    I do receive your offer'd love like love,
    And will not wrong it.

HAMLET: I embrace it freely;
    And will this brother's wager frankly play.
    Give us the foils. Come on.

LAERTES: Come, one for me.

HAMLET: I'll be your foil, Laertes; in mine ignorance
    Your skill shall, like a star i' th' darkest night,
    Stick fiery off indeed.

LAERTES: You mock me, sir.

HAMLET: No, by this hand.
KING: Give them the foils, young Osric. Cousin Hamlet,
    You know the wager?
HAMLET: Very well, my lord;
    Your Grace has laid the odds a' th' weaker side.
KING: I do not fear it: I have seen you both;
    But since he's better'd, we have therefore odds.
LAERTES: This is too heavy; let me see another.
HAMLET: This likes me well. These foils have all a length?
      [*They prepare to play.*]
OSRIC: Ay, my good lord.
KING: Set me the stoups of wine upon that table.
    If Hamlet give the first or second hit,
    Or quit in answer of the third exchange,
    Let all the battlements their ordnance fire;
    The King shall drink to Hamlet's better breath,
    And in the cup an union shall he throw,
    Richer than that which four successive kings
    In Denmark's crown have worn. Give me the cups;
    And let the kettle to the trumpet speak,
    The trumpet to the cannoneer without,
    The cannons to the heavens, the heaven to earth,
    'Now the King drinks to Hamlet.' Come, begin—
    And you, the judges, bear a wary eye.
HAMLET: Come on, sir.
LAERTES: Come, my lord.   [*They play.*]
HAMLET: One.
LAERTES: No.
HAMLET: Judgement?
OSRIC: A hit, a very palpable hit.
LAERTES: Well, again.
KING: Stay, give me drink. Hamlet, this pearl is thine;
    Here's to thy health. [*Drum, trumpets, and shot.*] Give him the cup.
HAMLET: I'll play this bout first; set it by awhile.
    Come. [*They play.*] Another hit; what say you?
LAERTES: A touch, a touch, I do confess't.
KING: Our son shall win.
QUEEN: He's fat, and scant of breath.
    Here, Hamlet, take my napkin, rub thy brows.
    The Queen carouses to thy fortune, Hamlet.
HAMLET: Good madam!
KING: Gertrude, do not drink.
QUEEN: I will, my lord; I pray you pardon me.

KING: *[aside]* It is the poison'd cup; it is too late.

HAMLET: I dare not drink yet, madam; by and by.

QUEEN: Come, let me wipe thy face.

LAERTES: My lord, I'll hit him now.

KING: I do not think't.

LAERTES: *[aside]* And yet it is almost against my conscience.

HAMLET: Come, for the third. Laertes, you do but dally;
    I pray you pass with your best violence;
    I am afeard you make a wanton of me.

LAERTES: Say you so? Come on.   *[They play.]*

OSRIC: Nothing, neither way.

LAERTES: Have at you now!

        [LAERTES wounds HAMLET: then, in scuffling, they change rapiers, and
        HAMLET wounds LAERTES.]

KING: Part them; they are incens'd.

HAMLET: Nay, come again.   *[The QUEEN falls.]*

OSRIC: Look to the Queen there, ho!

HORATIO: They bleed on both sides. How is it, my lord?

OSRIC: How is't, Laertes?

LAERTES: Why, as a woodcock, to mine own springe, Osric;
    I am justly kill'd with mine own treachery.

HAMLET: How does the Queen?

KING: She swoons to see them bleed.

QUEEN: No, no, the drink, the drink! O my dear Hamlet!
    The drink, the drink! I am poison'd   *[dies]*

HAMLET: O, villainy! Ho! let the door be lock'd.
    Treachery! seek it out.   *[LAERTES falls.]*

LAERTES: It is here, Hamlet. Hamlet, thou art slain;
    No med'cine in the world can do thee good;
    In thee there is not half an hour's life;
    The treacherous instrument is in thy hand,
    Unbated and envenom'd. The foul practice
    Hath turn'd itself on me; lo, here I lie,
    Never to rise again. Thy mother's poison'd.
    I can no more. The King, the King's to blame.

HAMLET: The point envenom'd too!
    Then, venom, to thy work.   *[stabs the KING]*

ALL: Treason! treason!

KING: O, yet defend me, friends; I am but hurt.

HAMLET: Here, thou incestuous, murd'rous, damned Dane,
    Drink off this potion. Is thy union here?
    Follow my mother.   *[KING dies.]*

LAERTES: He is justly serv'd:
    It is a poison temper'd by himself.

Exchange forgiveness with me, noble Hamlet.
Mine and my father's death come not upon thee,
Nor thine on me!   *[dies]*

HAMLET: Heaven make thee free of it! I follow thee.
I am dead, Horatio. Wretched Queen, adieu!
You that look pale and tremble at this chance,
That are but mutes or audience to this act,
Had I but time, as this fell sergeant Death
Is strict in his arrest, O, I could tell you—
But let it be. Horatio, I am dead:
Thou livest; report me and my cause aright
to the unsatisfied.

HORATIO: Never believe it.
I am more an antique Roman than a Dane;
Here's yet some liquor left.

HAMLET: As th'art a man,
Give me the cup. Let go. By heaven, I'll ha't.
O good Horatio, what a wounded name,
Things standing thus unknown, shall live behind me!
If thou didst ever hold me in thy heart,
Absent thee from felicity awhile,
And in this harsh world draw thy breath in pain,
To tell my story. [*March afar off, and shot within.*] What warlike noise is
        this?

OSRIC: Young Fortinbras, with conquest come from Poland,
To th' ambassadors of England gives
This warlike volley.

HAMLET: O, I die, Horatio!
The potent poison quite o'er-crows my spirit.
I cannot live to hear the news from England,
But I do prophesy th' election lights
On Fortinbras; he has my dying voice.
So tell him, with th' occurrents, more and less,
Which have solicited—the rest is silence.   *[dies]*

HORATIO: Now cracks a noble heart. Good night, sweet prince,
And flights of angels sing thee to thy rest!   *[March within.]*
Why does the drum come hither?
    [*Enter* FORTINBRAS *and* ENGLISH AMBASSADORS, *with drum, colours, and*
    attendants.]

FORTINBRAS: Where is this sight?

HORATIO: What is it you would see?
If aught of woe or wonder, cease your search.

FORTINBRAS: This quarry cries on havoc. O proud death,
What feast is toward in thine eternal cell

That thou so many princes at a shot
So bloodily hast struck?
FIRST AMBASSADOR: The sight is dismal;
And our affairs from England come too late:
The ears are senseless that should give us hearing
To tell him his commandment is fulfill'd
That Rosencrantz and Guildenstern are dead.
Where should we have our thanks?
HORATIO: Not from his mouth,
Had it th' ability of life to thank you:
He never gave commandment for their death.
But since, so jump upon this bloody question,
You from the Polack wars, and you from England,
Are here arrived, give order that these bodies
High on a stage be placed to the view;
And let me speak to th' yet unknowing world
How these things came about. So shall you hear
Of carnal, bloody, and unnatural acts;
Of accidental judgments, casual slaughters;
Of deaths put on by cunning and forc'd cause;
And, in this upshot, purposes mistook
Fall'n on th' inventors' heads—all this can I
Truly deliver.
FORTINBRAS: Let us haste to hear it,
And call the noblest to the audience.
For me, with sorrow I embrace my fortune;
I have some rights to memory in this kingdom,
Which now to claim my vantage doth invite me.
HORATIO: Of that I shall have also cause to speak,
And from his mouth whose voice will draw on more.
But let this same be presently perform'd,
Even while men's minds are wild, lest more mischance
On plots and errors happen.
FORTINBRAS: Let four captains
Bear Hamlet like a soldier to the stage;
For he was likely, had he been put on,
To have prov'd most royal; and for his passage
The soldier's music and the rite of war
Speak loudly for him.
Take up the bodies. Such a sight as this
Becomes the field, but here shows much amiss.
Go, bid the soldiers shoot.
          [*Exeunt marching. A peal of ordnance shot off.*]

Molière

Tartuffe or The Imposter

Translated by John Wood

CHARACTERS IN THE PLAY

MADAME PERNELLE, *mother of Orgon*
ORGON
ELMIRE, *his wife*
DAMIS, *his son*
MARIANE, *his daughter,*
   in love with Valère
VALÈRE, *in love with Mariane*

CLÉANTE, *brother-in-law of Orgon*
TARTUFFE, *a hypocrite*
DORINE, *maid to Mariane*
MR LOYAL, *a tipstaff*
FLIPOTE, *maid to Madame Pernelle*
AN OFFICER

THE SCENE *is* ORGON'S *house in Paris.*

ACT I

[*Enter* MADAME PERNELLE *and* FLIPOTE, ELMIRE, MARIANE, CLÉANTE, DAMIS, DORINE.]

MADAME PERNELLE: Come, Flipote, come along. Let me be getting away from them.

ELMIRE: You walk so fast one can hardly keep up with you.

MADAME PERNELLE: Never mind, my dear, never mind! Don't come any further. I can do without all this politeness.

ELMIRE: We are only paying you the respect that is due to you. Why must you be in such a hurry to go, mother?

MADAME PERNELLE: Because I can't bear to see the goings-on in this house and because there's no consideration shown to me at all. I have had a very unedifying visit indeed! All my advice goes for nothing here. There's no respect paid to anything. Everybody airs his opinions—the place is a veritable Bedlam!

DORINE: If . . .

MADAME PERNELLE: For a servant you have a good deal too much to say for yourself, my girl. You don't know your place. You give your opinion on everything.

DAMIS: But . . .

MADAME PERNELLE: You, my lad, are just a plain fool. I'm your grandmother and I'm telling you so! I warned your father a hundred times over that you showed all the signs of turning out badly and bringing him nothing but trouble.

MARIANE: I think . . .

MADAME PERNELLE: Oh Lord, yes! You are his little sister, and you put on your demure looks as if butter wouldn't melt in your mouth—but it's just as they say, 'Still waters run deep.' I hate to think of what you do on the sly.

ELMIRE: But mother . . .

MADAME PERNELLE: My dear, if you'll allow me to say so you go about these things in the wrong way entirely. You ought to set them an example. Their own mother did very much better. You are extravagant. It distresses me to see the way you go about dressed like a duchess. A woman who's concerned only with pleasing her husband has no need for so much finery, my dear.

CLÉANTE: Oh come, after all madam . . .

MADAME PERNELLE: As for you, sir, I have the greatest esteem, affection, and respect for you as the brother of Elmire but if I were in her husband's place I should entreat you never to set foot in the house. You keep on advocating a way of life which no respectable people should follow. If I speak a little bluntly—well, that's my way. I don't mince matters. I say what I think.

DAMIS: Your Mr Tartuffe is undoubtedly a very lucky man . . .

MADAME PERNELLE: He's a *good* man and people would do well to listen to him. It enrages me to hear him criticized by a dolt such as you.

DAMIS: What! Am I to allow a sanctimonious bigot to come and usurp tyrannical authority here in the very house? Are we to have no pleasure at all unless his lordship deigns to approve?

DORINE: If we took notice of him we should never be able to do anything without committing a sin. He forbids everything—pious busybody that he is!

MADAME PERNELLE: And whatever he forbids deserves to be forbidden. He means to lead you along the road to Salvation. My son ought to make you all love him.

DAMIS: No, grandmother, neither my father nor anyone else could make me have any liking for him. It would be hypocrisy for me to say anything else. His behaviour infuriates me at every turn. I can only see one end to it. It'll come to a row between this scoundrel and me. It's bound to.

DORINE: It really is a scandalous thing to see a mere nobody assuming a position of authority in the house, a beggar without shoes to his feet when he first came, all the clothes he had to his back not worth sixpence, and getting so far above himself as to interfere with everything and behave as if he were the master.

MADAME PERNELLE: Mercy on us! It would be a lot better if the whole place *were* under his pious instruction.

DORINE: You imagine he's a saint but believe me, he's nothing but a hypocrite!

MADAME PERNELLE: Listen to her talking!

DORINE: I wouldn't trust myself with him without good security or his man Laurence either.

MADAME PERNELLE: I don't know what the servant is really like, but the master's a good man, that I *will* warrant. The only reason you dislike him and are so set against him is that he tells you all the truth about yourselves: it's sin that rouses his wrath. Everything he does is done in the cause of the Lord.

DORINE: Hm! Then why is it—particularly just recently—that he can't bear to have anyone coming about the place? What is there sinful in calling on someone in an ordinary straightforward way that he should make such a hullabaloo about it? Shall I tell you what I think—between ourselves— [*she indicates* ELMIRE] I believe he's jealous on account of the mistress. Upon my word I do!

MADAME PERNELLE: Hold your tongue and mind what you are saying! He's not the only one who takes exception to visitors. All these people coming here and causing a disturbance, carriages for ever standing at the door, and swarms of noisy footmen and lackeys make a bad impression on the whole neighbourhood. I'm willing to believe that there's no harm in it really, but it sets people talking and that's not a good thing.

CLÉANTE: And do you propose, madam, to stop people talking? It would be a poor affair if we had to give up our best friends for fear of the silly things that people might say about us and even if we did, do you think you could shut everybody's mouth? There's no defence against malicious tongues, so let's pay no heed to their tittle-tattle; let us try to live virtuously and leave the gossips to say what they will.

DORINE: It's our neighbour, Daphne, and that little husband of hers who have been speaking ill of us, isn't it? Folk whose own behaviour is most ridiculous are always to the fore in slandering others. They never miss a chance of seizing on the least glimmering suspicion of an affair, of gleefully spreading the news and twisting things the way they want folk to believe. They think they can justify their own goings-on by painting other people's behaviour in the same colours as their own and so hope to give an air of innocence to their intrigues or throw on other people some share of the criticism their own actions only too well deserve.

MADAME PERNELLE: All this talk is beside the point. Everybody knows that Orante's life is an example to everybody. She's a God-fearing woman and I hear she strongly condemns the company that comes here.

DORINE:[1] She's a wonderful example—a really good woman! It's quite true that she leads a strict sort of life but it's age that has made her turn pious. We all know that she's virtuous only because she has no alternative. So long as she was able to attract men's attentions she enjoyed herself to the full, but now that she finds her eyes losing their lustre she resolves to renounce

---

[1] This is one of the speeches thought to have been originally given to Cléante.

the world which is slipping away from her and conceal the fading of her charms beneath an elaborate pretence of high principles. That's what coquettes come to in the end. It's hard for them to see their admirers desert them. Left alone and unhappy, the only course left to them is to turn virtuous. Their righteous severity condemns everything and forgives nothing. They rail against other people's way of life—not in the interests of righteousness but from envy—because they can't bear that anyone else should enjoy the pleasures which age had left them no power to enjoy.

MADAME PERNELLE: [*to* ELMIRE] These, daughter, are the sort of idle stories they serve up to please you. I have to hold my tongue when I'm at your house for Mistress Chatterbox here holds forth all day long. Nevertheless I will have my turn. What I say is that it was the wisest thing my son ever did to take into his house this holy man whom the Lord sent just when he was needed, to reclaim your minds from error. For the good of your souls you should hearken to him for he reproves nothing but what is deserving of reproof. This giddy round of balls, assemblies, and routs is all a device of the Evil One. In such places one never hears a word of godliness, nothing but idle chatter, singing, and nonsensical rigamaroles: often enough the neighbours come in for their share and slander and gossip go the rounds. Even sensible heads are turned in the turmoil of that sort of gathering, a thousand idle tongues get busy about nothing and, as a learned doctor said the other day, it becomes a veritable tower of Babylon where everybody babbles never-endingly—but to come to the point I was making. [*pointing to* CLÉANTE] What! The gentleman is sniggering already is he? Go find a laughing-stock elsewhere and don't—[*to* ELMIRE] Daughter, good-bye. I'll say no more, but I'd have you know I have even less opinion of this household than I had. It will be a long time before I set foot in here again. [*giving* FLIPOTE *a slap*] Hey you! What are you dreaming and gaping at? God bless my soul! I'll warm your ears for you. Come slut. Let's be off.

[*Exeunt all but* CLÉANTE *and* DORINE.]

CLÉANTE: I won't go out in case she starts on me again. How the old woman . . .

DORINE: It's a pity she can't hear you talking like that! She'd tell you what she thinks about you, and whether she's of an age that you can call her 'old woman' or not!

CLÉANTE: Didn't she get worked up against us—and all about nothing! How she dotes on her Tartuffe!

DORINE: Oh! It's nothing compared with her son. If you'd seen him you'd agree he was much worse. During the late disturbances he gained the reputation of being a reliable man and showed courage in the King's service, but since he took a fancy to Tartuffe he seems to have taken leave of his senses. He addresses him as brother and holds him a hundred times dearer than wife or mother, daughter or son. The man's the sole confidant of all his secrets and his trusted adviser in everything. He caresses and cossets him and he couldn't show more tenderness to a mistress. He insists on his taking the place of honour at table, and delights in seeing him devour enough for half a dozen. He has to have all the tit-bits and if he happens to belch it's 'Lord, preserve you!'[2] In short, he's crazy about him. He's his all in all, his hero: he admires everything he does, quotes him at every turn, his every trivial action is wonderful and every word he utters an oracle. As for Tartuffe, he knows his weakness and means to make use of it. He has a hundred ways of deceiving him, gets money out of him constantly by means of canting humbug, and assumes the right to take us to task. Even his lout of a servant has taken to instructing us, comes and harangues us with wild fanatical eyes, and throws away our ribbons, patches, and paint. The other day the dog tore up with his own hands a handkerchief he found in the *Flowers of Sanctity*. He said it was a dreadful thing to sully sacred things with the devil's trappings.

    [*Re-enter* ELMIRE *and* MARIANE.]

ELMIRE: You are lucky to have missed the harangue she delivered at the gate. But I caught sight of my husband and as he didn't see me I'll go and wait for him upstairs.

CLÉANTE: I'll await him here to save time. I only want to say good morning.

    [*Exeunt* ELMIRE *and* MARIANE.]

DAMIS: Have a word with him about my sister's marriage. I suspect that Tartuffe is opposing it and that it's he who is driving my father to these evasions. You know how closely concerned I am. Valère and my sister are in love and I, as you know, am no less in love with his sister, and if . . .

DORINE: Here he comes.

    [*Enter* ORGON.]

ORGON: Ah, good morning, brother.

CLÉANTE: I was just going. I'm glad to see you back again. There isn't much life in the countryside just now.

ORGON: Dorine—[*to* CLÉANTE] a moment brother, please—excuse me if I ask the news of the family first and set my mind at rest. [*to* DORINE] Has everything gone well the few days I've been away? What have you been doing? How is everyone?

DORINE: The day before yesterday the mistress was feverish all day. She had a dreadful headache.

ORGON: And Tartuffe?

DORINE: Tartuffe? He's very well: hale and hearty; in the pink.

ORGON: Poor fellow!

DORINE: In the evening she felt faint and couldn't touch anything, her headache was so bad.

ORGON: And Tartuffe?

DORINE: He supped with her. She ate nothing but he very devoutly devoured a couple of partridges and half a hashed leg of mutton.

ORGON: Poor fellow!

DORINE: She never closed her eyes all through the night. She was too feverish to sleep and we had to sit up with her until morning.

ORGON: And Tartuffe?

  2 *Molière's note*. It is a servant speaking.

DORINE: Feeling pleasantly drowsy, he went straight to his room, jumped into a nice warm bed, and slept like a top until morning.

ORGON: Poor fellow!

DORINE: Eventually she yielded to our persuasions, allowed herself to be bled, and soon felt much relieved.

ORGON: And Tartuffe?

DORINE: He dutifully kept up his spirits, and took three or four good swigs of wine at breakfast to fortify himself against the worst that might happen and to make up for the blood the mistress had lost.

ORGON: Poor fellow!

DORINE: They are both well again now so I'll go ahead and tell the mistress how glad you are to hear that she's better.

    [*Exit.*]

CLÉANTE. She's laughing at you openly, brother, and, though I don't want to anger you, I must admit that she's right. Did anyone ever hear of such absurd behaviour? Can the man really have gained such influence over you as to make you forget everything else, so that after having rescued him from poverty you should be ready to . . .

ORGON: Enough brother! You don't know the man you are talking about.

CLÉANTE: I grant you I don't know him, but then, to see what sort of fellow he is, one need only . . .

ORGON: Brother, you would be charmed with him if you knew him. You would be delighted beyond measure . . . he's a man who . . . who . . . ah! a man . . . in short, a man! Whoever follows his precepts enjoys a profound peace of mind and looks upon the world as so much ordure. Yes, under his influence I'm becoming another man. He's teaching me how to forgo affection and free myself from all human ties. I could see brother, children, mother, wife, all perish without caring that much!

CLÉANTE: Very humane sentiments, I must say, brother!

ORGON: Ah! Had you seen how I first met him you would have come to feel for him as I do. Every day he used to come to church and modestly fall on his knees just beside me. He would draw the eyes of the whole congregation by the fervour with which he poured forth his prayers, sighing, groaning, kissing the ground in transports of humility. When I went out he would step in front of me to offer me the Holy water at the door. Having learned from his servant—a man who follows his example in every way—who he was and how needy his condition, I offered him alms, but he would always modestly return a part. 'Too much,' he'd say, 'too much by half. I'm not worthy of your pity.' When I wouldn't have it back he'd go and bestow it on the poor before my very eyes. At length Heaven inspired me to give him shelter in my house, since when all things seem to prosper here. He keeps a reproving eye upon everything and, mindful of my honour, his concern for my interests extends even to my wife. He warns me of those who make eyes at her and is ten times more jealous for her than I am myself. You wouldn't believe the lengths to which his piety extends: the most trivial failing on his own part he accounts a sin: the slightest thing may suffice to shock his conscience—so much so that the other day he was full of self-reproach for having caught a flea while at his prayers and killed it with too much vindictiveness.

CLÉANTE: Gad! You are crazy, brother, that's what I think—or are you trying to pull my leg with a tale like this? What do you intend all this foolery . . .

ORGON: Brother, what you are saying savours of atheism. You *are* somewhat tainted with it at heart. As I have warned you a dozen times you'll bring some serious trouble upon yourself.

CLÉANTE: That's the way your sort of people usually talk. You would have everyone as purblind as yourselves. If one sees things clearly one's an atheist: whoever doesn't bow the knee to pious flummery is lacking in faith and respect for sacred things. No, no! Your threats don't frighten me! I know what I'm talking about and Heaven sees what's in my heart. We are not all duped by humbugs. Devotion, like courage, may be counterfeit. Just as, when honour puts men to the test, the truly brave are not those who make the biggest noise, so the truly pious, whose example we should ever follow, are not those who make the greatest show. What! Would you make no distinction between hypocrisy and true religion? Would you class both together, describe them in the same terms, respect the mask as you would the face itself, treat artifice and sincerity alike, confound appearance and reality, accept the shadow for the substance, base coin for true? Men, in the main, are strangely made. They can never strike the happy mean: the bounds of reason seem too narrow for them: they must needs overact whatever part they play and often ruin the noblest things because they will go to extremes and push them too far. This, brother, is all by the way—

ORGON: Yes, yes, there's no doubt you are a most reverend doctor. You have a monopoly of knowledge, you are unique in wisdom and enlightenment, Sir Oracle, the Cato of our age. In comparison the rest of us are fools—

CLÉANTE: No brother. I'm no reverend doctor; I've no monopoly of knowledge. I merely claim to be able to discriminate between false and true. Just as I know no kind of man more estimable than those who are genuinely religious, nothing in the whole world nobler or finer than the holy fervour of true piety, so I know nothing more odious than those whited sepulchres of specious zeal, those charlatans, those professional zealots, who with sacrilegious and deceitful posturings abuse and mock to their heart's content everything which men hold most sacred and holy; men who put self-interest first, who trade and traffic in devotion, seek to acquire credit and dignities by turning up their eyes in transports of simulated zeal. I mean the people who tread with such extraordinary ardour the godly road to fortune, burning with devotion but seeking material advantage, preaching daily the virtues of solitude and retirement while following the life of courts, shaping their zeal to their vices, quick, revengeful, faithless, scheming, who when they wish to destroy, hide their vindictive pride under the cloak of religion. They are the more dangerous in that they turn against us in their bitter rage the very weapons which men revere and use the passion for which they are respected to destroy us with a consecrated blade. One sees all too much of falsehood such as this. Yet the truly devout are easy to recognize. Our own age offers us many a glorious example, brother. Look at Ariston, Periander, Oronte, Alcidamus, Polydore, Clitander! Their claims no one can deny: theirs is no braggart virtue, no intolerable ostentation of piety; their religion is gentle and humane: they don't censure our actions: they would consider such strictures arrogant: leaving pride of eloquence to others they rebuke our conduct by their own: they don't assume from appearances that others are in fault: they are always ready to think well of people. No '*cabales*' for them, no intrigues! their whole concern is to live virtuously: they show no anger against sinners: they reserve their hate for sin itself: nor do they take upon themselves the interests of Heaven with a zeal beyond anything that Heaven itself displays. These are my sort of men: this is how one should conduct oneself: this is the example one should follow! Your man, however, is of another kind. You vaunt his zeal in all good faith but I think you are deceived by false appearances.

ORGON: My dear brother-in-law, have you finished?

CLÉANTE: Yes.

ORGON: [*going*] I'm much obliged to you.

CLÉANTE: One word, brother, please. Let us leave this topic. You remember that you promised Valère your daughter's hand?

ORGON: Yes.

CLÉANTE: And you named a day for the happy event.

ORGON: True.

CLÉANTE: Why then defer the ceremony?

ORGON: I don't know.

CLÉANTE: Have you something else in mind?

ORGON: Maybe.

CLÉANTE: Do you intend to break your word?

ORGON: I never said so.

CLÉANTE: There is nothing, I believe, to prevent your keeping your promise.

ORGON: That's as may be.

CLÉANTE: Why such circumspection in giving an answer? Valère has asked me to come and see you.

ORGON: God be praised!

CLÉANTE: What am I to tell him?

ORGON: Whatever you please.

CLÉANTE: But I need to know your intentions. What do you mean to do?

ORGON: The will of Heaven.

CLÉANTE: But, speaking seriously, Valère has your promise—are you standing to it or not?

ORGON: Good-bye. [*Exit.*]

CLÉANTE: I fear he is going to be disappointed in his love. I must warn him of the way things are going.

ACT II

[ORGON, MARIANE]

ORGON: Mariane.

MARIANE: Yes, father.

ORGON: Come here. I want a word with you in private.

MARIANE: What are you looking for? [*He is looking into a closet.*]

ORGON: I'm looking to see that there's no one to overhear us. This little place is just right for eavesdropping. Now, we are all right. I've always known that you have an obedient disposition, Mariane, and you've always been very dear to me.

MARIANE: I am very grateful for your fatherly affection.

ORGON: I'm pleased to hear you say so, my girl—and if you want to deserve it you should be at pains to do what I want.

MARIANE: That is my most earnest wish.

ORGON: Very well. What have you to say about our guest, Tartuffe?

MARIANE: What have I to say?

ORGON: Yes, you! Mind how you answer.

MARIANE: Oh dear! I'll say anything you like about him.

[*Enter* DORINE, *unobserved; she takes up her position behind* ORGON.]

ORGON: That's very sensible. Then let me hear you say, my dear, that he is a wonderful man, that you love him, and you'd be glad to have me choose him for your husband. Eh?

[MARIANE *starts in surprise.*]

MARIANE: Eh?

ORGON: What's the matter?

MARIANE: *What* did you say?

ORGON: What?

MARIANE: I must have misheard you.

ORGON: How d'ye mean?

MARIANE: Who is it, father, I'm to say I love and be glad to have you choose as my husband?

ORGON: Tartuffe!

MARIANE: But, father, I assure you I don't feel like that at all. Why make me tell such an untruth?

ORGON: But I mean it to be the truth and it's sufficient for you that it's what I have decided.

MARIANE: What, father! You really want me to . . .

ORGON: My intention, my girl, is that you should marry Tartuffe and make him one of the family. He shall be your husband. I have made up my mind about that and it's for me to decide . . . [*seeing* DORINE] What are *you* doing here? You must be mighty curious, my lass, to come eavesdropping like that.

DORINE: I don't really know master how the rumour arose—whether it's guess-work or coincidence, but when I heard about this marriage I treated it as a joke.

ORGON: Why? Is it unbelievable?

DORINE: So much so that I *won't* believe it though you tell me yourself.

ORGON: I know how to make you believe it.

DORINE: Yes, yes, but you are telling us it as a joke.

ORGON: I'm telling you what's going to happen and before long too!

DORINE: Oh, rubbish!

ORGON: [*to* MARIANE] It's no joking matter I tell you!

DORINE: No! Don't you believe your Papa! He's teasing!

ORGON: I'm telling you . . .

DORINE: It's no good. We shan't believe you.

ORGON: If I once get annoyed.

DORINE: All right! We believe you then and so much the worse for you. Why! How can you, master! You with all the appearance of a sensible man—and a venerable beard like you have—how can you be so silly as to . . .

ORGON: Listen! You have got into the habit of taking liberties lately. I tell you, my girl, I don't like it at all!

DORINE: Do let us discuss it without getting cross, master, please. You really must have made it all up for a joke. Your daughter isn't at all the right person to marry a bigot and he ought to have other things to think about. Anyhow, what use is such an alliance to you? With all the money you have why go and choose a beggar for a son-in-law?

ORGON: Be quiet! If he's poor that's all the more reason for respecting him. Understand that! His is an honourable poverty. That's beyond question. It should raise him above material consequence for he's allowed himself to be deprived of his means by his indifference to temporal matters and his unswerving attachment to the things which are eternal. My help may be able to afford him the means to escape from embarrassment and enter into his own possessions again—lands which are quite well known in his part of the country. Moreover, whatever his present condition may appear to be, he's certainly a gentleman.

DORINE: Yes. That's what *he* says, but that kind of boasting doesn't go well with his piety. A man who chooses the saintly life shouldn't crack up his birth and family so much. The humble ways of piety don't go well with such-like ambitions. Why take pride in that sort of thing? But there, you'd rather not discuss that. Let's leave the question of his family and talk about the man himself! Could you really bear to hand over your daughter to a fellow like that? Shouldn't you consider what's due to her and what the consequences of such a marriage might be! Let me tell you that when a girl isn't allowed her own choice in marriage her virtue's in jeopardy: her resolve to live as a good woman depends on the qualities of the husband she's given. Those whose wives are unfaithful have often made them what they are. There are some husbands it's not easy to remain faithful to and whoever gives a girl a husband she detests is responsible to Heaven for the sins she commits. Just think then what perils this scheme of yours may involve you in!

ORGON: [*to* MARIANE] Well, I declare, I have to take lessons from her as to how to do my own business!

DORINE: You couldn't do better than follow my advice.

ORGON: Let's waste no more time on such nonsense, my girl. I'm your father and I know what's good for you. I had promised you to Valère, but apart from the fact that he's said to be a bit of a gambler I suspect him of being a free thinker. I don't see him at church much.

DORINE: I suppose you'd have him run there at the very moment you get there yourself like some folk who only go there to be noticed.

ORGON: I'm not asking for your opinion. [*to* MARIANE] Moreover Tartuffe stands well with Heaven and that surpasses all earthly riches. This marriage will give you everything you could wish for, a perpetual source of pleasure and delight. You'll live together loving and faithful just like two babes—like a pair of turtle doves. No differences will ever arise between you and you'll be able to do just what you like with him.

DORINE: Will she? She won't do anything with him but make him a cuckold, believe me!

ORGON: Sh! What a way to talk!

DORINE: I tell you he has all the looks of one—he's born to it, master, and all your daughter's virtue couldn't prevent it.

ORGON: Stop interrupting me! Just hold your tongue and don't be for ever putting your nose in where you have no business.

DORINE: I'm only telling you for your own good, master.
[*Every time he turns to speak to his daughter she interrupts.*]

ORGON: You don't need to trouble. Just be quiet!

DORINE: If it wasn't that I'm fond of you . . .

ORGON: I don't *want* you to be fond of me.

DORINE: Yes, but I'm *determined* to be fond of you—whether *you* like it or not.

ORGON: Tcha!

DORINE: I'm concerned for your good name, and I won't have you making yourself the butt of everyone's gibes.

ORGON: Will you never be quiet?

DORINE: I could never forgive myself if I let you make such an alliance.

ORGON: Will you be quiet, you reptile, with your impudent . . .

DORINE: Ah! Fancy a godly man like you getting angry!

ORGON: Yes! This ridiculous nonsense is more than my temper can stand. I insist on your holding your tongue.

DORINE: Right, but I shan't *think* any the less because I don't say anything.

ORGON: Think if you like but take care you don't talk or . . . that's enough.
[*turning to* MARIANE] I've weighed everything carefully as a wise man should . . .

DORINE: It's maddening not to be able to speak. [*She stops as he turns his head.*]

ORGON: Without his being exactly a beauty Tartuffe's looks are . . .

DORINE: Yes! A lovely mug hasn't he?

ORGON: Such . . . that even if his other advantages don't appeal to you . . .
[ORGON *turns and faces* DORINE, *looking at her with arms folded.*]

DORINE: She *would* be well off wouldn't she? If *I* were in her place no man would marry me against my will—not with impunity. I would show him, ay, and soon after the ceremony too, that a woman has always ways and means of getting her own back.

ORGON: So what I say hasn't any effect on you at all?

DORINE: What are you grumbling about? I'm not talking to you.

ORGON: Then what *are* you doing?

DORINE: I'm talking to myself.

ORGON: Very well. [*aside*] I shall have to give her a back-hander for her impudence yet. [*He stands ready to box her ears.* DORINE *every time he looks at her stands rigid and without speaking.*] You can't do otherwise, my girl, than approve what I have in mind for you . . . and believe that the husband . . . I have chosen for you . . . [*to* DORINE] Why aren't you talking to yourself now?

DORINE: I've nothing to say to myself.

ORGON: Not a word even?

DORINE: Not a word thank you!

ORGON: But I was waiting for you . . .

DORINE: I'm not so silly as that!

ORGON: Well now, my girl, you must show how obedient you are and fall in with my choice.

DORINE: [*running away*] I'd scorn to take such a husband! [*He takes a slap at her and misses.*]

ORGON: She's a thorough pest is that girl of yours! If I live with her any longer I shall do something I shall be sorry for. I'm in no state to go on now. I'm so incensed at her impudence I shall have to go outside to recover myself.

     [*Exit* ORGON.]

DORINE: Have you lost your tongue? Do I have to do all the talking for you? Fancy letting him put a ridiculous proposal like that to you and never saying a word in reply!

MARIANE: What would you have me do in face of the absolute power of my father?

DORINE: Whatever is needed to ward off the danger.

MARIANE: But what?

DORINE: Tell him one can't love at another's bidding; that you'll marry to suit yourself, not him; that *you* are the person concerned and therefore it's *you* the husband has to please not him; and that, if he has such a fancy for his precious Tartuffe, he can marry him himself and there's nothing to stop him.

MARIANE: I confess that a father's authority is such that I have never had the temerity to say anything.

DORINE: Well, let us get down to business. Valère has made proposals for you. I ask you, *do* you love him or don't you?

MARIANE: You do my love great injustice, Dorine. How can you ask such a question? Haven't I opened my heart to you many and many a time? Don't you know how much I love him?

DORINE: How do I know that you meant what you said or that the young man really appeals to you?

MARIANE: You do me grievous wrong to doubt it, Dorine. I've shown my true feelings all too clearly.

DORINE: So you *do* love him, then?

MARIANE: Indeed I do.

DORINE: And, so far as you know, he loves you too?

MARIANE: I believe so.

DORINE: And you both want to be married?

MARIANE: Assuredly!

DORINE: Then what do you mean to do about this other proposal?

MARIANE: To die by my own hand if they force me to submit to it.

DORINE: Splendid! That's something I never thought of! You only need die and you are finished with your troubles. There's no doubt that's a wonderful remedy. That sort of talk infuriates me!

MARIANE: Oh dear, you are tiresome, Dorine. You have no sympathy at all for other people's troubles.

DORINE: I've no sympathy with folk who talk nonsense and are as faint-hearted as you are when it comes to the point.

MARIANE: But what do you expect me to do? If I'm timid . . .

DORINE: What lovers need is determination.

MARIANE: And have I wavered in my love for Valère? Surely it's for him to deal with my father.

DORINE: What! If your father's the fantastic creature he is—if he's plumb crazy over his precious Tartuffe and breaks his promise about the marriage he had decided on, is your lover to be blamed?

MARIANE: But can I reveal by flat refusal and open defiance how much I'm in love? Can I, whatever Valère's qualities may be, abandon the modesty of my sex and my filial duty? Do you want me to expose my feelings for all the world to see and . . .

DORINE: No. No. I don't want anything. I see that you want to marry Mr Tartuffe and, now I come to think about it, it would be wrong of me to dissuade you from such an alliance. Why should I oppose your inclinations? It's a most suitable match. Mr Tartuffe! Ha! Ha! It's not an offer to be despised, is it? Come to think of it Mr Tartuffe's a fine fellow. It's no small honour to be his better half. Everybody defers to him already. He's a man of family—where he comes from, and a fine looking fellow to boot—with his red ears and his red face. You would be sure to live happily with a husband like that.

MARIANE: Heavens!

DORINE: How delightful to be married to such a fine-looking husband!

MARIANE: Oh, please stop talking like this, and suggest some means of avoiding the marriage. It's enough. I give in. I'm ready for anything.

DORINE: No. No, a daughter must do as her father tells her even if he wants her to marry a monkey. You are very lucky. What are you complaining of? You'll be carted off to his little provincial town, and find it swarming with his relations. What fun you'll have meeting them all! You'll be taken straight into local society, visit the bailiff's wife and the councillor's lady, and they'll accord you the honour of letting you sit down with them as an equal, perhaps! In carnival time you'll be able to look forward to a ball with a grand orchestra, to wit a couple of bagpipes, and now and again Fagotin the monkey, and a marionette show. If only your husband . . .

MARIANE: Oh! I can't endure it! Why don't you help me?

DORINE: No, you must excuse me!

MARIANE: Oh, Dorine, *please* . . .

DORINE: No it must go through now—you deserve it!

MARIANE: Dear Dorine . . .

DORINE: No.

MARIANE: If my confessions of love . . .

DORINE: No. Tartuffe is your man, you shall have your fill of him.

MARIANE: You know that I've always trusted in you. Help me to . . .

DORINE: No, no! I give you my word—you shall be thoroughly Tartuffed!

MARIANE: Very well, since my miserable lot doesn't move you, leave me alone with my despair. There my heart will find relief. I have one infallible remedy for my troubles. [*She makes to go.*]

DORINE: Hey there! Come back. I won't be angry any more. I must take pity on you in spite of everything.

MARIANE: I assure you, Dorine, if they put me to this cruel torment it will be the death of me.

DORINE: Don't distress yourself. We'll find some means of preventing it. But here comes your Valère.

    [*Enter* VALÈRE.]

VALÈRE: I have just heard a fine piece of news. Something I was quite unaware of!

MARIANE: What is it?

VALÈRE: That you are to marry Tartuffe.

MARIANE: That is certainly my father's intention.

VALÈRE: But your father . . .

MARIANE: He's changed his mind. He has just put the new proposal to me now.

VALÈRE: What, seriously?

MARIANE: Yes, seriously. He's determined on the match.

VALÈRE: And what is your intention?

MARIANE: I don't know.

VALÈRE: That's a fine answer! You don't know?

MARIANE: No.

VALÈRE: No?

MARIANE: What do you advise me to do?

VALÈRE: What do I advise you to do? I advise you to take him!

MARIANE: *You* advise me to do that?

VALÈRE: Yes.

MARIANE: You really mean it?

VALÈRE: Of course. It's a splendid offer—one well worth considering.

MARIANE: Very well, sir. I'll take your advice.

VALÈRE: I don't doubt you'll find little difficulty in doing so.

MARIANE: No more than you in offering it.

VALÈRE: I gave it to please you.

MARIANE: And I'll follow it—to please you.

DORINE: [*aside*] We'll see what will come of this!

VALÈRE: So this is how you love me! You were deceiving me when . . .

MARIANE: Don't let us talk of that please! You told me frankly that I should accept the husband I was offered. Well then, that's just what I intend to do—since you give me such salutary advice.

VALÈRE: Don't make what I said your excuse! You had already made up your mind. You're just seizing on a frivolous pretext to justify breaking your word.

MARIANE: That's true. You put it very well.

VALÈRE: Of course! You never really loved me at all.

MARIANE: Alas! You may think so if you like.

VALÈRE: Yes, yes. I may indeed: but I may yet forestall your design. I know on whom to bestow both my hand and my affections.

MARIANE: Oh! I don't doubt that in the least, and the love which your good qualities inspire . . .

VALÈRE: Good Lord! Let's leave my good qualities out of it. They are slight enough and your behaviour is proof of it. But I know someone who will, I hope, consent to repair my loss once she knows I am free.

MARIANE: Your loss is little enough and, no doubt, you'll easily be consoled by the change.

VALÈRE: I shall do what I can you may be sure. To find oneself jilted is a blow to one's pride. One must do one's best to forget it and if one doesn't succeed, at least one must pretend to, for to love where one's love is scorned is an unpardonable weakness.

MARIANE: A very elevated and noble sentiment, I'm sure.

VALÈRE: Of course and one that everyone must approve. Would you have me languish for you indefinitely, see you throw yourself into the arms of another and yet not bestow elsewhere the heart that you spurn?

MARIANE: On the contrary, that is just what I want. I only wish it were done already.

VALÈRE: That's what you would like?

MARIANE: Yes.

VALÈRE: You have insulted me sufficiently. You shall have your wish . . . [*makes a move to go*] and immediately!

MARIANE: Very well.

VALÈRE: [*turning back*] At least remember that it is you yourself who are driving me to this extremity.

MARIANE: Yes.

VALÈRE: And that in what I am doing, I only am following your example.

MARIANE: My example, so be it!

VALÈRE: Very well! You shall have just what you asked for.

MARIANE: So much the better!

VALÈRE: You'll never see me again.

MARIANE: Capital!

VALÈRE: [*goes but when he reaches the door he returns*] Eh?

MARIANE: What?

VALÈRE: Didn't you call?

MARIANE: Me? You are dreaming.

VALÈRE: Good. I'm going then. Good-bye!

MARIANE: Good-bye!

DORINE: I think you must be out of your senses to behave in this absurd fashion. I've let you go on squabbling to see how far you would go. Here, Mr Valère! [*She takes him by the arm.* VALÈRE *pretends to resist.*]

VALÈRE: What do you want, Dorine?

DORINE: Come here!

VALÈRE: No, no. I'm too angry. Don't try to prevent me doing what she wants.

DORINE: Stop!

VALÈRE: No, no. It's all settled.

DORINE: Ah!

MARIANE: He can't bear the sight of me. He's going because I'm here. I'd better get out of his sight.

> [DORINE *leaves* VALÈRE *and runs to* MARIANE.]

DORINE: The other one now! Where are you off to?

MARIANE: Let me go!

DORINE: Come back!

MARIANE: No, no, Dorine. It's no good your trying to stop me.

VALÈRE: I can see that she hates the very sight of me. Far better I should spare her the embarrassment.

DORINE: [*leaving* MARIANE *and running to* VALÈRE] You again. The devil take you before I let you go. Stop this silly nonsense and come here both of you. [*She drags them both in.*]

VALÈRE: What are you trying to do?

MARIANE: What do you want?

DORINE: To bring you together again and get you out of this mess. [*to* VALÈRE] You must be crazy to quarrel like this!

VALÈRE: Didn't you hear how she spoke to me?

DORINE: You must be out of your mind to get so annoyed.

MARIANE: But didn't you see what happened? Didn't you see how he treated me?

DORINE: [*to* VALÈRE] Sheer silliness on both sides. She wants nothing better than to be yours—I can witness. [*to* MARIANE] He loves nobody but you and desires nothing better than to be your husband—I'll stake my life on it.

MARIANE: Then why did he give me the advice he did?

VALÈRE: Why did you ask me for advice on such a question?

DORINE: You are both quite mad. Here—give me your hands, both of you. [*to* VALÈRE] Come along, you.

VALÈRE: [*giving his hand to* DORINE] What good will that do?

DORINE: [*to* MARIANE] Now yours.

MARIANE: [*giving her hand*] What's the use?

DORINE: Heavens! Be quick. Come on! You love each other better than you think.

VALÈRE: [*to* MARIANE] Come, don't do it with such an ill grace. Don't look at a fellow as if you hated him. [MARIANE *turns toward* VALÈRE *and gives a little smile.*]

DORINE: The truth is all lovers are a bit touched!

VALÈRE: Ah! But hadn't I some cause for complaint? You must admit it was cruel of you to take such pleasure in giving me such a horrible piece of news.

MARIANE: But you—aren't you the most ungrateful of men?

DORINE: Let's leave the argument to another time and think how we can prevent this dreadful marriage . . .

MARIANE: Tell us what we are to do.

DORINE: We'll try everything we can. Your father can't be serious and it's all sheer rubbish, but you had better pretend to fall in with his nonsense and give the appearance of consenting so that if it comes to the point you'll more easily be able to delay the marriage. If we can only gain time we may set everything right. You can complain of a sudden illness that will necessitate delay; another time you can have recourse to bad omens—such as having met a corpse or broken a mirror or dreamt of muddy water. Finally, the great thing is that they can't make you his wife unless you answer 'I will'. But I think, as a precaution, you had better not be found talking together. [*to* VALÈRE] Off you go and get all your friends to use their influence with her father to stand by his promise. We must ask his brother to try once again, and see if we can get the stepmother on our side. Good-bye.

VALÈRE: [*to* MARIANE] Whatever schemes we may devise you are the one I really count on.

MARIANE: [*to* VALÈRE] I can't answer for what my father decides but I will never marry anyone but Valère.

VALÈRE: Ah, how happy you make me! Whatever they may venture to . . .

DORINE: Ah? Lovers are never tired of blathering! Be off, I tell you.

VALÈRE: [*making to go, then turning back*] Still . . .

DORINE: What a talker you are! [*pushing them both out*] You go this way and you that. Be off!

ACT III

DAMIS: May I be struck dead on the spot—call me the most miserable black-guard alive if I let either fear or favour prevent me—if I don't think out some master stroke!

DORINE: For goodness sake, don't get so excited! Your father has only just mentioned it. People don't do everything they intend to. There's a deal of difference between talking about a thing and doing it.

DAMIS: I must put a stop to the dog's machinations! I'll have something to say to him!

DORINE: Oh, go easy! Leave your stepmother to deal with both him and your father. She has some influence with Tartuffe. He takes notice of her. I'm not sure that he isn't sweet on her. I wish to Heaven he were! That would be a lark! As a matter of fact it's on your account that she's sent for him: she intends to sound him about this marriage you are so worried about: she means to find out what he has in mind and make him see what trouble it would cause in the family if he encouraged the idea. His servant said he was at his prayers so I wasn't able to see him, but he said he'd be coming down soon. So please go away and leave me to wait for him.

DAMIS: I'll be present at the interview.

DORINE: No. They must be alone.

DAMIS: I won't say a word.

DORINE: That's what *you* think! We all know how excitable you are and that's just the way to spoil everything. Off you go.

DAMIS: No I must see it. I won't lose my temper.

DORINE: How tiresome you are. Here he comes. Do go.

    [*Enter* TARTUFFE.]

TARTUFFE: [*seeing* DORINE] Laurent, put away my hair shirt and my scourge and continue to pray Heaven to send you grace. If anyone asks for me I'll be with the prisoners distributing alms.

DORINE: The impudent hypocrite!

TARTUFFE: What do you want?

DORINE: I'm to tell you . . .

TARTUFFE: For Heaven's sake! Before you speak, I pray you take this handkerchief. [*Takes handkerchief from his pocket.*]

DORINE: Whatever do you mean?

TARTUFFE: Cover your bosom. I can't bear to see it. Such pernicious sights give rise to sinful thoughts.

DORINE: You're mighty susceptible to temptation then! The flesh must make a great impression on you! I really don't know why you should get so excited. I can't say that I'm so easily roused. I could see you naked from head to foot and your whole carcass wouldn't tempt me in the least.

TARTUFFE: Pray, speak a little more modestly or I shall have to leave the room.

DORINE: No. No. *I'm* leaving *you*. All I have to say is that the mistress is coming down and would like a word with you.

TARTUFFE: Ah! Most willingly.

DORINE: [*aside*] That changes his tune. Upon my word I'm convinced there is something in what I said.

TARTUFFE: Will she be long?

DORINE: I think I hear her now. Yes, here she comes. I'll leave you together.

    [*Exit* DORINE. *Enter* ELMIRE.]

TARTUFFE: May the bounty of Heaven ever bestow on you health of body and of mind, and extend you blessings commensurate with the prayers of the most humble of its devotees!

ELMIRE: I'm very grateful for these pious wishes. Let us sit down. We shall be more comfortable.

TARTUFFE: Do you feel better of your indisposition?

ELMIRE: Very much. The feverishness soon left me.

TARTUFFE: My prayers have too little merit to have obtained this favour from on high; yet all the petitions I have addressed to Heaven have been concerned with your recovery.

ELMIRE: You are too solicitous on my behalf.

TARTUFFE: One cannot be too solicitous for your precious health. I would have sacrificed my own life for the sake of yours.

ELMIRE: That is carrying Christian charity rather far but I'm truly grateful for your kindness.

TARTUFFE: I do far less for you than you deserve.

ELMIRE: I wanted to speak to you in private on a certain matter. I'm pleased that no one can overhear us.

TARTUFFE: I too am delighted. I need hardly say how pleased I am to find myself alone with you. It's an opportunity which I have besought Heaven to accord me—vainly until this moment.

ELMIRE: What I want is that you should speak frankly and conceal nothing from me.

TARTUFFE: And my sole desire is that you should accord me the singular favour of allowing me to express all that is in my heart and assure you that anything I have said against those who were paying homage to your charms was not spoken in malice against you but rather that the intensity of my pious zeal and pure . . .

ELMIRE: I take it in that sense and believe that it arises from your concern for my salvation.

TARTUFFE: That is indeed so, madam, and such is the fervour of my . . . [*Squeezing her fingers.*]

ELMIRE: Oh! You're hurting me . . .

TARTUFFE: It comes from excess of devotion. I never intended to hurt you. [*Putting his hand upon her knee*] I would rather . . .

ELMIRE: What is your hand doing there?

TARTUFFE: I'm feeling your dress. How soft the material is!

ELMIRE: Please don't. I'm dreadfully ticklish.

[*She pushes back her chair.* TARTUFFE *brings his closer.*]

TARTUFFE: What marvellous lace! They do wonderful work nowadays. Things are so much better made than they used to be.

ELMIRE: Very true, but let us return to our business. They say my husband intends to break his promise to Valère and give his daughter to you. Tell me, is it true?

TARTUFFE: He did mention something about it, but to tell the truth, madam, that isn't the happiness I aspire to. All my hopes of felicity lie in another direction.

ELMIRE: That's because you have no interest in temporal things.

TARTUFFE: *My* breast does not enclose a heart of flint!

ELMIRE: I'm sure your thoughts are all turned Heavenward. Your desires are not concerned with anything here below.

TARTUFFE: A passion for the beauties which are eternal does not preclude a temporal love. Our senses can and do respond to those most perfect works of Heaven's creation, whose charms are exemplified in beings such as you and embodied in rarest measure in yourself. Heaven has lavished upon you a beauty that dazzles the eyes and moves the hearts of men. I never look upon your flawless perfections without adoring in you the great Author of all nature and feeling my heart filled with ardent love for that fair form in which He has portrayed Himself. At first I feared lest this secret passion which consumes me might be some subtle snare of the accursed one. I even resolved to avoid your sight, believing you to be an obstacle to my salvation; but at length I came to realize, O fairest among women, that there need be nothing culpable in my passion and that I could reconcile it with virtue. Since then I have surrendered to it heart and soul. It is, I admit, no small presumption on my part to address to you this offer of my love, but I rely upon your generosity and in no wise upon my own unworthy self: my hopes, my happiness, my peace are in your keeping: on you my bliss or future misery depends: my future hangs on your decree: make me for ever happy if such be your will, wretched if you would have it so.

ELMIRE: A very gallant declaration but a little surprising I must confess! It seems to me you ought to steel yourself more firmly against temptation and consider more deeply what you are about. A pious man like you, a holy man whom everyone . . .

TARTUFFE: Ah! But I'm not less a man for being devout! Confronted by your celestial beauty one can but let love have its way and make no demur. I realize that such a declaration coming from me may well seem strange but, after all, madam, I'm not an angel. If you condemn this declaration of mine you must lay the blame on your own enchanting loveliness. From the first moment that I beheld its more than mortal splendours you have ruled supreme in my affection. Those glances, goddess-like and gracious beyond all description, broke down my stubborn heart's resistance, surmounted every obstacle, prayers, fasting, tears, and turned all my thoughts to love of you. My eyes, my sighs, have told you a thousand times what I am now seeking to express in words. If you should turn a kindly eye upon the tribulations of your unworthy slave, if in your generosity you should choose to afford me consolation and deign to notice my insignificance, then I would offer you for ever, O miracle of loveliness, a devotion beyond compare. Moreover, your honour runs no risk with me; at my hands you need fear no danger of disgrace; these courtly gallants that women are so fond of noise their deeds abroad; they are for ever bragging of their conquests, never receiving a favour but they must divulge it, profaning with blabbing tongues (which folk still put their trust in) the altar to which they bring their offerings. But men of our sort burn with discreeter fires; our secrets are for ever sure; our concern for our own reputation is a safeguard for those we love, and to those who trust us we offer love without scandal, satisfaction without fear.

ELMIRE: I have listened to what you say and your eloquence has made your meaning sufficiently clear, but are you not afraid that I might take it into my head to tell my husband of this charming declaration of yours and that such a disclosure might impair his friendly feelings for you?

TARTUFFE: I know you are too kind, that you will pardon my temerity, condone as human frailty the transports of a passion which offends you, and, when you consult your glass, reflect that I'm not blind and that a man is but flesh and blood.

ELMIRE: Others might perhaps take a different course but I prefer to show discretion. I shall say nothing to my husband, but in return I must ask one thing of you—that you give your support openly and sincerely to the marriage of Valère and Mariane, renounce the exercise of that improper influence by which you have sought to promote your own hopes at the expense of another and . . .

DAMIS: [*coming out of the closet where he has been hidden*] No, no! This must be made known! I was in there and heard everything. Heaven's mercy has brought me here to confound the arrogance of a villain who intends me harm: it has offered me the opportunity to be revengèd upon his insolence and hypocrisy, to undeceive my father, and lay bare the soul of this scoundrel who talks to you of love!

ELMIRE: No, Damis, it is sufficient that he should mend his ways and endeavour to deserve the pardon I have promised him. I have given my word so don't make me break it. I'm not one to make a fuss: a wife makes light of follies such as these and never troubles her husband with them.

DAMIS: You may have your reasons for doing this but I have mine for doing otherwise. Your wish to spare him is absurd. He has already triumphed sufficiently over my just resentment with his insolence and humbug and made enough trouble among us. The scoundrel has ruled my father long enough and thwarted my love as well as Valère's. My father must be shown what a perfidious wretch he is and Providence now offers a simple means of doing it. I'm answerable to Heaven for this opportunity and it's too favourable to be neglected. Not to make use of it would be to deserve to lose it.

ELMIRE: Damis . . .

DAMIS: No. Pardon me—I must trust to my own judgement. I'm overjoyed. Nothing you say can dissuade me from the pleasure of revenge. I'll finish the business without more ado, and [*seeing* ORGON] here comes the instrument of my satisfaction.

[*Enter* ORGON.]

DAMIS: We have interesting news for you father. Something has just occurred which will astonish you. You are well repaid for your kindness! The gentleman sets a very high value on the consideration you have shown for him! He has just been demonstrating his passionate concern for you and he stops at nothing less than dishonouring your bed. I have just overheard him making a disgraceful declaration of his guilty passion for your wife. She in kind-heartedness and over-anxiety to be discreet was all for keeping it secret but I can't condone such shameless behaviour. I consider it would be a gross injustice to you to keep it from you.

ELMIRE: Well, I still think a wife shouldn't disturb her husband's peace of mind by repeating such silly nonsense to him; one's honour is in no wise involved. It's sufficient that we women should know how to defend ourselves. That's what I think and if you had taken notice of me you would not have said anything at all. [*Exit.*]

ORGON: Oh Heavens! Can what they say be true?

TARTUFFE: Yes, brother, I am a guilty wretch, a miserable sinner steeped in iniquity, the greatest villain that ever existed; not a moment of my life but is sullied with some foul deed: it's a succession of wickedness and corruption. I see now that Heaven is taking this opportunity of chastising me for my sins. Whatever crime I may be charged with, far be it from me to take pride in denying it! Believe what they tell you. Set no bounds to your resentment! Hound me like a felon from your doors! Whatever shame is heaped upon me I shall have deserved much more.

ORGON: [*to his son*] Ah! Miscreant! How dare you seek to tarnish his unspotted virtue with this false accusation?

DAMIS: What! Can a pretence of meekness from this hypocrite make you deny . . .

ORGON: Silence! You accursed plague!

TARTUFFE: Ah, let him speak. You do wrong to accuse him. You would do better to believe what he tells you. Why should you take such a favourable view of me? After all, do you know what I am capable of? Why should you trust appearances? Do you think well of me because of what I seem to be? No, no, you are letting yourself be deceived by outward show. I am, alas, no better than they think; everyone takes me for a good man but the truth is I'm good for nothing. [*speaking to* DAMIS] Yes, my son, speak freely, call me deceitful, infamous, abandoned, thief, murderer, load me with names yet more detestable, I'll not deny them. I've deserved them all, and on my knees I'll suffer the ignominy, in expiation of my shameful life.

ORGON: [*to* TARTUFFE] Brother, this is too much. [*to his son*] Doesn't your heart relent, you dog!

DAMIS: What! Can what he says so far prevail with you that . . .

ORGON: [*raising up* TARTUFFE] Silence you scoundrel! [*to* TARTUFFE] Rise brother—I beg you. [*to his son*] You scoundrel!

DAMIS: He may—

ORGON: Silence!

DAMIS: This is beyond bearing! What! I'm to . . .

ORGON: Say another word and I'll break every bone in your body!

TARTUFFE: In God's name, brother, calm yourself. I would rather suffer any punishment than he should receive the slightest scratch on my account.

ORGON: [*to his son*] Ungrateful wretch!

TARTUFFE: Leave him in peace! If need be, I'll ask your pardon for him on my knees . . .

ORGON: [*to* TARTUFFE] Alas! What are you thinking of? [*to his son*] See how good he is to you, you dog!

DAMIS: Then . . .

ORGON: Enough!

DAMIS: What! Can't I . . .

ORGON: Enough, I say! I know too well why you attack him. You hate him. Every one of you, wife, children, servants, all are in full cry against him. You use every impudent means to drive this devout and holy person from my house: but the more you strive to banish him the more determined I am not to let him go. I'll hasten his marriage with my daughter and confound the pride of the whole family.

DAMIS: You mean to make her accept his hand?

ORGON: Yes, you scoundrel, and this very evening to spite you all. Ah! I defy the lot of you. I'll have you know that I'm the master and I'll be obeyed. Come, retract your accusation instantly, you wretch! Down on your knees and beg forgiveness!

DAMIS: Who? Me? Of a villain whose impostures . . .

ORGON: So you refuse, you scoundrel, do you? And abuse him too! A stick!

Give me a stick! [*to* TARTUFFE] Don't try to restrain me! [*to his son*] Out of my house this instant and never darken my doors again!

DAMIS: Yes, I'll go but . . .

ORGON: Out! Leave the house! Be off! I disinherit you, you dog! And take my curse into the bargain.

> [*Exit* DAMIS.]

ORGON: What a way to insult a holy man!

TARTUFFE: May Heaven forgive him the sorrow that he causes me! Ah, if you only knew how much it grieves me to see them try to blacken me in my brother's esteem—

ORGON: Alas!

TARTUFFE: The mere thought of such ingratitude is unbearable to me . . . it horrifies me . . . it wrings my heart so that I cannot speak . . . it will be the death of me.

ORGON: [*weeping, runs to the door through which he drove forth his son*] Scoundrel! I'm sorry I kept my hands off you and didn't fell you on the spot! [*to* TARTUFFE] Compose yourself brother. Don't give way to your feelings.

TARTUFFE: Let us put an end to these painful dissensions. When I see what troubles I cause here I feel that I must leave you, brother.

ORGON: What! Are you mad?

TARTUFFE: They hate me. I see now they are trying to make you doubt my sincerity.

ORGON: What does it matter? Do you think I listen to them?

TARTUFFE: But they'll not fail to try again. These same reports you have rejected now you may believe another time.

ORGON: No, brother, never!

TARTUFFE: Ah, brother, a wife can easily influence her husband's mind.

ORGON: No. No!

TARTUFFE: Let me go and by going hence remove all occasion for them to attack me.

ORGON: No. No. You shall stay. My very life depends upon it.

TARTUFFE: Well then if it be so, I must sacrifice myself. But if you would only . . .

ORGON: Yes?

TARTUFFE: Let it be so. We'll speak of it no more but I know now what I must do. Reputation is a brittle thing: friendship requires that I should forestall every whisper, every shadow of suspicion. I must forswear the company of your wife and you will never see . . .

ORGON: No! You *shall* see her in spite of them all. Nothing gives me greater joy than to annoy them. You shall appear with her constantly and—to show my defiance, I'll make you my sole heir. I'll make a gift to you in due form of all my goods here and now. My true, dear, friend whom I now take as my son-in-law, you are dearer to me than son or wife or kin. Will you not accept what I am offering you?

TARTUFFE: Heaven's will be done in all things.

ORGON: Poor fellow! Let us go and draft the document at once. And let the whole envious pack of them burst with their own vexation at the news!

ACT IV

[CLÉANTE, TARTUFFE]

CLÉANTE: Yes, everyone is talking about it and, believe me, the sensation the news has made has done your reputation no good. This is an opportune time to tell you briefly and bluntly what I think about it. I won't go into details of the reports that are going about; setting them on one side and taking the matter at its worst, let us suppose that Damis did behave badly and that you were accused unjustly. Wouldn't it be the Christian thing to pardon the offence and forgo your revenge? Can you allow a son to be turned out of his father's house because of your quarrel with him? I tell you again—and I'm speaking frankly—that everybody thinks it shocking —people of all sorts, high and low alike. If you'll take notice of me you'll come to terms and not push things to extremes. Sacrifice your resentment as a Christian should and reconcile the son to his father again.

TARTUFFE: Alas! For my own part, I would willingly do so. I harbour no resentment against him, sir. I forgive him everything. I don't blame him at all. I would do anything I could for him and gladly, but the interests of Heaven forbid it. If he comes back here, then I must go. After such unheard-of behaviour any further relations between us would create a scandal. God knows what people might think of it! They would impute it to purely material considerations on my part and say that, knowing I was guilty, I feigned a charitable concern for my accuser; that in my heart of hearts I was afraid of him, and sought an arrangement with him to keep his mouth shut.

CLÉANTE: That's just putting me off with specious excuses. Your arguments are all too far fetched. Why should you take upon yourself the interests of religion? Can't God punish the guilty without assistance from us? Leave Him to look after his own vengeance. Remember rather that He ordains that we should forgive those who offend against us. When you are following orders from on high why worry about human judgements? What! Lose the glory of doing a good deed for trivial considerations of what people may think! No. No. Let us just obey Heaven's commands and not bother our heads about anything else.

TARTUFFE: I have already said I forgive him. That's doing what Heaven commands, but Heaven doesn't command me to live with him after the scandal and the insults put on me today.

CLÉANTE: And does it command you to lend an ear to his father's fantastic caprices? Or to accept the gift of possessions to which you have no rightful claim?

TARTUFFE: People who know me will not suspect me of self-interest. Worldly wealth makes little appeal to me. Its tawdry glitter doesn't dazzle me. If I resolve to accept the gift the father insists on offering me it's only because I fear that such possessions may fall into unworthy hands or pass to people who will use them for evil purposes and not employ them as I intend to do, to the glory of God and the good of my neighbour.

CLÉANTE: My good sir, put aside these delicate scruples! They'll get you into trouble with the rightful heir. Let him enjoy his possessions at his own peril without worrying your head about it; consider how much better it would be that he should make ill use of them than that you should find yourself accused of defrauding him! I'm only surprised that you could permit such a proposal without embarrassment. Does any of the maxims of true piety enjoin one to plunder a lawful heir? If Heaven has really inspired you with an insurmountable inability to live in the same house as Damis, wouldn't it be better that you should prudently withdraw rather than let a son be hounded from his father's house on your account in the fact of all right and reason? Believe me, that would be showing some sense of decency and . . .

TARTUFFE: It is now half past three, sir. Certain pious obligations require my presence upstairs without delay. Excuse my leaving you so soon.

[*Exit* TARTUFFE.]

CLÉANTE: Ah!

[*Enter* ELMIRE, MARIANE, DORINE.]

DORINE: Please join with us in trying to help her, Sir. She's in dreadful distress. The betrothal her father has arranged for this evening has reduced her to despair. Here he comes. I beseech you, give us your help. Let us try by hook or crook to frustrate this wretched scheme which is worrying us all.

ORGON: Ah! I'm pleased to find you all here. [*to* MARIANE] I have something in this document to please you. You know what it is.

MARIANE: [*on her knees*] Father, in the name of Heaven which is witness to my unhappiness, and by everything that can move your heart, forgo your rights as a father and absolve me from the dire necessity of obeying you in this matter. Don't drive me, by harsh insistence on your rights, to complain to Heaven of being your daughter; don't condemn to misery the life you have bestowed upon me. If, contrary to the one dear hope I cherished, you now forbid me to give myself to the man I love, save me at least—on my knees I implore you—from the torment of belonging to a man I abhor! Don't drive me to some act of desperation by pushing your authority to the extreme.

ORGON: [*moved*] Steel your heart, man, now! No human weakness!

MARIANE: Your affection for him doesn't trouble me: show it to the full; give him your wealth and, if that's not enough, let him have mine. I consent with all my heart and freely give it to you, but at least don't include me with it. Rather let me spend such sad days as may remain to me within the austere walls of a convent.

ORGON: Oh yes! Of course, girls are all for going into convents as soon as their fathers' wishes conflict with their wanton designs! Get up! The harder you find it to accept him the better for your soul! Marry and mortify the flesh but don't plague me any more with your bawling and crying!

DORINE: But what . . .

ORGON: You be quiet! Mind your own business. I absolutely forbid you to say a single word.

CLÉANTE: If I might be allowed to offer you a word of advice . . .

ORGON: Brother, your advice is always excellent, most cogent, and I value it extremely, but I hope you will allow me to manage without it!

ELMIRE: [*to her husband*] I am at a loss to know what to say after what we have seen; I can only marvel at your blindness. You must be bewitched by the man—infatuated—to deny the truth of what we told you today.

ORGON: With all due deference to you I judge things as I see them. I know your indulgence for that worthless son of mine. You were afraid to admit that he had played a trick on this unfortunate man. But you took it too calmly for me to believe you. Had the accusation been true you would have been in a very different state of mind.

ELMIRE: Why should a woman have to behave as if her honour is imperilled by a mere declaration of love? Is there no answering but with blazing eyes and furious tongue? For my part I just laugh at such advances. I don't like all this fuss at all. I would rather we protected our good name by less violent means. I have no use for virtuous harridans who defend their honour with tooth and claw and scratch a man's eyes out at the slightest word. Heaven preserve me from that sort of rectitude! No woman need be a dragon of vindictiveness. A snub coolly and discreetly given is, I think, sufficiently effective in rebuffing advances.

ORGON: All the same, I know where I stand and I'm not going to be put off.

ELMIRE: I wonder more and more at this strange infatuation, but what would you say if I were actually to show you that we are telling you the truth.

ORGON: Show me?

ELMIRE: Yes.

ORGON: Rubbish!

ELMIRE: Supposing I could contrive a means of letting you see with your own eyes.

ORGON: The very idea!

ELMIRE: What a man you are! Do at least give an answer. I'm not asking you to take my word for it. Supposing that I arranged for you to see and hear everything from some point of vantage, what would you say then about this Godly man of yours?

ORGON: I should say nothing—because it just can't be done.

ELMIRE: This delusion has lasted too long. I have had enough of being accused of deceiving you. It's necessary now for my own satisfaction that I make you a witness to the truth of everything I have said and without more ado.

ORGON: Very well. I'll take you at your word. We'll see what you can do. Let me see how you make good your promise.

ELMIRE: [*to* DORINE] Ask him to come here.

DORINE: He's cunning. He may be difficult to catch.

ELMIRE: No. People are easily taken in by what they love and vanity predisposes them to deception. Have him come down. [*to* CLÉANTE *and* MARIANE] You two must retire.

[*Exeunt.*]

ELMIRE: Help me to bring the table up. Now get under it.

ORGON: What!

ELMIRE: It's essential that you should be completely hidden.

ORGON: But why under the table?

ELMIRE: Oh, for Heaven's sake leave it to me! I know what I'm doing. You shall see in due course. Get under there and, mind now, take care that he doesn't see or hear you.

ORGON: You are asking a good deal of me, I must say, but I suppose I must see it through now.

ELMIRE: I don't think you'll have any cause to complain but I'm going to play a rather unusual role. Don't be shocked. [ORGON *is under the table*.] I must be allowed to say whatever I like—it will be to convince you as I promised. Since you reduce me to it, I intend to coax this hypocrite to drop his mask, to flatter his impudent desires and encourage his audacity. I shall lead him on merely for the purpose of opening your eyes and exposing him completely. I can stop as soon as you say you give in: things will only go so far as you wish them to go: it will be for you to call a halt to his insensate passion just as soon as you think he has gone far enough: you can spare your poor wife by exposing her to no more than is necessary to disabuse you. It's your affair, and it will be for you to decide . . . but here he comes. Keep in and take care not to be seen.
[*Enter* TARTUFFE.]

TARTUFFE: I was informed that you wished to speak to me here.

ELMIRE: Yes, I have a secret to tell you—but shut the door before I begin and have a good look round in case we should be overheard. We don't want another business like this morning's. I was never so surprised in my life. Damis made me terribly frightened on your account. You must have seen what efforts I made to check him and quieten him down. The truth is I was so taken aback that it never entered my head to deny his accusations, but there—thank Heaven it all turned out for the best! We are much more secure now in consequence. Your reputation saved us. My husband is incapable of thinking ill of you. He insists on our being together to show his contempt for idle rumour. So now I can be in here with you without fear of reproach and can reveal to you that I'm perhaps only too ready to welcome your love.

TARTUFFE: I find it difficult to follow your meaning, madam. Only a while ago you spoke very differently.

ELMIRE: How little you know the heart of woman if such a rebuff has offended you! How little you understand what we mean to convey when we defend ourselves so feebly! At such moments our modesty and the tender sentiments you arouse in us are still in conflict. However compelling the arguments of passion may be we are still too diffident to confess it: we shrink from an immediate avowal but our manner sufficiently reveals that in our heart of hearts we surrender: though our lips must in honour deny our true feelings, such refusals in fact promise everything. I realize that I am making a very frank admission: it shows little regard for womanly modesty but since I *am* speaking—should I have been so anxious to restrain Damis, should I have listened so indulgently, do you think, to your declaration of love, should I have taken it as I did if I had not welcomed it? Moreover, when I sought to make you renounce the marriage which had just been announced what was that intended to convey to you, if not that I took an interest in you and regretted the conclusion of a marriage which would force me to share an affection I wanted entirely to myself?

TARTUFFE: Ah, Madam, it is indeed delightful to hear such words from the lips of one I love! The honey of your words sets coursing through my whole being sensations more delicious than I have ever known before. My supreme concern is to find favour in your eyes. My hopes of bliss lie in your love. Yet you must forgive me if my heart still dares to entertain some doubt of its own felicity. Suppose what you are saying proved to be no more than a virtuous stratagem to induce me to abandon this impending marriage. If I may be allowed to put the matter frankly, I'll never trust these promises until I have been vouchsafed some small foretaste of the favours for which I yearn—that alone will reassure me and give me absolute confidence in your intentions towards me.

ELMIRE: [*coughing to attract her husband's attention*] Why must you go so fast? Would you have me reveal at once all that I feel for you? I have overstepped the bounds of modesty in confessing my feelings and yet it isn't enough for you! Can there be no satisfying you without going to ultimate lengths?

TARTUFFE: The less one deserves the less one dares to hope, and words are poor assurances of love. One cannot but mistrust a prospect of felicity: one must enjoy it before one can believe in it. Knowing how little I deserve your favours I doubt the outcome of my own temerity. I'll believe nothing until you give me proofs tangible enough to satisfy my passion.

ELMIRE: Heavens! What an importunate lover you are! I just don't know where I am. You quite overwhelm me—is there no denying you? Is there no evading your demands? Won't you even allow me a breathing space? How can you be so insistent, so peremptory, so merciless? How can you take such advantage of one's fondness for you?

TARTUFFE: But if you look upon my advances with a favourable eye, why refuse me convincing proof?

ELMIRE: How can I consent to what you ask without offending Him whose name is ever on your lips?

TARTUFFE: If fear of Heaven is the only obstacle to my passion that is a barrier I can easily remove. That need not restrain you.

ELMIRE: But they threaten us with the wrath of Heaven.

TARTUFFE: I can dissipate these foolish fears for you. I know the way to remove such scruples. It is true that certain forms of indulgence[3] are forbidden but there are ways and means of coming to terms with Heaven, of easing the restraints of conscience according to the exigencies of the case, of redressing the evil of the action by the purity of the intention. I can instruct you in these secrets, Madam. Only allow yourself to be led by me. Satisfy my desires and have not the slightest fear. I will answer for everything and take the sin upon myself. You have a bad cough, Madam.

ELMIRE: Yes! I'm in great distress.

[3] *Molière's footnote:* "It is a scoundrel speaking"

TARTUFFE: Would you care for a little of this liquorice?

ELMIRE: It's a most obstinate cold. I fear that all the liquorice in the world won't help me now.

TARTUFFE: It is certainly very trying.

ELMIRE: More so than I can say.

TARTUFFE: As I was saying then, your scruples can easily be removed. You are assured of absolute secrecy with me and the harm of any action lies only in its being known. The public scandal is what constitutes the offence: sins sinned in secret are no sins at all.

ELMIRE: [*after coughing again*] Very well then, I see that I must make up my mind to yield and consent to accord you everything you wish. It's no use hoping that anything less will satisfy or convey conviction. It's hard indeed to go to such lengths: it's very much against my will that I do so but since, it seems, I *have* to do it, since I'm not believed in spite of all I've said, since proofs still more convincing are required—I must resign myself to doing what's required of me. But if in consenting I offend, so much the worse for him who forces me to such extremity. The fault can surely not be accounted mine.

TARTUFFE: Yes, Madam, upon me be it and . . .

ELMIRE: Just open the door a moment and make sure that my husband isn't in the gallery.

TARTUFFE: Why worry about him? Between ourselves—he's a fellow one can lead by the nose. He glories in our association. I've got him to the stage where though he saw everything with his own eyes he wouldn't believe it.

ELMIRE: All the same, do go out a moment, please, and have a good look round.

ORGON: [*coming out from under the table*] Yes! I must admit it! The man's an abominable scoundrel! I can't get over it! I'm in a daze.

ELMIRE: But why come out so soon? You can't mean what you say! Get under the table again! It's not time yet. Wait till the very end and make quite sure. Don't trust to mere conjecture.

ORGON: No! No! Hell itself never produced anything more wicked.

ELMIRE: Good Heavens! You mustn't believe as easily as that. Wait until you are utterly convinced before you give in. Don't be too hasty! You might be mistaken! [*She puts her husband behind her.*]

[*Re-enter* TARTUFFE.]

TARTUFFE: Everything favours me, Madam. I've looked in all the rooms. There's no one there and now my rapture . . .

ORGON: [*stopping him*] Steady! You are letting your amorous desires run away with you. You shouldn't get so excited! Ah ha, my godly friend, you would deceive me, would you? How you give way to temptation! You meant to marry my daughter and yet you coveted my wife! For a long time I couldn't believe that it was really true and thought to hear you change your tune: but the proof has gone far enough. I'm convinced, and, for my part, I ask nothing further.

ELMIRE: [*to* TARTUFFE] It was very disagreeable to me to do it. I was driven to treat you like this.

TARTUFFE: [*to* ORGON] What! You believe . . .

ORGON: Come, let's have no more of it, please. Get out of the house without more ado.

TARTUFFE: My intention . . .

ORGON: That sort of talk won't do now. You must leave the house forthwith.

TARTUFFE: You are the one who must leave the house—you who talk as if you were master. This house is mine and I'll have you realize it. What's more, I'll show you how vainly you resort to these devices for picking a quarrel with me. You little know what you are doing when you insult me. I have the means to confound and punish your imposture, avenge the affront to Heaven, and make those who talk of making me leave the house regret it.

[*Exit* TARTUFFE.]

ELMIRE: What is he talking about? What does he mean?

ORGON: Alas! I don't know what to do. This is no laughing matter.

ELMIRE: Why? What . . .

ORGON: What he said makes me realize my mistake. My deed of gift begins to worry me.

ELMIRE: Your deed of gift . . . ?

ORGON: Yes, there's no going back upon it now, but there's something else that worries me.

ELMIRE: What is it?

ORGON: I'll tell you everything but I must go at once and see whether a certain casket is still upstairs.

ACT V

[ORGON, CLÉANTE]

CLÉANTE: Where are you off to?

ORGON: Alas! How do I know?

CLÉANTE: The first thing is to consider what's to be done.

ORGON: It's the casket that's worrying me. I'm more concerned about that than anything else.

CLÉANTE: Is there some important secret about the casket?

ORGON: Argas, my lamented friend, left it with me for safe keeping. He put it into my hands himself in the greatest secrecy. He selected me for this when he fled the country. It contains documents on which, he told me, his life and property depended.

CLÉANTE: Then why did you trust them to someone else?

ORGON: Because of a scruple of conscience. I went straight to this scoundrel and took him into my confidence. He persuaded me that it was better to let him have the casket for safe keeping so that in case of inquiry I could deny that I had it, and yet safeguard my conscience so far as giving false testimony was concerned.

CLÉANTE: You're in a difficult position it seems to me. Both the deed of gift and your action in confiding the casket to him were, if I may say so, very ill considered; he's in a position to lead you a pretty dance! What's more it was most imprudent to provoke him when he has such a hold upon you. You ought to have been more conciliatory in dealing with him.

ORGON: What! A fellow who could hide such double dealing, such wickedness, under the outward semblance of ardent piety, a man whom I took into my house as a penniless beggar . . . No, that's finished with: I'll have no more to do with godly men. I'll hold them in utter abhorrence in future. I'll consider nothing too bad for them!

CLÉANTE: There you go again! No moderation in anything! You are incapable of being temperate and sensible; you seem to have no idea of behaving reasonably. You must always be rushing from one extreme to the other. You see your mistake now; you've learned that you were taken in by an assumed piety; but what's the good of correcting one error by an even greater one, and failing to make a distinction between a scoundrelly good for nothing and genuinely good men? Because an audacious rogue has deceived you by a pretentious assumption of virtue and piety must you go and think everybody is like him and that there are no truly devout people nowadays? Leave such foolish inferences to the unbelievers; distinguish between virtue and the outward appearance of it, don't be so hasty in bestowing your esteem, and keep a sense of proportion. Be on your guard if you can against paying deference to imposture but say nothing against true devotion, and if you must run to extremes, better err on the same side as you did before.

[*Enter* DAMIS.]

DAMIS: Is it true, father, that this scoundrel is threatening you, that he's insensible to every benefit, and that in his wicked and outrageous pride he is turning your own generosity against you?

ORGON: It is, my son, and a dreadful grief it is to me too.

DAMIS: Leave it to me! I'll crop his ears for him. No half-measures with a rascal like that! I'll undertake to rid you of him without delay. I'll settle the business! I'll deal with him.

CLÉANTE: That's typical young man's talk. Moderate your feelings for goodness sake! We live in an age and under a government where it goes ill with those who resort to violence.

[*Enter* MADAME PERNELLE.]

MADAME PERNELLE: What's all this? What are these strange goings-on I have been hearing about?

ORGON: Ay! Strange indeed and I've seen them with my own eyes too. This is the reward I get for my pains. In sheer kindness of heart I relieve a man in his misery, receive him into my house, treat him like a brother, load him with kindness, give him my daughter, everything I possess, and what does the infamous scoundrel do but foully endeavour to seduce my wife! Not content with that he has the audacity to turn my own benevolence against me and threatens to ruin me with the weapons my own unwise generosity has put into his hand, deprive me of my possessions, and reduce me to the beggary from which I rescued him.

DORINE: Poor fellow!

MADAME PERNELLE: My son, I just can't believe that he has been guilty of such wickedness.

ORGON: How d'ye mean?

MADAME PERNELLE: People are always envious of the righteous.

ORGON: Whatever are you talking about, mother?

MADAME PERNELLE: I mean that there are queer goings-on in this house and I know very well how much they hate him.

ORGON: What has their hatred to do with what I'm telling you?

MADAME PERNELLE: I told you a hundred times when you were a little boy.

> 'Virtue, on earth, is persecuted ever
> The envious die, but envy never.'

ORGON: But what has this to do with what has happened?

MADAME PERNELLE: They'll have made up a hundred idle tales about him.

ORGON: I've already told you that *I saw it all myself.*

MADAME PERNELLE: There are no limits to the malice of slanderous tongues.

ORGON: You'll make me swear, mother, I've told you I saw his wickedness with my own eyes.

MADAME PERNELLE: Malicious tongues spread their poison abroad and nothing here below is proof against them.

ORGON: This is ridiculous talk. I *saw* him, I tell you, *saw him* with my own eyes! When I say I saw him I mean I really did see it! Must I go on saying it? How many times am I to tell you? Must I bawl it at the top of my voice?

MADAME PERNELLE: Good Heavens, appearances can often be deceptive. One shouldn't judge by what one sees.

ORGON: You'll drive me mad!

MADAME PERNELLE: It's human nature to think evil of people. Goodness is often misinterpreted.

ORGON: Am I to interpret it as kindly solicitude when I see him trying to kiss my wife?

MADAME PERNELLE: One ought never to make accusations without just cause. You should have waited until you were quite certain of his intentions.

ORGON: What the devil! How was I to be more certain? I should have waited, should I, until he . . . You'll drive me to say something I shouldn't.

MADAME PERNELLE: No, no! He's far too good a man. I just can't imagine he meant to do what you are saying he did.

ORGON: Look here! If you weren't my mother—I don't know what I wouldn't say to you—I'm so angry.

DORINE: Serves you right, master; it's the way of the world. *You* refused to believe once and now she won't believe you.

CLÉANTE: We are wasting time with this nonsense which we ought to be using for making plans. We can't afford to go to sleep in face of the scoundrel's threats.

DAMIS: Why! Do you think he'll really have the audacity to carry them out?

ELMIRE: I can't think he would have a case. His ingratitude is too glaring.

CLÉANTE: I shouldn't rely on that. He'll find means to justify whatever he does to you. Intrigue has landed people in difficulties on less evidence than this before now. I repeat what I said before: when he was in so strong a position as he is, you should never have provoked him so far.

ORGON: True. But what could I do? The audacity of the villain was such that I wasn't master of my feelings.

CLÉANTE: I only wish we could patch up some sort of reconciliation.

ELMIRE: Had I known what a strong position he was in I would never have been a party to making such a fuss . . .

ORGON: [*to* DORINE] What does *this* fellow want? Go at once and see. I'm in a fine state for anyone to come to see me.

[*Enter* MR LOYAL.]

MR LOYAL: Good afternoon, dear sister. Pray let me speak with the master.

DORINE: He has company. I don't suppose he can see anyone just now.

MR LOYAL: I'm not for being troublesome. I don't think he'll find *my* visit unsatisfactory. He'll be pleased with what I've come about.

DORINE: Your name?

MR LOYAL: Just tell him that I'm here on behalf of Mr Tartuffe and for his own good.

DORINE: [*to* ORGON] It's a man who's come on behalf of Mr Tartuffe. He's very civil about it. He says that his business is something that you will be pleased to hear.

CLÉANTE: [*to* ORGON] We must see who the man is and what he wants.

ORGON: Perhaps he's come to reconcile us. How should I behave to him?

CLÉANTE: Don't show your resentment. If he's for coming to an agreement you must listen to him.

MR LOYAL: How d'ye do, sir. May Heaven bless you and confound all who seek to do you harm.

ORGON: [*aside to* CLÉANTE] This civil beginning confirms my impression. It means a reconciliation.

MR LOYAL: I have always been very devoted to your family. I was once in your father's service.

ORGON: I'm sorry not to recognize you. You must forgive me but I don't know your name.

MR LOYAL: Loyal's the name. Norman by birth and bailiff to the court; and let them envy me that want to. I can rightly claim to have discharged my duty with credit this forty year now, Heaven be praised, and now I've come, sir, to serve this writ upon you, excusing the liberty.

ORGON: What! You've come to . . .

MR LOYAL: Now take it quiet, sir. It's only a writ, an order to quit the house at once, you and yours, bag and baggage, and make way for others, without delay and without fail as herein provided.

ORGON: What, me? Leave the house?

MR LOYAL: That's it, sir, if you don't mind. This house is now, as you be duly aware, good Mr Tartuffe's and no argument about it. He's lord and master of your possessions from now on by virtue of the deed that I be the bearer of. It's in due form and there's no disputing it.

DAMIS: What marvellous impudence!

MR LOYAL: [*to* DAMIS] I want nothing to do with you, sir. It's this gentleman I'm dealing with. He's reasonable and good to deal with and he knows too well what a good man's duty is to want to interfere with the course of justice.

ORGON: But . . .

MR LOYAL: Yes sir. I know you'd never resist authority, not on any consideration. You'll allow me to carry out my orders as a gentleman should.

DAMIS: You may as easily find yourself getting a hiding for all your black gown,
Mr Bailiff.

MR LOYAL: Ask your son to hold his tongue, sir, or retire. I should be very
sorry to have to report you.

DORINE: He should be *Dis*loyal, not Loyal, by the look of him.

MR LOYAL: I have a soft spot for godly men, sir, and I only took service of this
writ in consideration for you sir, and just to be helpful and to stop the
job falling to anybody who mightn't have the same feeling for you that
I have and wouldn't have gone about things so considerate-like.

ORGON: And what could be worse than ordering a man out of his own house?

MR LOYAL: We are giving you time. I'll give a stay of execution till tomorrow.
I'll just come and pass the night here with a dozen or so of my men
without fuss or scandal. I must ask for the keys as a matter of form, of
course, before you go to bed. I'll take pains not to disturb your rest and
I'll see that there's nothing that isn't as it should be. But tomorrow
morning you'll have to look slippy and clear everything out of here down
to the last article. My men will help you. I've picked a handy lot so that
they can get everything out for you. Nobody could treat you fairer than
that and, seeing as I'm showing you every consideration, I ask the same
from you, sir—that is, that you won't do nothing to hinder me in dis-
charge of my duty.

ORGON: [*aside*] I'd willingly give the last hundred louis I possess for the
pleasure of landing him a punch on his ugly snout!

CLÉANTE: [*whispers to* ORGON] Steady. Don't do anything foolish.

DAMIS: I can hardly restrain myself before such unheard-of insolence. I'm
itching to be at him.

DORINE: That broad back of yours could do with a good dusting, Mr Loyal.

MR LOYAL: I could get you into trouble for talking like that, my lass. The law
applies to women as well, you know.

CLÉANTE: [*to* LOYAL] That's enough, sir. We'll leave it at that. Give us the
document and go.

MR LOYAL: Good day then. The Lord be with you all.

    [*Exit* MR LOYAL.]

ORGON: Ay, and the Devil take you and him who sent you! Well mother, you
see now whether I was right or not. On the other point you can judge
from the writ. Do you realize now what a rascal he is?

MADAME PERNELLE: I don't know whether I'm on my head or my heels.

DORINE: You have no cause for complaint and no right to blame him. It all
fits in with his pious intentions; it's all part of his love for his neighbour.
He knows how possessions corrupt a man and it's pure charity on his part
to rob you of everything that might stand in the way of your salvation.

ORGON: Be quiet! I'm always having to remind you!

CLÉANTE: Let us go and take counsel on what course to follow.

ELMIRE: Go and expose the ungrateful scoundrel! This last act of his must invalidate the deed of gift. His treachery must appear too obvious to permit him the success we fear.

[*Enter* VALÈRE.]

VALÈRE: I'm very sorry to bring you bad news, sis, but I'm obliged to do so because you are in most urgent danger. A very close friend who knows the interest I have reason to take in your welfare has violated the secrecy due to affairs of state and sent me intelligence, in confidence. The purport of it is that you must fly immediately. The scoundrel, who has so long imposed upon you, denounced you to the King an hour ago and, among various charges made against you, put into his hands a casket which belonged to a disaffected person whose secrets he contends you have kept in breach of your duty as a subject. I know no particulars of the offence with which you are charged but a warrant has been issued for your arrest and to ensure effective service of it Tartuffe himself is commanded to accompany the person who is to apprehend you.

CLÉANTE: And so he strengthens his hand! That's how he means to make himself master of your possessions.

ORGON: I must admit, the man really is a brute!

VALÈRE: The slightest delay may be fatal to you. I have my carriage at the door to take you away, and a thousand guineas which I have brought for you. We must lose no time: this is a shattering blow—there's no avoiding it except by flight. I offer you my services to conduct you to some place of safety. I'll stay with you until you are out of danger.

ORGON: Alas! How can I repay your kindness? But I must leave my thanks to another time. May Heaven allow me some day to return this service! Farewell! Take care all of you . . .

CLÉANTE: Go at once, brother. We'll see that everything necessary is done.

[*Enter* TARTUFFE *and an* OFFICER.]

TARTUFFE: Gently, sir, gently, don't run so fast. You don't need to go very far to find a lodging. You are a prisoner in the King's name.

ORGON: Villain! To keep this trick to the last! This is the blow whereby you finish me, the master stroke of all your perfidy!

TARTUFFE: Your insults are powerless to move me. I am schooled to suffer everything in the cause of Heaven.

CLÉANTE: Remarkable meekness indeed!

DAMIS: How impudently the dog makes mockery of Heaven.

TARTUFFE: Not all your rage can move me. I have no thought for anything but to fulfil my duty.

MARIANE: What credit can you hope to reap from this? How can you regard such employment as honourable?

TARTUFFE: Any employment must needs be honourable which proceeds from that authority which sent me hither.

ORGON: And do you not remember, ungrateful wretch, that it was my charitable hand which rescued you from indigence?

TARTUFFE: Yes, I am mindful of the assistance I received from you, but my first duty is to the interests of my King and that sacred obligation is so strong as to extinguish in me all gratitude to you. To that allegiance I would sacrifice friends, wife, kinsmen, and myself with them.

ELMIRE: Impostor!

DORINE: How cunningly he cloaks his villainies with the mantle of all that we most revere!

CLÉANTE: If this consuming zeal of which you boast is as great as you say, why didn't it come to light until he had caught you making love to his wife? Why didn't it occur to you to denounce him until your attempt to dishonour him had forced him to turn you out? If I mention the gift it isn't to deter you from doing your duty but, nevertheless, if you want to treat him as a criminal now, why did you consent to accept anything from him before?

TARTUFFE: Pray deliver me from this futile clamour, sir! Proceed to the execution of your orders.

OFFICER: Yes. I have indeed waited too long already and you do well to recall me to my duty. In fulfilment of my instructions I command you to accompany me forthwith to the prison in which you are to be lodged.

TARTUFFE: What? Me, sir?

OFFICER: Yes, you.

TARTUFFE: But why to prison?

OFFICER: I am not accountable to you. [*to* ORGON] Calm your fears, sir. We live under the rule of a prince inimical to fraud, a monarch who can read men's hearts, whom no impostor's art deceives. The keen discernment of that lofty mind at all times sees things in their true perspective; nothing can disturb the firm constancy of his judgement nor lead him into error. On men of worth he confers immortal glory but his favour is not shown indiscriminately: his love for good men and true does not preclude a proper detestation of those who are false. This man could never deceive him—he has evaded more subtle snares than his. From the outset he discerned to the full the baseness of the villain's heart and in coming to accuse you he betrayed himself and by a stroke of supreme justice revealed himself as a notorious scoundrel of whose activities under another name His Majesty was already informed. The long history of his dark crimes would fill volumes. In short, the King, filled with detestation for his base ingratitude and wickedness to you, added this to his other crimes and only put me under his orders to see to what lengths his impudence would go and to oblige him to give you full satisfaction. All documents he says he has of yours I am to take from him in your presence and restore them to you and His Majesty annuls by act of sovereign prerogative the deed of gift of your possessions that you made to him. Moreover, he pardons you that clandestine offence in which the flight of your friend involved you: this clemency he bestows upon you in recognition of your former loyal service and to let you see that he can reward a good action when least expected, that he is never insensible to true merit and chooses rather to remember good than ill.

DORINE: Heaven be praised!

MADAME PERNELLE: Now I can breathe again.

ELMIRE: A happy end to all our troubles!

MARIANE: Who could have foretold this?

ORGON: [*to* TARTUFFE] So you see, you villain, you . . .

CLÉANTE: Ah! Brother forbear. Do not stoop to such indignity. Leave the unhappy creature to his fate. Add nothing to the remorse which must now overwhelm him. Rather hope that he may henceforward return to the paths of virtue, reform his life, learn to detest his vices, and so earn some mitigation of the justice of the King. Meanwhile, for your own part, you must go on your knees and render appropriate thanks for the benevolence His Majesty has shown to you.

ORGON: Yes, that's well said. Let us go and offer him our humble thanks for all his generosity to us. Then, that first duty done, we have another to perform—to crown the happiness of Valère, a lover who has proved both generous and sincere.

Richard Brinsley Sheridan

The School for Scandal

CHARACTERS

SIR PETER TEAZLE

SIR OLIVER SURFACE

JOSEPH SURFACE

CHARLES SURFACE

CARELESS

SNAKE

SIR BENJAMIN BACKBITE

CRABTREE

ROWLEY

MOSES

TRIP

SIR HARRY BUMPER

LADY TEAZLE

MARIA

LADY SNEERWELL

MRS. CANDOUR

Gentlemen, Maid,
and Servants

THE SCENE *is London in the 1770's.*

PROLOGUE

[*Written by* MR. GARRICK. *Spoken by* SIR PETER TEAZLE.]
A School for Scandal! tell me, I beseech you,
Needs there a school this modish art to teach you?
No need of lessons now, the knowing think;
We might as well be taught to eat and drink.
Caused by a dearth of scandal, should the vapors
Distress our fair ones—let them read the papers;
Their powerful mixtures such disorders hit;
Crave what you will—there's *quantum sufficit.*
"Lord!" cries my Lady Wormwood (who loves tattle,
And puts much salt and pepper in her prattle),
Just risen at noon, all night at cards when threshing
Strong tea and scandal—"Bless me, how refreshing!
Give me the papers, Lisp—how bold and free! (*sips*)
Last night Lord L. (*sips*) *was caught with Lady D.*
For aching heads what charming sal volatile! (*sips*)
If Mrs. B. will still continue flirting,
We hope she'll DRAW, *or we'll* UNDRAW *the curtain.*
Fine satire, poz—in public all abuse it,
But, by ourselves (*sips*), our praise we can't refuse it.
Now, Lisp, read you—there at that dash and star."
"Yes, ma'am—*A certain Lord had best beware,*
Who lives not twenty miles from Grosvenor Square;
For should he Lady W. find willing,

W*ormwood is bitter*"—"Oh! that's me! the villian!
Throw it behind the fire, and never more
Let that vile paper come within my door."
Thus at our friends we laugh, who feel the dart;
To reach our feelings, we ourselves must smart.
Is our young bard so young, to think that he
Can stop the full spring-tide of calumny?
Knows he the world so little, and its trade?
Alas! the devil's sooner raised than laid.
So strong, so swift, the monster there's no gagging:
Cut Scandal's head off, still the tongue is wagging.
Proud of your smiles once lavishly bestowed,
Again our young Don Quixote takes the road;
To show his gratitude he draws his pen,
And seeks his hydra, Scandal, in his den.
For your applause all perils he would through—
He'll fight—thats *write*—a cavalliero true,
Till every drop of blood—that's *ink*—is spilt for you.

ACT I

SCENE I——LADY SNEERWELL'S *dressing-room.*

[LADY SNEERWELL *at her dressing-table;* SNAKE *drinking chocolate.*]

LADY SNEERWELL: The paragraphs, you say, Mr. Snake, were all inserted?

SNAKE: They were, madam; and, as I copied them myself in a feigned hand, there can be no suspicion whence they came.

LADY SNEERWELL: Did you circulate the report of Lady Brittle's intrigue with Captain Boastall?

SNAKE: That's in as fine a train as your ladyship could wish. In the common course of things, I think it must reach Mrs. Clackitt's ears within four-and-twenty hours; and then, you know, the business is as good as done.

LADY SNEERWELL: Why, truly, Mrs. Clackitt has a very pretty talent, and a great deal of industry.

SNAKE: True, madam, and has been tolerably successful in her day. To my knowledge, she has been the cause of six matches being broken off, and three sons being disinherited; of four forced elopements, and as many close confinements; nine separate maintenances, and two divorces. Nay, I have more than once traced her causing a *tête-à-tête* in the *Town and Country Magazine,* when the parties, perhaps, had never seen each other's face before in the course of their lives.

LADY SNEERWELL: She certainly has talents, but her manner is gross.

SNAKE: 'Tis very true. She generally designs well, has a free tongue and a bold invention; but her coloring is too dark, and her outlines often extravagant. She wants that delicacy of tint, and mellowness of sneer, which distinguish your ladyship's scandal.

LADY SNEERWELL: You are partial, Snake.

SNAKE: Not in the least; everybody allows that Lady Sneerwell can do more with a word or look than many can with the most labored detail, even when they happen to have a little truth on their side to support it.

LADY SNEERWELL: Yes, my dear Snake; and I am no hypocrite to deny the satisfaction I reap from the success of my efforts. Wounded myself in the early part of my life, by the envenomed tongue of slander, I confess I have since known no pleasure equal to the reducing others to the level of my own injured reputation.

SNAKE: Nothing can be more natural. But, Lady Sneerwell, there is one affair in which you have lately employed me, wherein, I confess, I am at a loss to guess your motives.

LADY SNEERWELL: I conceive you mean with respect to my neighbor, Sir Peter Teazle, and his family?

SNAKE: I do. Here are two young men, to whom Sir Peter has acted as kind of guardian since their father s death; the eldest possessing the most amiable character, and universally well spoken of—the youngest, the most dissipated and extravagant young fellow in the kingdom, without friends or character: the former an avowed admirer of your ladyship, and apparently your favorite; the latter attached to Maria, Sir Peter's ward, and confessedly beloved by her. Now, on the face of these circumstances, it is utterly unaccountable to me why you, the widow of a city knight, with a good jointure, should not close with the passion of a man of such character and expectations as Mr. Surface; and more so, why you should be so uncommonly earnest to destroy the mutual attachment subsisting between his brother Charles and Maria.

LADY SNEERWELL: Then, at once to unravel this mystery, I must inform you that love has no share whatever in the intercourse between Mr. Surface and me.

SNAKE: No!

LADY SNEERWELL: His real attachment is to Maria or her fortune; but, finding in his brother a favorite rival, he has been obliged to mask his pretensions and profit by my assistance.

SNAKE: Yet still I am more puzzled why you should interest yourself in his success.

LADY SNEERWELL: Heavens! how dull you are! Cannot you surmise the weakness which I hitherto, through shame, have concealed even from you? Must I confess that Charles—that libertine, that extravagant, that bankrupt in fortune and reputation—that he it is for whom I am thus anxious and malicious, and to gain whom I would sacrifice everything?

SNAKE: Now, indeed, your conduct appears consistent; but how came you and Mr. Surface so confidential?

LADY SNEERWELL: For our mutual interest. I have found him out a long time since. I know him to be artful, selfish, and malicious—in short, a sentimental knave; while with Sir Peter, and indeed with all his acquaintance, he passes for a youthful miracle of prudence, good sense, and benevolence.

SNAKE: Yes! yet Sir Peter vows he has not his equal in England; and, above all, he praises him as a man of sentiment.

LADY SNEERWELL: True; and with the assistance of his sentiment and hypocrisy he has brought Sir Peter entirely into his interest with regard to Maria; while poor Charles has no friend in the house—though, I fear, he has a powerful one in Maria's heart, against whom we must direct our schemes.

[*Enter* SERVANT.]

SERVANT: Mr. Surface.

LADY SNEERWELL: Show him up.

[*Exit* SERVANT.]

He generally calls about this time. I don't wonder at people giving him to me for a lover.

[*Enter* JOSEPH SURFACE.]

JOSEPH SURFACE: My dear Lady Sneerwell, how do you do today? Mr. Snake, your most obedient.

LADY SNEERWELL: Snake has just been rallying me on our mutual attachment; but I have informed him of our real views. You know how useful he has been to us; and, believe me, the confidence is not ill placed.

JOSEPH SURFACE: Madam, it is impossible for me to suspect a man of Mr. Snake's sensibility and discernment.

LADY SNEERWELL: Well, well, no compliments now; but tell me when you saw your mistress, Maria—or, what is more material to me, your brother.

JOSEPH SURFACE: I have not seen either since I left you; but I can inform you that they never meet. Some of your stories have taken a good effect on Maria.

LADY SNEERWELL: Ah, my dear Snake! the merit of this belongs to you. But do your brother's distresses increase?

JOSEPH SURFACE: Every hour. I am told he has had another execution in the house yesterday. In short, his dissipation and extravagance exceed anything I have ever heard of.

LADY SNEERWELL: Poor Charles!

JOSEPH SURFACE: True, madam; notwithstanding his vices one can't help feeling for him. Poor Charles! I'm sure I wish it were in my power to be of any essential service to him; for the man who does not share in the distresses of a brother, even though merited by his own misconduct, deserves—

LADY SNEERWELL: O Lud! you are going to be moral and forget that you are among friends.

JOSEPH SURFACE: Egad, that's true! I'll keep that sentiment till I see Sir Peter. However, it is certainly a charity to rescue Maria from such a libertine, who, if he is to be reclaimed, can be so only by a person of your ladyship's superior accomplishments and understanding.

SNAKE: I believe, Lady Sneerwell, here's company coming. I'll go and copy the letter I mentioned to you. Mr. Surface, your most obedient.

JOSEPH SURFACE: Sir, your very devoted.

[*Exit* SNAKE.]

Lady Sneerwell, I am very sorry you have put any further confidence in that fellow.

LADY SNEERWELL: Why so?

JOSEPH SURFACE: I have lately detected him in frequent conference with old

Rowley, who was formerly my father's steward and has never, you know, been a friend of mine.

LADY SNEERWELL: And do you think he would betray us?

JOSEPH SURFACE: Nothing more likely: take my word for't, Lady Sneerwell, that fellow hasn't virtue enough to be faithful even to his own villainy. Ah, Maria!

[*Enter* MARIA.]

LADY SNEERWELL: Maria, my dear, how do you do? What's the matter?

MARIA: Oh! there's that disagreeable lover of mine, Sir Benjamin Backbite, has just called at my guardian's with his odious uncle, Crabtree; so I slipped out and ran hither to avoid them.

LADY SNEERWELL: Is that all?

JOSEPH SURFACE: If my brother Charles had been of the party, madam, perhaps you would not have been so much alarmed.

LADY SNEERWELL: Nay, now you are severe; for I dare swear the truth of the matter is, Maria heard you were here. But, my dear, what has Sir Benjamin done that you should avoid him so?

MARIA: Oh, he has done nothing—but 'tis for what he has said. His conversation is a perpetual libel on all his acquaintance.

JOSEPH SURFACE: Ay, and the worst of it is, there is no advantage in not knowing him, for he'll abuse a stranger just as soon as his best friend; and his uncle's as bad.

LADY SNEERWELL: Nay, but we should make allowance; Sir Benjamin is a wit and a poet.

MARIA: For my part, I own, madam, wit loses its respect with me when I see it in company with malice. What do you think, Mr. Surface?

JOSEPH SURFACE: Certainly, madam. To smile at the jest which plants a thorn in another's breast is to become a principal in the mischief.

LADY SNEERWELL: Psha! there's no possibility of being witty without a little ill nature. The malice of a good thing is the barb that makes it stick. What's your opinion, Mr. Surface?

JOSEPH SURFACE: To be sure, madam; that conversation, where the spirit of raillery is suppressed, will ever appear tedious and insipid.

MARIA: Well, I'll not debate how far scandal may be allowable; but in a man, I am sure, it is always contemptible. We have pride, envy, rivalship, and a thousand motives to depreciate each other; but the male slanderer must have the cowardice of a woman before he can traduce one.

[*Enter* SERVANT.]

SERVANT: Madam, Mrs. Candour is below, and, if your ladyship's at leisure, will leave her carriage.

LADY SNEERWELL: Beg her to walk in.

[*Exit* SERVANT.]

Now, Maria, here is a character to your taste; for, though Mrs. Candour is a little talkative, everybody knows her to be the best natured and best sort of woman.

MARIA: Yes, with a very gross affection of good nature and benevolence, she does more mischief than the direct malice of old Crabtree.

JOSEPH SURFACE: I'faith that's true, Lady Sneerwell: whenever I hear the current running against the characters of my friends, I never think them in such danger as when Candour undertakes their defence.

LADY SNEERWELL: Hush!—here she is!

[*Enter* MRS. CANDOUR.]

MRS. CANDOUR: My dear Lady Sneerwell, how have you been this century?—Mr. Surface, what news do you hear?—though indeed it is no matter, for I think one hears nothing else but scandal.

JOSEPH SURFACE: Just so, indeed, ma'am.

MRS. CANDOUR: Oh, Maria! child—what, is the whole affair off between you and Charles? His extravagance, I presume—the town talks of nothing else.

MARIA: I am very sorry, ma'am, the town has so little to do.

MRS. CANDOUR: True, true, child: but there's no stopping people's tongues. I own I was hurt to hear it, as I indeed was to learn, from the same quarter, that your guardian, Sir Peter, and Lady Teazle have not agreed lately as well as could be wished.

MARIA: 'Tis strangely impertinent for people to busy themselves so.

MRS. CANDOUR: Very true, child; but what's to be done? People will talk—there's no preventing it. Why, it was but yesterday I was told that Miss Gadabout had eloped with Sir Filagree Flirt. But, Lord! there's no minding what one hears; though, to be sure, I had this from very good authority.

MARIA: Such reports are highly scandalous.

MRS. CANDOUR: So they are, child—shameful, shameful! But the world is so censorious, no character escapes. Lord, now who would have suspected your friend, Miss Prim, of an indiscretion? Yet such is the ill nature of people that they say her uncle stopped her last week just as she was stepping into the York diligence with her dancing-master.

MARIA: I'll answer for't there are no grounds for that report.

MRS. CANDOUR: Ah, no foundation in the world, I dare swear: no more, probably, than for the story circulated last month, of Mrs. Festino's affair with Colonel Cassino—though, to be sure, that matter was never rightly cleared up.

JOSEPH SURFACE: The license of invention some people take is monstrous indeed.

MARIA: 'Tis so; but, in my opinion, those who report such things are equally culpable.

MRS. CANDOUR: To be sure they are; tale bearers are as bad as the tale makers—'tis an old observation and a very true one: but what's to be done, as I said before? how will you prevent people from talking? Today, Mrs. Clackitt assured me Mr. and Mrs. Honeymoon were at last become mere man and wife like the rest of their acquaintance. She likewise hinted that a certain widow in the next street had got rid of her dropsy and recovered her shape in a most surprising manner. And at the same time Miss Tattle, who was by, affirmed that Lord Buffalo had discovered his lady at a house of no extraordinary fame; and that Sir Harry Bouquet and Tom Saunter were to measure swords on a similar provocation. But, Lord, do you think

I would report these things! No, no! tale bearers, as I said before, are just as bad as the tale makers.

JOSEPH SURFACE: Ah! Mrs. Candour, if everybody had your forbearance and good nature!

MRS. CANDOUR: I confess, Mr. Surface, I cannot bear to hear people attacked behind their backs; and when ugly circumstances come out against our acquaintance, I own I always love to think the best. By-the-bye, I hope 'tis not true that your brother is absolutely ruined?

JOSEPH SURFACE: I am afraid his circumstances are very bad indeed, ma'am.

MRS. CANDOUR: Ah!—I heard so—but you must tell him to keep up his spirits; everybody almost is in the same way: Lord Spindle, Sir Thomas Splint, Captain Quinze, and Mr. Nickit—all up, I hear, within this week; so, if Charles is undone, he'll find half his acquaintance ruined too; and that, you know, is a consolation.

JOSEPH SURFACE: Doubtless, ma'am—a very great one.

[*Enter* SERVANT.]

SERVANT: Mr. Crabtree and Sir Benjamin Backbite.

[*Exit* SERVANT.]

LADY SNEERWELL: So, Maria, you see your lover pursues you; positively you shan't escape.

[*Enter* CRABTREE *and* SIR BENJAMIN BACKBITE.]

CRABTREE: Lady Sneerwell, I kiss your hand. Mrs. Candour, I don't believe you are acquainted with my nephew, Sir Benjamin Backbite? Egad, ma'am, he has a pretty wit and is a pretty poet too. Isn't he, Lady Sneerwell?

SIR BENJAMIN: Oh, fie, uncle!

CRABTREE: Nay, egad it's true: I back him at a rebus or a charade against the best rhymer in the kingdom. Has your ladyship heard the epigram he wrote last week on Lady Frizzle's feather catching fire?—Do, Benjamin, repeat it, or the charade you made last night extempore at Mrs. Drowzie's *conversazione*. Come now; your first is the name of a fish, your second a great naval commander, and—

SIR BENJAMIN: Uncle, now—prithee—

CRABTREE: I'faith, ma'am, 'twould surprise you to hear how ready he is at all these sort of things.

LADY SNEERWELL: I wonder, Sir Benjamin, you never publish anything.

SIR BENJAMIN: To say truth, ma'am, 'tis very vulgar to print; and, as my little productions are mostly satires and lampoons on particular people, I find they circulate more by giving copies in confidence to the friends of the parties. However, I have some love elegies, which, when favored with this lady's smiles, I mean to give the public.

CRABTREE: [*to* MARIA] 'Fore heaven, ma'am, they'll immortalize you—you will be handed down to posterity like Petrarch's Laura, or Waller's Sacharissa.

SIR BENJAMIN: [*to* MARIA] Yes, madam, I think you will like them when you shall see them on a beautiful quarto page, where a neat rivulet of text shall meander through a meadow of margin. 'Fore gad, they will be the most elegant things of their kind!

CRABTREE: But, ladies, that's true—have you heard the news?

MRS. CANDOUR: What, sir, do you mean the report of—

CRABTREE: No, ma'am, that's not it. Miss Nicely is going to be married to her own footman.

MRS. CANDOUR: Impossible!

CRABTREE: Ask Sir Benjamin.

SIR BENJAMIN: 'Tis very true, ma'am: everything is fixed and the wedding liveries bespoke.

CRABTREE: Yes—and they do say there were pressing reasons for it.

LADY SNEERWELL: Why, I have heard something of this before.

MRS. CANDOUR: It can't be—and I wonder any one should believe such a story of so prudent a lady as Miss Nicely.

SIR BENJAMIN: O lud! ma'am, that's the very reason 'twas believed at once. She has always been so cautious and so reserved, that everybody was sure there was some reason for it at bottom.

MRS. CANDOUR: Why, to be sure, a tale of scandal is as fatal to the credit of a prudent lady of her stamp as a fever is generally to those of the strongest constitution. But there is a sort of puny, sickly reputation, that is always ailing, yet will outlive the robuster characters of a hundred prudes.

SIR BENJAMIN: True, madam, there are valetudinarians in reputation as well as constitution, who, being conscious of their weak part, avoid the least breath of air and supply their want of stamina by care and circumspection.

MRS. CANDOUR: Well, but this may be all a mistake. You know, Sir Benjamin, very trifling circumstances often give rise to the most injurious tales.

CRABTREE: That they do, I'll be sworn, ma'am. Did you ever hear how Miss Piper came to lose her lover and her character last summer at Tunbridge? Sir Benjamin, you remember it?

SIR BENJAMIN: Oh, to be sure!—the most whimsical circumstance.

LADY SNEERWELL: How was it, pray?

CRABTREE: Why, one evening at Mrs. Ponto's assembly, the conversation happened to turn on the breeding Nova Scotia sheep in this country. Says a young lady in company, "I have known instances of it; for Miss Letitia Piper, a first cousin of mine, had a Nova Scotia sheep that produced her twins." "What!" cries the Lady Dowager Dundizzy [who you know is as deaf as a post], "has Miss Piper had twins?" This mistake, as you may imagine, threw the whole company into a fit of laughter. However, 'twas the next morning everywhere reported, and in a few days believed by the whole town, that Miss Letitia Piper had actually been brought to bed of a fine boy and a girl: and in less than a week there were some people who could name the father, and the farm-house where the babies were put to nurse.

LADY SNEERWELL: Strange, indeed!

CRABTREE: Matter of fact, I assure you. O lud! Mr. Surface, pray is it true that your uncle, Sir Oliver, is coming home?

JOSEPH SURFACE: Not that I know of, indeed, sir.

CRABTREE: He has been in the East Indies a long time. You can scarcely remember him, I believe? Sad comfort, whenever he returns, to hear how your brother has gone on!

JOSEPH SURFACE: Charles has been imprudent, sir, to be sure; but I hope no busy people have already prejudiced Sir Oliver against him. He may reform.

SIR BENJAMIN: To be sure he may. For my part I never believed him to be so utterly void of principle as people say; and though he has lost all his friends, I am told nobody is better spoken of by the Jews.

CRABTREE: That's true, egad, nephew. If the old Jewry was a ward, I believe Charles would be an alderman: no man more popular there, 'fore gad! I hear he pays as many annuities as the Irish tontine; and that whenever he is sick they have prayers for the recovery of his health in all the synagogues.

SIR BENJAMIN: Yet no man lives in greater splendor. They tell me, when he entertains his friends he will sit down to dinner with a dozen of his own securities, have a score of tradesmen in the ante-chamber, and an officer behind every guest's chair.

JOSEPH SURFACE: This may be entertainment to you gentlemen, but you pay very little regard to the feelings of a brother.

MARIA: [*aside*] Their malice is intolerable!—[*aloud*] Lady Sneerwell, I must wish you a good morning: I'm not very well.
    [*Exit* MARIA.]

MRS. CANDOUR: O dear! she changes color very much.

LADY SNEERWELL: Do, Mrs. Candour, follow her; she may want assistance.

MRS. CONDOUR: That I will, with all my soul, ma'am. Poor dear girl, who knows what her situation may be!
    [*Exit.*]

LADY SNEERWELL: 'Twas nothing but that she could not bear to hear Charles reflected on, notwithstanding their difference.

SIR BENJAMIN: The young lady's *penchant* is obvious.

CRABTREE: But, Benjamin, you must not give up the pursuit for that: follow her and put her into good humor. Repeat her some of your own verses. Come, I'll assist you.

SIR BENJAMIN: Mr. Surface, I did not mean to hurt you; but depend on't your brother is utterly undone.

CRABTREE: O lud, ay! undone as ever man was—can't raise a guinea!

SIR BENJAMIN: And everything sold, I'm told, that was movable.

CRABTREE: I have seen one that was at his house. Not a thing left but some empty bottles that were overlooked and the family pictures which I believe are framed in the wainscots.

SIR BENJAMIN: [*going*] And I'm very sorry also to hear some bad stories against him.

CRABTREE: Oh, he has done many mean things, that's certain.

SIR BENJAMIN: [*going*] But, however, as he's your brother—

CRABTREE: We'll tell you all another opportunity.
    [*Exeunt* CRABTREE *and* SIR BENJAMIN.]

LADY SNEERWELL: Ha, ha! 'tis very hard for them to leave a subject they have not quite run down.

JOSEPH SURFACE: And I believe the abuse was no more acceptable to your ladyship than to Maria.

LADY SNEERWELL: I doubt her affections are further engaged than we imagine.

But the family are to be here this evening, so you may as well dine where you are and we shall have an opportunity of observing further. In the meantime, I'll go and plot mischief and you shall study sentiment.

SCENE II——SIR PETER TEAZLE's *House.*

SIR PETER: When an old bachelor marries a young wife, what is he to expect? 'Tis now six months since Lady Teazle made me the happiest of men— and I have been the most miserable dog ever since! We tiffed a little going to church and fairly quarrelled before the bells had done ringing. I was more than once nearly choked with gall during the honeymoon, and had lost all comfort in life before my friends had done wishing me joy. Yet I chose with caution—a girl bred wholly in the country, who never knew luxury beyond one silk gown, nor dissipation above the annual gala of a race ball. Yet she now plays her part in all the extravagant fopperies of fashion and the town, with as ready a grace as if she never had seen a bush or a grass-plot out of Grosvenor Square! I am sneered at by all my acquaintance and paragraphed in the newspapers. She dissipates my fortune, and contradicts all my humors; yet the worst of it is, I doubt I love her, or I should never bear all this. However, I'll never be weak enough to own it.

[*Enter* ROWLEY.]

ROWLEY: Oh! Sir Peter, your servant: how is it with you, sir?

SIR PETER: Very bad, Master Rowley, very bad. I meet with nothing but crosses and vexations.

ROWLEY: What can have happened to trouble you since yesterday?

SIR PETER: A good question to a married man!

ROWLEY: Nay, I'm sure, Sir Peter, your lady can't be the cause of your uneasiness.

SIR PETER: Why, has anybody told you she was dead?

ROWLEY: Come, come, Sir Peter, you love her, notwithstanding your tempers don't exactly agree.

SIR PETER: But the fault is entirely hers, Master Rowley. I am myself the sweetest tempered man alive, and hate a teasing temper; and so I tell her a hundred times a day.

ROWLEY: Indeed!

SIR PETER: Ay; and what is very extraordinary, in all our disputes she is always in the wrong! But Lady Sneerwell and the set she meets at her house encourage the perverseness of her disposition. Then, to complete my vexation, Maria, my ward, whom I ought to have the power of a father over, is determined to turn rebel too and absolutely refuses the man whom I have long resolved on for her husband; meaning, I suppose, to bestow herself on his profligate brother.

ROWLEY: You know, Sir Peter, I have always taken the liberty to differ with you on the subject of these two young gentlemen. I only wish you may not be deceived in your opinion of the elder. For Charles, my life on't! he will retrieve his errors yet. Their worthy father, once my honored master, was, at his years, nearly as wild a spark; yet, when he died, he did not leave a more benevolent heart to lament his loss.

SIR PETER: You are wrong, Master Rowley. On their father's death, you know, I acted as a kind of guardian to them both till their uncle Sir Oliver's liberality gave them an early independence. Of course no person could have more opportunity of judging of their hearts, and I was never mistaken in my life. Joseph is indeed a model for the young men of the age. He is a man of sentiment and acts up to the sentiments he professes; but, for the other, take my word for't, if he had any grain of virtue by descent, he has dissipated it with the rest of his inheritance. Ah! my old friend Sir Oliver will be deeply mortified when he finds how part of his bounty has been misapplied.

ROWLEY: I am sorry to find you so violent against the young man, because this may be the most critical period of his fortune. I came hither with news that will surprise you.

SIR PETER: What! let me hear.

ROWLEY: Sir Oliver is arrived, and at this moment in town.

SIR PETER: How! you astonish me! I thought you did not expect him this month.

ROWLEY: I did not: but his passage has been remarkably quick.

SIR PETER: Egad, I shall rejoice to see my old friend. 'Tis sixteen years since we met. We have had many a day together: but does he still enjoin us not to inform his nephews of his arrival?

ROWLEY: Most strictly. He means, before it is known, to make some trial of their dispositions.

SIR PETER: Ah! There needs no art to discover their merits—however, he shall have his way; but, pray, does he know I am married?

ROWLEY: Yes, and will soon wish you joy.

SIR PETER: What, as we drink health to a friend in consumption! Ah, Oliver will laugh at me. We used to rail at matrimony together, but he has been steady to his text. Well, he must be soon at my house, though—I'll instantly give orders for his reception. But, Master Rowley, don't drop a word that Lady Teazle and I ever disagree.

ROWLEY: By no means.

SIR PETER: For I should never be able to stand Noll's jokes; so I'll have him think, Lord forgive me! that we are a very happy couple.

ROWLEY: I understand you: but then you must be very careful not to differ while he is in the house with you.

SIR PETER: Egad, and so we must—and that's impossible. Ah! Master Rowley, when an old bachelor marries a young wife, he deserves—no—the crime carries its punishment along with it.

ACT II

SCENE I——SIR PETER TEAZLE'S *House.*

[SIR PETER *and* LADY TEAZLE.]

SIR PETER: Lady Teazle, Lady Teazle, I'll not bear it!

LADY TEAZLE: Sir Peter, Sir Peter, you may bear it or not as you please; but I ought to have my own way in everything, and what's more, I will too. What though I was educated in the country, I know very well that women of fashion in London are accountable to nobody after they are married.

SIR PETER: Very well, ma'am, very well; so a husband is to have no influence, no authority?

LADY TEAZLE: Authority! No, to be sure. If you wanted authority over me, you should have adopted me and not married me: I am sure you were old enough.

SIR PETER: Old enough! ay, there it is! Well, well, Lady Teazle, though my life may be made unhappy by your temper, I'll not be ruined by your extravagance!

LADY TEAZLE: My extravagance! I'm sure I'm not more extravagant than a woman of fashion ought to be.

SIR PETER: No, no, madam, you shall throw away no more sums on such unmeaning luxury. 'Slife! to spend as much to furnish your dressing-room with flowers in winter as would suffice to turn the Pantheon into a greenhouse, and give a *fête champêtre* at Christmas.

LADY TEAZLE: And am I to blame, Sir Peter, because flowers are dear in cold weather? You should find fault with the climate, and not with me. For my part, I'm sure I wish it was spring all the year round and that roses grew under our feet!

SIR PETER: Oons! madam—if you had been born to this, I shouldn't wonder at your talking thus; but you forget what your situation was when I married you.

LADY TEAZLE: No, no, I don't; 'twas a very disagreeable one, or I should never have married you.

SIR PETER: Yes, yes, madam, you were then in somewhat a humbler style—the daughter of a plain country squire. Recollect, Lady Teazle, when I saw you first sitting at your tambour in a pretty figured linen gown with a bunch of keys at your side, your hair combed smooth over a roll and your apartment hung round with fruits in worsted of your own working.

LADY TEAZLE: Oh, yes! I remember it very well, and a curious life I led. My daily occupation to inspect the dairy, superintend the poultry, make extracts from the family receipt-book, and comb my aunt Deborah's lapdog.

SIR PETER: Yes, yes, ma'am, 'twas so indeed.

LADY TEAZLE: And then, you know, my evening amusements! To draw patterns for ruffles, which I had not the materials to make up; to play Pope Joan with the Curate; to read a sermon to my aunt; or to be stuck down to an old spinet to strum my father to sleep after a fox-chase.

SIR PETER: I am glad you have so good a memory. Yes, madam, these were the recreations I took you from; but now you must have your coach—*vis-à-vis* —and three powdered footmen before your chair; and, in the summer, a pair of white cats to draw you to Kensington Gardens. No recollection, I suppose, when you were content to ride double, behind the butler, on a docked coach-horse?

LADY TEAZLE: No—I swear I never did that; I deny the butler and the coach-horse.

SIR PETER: This, madam, was your situation; and what have I done for you? I have made you a woman of fashion, of fortune, of rank—in short, I have made you my wife.

LADY TEAZLE: Well, then, and there is but one thing more you can make me to add to the obligation, that is—

SIR PETER: My widow, I suppose?

LADY TEAZLE: Hem! hem!

SIR PETER: I thank you, madam—but don't flatter yourself; for, though your ill-conduct may disturb my peace it shall never break my heart, I promise you. However, I am equally obliged to you for the hint.

LADY TEAZLE: Then why will you endeavor to make yourself so disagreeable to me and thwart me in every little elegant expense?

SIR PETER: 'Slife, madam, I say; had you any of these little elegant expenses when you married me?

LADY TEAZLE: Lud, Sir Peter! would you have me be out of the fashion?

SIR PETER: The fashion, indeed! what had you to do with the fashion before you married me?

LADY TEAZLE: For my part, I should think you would like to have your wife thought a woman of taste.

SIR PETER: Ay—there again—taste! Zounds! madam, you had no taste when you married me!

LADY TEAZLE: That's very true, indeed, Sir Peter! and after having married you, I should never pretend to taste again, I allow. But now, Sir Peter, since we have finished our daily jangle, I presume I may go to my engagement at Lady Sneerwell's?

SIR PETER: Ay, there's another precious circumstance—a charming set of acquaintance you have made there!

LADY TEAZLE: Nay, Sir Peter, they are all people of rank and fortune and remarkably tenacious of reputation.

SIR PETER: Yes, egad, they are tenacious of reputation with a vengeance; for they don't choose anybody should have a character but themselves! Such a crew! Ah! many a wretch has rid on a hurdle who has done less mischief than these utterers of forged tales, coiners of scandal, and clippers of reputation.

LADY TEAZLE: What, would you restrain the freedom of speech?

SIR PETER: Ah! they have made you just as bad as any one of the society.

LADY TEAZLE: Why, I believe I do bear a part with a tolerable grace. But I vow I bear no malice against the people I abuse: when I say an ill natured thing, 'tis out of pure good humor; and I take it for granted they deal exactly in the same manner with me. But, Sir Peter, you know you promised to come to Lady Sneerwell's too.

SIR PETER: Well, well, I'll call in just to look after my own character.

LADY TEAZLE: Then, indeed, you must make haste after me or you'll be too late. So goodbye to ye.

[*Exit* LADY TEAZLE.]

SIR PETER: So—I have gained much by my intended expostulation! Yet with what a charming air she contradicts everything I say, and how pleasantly she shows her contempt for my authority! Well, though I can't make her love me, there is great satisfaction in quarrelling with her; and I think she never appears to such advantage as when she is doing everything in her power to plague me.

SCENE II——LADY SNEERWELL'S House.

[LADY SNEERWELL, MRS. CANDOUR, CRABTREE, SIR BENJAMIN BACKBITE *and* JOSEPH SURFACE.]

LADY SNEERWELL: Nay, positively, we will hear it.

JOSEPH SURFACE: Yes, yes, the epigram, by all means.

SIR BENJAMIN: O plague on't, uncle! 'tis mere nonsense.

CRABTREE: No, no; 'fore gad, very clever for an extempore!

SIR BENJAMIN: But, ladies, you should be acquainted with the circumstance. You must know, that one day last week as Lady Betty Curricle was taking the dust in Hyde Park, in a sort of duodecimo phaeton, she desired me to write some verses on her ponies; upon which, I took out my pocket-book, and in one moment produced the following:—

> Sure never we seen two such beautiful ponies;
> Other horses are clowns, but these macaronies:
> To give them this title I am sure can't be wrong.
> Their legs are so slim, and their tails are so long.

CRABTREE: There, ladies, done in the smack of a whip, and on horseback too.

JOSEPH SURFACE: A very Phœbus mounted—indeed, Sir Benjamin!

SIR BENJAMIN: Oh dear, sir!—trifles—trifles.

[*Enter* LADY TEAZLE *and* MARIA.]

MRS. CANDOUR: I must have a copy.

LADY SNEERWELL: Lady Teazle, I hope we shall see Sir Peter?

LADY TEAZLE: I believe he'll wait on your ladyship presently.

LADY SNEERWELL: Maria, my love, you look grave. Come, you shall sit down to piquet with Mr. Surface.

MARIA: I take very little pleasure in cards—however, I'll do as your ladyship pleases.

LADY TEAZLE: [*aside*] I am surprised Mr. Surface should sit down with her; I thought he would have embraced this opportunity of speaking to me before Sir Peter came.

MRS. CANDOUR: Now, I'll die; but you are so scandalous, I'll forswear your society.

LADY TEAZLE: What's the matter, Mrs. Candour?

MRS. CANDOUR: They'll not allow our friend Miss Vermillion to be handsome.

LADY SNEERWELL: Oh, surely she is a pretty woman.

CRABTREE: I am very glad you think so, ma'am.

MRS. CANDOUR: She has a charming fresh color.

LADY TEAZLE: Yes, when it is fresh put on.

MRS. CANDOUR: Oh, fie! I'll swear her color is natural: I have seen it come and go!

LADY TEAZLE: I dare swear you have, ma'am: it goes off at night and comes again in the morning.

SIR BENJAMIN: True, ma'am, it not only comes and goes; but, what's more, egad, her maid can fetch and carry it!

MRS. CANDOUR: Ha! ha! ha! how I hate to hear you talk so! But surely, now, her sister is, or was, very handsome.

CRABTREE: Who? Mrs. Evergreen? O Lord! she's six-and-fifty if she's an hour!

MRS. CANDOUR: Now positively you wrong her; fifty-two or fifty-three is the utmost—and I don't think she looks more.

SIR BENJAMIN: Ah! there's no judging by her looks, unless one could see her face.

LADY SNEERWELL: Well, well, if Mrs. Evergreen does take some pains to repair the ravages of time, you must allow she effects it with great ingenuity; and surely that's better than the careless manner in which the widow Ochre caulks her wrinkles.

SIR BENJAMIN: Nay, now, Lady Sneerwell, you are severe upon the widow. Come, come, 'tis not that she paints so ill—but, when she has finished her face, she joins it on so badly to her neck, that she looks like a mended statue, in which the connoisseur may see at once that the head's modern, though the trunk's antique!

CRABTREE: Ha! ha! ha! well said, nephew!

MRS. CANDOUR: Ha! ha! ha! Well, you make me laugh; but I vow I hate you for it. What do you think of Miss Simper?

SIR BENJAMIN: Why, she has very pretty teeth.

LADY TEAZLE: Yes; and on that account, when she is neither speaking nor laughing [which very seldom happens], she never absolutely shuts her mouth, but leaves it always on ajar, as it were—thus.
     [*Shows her teeth.*]

MRS. CANDOUR: How can you be so ill natured?

LADY TEAZLE: Nay, I allow even that's better than the pains Mrs. Prim takes to conceal her losses in front. She draws her mouth till it positively resembles the aperture of a poor's-box, and all her words appear to slide out edgewise, as it were—thus: *How do you do, madam? Yes, madam.*

LADY SNEERWELL: Very well, Lady Teazle; I see you can be a little severe.

LADY TEAZLE: In defence of a friend it is but justice. But here comes Sir Peter to spoil our pleasantry.
     [*Enter* SIR PETER.]

SIR PETER: Ladies, your most obedient—[*aside*] Mercy on me, here is the whole set! a character dead at every word, I suppose.

MRS. CANDOUR: I am rejoiced you are come, Sir Peter. They have been so censorious—and Lady Teazle as bad as any one.

SIR PETER: That must be very distressing to you, Mrs. Candour, I dare swear.

MRS. CANDOUR: Oh, they will allow good qualities to nobody; not even good nature to our friend Mrs. Pursy.

LADY TEAZLE: What, the fat dowager who was at Mrs. Quadrille's last night?

MRS. CANDOUR: Nay, her bulk is her misfortune; and, when she takes so much pains to get rid of it, you ought not to reflect on her.

LADY SNEERWELL: That's very true, indeed.

LADY TEAZLE: Yes, I know she almost lives on acids and small whey; laces herself by pulleys; and often, in the hottest noon in summer, you may see her on a little squat pony, with her hair plaited up behind like a drummer's and puffing round the Ring on a full trot.

MRS. CANDOUR: I thank you, Lady Teazle, for defending her.

SIR PETER: Yes, a good defence, truly.

MRS. CANDOUR: Truly, Lady Teazle is as censorious as Miss Sallow.

CRABTREE: Yes, and she is a curious being to pretend to be censorious—an awkward gawky, without any one good point under heaven.

MRS. CANDOUR: Positively you shall not be so very severe. Miss Sallow is a near relation of mine by marriage, and, as for her person, great allowance is to be made; for, let me tell you, a woman labors under many disadvantages who tries to pass for a girl of six-and-thirty.

LADY SNEERWELL: Though, surely, she is handsome still—and for the weakness in her eyes, considering how much she reads by candlelight, it is not to be wondered at.

MRS. CANDOUR: True; and then as to her manner, upon my word, I think it is particularly graceful, considering she never had the least education; for you know her mother was a Welsh milliner, and her father a sugar-baker at Bristol.

SIR BENJAMIN: Ah! you are both of you too good natured!

SIR PETER: [aside] Yes, damned good natured! This their own relation! mercy on me!

MRS. CANDOUR: For my part, I own I cannot bear to hear a friend ill spoken of.

SIR PETER: No, to be sure.

SIR BENJAMIN: Oh! you are of a moral turn. Mrs. Candour and I can sit for an hour and hear Lady Stucco talk sentiment.

LADY TEAZLE: Nay, I vow Lady Stucco is very well with the dessert after dinner; for she's just like the French fruit one cracks for mottoes—made up of paint and proverb.

MRS. CANDOUR: Well, I will never join in ridiculing a friend; and so I constantly tell my cousin Ogle, and you all know what pretensions she has to be critical on beauty.

CRABTREE: Oh, to be sure! she has herself the oddest countenance that ever was seen; 'tis a collection of features from all the different countries of the globe.

SIR BENJAMIN: So she has, indeed—an Irish front—

CRABTREE: Caledonian locks—

SIR BENJAMIN: Dutch nose—

CRABTREE: Austrian lips—

SIR BENJAMIN: Complexion of a Spaniard—

CRABTREE: And teeth *à la Chinoise*—

SIR BENJAMIN: In short, her face resembles a *table d'hôte* at Spa—where no two guests are of a nation—

CRABTREE: Or a congress at the close of a general war—wherein all the members, even to her eyes, appear to have a different interest, and her nose and chin are the only parties likely to join issue.

MRS. CANDOUR: Ha! ha! ha!

SIR PETER: [*aside*] Mercy on my life!—a person they dine with twice a week!

LADY SNEERWELL: Go—go—you are a couple of provoking toads.

MRS. CANDOUR: Nay, but I vow you shall not carry the laugh off so—for give me leave to say, that Mrs. Ogle—

SIR PETER: Madam, madam, I beg your pardon—there's no stopping these good gentlemen's tongues. But when I tell you, Mrs. Candour, that the lady they are abusing is a particular friend of mine, I hope you'll not take her part.

LADY SNEERWELL: Ha! ha! ha! well said, Sir Peter! but you are a cruel creature —too phlegmatic yourself for a jest, and too peevish to allow wit in others.

SIR PETER: Ah, madam, true wit is more nearly allied to good nature than your ladyship is aware of.

LADY TEAZLE: True, Sir Peter: I believe they are so near akin that they can never be united.

SIR BENJAMIN: Or rather, madam, I suppose them man and wife because one seldom sees them together.

LADY TEAZLE: But Sir Peter is such an enemy to scandal, I believe he would have it put down by Parliament.

SIR PETER: 'Fore heaven, madam, if they were to consider the sporting with reputation of as much importance as poaching on manors, and pass an act for the preservation of fame, I believe many would thank them for the bill.

LADY SNEERWELL: O Lud! Sir Peter; would you deprive us of our privileges?

SIR PETER: Ay, madam; and then no person should be permitted to kill characters and run down reputations, but qualified old maids and disappointed widows.

LADY SNEERWELL: Go, you monster!

MRS. CANDOUR: But, surely, you would not be quite so severe on those who only report what they hear?

SIR PETER: Yes, madam, I would have law merchant for them too; and in all cases of slander currency, whenever the drawer of the lie was not to be found, the injured parties should have a right to come on any of the indorsers.

CRABTREE: Well, for my part, I believe there never was a scandalous tale without some foundation.

LADY SNEERWELL: Come, ladies, shall we sit down to cards in the next room?

[*Enter* SERVANT, *who whispers to* SIR PETER.]

SIR PETER: I'll be with them directly.

[*Exit* SERVANT.]

[*aside*] I'll get away unperceived.

LADY SNEERWELL: Sir Peter, you are not going to leave us?

SIR PETER: Your ladyships must excuse me: I'm called away by particular business. But I leave my character behind me.

[*Exit* SIR PETER.]

SIR BENJAMIN: Well—certainly, Lady Teazle, that lord of yours is a strange being. I could tell you some stories of him would make you laugh heartily if he were not your husband.

LADY TEAZLE: Oh, pray don't mind that; come, do let's hear them.

[*Exeunt all but* JOSEPH SURFACE *and* MARIA.]

JOSEPH SURFACE: Maria, I see you have no satisfaction in this society.

MARIA: How is it possible I should? If to raise malicious smiles at the infirmities or misfortunes of those who have never injured us be the province of wit or humor, Heaven grant me a double portion of dullness!

JOSEPH SURFACE: Yet they appear more ill natured than they are; they have no malice at heart.

MARIA: Then is their conduct still more contemptible; for in my opinion, nothing could excuse the intemperance of their tongues but a natural and uncontrollable bitterness of mind.

JOSEPH SURFACE: Undoubtedly, madam; and it has always been a sentiment of mine to propagate a malicious truth wantonly is more despicable than to falsify from revenge. But can you, Maria, feel thus for others, and be unkind to me alone? Is hope to be denied the tenderest passion?

MARIA: Why will you distress me by renewing this subject?

JOSEPH SURFACE: Ah, Maria! you would not treat me thus, and oppose your guardian, Sir Peter's will, but that I see that profligate Charles is still a favored rival.

MARIA: Ungenerously urged! But whatever my sentiments are for that unfortunate young man, be assured I shall not feel more bound to give him up, because his distresses have lost him the regard even of a brother.

JOSEPH SURFACE: Nay, but, Maria, do not leave me with a frown: by all that's honest, I swear—

    [*He kneels. Enter* LADY TEAZLE.]

    [*aside*] Gad's life, here's Lady Teasle.—[*aloud to* MARIA] You must not— no, you shall not—for, though I have the greatest regard for Lady Teazle—

MARIA: Lady Teazle!

JOSEPH SURFACE: Yet were Sir Peter to suspect—

LADY TEAZLE: [*coming forward*] What is this, pray? Do you take her for me?— Child, you are wanted in the next room.—

    [*Exit* MARIA.]

    What is all this, pray?

JOSEPH SURFACE: Oh, the most unlucky circumstance in nature! Maria has somehow suspected the tender concern I have for your happiness, and threatened to acquaint Sir Peter with her suspicions, and I was just endeavoring to reason with her when you came in.

LADY TEAZLE: Indeed! but you seemed to adopt a very tender mode of reasoning —do you usually argue on your knees?

JOSEPH SURFACE: Oh, she's a child and I thought a little bombast—but, Lady Teazle, when are you to give me your judgment on my library, as you promised?

LADY TEAZLE: No, no; I begin to think it would be imprudent, and you know I admit you as a lover no farther than fashion requires.

JOSEPH SURFACE: True—a mere Platonic cicisbeo, what every wife is entitled to.

LADY TEAZLE: Certainly, one must not be out of the fashion. However, I have so many of my country prejudices left that, though Sir Peter's ill humor may vex me ever so, it never shall provoke me to—

JOSEPH SURFACE: The only revenge in your power. Well, I applaud your moderation.

LADY TEAZLE: Go—you are an insinuating wretch! But we shall be missed—let us join the company.

JOSEPH SURFACE: But we had best not return together.

LADY TEAZLE: Well, don't stay; for Maria shan't come to hear any more of your reasoning, I promise you. [*Exit.*]

JOSEPH SURFACE: A curious dilemma, truly, my politics have run me into! I wanted, at first, only to ingratiate myself with Lady Teazle, that she might not be my enemy with Maria; and I have, I don't know how, become her serious lover. Sincerely I begin to wish I had never made such a point of gaining so very good a character; for it has led me into so many cursed rogueries that I doubt I shall be exposed at last.

SCENE III——SIR PETER TEAZLE'S *House.*

[SIR OLIVER SURFACE *and* ROWLEY.]

SIR OLIVER: Ha! ha! ha! so my old friend is married, hey?—a young wife out of the country. Ha! ha! ha! that he should have stood bluff to old bachelor so long and sink into a husband at last!

ROWLEY: But you must not rally him on the subject, Sir Oliver; 'tis a tender point, I assure you, though he has been married only seven months.

SIR OLIVER: Then he has been just half a year on the stool of repentance!— Poor Peter! But you say he has entirely given up Charles—never sees him, hey?

ROWLEY: His prejudice against him is astonishing, and I am sure greatly increased by a jealousy of him with Lady Teazle, which he has industriously been led into by a scandalous society in the neighborhood, who have contributed not a little to Charles's ill name. Whereas the truth is, I believe, if the lady is partial to either of them, his brother is the favorite.

SIR OLIVER: Ay, I know there are a set of malicious, prating, prudent gossips, both male and female, who murder characters to kill time, and will rob a young fellow of his good name before he has years to know the value of it. But I am not to be prejudiced against my nephew by such, I promise you! No, no; if Charles has done nothing false or mean, I shall compound for his extravagance.

ROWLEY: Then, my life on't, you will reclaim him. Ah, sir, it gives me new life to find that your heart is not turned against him, and that the son of my good old master has one friend, however, left.

SIR OLIVER: What! shall I forget, Master Rowley, when I was at his years myself? Egad, my brother and I were neither of us very prudent youths; and yet, I believe, you have not seen many better men than your old master was?

ROWLEY: Sir, 'tis this reflection gives me assurance that Charles may yet be a credit to his family. But here comes Sir Peter.

SIR OLIVER: Egad, so he does! Mercy on me, he's greatly altered, and seems to have a settled married look! One may read *husband* in his face at this distance! [*Enter* SIR PETER.]

SIR PETER: Ha! Sir Oliver—my old friend! Welcome to England a thousand times!

SIR OLIVER: Thank you, thank you, Sir Peter! and i'faith I am glad to find you well, believe me!

SIR PETER: Oh! 'tis a long time since we met—fifteen years, I doubt, Sir Oliver, and many a cross accident in the time.

SIR OLIVER: Ay, I have had my share. But, what! I find you are married, hey, my old boy? Well, well, it can't be helped; and so—I wish you joy with all my heart!

SIR PETER: Thank you, thank you, Sir Oliver.—Yes, I have entered into—the happy state; but we'll not talk of that now.

SIR OLIVER: True, true, Sir Peter; old friends should not begin on grievances at first meeting. No, no, no.

ROWLEY: [*aside to* SIR OLIVER] Take care, pray, sir.

SIR OLIVER: Well, so one of my nephews is a wild rogue, hey?

SIR PETER: Wild! Ah! my old friend. I grieve for your disappointment there; he's a lost young man, indeed. However, his brother will make you amends; Joseph is, indeed, what a youth should be—everyone in the world speaks well of him.

SIR OLIVER: I am sorry to hear it; he has too good a character to be an honest fellow. Everyone speaks well of him! Psha! then he has bowed as low to knaves and fools as to the honest dignity of genius and virtue.

SIR PETER: What, Sir Oliver! do you blame him for not making enemies?

SIR OLIVER: Yes, if he has merit enough to deserve them.

SIR PETER: Well, well—you'll be convinced when you know him. 'Tis edification to hear him converse; he professes the noblest sentiments.

SIR OLIVER: Oh, plague of his sentiments! If he salutes me with a scrap of morality in his mouth. I shall be sick directly. But, however, don't mistake me, Sir Peter; I don't mean to defend Charles's errors: but, before I form my judgment of either of them, I intend to make a trial of their hearts; and my friend Rowley and I have planned something for the purpose.

ROWLEY: And Sir Peter shall own for once he has been mistaken.

SIR PETER: Oh, my life on Joseph's honor!

SIR OLIVER: Well—come, give us a bottle of good wine, and we'll drink the lad's health and tell you our scheme.

SIR PETER: *Allons*, then!

SIR OLIVER: And don't, Sir Peter, be so severe against your old friend's son. Odds my life! I am not sorry that he has run out of the course a little. For my part, I hate to see prudence clinging to the green suckers of youth; 'tis like ivy round a sapling, and spoils the growth of the tree.

ACT III

SCENE I——SIR PETER TEAZLE'S *House.*

[SIR PETER TEAZLE, SIR OLIVER SURFACE, *and* ROWLEY.]

SIR PETER: Well, then, we will see this fellow first and have our wine afterwards. But how is this, Master Rowley? I don't see the jet of your scheme.

ROWLEY: Why, sir, this Mr. Stanley, whom I was speaking of, is nearly related to them by their mother. He was once a merchant in Dublin, but has been ruined by a series of undeserved misfortunes. He has applied, by letter, since his confinement, both to Mr. Surface and Charles. From the former he has received nothing but evasive promises of future service, while Charles has done all that his extravagance has left him power to do; and he is, at this time, endeavoring to raise a sum of money, part of which, in the midst of his own distresses, I know he intends for the service of poor Stanley.

SIR OLIVER: Ah, he is my brother's son.

SIR PETER: Well, but how is Sir Oliver personally to—

ROWLEY: Why, sir. I will inform Charles and his brother that Stanley has obtained permission to apply personally to his friends; and, as they have neither of them ever seen him, let Sir Oliver assume his character, and he will have a fair opportunity of judging, at least, of the benevolence of their dispositions; and believe me, sir, you will find in the youngest brother one who, in the midst of folly and dissipation, has still, as our immortal bard expresses it,—

> a tear for pity, and a hand
> Open as day, for melting charity.

SIR PETER: Psha! What signifies his having an open hand or purse either, when he has nothing left to give? Well, well, make the trial, if you please. But where is the fellow whom you brought for Sir Oliver to examine relative to Charles's affairs?

ROWLEY: Below, waiting his commands, and no one can give him better intelligence.—This, Sir Oliver, is a friendly Jew, who, to do him justice, has done everything in his power to bring your nephew to a proper sense of his extravagance.

SIR PETER: Pray let us have him in.

ROWLEY: [*calls to* SERVANT] Desire Mr. Moses to walk upstairs.

SIR PETER: But, pray, why should you suppose he will speak the truth?

ROWLEY: Oh, I have convinced him that he has no chance of recovering certain sums advanced to Charles but through the bounty of Sir Oliver, who he knows is arrived; so that you may depend on his fidelity to his own interests. I have also another evidence in my power, one Snake, whom I have detected in a matter little short of forgery and shall shortly produce to remove some of your prejudices, Sir Peter, relative to Charles and Lady Teazle.

SIR PETER: I have heard too much on that subject.

ROWLEY: Here comes the honest Israelite.

[*Enter* MOSES.]

—This is Sir Oliver.

SIR OLIVER: Sir, I understand you have lately had great dealings with my nephew Charles.

MOSES: Yes, Sir Oliver, I have done all I could for him; but he was ruined before he came to me for assistance.

SIR OLIVER: That was unlucky, truly; for you have had no opportunity of showing your talents.

MOSES: None at all; I hadn't the pleasure of knowing his distresses till he was some thousands worse than nothing.

SIR OLIVER: Unfortunate, indeed! But I suppose you have done all in your power for him, honest Moses?

MOSES: Yes, he knows that. This very evening I was to have brought him a gentleman from the city, who does not know him, and will, I believe, advance him some money.

SIR PETER: What, one Charles has never had money from before?

MOSES: Yes, Mr. Premium, of Crutched Friars, formerly a broker.

SIR PETER: Egad, Sir Oliver, a thought strikes me!—Charles, you say, does not know Mr. Premium?

MOSES: Not at all.

SIR PETER: Now then, Sir Oliver, you may have a better opportunity of satisfying yourself than by an old romancing tale of a poor relation. Go with my friend Moses and represent Premium, and then, I'll answer for it, you'll see your nephew in all his glory.

SIR OLIVER: Egad, I like this idea better than the other and I may visit Joseph afterwards as old Stanley.

SIR PETER: True—so you may.

ROWLEY: Well, this is taking Charles rather at a disadvantage, to be sure. However, Moses, you understand Sir Peter, and will be faithful.

MOSES: You may depend upon me.—This is near the time I was to have gone.

SIR OLIVER: I'll accompany you as soon as you please, Moses—But hold! I have forgot one thing—how the plague shall I be able to pass for a Jew?

MOSES: There's no need—the principal is Christian.

SIR OLIVER: Is he? I'm very sorry to hear it. But, then again, an't I rather too smartly dressed to look like a money-lender?

SIR PETER: Not at all; 'twould not be out of character, if you went in your carriage—would it, Moses?

MOSES: Not in the least.

SIR OLIVER: Well, but how must I talk? there's certainly some cant of usury and mode of treating that I ought to know.

SIR PETER: Oh, there's not much to learn. The great point, as I take it, is to be exorbitant enough in your demands. Hey, Moses?

MOSES: Yes, that's a very great point.

SIR OLIVER: I'll answer for't I'll not be wanting in that. I'll ask him eight or ten per cent on the loan, at least.

MOSES: If you ask him no more than that, you'll be discovered immediately.

SIR OLIVER: Hey! what, the plague! how much then?

MOSES: That depends upon the circumstances. If he appears not very anxious for the supply, you should require only forty or fifty per cent; but if you find him in great distress, and want the moneys very bad, you may ask double.

SIR PETER: A good honest trade you're learning, Sir Oliver!

SIR OLIVER: Truly I think so—and not unprofitable.

MOSES: Then, you know, you haven't the moneys yourself, but are forced to borrow them for him of a friend.

SIR OLIVER: Oh! I borrow it of a friend, do I?

MOSES: And your friend is an unconscionable dog: but you can't help that.

SIR OLIVER: My friend an unconscionable dog, is he?

MOSES: Yes, and he himself has not the moneys by him, but is forced to sell stocks at a great loss.

SIR OLIVER: He is forced to sell stocks at a great loss, is he? Well, that's very kind of him.

SIR PETER: I'faith, Sir Oliver—Mr. Premium, I mean—you'll soon be master of the trade. But, Moses! would not you have him run out a little against the Annuity Bill? That would be in character, I should think.

MOSES: Very much.

ROWLEY: And lament that a young man now must be at years of discretion before he is suffered to ruin himself?

MOSES: Ay, great pity!

SIR PETER: And abuse the public for allowing merit to an act whose only object is to snatch misfortune and imprudence from the rapacious grip of usury, and give the minor a chance of inheriting his estate without being undone by coming into possession.

SIR OLIVER: So, so—Moses shall give me further instructions as we go together.

SIR PETER: You will not have much time, for your nephew lives hard by.

SIR OLIVER: Oh, never fear! my tutor appears so able, that though Charles lived in the next street, it must be my own fault if I am not a complete rogue before I turn the corner.

[*Exit with* MOSES.]

SIR PETER: So, now, I think Sir Oliver will be convinced; you are partial, Rowley, and would have prepared Charles for the other plot.

ROWLEY: No, upon my word, Sir Peter.

SIR PETER: Well, go bring me this Snake, and I'll hear what he has to say presently. I see Maria and want to speak with her.

[*Exit* ROWLEY.]

I should be glad to be convinced my suspicions of Lady Teazle and Charles were unjust. I have never yet opened my mind on this subject to my friend Joseph—I am determined I will do it—he will give me his opinion sincerely.

[*Enter* MARIA.]

So, child, has Mr. Surface returned with you?

MARIA: No, sir; he was engaged.

SIR PETER: Well, Maria, do you not reflect, the more you converse with that amiable young man, what return his partiality for you deserves?

MARIA: Indeed, Sir Peter, your frequent importunity on this subject distresses me extremely—you compel me to declare, that I know no man who has ever paid me a particular attention whom I would not prefer to Mr. Surface.

SIR PETER: So—here's perverseness! No, no, Maria, 'tis Charles only whom you would prefer. 'Tis evident his vices and follies have won your heart.

MARIA: This is unkind sir. You know I have obeyed you in neither seeing nor corresponding with him: I have heard enough to convince me that he is unworthy my regard. Yet I cannot think it culpable, if, while my understanding severely condemns his vices, my heart suggests some pity for his distresses.

SIR PETER: Well, well, pity him as much as you please; but give your heart and hand to a worthier object.

MARIA: Never to his brother!

SIR PETER: Go, perverse and obstinate! But take care, madam; you have never yet known what the authority of a guardian is. Don't compel me to inform you of it.

MARIA: I can only say, you shall not have just reason. 'Tis true, by my father's will I am for a short period bound to regard you as his substitute; but must cease to think you so, when you would compel me to be miserable.

[*Exit* MARIA.]

SIR PETER: Was ever man so crossed as I am, everything conspiring to fret me! I had not been involved in matrimony a fortnight, before her father, a hale and hearty man, died, on purpose, I believe, for the pleasure of plaguing me with the care of his daughter.

[LADY TEAZLE *sings without.*]

But here comes my helpmate! She appears in great good humor. How happy I should be if I could tease her into loving me, though but a little!

[*Enter* LADY TEAZLE.]

LADY TEAZLE: Lud! Sir Peter, I hope you haven't been quarrelling with Maria? It is not using me well to be ill humored when I am not by.

SIR PETER: Ah, Lady Teazle, you might have the power to make me good humored at all times.

LADY TEAZLE: I am sure I wish I had; for I want you to be in a charming sweet temper at this moment. Do be good humored now, and let me have two hundred pounds, will you?

SIR PETER: Two hundred pounds; what, an't I to be in a good humor without paying for it! But speak to me thus, and i'faith there's nothing I could refuse you. You shall have it; but seal me a bond for the repayment.

LADY TEAZLE: Oh, no—there—my note of hand will do as well. [*Offering her hand.*]

SIR PETER: And you shall no longer reproach me with not giving you an independent settlement. I mean shortly to surprise you; but shall we always live thus, hey?

LADY TEAZLE: If you please; I'm sure I don't care how soon we leave off quarrelling, provided you'll own you were tired first.

SIR PETER: Well—then let our future contest be, who shall be most obliging.

LADY TEAZLE: I assure you, Sir Peter, good nature becomes you. You look now as you did before we were married, when you used to walk with me under the elms, and tell me stories of what a gallant you were in your youth, and chuck me under the chin, you would; and ask me if I thought I could love an old fellow who would deny me nothing—didn't you?

SIR PETER: Yes, yes, and you were as kind and attentive—

LADY TEAZLE: Ay, so I was, and would always take your part, when my acquaintance used to abuse you, and turn you into ridicule.

SIR PETER: Indeed!

LADY TEAZLE: Ay, and when my cousin Sophy has called you a stiff, peevish old bachelor, and laughed at me for thinking of marrying one who might be my father, I have always defended you, and said, I didn't think you so ugly by any means, and that I dared say you'd make a very good sort of a husband.

SIR PETER: And you prophesied right; and we shall now be the happiest couple—

LADY TEAZLE: And never differ again?

SIR PETER: No, never—though at the same time, indeed, my dear lady Teazle, you must watch your temper very seriously; for in all our little quarrels, my dear, if you recollect, my love, you always began first.

LADY TEAZLE: I beg your pardon, my dear Sir Peter: indeed, you always gave the provocation.

SIR PETER: Now, see, my angel! take care—contradicting isn't the way to keep friends.

LADY TEAZLE: Then, don't you begin it, my love!

SIR PETER: There now! you—you are going on. You don't perceive, my life, that you are just doing the very thing which you know always makes me angry.

LADY TEAZLE: Nay, you know if you will be angry without any reason, my dear—

SIR PETER: There! now you want to quarrel again.

LADY TEAZLE: No, I'm sure I don't; but, if you will be so peevish—

SIR PETER: There now! who begins first?

LADY TEAZLE: Why, you to be sure. I said nothing—but there's no bearing your temper.

SIR PETER: No, no madam: the fault's in your own temper.

LADY TEAZLE: Ay, you are just what my cousin Sophy said you would be.

SIR PETER: Your cousin Sophy is a forward, impertinent gypsy.

LADY TEAZLE: You are a great bear, I am sure, to abuse my relations.

SIR PETER: Now may all the plagues of marriage be doubled on me if ever I try to be friends with you any more!

LADY TEAZLE: So much the better.

SIR PETER: No, no, madam. 'Tis evident you never cared a pin for me, and I was a madman to marry you—a pert, rural coquette, that had refused half the honest squires in the neighborhood!

LADY TEAZLE: And I am sure I was a fool to marry you—an old dangling bachelor, who was single at fifty, only because he never could meet with any one who would have him.

SIR PETER: Ay, ay, madam; but you were pleased enough to listen to me: you never had such an offer before.

LADY TEAZLE: No! didn't I refuse Sir Tivy Terrier, who everybody said would have been a better match? for his estate is just as good as yours, and he has broke his neck since we have been married.

SIR PETER: I have done with you, madam! You are an unfeeling, ungrateful— but there's an end of everything. I believe you capable of everything that is bad. Yes, madam, I now believe the reports relative to you and Charles, madam. Yes, madam, you and Charles are, not without grounds—

LADY TEAZLE: Take care, Sir Peter! you had better not insinuate any such thing! I'll not be suspected without cause, I promise you.

SIR PETER: Very well, madam! very well! a separate maintenance as soon as you please. Yes, madam, or a divorce! I'll make an example of myself for the benefit of all old bachelors. Let us separate, madam.

LADY TEAZLE: Agreed! agreed! And now, my dear Sir Peter, we are of a mind once more, we may be the happiest couple, and never differ again, you know: ha! ha! ha! Well, you are going to be in a passion, I see, and I shall only interrupt you—so, bye! Bye!

[*Exit* LADY TEAZLE.]

SIR PETER: Plagues and tortures! can't I make her angry either! Oh, I am the most miserable fellow! But I'll not bear her presuming to keep her temper: no! she may break my heart, but she shan't keep her temper.

SCENE II——CHARLES SURFACE'S *House.*

[TRIP, MOSES, *and* SIR OLIVER SURFACE.]

TRIP: Here, Master Moses! if you'll stay a moment; I'll try whether—what's the gentleman's name?

SIR OLIVER: [*aside to* MOSES] Mr. Moses, what is my name?

MOSES: Mr. Premium.

TRIP: Premium—very well.

[*Exit, taking snuff.*]

SIR OLIVER: To judge by the servants, one wouldn't believe the master was ruined. But what!—sure, this was my brother's house?

MOSES: Yes, sir; Mr. Charles bought it of Mr. Joseph, with the furniture, pictures, etc., just as the old gentleman left it. Sir Peter thought it a piece of extravagance in him.

SIR OLIVER: In my mind, the other's economy in selling it to him was more reprehensible by half.

[*Re-enter* TRIP.]

TRIP: My master says you must wait, gentlemen: he has company, and can't speak with you yet.

SIR OLIVER: If he knew who it was wanted to see him, perhaps he would not send a message?

TRIP: Yes, yes, sir; he knows you are here—I did not forget little Premium: no, no, no.

SIR OLIVER: Very well; and I pray, sir, what may be your name?

TRIP: Trip, sir; my name is Trip, at your service.

SIR OLIVER: Well, then, Mr. Trip, you have a pleasant sort of place here, I guess?

TRIP: Why, yes—here are three or four of us to pass our time agreeably enough; but then our wages are sometimes a little in arrear—and not very great either—but fifty pounds a year, and find our own bags and bouquets.

SIR OLIVER: [*aside*] Bags and bouquets! halters and bastinadoes!

TRIP: And *à propos*, Moses, have you been able to get me that little bill dis-
counted?

SIR OLIVER: [*aside*] Wants to raise money, too!—mercy on me! Has his distresses too, I warrant, like a lord, and affects creditors and duns.

MOSES: 'Twas not to be done, indeed, Mr. Trip.

TRIP: Good lack, you surprise me! My friend Brush has indorsed it, and I
thought when he put his name at the back of a bill 'twas the same as cash.

MOSES: No, 'twouldn't do.

TRIP: A small sum—but twenty pounds. Hark'ee, Moses, do you think you
couldn't get it me by way of annuity?

SIR OLIVER: [*aside*] An annuity! ha! ha! a footman raise money by way of
annuity. Well done, luxury, egad!

MOSES: Well, but you must insure your place.

TRIP: Oh, with all my heart! I'll insure my place and my life too, if you please.

SIR OLIVER: [*aside*] It's more than I would your neck.

MOSES: But is there nothing you could deposit?

TRIP: Why, nothing capital of my master's wardrobe has dropped lately; but
I could give you a mortgage on some of his winter clothes, with equity of
redemption before November—or you shall have the reversion of the
French velvet, or a post-obit on the blue and silver. These, I should think,
Moses, with a few pair of point ruffles, as a collateral security—hey, my
little fellow?

MOSES: Well, well.

[*Bell rings.*]

TRIP: Egad. I heard the bell! I believe, gentlemen, I can now introduce you.
Don't forget the annuity, little Moses! This way gentlemen, I'll insure my
place, you know.

SIR OLIVER: [*aside*] If the man be a shadow of the master, this is the temple
of dissipation indeed!

[*Exeunt.*]

SCENE III——*Another room.*

[CHARLES SURFACE, CARELESS, SIR HARRY BUMPER, *and Others, at a
table with wine, etc.*]

CHARLES SURFACE: 'Fore heaven, 'tis true! there's the great degeneracy of the
age. Many of our acquaintance have taste, spirit, and politeness; but
plague on't they won't drink.

CARELESS: It is so, indeed, Charles! they give in to all the substantial luxuries
of the table, and abstain from nothing but wine and wit. Oh, certainly
society suffers by it intolerably! for now, instead of the social spirit of
raillery that used to mantle over a glass of bright Burgundy, their conversation is become just like the Spa-water they drink, which has all the
pertness and flatulency of champagne, without its spirit or flavor.

FIRST GENTLEMAN: But what are they to do who love play better than wine?

CARELESS: True! there's Sir Harry diets himself for gaming, and is now under
a hazard regimen.

CHARLES SURFACE: Then he'll have the worst of it. What! you wouldn't train a horse for the course by keeping him from corn? For my part, egad, I'm never so successful as when I am a little merry. Let me throw on a bottle of champagne and I never lose—at least I never feel my losses, which is exactly the same thing.

SECOND GENTLEMAN: Ay, that I believe.

CHARLES SURFACE: And then, what man can pretend to be a believer in love who is an abjurer of wine? 'Tis the test by which the lover knows his own heart. Fill a dozen bumpers to a dozen beauties, and she that floats at the top is the maid that has bewitched you.

CARELESS: Now then, Charles, be honest, and give us your real favorite.

CHARLES SURFACE: Why, I have withheld her only in compassion to you. If I toast her, you must give her a round of her peers, which is impossible— on earth.

CARELESS: Oh, then we'll find some canonized vestals or heathen goddesses that will do, I warrant!

CHARLES SURFACE: Here then, bumpers, you rogues! bumpers! Maria! Maria—

SIR HARRY: Maria who?

CHARLES SURFACE: Oh, damn the surname—'tis too formal to be registered in Love's calendar—but now, Sir Harry, beware, we must have beauty super-lative.

CARELESS: Nay, never study, Sir Harry: we'll stand to the toast, though your mistress should want an eye, and you know you have a song will excuse you.

SIR HARRY: Egad, so I have! and I'll give him the song instead of the lady. [*Sings.*]

Here's to the maiden of bashful fifteen;
 Here's to the widow of fifty;
Here's to the flaunting extravagant quean,
 And here's to the housewife that's thrifty.

Chorus Let the toast pass,
   Drink to the lass,
I'll warrant she'll prove an excuse for a glass!

Here's to the charmer whose dimples we prize;
 Now to the maid who has none, sir;
Here's to the girl with a pair of blue eyes,
 And here's to the nymph with but one, sir.

Chorus Let the toast pass,
   Drink to the lass,
I'll warrant she'll prove an excuse for a glass.

Here's to the maid with bosom of snow;
 Now to her that's as brown as a berry;
Here's to the wife with a face full of woe,
 And now to the damsel that's merry.

Chorus   Let the toast pass,
         Drink to the lass,
I'll warrant she'll prove an excuse for a glass.

For let 'em be clumsy, or let 'em be slim,
   Young or ancient, I care not a feather;
So fill a pint bumper quite up to the brim,
   And let us e'en toast them together.

Chorus   Let the toast pass,
         Drink to the lass,
I'll warrant she'll prove an excuse for a glass.

ALL: Bravo! Bravo!
      [*Enter* TRIP, *and whispers to* CHARLES SURFACE.]
CHARLES SURFACE: Gentlemen, you must excuse me a little. Careless, take the chair, will you?
CARELESS: Nay, prithee, Charles, what now? This is one of your peerless beauties, I suppose, has dropped in by chance?
CHARLES SURFACE: No, faith! To tell you the truth, 'tis a Jew and a broker, who are come by appointment.
CARELESS: Oh, damn it! let's have the Jew in.
FIRST GENTLEMAN: Ay, and the broker too, by all means.
SECOND GENTLEMAN: Yes, yes, the Jew, and the broker!
CHARLES SURFACE: Egad, with all my heart!— Trip, bid the gentlemen walk in.
      [*Exit* TRIP.]
Though there's one of them a stranger I can tell you.
CARELESS: Charles, let us give them some generous Burgundy and perhaps they'll grow conscientious.
CHARLES SURFACE: Oh, hang 'em, no! wine does but draw forth a man's natural qualities; and to make them drink would only be to whet their knavery.
      [*Enter* TRIP, *with* SIR OLIVER SURFACE *and* MOSES.]
CHARLES SURFACE: So, honest Moses; walk in, pray, Mr. Premium—that's the gentleman's name, isn't it, Moses?
MOSES: Yes, sir.
CHARLES SURFACE: Set chairs, Trip.—Sit down, Mr. Premium. Glasses, Trip.— Sit down, Moses.—Come, Mr. Premium, I'll give you a sentiment; here's *Success to usury!*—Moses, fill the gentleman a bumper.
MOSES: Success to usury! [*Drinks.*]
CARELESS: Right, Moses—usury is prudence and industry, and deserves to succeed.
SIR OLIVER: Then here's—all the success it deserves! [*Drinks.*]
CARELESS: No, no, that won't do! Mr. Premium, you have demurred at the toast, and must drink it in a pint bumper.
FIRST GENTLEMAN: A pint bumper, at least!
MOSES: Oh, pray, sir, consider—Mr. Premium's a gentleman.

CARELESS: And therefore loves good wine.

SECOND GENTLEMAN: Give Moses a quart glass—this is mutiny, and a high contempt for the chair.

CARELESS: Here now for't! I'll see justice done, to the last drop of my bottle.

SIR OLIVER: Nay, pray, gentlemen—I did not expect this usage.

CHARLES SURFACE: No, hang it, you shan't; Mr. Premium's a stranger.

SIR OLIVER: [*aside*] Odd! I wish I was well out of their company.

CARELESS: Plague on 'em then! if they won't drink, we'll not sit down with them. Come, Harry, the dice are in the next room.—Charles, you'll join us when you have finished your business with the gentlemen?

CHARLES SURFACE: I will! I will!

[*Exeunt* GENTLEMEN.]

Careless!

CARELESS: [*returning*] Well?

CHARLES SURFACE: Perhaps I may want you.

CARELESS: Oh, you know I am always ready: word, note, or bond. 'tis all the same to me. [*Exit.*]

MOSES: Sir, this is Mr. Premium, a gentleman of the strictest honor and secrecy; and always performs what he undertakes. Mr. Premium, this is—

CHARLES SURFACE: Psha! have done. Sir, my friend Moses is a very honest fellow, but a little slow at expression: he'll be an hour giving us our titles. Mr. Premium, the plain state of the matter is this: I am an extravagant young fellow who wants to borrow money; you I take to be a prudent old fellow, who has got money to lend. I am blockhead enough to give fifty per cent sooner than not have it! and you, I presume, are rogue enough to take a hundred if you can get it. Now, sir, you see we are acquainted at once, and may proceed to business without further ceremony.

SIR OLIVER: Exceeding frank, upon my word. I see, sir, you are not a man of many compliments.

CHARLES SURFACE: Oh, no, sir! plain dealing in business I always think best.

SIR OLIVER: Sir, I like you the better for it. However, you are mistaken in one thing. I have no money to lend, but I believe I could procure some of a friend; but then he's an unconscionable dog. Isn't he, Moses? And must sell stock to accommodate you. Mustn't he, Moses?

MOSES: Yes, indeed! You know I always speak the truth, and scorn to tell a lie!

CHARLES SURFACE: Right. People that speak truth generally do. But these are trifles, Mr. Premium. What! I know money isn't to be bought without paying for't!

SIR OLIVER: Well, but what security could you give? You have no land, I suppose?

CHARLES SURFACE: Not a mole-hill, nor a twig, but what's in the bough-pots out of the window!

SIR OLIVER: Nor any stock, I presume?

CHARLES SURFACE: Nothing but live stock—and that's only a few pointers and ponies. But pray, Mr. Premium, are you acquainted at all with any of my connections?

SIR OLIVER: Why, to say the truth, I am.

CHARLES SURFACE: Then you must know that I have a devilish rich uncle in the East Indies, Sir Oliver Surface, from whom I have the greatest expectations?

SIR OLIVER: That you have a wealthy uncle, I have heard; but how your expectations will turn out is more, I believe, than you can tell.

CHARLES SURFACE: Oh, no!—there can be no doubt. They tell me I'm a prodigious favorite, and that he talks of leaving me everything.

SIR OLIVER: Indeed! this is the first I've heard of it.

CHARLES SURFACE: Yes, yes, 'tis just so. Moses knows 'tis true; don't you, Moses?

MOSES: Oh, yes! I'll swear to't.

SIR OLIVER: [*aside*] Egad, they'll persuade me presently I'm at Bengal.

CHARLES SURFACE: Now I propose, Mr. Premium, if it's agreeable to you, a post-orbit on Sir Oliver's life: though at the same time the old fellow has been so liberal with me, that I give you my word, I should be very sorry to hear that anything had happened to him.

SIR OLIVER: Not more than I should, I assure you. But the bond you mention happens to be just the worst security you could offer me—for I might live to be a hundred and never see the principal.

CHARLES SURFACE: Oh, yes, you would! the moment Sir Oliver dies, you know, you would come on me for the money.

SIR OLIVER: Then I believe I should be the most unwelcome dun you ever had in your life.

CHARLES SURFACE: What! I suppose you're afraid that Sir Oliver is too good a life?

SIR OLIVER: No, indeed I am not; though I have heard he is as hale and healthy as any man of his years in Christendom.

CHARLES SURFACE: There again, now, you are misinformed. No, no, the climate has hurt him considerably, poor uncle Oliver. Yes, yes, he breaks apace, I'm told—and is so much altered lately that his nearest relations would not know him.

SIR OLIVER: No! Ha! ha ha! so much altered lately that his nearest relation would not know him! Ha! ha! ha! egad—ha! ha!

CHARLES SURFACE: Ha! ha!—you're glad to hear that, little Premium.

SIR OLIVER: No, no, I'm not.

CHARLES SURFACE: Yes, yes, you are—ha! ha! ha!—you know that mends your chance.

SIR OLIVER: But I'm told Sir Oliver is coming over; nay, some say he has actually arrived.

CHARLES SURFACE: Psha! sure I must know better than you whether he's come or not. No, no, rely on't he's at this moment at Calcutta. Isn't he, Moses?

MOSES: Oh, yes, certainly.

SIR OLIVER: Very true, as you say, you must know better than I, though I have it from a pretty good authority. Haven't I, Moses?

MOSES: Yes, most undoubted!

SIR OLIVER: But, sir, as I understand you want a few hundreds immediately, is there nothing you could dispose of?

CHARLES SURFACE: How do you mean?

SIR OLIVER: For instance, now, I have heard that your father left behind him a great quantity of massy old plate.

CHARLES SURFACE: O lud, that's gone long ago. Moses can tell you how better than I can.

SIR OLIVER: [*aside*] Good lack! all the family race-cups and corporation-bowls! [*aloud*] Then it was also supposed that his library was one of the most valuable and compact.

CHARLES SURFACE: Yes, yes, so it was—vastly too much for a private gentleman. For my part, I was always of a communicative disposition, so I thought it a shame to keep so much knowledge to myself.

SIR OLIVER: [*aside*] Mercy upon me! learning that had run in the family like an heirloom!—[*aloud*] Pray, what has become of the books?

CHARLES SURFACE: You must inquire of the auctioneer, Master Premium, for I don't believe even Moses can direct you.

MOSES: I know nothing of books.

SIR OLIVER: So, so, nothing of the family property left, I suppose?

CHARLES SURFACE: Not much, indeed; unless you have a mind to the family pictures. I have got a room full of ancestors above; and if you have a taste for old paintings, egad, you shall have 'em a bargain!

SIR OLIVER: Hey! what the devil! sure, you wouldn't sell your forefathers, would you?

CHARLES SURFACE: Every man of them, to the best bidder.

SIR OLIVER: What! your great-uncles and aunts?

CHARLES SURFACE: Ay, and my great-grandfathers and grandmothers too.

SIR OLIVER: [*aside*] Now I give him up!—[*aloud*] What the plague, have you no bowels for your own kindred? Odd's life! do you take me for Shylock in the play, that you would raise money of me on your own flesh and blood?

CHARLES SURFACE: Nay, my little broker, don't be angry. What need you care, if you have your money's worth?

SIR OLIVER: Well, I'll be the purchaser. I think I can dispose of the family canvas.—[*aside*] Oh, I'll never forgive him this! never!

[*Enter* CARELESS.]

CARELESS: Come, Charles, what keeps you?

CHARLES SURFACE: I can't come yet. I'faith, we are going to have a sale above stairs; here's little Premium will buy all my ancestors!

CARELESS: Oh, burn your ancestors!

CHARLES SURFACE: No, he may do that afterwards, if he pleases. Stay, Careless, we want you: egad, you shall be auctioneer—so come along with us.

CARELESS: Oh, have with you, if that's the case. I can handle a hammer as well as a dice box!

SIR OLIVER: [*aside*] Oh, the profligates!

CHARLES SURFACE: Come, Moses, you shall be appraiser, if we want one. Gad's life, little Premium, you don't seem to like the business?

SIR OLIVER: Oh, yes, I do, vastly! Ha! ha! ha! yes, yes, I think it a rare joke to sell one's family by auction—ha! ha!—[*aside*] Oh, the prodigal!

CHARLES SURFACE: To be sure! when a man wants money, where the plague should be get assistance if he can's make free with his own relations? [*Exeunt.*]

ACT IV

SCENE I——*Picture Room at* CHARLES'S.

[*Enter* CHARLES SURFACE, SIR OLIVER SURFACE, MOSES, *and* CARELESS.]

CHARLES SURFACE: Walk in, gentlemen, pray walk in—here they are, the family of the Surfaces up to the Conquest.

SIR OLIVER: And, in my opinion, a goodly collection.

CHARLES SURFACE: Ay, ay, these are done in the true spirit of portrait-painting; no *volontière grace* or expression. Not like the works of your modern Raphaels, who give you the strongest resemblance, yet contrive to make your portrait independent of you; so that you may sink the original and not hurt the picture. No, no; the merit of these is the inveterate likeness —all stiff and awkward as the originals, and like nothing in human nature besides.

SIR OLIVER: Ah! we shall never see such figures of men again.

CHARLES SURFACE: I hope not. Well, you see, Master Premium, what a domestic character I am; here I sit of an evening surrounded by my family. But come, get to your pulpit, Mr. Auctioneer; here's an old gouty chair of my grandfather's will answer the purpose.

CARELESS: Ay, ay, this will do. But, Charles, I haven't a hammer; and what's an auctioneer without his hammer?

CHARLES SURFACE: Egad, that's true. What parchment have we here? Oh, our genealogy in full. Here, Careless, you shall have no common bit of mahogany, here's the family tree for you, you rogue! This shall be your hammer, and now you may knock down my ancestors with their own pedigree.

SIR OLIVER: [*aside*] What an unnatural rogue!—an *ex post facto* parricide!

CARELESS: Yes, yes, here's a list of your generation indeed;—faith, Charles, this is the most convenient thing you could have found for the business, for 'twill not only serve as a hammer, but a catalogue into the bargain. Come, begin—A-going, a-going a-going!

CHARLES SURFACE: Bravo, Careless! Well, here's my great uncle, Sir Richard Raveline, a marvelous good general in his day, I assure you. He served in all the Duke of Marlborough's wars, and got that cut over his eye at the battle of Malplaquet. What say you, Mr. Premium? look at him—there's a hero! not cut out of his feathers, as your modern clipped captains are, but enveloped in wig and regimentals as a general should be. What do you bid?

MOSES: Mr. Premium would have you speak.

CHARLES SURFACE: Why, then he shall have him for ten pounds, and I'm sure that's not dear for a staff-officer.

SIR OLIVER: [*aside*] Heaven deliver me! his famous uncle Richard for ten pounds!—[*aloud*] Very well, sir. I take him at that.

CHARLES SURFACE: Careless, knock down my uncle Richard.—Here, now, is a maiden sister of his, my great-aunt Deborah, done by Kneller, in his best manner, and a very formidable likeness. There she is, you see, a shepherdess feeding her flock. You shall have her for five pounds ten—the sheep are worth the money.

SIR OLIVER: [*aside*] Ah! poor Deborah! a woman who set such a value on herself!—[*aloud*] Five pounds ten—she's mine.

CHARLES SURFACE: Knock down my aunt Deborah! Here, now, are two that were a sort of cousins of theirs—You see, Moses, these pictures were done some time ago, when beaux wore wigs, and the ladies their own hair.

SIR OLIVER: Yes, truly, head-dresses appear to have been a little lower in those days.

CHARLES SURFACE: Well, take that couple for the same.

MOSES: 'Tis a good bargain.

CHARLES SURFACE: Careless—this, now, is a grandfather of my mother's, a learned judge, well known on the western circuit.—What do you rate him at, Moses?

MOSES: Four guineas.

CHARLES SURFACE: Four guineas! Gad's life, you don't bid me the price of his wig.—Mr. Premium, you have more respect for the wool-sack, do let us knock his Lordship down at fifteen.

SIR OLIVER: By all means.

CARELESS: Gone!

CHARLES SURFACE: And there are two brothers of his, William and Walter Blunt, Esquires, both members of Parliament, and noted speakers; and, what's very extraordinary, I believe, this is the first time they were ever bought or sold.

SIR OLIVER: That is very extraordinary, indeed! I'll take them at your own price, for the honor of Parliament.

CARELESS: Well said, little Premium! I'll knock them down at forty.

CHARLES SURFACE: Here's a jolly fellow—I don't know what relation, but he was mayor of Manchester: take him at eight pounds.

SIR OLIVER: No, no, six will do for the mayor.

CHARLES SURFACE: Come, make it guineas, and I'll throw you the two aldermen there into the bargain.

SIR OLIVER: They're mine.

CHARLES SURFACE: Careless, knock down the mayor and aldermen. But, plague on't! we shall be all day retailing in this manner; do let us deal wholesale: what say you, little Premium? Give me three hundred pounds for the rest of the family in the lump.

CARELESS: Ay, ay, that will be the best way.

SIR OLIVER: Well, well, anything to accommodate you; they are mine. But there is one portrait which you have always passed over.

CARELESS: What, that ill-looking little fellow over the settee?

SIR OLIVER: Yes, sir, I mean that; though I don't think him so ill-looking a little fellow, by any means.

CHARLES SURFACE: What, that? Oh; that's my uncle Oliver! 'Twas done before he went to India.

CARELESS: Your uncle Oliver! Gad, then you'll never be friends, Charles. That, now, to me, is as stern a looking rogue as ever I saw; an unforgiving eye, and a damned disinheriting countenance! an inveterate knave, depend on't. Don't you think so little Premium?

SIR OLIVER: Upon my soul, sir, I do not; I think it is as honest a looking face as any in the room, dead or alive. But I suppose uncle Oliver goes with the rest of the lumber?

CHARLES SURFACE: No, hang it! I'll not part with poor Noll. The old fellow has been very good to me, and, egad, I'll keep his picture while I've a room to put it in.

SIR OLIVER: [*aside*] The rogue's my nephew after all!—[*aloud*] But, sir, I have somehow taken a fancy to that picture.

CHARLES SURFACE: I'm sorry for't, for you certainly will not have it. Oons, haven't you got enough of them?

SIR OLIVER: [*aside*] I forgive him everything!—[*aloud*] But, sir, when I take a whim in my head, I don't value money. I'll give you as much for that as for all the rest.

CHARLES SURFACE: Don't tease me, master broker; I tell you I'll not part with it, and there's an end of it.

SIR OLIVER: [*aside*] How like his father the dog is!—[*aloud*] Well, well, I have done.—[*aside*] I did not perceive it before, but I think I never saw such a striking resemblance.—[*aloud*] Here is a draught for your sum.

CHARLES SURFACE: Why, 'tis for eight hundred pounds!

SIR OLIVER: You will not let Sir Oliver go?

CHARLES SURFACE: Zounds! no! I tell you, once more.

SIR OLIVER: Then never mind the difference, we'll balance that another time. But give me your hand on the bargain; you are an honest fellow, Charles —I beg pardon, sir, for being so free.—Come, Moses.

CHARLES SURFACE: Egad, this is a whimsical old fellow!—But hark'ee, Premium, you'll prepare lodgings for these gentlemen.

SIR OLIVER: Yes, yes, I'll send for them in a day or two.

CHARLES SURFACE: But hold; do now send a genteel conveyance for them, for, I assure you, they were most of them used to ride in their own carriages.

SIR OLIVER: I will, I will—for all but Oliver.

CHARLES SURFACE: Ay, all but the little nabob.

SIR OLIVER: You're fixed on that?

CHARLES SURFACE: Peremptorily.

SIR OLIVER: [*aside*] A dear extravagant rogue!—[*aloud*] Good day!—Come, Moses.—[*aside*] Let me hear now who dares call him profligate!
        [*Exeunt* SIR OLIVER *and* MOSES.]

CARELESS: Why, this is the oddest genius of the sort I ever met with!

CHARLES SURFACE: Egad, he's the prince of brokers, I think. I wonder how the devil Moses got acquainted with so honest a fellow.—Ha! here's Rowley. —Do, Careless, say I'll join the company in a few moments.

CARELESS: I will—but don't let that old blockhead persuade you to squander any of that money on old musty debts, or any such nonsense; for tradesmen, Charles, are the most exorbitant fellows.

CHARLES SURFACE: Very true, and paying them is only encouraging them.

CARELESS: Nothing else.

CHARLES SURFACE: Ay, ay, never fear.—

> [*Exit* CARELESS.]

So! this was an odd old fellow, indeed. Let me see, two-thirds of this is mine by right: five hundred and thirty odd pounds. 'Fore heaven! I find one's ancestors are more valuable relations than I took them for!—Ladies and gentlemen, your most obedient and very grateful servant.

> [*Bows to the pictures. Enter* ROWLEY.]

Ha! old Rowley! egad, you are just come in time to take leave of your old acquaintance.

ROWLEY: Yes, I heard they were a-going. But I wonder you can have such spirits under so many distresses.

CHARLES SURFACE: Why, there's the point! my distresses are so many that I can't afford to part with my spirits; but I shall be rich and splenetic, all in good time. However, I suppose you are surprised that I am not more sorrowful at parting with so many near relations; to be sure, 'tis very affecting; but you see they never move a muscle, so why should I?

ROWLEY: There's no making you serious a moment.

CHARLES SURFACE: Yes, faith, I am so now. Here, my honest Rowley, here, get me this changed directly and take a hundred pounds of it immediately to old Stanley.

ROWLEY: A hundred pounds! Consider only—

CHARLES SURFACE: Gad's life, don't talk about it! poor Stanley's wants are pressing, and, if you don't make haste, we shall have some one call that has a better right to the money.

ROWLEY: Ah! there's the point! I never will cease dunning you with the old proverb—

CHARLES SURFACE: "Be just before you're generous."—Why, so I would if I could; but Justice is an old lame, hobbling beldame, and I can't get her to keep pace with Generosity, for the soul of me.

ROWLEY: Yet, Charles, believe me, one hour's reflection—

CHARLES SURFACE: Ay, ay, it's very true; but, hark'ee, Rowley, while I have, by Heaven I'll give; so, damn your economy! and now for hazard. [*Exeunt.*]

SCENE II——*The parlor.*

> [*Enter* SIR OLIVER SURFACE *and* MOSES.]

MOSES: Well, sir, I think, as Sir Peter said, you have seen Mr. Charles in high glory; 'tis great pity he's so extravagant.

SIR OLIVER: True, but he would not sell my picture.

MOSES: And loves wine and women so much.

SIR OLIVER: But he would not sell my picture.

MOSES: And games so deep.

SIR OLIVER: But he would not sell my picture. Oh, here's Rowley.

> [*Enter* ROWLEY.]

ROWLEY: So, Sir Oliver, I find you have made a purchase—

SIR OLIVER: Yes, yes, our young rake has parted with his ancestors like old tapestry.

ROWLEY: And here has he commissioned me to re-deliver you part of the purchase-money—I mean, though, in your necessitous character of old Stanley.

MOSES: Ah! there is the pity of all; he is so damned charitable.

ROWLEY: And I left a hosier and two tailors in the hall, who I'm sure, won't be paid, and this hundred would satisfy them.

SIR OLIVER: Well, well I'll pay his debts, and his benevolence too. But now I am no more a broker, and you shall introduce me to the elder brother as old Stanley.

ROWLEY: Not yet awhile; Sir Peter, I know, means to call there about this time.
[*Enter* TRIP.]

TRIP: Oh, gentlemen, I beg pardon for not showing you out; this way—Moses, a word.
[*Exit with* MOSES.]

SIR OLIVER: There's a fellow for you! Would you believe it, that puppy intercepted the Jew on our coming, and wanted to raise money before he got to his master!

ROWLEY: Indeed.

SIR OLIVER: Yes, they are now planning an annuity business. Ah, Master Rowley, in my days servants were content with the follies of their masters when they were worn a little threadbare; but now they have their vices, like their birthday clothes, with the gloss on. [*Exeunt.*]

SCENE III——A *Library in* JOSEPH SURFACE's *House.*

JOSEPH SURFACE: No letter from Lady Teazle?

SERVANT: No, sir.

JOSEPH SURFACE: [*aside*] I am surprised she has not sent, if she is prevented from coming. Sir Peter certainly does not suspect me. Yet I wish I may not lose the heiress through the scrape I have drawn myself into with the wife. However, Charles's imprudence and bad character are great points in my favor.
[*Knocking.*]

SERVANT: Sir, I believe that must be Lady Teazle.

JOSEPH SURFACE: Hold! See whether it is or not before you go to the door. I have a particular message for you if it should be my brother.

SERVANT: 'Tis her ladyship, sir; she always leaves the chair at the milliner's in the next street.

JOSEPH SURFACE: Stay, stay! Draw that screen before the window—that will do. My opposite neighbor is a maiden lady of so curious a temper.
[*Servant draws the screen, and exits.*]
I have a difficult hand to play in this affair. Lady Teazle has lately suspected my views on Maria; but she must by no means be let into that secret—at least, till I have her more in my power.
[*Enter* LADY TEAZLE.]

LADY TEAZLE: What, sentiment in soliloquy now? Have you been very impatient? O lud! don't pretend to look grave. I vow I couldn't come before.

JOSEPH SURFACE: O madam, punctuality is a species of constancy very unfashionable in a lady of quality.

LADY TEAZLE: Upon my word, you ought to pity me. Do you know Sir Peter is grown so ill-natured to me of late, and so jealous of Charles too—that's the best of the story, isn't it?

JOSEPH SURFACE: [*aside*] I am glad my scandalous friends keep that up.

LADY TEAZLE: I am sure I wish he would let Maria marry him, and then perhaps he would be convinced; don't you, Mr. Surface?

JOSEPH SURFACE: [*aside*] Indeed I do not.—[*aloud*] Oh, certainly I do! for then my dear Lady Teazle would also be convinced how wrong her suspicions were of my having any design on the silly girl.

LADY TEAZLE: Well, well, I'm inclined to believe you. But isn't it provoking to have the most ill-natured things said at one? And there's my friend Lady Sneerwell has circulated I don't know how many scandalous tales of me, and all without any foundation, too; that's what vexes me.

JOSEPH SURFACE: Ay, madam, to be sure, that is the provoking circumstance—without foundation. Yes, yes, there's the mortification, indeed; for, when a scandalous story is believed against one, there certainly is no comfort like the consciousness of having deserved it.

LADY TEAZLE: No, to be sure, then I'd forgive their malice; but to attack me, who am really so innocent, and who never say an ill-natured thing of anybody—that is, of any friend; and then Sir Peter, too, to have him so peevish, and so suspicious, when I know the integrity of my own heart—indeed 'tis monstrous!

JOSEPH SURFACE: But, my dear Lady Teazle, 'tis your own fault if you suffer it. When a husband entertains a groundless suspicion of his wife, and withdraws his confidence from her, the original compact is broken, and she owes it to the honor of her sex to endeavor to outwit him.

LADY TEAZLE: Indeed! So that, if he suspects me without cause, it follows, that the best way of curing his jealousy is to give him reason for't?

JOSEPH SURFACE: Undoubtedly—for your husband should never be deceived in you: and in that case it becomes you to be frail in compliment to his discernment.

LADY TEAZLE: To be sure, what you say is very reasonable, and when the consciousness of my innocence—

JOSEPH SURFACE: Ah, my dear madam, there is the great mistake; 'tis this very conscious innocence that is of the greatest prejudice to you. What is it makes you negligent of forms, and careless of the world's opinion? why, the consciousness of your own innocence. What makes you thoughtless in your conduct and apt to run into a thousand little imprudences? why, the consciousness of your own innocence. What makes you impatient of Sir Peter's temper, and outrageous at his suspicions? why, the consciousness of your innocence.

LADY TEAZLE: 'Tis very true!

JOSEPH SURFACE: Now, my dear Lady Teazle, if you would but once make a trifling *faux pas*, you can't conceive how cautious you would grow, and how ready to humor and agree with your husband.

LADY TEAZLE: Do you think so?

JOSEPH SURFACE: Oh, I'm sure on't! and then you would find all scandal would cease at once, for—in short, your character at present is like a person in a plethora, absolutely dying from too much health.

LADY TEAZLE: So, so; then I perceive your prescription is that I must sin in my own defence, and part with my virtue to preserve my reputation?

JOSEPH SURFACE: Exactly so, upon my credit, ma'am.

LADY TEAZLE: Well, certainly this is the oddest doctrine, and the newest receipt for avoiding calumny.

JOSEPH SURFACE: An infallible one, believe me. Prudence, like experience, must be paid for.

LADY TEAZLE: Why, if my understanding were once convinced—

JOSEPH SURFACE: Oh, certainly, madam, your understanding should be convinced. Yes, yes—Heaven forbid I should persuade you to do anything you thought wrong. No, no, I have too much honor to desire it.

LADY TEAZLE: Don't you think we may as well leave honor out of the argument? [*rises*]

JOSEPH SURFACE: Ah, the ill effects of your country education, I see, still remain with you.

LADY TEAZLE: I doubt they do, indeed; and I will fairly own to you, that if I could be persuaded to do wrong, it would be by Sir Peter's ill usage sooner than your honorable logic, after all.

JOSEPH SURFACE: Then, by this hand, which he is unworthy of—[*taking her hand*]

[*Enter* SERVANT.]

'Sdeath, you blockhead—what do you want?

SERVANT: I beg your pardon, sir, but I thought you would not choose Sir Peter to come up without announcing him.

JOSEPH SURFACE: Sir Peter!—Oons—the devil!

LADY TEAZLE: Sir Peter! O lud! I'm ruined! I'm ruined!

SERVANT: Sir, 'twasn't I let him in.

LADY TEAZLE: Oh! I'm quite undone! What will become of me now, Mr. Logic?—Oh! mercy, he's on the stairs—I'll get behind here—and if ever I'm so imprudent again—[*Goes behind the screen.*]

JOSEPH SURFACE: Give me that book.

[*Sits down.* SERVANT *pretends to adjust his chair. Enter* SIR PETER TEAZLE.]

SIR PETER: Ay, ever improving himself. Mr. Surface, Mr. Surface—

JOSEPH SURFACE: Oh, my dear Sir Peter, I beg your pardon. [*Gaping, throws away the book.*] I have been dozing over a stupid book. Well, I am much obliged to you for this call. You haven't been here, I believe, since I fitted up this room. Books, you know, are the only things I am a coxcomb in.

SIR PETER: 'Tis very neat indeed. Well, well, that's proper; and you can make even your screen a source of knowledge—hung, I perceive, with maps.

JOSEPH SURFACE: Oh, yes, I find great use in that screen.

SIR PETER: I dare say you must, certainly, when you want to find anything in a hurry.

JOSEPH SURFACE: [aside] Ay, or to hide anything in a hurry either.

SIR PETER: Well, I have a little private business—

JOSEPH SURFACE: [to SERVANT] You need not stay.

SERVANT: No, sir.

[Exit SERVANT.]

JOSEPH SURFACE: Here's a chair, Sir Peter—I beg—

SIR PETER: Well, now we are alone, there is a subject, my dear friend, on which I wish to unburden my mind to you—a point of the greatest moment to my peace; in short, my good friend, Lady Teazle's conduct of late has made me very unhappy.

JOSEPH SURFACE: Indeed! I am very sorry to hear it.

SIR PETER: Yes, 'tis but too plain she has not the least regard for me; but, what's worse, I have pretty good authority to suppose she has formed an attachment to another.

JOSEPH SURFACE: Indeed! you astonish me!

SIR PETER: Yes! and, between ourselves, I think I've discovered the person.

JOSEPH SURFACE: How! you alarm me exceedingly.

SIR PETER: Ay, my dear friend, I knew you would sympathize with me!

JOSEPH SURFACE: Yes, believe me, Sir Peter, such a discovery would hurt me just as much as it would you.

SIR PETER: I am convinced of it. Ah! it is a happiness to have a friend whom we can trust even with one's family secrets. But have you no guess who I mean?

JOSEPH SURFACE: I haven't the most distant idea. It can't be Sir Benjamin Backbite!

SIR PETER: Oh, no! what say you to Charles?

JOSEPH SURFACE: My brother! impossible!

SIR PETER: Oh, my dear friend, the goodness of your own heart misleads you. You judge of others by yourself.

JOSEPH SURFACE: Certainly, Sir Peter, the heart that is conscious of its own integrity is ever slow to credit another's treachery.

SIR PETER: True; but your brother has no sentiment—you never hear him talk so.

JOSEPH SURFACE: Yet I can't but think Lady Teazle herself has too much principle.

SIR PETER: Ay; but what is principle against the flattery of a handsome, lively young fellow?

JOSEPH SURFACE: That's very true.

SIR PETER: And then, you know, the difference of our ages makes it very improbable that she should have any great affection for me; and if she were to be frail, and I were to make it public, why the town would only laugh at me, the foolish old bachelor who had married a girl.

JOSEPH SURFACE: That's true, to be sure—they would laugh.

SIR PETER: Laugh! ay, and make ballads, and paragraphs, and the devil knows what of me.

JOSEPH SURFACE: No, you must never make it public.

SIR PETER: But then again—that the nephew of my old friend, Sir Oliver, should be the person to attempt such a wrong, hurts me more nearly.

JOSEPH SURFACE: Ay, there's the point. When ingratitude barbs the dart of injury, the wound has double danger in it.

SIR PETER: Ay—I that was, in a manner, left his guardian, in whose house he had been so often entertained, who never in my life denied him—my advice!

JOSEPH SURFACE: Oh, 'tis not to be credited! There may be a man capable of such baseness, to be sure; but, for my part, till you can give me positive proofs, I cannot but doubt it. However, if it should be proved on him, he is no longer a brother of mine—I disclaim kindred with him: for the man who can break the laws of hospitality and tempt the wife of his friend, deserves to be branded as the pest of society.

SIR PETER: What a difference there is between you! What noble sentiments!

JOSEPH SURFACE: Yet I cannot suspect Lady Teazle's honor.

SIR PETER: I am sure I wish to think well of her, and to remove all ground of quarrel between us. She has lately reproached me more than once with having made no settlement on her; and, in our last quarrel, she almost hinted that she should not break her heart if I was dead. Now, as we seem to differ in our ideas of expense, I have resolved she shall have her own way and be her own mistress in that respect for the future; and, if I were to die, she will find I have not been inattentive to her interest while living. Here, my friend, are the drafts of two deeds, which I wish to have your opinion on. By one, she will enjoy eight hundred a year independent while I live; and by the other, the bulk of my fortune at my death.

JOSEPH SURFACE: This conduct, Sir Peter, is indeed truly generous. [*aside*] I wish it may not corrupt my pupil.

SIR PETER: Yes, I am determined she shall have no cause to complain, though I would not have her acquainted with the latter instance of my affection yet awhile.

JOSEPH SURFACE: [*aside*] Nor I, if I could help it.

SIR PETER: And now, my dear friend, if you please, we will talk over the situation of your hopes with Maria.

JOSEPH SURFACE: [*softly*] Oh, no, Sir Peter; another time, if you please.

SIR PETER: I am sensibly chagrined at the little progress you seem to make in her affections.

JOSEPH SURFACE: [*softly*] I beg you will not mention it. What are my disappointments when your happiness is in debate! [*aside*] 'Sdeath, I shall be ruined every way!

SIR PETER: And though you are averse to my acquainting Lady Teazle with your passion, I'm sure she's not your enemy in the affair.

JOSEPH SURFACE: Pray, Sir Peter, now oblige me. I am really too much affected by the subject we have been speaking of to bestow a thought on my own

concerns. The man who is entrusted with his friend's distress can never—
[*Enter* SERVANT.]
Well, sir?

SERVANT: Your brother, sir, is speaking to a gentleman in the street, and says he knows you are within.

JOSEPH SURFACE: 'Sdeath, blockhead, I'm not within—I'm out for the day.

SIR PETER: Stay—hold—a thought has struck me: you shall be at home.

JOSEPH SURFACE: Well, well, let him up.
[*Exit* SERVANT.]
[*aside*] He'll interrupt Sir Peter, however.

SIR PETER: Now, my good friend, oblige me, I entreat you. Before Charles comes, let me conceal myself somewhere, then do you tax him on the point we have been talking, and his answer may satisfy me at once.

JOSEPH SURFACE: Oh, fie, Sir Peter! would you have me join in so mean a trick? —to trepan my brother too?

SIR PETER: Nay, you tell me you are sure he is innocent; if so, you do him the greatest service by giving him an opportunity to clear himself, and you will set my heart at rest. Come, you shall not refuse me: here, behind the screen will be—Hey! what the devil! there seems to be one listener here already—I'll swear I saw a petticoat!

JOSEPH SURFACE: Ha! ha! ha! Well, this is ridiculous enough. I'll tell you, Sir Peter, though I hold a man of intrigue to be a most despicable character, yet you know, it does not follow that one is to be an absolute Joseph either! Hark'ee, 'tis a little French milliner, a silly rogue that plagues me; and having some character to lose, on your coming, sir, she ran behind the screen.

SIR PETER: Ah, you rogue—But, egad, she has overheard all I have been saying of my wife.

JOSEPH SURFACE: Oh, 'twill never go any farther, you may depend upon it!

SIR PETER: No! then, faith, let her hear it out.—Here's a closet will do as well.

JOSEPH SURFACE: Well, go in there.

SIR PETER: Sly rogue; sly rogue! [*Goes into the closet.*]

JOSEPH SURFACE: A narrow escape, indeed! and a curious situation I'm in, to part man and wife in this manner.

LADY TEAZLE: [*peeping*] Couldn't I steal off?

JOSEPH SURFACE: Keep close, my angel.

SIR PETER: [*peeping*] Joseph, tax me home!

JOSEPH SURFACE: Back, my dear friend!

LADY TEAZLE: [*peeping*] Couldn't you lock Sir Peter in?

JOSEPH SURFACE: Be still, my life!

SIR PETER: [*peeping*] You're sure the little milliner won't blab?

JOSEPH SURFACE: In, in, my dear Sir Peter!—'Fore gad, I wish I had a key to the door!
[*Enter* CHARLES SURFACE.]

CHARLES SURFACE: Holla! brother, what has been the matter? Your fellow would not let me up at first. What! have you had a Jew or a wench with you?

JOSEPH SURFACE: Neither, brother, I assure you.

CHARLES SURFACE: But what has made Sir Peter steal off? I thought he had been with you.

JOSEPH SURFACE: He was, brother; but, hearing you were coming, he did not choose to stay.

CHARLES SURFACE: What! was the old gentleman' afraid I wanted to borrow money of him!

JOSEPH SURFACE: No, sir: but I am sorry to find, Charles, you have lately given that worthy man grounds for great uneasiness.

CHARLES SURFACE: Yes, they tell me I do that to a great many worthy men. But how so, pray?

JOSEPH SURFACE: To be plain with you, brother, he thinks you are endeavoring to gain Lady Teazle's affections from him.

CHARLES SURFACE: Who, I? O lud! not I, upon my word.—Ha! ha! ha! ha! so the old fellow has found out that he has got a young wife, has he?—or, what's worse, Lady Teazle has found out she has an old husband?

JOSEPH SURFACE: This is no subject to jest on, brother. He who can laugh—

CHARLES SURFACE: True, true, as you were going to say—then, seriously, I never had the least idea of what you charge me with, upon my honor.

JOSEPH SURFACE: [*in a loud voice*] Well, it will give Sir Peter great satisfaction to hear this.

CHARLES SURFACE: To be sure, I once thought the lady seemed to have taken a fancy to me; but, upon my soul, I never gave her the least encouragement. Besides, you know my attachment to Maria.

JOSEPH SURFACE: But sure, brother, even if Lady Teazle had betrayed the fondest partiality for you—

CHARLES SURFACE: Why, look'ee, Joseph, I hope I shall never deliberately do a dishonorable action; but if a pretty woman were purposely to throw herself in my way—and that pretty woman married to a man old enough to be her father—

JOSEPH SURFACE: Well!

CHARLES SURFACE: Why, I believe I should be obliged to borrow a little of your morality, that's all. But, brother, do you know now that you surprise me exceedingly by naming me with Lady Teazle; for i'faith, I always understood you were her favorite.

JOSEPH SURFACE: Oh, for shame, Charles! This retort is foolish.

CHARLES SURFACE: Nay, I swear I have seen you exchange such significant glances—

JOSEPH SURFACE: Nay, nay, sir, this is no jest.

CHARLES SURFACE: Egad, I'm serious! Don't you remember one day when I called here—

JOSEPH SURFACE: Nay, prithee, Charles—

CHARLES SURFACE: And found you together—

JOSEPH SURFACE: Zounds, sir, I insist—

CHARLES SURFACE: And another time, when your servant—

JOSEPH SURFACE: Brother, brother, a word with you! [*aside*] Gad, I must stop him.

CHARLES SURFACE: Informed, I say, that—

JOSEPH SURFACE: Hush, I beg your pardon, but Sir Peter has overheard all we have been saying. I knew you would clear yourself, or I should not have consented.

CHARLES SURFACE: How, Sir Peter! Where is he?

JOSEPH SURFACE: Softly, there! [*Points to the closet.*]

CHARLES SURFACE: Oh, 'fore Heaven, I'll have him out. Sir Peter, come forth!

JOSEPH SURFACE: No, no—

CHARLES SURFACE: I say, Sir Peter, come into court. [*Pulls in* SIR PETER.]
What! my old guardian!—What! turn inquisitor and take evidence incog.?

SIR PETER: Give me your hand, Charles—I believe I have suspected you wrongfully; but you mustn't be angry with Joseph—'twas my plan!

CHARLES SURFACE: Indeed!

SIR PETER: But I acquit you. I promise you I don't think near so ill of you as I did. What I have heard has given me great satisfaction.

CHARLES SURFACE: Egad, then 'twas lucky you didn't hear any more. Wasn't it, Joseph?

SIR PETER: Ah! you would have retorted on him.

CHARLES SURFACE: Ah, ay, that was a joke.

SIR PETER: Yes, yes, I know his honor too well.

CHARLES SURFACE: But you might as well have suspected him as me in this matter, for all that. Mightn't he, Joseph?

SIR PETER: Well, well, I believe you.

JOSEPH SURFACE: [*aside*] Would they were both out of the room!

SIR PETER: And in future, perhaps, we may not be such strangers.
[*Enter* SERVANT *and whispers to* JOSEPH SURFACE.]

JOSEPH SURFACE: Gentlemen, I beg pardon—I must wait on you downstairs; here's a person come on particular business.

CHARLES SURFACE: Well, you can see him in another room. Sir Peter and I have not met a long time, and I have something to say to him.

JOSEPH SURFACE: [*aside*] They must not be left together—[*aloud*] I'll send Lady Sneerwell away, and return directly. [*aside to* SIR PETER] Sir Peter, not a word of the French milliner.

SIR PETER: [*aside to* JOSEPH SURFACE] I! not for the world!—
[*Exit* JOSEPH SURFACE.]
Ah, Charles, if you associated more with your brother, one might indeed hope for your reformation. He is a man of sentiment. Well, there is nothing in the world so noble as a man of sentiment.

CHARLES SURFACE: Psha! he is too moral by half; and so apprehensive of his good name, as he calls it, that I suppose he would as soon let a priest into his house as a wench.

SIR PETER: No, no—come, come,—you wrong him. No, no, Joseph is no rake, but he is no such saint either, in that respect. [*aside*] I have a great mind to tell him—we should have such a laugh at Joseph.

CHARLES SURFACE: Oh, hang him! he's a very anchorite, a young hermit!

SIR PETER: Hark'ee—you must not abuse him: he may chance to hear of it again I promise you.

CHARLES SURFACE: Why, you won't tell him?

SIR PETER: No—but—this way. [*aside*] Egad, I'll tell him. [*aloud*] Hark'ee, have you a mind to have a good laugh at Joseph?

CHARLES SURFACE: I should like it of all things.

SIR PETER: Then, i'faith, we will! I'll be quit with him for discovering me. He had a girl with him when I called.

CHARLES SURFACE: What! Joseph? you jest.

SIR PETER: Hush!—a little French milliner—and the best of the jest is—she's in the room now.

CHARLES SURFACE: The devil she is!

SIR PETER: Hush! I tell you. [*Points to the screen.*]

CHARLES SURFACE: Behind the screen! S'life, let's unveil her!

SIR PETER: No, no, he's coming. You shan't, indeed!

CHARLES SURFACE: Oh, egad, we'll have a peep at the little milliner!

SIR PETER: Not for the world!—Joseph will never forgive me.

CHARLES SURFACE: I'll stand by you—

SIR PETER: Odds, here he is!

[JOSEPH SURFACE *enters just as* CHARLES *throws down the screen.*]

CHARLES SURFACE: Lady Teazle, by all that's wonderful!

SIR PETER: Lady Teazle, by all that's damnable!

CHARLES SURFACE: Sir Peter, this is one of the smartest French milliners I ever saw. Egad, you seem all to have been diverting yourselves here at hide and seek, and I don't see who is out of the secret. Shall I beg your ladyship to inform me? Not a word!—Brother, will you be pleased to explain this matter? What! is Morality Dumb too?—Sir Peter, though I found you in the dark, perhaps you are not so now! All mute! Well—though I can make nothing of the affair, I suppose you perfectly understand one another; so I'll leave you to yourselves. [*going*] Brother, I'm sorry to find you have given that worthy man grounds for so much uneasiness.—Sir Peter! there's nothing in the world so noble as a man of sentiment.

[*Exit* CHARLES SURFACE. *They stand for some time looking at each other.*]

JOSEPH SURFACE: Sir Peter—notwithstanding—I confess—that appearances are against me—if you will afford me your patience—I make no doubt—but I shall explain everything to your satisfaction.

SIR PETER: If you please, sir.

JOSEPH SURFACE: The fact is, sir, that Lady Teazle, knowing my pretensions to your ward Maria—I say, sir, Lady Teazle, being apprehensive of the jealousy of your temper—and knowing my friendship to the family—she, sir, I say—called here—in order that—I might explain these pretensions—but on your coming—being apprehensive—as I said—of your jealousy—she withdrew—and this, you may depend on it, is the whole truth of the matter.

SIR PETER: A very clear account, upon my word; and I dare swear the lady will vouch for every article of it.

LADY TEAZLE: For not one word of it, Sir Peter!

SIR PETER: How! don't you think it worth while to agree in the lie?

LADY TEAZLE: There is not one syllable of truth in what that gentleman has told you.

SIR PETER: I believe you, upon my soul, ma'am!

JOSEPH SURFACE: [*aside to* LADY TEAZLE] 'Sdeath, madam, will you betray me?

LADY TEAZLE: Good Mr. Hypocrite, by your leave, I'll speak for myself.

SIR PETER: Ay, let her alone, sir; you'll find she'll make out a better story than you, without prompting.

LADY TEAZLE: Hear me, Sir Peter! I came here on no matter relating to your ward, and even ignorant of this gentleman's pretensions to her. But I came, seduced by his insidious arguments, at least to listen to his pretended passion, if not to sacrifice your honor to his baseness.

SIR PETER: Now, I believe, the truth is coming, indeed!

JOSEPH SURFACE: The woman's mad!

LADY TEAZLE: No, sir; she has recovered her senses, and your own arts have furnished her with the means. Sir Peter, I do not expect you to credit me —but the tenderness you express for me, when I am sure you could not think I was a witness to it, has penetrated so to my heart, that had I left the place without the shame of this discovery, my future life should have spoken the sincerity of my gratitude. As for that smooth-tongued hypocrite, who would have seduced the wife of his too credulous friend, while he affected honorable addresses to his ward—I behold him now in a light so truly despicable that I shall never again respect myself for having listened to him.

[*Exit* LADY TEAZLE.]

JOSEPH SURFACE: Notwithstanding all this, Sir Peter, Heaven knows—

SIR PETER: That you are a villain! and so I leave you to your conscience.

JOSEPH SURFACE: You are too rash, Sir Peter; you shall hear me. The man who shuts out conviction by refusing to—

[*Exeunt,* JOSEPH SURFACE *talking.*]

ACT V

SCENE I——*The Library in* JOSEPH SURFACE'S *House.*

[JOSEPH SURFACE *and* SERVANT.]

JOSEPH SURFACE: Mr. Stanley! and why should you think I would see him? you must know he comes to ask something.

SERVANT: Sir, I should not have let him in, but that Mr. Rowley came to the door with him.

JOSEPH SURFACE: Psha! blockhead! to suppose that I should now be in a temper to receive visits from poor relations!—Well, why don't you show the fellow up?

SERVANT: I will, sir.—Why, sir it was not my fault that Sir Peter discovered my lady—

JOSEPH SURFACE: Go, fool!

[*Exit* SERVANT.]

Sure fortune never played a man of my policy such a trick before! My character with Sir Peter, my hopes with Maria, destroyed in a moment!

I'm in a rare humor to listen to other people's distresses! I shan't be able to bestow even a benevolent sentiment on Stanley.—So! here he comes, and Rowley with him. I must try to recover myself, and put a little charity in my face, however.

[*Exit. Enter* SIR OLIVER SURFACE *and* ROWLEY.]

SIR OLIVER: What! does he avoid us? That was he, was it not?

ROWLEY: It was, sir. But I doubt you are coming a little too abruptly. His nerves are so weak that the sight of a poor relation may be too much for him. I should have gone first to break it to him.

SIR OLIVER: Oh, plague of his nerves! Yet this is he whom Sir Peter extols as a man of the most benevolent way of thinking!

ROWLEY: As to his way of thinking, I cannot pretend to decide; for, to do him justice, he appears to have as much speculative benevolence as any private gentleman in the kingdom, though he is seldom so sensual as to indulge himself in the exercise of it.

SIR OLIVER: Yet he has a string of charitable sentiments at his fingers' ends.

ROWLEY: Or, rather, at his tongue's end, Sir Oliver; for I believe there is no sentiment he has such faith in as that "Charity begins at home."

SIR OLIVER: And his, I presume, is of that domestic sort which never stirs abroad at all.

ROWLEY: I doubt you'll find it so;—but he's coming. I mustn't seem to interrupt you; and you know, immediately as you leave him, I come in to announce your arrival in your real character.

SIR OLIVER: True; and afterwards you'll meet me at Sir Peter's.

ROWLEY: Without losing a moment.

[*Exit* ROWLEY.]

SIR OLIVER: I don't like the complaisance of his features.

[*Enter* JOSEPH SURFACE.]

JOSEPH SURFACE: Sir, I beg you ten thousand pardons for keeping you a moment waiting.—Mr. Stanley, I presume.

SIR OLIVER: At your service.

JOSEPH SURFACE: Sir, I beg you will do me the honor to sit down—I entreat you, sir.

SIR OLIVER: Dear sir—there's no occasion. [*aside*] Too civil by half!

JOSEPH SURFACE: I have not the pleasure of knowing you, Mr. Stanley; but I am extremely happy to see you look so well. You were nearly related to my mother, I think, Mr. Stanley?

SIR OLIVER: I was, sir; so nearly that my present poverty, I fear, may do discredit to her wealthy children, else I should not have presumed to trouble you.

JOSEPH SURFACE: Dear sir, there needs no apology: he that is in distress, though a stranger, has a right to claim kindred with the wealthy. I am sure I wish I was one of that class, and had it in my power to offer you even a small relief.

SIR OLIVER: If your uncle, Sir Oliver, were here, I should have a friend.

JOSEPH SURFACE: I wish he was, sir, with all my heart: you should not want an advocate with him, believe me, sir.

SIR OLIVER: I should not need one—my distresses would recommend me. But I imagined his bounty would enable you to become the agent of his charity.

JOSEPH SURFACE: My dear sir, you were strangely misinformed. Sir Oliver is a worthy man, a very worthy man, but avarice, Mr. Stanley, is the vice of age. I will tell you, my good sir, in confidence, what he has done for me has been a mere nothing; though, people, I know, have thought otherwise; and, for my part, I never choose to contradict the report.

SIR OLIVER: What! has he never transmitted you bullion—rupees—pagodas?

JOSEPH SURFACE: Oh, dear sir, nothing of the kind; No, no; a few presents now and then—china, shawls, congou tea, avadavats,[1] and Indian crackers[2]— little more, believe me.

SIR OLIVER: [*aside*] Here's gratitude for twelve thousand pounds!—Avadavats and Indian crackers!

JOSEPH SURFACE: Then, my dear sir, you have heard, I doubt not, of the extravagance of my brother; there are very few would credit what I have done for that unfortunate young man.

SIR OLIVER: [*aside*] Not I, for one!

JOSEPH SURFACE: The sums I have lent him! Indeed I have been exceedingly to blame; it was an amiable weakness; however, I don't pretend to defend it—and now I feel it doubly culpable, since it has deprived me of the pleasure of serving you, Mr. Stanley, as my heart dictates.

SIR OLIVER: [*aside*] Dissembler! [*aloud*] Then, sir, you can't assist me?

JOSEPH SURFACE: At present, it grieves me to say, I cannot; but, whenever I have the ability, you may depend upon hearing from me.

SIR OLIVER: I am extremely sorry—

JOSEPH SURFACE: Not more than I, believe me; to pity, without the power to relieve, is still more painful than to ask and be denied.

SIR OLIVER: Kind sir, your most obedient humble servant.

JOSEPH SURFACE: You leave me deeply affected, Mr. Stanley.—William, be ready to open the door.

SIR OLIVER: Oh, dear sir, no ceremony.

JOSEPH SURFACE: Your very obedient.

SIR OLIVER: Sir, your most obsequious.

JOSEPH SURFACE: You may depend upon hearing from me, whenever I can be of service.

SIR OLIVER: Sweet sir, you are too good.

JOSEPH SURFACE: In the meantime I wish you health and spirits.

SIR OLIVER: Your ever grateful and perpetual humble servant.

JOSEPH SURFACE: Sir, yours as sincerely.

SIR OLIVER: [*aside*] Charles!—you are my heir.
[*Exit* SIR OLIVER.]

JOSEPH SURFACE: This is one bad effect of a good character; it invites application from the unfortunate, and there needs no small degree of address to gain the reputation of benevolence without incurring the expense. The

---

[1] *Avadavats:* Small songbirds from India.
[2] *Indian crackers:* firecrackers.

silver ore of pure charity is an expensive article in the catalogue of a man's
good qualities; whereas the sentimental French plate I use instead of it
makes just as good a show, and pays no tax.

[*Enter* ROWLEY.]

ROWLEY: Mr. Surface, your servant: I was apprehensive of interrupting you,
though my business demands immediate attention, as this note will inform
you.

JOSEPH SURFACE: Always happy to see Mr. Rowley.—[*reads*] Sir Oliver Surface!
My uncle arrived!

ROWLEY: He is, indeed: we have just parted—quite well, after a speedy voyage,
and impatient to embrace his worthy nephew.

JOSEPH SURFACE: I am astonished!—William! stop Mr. Stanley, if he's not
gone.

ROWLEY: Oh, he's out of reach, I believe.

JOSEPH SURFACE: Why did you not let me know this when you came in together?

ROWLEY: I thought you had particular business. But I must be gone to inform
your brother and appoint him here to meet your uncle. He will be with
you in a quarter of an hour.

JOSEPH SURFACE: So he says. Well, I am strangely overjoyed at his coming.—
[*aside*] Never, to be sure, was anything so damned unlucky!

ROWLEY: You will be delighted to see how well he looks.

JOSEPH SURFACE: Oh! I'm overjoyed to hear it. [*aside*]—Just at this time!

ROWLEY: I'll tell him how impatiently you expect him.

JOSEPH SURFACE: Do, do; pray give my best duty and affection. Indeed, I cannot express the sensations I feel at the thought of seeing him.

[*Exit* ROWLEY.]

Certainly his coming just at this time is the cruellest piece of ill fortune.
[*Exit.*]

SCENE II——SIR PETER TEAZLE'S *House.*

[*Enter* MRS. CANDOUR *and* MAID.]

MAID: Indeed, ma'am, my lady will see nobody at present.

MRS. CANDOUR: Did you tell her it was her friend Mrs. Candour?

MAID: Yes, ma'am; but she begs you will excuse her.

MRS. CANDOUR: Do go again; I shall be glad to see her, if it be only for a
moment, for I am sure she must be in great distress.

[*Exit* MAID.]

Dear heart, how provoking! I'm not mistress of half the circumstances!
We shall have the whole affair in the newspapers, with the names of the
parties at length, before I have dropped the story at a dozen houses.

[*Enter* SIR BENJAMIN BACKBITE.]

Oh, dear Sir Benjamin! you have heard, I suppose—

SIR BENJAMIN: Of Lady Teazle and Mr. Surface—

MRS. CANDOUR: And Sir Peter's discovery—

SIR BENJAMIN: Oh, the strangest piece of business, to be sure!

MRS. CANDOUR: Well, I never was so surprised in my life. I am so sorry for all parties, indeed.

SIR BENJAMIN: Now, I don't pity Sir Peter at all: he was so extravagantly partial to Mr. Surface.

MRS. CANDOUR: Mr. Surface! Why, 'twas with Charles Lady Teazle was detected.

SIR BENJAMIN: No, no, I tell you: Mr. Surface is the gallant.

MRS. CANDOUR: No such thing! Charles is the man. 'Twas Mr. Surface brought Sir Peter on purpose to discover them.

SIR BENJAMIN: I tell you I had it from one—

MRS. CANDOUR: And I have it from one—

SIR BENJAMIN: Who had it from one, who had it—

MRS. CANDOUR: From one immediately—But here comes Lady Sneerwell; perhaps she knows the whole affair.

[*Enter* LADY SNEERWELL.]

LADY SNEERWELL: So, my dear Mrs. Candour, here's a sad affair of our friend Lady Teazle!

MRS. CANDOUR: Ay, my dear friend, who would have thought—

LADY SNEERWELL: Well, there is no trusting to appearances; though indeed, she was always too lively for me.

MRS. CANDOUR: To be sure, her manners were a little too free; but then she was so young!

LADY SNEERWELL: And had, indeed, some good qualities.

MRS. CANDOUR: So she had, indeed. But have you heard the particulars?

LADY SNEERWELL: No; but everybody says that Mr. Surface—

SIR BENJAMIN: Ay, there; I told you Mr. Surface was the man.

MRS. CANDOUR: No, no: indeed the assignation was with Charles.

LADY SNEERWELL: With Charles! You alarm me, Mrs. Candour.

MRS. CANDOUR: Yes, yes: he was the lover. Mr. Surface, to do him justice, was only the informer.

SIR BENJAMIN: Well, I'll not dispute with you, Mrs Candour; but, be it which it may, I hope that Sir Peter's wound will not—

MRS. CANDOUR: Sir Peter's wound! Oh, mercy! I didn't hear a word of their fighting.

LADY SNEERWELL: Nor I, a syllable.

SIR BENJAMIN: No! what, no mention of the duel?

MRS. CANDOUR: Not a word.

SIR BENJAMIN: Oh yes: they fought before they left the room.

LADY SNEERWELL: Pray let us hear.

MRS. CANDOUR: Ay, do oblige us with the duel.

SIR BENJAMIN: "Sir," says Sir Peter, immediately after the discovery, "you are a most ungrateful fellow."

MRS. CANDOUR: Ay, to Charles—

SIR BENJAMIN: No, no—to Mr. Surface—"a most ungrateful fellow; and old as I am, sir," says he, "I insist on immediate satisfaction."

MRS. CANDOUR: Ay, that must have been to Charles; for 'tis very unlikely Mr. Surface should fight in his own house.

SIR BENJAMIN: 'Gad's life, ma'am, not at all—"giving me immediate satisfac-
tion"—On this, ma'am, Lady Teazle, seeing Sir Peter in such danger,
ran out of the room in strong hysterics, and Charles after her, calling out
for hartshorn and water; then, madam, they began to fight with swords—
      [*Enter* CRABTREE.]
CRABTREE: With pistols, nephew—pistols! I have it from undoubted authority.
MRS. CANDOUR: Oh, Mr. Crabtree, then it is all true!
CRABTREE: Too true, indeed, madam, and Sir Peter is dangerously wounded—
SIR BENJAMIN: By a thrust in *seconde* quite through his left side—
CRABTREE: By a bullet lodged in the thorax.
MRS. CANDOUR: Mercy on me! Poor Sir Peter!
CRABTREE: Yes, madam; though Charles would have avoided the matter, if he
could.
MRS. CANDOUR: I knew Charles was the person.
SIR BENJAMIN: My uncle, I see, knows nothing of the matter.
CRABTREE: But Sir Peter taxed him with the basest ingratitude—
SIR BENJAMIN: That I told you, you know—
CRABTREE: Do, nephew, let me speak!—and insisted on immediate—
SIR BENJAMIN: Just as I said—
CRABTREE: Odds life, nephew, allow others to know something too! A pair of
pistols lay on the bureau (for Mr. Surface, it seems, had come home the
night before late from Salthill where he had been to see the Montem
with a friend who has a son at Eton) so, unluckily, the pistols were left
charged.
SIR BENJAMIN: I heard nothing of this.
CRABTREE: Sir Peter forced Charles to take one, and they fired, it seems, pretty
nearly together. Charles's shot took effect, as I tell you, and Sir Peter's
missed; but, what is very extraordinary, the ball struck against a little
bronze Shakespeare that stood over the fireplace, grazed out of the window
at a right angle, and wounded the postman who was just coming to the
door with a double letter from Northamptonshire.
SIR BENJAMIN: My uncle's account is more circumstantial, I confess; but I
believe mine is the true one for all that.
LADY SNEERWELL: [*aside*] I am more interested in this affair than they imagine,
and must have better information.
      [*Exit* LADY SNEERWELL.]
SIR BENJAMIN: Ah! Lady Sneerwell's alarm is very easily accounted for.
CRABTREE: Yes, yes, they certainly do say—but that's neither here nor there.
MRS. CANDOUR: But, pray, where is Sir Peter at present?
CRABTREE: Oh! they brought him home, and he is now in the house, though
the servants are ordered to deny him.
MRS. CANDOUR: I believe so, and Lady Teazle, I suppose, attending him.
CRABTREE: Yes, yes; and I saw one of the faculty enter just before me.
SIR BENJAMIN: Hey! who comes here?
CRABTREE: Oh, this is he: the physician, depend on't.
MRS. CANDOUR: Oh, certainly; it must be the physician; and now we shall know.
      [*Enter* SIR OLIVER SURFACE.]

CRABTREE: Well, doctor, what hopes?

MRS. CANDOUR: Ay, doctor, how's your patient?

SIR BENJAMIN: Now, doctor, isn't it a wound with a smallsword?

CRABTREE: A bullet lodged in the thorax, for a hundred!

SIR OLIVER: Doctor! a wound with a smallsword; and a bullet in the thorax?— Oons! are you mad, good people?

SIR BENJAMIN: Perhaps, sir, you are not a doctor?

SIR OLIVER: Truly, I am to thank you for my degree, if I am.

CRABTREE: Only a friend of Sir Peter's, then, I presume. But, sir, you must have heard of his accident?

SIR OLIVER: Not a word!

CRABTREE: Not of his being dangerously wounded?

SIR OLIVER: The devil he is!

SIR BENJAMIN: Run through the body—

CRABTREE: Shot in the breast—

SIR BENJAMIN: By one Mr. Surface—

CRABTREE: Ay, the younger.

SIR OLIVER: Hey! what the plague! you seem to differ strangely in your accounts: however, you agree that Sir Peter is dangerously wounded.

SIR BENJAMIN: Oh, yes, we agree there.

CRABTREE: Yes, yes, I believe there can be no doubt in that.

SIR OLIVER: Then, upon my word, for a person in that situation, he is the most imprudent man alive; for here he comes, walking as if nothing at all was the matter.

[*Enter* SIR PETER TEAZLE.]

Odds heart, Sir Peter! you are come in good time, I promise you; for we had just given you over!

SIR BENJAMIN: [*aside to* CRABTREE] Egad, uncle, this is the most sudden recovery!

SIR OLIVER: Why, man! what do you do out of bed with a smallsword through your body and a bullet lodged in your thorax?

SIR PETER: A smallsword and a bullet?

SIR OLIVER: Ay; these gentlemen would have killed you without law or physic, and wanted to dub me a doctor, to make me an accomplice.

SIR PETER: Why, what is all this?

SIR BENJAMIN: We rejoice, Sir Peter, that the story of the duel is not true and are sincerely sorry for your other misfortune.

SIR PETER: [*aside*] So, so; all over the town already.

CRABTREE: Though, Sir Peter, you were certainly vastly to blame to marry at your years.

SIR PETER: Sir, what business is that of yours?

MRS. CANDOUR: Though, indeed, as Sir Peter made so good a husband, he's very much to be pitied.

SIR PETER: Plague on your pity, ma'am! I desire none of it.

SIR BENJAMIN: However, Sir Peter, you must not mind the laughing and jests you will meet with on the occasion.

SIR PETER: Sir, sir! I desire to be master in my own house.

CRABTREE: 'Tis no uncommon case, that's one comfort.

SIR PETER: I insist on being left to myself. Without ceremony, I insist on your leaving my house directly!

MRS. CANDOUR: Well, well, we are going; and depend on't, we'll make the best report of it we can.

[*Exit* MRS. CANDOUR.]

SIR PETER: Leave my house!

CRABTREE: And tell how hardly you've been treated!

[*Exit* CRABTREE.]

SIR PETER: Leave my house!

SIR BENJAMIN: And how patiently you bear it.

[*Exit* SIR BENJAMIN.]

SIR PETER: Fiends! vipers! furies! Oh! that their own venom would choke them!

SIR OLIVER: They are very provoking indeed, Sir Peter.

[*Enter* ROWLEY.]

ROWLEY: I heard high words: what has ruffled you, sir?

SIR PETER: Psha! what signifies asking? Do I ever pass a day without my vexations?

ROWLEY: Well, I'm not inquisitive.

SIR OLIVER: Well, Sir Peter, I have seen both my nephews in the manner we proposed.

SIR PETER: A precious couple they are!

ROWLEY: Yes, and Sir Oliver is convinced that your judgment was right, Sir Peter.

SIR OLIVER: Yes, I find Joseph is indeed the man, after all.

ROWLEY: Ay, as Sir Peter says, he is a man of sentiment.

SIR OLIVER: And acts up to the sentiments he professes.

ROWLEY: It certainly is edification to hear him talk.

SIR OLIVER: Oh, he's a model for the young men of the age! But how's this, Sir Peter? you don't join us in your friend Joseph's praise, as I expected.

SIR PETER: Sir Oliver, we live in a damned wicked world, and the fewer we praise the better.

ROWLEY: What! do you say so, Sir Peter, who were never mistaken in your life?

SIR PETER: Psha! plague on you both! I see by your sneering you have heard the whole affair. I shall go mad among you!

ROWLEY: Then, to fret you no longer, Sir Peter, we are indeed acquainted with it all. I met Lady Teazle coming from Mr. Surface's so humbled, that she deigned to request me to be her advocate with you.

SIR PETER: And does Sir Oliver know all this?

SIR OLIVER: Every circumstance.

SIR PETER: What, of the closet and the screen, hey?

SIR OLIVER: Yes, yes, and the little French milliner. Oh, I have been vastly diverted with the story! ha! ha! ha!

SIR PETER: 'Twas very pleasant.

SIR OLIVER: I never laughed more in my life, I assure you: ha! ha! ha!

SIR PETER: Oh, vastly diverting! ha! ha! ha!

ROWLEY: To be sure, Joseph with his sentiments! ha! ha! ha!

SIR PETER: Yes, yes, his sentiments! ha! ha! ha! Hyprocritical villain!

SIR OLIVER: Ay, and the rogue Charles to pull Sir Peter out of the closet: ha! ha! ha!

SIR PETER: Ha! ha! 'twas devilish entertaining, to be sure!

SIR OLIVER: Ha! ha! ha! Egad, Sir Peter, I should like to have seen your face when the screen was thrown down: ha! ha.

SIR PETER: Yes, yes, my face when the screen was thrown down: ha! ha! ha! Oh, I must never show my head again!

SIR OLIVER: But come, come, it isn't fair to laugh at you neither, my old friend; though, upon my soul, I can't help it.

SIR PETER: Oh, pray, don't restrain your mirth on my account: it does not hurt me at all! I laugh at the whole affair myself. Yes, yes, I think being a standing jest for all one's acquaintance a very happy situation. Oh, yes, and then of a morning to read the paragraphs about Mr. S—, Lady T—, and Sir P—, will be so entertaining!

ROWLEY: Without affection, Sir Peter, you may despise the ridicule of fools. But I see Lady Teazle going towards the next room, I am sure you must desire a reconciliation as earnestly as she does.

SIR OLIVER: Perhaps my being here prevents her coming to you. Well, I'll leave honest Rowley to mediate between you; but he must bring you all presently to Mr. Surface's where I am now returning, if not to reclaim a libertine, at least to expose hypocrisy.

SIR PETER: Ah, I'll be present at your discovering yourself there with all my heart; though 'tis a vile unlucky place for discoveries.

ROWLEY: We'll follow.

[*Exit* SIR OLIVER.]

SIR PETER: She is not coming here, you see, Rowley.

ROWLEY: No, but she has left the door of that room open, you perceive. See, she is in tears.

SIR PETER: Certainly a little mortification appears very becoming in a wife. Don't you think it will do her good to let her pine a little?

ROWLEY: Oh, this is ungenerous in you!

SIR PETER: Well, I know not what to think. You remember the letter I found of hers evidently intended for Charles!

ROWLEY: A mere forgery, Sir Peter! laid in your way on purpose. This is one of the points which I intend Snake shall give you conviction of.

SIR PETER: I wish I were once satisfied of that. She looks this way. What a remarkably elegant turn of the head she has! Rowley, I'll go to her.

ROWLEY: Certainly.

SIR PETER: Though, when it is known that we are reconciled, people will laugh at me ten times more.

ROWLEY: Let them laugh, and retort their malice only by showing them you are happy in spite of it.

SIR PETER: I'faith, so I will! and, if I'm not mistaken, we may yet be the happiest couple in the country.

ROWLEY: Nay, Sir Peter, he is who once lays aside suspicion—

SIR PETER: Hold, Master Rowley! if you have any regard for me, never let me hear you utter anything like a sentiment. I have had enough of them to serve me the rest of my life.

SCENE III——*The Library in* JOSEPH SURFACE'S *House.*

[JOSEPH SURFACE *and* LADY SNEERWELL.]

LADY SNEERWELL: Impossible! Will not Sir Peter immediately be reconciled to Charles, and of course no longer oppose his union with Maria? The thought is distraction to me.

JOSEPH SURFACE: Can passion furnish a remedy?

LADY SNEERWELL: No, nor cunning either. Oh, I was a fool, an idiot, to league with such a blunderer!

JOSEPH SURFACE: Sure, Lady Sneerwell, I am the greatest sufferer; yet you see I bear the accident with calmness.

LADY SNEERWELL: Because the disappointment doesn't reach your heart; your interest only attached you to Maria. Had you felt for her what I have for that ungrateful libertine, neither your temper nor hypocrisy could prevent your showing the sharpness of your vexation.

JOSEPH SURFACE: But why should your reproaches fall on me for this disappointment?

LADY SNEERWELL: Are you not the cause of it? Had you not a sufficient field for your roguery in imposing upon Sir Peter, and supplanting your brother, but you must endeavor to seduce his wife? I hate such an avarice of crimes; 'tis an unfair monopoly, and never prospers.

JOSEPH SURFACE: Well, I admit I have been to blame. I confess I deviated from the direct road of wrong, but I don't think we're so totally defeated neither.

LADY SNEERWELL: No?

JOSEPH SURFACE: You tell me you have made a trial of Snake since we met, and that you still believe him faithful to us?

LADY SNEERWELL: I do believe so.

JOSEPH SURFACE: And that he has undertaken, should it be necessary, to swear and prove that Charles is at this time contracted by vows and honor to your ladyship, which some of his former letters to you will serve to support?

LADY SNEERWELL: This, indeed, might have assisted.

JOSEPH SURFACE: Come, come; it is not too late yet.

[*Knocking at the door.*]

But hark! this is probably my uncle, Sir Oliver: retire to that room; we'll consult further when he's gone.

LADY SNEERWELL: Well, but if he should find you out too?

JOSEPH SURFACE: Oh, I have no fear of that. Sir Peter will hold his tongue for his own credit's sake—and you may depend on it I shall soon discover Sir Oliver's weak side!

LADY SNEERWELL: I have no diffidence of your abilities! only be constant to one roguery at a time.

[*Exit* LADY SNEERWELL.]

JOSEPH SURFACE: I will, I will! So! 'tis confounded hard, after such bad fortune, to be baited by one's confederate in evil. Well, at all events, my character is so much better than Charles's that I certainly—hey!—what—this is not Sir Oliver, but old Stanley again. Plague on't that he should return to tease me just now! I shall have Sir Oliver come and find him here—and—

[*Enter* SIR OLIVER SURFACE.]

Gad's life, Mr. Stanley, why have you come back to plague me at this time? You must not stay now, upon my word.

SIR OLIVER: Sir, I hear your uncle Oliver is expected here, and though he has been so penurious to you, I'll try what he'll do for me.

JOSEPH SURFACE: Sir, 'tis impossible for you to stay now, so I must beg—Come any other time, and I promise you, you shall be assisted.

SIR OLIVER: No: Sir Oliver and I must be acquainted.

JOSEPH SURFACE: Zounds, sir! then I insist on your quitting the room directly.

SIR OLIVER: Nay, sir—

JOSEPH SURFACE: Sir, I insist on't!—Here, William! show this gentleman out. Since you compel me, sir not one moment—this is such insolence!

[*Going to push him out. Enter* CHARLES SURFACE.]

CHARLES SURFACE: Heyday! what's the matter now? What the devil have you got hold of my little broker here? Zounds, brother, don't hurt little Premium. What's the matter, my little fellow?

JOSEPH SURFACE: So! he has been with you, too, has he?

CHARLES SURFACE: To be sure he has. Why, he's as honest a little—But sure, Joseph, you have not been borrowing money too, have you?

JOSEPH SURFACE: Borrowing! no! But, brother, you know we expect Sir Oliver here every—

CHARLES SURFACE: O gad, that's true! Noll mustn't find the little broker here, to be sure.

JOSEPH SURFACE: Yet, Mr. Stanley insists—

CHARLES SURFACE: Stanley! why his name's Premium.

JOSEPH SURFACE: No, sir, Stanley.

CHARLES SURFACE: No, no, Premium.

JOSEPH SURFACE: Well, no matter which—but—

CHARLES SURFACE: Ay, ay, Stanley or Premium, 'tis the same thing, as you say; for I suppose he goes by half a hundred names, besides A.B. at the coffee-house.

[*Knocking.*]

JOSEPH SURFACE: 'Sdeath! here's Sir Oliver at the door. Now I beg, Mr. Stanley—

CHARLES SURFACE: Ay, ay, and I beg, Mr. Premium—

SIR OLIVER: Gentlemen—

JOSEPH SURFACE: Sir, by heaven you shall go!

CHARLES SURFACE: Ay, out with him, certainly!

SIR OLIVER: This violence—

JOSEPH SURFACE: Sir, 'tis your own fault.

CHARLES SURFACE: Out with him, to be sure!

[*Both forcing* SIR OLIVER *out. Enter* SIR PETER *and* LADY TEAZLE, MARIA, *and* ROWLEY.]

SIR PETER: My old friend, Sir Oliver—hey! What in the name of wonder!— here are dutiful nephews—assault their uncle at first visit!

LADY TEAZLE: Indeed, Sir Oliver, 'twas well we came in to rescue you.

ROWLEY: Truly it was; for I perceive, Sir Oliver, the character- of old Stanley was no protection to you.

SIR OLIVER: Nor of Premium either: the necessities of the former could not extort a shilling from that benevolent gentleman; and now, egad, I stood a chance of faring worse than my ancestors and being knocked down without being bid for.

JOSEPH SURFACE: Charles!

CHARLES SURFACE: Joseph!

JOSEPH SURFACE: 'Tis now complete!

CHARLES SURFACE: Very!

SIR OLIVER: Sir Peter, my friend, and Rowley too—look on that elder nephew of mine. You know what he has already received from my bounty; and you also know how gladly I would have regarded half my fortune as held in trust for him? judge, then, my disappointment in discovering him to be destitute of truth, charity, and gratitude!

SIR PETER: Sir Oliver, I should be more surprised at this declaration, if I had not myself found him to be mean, treacherous, and hypocritical.

LADY TEAZLE: And if the gentleman pleads not guilty to these, pray let him call me to his character.

SIR PETER: Then, I believe, we need add no more: if he knows himself, he will consider it as the most perfect punishment that he is known to the world.

CHARLES SURFACE: [*aside*] If they talk this way to Honesty, what will they say to me, by-and-by?

SIR OLIVER: As for that prodigal, his brother, there—

CHARLES SURFACE: [*aside*] Ay, now comes my turn: the damned family pictures will ruin me!

JOSEPH SURFACE: Sir Oliver—uncle, will you honor me with a hearing?

CHARLES SURFACE: [*aside*] Now, if Joseph would make one of his long speeches, I might recollect myself a little.

SIR OLIVER: [*to* JOSEPH] I suppose you would undertake to justify yourself entirely?

JOSEPH SURFACE: I trust I could.

SIR OLIVER: [*to* CHARLES] Well, sir!—and you could justify yourself too, I suppose?

CHARLES SURFACE: Not that I know of, Sir Oliver.

SIR OLIVER: What!—Little Premium has been let too much into the secret, I suppose?

CHARLES SURFACE: True, sir; but they were family secrets, and should not be mentioned again, you know.

ROWLEY: Come, Sir Oliver, I know you cannot speak of Charles's follies with anger.

SIR OLIVER: Odd's heart, no more I can; nor with gravity either. Sir Peter, do you know the rogue bargained with me for all his ancestors; sold me judges and generals by the foot, and maiden aunts as cheap as broken china.

CHARLES SURFACE: To be sure, Sir Oliver, I did make a little free with the family canvas, that's the truth on't. My ancestors may rise in judgment against me, there's no denying it; but believe me sincere when I tell you —and upon my soul I would not say so if I was not—that if I do not appear mortified at the exposure of my follies, it is because I feel at this moment the warmest satisfaction at seeing you, my liberal benefactor.

SIR OLIVER: Charles, I believe you. Give me your hand again: the ill looking little fellow over the settee has made your peace.

CHARLES SURFACE: Then, sir, my gratitude to the original is still increased.

LADY TEAZLE: Yet, I believe, Sir Oliver, here is one whom Charles is still more anxious to be reconciled to.

[*Pointing to* MARIA.]

SIR OLIVER: Oh, I have heard of his attachment there; and, with the young lady's pardon, if I construe right—that blush—

SIR PETER: Well, child, speak your sentiments.

MARIA: Sir, I have little to say, but I shall rejoice to hear that he is happy; for me, whatever claim I had to his attention, I willingly resign to one who has a better title.

CHARLES SURFACE: How, Maria!

SIR PETER: Heyday! what's the mystery now? While he appeared an incorrigible rake, you would give your hand to no one else; and now that he is likely to reform I'll warrant you won't have him.

MARIA: His own heart and Lady Sneerwell know the cause.

CHARLES SURFACE: Lady Sneerwell!

JOSEPH SURFACE: Brother, it is with great concern I am obliged to speak on this point, but my regard to justice compels me, and Lady Sneerwell's injuries can no longer be concealed.

[*Opens the door. Enter* LADY SNEERWELL.]

SIR PETER: So! another French milliner! Egad, he has one in every room in the house, I suppose!

LADY SNEERWELL: Ungrateful Charles! Well may you be surprised, and feel for the indelicate situation your perfidy has forced me into.

CHARLES SURFACE: Pray, uncle, is this another plot of yours? For, as I have life, I don't understand it.

JOSEPH SURFACE: I believe, sir, there is but the evidence of one person more necessary to make it extremely clear.

SIR PETER: And that person, I imagine, is Mr. Snake. Rowley, you were perfectly right to bring him with us, and pray let him appear.

ROWLEY: Walk in, Mr. Snake.

[*Enter* SNAKE.]

I thought his testimony might be wanted; however, it happens unluckily, that he comes to confront Lady Sneerwell, not to support her.

LADY SNEERWELL: A villain! Treacherous to me at last! Speak, fellow, have you too conspired against me?

SNAKE: I beg your ladyship ten thousand pardons: you paid me extremely liberally for the lie in question; but I unfortunately have been offered double to speak the truth.

SIR PETER: Plot and counterplot, egad!

LADY SNEERWELL: The torments of shame and disappointment on you all!

LADY TEAZLE: Hold, Lady Sneerwell—before you go, let me thank you for the trouble you and that gentleman have taken in writing letters from me to Charles, and answering them yourself; and let me also request you to make my respects to the scandalous college, of which you are president, and inform them that Lady Teazle, licentiate, begs leave to return the diploma they granted her, as she leaves off practice and kills characters no longer.

LADY SNEERWELL: You too, madam!—provoking—insolent! May your husband live these fifty years!

[*Exit* LADY SNEERWELL.]

SIR PETER: Oons! what a fury!

LADY TEAZLE: A malicious creature, indeed!

SIR PETER: Hey! not for her last wish?

LADY TEAZLE: Oh, no!

SIR OLIVER: Well, sir, and what have you to say now?

JOSEPH SURFACE: Sir, I am so confounded, to find that Lady Sneerwell could be guilty of suborning Mr. Snake in this manner, to impose on us all, that I know not what to say: however, lest her revengeful spirit should prompt her to injure my brother, I had certainly better follow her directly.

[*Exit* JOSEPH SURFACE.]

SIR PETER: Moral to the last drop!

SIR OLIVER: Ay, and marry her, Joseph, if you can. Oil and vinegar—egad, you'll do very well together.

ROWLEY: I believe we have no more occasion for Mr. Snake at present?

SNAKE: Before I go, I beg pardon once for all, for whatever uneasiness I have been the humble instrument of causing to the parties present.

SIR PETER: Well, well, you have made atonement by a good deed at last.

SNAKE: But I must request of the company, that it shall never be known.

SIR PETER: Hey! what the plague! are you ashamed of having done a right thing once in your life?

SNAKE: Ah, sir, consider—I live by the badness of my character; I have nothing but my infamy to depend on; and, if it were once known that I had been betrayed into an honest action, I should lose every friend I have in the world.

SIR OLIVER: Well, well—we'll not traduce you by saying anything in your praise, never fear.

[*Exit* SNAKE.]

SIR PETER: There's a precious rogue!

LADY TEAZLE: See, Sir Oliver, there needs no persuasion now to reconcile your nephew and Maria.

SIR OLIVER: Ay, ay, that's as it should be; and, egad, we'll have the wedding tomorrow morning.

CHARLES SURFACE: Thank you, dear uncle.

SIR PETER: What, you rogue! don't you ask the girl's consent first?

CHARLES SURFACE: Oh, I have done that a long time—a minute ago—and she has looked yes.

MARIA: For shame, Charles!—I protest, Sir Peter, there has not been a word—

SIR OLIVER: Well, then, the fewer the better: may your love for each other never know abatement.

SIR PETER: And may you live as happily together as Lady Teazle and I intend to do!

CHARLES SURFACE: Rowley, my old friend, I am sure you congratulate me; and I suspect that I owe you much.

SIR OLIVER: You do, indeed, Charles.

ROWLEY: If my efforts to serve you had not succeeded, you would have been in my debt for the attempt—but deserve to be happy—and you overpay me.

SIR PETER: Ay, honest Rowley always said you would reform.

CHARLES SURFACE: Why as to reforming, Sir Peter, I'll make no promises, and that I take to be a proof that I intend to set about it. But here shall be my monitor—my gentle guide.—Ah! can I leave the virtuous path those eyes illumine?

> Though thou, dear maid, shouldst wave thy beauty's sway,
> Thou still must rule, because I will obey:
> An humble fugitive from Folly view,
> No sanctuary near but Love—and you: [*To the audience.*]
> *You* can, indeed, each anxious fear remove,
> For even Scandal dies, if you approve.

EPILOGUE

[*Written by* MR. COLMAN.]
[*Spoken by* LADY TEAZLE.]

> I, who was late so volatile and gay,
> Like a trade-wind must now blow all one way,
> Bend all my cares, my studies, and my vows,
> To one dull rusty weathercock—my spouse!
> So wills our virtuous bard—the motley Bayes   5
> Of crying epilogues and laughing plays!
> Old bachelors, who marry smart young wives—
> Learn from our play to regulate your lives:
> Each bring his dear to town, all faults upon her—
> London will prove the very source of honor.   10
> Plunged fairly in, like a cold bath it serves,
> When principles relax, to brace the nerves.
> Such is my case; and yet I must deplore
> That the gay dream of dissipation's o'er.
> And say, ye fair! was ever lively wife,   15
> Born with a genius for the highest life,

Like me untimely blasted in her bloom,
Like me condemned to such a dismal doom?
Save money—when I just knew how to waste it!
Leave London—just as I began to taste it!   20
Must I then watch the early-crowing cock,
The melancholy ticking of a clock;
In a lone rustic hall for ever pounded,
With dogs, cats, rats, and squalling brats surrounded?
With humble curate can I now retire,   25
(While good Sir Peter boozes with the squire,)
And at backgammon mortify my soul,
That pants for loo, or flutters at a vole.
Seven's the main! Dear sound that must expire,
Lost at hot cockles round a Christmas fire;   30
The transient hour of fashion too soon spent,
Farewell the tranquil mind, farewell content!
Farewell the pluméd head, the cushioned tête,
That takes the cushion from its proper seat!
That spirit-stirring drum—card drums I mean,   35
Spadille—odd trick—pam—basto—king and queen!
And you, ye knockers that with brazen throat
The welcome visitors' approach denote;
Farewell all quality of high renown,
Pride, pomp, and circumstance of glorious town!   40
Farewell! your revels I partake no more,
And Lady Teazle's occupation's o'er!
All this I told our bard; he smiled, and said 'twas clear,
I ought to play deep tragedy next year.
Meanwhile he drew wise morals from his play,   45
And in these solemn periods stalked away:—
"Blessed were the fair like you; her faults who stopped.
And closed her follies when the curtain dropped!
No more in vice or error to engage,
Or play the fool at large on life's great stage."   50

Henrik Ibsen

The Wild Duck

Translated by William Archer

PERSONS OF THE PLAY

WERLE, *a merchant*

GREGERS WERLE, *his son*

OLD EKDAL

HIALMAR EKDAL, *his son, a
photographer*

GINA EKDAL, *Hialmar's wife*

HEDVIG, *their daughter, a girl of
fourteen*

MRS SORBY, *Werle's housekeeper*

RELLING, *a doctor*

MOLVIK, *a student of theology*

GRABERG, *Werle's bookkeeper*

PETTERSEN, *Werle's servant*

JENSEN, *a hired waiter*

A FLABBY GENTLEMAN

A THIN-HAIRED GENTLEMAN

A SHORTSIGHTED GENTLEMAN

SIX OTHER GENTLEMEN, *guests at
Werle's dinner party*

SEVERAL HIRED WAITERS

The action takes place in the home of
WERLE *and the studio of* HIALMAR EKDAL.

ACT I

SCENE——*At* WERLE'S *house. A richly and comfortably furnished study; book-
cases and upholstered furniture; a writing table, with papers and documents,
in the center of the room; lighted lamps with green shades, giving a subdued
light. At the back open folding doors with curtains drawn back. Within is
seen a large and handsome room, brilliantly lighted with lamps and branch-
ing candlesticks. In front, on the right (in the study), a small baize door
leads into* WERLE'S *office. On the left, in front, a fireplace with a glowing
coal fire and farther back a double door leading into the dining room.*

> [WERLE'S *servant,* PETTERSEN, *in livery, and* JENSEN, *the hired waiter,
in black, are putting the study in order. In the large room two or
three other hired waiters are moving about arranging things and
lighting more candles. From the dining room the hum of conversation and laughter of many voices are heard; a glass is tapped with a
knife; silence follows, and a toast is proposed; shouts of "Bravo!" and
then again a buzz of conversation.*]

285

PETTERSEN: [*lights a lamp on the chimney place and places a shade over it*] Listen to them, Jensen! Now the old man's on his legs giving a long speech about Mrs Sorby.

JENSEN: [*pushing forward an armchair*] Is it true, what folks say, that they're—very good friends, eh?

PETTERSEN: Lord knows.

JENSEN: I've heard tell as he's been a lively customer in his day.

PETTERSEN: May be.

JENSEN: And he's giving this spread in honor of his son, they say.

PETTERSEN: Yes. His son came home yesterday.

JENSEN: This is the first time I ever heard as Mr Werle had a son.

PETTERSEN: Oh yes, he has a son right enough. But he's a fixture, as you might say, up at the Höidal works. He's never once come to town all the years I've been in service here.

A WAITER: [*in the doorway of the other room*] Pettersen, here's an old fellow wanting—

PETTERSEN: [*mutters*] The devil—who's this now?

[OLD EKDAL *appears from the right, in the inner room. He is dressed in a threadbare overcoat with a high collar; he wears woolen mittens and carries in his hand a stick and a fur cap. Under his arm a brown paper parcel. Dirty red-brown wig and small gray mustache.*]

PETTERSEN: [*goes toward him*] Good lord!—what do you want here?

EKDAL: [*in the doorway*] Must get into the office, Pettersen.

PETTERSEN: The office was closed an hour ago, and—

EKDAL: So they told me at the front door. But Graberg's in there still. Let me slip in this way, Pettersen; there's a good fellow. [*Points toward the baize door.*] It's not the first time I've come this way.

PETTERSEN: Well, you may pass. [*opens the door*] But mind you go out again the proper way, for we've got company.

EKDAL: I know, I know—h'm! Thanks, Pettersen, good old friend! Thanks! [*mutters softly*] Ass! [*He goes into the office;* PETTERSEN *shuts the door after him.*]

JENSEN: Is he one of the office people?

PETTERSEN: No, he's only an outside hand that does odd jobs of copying. But he's been a topnotcher in his day, has old Ekdal.

JENSEN: You can see he's been through a lot.

PETTERSEN: Yes; he was an army officer, you know.

JENSEN: You don't say so?

PETTERSEN: No mistake about it. But then he went into the timber trade or something of the sort. They say he once played Mr Werle a very nasty trick. They were partners in the Höidal works at the time. Oh, I know old Ekdal well, I do. Many a nip of bitters and bottle of ale we two have drunk at Madam Eriksen's.

JENSEN: He don't look as if he'd much to stand treat with.

PETTERSEN: Why, bless you, Jensen, it's me that stands treat. I always think there's no harm in being a bit civil to folks that have seen better days.

JENSEN: Did he go bankrupt then?

PETTERSEN: Worse than that. He went to jail.

JENSEN: To jail!

PETTERSEN: Or perhaps it was the penitentiary. [*listens*] Sh! They're leaving the table.

> [*The dining-room door is thrown open from within by a couple of waiters.* MRS SORBY *comes out conversing with two gentlemen. Gradually the whole company follows, among them* WERLE. *Last come* HIALMAR EKDAL *and* GREGERS WERLE.]

MRS SORBY: [*in passing, to the servant*] Tell them to serve the coffee in the music room, Pettersen.

PETTERSEN: Very well, madam.

> [*She goes with the two gentlemen into the inner room and thence out to the right.* PETTERSEN *and* JENSEN *go out the same way.*]

A FLABBY GENTLEMAN: [*to a* THIN-HAIRED GENTLEMAN] Whew! What a dinner! It was no joke to do it justice.

THE THIN-HAIRED GENTLEMAN: Oh, with a little good will one can get through a lot in three hours.

THE FLABBY GENTLEMAN: Yes, but afterward, afterward, my dear Chamberlain!

A THIRD GENTLEMAN: I hear the coffee and liqueur are to be served in the music room.

THE FLABBY GENTLEMAN: Bravo! Then perhaps Mrs Sorby will play us something.

THE THIN-HAIRED GENTLEMAN: [*in a low voice*] I hope Mrs Sorby doesn't play us a tune we don't like, one of these days!

THE FLABBY GENTLEMAN: Oh no, Bertha will never turn against her old friends.

> [*They laugh and pass into the inner room.*]

WERLE: [*in a low voice, dejectedly*] I don't think anybody noticed it, Gregers.

GREGERS: [*looks at him*] Noticed what?

WERLE: Didn't you notice it either?

GREGERS: What do you mean?

WERLE: We were thirteen at table.

GREGERS: Really? Were there thirteen of us?

WERLE: [*glances toward* HIALMAR EKDAL] Our usual party is twelve. [*to the others*] This way, gentlemen!

> [WERLE *and the others, all except* HIALMAR *and* GREGERS, *go out by the back, to the right.*]

HIALMAR: [*who has overheard the conversation*] You ought not to have invited me, Gregers.

GREGERS: What! Not ask my best and only friend to a party supposed to be in my honor?

HIALMAR: But I don't think your father likes it. You see, I am quite outside his circle.

GREGERS: So I hear. But I wanted to see you and have a talk with you, and I certainly shan't be staying long. Ah, we two old schoolfellows have drifted apart from each other. It must be sixteen or seventeen years since we met.

HIALMAR: Is it so long?

GREGERS: It is. Well, how goes it with you? You look well. You have put on flesh and grown almost stout.

HIALMAR: Well, "stout" is scarcely the word, but I daresay I look a little more of a man than I used to.

GREGERS: Yes, you do; your outer man is in first-rate condition.

HIALMAR: [*in a tone of gloom*] Ah, but the inner man! That is a very different matter, I can tell you! Of course you know of the terrible catastrophe that has befallen me since last we met.

GREGERS: [*more softly*] How are things going with your father now?

HIALMAR: Don't let us talk of it, old fellow. Of course my poor unhappy father lives with me. He hasn't another soul in the world to care for him. But you can understand that this is a miserable subject for me. Tell me, rather, how you have been getting on up at the works.

GREGERS: I have had a delightfully lonely time of it—plenty of leisure to think and think about things. Come over here; we may as well make ourselves comfortable.

    [*He seats himself in an armchair by the fire and draws* HIALMAR *down into another alongside of it.*]

HIALMAR: [*sentimentally*] After all, Gregers, I thank you for inviting me to your father's table; for I take it as a sign that you have got over your feeling against me.

GREGERS: [*surprised*] How could you imagine I had any feeling against you?

HIALMAR: You had at first, you know.

GREGERS: How at first?

HIALMAR: After the great misfortune. It was natural enough that you should. Your father was within an ace of being drawn into that—well, that terrible business.

GREGERS: Why should that give me any feeling against you? Who can have put that into your head?

HIALMAR: I know it did, Gregers; your father told me so himself.

GREGERS: [*starts*] My father! Oh, indeed. H'm. Was that why you never let me hear from you?—not a single word.

HIALMAR: Yes.

GREGERS: Not even when you made up your mind to become a photographer?

HIALMAR: Your father said I had better not write to you at all, about anything.

GREGERS: [*looking straight before him*] Well, well, perhaps he was right. But tell me now, Hialmar: are you pretty well satisfied with your present position?

HIALMAR: [*with a little sigh*] Oh yes, I am; I have really no cause to complain. At first, as you may guess, I felt it a little strange. It was such a totally new state of things for me. But of course my whole circumstances were totally changed. Father's utter, irretrievable ruin—the shame and disgrace of it, Gregers—

GREGERS: [*affected*] Yes, yes; I understand.

HIALMAR: I couldn't think of remaining at college; there wasn't a shilling to spare; on the contrary, there were debts—mainly to your father, I believe—

GREGERS: H'm.

HIALMAR: In short, I thought it best to break, once for all, with my old surroundings and associations. It was your father that specially urged me to it, and since he interested himself so much in me—

GREGERS: My father did?

HIALMAR: Yes, you surely knew that, didn't you? Where do you suppose I found the money to learn photography and to furnish a studio and make a start? All that costs money, I can tell you.

GREGERS: And my father provided it?

HIALMAR: Yes, my dear fellow, didn't you know? I understood him to say he had written to you about it.

GREGERS: Not a word about his part in the business. He must have forgotten it. Our correspondence has always been purely a business one. So it was my father that—

HIALMAR: Yes, certainly. He didn't wish it to be generally known, but he it was. And of course it was he, too, that put me in a position to marry. Don't you—don't you know about that either?

GREGERS: No, I haven't heard a word of it. [*shakes him by the arm*] But, my dear Hialmar, I can't tell you what pleasure all this gives me—pleasure and self-reproach. I have perhaps done my father injustice after all—in some things. This proves that he has a heart. It shows a sort of compunction—

HIALMAR: Compunction?

GREGERS: Yes, yes—whatever you like to call it. Oh, I can't tell you how glad I am to hear this of Father. So you are a married man, Hialmar! That is further than I shall ever get. Well, I hope you are happy in your married life?

HIALMAR: Yes, thoroughly happy. She is as good and capable a wife as any man could wish for. And she is by no means without culture.

GREGERS: [*rather surprised*] No, of course not.

HIALMAR: You see, life is itself an education. Her daily intercourse with me— And then we know one or two rather remarkable men who come a good deal about us. I assure you, you would hardly know Gina again.

GREGERS: Gina?

HIALMAR: Yes; had you forgotten that her name was Gina?

GREGERS: Whose name? I haven't the slightest idea—

HIALMAR: Don't you remember that she used to be in service here?

GREGERS: [*looks at him*] Is it Gina Hansen?

HIALMAR: Yes, of course it is Gina Hansen.

GREGERS: —who kept house for us during the last year of my mother's illness?

HIALMAR: Yes, exactly. But, my dear friend, I'm quite sure your father told you that I was married.

GREGERS: [*who has risen*] Oh yes, he mentioned it, but not that— [*walking about the room*] Stay—perhaps he did—now that I think of it. My father always writes such short letters. [*half seats himself on the arm of the chair*] Now tell me, Hialmar—this is interesting—how did you come to know Gina—your wife?

HIALMAR: The simplest thing in the world. You know Gina did not stay here long; everything was so much upset at that time, owing to your mother's illness and so forth, that Gina was not equal to it all; so she gave notice and left. That was the year before your mother died—or it may have been the same year.

GREGERS: It was the same year. I was up at the works then. But afterward?

HIALMAR: Well, Gina lived at home with her mother, Madam Hansen, an excellent, hard-working woman who kept a little eating house. She had a room to let too, a very nice comfortable room.

GREGERS: And I suppose you were lucky enough to secure it?

HIALMAR: Yes; in fact, it was your father that recommended it to me. So it was there, you see, that I really came to know Gina.

GREGERS: And then you got engaged?

HIALMAR: Yes. It doesn't take young people long to fall in love—h'm.

GREGERS: [*rises and moves about a little*] Tell me: was it after your engagement —was it then that my father— I mean was it then that you began to take up photography?

HIALMAR: Yes, precisely. I wanted to make a start and to set up house as soon as possible, and your father and I agreed that this photography business was the readiest way. Gina thought so too. Oh, and there was another thing in its favor, by the bye; it happened luckily, that Gina had learned to retouch.

GREGERS: That chimed in marvelously.

HIALMAR: [*pleased, rises*] Yes, didn't it? Don't you think it was a marvelous piece of luck?

GREGERS: Oh, unquestionably. My father seems to have been almost a kind of providence to you.

HIALMAR: [*with emotion*] He did not forsake his old friend's son in the hour of his need. For he has a heart, you see.

MRS SORBY: [*enters arm in arm with* WERLE] Nonsense, my dear Mr Werle; you mustn't stay there any longer staring at all the lights. It's very bad for you.

WERLE: [*lets go her arm and passes his hand over his eyes*] I daresay you are right.

[PETTERSEN *and* JENSEN *carry round refreshment trays.*]

MRS SORBY: [*to the guests in the other room*] This way, if you please, gentlemen. Whoever wants a glass of punch must be so good as to come in here.

THE FLABBY GENTLEMAN: [*comes up to* MRS SORBY] Surely it isn't possible that you have suspended our cherished right to smoke?

MRS SORBY: Yes, No smoking here, in Mr Werle's sanctum, Chamberlain.

THE THIN-HAIRED GENTLEMAN: When did you enact these stringent amendments on the cigar law, Mrs Sorby?

MRS SORBY: After the last dinner, Chamberlain, when certain persons permitted themselves to overstep the mark.

THE THIN-HAIRED GENTLEMAN: And may one never overstep the mark a little bit, Madame Bertha? Not the least little bit?

MRS SORBY: Not in any respect whatsoever, Mr Balle.

[*Most of the guests have assembled in the study; servants hand round glasses of punch.*]

WERLE: [*to* HIALMAR, *who is studying beside a table*] What are you studying so intently, Ekdal?

HIALMAR: Only an album, Mr Werle.

THE THIN-HAIRED GENTLEMAN: [*who is wandering about*] Ah, photographs! They are quite in your line of course.

THE FLABBY GENTLEMAN: [*in an armchair*] Haven't you brought any of your own with you?

HIALMAR: No, I haven't.

THE FLABBY GENTLEMAN: You ought to have; it's very good for the digestion to sit and look at pictures.

THE THIN-HAIRED GENTLEMAN: And it contributes to the entertainment, you know.

THE SHORTSIGHTED GENTLEMAN: And all contributions are thankfully received.

MRS SORBY: The chamberlains think that when one is invited out to dinner one ought to exert oneself a little in return, Mr Ekdal.

THE FLABBY GENTLEMAN: Where one dines so well, that duty becomes a pleasure.

THE THIN-HAIRED GENTLEMAN: And when it's a case of the struggle for existence, you know—

MRS SORBY: I quite agree with you!

[*They continue the conversation with laughter and joking.*]

GREGERS: [*softly*] You must join in, Hialmar.

HIALMAR: [*writhing*] What am I to talk about?

THE FLABBY GENTLEMAN: Don't you think, Mr Werle, that Tokay may be considered one of the more wholesome sorts of wine?

WERLE: [*by the fire*] I can answer for the Tokay you had today, at any rate; it's one of the very finest seasons. Of course you would notice that.

THE FLABBY GENTLEMAN: Yes, it had a remarkably delicate flavor.

HIALMAR: [*shyly*] Is there any difference between the seasons?

THE FLABBY GENTLEMAN: [*laughs*] Come! That's good!

WERLE: [*smiles*] It really doesn't pay to set fine wine before you.

THE THIN-HAIRED GENTLEMAN: Tokay is like photographs, Mr Ekdal; they both need sunshine. Am I not right?

HIALMAR: Yes, light is important, no doubt.

MRS SORBY: And it's exactly the same with the chamberlains—they, too, depend very much on sunshine, as the saying is.

THE THIN-HAIRED GENTLEMAN: Oh, shame! That's a very threadbare joke!

THE SHORTSIGHTED GENTLEMAN: Mrs Sorby is coming out—

THE FLABBY GENTLEMAN: —and at our expense too. [*holds up his finger reprovingly*] Oh, Madame Bertha, Madame Bertha!

MRS SORBY: Yes, and there's not the least doubt that the seasons differ greatly. The old vintages are the finest.

THE SHORTSIGHTED GENTLEMAN: Do you count me among the old vintages?

MRS SORBY: Oh, far from it.

THE THIN-HAIRED GENTLEMAN: There now! But me, dear Mrs Sorby—

THE FLABBY GENTLEMAN: Yes, and me? What vintage should you say that we belong to?

MRS SORBY: Why, to the sweet vintages, gentlemen. [*She sips a glass of punch. The gentlemen laugh and flirt with her.*]

WERLE: Mrs Sorby can always find a loophole—when she wants to. Fill your glasses, gentlemen! Pettersen, will you see to it? Gregers, suppose we have a glass together. [GREGERS *does not move.*] Won't you join us, Ekdal? I found no opportunity of drinking with you at table.

[GRABERG, *the bookkeeper, looks in at the baize door.*]

GRABERG: Excuse me, sir, but I can't get out.

WERLE: Have you been locked in again?

GRABERG: Yes, and Flakstad has carried off the keys.

WERLE: Well, you can pass out this way.

GRABERG: But there's someone else—

WERLE: All right; come through, both of you. Don't be afraid.

[GRABERG *and* OLD EKDAL *come out of the office.*]

WERLE: [*involuntarily*] Ugh!

[*The laughter and talk among the guests cease.* HIALMAR *starts at the sight of his father, puts down his glass and turns toward the fireplace.*]

EKDAL: [*does not look up but makes little bows to both sides as he passes, murmuring*] Beg pardon, come the wrong way. Door locked—door locked. Beg pardon.

[*He and* GRABERG *go out by the back, to the right.*]

WERLE: [*between his teeth*] That idiot Graberg.

GREGERS: [*open-mouthed and staring, to* HIALMAR] Why, surely that wasn't—

THE FLABBY GENTLEMAN: What's the matter? Who was it?

GREGERS: Oh, nobody; only the bookkeeper and someone with him.

THE SHORTSIGHTED GENTLEMAN: [*to* HIALMAR] Did you know that man?

HIALMAR: I don't know—I didn't notice—

THE FLABBY GENTLEMAN: What the devil has come over everyone? [*He joins another group who are talking softly.*]

MRS SORBY: [*whispers to the* SERVANT] Give him something to take with him—something good, mind.

PETTERSEN: [*nods*] I'll see to it.

[*Goes out.*]

GREGERS: [*softly and with emotion, to* HIALMAR] So that was really he!

HIALMAR: Yes.

GREGERS: And you could stand there and deny that you knew him.

HIALMAR: [*whispers vehemently*] But how could I—

GREGERS: —acknowledge your own father?

HIALMAR: [*with pain*] Oh, if you were in my place—

[*The conversation among the guests, which has been carried on in a low tone, now swells into constrained joviality.*]

THE THIN-HAIRED GENTLEMAN: [*approaching* HIALMAR *and* GREGERS *in a friendly manner*] Ah! Reviving old college memories, eh? Don't you smoke, Mr Ekdal? May I give you a light? Oh, by the bye, we mustn't—

HIALMAR: No, thank you, I won't—

THE FLABBY GENTLEMAN: Haven't you a nice little poem you could recite to us, Mr Ekdal? You used to recite so charmingly.

HIALMAR: I am sorry, I can't remember anything.

THE FLABBY GENTLEMAN: Oh, that's a pity. Well, what shall we do, Balle?
[*Both gentlemen move away and pass into the other room.*]

HIALMAR: [*gloomily*] Gregers—I am going! When a man has felt the crushing hand of Fate, you see— Say good-by to your father for me.

GREGERS: Yes, yes. Are you going straight home?

HIALMAR: Yes. Why?

GREGERS: Oh, because I may perhaps look in on you later.

HIALMAR: No, you mustn't do that. You must not come to my home. Mine is a melancholy abode, Gregers; especially after a splendid banquet like this. We can always arrange to meet somewhere in the town.

MRS SORBY: [*who has quietly approached*] Are you going, Ekdal?

HIALMAR: Yes.

MRS SORBY: Remember me to Gina.

HIALMAR: Thanks.

MRS SORBY: And say I am coming up to see her one of these days.

HIALMAR: Yes, thank you. [*to* GREGERS] Stay here; I will slip out unobserved.
[*He saunters away, then into the other room and so out to the right.*]

MRS SORBY: [*softly to the* SERVANT, *who has come back*] Well, did you give the old man something?

PETTERSEN: Yes; I sent him off with a bottle of brandy.

MRS SORBY: Oh, you might have thought of something better than that.

PETTERSEN: Oh no, Mrs Sorby; brandy is what he likes best in the world.

THE FLABBY GENTLEMAN: [*in the doorway with a sheet of music in his hand*] Shall we play a duet, Mrs Sorby?

MRS SORBY: Yes, suppose we do.

THE GUESTS: Bravo, bravo!
[*She goes with all the guests through the back room out to the right.* GREGERS *remains standing by the fire.* WERLE *is looking for something on the writing table and appears to wish that* GREGERS *would go; as* GREGERS *does not move* WERLE *goes toward the door.*]

GREGERS: Father, won't you stay a moment?

WERLE: [*stops*] What is it?

GREGERS: I must have a word with you.

WERLE: Can't it wait until we are alone?

GREGERS: No, it can't, for perhaps we shall never be alone together.

WERLE: [*drawing nearer*] What do you mean by that?
[*During what follows the pianoforte is faintly heard from the distant music room.*]

GREGERS: How has that family been allowed to go so miserably to the wall?

WERLE: You mean the Ekdals, I suppose.

GREGERS: Yes, I mean the Ekdals. Lieutenant Ekdal was once so closely associated with you.

WERLE: Much too closely; I have felt that to my cost for many a year. It is thanks to him that I—yes I—have had a kind of slur cast upon my reputation.

GREGERS: [*softly*] Are you sure that he alone was to blame?

WERLE: Who else do you suppose?

GREGERS: You and he acted together in that affair of the forests—

WERLE: But was it not Ekdal that drew the map of the tracts we had bought— that fraudulent map! It was he who felled all that timber illegally on government ground. In fact, the whole management was in his hands. I was quite in the dark as to what Lieutenant Ekdal was doing.

GREGERS: Lieutenant Ekdal himself seems to have been very much in the dark as to what he was doing.

WERLE: That may be. But the fact remains that he was found guilty and I acquitted.

GREGERS: Yes, I know that nothing was proved against you.

WERLE: Acquittal is acquittal. Why do you rake up these old miseries that turned my hair gray before its time? Is that the sort of thing you have been brooding over up there, all these years? I can assure you, Gregers, here in the town the whole story has been forgotten long ago—as far as I am concerned.

GREGERS: But that unhappy Ekdal family—

WERLE: What would you have me do for the people? When Ekdal came out of prison he was a broken-down being, past all help. There are people in the world who dive to the bottom the moment they get a couple of slugs in their body and never come to the surface again. You may take my word for it, Gregers, I have done all I could without positively laying myself open to all sorts of suspicion and gossip.

GREGERS: Suspicion? Oh, I see.

WERLE: I have given Ekdal copying to do for the office, and I pay him far, far more for it than his work is worth.

GREGERS: [*without looking at him*] H'm; that I don't doubt.

WERLE: You laugh? Do you think I am not telling you the truth? Well, I certainly can't refer you to my books, for I never enter payments of that sort.

GREGERS: [*smiles coldly*] No, there are certain payments it is best to keep no account of.

WERLE: [*taken aback*] What do you mean by that?

GREGERS: [*mustering up courage*] Have you entered what it cost you to have Hialmar Ekdal taught photography?

WERLE: I? How "entered" it?

GREGERS: I have learned that it was you who paid for his training. And I have learned, too, that it was you who enabled him to set up house so comfortably.

WERLE: Well, and yet you talk as though I had done nothing for the Ekdals! I can assure you these people have cost me enough in all conscience.

GREGERS: Have you entered any of these expenses in your books?

WERLE: Why do you ask?

GREGERS: Oh, I have my reasons. Now tell me: when you interested yourself so warmly in your old friend's son—it was just before his marriage, was it not?

WERLE: Why, deuce take it—after all these years how can I—

GREGERS: You wrote me a letter about that time—a business letter, of course—and in a postscript you mentioned—quite briefly—that Hialmar Ekdal had married a Miss Hansen.

WERLE: Yes, that was quite right. That was her name.

GREGERS: But you did not mention that this Miss Hansen was Gina Hansen—our former housekeeper.

WERLE: [*with a forced laugh of derision*] No; to tell the truth, it didn't occur to me that you were so particularly interested in our former housekeeper.

GREGERS: Nor was I. But [*lowers his voice*] there were others in this house who were particularly interested in her.

WERLE: What do you mean by that? [*flaring up*] You are not alluding to me, I hope?

GREGERS: [*softly but firmly*] Yes, I am alluding to you.

WERLE: And you dare— You presume to— How can that ungrateful hound—that photographer fellow—how dare he go making such insinuations!

GREGERS: Hialmar has never breathed a word about this. I don't believe he has the faintest suspicion of such a thing.

WERLE: Then where have you got it from? Who can have put such notions in your head?

GREGERS: My poor unhappy mother told me, the very last time I saw her.

WERLE: Your mother! I might have known as much! You and she—you always stuck together. It was she who turned you against me from the first.

GREGERS: No, it was all that she had to suffer and submit to, until she broke down and came to such a pitiful end.

WERLE: Oh, she had nothing to suffer or submit to; not more than most people, at all events. But there's no getting on with morbid, overstrained creatures—that I have learned to my cost. And you could go on nursing such a suspicion—burrowing into all sorts of slanders against your own father! I must say, Gregers, I really think at your age you might find something more useful to do.

GREGERS: Yes, it is high time.

WERLE: Then perhaps your mind would be easier than it seems to be now. What can be your object in remaining up at the works year out and year in, drudging away like a common clerk and not drawing a farthing more than the ordinary monthly wage? It is downright folly.

GREGERS: Ah, if I were only sure of that.

WERLE: I understand you well enough. You want to be independent; you won't be beholden to me for anything. Well, now there happens to be an opportunity for you to become independent, your own master in everything.

GREGERS: Indeed? In what way?

WERLE: When I wrote you insisting on your coming to town at once—h'm—

GREGERS: Yes, what is it you really want of me? I have been waiting all day to know.

WERLE: I want to propose that you should enter the firm as partner.

GREGERS: I! Join your firm? As partner?

WERLE: Yes. It would not involve our being constantly together. You could take over the business here in town, and I would move up to the works.

GREGERS: You would?

WERLE: The fact is, I am not so fit for work as I once was. I am obliged to spare my eyes, Gregers; they have begun to trouble me.

GREGERS: They have always been weak.

WERLE: Not as they are now. And besides, circumstances might possibly make it desirable for me to live up there—for a time, at any rate.

GREGERS: That is certainly quite a new idea to me.

WERLE: Listen, Gregers, there are many things that stand between us; but we are father and son after all. We ought surely to be able to come to some sort of understanding with each other.

GREGERS: Outwardly, you mean, of course?

WERLE: Well, even that would be something. Think it over, Gregers. Don't you think it ought to be possible? Eh?

GREGERS: [*looking at him coldly*] There is something behind all this.

WERLE: How so?

GREGERS: You want to make use of me in some way.

WERLE: In such a close relationship as ours the one can always be useful to the other.

GREGERS: Yes, so people say.

WERLE: I want very much to have you at home with me for a time. I am a lonely man, Gregers; I have always felt lonely all my life through, but most of all now that I am getting up in years. I feel the need of someone about me—

GREGERS: You have Mrs Sorby.

WERLE: Yes, I have her, and she has become, I may say, almost indispensable to me. She is lively and even tempered; she brightens up the house; and that is a very great thing for me.

GREGERS: Well, then, you have everything as you wish it.

WERLE: Yes, but I am afraid it can't last. A woman so situated may easily find herself in a false position in the eyes of the world. For that matter, it does a man no good either.

GREGERS: Oh, when a man gives such dinners as you give he can risk a great deal.

WERLE: Yes, but how about the woman, Gregers? I fear she won't accept the situation much longer, and even if she did—even if, out of attachment to me, she were to take her chance of gossip and scandal and all that—do you think, Gregers, you with your strong sense of justice—

GREGERS: [*interrupts him*] Tell me in one word: are you thinking of marrying her?

WERLE: Suppose I were thinking of it? What then?

GREGERS: That's what I say: What then?

WERLE: Should you be inflexibly opposed to it?

GREGERS: Not at all. Not by any means.

WERLE: I was not sure whether your devotion to your mother's memory—

GREGERS: I am not overstrained.

WERLE: Well, whatever you may or not be, at all events you have lifted a great weight from my mind. I am extremely pleased that I can reckon on your concurrence in this matter.

GREGERS: [*looking intently at him*] Now I see the use you want to put me to.

WERLE: Use to put you to? What an expression!

GREGERS: Oh, don't let us be nice in our choice of words—not when we are alone together, at any rate. [*with a short laugh*] Well, well. So this is what made it absolutely essential that I should come to town in person. For the sake of Mrs Sorby we are to get up a pretense at family life in the house— a tableau of filial affection. That will be something new, indeed.

WERLE: How dare you speak in that tone!

GREGERS: Was there ever any family life here? Never since I can remember. But now, your plans demand something of the sort. No doubt it will have an excellent effect when it is reported that the son has hastened home, on the wings of filial piety, to the gray-haired father's wedding feast. What will then remain of all the rumors as to the wrongs the poor dead mother had to submit to? Not a scrap. Her son annihilates them at one stroke.

WERLE: Gregers—I believe there is no one in the world you detest as you do me.

GREGERS: [*softly*] I have seen you at too close quarters.

WERLE: You have seen me with your mother's eyes. [*lowers his voice a little*] But you should remember that her eyes were—clouded now and then.

GREGERS: [*quivering*] I see what you are hinting at. But who was to blame for mother's unfortunate weakness? Why, you and all those— The last of them was this woman that you palmed off upon Hialmar Ekdal when you were— Ugh!

WERLE: [*shrugs his shoulders*] Word for word as if it were your mother speaking!

GREGERS: [*without heeding*] And there he is now, with his great, confiding child-like mind, compassed about with all this treachery—living under the same roof with such a creature and never dreaming that what he calls his home is built up on a lie! [*comes a step nearer*] When I look back upon your past I seem to see a battlefield with shattered lives on every hand.

WERLE: I begin to think that the chasm that divides us is too wide.

GREGERS: [*bowing with self-command*] So I have observed, and therefore I take my hat and go.

WERLE: You are going? Out of the house?

GREGERS: Yes. For at last I see my mission in life.

WERLE: What mission?

GREGERS: You would only laugh if I told you.

WERLE: A lonely man doesn't laugh so easily, Gregers.

GREGERS: [*pointing toward the background*] Look, Father—the chamberlains are playing blindman's buff with Mrs Sorby. Good night and good-by.

[*He goes out by the back to the right. Sound of laughter and merriment from the company, who are now visible in the outer room.*]

WERLE: [*muttering contemptuously after* GREGERS] Ha! Poor wretch—and he says he is not overstrained!

ACT II

SCENE——HIALMAR EKDAL'S *studio, a good-sized room, evidently in the top story of the building. On the right a sloping roof of large panes of glass half covered by a blue curtain. In the right-hand corner, at the back, the entrance door; farther forward, on the same side, a door leading to the sitting room. Two doors on the opposite side and between them an iron stove. At the back a wide double sliding door. The studio is plainly but comfortably furnished. Between the door on the right, standing out a little from the wall, a sofa with a table and some chairs; on the table a lighted lamp with a shade; beside the stove an old armchair. Photographic instruments and apparatus of different kinds lying about the room. Against the back wall, to the left of the double door, stands a bookcase containing a few books, boxes and bottles of chemicals, instruments, tools and other objects. Photographs and small articles, such as camel's-hair pencils, paper and so forth, lie on the table.*

> [GINA EKDAL *sits on a chair by the table, sewing.* HEDVIG *is sitting on the sofa, with her hands shading her eyes and her thumbs in her ears, reading a book.*]

GINA: [*glances once or twice at* HEDVIG, *as if with secret anxiety, then says*] Hedvig!

> [HEDVIG *does not hear.*]

GINA: [*repeats more loudly*] Hedvig!

HEDVIG: [*takes away her hands and looks up*] Yes, Mother?

GINA: Hedvig dear, you mustn't sit reading any longer now.

HEDVIG: Oh, Mother, mayn't I read a little more? Just a little bit?

GINA: No, no, you must put away your book now. Father doesn't like it; he never reads himself in the evening.

HEDVIG: [*shuts the book*] No, Father doesn't care much about reading.

GINA: [*puts aside her sewing and takes up a lead pencil and a little account book from the table*] Can you remember how much we paid for the butter today?

HEDVIG: It was one crown sixty-five.

GINA: That's right. [*puts it down*] It's terrible what a lot of butter we get through in this house. Then there was the smoked sausage and the cheese —let me see [*writes*]—and the ham. [*adds up*] Yes, that makes just—

HEDVIG: And then the beer.

GINA: Yes, to be sure.[*writes*] How it do mount up! But we can't manage with no less.

HEDVIG: And then you and I didn't need anything hot for dinner, as Father was out.

GINA: No, that was so much to the good. And then I took eight crowns fifty for the photographs.

HEDVIG: Really! As much as that?

GINA: Exactly eight crowns fifty.

> [*Silence.* GINA *takes up her sewing again;* HEDVIG *takes paper and pencil and begins to draw, shading her eyes with her left hand.*]

HEDVIG: Isn't it jolly to think that Father is at Mr Werle's big dinner party?

GINA: You know he's not really Mr Werle's guest. It was the son invited him. [*after a pause*] We have nothing to do with that Mr Werle.

HEDVIG: I'm longing for Father to come home. He promised to ask Mrs Sorby for something nice for me.

GINA: Yes, there's plenty of good things in that house, I can tell you.

HEDVIG: [*goes on drawing*] And I believe I'm a little hungry too.
  [OLD EKDAL, *with the paper parcel under his arm and another parcel in his coat pocket, comes in by the entrance door.*]

GINA: How late you are today, Grandfather!

EKDAL: They had locked the office door. Had to wait in Graberg's room. And then they let me through—h'm.

HEDVIG: Did you get some more copying to do, Grandfather?

EKDAL: This whole packet. Just look.

GINA: That's fine.

HEDVIG: And you have another parcel in your pocket.

EKDAL: Eh? Oh, never mind, that's nothing. [*puts his stick away in a corner*] This work will keep me going a long time, Gina. [*opens one of the sliding doors in the back wall a little*] Hush! [*peeps into the room for a moment, then pushes the door carefully to again*] Hee-hee! They're fast asleep, all the lot of them. And she's gone into the basket herself. Hee-hee!

HEDVIG: Are you sure she isn't cold in that basket, Grandfather?

EKDAL: Not a bit of it! Cold? With all that straw? [*goes toward the farther door on the left*] There are matches in here, I suppose.

GINA: The matches is on the drawers.
  [EKDAL *goes into his room.*]

HEDVIG: It's nice that Grandfather has got all that copying.

GINA: Yes, poor old Father; it means a bit of pocket money for him.

HEDVIG: And he won't be able to sit the whole forenoon down at that horrid Madam Eriksen's.

GINA: No more he won't. [*short silence*]

HEDVIG: Do you suppose they are still at the dinner table?

GINA: Goodness knows; as like as not.

HEDVIG: Think of all the delicious things Father is having to eat! I'm certain he'll be in splendid spirits when he comes. Don't you think so, Mother?

GINA: Yes; and if only we could tell him that we'd rented the room—

HEDVIG: But we don't need that this evening.

GINA: Oh, we'd be none the worst of it, I can tell you. It's no use to us as it is.

HEDVIG: I mean we don't need it this evening, for Father will be in good humor at any rate. It is best to keep the renting of the room for another time.

GINA: [*looks across at her*] You like having some good news to tell Father when he comes home in the evening?

HEDVIG: Yes, for then things are pleasanter somehow.

GINA: [*thinking to herself*] Yes, yes, there's something in that.
  [OLD EKDAL *comes in again and is going out by the foremost door to the left.*]

GINA: [*half turning in her chair*] Do you want something in the kitchen, Grandfather?

EKDAL: Yes, yes, I do. Don't you trouble. [*Goes out.*]

GINA: He's not poking away at the fire, is he? [*waits a moment*] Hedvig, go and see what he's about.

[EKDAL *comes in again with a small jug of steaming hot water.*]

HEDVIG: Have you been getting some hot water, Grandfather?

EKDAL: Yes, hot water. Want it for something. Want to write, and the ink has got as thick as porridge—h'm.

GINA: But you'd best have your supper first, Grandfather. It's laid in there.

EKDAL: Can't be bothered with supper, Gina. Very busy, I tell you. No one's to come to my room. No one—h'm.

[*He goes into his room;* GINA *and* HEDVIG *look at each other.*]

GINA: [*softly*] Can you imagine where he's got money from?

HEDVIG: From Graberg, perhaps.

GINA: Not a bit of it. Graberg always sends the money to me.

HEDVIG: Then he must have got a bottle on credit somewhere.

GINA: Poor Grandfather, who'd give him credit?

[HIALMAR EKDAL, *in an overcoat and gray felt hat, comes in from the right.*]

GINA: [*throws down her sewing and rises*] Why, Ekdal, is that you already?

HEDVIG: [*at the same time jumping up*] Fancy your coming so soon, Father!

HIALMAR: [*taking off his hat*] Yes, most of the people were coming away.

HEDVIG: So early?

HIALMAR: Yes, it was a dinner party, you know. [*takes off his overcoat*]

GINA: Let me help you.

HEDVIG: Me too.

[*They draw off his coat;* GINA *hangs it up on the back wall.*]

HEDVIG: Were there many people there, Father?

HIALMAR: Oh no, not many. We had about twelve or fourteen at table.

GINA: And you had some talk with them all?

HIALMAR: Oh yes, a little; but Gregers took me up most of the time.

GINA: Is Gregers as ugly as ever?

HIALMAR: Well, he's not very much to look at. Hasn't the old man come home?

HEDVIG: Yes, Grandfather is in his room, writing.

HIALMAR: Did he say anything?

GINA: No, what should he say?

HIALMAR: Didn't he say anything about— I heard something about his having been with Graberg. I'll go in and see him for a moment.

GINA: No, no, better not.

HIALMAR: Why not? Did he say he didn't want me to go in?

GINA: I don't think he wants to see nobody this evening.

HEDVIG: [*making signs*] H'm—h'm!

GINA: [*not noticing*] He has been in to fetch hot water—

HIALMAR: Aha! Then he's—

GINA: Yes, I suppose so.

HIALMAR: Oh God! My poor old white-haired father! Well, well, there let him sit and get all the enjoyment he can.

[OLD EKDAL, *in an indoor coat and with a lighted pipe, comes from his room.*]

EKDAL: Got home? Thought it was you I heard talking.

HIALMAR: Yes, I have just come.

EKDAL: You didn't see me, did you?

HIALMAR: No, but they told me you had passed through—so I thought I would follow you.

EKDAL: H'm, good of you, Hialmar. Who were they, all those fellows?

HIALMAR: Oh, all sorts of people. There was Chamberlain Flor and Chamberlain Balle and Chamberlain Kaspersen and Chamberlain—this, that and the other—I don't know who all.

EKDAL: [*nodding*] Hear that, Gina! Chamberlains every one of them!

GINA: Yes, I hear as they're terrible genteel in that house nowadays.

HEDVIG: Did the chamberlains sing, Father? Or did they read aloud?

HIALMAR: No, they only talked nonsense. They wanted me to recite something for them, but I knew better than that.

EKDAL: You weren't to be persuaded, eh?

GINA: Oh, you might have done it.

HIALMAR: No; one mustn't be at everybody's beck and call. [*walks about the room*] That's not my way, at any rate.

EKDAL: No, no; Hialmar's not to be had for the asking, he isn't.

HIALMAR: I don't see why I should bother myself to entertain people on the rare occasions when I go into society. Let the others exert themselves. These fellows go from one great dinner table to the next and gorge and guzzle day out and day in. It's for them to bestir themselves and do something in return for all the good feeding they get.

GINA: But you didn't say that?

HIALMAR: [*humming*] Ho-ho-ho; I gave them a bit of my mind.

EKDAL: Not the chamberlains?

HIALMAR: Oh, why not? [*lightly*] After that we had a little discussion about Tokay.

EKDAL: Tokay! There's a fine wine for you!

HIALMAR: [*comes to a standstill*] It may be a fine wine. But of course you know the vintages differ; it all depends on how much sunshine the grapes have had.

GINA: Why, you know everything, Ekdal.

EKDAL: And did they argue that?

HIALMAR: They tried to, but they were requested to observe it was just the same with chamberlains—that with them, too, different batches were of different qualities.

GINA: What things you do think of!

EKDAL: Hee-hee! So they got that in their pipes too?

HIALMAR: Right in their teeth.

EKDAL: Do you hear that, Gina? He said it right in the very teeth of all the chamberlains.

GINA: Fancy! Right in their teeth!

HIALMAR: Yes, but I don't want it talked about. One doesn't speak of such things. The whole affair passed off quite amicably, of course. They were nice genial fellows; I didn't want to wound them—not I!

EKDAL: Right in their teeth, though!

HEDVIG: [*caressingly*] How nice it is to see you in a dress coat! It suits you so well, Father.

HIALMAR: Yes, don't you think so? And this one really fits to perfection. It fits almost as if it had been made for me—a little tight in the armholes, perhaps; help me, Hedvig. [*takes off the coat*] I think I'll put on my jacket. Where is my jacket, Gina?

GINA: Here it is. [*Brings the jacket and helps him.*]

HIALMAR: That's it! Don't forget to send the coat back to Molvik first thing tomorrow morning.

GINA: [*laying it away*] I'll be sure and see to it.

HIALMAR: [*stretching himself*] After all, there's a more homely feeling about this. A free-and-easy indoor costume suits my whole personality better. Don't you think so, Hedvig?

HEDVIG: Yes, Father.

HIALMAR: When I loosen my necktie into a pair of flowing ends—like this—eh?

HEDVIG: Yes, and that goes so well with your mustache and the sweep of your curls.

HIALMAR: I should not call them curls exactly; I should rather say locks.

HEDVIG: Yes, they are too big for curls.

HIALMAR: Locks describes them better.

HEDVIG: [*after a pause, twitching his jacket*] Father!

HIALMAR: Well, what is it?

HEDVIG: Oh, you know very well.

HIALMAR: No, really I don't.

HEDVIG: [*half laughing, half whispering*] Oh yes, Father; now don't tease me any longer!

HIALMAR: Why, what do you mean?

HEDVIG: [*shaking him*] Oh, what nonsense! Come, where are they, Father? All the good things you promised me, you know?

HIALMAR: Oh—if I haven't forgotten all about them!

HEDVIG: Now you're only teasing me, Father! Oh, it's too bad of you! Where have you put them?

HIALMAR: No, I positively forgot to get anything. But wait a little! I have something else for you, Hedvig.

[*Goes and searches in the pockets of the coat.*]

HEDVIG: [*skipping and clapping her hands*] Oh, Mother, Mother!

HIALMAR: [*with a paper*] Look, here it is.

GINA: There, you see; if you only give him time—

HEDVIG: That? Why, that's only a paper.

HIALMAR: That is the bill of fare, my dear; the whole bill of fare. Here you see "Menu"—that means bill of fare.

HEDVIG: Haven't you anything else?

HIALMAR: I forgot the other things, I tell you. But you may take my word for it, these dainties are very unsatisfying. Sit down at the table and read the bill of fare, and then I'll describe to you how the dishes taste. Here you are, Hedvig.

HEDVIG: [*gulping down her tears*] Thank you.

[*She seats herself but does not read;* GINA *makes signs to her;* HIALMAR *notices it.*]

HIALMAR: [*pacing up and down the room*] It's monstrous what absurd things the father of a family is expected to think of, and if he forgets the smallest trifle he is treated to sour faces at once. Well, well, one gets used to that too. [*stops near the stove by the old man's chair*] Have you peeped in there this evening, Father?

EKDAL: Yes, to be sure I have. She's gone into the basket.

HIALMAR: Ah, she has gone into the basket. Then she's beginning to get used to it.

EKDAL: Yes, just as I prophesied. But you know there are still a few little things—

HIALMAR: A few improvements, yes.

EKDAL: They've got to be made, you know.

HIALMAR: Yes, let us have a talk about the improvements, Father. Come, let us sit on the sofa.

EKDAL: All right. H'm—think I'll just fill my pipe first. Must clean it out too. H'm.

[*He goes into his room.*]

GINA: [*smiling to* HIALMAR] His pipe!

HIALMAR: Oh yes, yes, Gina; let him alone—the poor shipwrecked old man. Yes, these improvements—we had better get them out of the way tomorrow.

GINA: You'll hardly have time tomorrow, Ekdal.

HEDVIG: [*interposing*] Oh yes, he will, Mother!

GINA: —for remember them prints that has to be retouched; they've sent for them time after time.

HIALMAR: There now! Those prints again! I shall get them finished all right. Have any new orders come in?

GINA: No, worse luck; tomorrow I have nothing to do but those two sittings, you know.

HIALMAR: Nothing else? Oh no, if people won't set about things with a will—

GINA: But what more can I do? Don't I advertise in the papers as much as we can afford?

HIALMAR: Yes, the papers; you see how much good they do. And I suppose no one has been to look at the room either?

GINA: No, not yet.

HIALMAR: That was only to be expected. If people won't keep their eyes open— Nothing can be done without a real effort, Gina!

HEDVIG: [*going toward him*] Shall I fetch you the flute, Father?

HIALMAR: No; no flute for me; *I* want no pleasures in this world. [*pacing about*] Yes indeed, I will work tomorrow; you shall see if I don't. You may be sure I shall work as long as my strength holds out.

GINA: But, my dear good Ekdal, I didn't mean it in that way.

HEDVIG: Father, mayn't I bring in a bottle of beer?

HIALMAR: No, certainly not. I require nothing, nothing. [*comes to a standstill*] Beer? Was it beer you were talking about?

HEDVIG: [*cheerfully*] Yes, Father; beautiful fresh beer.

HIALMAR: Well—since you insist upon it, you may bring in a bottle.

GINA: Yes, do; and we'll be nice and cosy.

[HEDVIG *runs toward the kitchen door.*]

HIALMAR: [*by the stove, stops her, looks at her, puts his arm round her neck and presses her to him*] Hedvig, Hedvig!

HEDVIG: [*with tears of joy*] My dear, kind father!

HIALMAR: No, don't call me that. Here have I been feasting at the rich man's table—battening at the groaning board! And I couldn't even—

GINA: [*sitting at the table*] Oh, nonsense, nonsense, Ekdal.

HIALMAR: It's not nonsense! And yet you mustn't be too hard upon me. You know that I love you for all that.

HEDVIG: [*throwing her arms round him*] And we love you, oh, so dearly, Father!

HIALMAR: And if I am unreasonable once in a while—why, then—you must remember that I am a man beset by a host of cares. There, there! [*dries his eyes*] No beer at such a moment as this. Give me the flute.

[HEDVIG *runs to the bookcase and fetches it.*]

HIALMAR: Thanks! That's right. With my flute in my hand and you two at my side—ah!

[HEDVIG *seats herself at the table near* GINA; HIALMAR *paces backward and forward, pipes up vigorously and plays a Bohemian peasant dance, but in a slow plaintive tempo and with sentimental expression.*]

HIALMAR: [*breaking off the melody, holds out his left hand to* GINA *and says with emotion*] Our roof may be poor and humble, Gina, but it is home. And with all my heart I say: here dwells my happiness.

[*He begins to play again; almost immediately after a knocking is heard at the entrance door.*]

GINA: [*rising*] Hush, Ekdal—I think there's someone at the door.

HIALMAR: [*laying the flute on the bookcase*] There! Again!

[GINA *goes and opens the door.*]

GREGERS: [*in the passage*] Excuse me—

GINA: [*starting back slightly*] Oh!

GREGERS: —doesn't Mr Ekdal, the photographer, live here?

GINA: Yes, he does.

HIALMAR: [*going toward the door*] Gregers! You here after all? Well, come in then.

GREGERS: [*coming in*] I told you I would come and look you up.

HIALMAR: But this evening— Have you left the party?

GREGERS: I have left both the party and my father's house. Good evening, Mrs Ekdal. I don't know whether you recognize me?

GINA: Oh yes, it's not difficult to know young Mr Werle again.

GREGERS: No, I am like my mother, and no doubt you remember her.

HIALMAR: Left your father's house, did you say?

GREGERS: Yes, I have gone to a hotel.

HIALMAR: Indeed. Well, since you're here, take off your coat and sit down.

GREGERS: Thanks. [*He takes off his overcoat. He is now dressed in a plain gray suit of a countrified cut.*]

HIALMAR: Here on the sofa. Make yourself comfortable.

GREGERS: [*looking around him*] So these are your quarters, Hialmar—this is your home.

HIALMAR: This is the studio, as you see.

GINA: But it's the largest of our rooms, so we generally sit here.

HIALMAR: We used to live in a better place, but this flat has one great advantage: there are such capital outer rooms—

GINA: And we have a room on the other side of the passage that we can rent.

GREGERS: [*to* HIALMAR] Ah—so you have lodgers too?

HIALMAR: No, not yet. They're not so easy to find, you see; you have to keep your eyes open. [*to* HEDVIG] How about that beer, eh?

[HEDVIG *nods and goes out into the kitchen.*]

GREGERS: So that is your daughter?

HIALMAR: Yes, that is Hedvig.

GREGERS: And she is your only child?

HIALMAR: Yes, the only one. She is the joy of our lives, and [*lowering his voice*] at the same time our deepest sorrow, Gregers.

GREGERS: What do you mean?

HIALMAR: She is in serious danger of losing her eyesight.

GREGERS: Becoming blind?

HIALMAR: Yes. Only the first symptoms have appeared as yet, and she may not feel it much for some time. But the doctor has warned us. It is coming inexorably.

GREGERS: What a terrible misfortune! How do you account for it?

HIALMAR: [*sighs*] Hereditary, no doubt.

GREGERS: [*starting*] Hereditary?

GINA: Ekdal's mother had weak eyes.

HIALMAR: Yes, so my father says; I can't remember her.

GREGERS: Poor child! And how does she take it?

HIALMAR: Oh, you can imagine we haven't the heart to tell her of it. She dreams of no danger. Gay and careless and chirping like a little bird, she flutters onward into a life of endless night. [*overcome*] Oh, it is cruelly hard on me, Gregers.

[HEDVIG *brings a tray with beer and glasses which she sets upon the table.*]

HIALMAR: [*stroking her hair*] Thanks, thanks, Hedvig.

[HEDVIG *puts her arm around his neck and whispers in his ear.*]

HIALMAR: No, no bread and butter just now. [*looks up*] But perhaps you would like some, Gregers?

GREGERS: [*with a gesture of refusal*] No, no thank you.

HIALMAR: [*still melancholy*] Well, you can bring in a little all the same. If you have a crust, that is all I want. And plenty of butter on it, mind.

[HEDVIG *nods gaily and goes out into the kitchen again.*]

GREGERS: [*who has been following her with his eyes*] She seems quite strong and healthy otherwise.

GINA: Yes. In other ways there's nothing amiss with her, thank goodness.

GREGERS: She promises to be very like you, Mrs Ekdal. How old is she now?

GINA: Hedvig is close on fourteen; her birthday is the day after tomorrow.

GREGERS: She is pretty tall for her age then.

GINA: Yes, she's shot up wonderful this last year.

GREGERS: It makes one realize one's own age to see these young people growing up. How long is it now since you were married?

GINA: We've been married—let me see—just on fifteen years.

GREGERS: Is it so long as that?

GINA: [*becomes attentive, looks at him*] Yes, it is indeed.

HIALMAR: Yes, so it is. Fifteen years, all but a few months. [*changing his tone*] They must have been long years for you up at the works, Gregers.

GREGERS: They seemed long while I was living them; now they are over, I hardly know how the time has gone.

> [OLD EKDAL *comes from his room without his pipe but with his old-fashioned uniform cap on his head; his gait is somewhat unsteady.*]

EKDAL: Come now, Hialmar, let's sit down and have a good talk about this— h'm—what was it again?

HIALMAR: [*going toward him*] Father, we have a visitor here—Gregers Werle— I don't know if you remember him.

EKDAL: [*looking at* GREGERS, *who has risen*] Werle? Is that the son? What does he want with me?

HIALMAR: Nothing! It's me he has come to see.

EKDAL: Oh! Then there's nothing wrong?

HIALMAR: No, no, of course not.

EKDAL: [*with a large gesture*] Not that I'm afraid, you know; but—

GREGERS: [*goes over to him*] I bring you a greeting from your old hunting grounds, Lieutenant Ekdal.

EKDAL: Hunting grounds?

GREGERS: Yes, up in Höidal, about the works, you know.

EKDAL: Oh, up there. Yes, I knew all those places well in the old days.

GREGERS: You were a great sportsman then.

EKDAL: So I was, I don't deny it. You're looking at my uniform cap. I don't ask anybody's leave to wear it in the house. So long as I don't go out in the streets with it—

> [HEDVIG *brings a plate of bread and butter which she puts upon the table.*]

HIALMAR: Sit down, Father, and have a glass of beer. Help yourself, Gregers.

> [EKDAL *mutters and stumbles over to the sofa.* GREGERS *seats himself on the chair nearest to him,* HIALMAR *on the other side of* GREGERS. GINA *sits a little way from the table, sewing;* HEDVIG *stands beside her father.*]

GREGERS: Can you remember, Lieutenant Ekdal, how Hialmar and I used to come up and visit you in the summer and at Christmas?

EKDAL: Did you? No, no, no; I don't remember it. But, sure enough, I've been a tidy bit of sportsman in my day. I've shot bears too. I've shot nine of 'em no less.

GREGERS: [*looking sympathetically at him*] And now you never get any shooting?

EKDAL: Can't say that, sir. Get a shot now and then, perhaps. Of course not in the old way. For the woods, you see—the woods, the woods— [*drinks*] Are the woods fine up there now?

GREGERS: Not so fine as in your time. They have been thinned out a good deal.

EKDAL: Thinned? [*more softly and as if afraid*] It's dangerous work, that. Bad things come of it. The woods revenge themselves.

HIALMAR: [*filling up his glass*] Come—a little more, Father.

GREGERS: How can a man like you—such a man for the open air—live in the midst of a stuffy town, boxed within four walls?

EKDAL: [*laughs quietly and glances at* HIALMAR] Oh, it's not so bad here. Not at all so bad.

GREGERS: But don't you miss all the things that used to be a part of your very being—the cool sweeping breezes, the free life in the woods and on the uplands, among beasts and birds?

EKDAL: [*smiling*] Hialmar, shall we let him see it?

HIALMAR: [*hastily and a little embarrassed*] Oh no, no, Father; not this evening.

GREGERS: What does he want to show me?

HIALMAR: Oh, it's only something—you can see it another time.

GREGERS: [*continues, to the old man*] You see, I have been thinking, Lieutenant Ekdal, that you should come up with me to the works; I am sure to be going back soon. No doubt you could get some copying there too. And here you have nothing on earth to interest you—nothing to liven you up.

EKDAL: [*stares in astonishment at him*] Have I nothing on earth to—

GREGERS: Of course you have Hialmar, but then he has his own family. And a man like you, who has always had such a passion for what is free and wild—

EKDAL: [*thumps the table*] Hialmar, he shall see it!

HIALMAR: Oh, do you think it's worth while, Father? It's all dark.

EKDAL: Nonsense; it's moonlight. [*rises*] He shall see it, I tell you. Let me pass! Come on and help me, Hialmar.

HEDVIG: Oh yes, do, Father!

HIALMAR: [*rising*] Very well then.

GREGERS: [*to* GINA] What is it?

GINA: Oh, nothing so wonderful after all.

> [EKDAL *and* HIALMAR *have gone to the back wall and are each pushing back a side of the sliding door;* HEDVIG *helps the old man;* GREGERS *remains standing by the sofa;* GINA *sits still and sews. Through the open doorway a large, deep irregular garret is seen with odd nooks and corners, a couple of stovepipes running through it from rooms below. There are skylights through which clear moonbeams shine in on some parts of the great room; others lie in deep shadow.*]

EKDAL: [*to* GREGERS] You may come close up if you like.

GREGERS: [*going over to them*] Why, what is it?

EKDAL: Look for yourself, h'm.

HIALMAR: [*somewhat embarrassed*] This belongs to Father, you understand.

GREGERS: [*at the door, looks into the garret*] Why, you keep poultry, Lieutenant Ekdal.

EKDAL: Should think we did keep poultry. They've gone to roost now. But you should see our fowls by daylight, sir!

HEDVIG: And there's a—

EKDAL: Sh—sh! Don't say anything about it yet.

GREGERS: And you have pigeons too, I see.

EKDAL: Oh yes, haven't we just got pigeons! They have their nest boxes up there under the rooftree; for pigeons like to roost high, you see.

HIALMAR: They aren't all common pigeons.

EKDAL: Common! Should think not, indeed! We have tumblers and a pair of pouters too. But come here! Can you see that hutch down there by the wall?

GREGERS: Yes; what do you use it for?

EKDAL: That's where the rabbits sleep, sir.

GREGERS: Dear me, so you have rabbits too?

EKDAL: Yes, you may take my word for it, we have rabbits! He wants to know if we have rabbits, Hialmar! H'm! But now comes the thing, let me tell you! Here we have it! Move away, Hedvig. Stand here; that's right—and now look down there. Don't you see a basket with straw in it?

GREGERS: Yes. And I can see a fowl lying in the basket.

EKDAL: H'm—"a fowl"—

GREGERS: Isn't it a duck?

EKDAL: [*hurt*] Why, of course it's a duck.

HIALMAR: But what kind of a duck, do you think?

HEDVIG: It's not just a common duck.

EKDAL: Sh!

GREGERS: And it's not a Muscovy duck either.

EKDAL: No, Mr—Werle; it's not a Muscovy duck, for it's a wild duck!

GREGERS: Is it really? A wild duck?

EKDAL: Yes, that's what it is. That "fowl"—as you call it—is the wild duck. It's our wild duck, sir.

HEDVIG: My wild duck. It belongs to me.

GREGERS: And can it live up here in the garret? Does it thrive?

EKDAL: Of course it has a trough of water to splash about in, you know.

HIALMAR: Fresh water every other day.

GINA: [*turning toward* HIALMAR] But, my dear Ekdal, it's getting icy cold here.

EKDAL: H'm, we had better shut up then. It's as well not to disturb their night's rest too. Close up, Hedvig.

[HIALMAR *and* HEDVIG *push the garret doors together.*]

EKDAL: Another time you shall see her properly. [*seats himself in the armchair by the stove*] Oh, they're curious things, these wild ducks, I can tell you.

GREGERS: How did you manage to catch it, Lieutenant Ekdal?

EKDAL: *I* didn't catch it. There's a certain man in this town whom we have to thank for it.

GREGERS: [*starts slightly*] That man was not my father, was he?

EKDAL: You've hit it. Your father and no one else. H'm.

HIALMAR: Strange that you should guess that, Gregers.

GREGERS: You were telling me that you owed so many things to my father, and so I thought perhaps—

GINA: But we didn't get the duck from Mr Werle himself.

EKDAL: It's Hakon Werle we have to thank for her, all the same, Gina. [*to* GREGERS] He was shooting from a boat, you see, and he brought her down. But your father's sight is not very good now. H'm; she was only wounded.

GREGERS: Ah! She got a couple of slugs in her body, I suppose?

HIALMAR: Yes, two or three.

HEDVIG: She was hit under the wing so that she couldn't fly.

GREGERS: And I suppose she dived to the bottom, eh?

EKDAL: [*sleepily, in a thick voice*] Of course. Always do that, wild ducks do. They shoot to the bottom as deep as they can get, sir—and catch themselves in the tangle and seaweed—and all the devil's own mess that grows down there. And they never come up again.

GREGERS: But your wild duck came up again, Lieutenant Ekdal.

EKDAL: He had such an amazingly clever dog, your father had. And that dog—he dived in after the duck and fetched her up again.

GREGERS: [*who has turned to* HIALMAR] And then she was sent to you here?

HIALMAR: Not at once; at first your father took her home. But she wouldn't thrive there, so Pettersen was told to put an end to her.

EKDAL: [*half asleep*] H'm—yes—Pettersen—that ass—

HIALMAR: [*speaking more softly*] That was how we got her, you see; for Father knows Pettersen a little, and when he heard about the wild duck he got him to hand her over to us.

GREGERS: And now she thrives as well as possible in the garret there?

HIALMAR: Yes, wonderfully well. She has got fat. You see, she has lived in there so long now that she has forgotten her natural wild life, and it all depends on that.

GREGERS: You are right there, Hialmar. Be sure you never let her get a glimpse of the sky and the sea. But I mustn't stay any longer; I think your father is asleep.

HIALMAR: Oh, as for that—

GREGERS: But by the bye—you said you had a room to let—a spare room?

HIALMAR: Yes; what then? Do you know of anybody?

GREGERS: Can *I* have that room?

HIALMAR: You?

GINA: Oh no, Mr Werle, you—

GREGERS: May I have the room? If so, I'll take possession first thing tomorrow morning.

HIALMAR: Yes, with the greatest pleasure.

GINA: But, Mr Werle, I'm sure it's not at all the sort of room for you.

HIALMAR: Why, Gina! how can you say that?

GINA: Why, because the room's neither large enough nor light enough, and—

GREGERS: That really doesn't matter, Mrs Ekdal.

HIALMAR: I call it quite a nice room, and not at all badly furnished either.

GINA: But remember the pair of them underneath.

GREGERS: What pair?

GINA: Well, there's one as has been a tutor.

HIALMAR: That's Molvik—Mr Molvik, B.A.

GINA: And then there's a doctor by the name of Relling.

GREGERS: Relling? I know him a little; he practiced for a time up in Höidal.

GINA: They're a regular rackety pair, they are. As often as not they're out on the loose in the evenings, and then they come home at all hours, and they are not always just—

GREGERS: One soon gets used to that sort of thing. I daresay I shall be like the wild duck.

GINA: H'm; I think you ought to sleep upon it first, anyway.

GREGERS: You seem very unwilling to have me in the house, Mrs Ekdal.

GINA: Oh no! What makes you think that?

HIALMAR: Well, you really behave strangely about it, Gina. [to GREGERS] Then I suppose you intend to remain in town for the present?

GREGERS: [putting on his overcoat] Yes, now I intend to remain here.

HIALMAR: And yet not at your father's? What do you propose to do then?

GREGERS: Ah, if I only knew that, Hialmar, I shouldn't be so badly off! But when one has the misfortune to be called Gregers!—"Gregers"—and then "Werle" after it; did you ever hear of anything so hideous?

HIALMAR: Oh, I don't think so at all.

GREGERS: Ugh! Bah! I feel I should like to spit on the fellow that answers to such a name. But when a man is once for all doomed to be Gregers Werle —in this world—as I am—

HIALMAR: [laughs] Ha, ha! If you weren't Gregers Werle, what would you like to be?

GREGERS: If I should choose, I should like best to be a clever dog.

GINA: A dog!

HEDVIG: [involuntarily] Oh no!

GREGERS: Yes, an amazingly clever dog; one that goes to the bottom after wild ducks when they dive and catch themselves fast in tangle and seaweed down among the ooze.

HIALMAR: Upon my word now. Gregers—I don't in the least know what you are driving at.

GREGERS: Oh well, you might not be much the wiser if you did. It's understood, then, that I move in early tomorrow morning. [to GINA] I won't give you any trouble; I do everything for myself. [to HIALMAR] We will talk about the rest tomorrow. Good night, Mrs Ekdal. [nods to HEDVIG] Good night.

HEDVIG: Good night.

HIALMAR: [who has lighted a candle] Wait a moment; I must show you a light; the stairs are sure to be dark.

[GREGERS and HIALMAR go out by the passage door.]

GINA: [looking straight before her with her sewing in her lap] Wasn't that queer-like talk about wanting to be a dog?

HEDVIG: Do you know, Mother—I believe he meant something quite different by that.

GINA: Why, what should he mean?

HEDVIG: Oh, I don't know, but it seemed to me he meant something different from what he said—all the time.

GINA: Do you think so? Yes, it was sort of queer.

HIALMAR: [*comes back*] The lamp was still burning. [*puts out the candle and sets it down*] Ah, now one can get a mouthful of food at last. [*begins to eat the bread and butter*] Well, you see, Gina—if only you keep your eyes open—

GINA: How keep your eyes open?

HIALMAR: Why, haven't we at last had the luck to rent the room? And just think—to a person like Gregers—a good old friend.

GINA: Well, I don't know what to say about it.

HEDVIG: Oh, Mother, you'll see: it'll be such fun!

HIALMAR: You're very strange. You were so bent upon getting the room rented before, and now you don't like it.

GINA: Yes, I do, Ekdal; if it had only been to someone else. But what do you suppose Mr Werle will say?

HIALMAR: Old Werle? It doesn't concern him.

GINA: But surely you can see that there's something wrong between them again, or the young man wouldn't be leaving home. You know very well those two can't get on with each other.

HIALMAR: Very likely not, but—

GINA: And now Mr Werle may think it's you that has egged him on—

HIALMAR: Let him think so, then! Mr Werle has done a great deal for me; far be it from me to deny it. But that doesn't make me everlastingly dependent upon him.

GINA: But, my dear Ekdal, maybe Grandfather'll suffer for it. He may lose the little bit of work he gets from Graberg.

HIALMAR: I could almost say: so much the better! Is it not humiliating for a man like me to see his grayhaired father treated as a pariah? But now I believe the fullness of time is at hand. [*takes a fresh piece of bread and butter*] As sure as I have a mission in life, I mean to fulfill it now!

HEDVIG: Oh yes, Father, do!

GINA: Hush! Don't wake him!

HIALMAR: [*more softly*] I will fulfill it, I say. The day shall come when— And that is why I say it's a good thing we have rented the room, for that makes me more independent. The man who has a mission in life must be independent. [*by the armchair, with emotion*] Poor old white-haired Father! Rely on your Hialmar. He has broad shoulders—strong shoulders, at any rate. You shall yet wake up some fine day and— [*to* GINA] Do you not believe it?

GINA: [*rising*] Yes, of course I do, but in the meantime suppose we see about getting him to bed.

HIALMAR: Yes, come.

[*They take hold of the old man carefully.*]

ACT III

SCENE——HIALMAR EKDAL'S *studio. It is morning; the daylight shines through the large window in the slanting roof; the curtain is drawn back.*

[HIALMAR *is sitting at the table, busy retouching a photograph; several others lie before him. Presently* GINA, *wearing her hat and cloak, enters by the passage door; she has a covered basket on her arm.*]

HIALMAR: Back already, Gina?

GINA: Oh yes, one can't let the grass grow under one's feet. [*Sets her basket on a chair and takes off her things.*]

HIALMAR: Did you look in at Gregers' room?

GINA: Yes, I did. It's a rare sight, I can tell you; he's made a pretty mess to start off with.

HIALMAR: How so?

GINA: He was determined to do everything for himself, he said; so he sets to work to light the stove, and what must he do but screw down the damper till the whole room is full of smoke. Ugh! There was a smell fit to—

HIALMAR: Well, really!

GINA: But that's not the worst of it; for then he thinks he'll put out the fire and goes and empties his water jug into the stove and so makes the whole floor one filthy puddle.

HIALMAR: How annoying!

GINA: I've got the porter's wife to clear up after him, the pig! But the room won't be fit to live in till the afternoon.

HIALMAR: What's he doing with himself in the meantime?

GINA: He said he was going out for a little while.

HIALMAR: I looked in upon him too, for a moment—after you had gone.

GINA: So I heard. You've asked him to lunch.

HIALMAR: Just to a little bit of early lunch, you know. It's his first day—we can hardly do less. You've got something in the house, I suppose?

GINA: I shall have to find something or other.

HIALMAR: And don't cut it too fine, for I fancy Relling and Molvik are coming up too. I just happened to meet Relling on the stairs, you see; so I had to—

GINA: Oh, are we to have those two as well?

HIALMAR: Good lord—a couple more or less can't make any difference.

OLD EKDAL: [*opens his door and looks in*] I say, Hialmar— [*sees* GINA] Oh!

GINA: Do you want anything, Grandfather?

EKDAL: Oh no, it doesn't matter. H'm! [*Retires again.*]

GINA: [*takes up the basket*] Be sure you see that he doesn't go out.

HIALMAR: All right, all right. And, Gina, a little herring salad wouldn't be a bad idea. Relling and Molvik were out on the loose again last night.

GINA: If only they don't come before I'm ready for them—

HIALMAR: No, of course they won't; take your own time.

GINA: Very well, and meanwhile you can be working a bit.

HIALMAR: Well, I am working! I am working as hard as I can!

GINA: Then you'll have that job off your hands, you see. [*She goes out to the kitchen with her basket.* HIALMAR *sits for a time penciling away at the photograph in an indolent and listless manner.*]

EKDAL: [*peeps in, looks round the studio and says softly*] Are you busy?

HIALMAR: Yes, I'm toiling at these wretched pictures.

EKDAL: Well, well, never mind—since you're so busy—h'm!

[*He goes out again; the door stands open.*]

HIALMAR: [*continues for some time in silence, then he lays down his brush and goes over to the door*] Are you busy, Father?

EKDAL: [*in a grumbling tone within*] If you're busy, I'm busy too. H'm!

HIALMAR: Oh, very well then. [*Goes to his work again.*]

EKDAL: [*presently coming to the door again*] H'm; I say Hialmar, I'm not so very busy, you know.

HIALMAR: I thought you were writing.

EKDAL: Oh, devil take it! Can't Graberg wait a day or two? After all, it's not a matter of life and death.

HIALMAR: No, and you're not his slave either.

EKDAL: And about that other business in there—

HIALMAR: Just what I was .thinking of. Do you want to go in? Shall I open the door for you?

EKDAL: Well, it wouldn't be a bad notion.

HIALMAR: [*rises*] Then we'd have that off our hands.

EKDAL: Yes, exactly. It's got to be ready first thing tomorrow. It is tomorrow, isn't it? H'm?

HIALMAR: Yes, of course it's tomorrow.

[HIALMAR *and* EKDAL *push aside each his half of the sliding door. The morning sun is shining in through the skylights; some doves are flying about; others sit cooing upon the perches; the hens are heard clucking now and then further back in the garret.*]

HIALMAR: There; now you can get to work, Father.

EKDAL: [*goes in*] Aren't you coming too?

HIALMAR: Well, really, you know—I almost think—[*sees* GINA *at the kitchen door*] I? No; I haven't time; I must work— But now for our new contrivance—

[*He pulls a cord; a curtain slips down inside, the lower part consisting of a piece of old sailcloth, the upper part of a stretched fishing net. The floor of the garret is thus no longer visible.*]

HIALMAR: [*goes to the table*] So! Now perhaps I can sit in peace for a little while.

GINA: Is he rampaging in there again?

HIALMAR: Would you rather have him slip down to Madam Eriksen's? [*seats himself*] Do you want anything? You know you said—

GINA: I only wanted to ask if you think we can lay the table for lunch here?

HIALMAR: Yes; we have no early appointment, I suppose?

GINA: No, I expect no one today except those two sweethearts that are to be taken together.

HIALMAR: Why the devil couldn't they be taken together another day?

GINA: Don't you know, I told them to come in the afternoon, when you are having your nap.

HIALMAR: Oh, that's capital. Very well, let us have lunch here then.

GINA: All right, but there's no hurry about laying the cloth; you can have the table for a good while yet.

HIALMAR: Do you think I am not sticking to my work? I'm at it as hard as I can!

GINA: Then you'll be free later on, you know.

    [*Goes out into the kitchen again. Short pause.*]

EKDAL: [*in the garret doorway, behind the net*] Hialmar!

HIALMAR: Well?

EKDAL: Afraid we shall have to move the water trough after all.

HIALMAR: What else have I been saying all along?

EKDAL: H'm—h'm—h'm.

    [*Goes away from the door again.* HIALMAR *goes on working a little, glances toward the garret and half rises.* HEDVIG *comes in from the kitchen.*]

HIALMAR: [*sits down again hurriedly*] What do you want?

HEDVIG: I only wanted to come in beside you, Father.

HIALMAR: [*after a pause*] What makes you go prying around like that? Perhaps you are told to watch me?

HEDVIG: No, no.

HIALMAR: What is your mother doing out there?

HEDVIG: Oh, Mother's in the middle of making the herring salad. [*goes to the table*] Isn't there any little thing I could help you with, Father?

HIALMAR: Oh no. It is right that I should bear the whole burden—so long as my strength holds out. Set your mind at rest, Hedvig; if only your father keeps his health—

HEDVIG: Oh no, Father! You mustn't talk in that horrid way.

    [*She wanders about a little, stops by the doorway and looks into the garret.*]

HIALMAR: Tell me, what is he doing?

HEDVIG: I think he's making a new path to the water trough.

HIALMAR: He can never manage that by himself! And here am I doomed to sit!

HEDVIG: [*goes to him*] Let me take the brush, Father; I can do it quite well.

HIALMAR: Oh, nonsense; you will only hurt your eyes.

HEDVIG: Not a bit. Give me the brush.

HIALMAR: [*rising*] Well, it won't take more than a minute or two.

HEDVIG: Pooh, what harm can it do then? [*takes the brush*] There! [*seats herself*] I can begin upon this one.

HIALMAR: But mind you don't hurt your eyes! Do you hear? I won't be answerable; you do it on your own responsibility—understand that.

HEDVIG: [*retouching*] Yes, yes, I understand.

HIALMAR: You are quite clever at it, Hedvig. Only a minute or two, you know.

    [*He slips through by the edge of the curtain into the garret.* HEDVIG *sits at her work.* HIALMAR *and* EKDAL *are heard disputing inside.*]

HIALMAR: [*appears behind the net*] I say, Hedvig—give me those pliers that are lying on the shelf. And the chisel. [*turns away inside*] Now you shall see, Father. Just let me show you first what I mean!

[HEDVIG *has fetched the required tools from the shelf and hands them to him through the net.*]

HIALMAR: Ah, thanks. I didn't come a moment too soon.

[*Goes back from the curtain again; they are heard carpentering and talking inside.* HEDVIG *stands looking in at them. A moment later there is a knock at the passage door; she does not notice it.*]

GREGERS WERLE: [*bareheaded, in indoor dress, enters and stops near the door*] H'm!

HEDVIG: [*turns and goes toward him*] Good morning. Please come in.

GREGERS: Thank you. [*looking toward the garret*] You seem to have work-people in the house.

HEDVIG: No, it's only Father and Grandfather. I'll tell them you are here.

GREGERS: No, no, don't do that; I would rather wait a little. [*seats himself on the sofa.*]

HEDVIG: It looks so untidy here— [*Begins to clear away the photographs.*]

GREGERS: Oh, don't take them away. Are those prints that have to be finished off?

HEDVIG: Yes, they are a few I was helping Father with.

GREGERS: Please don't let me disturb you.

HEDVIG: Oh no.

[*She gathers the things to her and sits down to work;* GREGERS *looks at her meanwhile in silence.*]

GREGORS: Did the wild duck sleep well last night?

HEDVIG: Yes, I think so, thanks.

GREGERS: [*turning toward the garret*] It looks quite different by day from what it did last night in the moonlight.

HEDVIG: Yes, it changes ever so much. It looks different in the morning and in the afternoon, and it's different on rainy days from what it is in fine weather.

GREGERS: Have you noticed it?

HEDVIG: Yes, how could I help it?

GREGERS: Are you too fond of being in there with the wild duck?

HEDVIG: Yes, when I can manage it.

GREGERS: But I suppose you haven't much spare time; you go to school, no doubt.

HEDVIG: No, not now; Father is afraid of my hurting my eyes.

GREGERS: Oh, then he reads with you himself?

HEDVIG: Father has promised to read with me, but he has never had time yet.

GREGERS: Then is there nobody else to give you a little help?

HEDVIG: Yes, there is Mr Molvik, but he is not always exactly—quite—

GREGERS: Sober?

HEDVIG: Yes, I suppose that's it!

GREGERS: Why, then, you must have any amount of time on your hands. And in there I suppose it is a sort of world by itself?

HEDVIG: Oh yes, quite. And there are such lots of wonderful things.

GREGERS: Indeed?

HEDVIG: Yes, there are big cupboards full of books, and a great many of the books have pictures in them.

GREGERS: Aha!

HEDVIG: And there's an old bureau with drawers and flaps and a big clock with figures that go out and in. But the clock isn't going now.

GREGERS: So time has come to a standstill in there—in the wild duck's world?

HEDVIG: Yes. And then there's an old paintbox and things of that sort, and all the books.

GREGERS: And you read the books, I suppose.

HEDVIG: Oh yes, when I get the chance. Most of them are English, though, and I don't understand English. But then I look at the pictures. There is one great book called *Harrison's History of London*. It must be a hundred years old, and there are such heaps of pictures in it. At the beginning there is Death with an hourglass and a woman. I think that is horrid. But then there are all the other pictures of churches and castles and streets and great ships sailing on the sea.

GREGERS: But tell me, where did all those wonderful things come from?

HEDVIG: Oh, an old sea captain once lived here, and he brought them home with him. They used to call him "The Flying Dutchman." That was curious, because he wasn't a Dutchman at all.

GREGERS: Was he not?

HEDVIG: No. But at last he was drowned at sea, and so he left all those things behind him.

GREGERS: Tell me now—when you are sitting in there looking at the pictures don't you wish you could travel and see the real world for yourself?

HEDVIG: Oh no! I mean always to stay at home and help Father and Mother.

GREGERS: To retouch photographs?

HEDVIG: No, not only that. I should love above everything to learn to engrave pictures like those in the English books.

GREGERS: H'm. What does your father say to that?

HEDVIG: I don't think Father likes it; Father is strange about such things. Only think, he talks of my learning basketmaking! But I don't think that would be much good.

GREGERS: Oh no, I don't think so either.

HEDVIG: But Father was right in saying that if I had learned basketmaking I could have made the new basket for the wild duck.

GREGERS: So you could; and it was you that ought to have done it, wasn't it?

HEDVIG: Yes, for it's my wild duck.

GREGERS: Of course it is.

HEDVIG: Yes, it belongs to me. But I lend it to Father and Grandfather as often as they please.

GREGERS: Indeed? What do they do with it?

HEDVIG: Oh, they look after it and build places for it and so on.

GREGERS: I see; for no doubt the wild duck is by far the most distinguished inhabitant of the garret?

HEDVIG: Yes, indeed she is; for she is a real wild fowl, you know. And then she is so much to be pitied; she has no one to care for, poor thing.

GREGERS: She has no family, as the rabbits have.

HEDVIG: No. The hens too, many of them, were chickens together; but she has been taken right away from all her friends. And then there is so much that is strange about the wild duck. Nobody knows her, and nobody knows where she came from either.

GREGERS: And she has been down in the depths of the sea.

HEDVIG: [*with a quick glance at him, represses a smile and asks*] Why do you say "depths of the sea"?

GREGERS: What else should I say?

HEDVIG: You could say "the bottom of the sea."

GREGERS: Oh, can't I just as well say the depths of the sea?

HEDVIG: Yes, but it sounds so strange to me when other people speak of the depths of the sea.

GREGERS: Why? Tell me why?

HEDVIG: No, I won't; it's so stupid.

GREGERS: Oh no, I am sure it's not. Do tell me why you smiled.

HEDVIG: Well, this is the reason: whenever I come to realize suddenly—in a flash—what is in there, it always seems to me that the whole room and everything in it should be called "the depths of the sea." But that is so stupid.

GREGERS: You mustn't say that.

HEDVIG: Oh yes, for you know it is only a garret.

GREGERS: [*looks fixedly at her*] Are you so sure of that?

HEDVIG: [*astonished*] That it's a garret?

GREGERS: Are you quite certain of it?

[HEDVIG *is silent and looks at him open-mouthed.* GINA *comes in from the kitchen with the table things.*]

GREGERS: [*rising*] I have come in upon you too early.

GINA: Oh, you must be somewhere, and we're nearly ready now anyway. Clear the table, Hedvig.

[HEDVIG *clears away her things; she and* GINA *lay the cloth during what follows.* GREGERS *seats himself in the armchair and turns over an album.*]

GREGERS: I hear you can retouch, Mrs Ekdal.

GINA: [*with a side glance*] Yes, I can.

GREGERS: That was exceedingly lucky.

GINA: How—lucky?

GREGERS: Since Ekdal took to photography, I mean.

HEDVIG: Mother can take photographs too.

GINA: Oh yes, I had to learn that.

GREGERS: So it is really you that carry on the business, I suppose?

GINA: Yes, when Ekdal hasn't time himself—

GREGERS: He is a great deal taken up with his old father, I daresay.

GINA: Yes; and then you can't expect a man like Ekdal to do nothing but take pictures of Dick, Tom and Harry.

GREGERS: I quite agree with you, but having once gone in for the thing—

GINA: You can surely understand, Mr Werle, that Ekdal's not like one of your common photographers.

GREGERS: Of course not, but still—

[*A shot is fired within the garret.*]

GREGERS: [*starting up*] What's that?

GINA: Ugh! Now they're firing again!

GREGERS: Have they firearms in there?

HEDVIG: They are out shooting.

GREGERS: What! [*at the door of the garret*] Are you shooting, Hialmar?

HIALMAR: [*inside the net*] Are you there? I didn't know; I was so taken up—
[*to* HEDVIG] Why did you not let us know? [*Comes into the studio.*]

GREGERS: Do you go shooting in the garret?

HIALMAR: [*showing a double-barreled pistol*] Oh, only with this thing.

GINA: Yes, you and Grandfather will hurt yourselves someday with that there
pigstol.

HIALMAR: [*with irritation*] I believe I have told you that this kind of firearm
is called a pistol.

GINA: Oh, that doesn't make it much better that I can see.

GREGERS: So you have become a sportsman too, Hialmar?

HIALMAR: Only a little rabbit shooting now and then. Mostly to please Father,
you understand.

GINA: Men are strange beings; they must always have something to pervert
theirselves with.

HIALMAR: [*snappishly*] Just so; we must always have something to divert ourselves with.

GINA: Yes, that's just what I say.

HIALMAR: H'm. [*to* GREGERS] You see, the garret is fortunately so situated that
no one can hear us shooting. [*lays the pistol on the top shelf of the bookcase*] Don't touch the pistol, Hedvig! One of the barrels is loaded; remember that.

GREGERS: [*looking through the net*] You have a fowling piece too, I see.

HIALMAR: That is Father's old gun. It's of no use now. Something has gone
wrong with the lock. But it's fun to have it all the same, for we can take
it to pieces now and then and clean and grease it and screw it together
again. Of course it's mostly Father that fiddles with all that sort of thing.

HEDVIG: [*beside* GREGERS] Now you can see the wild duck properly.

GREGERS: I was just looking at her. One of her wings seems to me to droop a bit.

HEDVIG: Well, no wonder; her wing was broken, you know.

GREGERS: And she trails one foot a little. Isn't that so?

HIALMAR: Perhaps a very little bit.

HEDVIG: Yes, it was by that foot the dog took hold of her.

HIALMAR: But otherwise she hasn't the least thing the matter with her, and
that is simply marvelous for a creature that has a charge of shot in her body
and has been between a dog's teeth—

GREGERS: [*with a glance at* HEDVIG] —and that has lain in the depths of the sea
—so long.

HEDVIG: [*smiling*] Yes.

GINA: [*laying the table*] That blessed wild duck! What a lot of fuss you do make
over her.

HIALMAR: H'm—will lunch soon be ready?

GINA: Yes, directly. Hedvig, you must come and help me now.

[GINA *and* HEDVIG *go out into the kitchen.*]

HIALMAR: [*in a low voice*] I think you had better not stand there looking in at Father; he doesn't like it. [GREGERS *moves away from the garret door.*] Besides, I may as well shut up before the others come. [*claps his hands to drive the fowls back*] Shh—shh, in with you! [*draws up the curtain and pulls the doors together*] All the contrivances are my own invention. Its really quite amusing to have things of this sort to potter with and to put to rights when they get out of order. And its absolutely necessary too, for Gina objects to having rabbits and fowls in the studio.

GREGERS: To be sure, and I suppose the studio is your wife's special department?

HIALMAR: As a rule I leave the everyday details of business to her, for then I can take refuge in the parlor and give my mind to more important things.

GREGERS: What things are they Hialmar?

HIALMAR: I wonder you have not asked that question sooner. But perhaps you haven't heard of the invention?

GREGERS: The invention? No.

HIALMAR: Really? Haven't you? Oh no, out there in the wilds—

GREGERS: So you have invented something, have you?

HIALMAR: It is not quite completed yet, but I am working at it. You can easily imagine that when I resolved to devote myself to photography it wasn't simply with the idea of taking likenesses of all sorts of commonplace people.

GREGERS: No; your wife was saying the same thing just now.

HIALMAR: I swore that if I concentrated my powers to this handicraft I would so exalt it that it should become both an art and a science. And to that end I determined to make this great invention.

GREGERS: And what is the nature of the invention? What purpose does it serve?

HIALMAR: Oh, my dear fellow, you mustn't ask for details yet. It takes time, you see. And you must not think that my motive is vanity. It is not for my own sake that I am working. Oh no; it is my life's mission that stands before me night and day.

GREGERS: What is your life's mission?

HIALMAR: Do you forget the old man with the silver hair?

GREGERS: Your poor father? Well, but what can you do for him?

HIALMAR: I can raise up his self-respect from the dead by restoring the name of Ekdal to honor and dignity.

GREGERS: Then that is your life's mission?

HIALMAR: Yes. I will rescue the shipwrecked man. For shipwrecked he was, by the very first blast of the storm. Even while those terrible investigations were going on he was no longer himself. That pistol there—the one we used to shoot rabbits with—has played its part in the tragedy of the house of Ekdal.

GREGERS: The pistol? Indeed?

HIALMAR: When the sentence of imprisonment was passed—he had the pistol in his hand.

GREGERS: Had he?

HIALMAR: Yes, but he dared not use it. His courage failed him. So broken, so demoralized was he even then! Oh, can you understand it? He, a soldier; he, who had shot nine bears and who was descended from two lieutenant colonels—one after the other, of course. Can you understand it, Gregers?

GREGERS: Yes, I understand it well enough.

HIALMAR: I cannot. And once more the pistol played a part in the history of our house. When he had put on the gray clothes and was under lock and key— oh, that was a terrible time for me, I can tell you. I kept the blinds drawn down over both my windows. When I peeped out I saw the sun shining as if nothing had happened. I could not understand it. I saw people going along the street, laughing and talking about indifferent things. I could not understand it. It seemed to me that the whole of existence must be at a standstill—as if under an eclipse.

GREGERS: I felt that too, when my mother died.

HIALMAR: It was in such an hour that Hialmar Ekdal pointed the pistol at his own breast.

GREGERS: You, too, thought of—

HIALMAR: Yes.

GREGERS: But you did not fire?

HIALMAR: No. At the decisive moment I won the victory over myself. I remained in life. But I can assure you it takes some courage to choose life under circumstances like those.

GREGERS: Well, that depends on how you look at it.

HIALMAR: Yes indeed, it takes courage. But I am glad I was firm, for now I shall soon perfect my invention; and Doctor Relling thinks, as I do myself, that Father may be allowed to wear his uniform again. I will demand that as my sole reward.

GREGERS: So that is what he meant about his uniform?

HIALMAR: Yes, that is what he most yearns for. You can't think how my heart bleeds for him. Every time we celebrate any little family festival—Gina's and my wedding day or whatever it may be—in comes the old man in the lieutenant's uniform of happier days. But if he only hears a knock at the door—for he daren't show himself to strangers, you know—he hurries back to his room again as fast as his old legs can carry him. Oh, it's heart-rending for a son to see such things!

GREGERS: How long do you think it will take you to finish your invention?

HIALMAR: Come now, you mustn't expect me to enter into particulars like that. An invention is not a thing completely under one's own control. It depends largely on inspiration—on intuition—and it is almost impossible to predict when the inspiration may come.

GREGERS: But it's advancing?

HIALMAR: Yes, certainly it is advancing. I turn it over in my mind every day; I am full of it. Every afternoon, when I have had my dinner, I shut myself up in the parlor where I can ponder undisturbed. But I can't be goaded to it; it's not a bit of good. Relling says so too.

GREGERS: And you don't think that all that business in the garret draws you off and distracts you too much?

HIALMAR: No, no, no; quite the contrary. You mustn't say that. I cannot be everlastingly absorbed in the same laborious train of thought. I must have something alongside of it to fill up the time of waiting. The inspiration, the intuition, you see—when it comes it comes, and there's an end of it.

GREGERS: My dear Hialmar, I almost think you have something of the wild duck in you.

HIALMAR: Something of the wild duck? How do you mean?

GREGERS: You have dived down and caught yourself fast in the undergrowth.

HIALMAR: Are you alluding to the almost fatal shot that has broken my father's wing—and mine too?

GREGERS: Not exactly to that. I don't say that your wing has been broken, but you have strayed into a poisonous marsh, Hialmar; an insidious disease has taken hold of you, and you have sunk down to die in the dark.

HIALMAR: I? To die in the dark? Look here, Gregers, you must really stop talking such nonsense.

GREGERS: Don't be afraid; I shall find a way to help you up again. I, too, have a mission in life now; I found it yesterday.

HIALMAR: That's all very well, but you will please leave me out of it. I can assure you that—apart from my very natural melancholy, of course—I am as contented as anyone can wish to be.

GREGERS: Your contentment is an effect of the marsh poison.

HIALMAR: Now, my dear Gregers, pray do not go on about disease and poison; I am not used to that sort of talk. In my house nobody ever speaks to me about unpleasant things.

GREGERS: Ah, that I can easily believe.

HIALMAR: It's not good for me, you see. And there are no marsh poisons here, as you express it. The poor photographer's roof is lowly, I know—and my circumstances are narrow. But I am an inventor, and I am the bread-winner of a family. That exalts me above my mean surroundings. Ah, here comes lunch!

[GINA *and* HEDVIG *bring bottles of ale, a decanter of brandy, glasses, etc. At the same time* RELLING *and* MOLVIK *enter from the passage; they are both without hat or overcoat.* MOLVIK *is dressed in black.*]

GINA: [*placing the things upon the table*] Ah you two have come in the nick of time.

RELLING: Molvik got it into his head that he could smell herring salad, and then there was no holding him. Good morning again, Ekdal.

HIALMAR: Gregers, let me introduce you to Mr Molvik—Doctor— Oh, you know Relling, don't you?

GREGERS: Yes, slightly.

RELLING: Oh, Mr Werle junior! Yes, we two have had one or two little skirmishes up at the Höidal works. You've just moved in?

GREGERS: I moved in this morning.

RELLING: Molvik and I live right under you, so you haven't far to go for the doctor and the clergyman if you should need anything in that line.

GREGERS: Thanks; it's not quite unlikely, for yesterday we were thirteen at table.

HIALMAR: Oh, come now, don't let us get upon unpleasant subjects again!

RELLING: You may make your mind easy, Ekdal; I'll be hanged if the finger of fate points to you.

HIALMAR: I should hope not, for the sake of my family. But let us sit down now and eat and drink and be merry.

GREGERS: Shall we not wait for your father?

HIALMAR: No, his lunch will be taken in to him later. Come along!

> [*The men seat themselves at table and eat and drink.* GINA *and* HEDVIG *go in and out and wait upon them.*]

RELLING: Molvik was frightfully drunk yesterday, Mrs Ekdal.

GINA: Really? Yesterday again?

RELLING: Didn't you hear him when I brought him home last night?

GINA: No, I can't say I did.

RELLING: That was a good thing, for Molvik was disgusting last night.

GINA: Is that true, Molvik?

MOLVIK: Let us draw a veil over last night's proceedings. That sort of thing is totally foreign to my better self.

RELLING: [*to* GREGERS] It comes over him like a sort of possession, and then I have to go out on the loose with him. Mr Molvik is demonic, you see.

GREGERS: Demonic?

RELLING: Molvik is demonic, yes.

GREGERS: H'm

RELLING: And demonic natures are not made to walk straight through the world; they must meander a little now and then. Well, so you still stay up there at those horrible grimy works?

GREGERS: I have stayed there until now.

RELLING: And did you ever manage to collect that claim you went about presenting?

GREGERS: Claim? [*understands him*] Ah, I see.

HIALMAR: Have you been presenting claims, Gregers?

GREGERS: Oh, nonsense.

RELLING: Faith, but he has, though! He went round to all the cotters' cabins presenting something he called "the claim of the ideal."

GREGERS: I was young then.

RELLING: You're right; you were very young. And as for the claim of the ideal— you never got it honored while *I* was up there.

GREGERS: Nor since either.

RELLING: Ah, then you've learned to knock a little discount off, I expect.

GREGERS: Never, when I have a true man to deal with.

HIALMAR: No, I should think not, indeed. A little butter, Gina.

RELLING: And a slice of bacon for Molvik.

MOLVIK: Ugh! not bacon!

> [*A knock at the garret door.*]

HIALMAR: Open the door, Hedvig; Father wants to come out.

> [HEDVIG *goes over and opens the door a little way;* EKDAL *enters with a fresh rabbitskin; she closes the door after him.*]

EKDAL: Good morning, gentlemen! Good sport today. Shot a big one.

HIALMAR: And you've gone and skinned it without waiting for me!

EKDAL: Salted it too. It's good tender meat, is rabbit; it's sweet; it tastes like sugar. Good appetite to you, gentlemen! [*Goes into his room.*]

MOLVIK: [*rising*] Excuse me—I can't—I must get downstairs immediately—

RELLING: Drink some soda water, man!

MOLVIK: [*hurrying away*] Ugh—ugh. [*Goes out by the passage door.*]

RELLING: [*to* HIALMAR] Let us drain a glass to the old hunter.

HIALMAR: [*clinks glasses with him*] To the undaunted sportsman who has looked death in the face!

RELLING: To the gray-haired— [*drinks*] By the bye. is his hair gray or white?

HIALMAR: Something between the two, I fancy; for that matter, he has very few hairs left of any color.

RELLING: Well, well, one can get through the world with a wig. After all, you are a happy man, Ekdal; you have your noble mission to labor for—

HIALMAR: And I do labor, I can tell you.

RELLING: And then you have your excellent wife, shuffling quietly in and out in her felt slippers, with that seesaw walk of hers, and making everything cosy and comfortable about you.

HIALMAR: Yes, Gina [*nods to her*] you've been a good helpmate on the path of life.

GINA: Oh, don't sit there cricketizing me.

RELLING: And your Hedvig too, Ekdal!

HIALMAR: [*affected*] The child, yes! The child before everything! Hedvig, come here to me. [*strokes her hair*] What day is it tomorrow, eh?

HEDVIG: [*shaking him*] Oh no, you're not to say anything, Father.

HIALMAR: It cuts me to the heart when I think what a poor affair it will be; only a little festivity in the garret.

HEDVIG: Oh, but that's just what I like!

RELLING: Just you wait till the wonderful invention sees the light, Hedvig!

HIALMAR: Yes indeed—then you shall see! Hedvig, I have resolved to make your future secure. You shall live in comfort all your days. I will demand something or other—on your behalf. That shall be the poor inventor's sole reward.

HEDVIG: [*whispering, with her arms round his neck*] Oh, you dear, kind father!

RELLING: [*to* GREGERS] Come now, don't you find it pleasant, for once, to sit at a well-spread table in a happy family circle?

HIALMAR: Ah yes, I really prize these social hours.

GREGERS: For my part, I don't thrive in marsh vapors.

RELLING: Marsh vapors?

HIALMAR: Oh, don't begin with that stuff again!

GINA: Goodness knows there's no vapors in this house, Mr Werle; I give the place a good airing every blessed day.

GREGERS: [*leaves the table*] No airing you can give will drive out the taint I mean.

HIALMAR: Taint!

GINA: Yes, what do you say to that, Ekdal!

RELLING: Excuse me—may it not be you yourself that have brought the taint from those mines up there?

GREGERS: It is like you to call what I bring into this house a taint.

RELLING: [*goes up to him*] Look here, Mr Werle junior: I have a strong suspicion that you are still carrying about that "claim of the ideal" large as life in your coattail pocket.

GREGERS: I carry it in my breast.

RELLING: Well, wherever you carry it, I advise you not to come dunning us with it here as long as *I* am on the premises.

GREGERS: And if I do so nonetheless?

RELLING: Then you'll go headfirst down the stairs; now I've warned you.

HIALMAR: [*rising*] Oh, but, Relling—

GREGERS: Yes, you may turn me out.

GINA: [*interposing between them*] We can't have that, Relling. But I must say, Mr Werle, it ill becomes you to talk about vapors and taints after all the mess you made with your stove.

[*A knock at the passage door.*]

HEDVIG: Mother, there's somebody knocking.

HIALMAR: There now, we're going to have a whole lot of people!

GINA: I'll go. [*goes over and opens the door, starts and draws back*] Oh—oh dear!

[WERLE, *in a fur coat, advances one step into the room.*]

WERLE: Excuse me, but I think my son is staying here.

GINA: [*with a gulp*] Yes.

HIALMAR: [*approaching him*] Won't you do us the honor to—

WERLE: Thank you, I merely wish to speak to my son.

GREGERS: What is it? Here I am.

WERLE: I want a few words with you in your room.

GREGERS: In my room? Very well. [*about to go*]

GINA: No, no, your room's not in a fit state.

WERLE: Well, then, out in the passage here; I want to have a few words with you alone.

HIALMAR: You can have them here, sir. Come into the parlor, Relling.

[HIALMAR *and* RELLING *go off to the right;* GINA *takes* HEDVIG *with her into the kitchen.*]

GREGERS: [*after a short pause*] Well, now we are alone.

WERLE: From something you let fall last evening, and from your coming to lodge with the Ekdals, I can't help inferring that you intend to make yourself unpleasant to me in one way or another.

GREGERS: I intend to open Hialmar Ekdal's eyes. He shall see his position as it really is—that is all.

WERLE: Is that the mission in life you spoke of yesterday?

GREGERS: Yes. You have left me no other.

WERLE: Is it I, then, that have crippled your mind, Gregers?

GREGERS: You have crippled my whole life. I am not thinking of all that about Mother—but it's thanks to you that I am continually haunted and harassed by a guilty conscience.

WERLE: Indeed! It is your conscience that troubles you, is it?

GREGERS: I ought to have taken a stand against you when the trap was set for

Lieutenant Ekdal. I ought to have cautioned him, for I had a misgiving as to what was in the wind.

WERLE: Yes, that was the time to have spoken.

GREGERS: I did not dare to, I was so cowed and spiritless. I was mortally afraid of you—not only then, but long afterward.

WERLE: You have got over that fear now, it appears.

GREGERS: Yes, fortunately. The wrong done to old Ekdal, both by me and by others, can never be undone; but Hialmar I can rescue from all the false-hood and deception that are bringing him to ruin.

WERLE: Do you think that will be doing him a kindness?

GREGERS: I have not the least doubt of it.

WERLE: You think our worthy photographer is the sort of man to appreciate such friendly offices?

GREGERS: Yes, I do.

WERLE: H'm—we shall see.

GREGERS: Besides, if I am to go on living, I must try to find some cure for my sick conscience.

WERLE: It will never be sound. Your conscience has been sickly from child-hood. That is a legacy from your mother, Gregers—the only one she left you.

GREGERS: [*with a scornful half-smile*] Have you not yet forgiven her for the mistake you made in supposing she would bring you a fortune?

WERLE: Don't let us wander from the point. Then you hold to your purpose of setting young Ekdal upon what you imagine to be the right scent?

GREGERS: Yes, that is my fixed resolve.

WERLE: Well, in that case I might have spared myself this visit, for of course it is useless to ask whether you will return home with me?

GREGERS: Quite useless.

WERLE: And I suppose you won't enter the firm either?

GREGERS: No.

WERLE: Very good. But as I am thinking of marrying again, your share in the property will fall to you at once.

GREGERS: [*quickly*] No, I do not want that.

WERLE: You don't want it?

GREGERS: No, I dare not take it, for conscience' sake.

WERLE: [*after a pause*] Are you going up to the works again?

GREGERS: No; I consider myself released from your service.

WERLE: But what are you going to do?

GREGERS: Only fulfill my mission, nothing more.

WERLE: Well, but afterward? What are you going to live upon?

GREGERS: I have laid by a little out of my salary.

WERLE: How long will that last?

GREGERS: I think it will last my time.

WERLE: What do you mean?

GREGERS: I shall answer no more questions.

WERLE: Good-by, then, Gregers.

GREGORS: Good-by.

[WERLE *goes.*]

HIALMAR: [*peeping in*] He's gone, isn't he?

GREGERS: Yes.

[HIALMAR *and* RELLING *enter; also* GINA *and* HEDVIG *from the kitchen.*]

RELLING: That luncheon party was a failure.

GREGERS: Put on your coat, Hialmar; I want you to come for a long walk with me.

HIALMAR: With pleasure. What was it your father wanted? Had it anything to do with me?

GREGERS: Come along. We must have a talk. I'll go and put on my overcoat. [*Goes out by the passage door.*]

GINA: You shouldn't go out with him, Ekdal.

RELLING: No, don't you do it. Stay where you are.

HIALMAR: [*gets his hat and overcoat*] Oh, nonsense! When a friend of my youth feels impelled to open his mind to me in private—

RELLING: But devil take it—don't you see that the fellow's mad, cracked, demented!

GINA: There, what did I tell you! His mother before him had crazy fits like that sometimes.

HIALMAR: The more need for a friend's watchful eye. [*to* GINA] Be sure you have dinner ready in good time. Good-by for the present. [*Goes out by the passage door.*]

RELLING: It's a thousand pities the fellow didn't go to hell through one of the Höidal mines.

GINA: Good lord! What makes you say that?

RELLING: [*muttering*] Oh, I have my own reasons.

GINA: Do you think young Werle is really mad?

RELLING: No, worse luck; he's no madder than most other people. But one disease he has certainly got in his system.

GINA: What is it that's the matter with him?

RELLING: Well, I'll tell you, Mrs Ekdal. He is suffering from an acute attack of integrity.

GINA: Integrity?

HEDVIG: Is that a kind of disease?

RELLING: Yes, it's a national disease. but it only appears sporadically. [*nods to* GINA] Thanks for your hospitality. [*He goes out by the passage door.*]

GINA: [*moving restlessly to and fro*] Ugh, that Gregers Werle—he was always a wretched creature.

HEDVIG: [*standing by the table and looking searchingly at her*] I think all this is very strange.

ACT IV

SCENE——HIALMAR EKDAL's *studio. A photograph has just been taken; a camera with the cloth over it, a pedestal, two chairs, a folding table, etc., are standing out in the room. Afternoon light; the sun is going down; a little later it begins to grow dusk.*

[*Gina stands in the passage doorway with a little box and a wet glass plate in her hand and is speaking to somebody outside.*]

GINA: Yes, certainly. When I make a promise I keep it. The first dozen will be ready on Monday. Good afternoon.

[*Someone is heard going downstairs.* GINA *shuts the door, slips the plate into the box and puts it into the covered camera.*]

HEDVIG: [*comes in from the kitchen*] Are they gone?

GINA: [*tidying up*] Yes, thank goodness. I've got rid of them at last.

HEDVIG: But can you imagine why Father hasn't come home yet?

GINA: Are you sure he's not down in Relling's room?

HEDVIG: No, he's not; I ran down the kitchen stair just now and asked.

GINA: And his dinner standing and getting cold too.

HEDVIG: Yes, I can't understand it. Father's always so careful to be home for dinner!

GINA: Oh, he'll be here directly, you'll see.

HEDVIG: I wish he would come; everything seems so queer today.

GINA: [*calls out*] There he is!

[HIALMAR EKDAL *comes in at the passage door.*]

HEDVIG: [*going to him*] Father! Oh, what a time we've been waiting for you!

GINA: [*glancing sidelong at him*] You've been out a long time, Ekdal.

HIALMAR: [*without looking at her*] Rather long, yes.

[*He takes off his overcoat;* GINA *and* HEDVIG *go to help him; he motions them away.*]

GINA: Perhaps you've had dinner with Werle?

HIALMAR: [*hanging up his coat*] No.

GINA: [*going toward the kitchen door*] Then I'll bring some in for you.

HIALMAR: No; let the dinner alone. I want nothing to eat.

HEDVIG: [*going nearer to him*] Are you not well, Father?

HIALMAR: Well? Oh yes, well enough. We have had a tiring walk, Gregers and I.

GINA: You didn't ought to have gone so far, Ekdal; you're not used to it.

HIALMAR: H'm; there's many a thing a man must get used to in this world. [*wanders about the room*] Has anyone been here whilst I was out?

GINA: Nobody but the two sweethearts.

HIALMAR: No new orders?

GINA: No, not today.

HEDVIG: There will be some tomorrow, Father, you'll see.

HIALMAR: I hope there will, for tomorrow I am going to set to work in real earnest.

HEDVIG: Tomorrow! Don't you remember what day it is tomorrow?

HIALMAR: Oh yes, by the bye— Well, the day after, then. Henceforth I mean to do everything myself; I shall take all the work into my own hands.

GINA: Why, what can be the good of that. Ekdal? It'll only make your life a burden to you. I can manage the photography all right, and you can go on working at your invention.

HEDVIG: And think of the wild duck, Father. and all the hens and rabbits and—

HIALMAR: Don't talk to me of all that trash! From tomorrow I will never set foot in the garret again.

HEDVIG: Oh, but, Father, you promised that we should have a little party.

HIALMAR: H'm, true. Well, then, from the day after tomorrow. I should almost like to wring that cursed wild duck's neck!

HEDVIG: [*shrieks*] The wild duck!

GINA: Well, I never!

HEDVIG: [*shaking him*] Oh no, Father; you know it's my wild duck!

HIALMAR: That is why I don't do it. I haven't the heart to—for your sake, Hedvig. But in my inmost soul I feel that I ought to do it. I ought nòt to tolerate under my roof a creature that has been through those hands.

GINA: Why, good gracious, even if Grandfather did get it from that poor creature Pettersen—

HEDVIG: [*going after him*] But think of the wild duck—the poor wild duck!

HIALMAR: [*stops*] I tell you I will spare it—for your sake. Not a hair of its head shall be—I mean, it shall be spared. There are greater problems than that to be dealt with. But you should go out a little now, Hedvig, as usual; it is getting dusk enough for you now.

HEDVIG: No, I don't care about going out now.

HIALMAR: Yes, do; it seems to me your eyes are blinking a great deal; all these vapors in here are bad for you. The air is heavy under this roof.

HEDVIG: Very well then, I'll run down the kitchen stair and go for a little walk. My cloak and hat? Oh, they're in my own room. Father—be sure you don't do the wild duck any harm while I'm out.

HIALMAR: Not a feather of its head shall be touched. [*draws her to him*] You and I, Hedvig—we two—Well, go along.

   [HEDVIG *nods to her parents and goes out through the kitchen.*]

HIALMAR: [*walks about without looking up*] Gina.

GINA: Yes?

HIALMAR: From tomorrow—or say from the day after tomorrow—I should like to keep the household account book myself.

GINA: Do you want to keep the accounts too now?

HIALMAR: Yes; or to check the receipts at any rate.

GINA: Lord help us; that's soon done.

HIALMAR: One would hardly think so; at any rate you seem to make the money go a very long way. [*stops and looks at her*] How do you manage it?

GINA: It's because me and Hedvig, we need so little.

HIALMAR: Is it the case that Father is very liberally paid for the copying he does for Mr Werle?

GINA: I don't know as he gets anything out of the way. I don't know the rates for that sort of work.

HIALMAR: Well, what does he get, about? Let me hear!

GINA: Oh, it varies; I daresay it'll come to about as much as he costs us, with a little pocket money over.

HIALMAR: As much as he costs us! And you have never told me this before.

GINA: No, how could I tell you? It pleased you so much to think he got everything from you.

HIALMAR: And he gets it from Mr Werle.

GINA: Oh well, he has plenty and to spare, he has.

HIALMAR: Light the lamp for me, please!

GINA: [*lighting the lamp*] And of course we don't know as it's Mr Werle himself; it may be Graberg.

HIALMAR: Why attempt such an evasion?

GINA: I don't know; I only thought—

HIALMAR: H'm!

GINA: It wasn't me that got Grandfather that copying. It was Bertha, when she used to come about us.

HIALMAR: It seems to me your voice is trembling.

GINA: [*putting the lamp shade on*] Is it?

HIALMAR: And your hands are shaking, are they not?

GINA: [*firmly*] Come right out with it, Ekdal. What has he been saying about me?

HIALMAR: Is it true—can it be true that—that there was an—an understanding between you and Mr Werle while you were in service there?

GINA: That's not true. Not at that time. Mr Werle did come after me, that's a fact. And his wife thought there was something in it, and then she made such a hocus-pocus and hurly-burly, and she hustled me and bustled me about so that I left her service.

HIALMAR: But afterward, then?

GINA: Well. then I went home. And Mother—well, she wasn't the woman you took her for, Ekdal; she kept on worrying and worrying at me about one thing and another—for Mr Werle was a widower by that time.

HIALMAR: Well, and then?

GINA: I suppose you've got to know it. He gave me no peace until he'd had his way.

HIALMAR: [*striking his hands together*] And this is the mother of my child! How could you hide this from me?

GINA: Yes, it was wrong of me; I ought certainly to have told you long ago.

HIALMAR: You should have told me at the very first—then I should have known the sort of woman you were.

GINA: But would you have married me all the same?

HIALMAR: How can you dream that I would?

GINA: That's just why I didn't dare tell you anything then. For I'd come to care for you so much, you see, and I couldn't go and make myself utterly miserable.

HIALMAR: [*walks about*] And this is my Hedvig's mother! And to know that all I see before me [*kicks at chair*]—all that I call my home—I owe to a favored predecessor! Oh, that scoundrel Werle!

GINA: Do you repent of the fourteen—the fifteen years we've lived together?

HIALMAR: [*placing himself in front of her*] Have you not every day, every hour, repented of the spider's web of deceit you have spun around me? Answer me that! How could you help writhing with penitence and remorse?

GINA: Oh, my dear Ekdal, I've had all I could do to look after the house and get through the day's work.

HIALMAR: Then you never think of reviewing your past?

GINA: No; heaven knows I'd almost forgotten those old stories.

HIALMAR: Oh. this dull, callous contentment! To me there is something revolting about it. Think of it—never so much as a twinge of remorse!

GINA: But tell me, Ekdal—what would have become of you if you hadn't had a wife like me?

HIALMAR: Like you!

GINA: Yes; for you know I've always been a bit more practical and wide awake than you. Of course I'm a year or two older.

HIALMAR: What would have become of me!

GINA: You'd got into all sorts of bad ways when first you met me; that you can't deny.

HIALMAR: "Bad ways," do you call them? Little do you know what a man goes through when he is in grief and despair—especially a man of my fiery temperament.

GINA: Well, well, that may be so. And I've no reason to crow over you neither, for you turned a fine husband, that you did, as soon as ever you had a house and home of your own. And now we'd got everything so nice and cosy about us, and me and Hedvig was just thinking we'd soon be able to let ourselves go a bit in the way of both food and clothes.

HIALMAR: In the swamp of deceit, yes.

GINA: I wish to goodness that detestable thing had never set his foot inside our doors!

HIALMAR: And I, too, thought my home such a pleasant one. That was a delusion. Where shall I now find the elasticity of spirit to bring my invention into the world of reality? Perhaps it will die with me, and then it will be your past, Gina, that will have killed it.

GINA: [*nearly crying*] You mustn't say such things, Ekdal. Me, that has only wanted to do the best I could for you all my days!

HIALMAR: I ask you, what becomes of the breadwinner's dream? When I used to lie in there on the sofa and brood over my invention I had a clear enough presentiment that it would sap my vitality to the last drop. I felt even then that the day when I held the patent in my hand—that day— would bring my—release. And then it was my dream that you should live on after me, the dead inventor's well-to-do widow.

GINA: [*drying her tears*] No, you mustn't talk like that, Ekdal. May the Lord never let me see the day I am left a widow!

HIALMAR: Oh, the whole dream has vanished. It is all over now. All over!

[GREGERS WERLE *opens the passage door cautiously and looks in.*]

GREGERS: May I come in?

HIALMAR: Yes, come in.

GREGERS: [*comes forward, his face beaming with satisfaction, and holds out both his hands to them*] Well, dear friends! [*looks from one to the other and whispers to* HIALMAR] Have you not done it yet?

HIALMAR: [*aloud*] It is done.

GREGERS: It is?

HIALMAR: I have passed through the bitterest moments of my life.

GREGERS: But also, I trust, the most ennobling.

HIALMAR: Well, at any rate, we have got through it for the present.

GINA: God forgive you, Mr Werle.

GREGERS: [*in great surprise*] But I don't understand this.

HIALMAR: What don't you understand?

GREGERS: After so great a crisis—a crisis that is to be the starting point of an entirely new life—of a communion founded on truth and free from all taint of deception—

HIALMAR: Yes, yes, I know; I know that quite well.

GREGERS: I confidently expected, when I entered the room, to find the light of transfiguration shining upon me from both husband and wife. And now I see nothing but dullness, oppression, gloom—

GINA: Oh, is that it? [*takes off the lamp shade*]

GREGERS: You will not understand me, Mrs Ekdal. Ah well, you, I suppose, need time to— But you, Hialmar? Surely you feel a new consecration after the great crisis?

HIALMAR: Yes, of course I do. That is—in a sort of way.

GREGERS: For surely nothing in the world can compare with the joy of forgiving one who has sinned and raising her up to oneself in love.

HIALMAR: Do you think a man can so easily throw off the bitter cup I have drained?

GREGERS: No, not a common man, perhaps. But a man like you—

HIALMAR: Good God! I know that well enough. But you must keep me up to it, Gregers. It takes time, you know.

GREGERS: You have much of the wild duck in you, Hialmar.

[RELLING *has come in at the passage door.*]

RELLING: Oho! Is the wild duck to the fore again?

HIALMAR: Yes; Mr Werle's wing-broken victim.

RELLING: Mr Werle? So it's him you are talking about?

HIALMAR: Him and—ourselves.

RELLING: [*in an undertone to* GREGERS] May the devil take you!

HIALMAR: What is that you are saying?

RELLING: Only uttering a heartfelt wish that this quack would take himself off. If he stays here he is quite equal to making an utter mess of life for both of you.

GREGERS: These two will not make a mess of life, Mr Relling. Of course I won't speak for Hialmar—him we know. But she too, in her innermost heart, has certainly something loyal and sincere—

GINA: [*almost crying*] You might have let me alone for what I was then.

RELLING: [*to* GREGERS] Is it rude to ask what you really want in this house?

GREGERS: To lay the foundations of a true marriage.

RELLING: So you don't think Ekdal's marriage is good enough as it is?

GREGERS: No doubt it is as good a marriage as most others, worse luck. But a true marriage it has yet to become.

HIALMAR: You have never had eyes for the claims of the ideal, Relling.

RELLING: Rubbish, my boy! But excuse me, Mr Werle; how many—in round numbers—how many true marriages have you seen in the course of your life?

GREGERS: Scarcely a single one.

RELLING: Nor I either.

GREGERS: But I have seen innumerable marriages of the opposite kind. And it has been my fate to see at close quarters what ruin such a marriage can work in two human souls.

HIALMAR: A man's whole moral basis may give away beneath his feet; that is the terrible part of it.

RELLING: Well, I can't say I've ever been exactly married, so I don't pretend to speak with authority. But this I know, that the child enters into the marriage problem. And you must leave the child in peace.

HIALMAR: Oh—Hedvig! My poor Hedvig!

RELLING: Yes, you must be good enough to keep Hedvig outside of all this. You two are grown-up people; you are free, in God's name, to make what mess you please of your life. But you must deal cautiously with Hedvig, I tell you; otherwise you may do her a great injury.

HIALMAR: An injury!

RELLING: Yes, or she may do herself an injury—and perhaps others too.

GINA: How can you know that, Relling?

HIALMAR: Her sight is in no immediate danger, is it?

RELLING: I am not talking about her sight. Hedvig is at a critical age. She may be getting all sorts of mischief into her head.

GINA: That's true—I've noticed it already! She's taken to carrying on with the fire out in the kitchen. She calls it playing at house on fire. I'm often scared for fear she really sets fire to the house.

RELLING: You see, I thought as much.

GREGERS: [*to* RELLING] But how do you account for that?

RELLING: [*sullenly*] Her constitution's changing, sir.

HIALMAR: So long as the child has me—so long as *I* am above ground—
    [*A knock at the door.*]

GINA: Hush, Ekdal, there's someone in the passage. [*calls out*] Come in!
    [MRS SORBY, *in walking dress, comes in.*]

MRS SORBY: Good evening.

GINA: [*going toward her*] Is it really you, Bertha?

MRS SORBY: Yes, of course it is. But I'm disturbing you, I'm afraid.

HIALMAR: No, not at all; an emissary from that house—

MRS SORBY: [*to* GINA] To tell the truth, I hoped your menfolk would be out at this time. I just ran up to have a little chat with you and to say good-by.

GINA: Good-by? Are you going away then?

MRS SORBY: Yes, tomorrow morning—up to Höidal. Mr Werle started this afternoon. [*lightly to* GREGERS] He asked me to say good-by for him.

GINA: Only fancy!

HIALMAR: I say: beware!

GREGERS: I must explain the situation. My father and Mrs Sorby are going to be married.

HIALMAR: Going to be married!

GINA: Oh, Bertha! So it's come to that at last!

RELLING: [*his voice quivering a little*] This is surely not true?

MRS SORBY: Yes, my dear Relling, it's true enough.

RELLING: You are going to marry again?

MRS SORBY: Yes, it looks like it. Werle has got a special license, and we are going to be married quietly up at the works.

GREGERS: Then I must wish you all happiness, like a dutiful stepson.

MRS SORBY: Thank you very much—if you mean what you say. I certainly hope it will lead to happiness, both for Werle and for me.

RELLING: You have every reason to hope that. Mr Werle never gets drunk—so far as I know; and I don't suppose he's in the habit of thrashing his wives, like the late lamented horse doctor.

MRS SORBY: Come now, let Sorby rest in peace. He had his good points too.

RELLING: Mr Werle has better ones, I have no doubt.

MRS SORBY: He hasn't frittered away all that was good in him, at any rate. The man who does that must take the consequences.

RELLING: I shall go out with Molvik this evening.

MRS SORBY: You mustn't do that, Relling. Don't do it—for my sake.

RELLING: There's nothing else for it. [*to* HIALMAR] If you're going with us, come along.

GINA: No, thank you. Ekdal doesn't go in for that sort of dissertation.

HIALMAR: [*half aloud. in vexation*] Oh, do hold your tongue!

RELLING: Good-by, Mrs—Werle. [*Goes out through the passage door.*]

GREGERS: [*to* MRS SORBY] You seem to know Doctor Relling pretty intimately.

MRS SORBY: Yes, we have known each other for many years. At one time it seemed as if things might have gone further between us.

GREGERS: It was surely lucky for you that they did not.

MRS SORBY: You may well say that. But I have always been wary of acting on impulse. A woman can't afford absolutely to throw herself away.

GREGERS: Are you not in the least afraid that I may let my father know about this old friendship?

MRS SORBY: Why. of course I have told him all about it myself.

GREGERS: Indeed?

MRS SORBY: Your father knows every single thing that can, with any truth, be said about me. I have told him all; it was the first thing I did when I saw what was in his mind.

GREGERS: Then you have been franker than most people, I think.

MRS SORBY: I have always been frank. We women find that the best policy.

HIALMAR: What do you say to that, Gina?

GINA: Oh, we're not all alike, us women aren't. Some are made one way, some another.

MRS SORBY: Well, for my part, Gina, I believe it's wisest to do as I've done. And Werle has no secrets either, on his side. That's really the great bond between us, you see. Now he can talk to me as openly as a child. He has never had the chance to do that before. Fancy a man like him, full of health and vigor, passing his whole youth and the best years of his life in listening to nothing but penitential sermons! And very often the sermons had for their text the most imaginary offenses—at least so I understand.

GINA: That's true enough.

GREGERS: If you ladies are going to follow up this topic, I had better withdraw.

MRS SORBY: You can stay as far as that's concerned. I shan't say a word more. But I wanted you to know that I had done nothing secretly or in an underhand way. I may seem to have come in for a great piece of luck, and so I have, in a sense. But after all, I don't think I am getting any more than I am giving. I shall stand by him always, and I can tend and care for him as no one else can, now that he is getting helpless.

HIALMAR: Getting helpless?

GREGERS: [*to* MRS SORBY] Hush, don't speak of that here.

MRS SORBY: There is no disguising it any longer, however much he would like to. He is going blind.

HIALMAR: [*starts*] Going blind? That's strange. He, too, going blind!

GINA: Lots of people do.

MRS SORBY: And you can imagine what that means to a businessman. Well, I shall try as well as I can to make my eyes take the place of his. But I mustn't stay any longer; I have heaps of things to do. Oh, by the bye, Ekdal, I was to tell you that if there is anything Werle can do for you, you must just apply to Graberg.

GREGERS: That offer I am sure Hialmar Ekdal will decline with thanks.

MRS SORBY: Indeed? I don't think he used to be so—

GINA: No, Bertha, Ekdal doesn't need anything from Mr Werle now.

HIALMAR: [*slowly and with emphasis*] Will you present my compliments to your future husband and say that I intend very shortly to call upon Mr Graberg—

GREGERS: What! You don't really mean that?

HIALMAR: To call upon Mr Graberg, I say, and obtain an account of the sum I owe his principal. I will pay that debt of honor—ha, ha, ha! a debt of honor, let us call it! In any case I will pay the whole with five per cent interest.

GINA: But, my dear Ekdal, God knows we haven't got the money to do it.

HIALMAR: Be good enough to tell your future husband that I am working assiduously at my invention. Please tell him that what sustains me in this laborious task is the wish to free myself from a torturing burden of debt. That is my reason for proceeding with the invention. The entire profits shall be devoted to releasing me from my pecuniary obligations to your future husband.

MRS SORBY: Something has happened here.

HIALMAR: Yes, you are right.

MRS SORBY: Well, good-by. I had something else to speak to you about, Gina, but it must keep till another time. Good-by.

> [HIALMAR *and* GREGERS *bow silently.* GINA *follows* MRS SORBY *to the door.*]

HIALMAR: Not beyond the threshold, Gina!

> [MRS SORBY *goes;* GINA *shuts the door after her.*]

HIALMAR: There now, Gregers, I have got that burden of debt off my mind.

GREGERS: You soon will, at all events.

HIALMAR: I think my attitude may be called correct.

GREGERS: You are the man I have always taken you for.

HIALMAR: In certain cases it is impossible to disregard the claim of the ideal. Yet, as the breadwinner of a family, I cannot but writhe and groan under it. I can tell you it is no joke for a man without capital to attempt the repayment of a long-standing obligation over which, so to speak, the dust of oblivion has gathered. But it cannot be helped; the man in me demands his rights.

GREGERS: [*laying his hand on* HIALMAR'S *shoulder*] My dear Hialmar—was it not a good thing I came?

HIALMAR: Yes.

GREGERS: Are you not glad to have had your true position made clear to you?

HIALMAR: [*somewhat impatiently*] Yes, of course I am. But there is one thing that is revolting to my sense of justice.

GREGERS: And what is that?

HIALMAR: It is that— But I don't know whether I ought to express myself so unreservedly about your father.

GREGERS: Say what you please so far as I am concerned.

HIALMAR: Well, then, is it not exasperating to think that it is not I, but he, who will realize the true marriage?

GREGERS: How can you say such a thing?

HIALMAR: Because it is clearly the case. Isn't the marriage between your father and Mrs Sorby founded upon complete confidence, upon entire and unreserved candor on both sides? They hide nothing from each other, they keep no secrets in the background; their relation is based, if I may put it so, on mutual confession and absolution.

GREGERS: Well, what then?

HIALMAR: Well, is not that the whole thing? Did you not yourself say that this was precisely the difficulty that had to be overcome in order to found a true marriage?

GREGERS: But this is a totally different matter, Hialmar. You surely don't compare either yourself or your wife with those two— Oh, you understood me well enough.

HIALMAR: Say what you like, there is something in all this that hurts and offends my sense of justice. It really looks as if there were no just Providence to rule the world.

GINA: Oh no, Ekdal; for God's sake don't say such things.

GREGERS: H'm; don't let us get upon those questions.

HIALMAR: And yet, after all, I cannot but recognize the guiding finger of Fate. He is going blind.

GINA: Oh, you can't be sure of that.

HIALMAR: There is no doubt about it. At all events there ought not to be, for in that very fact lies the righteous retribution. He has hoodwinked a confiding fellow creature in days gone by—

GREGERS: I fear he has hoodwinked many.

HIALMAR: And now comes inexorable, mysterious Fate and demands Werle's own eyes.

GINA: Oh, how dare you say such dreadful things! You make me quite scared.

HIALMAR: It is profitable, now and then, to plunge deep into the night side of existence.

[HEDVIG, *in her hat and cloak, comes in by the passage door. She is pleasurably excited and out of breath.*]

GINA: Are you back already?

HEDVIG: Yes, I didn't care to go any farther. It was a good thing, too, for I've just met someone at the door.

HIALMAR: It must have been that Mrs Sorby.

HEDVIG: Yes.

HIALMAR: [*walks up and down*] I hope you have seen her for the last time.

[*Silence.* HEDVIG, *discouraged, looks first at one and then at the other, trying to divine their frame of mind.*]

HEDVIG: [*approaching, coaxingly*] Father.

HIALMAR: Well—what is it, Hedvig?

HEDVIG: Mrs Sorby had something with her for me.

HIALMAR: [*stops*] For you?

HEDVIG: Yes. Something for tomorrow.

GINA: Bertha has always given you some little thing on your birthday.

HIALMAR: What is it?

HEDVIG: Oh, you mustn't see it now. Mother is to give it to me tomorrow morning before I'm up.

HIALMAR: What is all this hocus-pocus that I am to be in the dark about?

HEDVIG: [*quickly*] Oh no, you may see it if you like. It's a big letter. [*takes the letter out of her cloak pocket*]

HIALMAR: A letter too?

HEDVIG: Yes, it is only a letter. The rest will come afterward, I suppose. But fancy—a letter! I've never had a letter before. And there's "Miss" written upon it. [*reads*] "Miss Hedvig Ekdal." Only think—that's me!

HIALMAR: Let me see that letter.

HEDVIG: [*hands it to him*] There it is.

HIALMAR: That is Mr Werle's hand.

GINA: Are you sure of that, Ekdal?

HIALMAR: Look for yourself.

GINA: Oh, what do I know about suchlike things?

HIALMAR: Hedvig, may I open the letter—and read it?

HEDVIG: Yes, of course you may, if you want to.

GINA: No, not tonight, Ekdal; it's to be kept till tomorrow.

HEDVIG: [*softly*] Oh, can't you let him read it! It's sure to be something good, and then Father will be glad and everything will be nice again.

HIALMAR: I may open it then?

HEDVIG: Yes, do, Father. I'm so anxious to know what it is.

HIALMAR: Well and good. [*opens the letter, takes out a paper, reads it through and appears bewildered.*] What is this?

GINA: What does it say?

HEDVIG: Oh yes, Father—tell us!

HIALMAR: Be quiet. [*Reads it through again; he has turned pale but says with self-control.*] It is a deed of gift, Hedvig.

HEDVIG: Is it? What sort of gift am I to have?

HIALMAR: Read for yourself.

[HEDVIG *goes over and reads for a time by the lamp.*]

HIALMAR: [*half aloud, clenching his hands*] The eyes! The eyes—and then that letter!

HEDVIG: [*leaves off reading*] Yes, but it seems to me that it's Grandfather that's to have it.

HIALMAR: [*takes letter from her*] Gina—can you understand this?

GINA: I know nothing whatever about it; tell me what's the matter.

HIALMAR: Mr Werle writes to Hedvig that her old grandfather need not trouble himself any longer with the copying but that he can henceforth draw on the office for a hundred crowns a month—

GREGERS: Aha!

HEDVIG: A hundred crowns, Mother! I read that.

GINA: What a good thing for Grandfather!

HIALMAR: —a hundred crowns a month so long as he needs it—that means, of course, so long as he lives.

GINA: Well, so he's provided for, poor dear.

HIALMAR: But there is more to come. You didn't read that, Hedvig. Afterward this gift is to pass on to you.

HEDVIG: To me! The whole of it?

HIALMAR: He says that the same amount is assured to you for the whole of your life. Do you hear that, Gina?

GINA: Yes, I hear.

HEDVIG: Fancy—all that money for me! [*shakes him*] Father, Father, aren't you glad?

HIALMAR: [*eluding her*] Glad! [*walks about*] Oh, what vistas—what perspectives open up before me! It is Hedvig, Hedvig that he showers these benefactions upon!

GINA: Yes, because it's Hedvig's birthday.

HEDVIG: And you'll get it all the same, Father! You know quite well I shall give all the money to you and Mother.

HIALMAR: To Mother, yes! There we have it.

GREGERS: Hialmar, this is a trap he is setting for you.

HIALMAR: Do you think it's another trap?

GREGERS: When he was here this morning he said: Hialmar Ekdal is not the man you imagine him to be.

HIALMAR: Not the man—

GREGERS: That you shall see, he said.

HIALMAR: He meant you should see that I would let myself be bought off!

HEDVIG: Oh, Mother, what does all this mean?

GINA: Go and take off your things.

[HEDVIG *goes out by the kitchen door, half crying.*]

GREGERS: Yes, Hialmar—now is the time to show who was right, he or I.

HIALMAR: [*slowly tears the paper across, lays both pieces on the table and says*] Here is my answer.

GREGERS: Just what I expected.

HIALMAR: [*goes over to* GINA, *who stands by the stove and says in a low voice*] Now please make a clean breast of it. If the connection between you and him was quite over when you—came to care for me, as you call it—why did he place us in a position to marry?

GINA: I suppose he thought as he could come and go in our house.

HIALMAR: Only that? Was he not afraid of a possible contingency?

GINA: I don't know what you mean.

HIALMAR: I want to know whether—your child has the right to live under my roof.

GINA: [*draws herself up; her eyes flash*] You ask that!

HIALMAR: You shall answer me this one question: Does Hedvig belong to me—or—? Well?

GINA: [*looking at him with cold defiance*] I don't know.

HIALMAR: [*quivering a little*] You don't know!

GINA: How should *I* know. A creature like me—

HIALMAR: [*quietly turning away from her*] Then I have nothing more to do in this house.

GREGERS: Take care, Hialmar! Think what you are doing!

HIALMAR: [*puts on his overcoat*] In this case there is nothing for a man like me to think twice about.

GREGERS: Yes indeed, there are endless things to be considered. You three must be together if you are to attain the true frame of mind for self-sacrifice and forgiveness.

HIALMAR: I don't want to attain it. Never, never! My hat! [*takes his hat*] My home has fallen into ruins about me. [*bursts into tears*] Gregers, I have no child!

HEDVIG: [*who has opened the kitchen door*] What is that you're saying? [*coming to him*] Father, Father!

GINA: There, you see!

HIALMAR: Don't come near me, Hedvig! Keep far away. I cannot bear to see you. Oh! those eyes! Good-by.

            [*Makes for the door.*]

HEDVIG: [*clinging close to him and screaming loudly*] No! No! Don't leave me!

GINA: [*cries out*] Look at the child, Ekdal! Look at the child!

HIALMAR: I will not! I cannot! I must get out—away from all this! [*He tears himself away from* HEDVIG *and goes out by the passage door.*]

HEDVIG: [*with despairing eyes*] He is going away from us, Mother! He is going away from us! He will never come back again!

GINA: Don't cry, Hedvig. Father's sure to come back again.

HEDVIG: [*throws herself sobbing on the sofa*] No, no, he'll never come home to us any more.

GREGERS: Do you believe I meant all for the best, Mrs Ekdal?

GINA: Yes, I daresay you did, but God forgive you all the same.

HEDVIG: [*lying on the sofa*] Oh, this will kill me! What have I done to him? Mother, you must fetch him home again!

GINA: Yes, yes, yes; only be quiet, and I'll go out and look for him. [*puts on her outdoor things*] Perhaps he's gone into Relling's. But you mustn't lie there and cry. Promise me!

HEDVIG: [*weeping convulsively*] Yes, I'll stop, I'll stop; if only Father comes back!

GREGERS: [*to* GINA, *who is going*] After all, had you not better leave him to fight out his bitter fight to the end?

GINA: Oh, he can do that afterward. First of all we must get the child quieted. [*Goes out by the passage door.*]

HEDVIG: [*sits up and dries her tears*] Now you must tell me what all this means. Why doesn't Father want me any more?

GREGERS: You mustn't ask that till you are a big girl—quite grown up.

HEDVIG: [*sobs*] But I can't go on being as miserable as this till I'm grown up. I think I know what it is. Perhaps I'm not really Father's child.

GREGERS: [*uneasily*] How could that be?

HEDVIG: Mother might have found me. And perhaps Father has just found out; I've read of such things.

GREGERS: Well, but if it were so—

HEDVIG: I think he might be just as fond of me for all that. Yes, fonder almost. We got the wild duck as a present, you know, and I love it so dearly all the same.

GREGERS: [*turning the conversation*] Ah, the wild duck, by the bye! Let us talk about the wild duck a little, Hedvig.

HEDVIG: The poor wild duck! He doesn't want to see it any more either. Only think, he wanted to wring its neck!

GREGERS: Oh, he won't do that.

HEDVIG: No, but he said he would like to. And I think it was horrid of Father to say it, for I pray for the wild duck every night and ask that it may be preserved from death and all that is evil.

GREGERS: [*looking at her*] Do you say your prayers every night?

HEDVIG: Yes.

GREGERS: Who taught you to do that?

HEDVIG: I myself—one time when Father was very ill and said that death was staring him in the face.

GREGERS: Well?

HEDVIG: Then I prayed for him as I lay in bed, and since then I have always kept it up.

GREGERS: And now you pray for the wild duck too?

HEDVIG: I thought it best to bring in the wild duck, for she was so weak at first.

GREGERS: Do you pray in the morning too?

HEDVIG: No, of course not.

GREGERS: Why not in the morning as well?

HEDVIG: In the morning it's light, you know, and there's nothing in particular to be afraid of.

GREGERS: And your father was going to wring the neck of the wild duck that you love so dearly?

HEDVIG: No; he said he ought to wring its neck but he would spare it for my sake, and that was kind of Father.

GREGERS: [*coming a little nearer*] But suppose you were to sacrifice the wild
duck of your own free will for his sake?

HEDVIG: [*rising*] The wild duck!

GREGERS: Suppose you were to make a free-will offering, for his sake, of the
dearest treasure you have in the world?

HEDVIG: Do you think that would do any good?

GREGERS: Try it, Hedvig.

HEDVIG: [*softly, with flashing eyes*] Yes, I will try it.

GREGERS: Have you really the courage for it, do you think?

HEDVIG: I'll ask Grandfather to shoot the wild duck for me.

GREGERS: Yes, do. But not a word to your mother about it.

HEDVIG: Why not?

GREGERS: She doesn't understand us.

HEDVIG: The wild duck! I'll try it tomorrow morning.

> [GINA *comes in by the passage door.*]

HEDVIG: [*going toward her*] Did you find him, Mother?

GINA: No, but I heard as he had called and taken Relling with him.

GREGERS: Are you sure of that?

GINA: Yes, the porter's wife said so. Molvik went with them too, she said.

GREGERS: This evening, when his mind so sorely needs to wrestle in solitude!

GINA: [*takes off her things*] Yes, men are strange creatures, so they are. The
Lord only knows where Relling has dragged him to! I ran over to Madam
Eriksen's, but they weren't there.

HEDVIG: [*struggling to keep back her tears*] Oh, if he should never come home
any more!

GREGERS: He will come home again. I shall have news to give him tomorrow,
and then you shall see how he comes home. You may rely upon that,
Hedvig, and sleep in peace. Good night. [*He goes out by the passage door.*]

HEDVIG: [*throws herself sobbing on* GINA's *neck*] Mother, Mother!

GINA: [*pats her shoulder and sighs*] Ah yes, Relling was right, he was. That's
what comes of it when crazy creatures go about presenting the claim of
the—what-you-may-call-it.

ACT V

SCENE——HIALMAR EKDAL'S *studio. Cold gray morning light. Wet snow lies
upon the large panes of the sloping roof window.*

> [GINA *comes from the kitchen with an apron and bib on and carrying
> a dusting brush and a duster; she goes toward the sitting-room door.
> At the same moment* HEDVIG *comes hurriedly in from the passage.*]

GINA: [*stops*] Well?

HEDVIG: Oh, Mother, I almost think he's down at Relling's—

GINA: There, you see!

HEDVIG: —because the porter's wife says she could hear that Relling had two
people with him when he came home last night.

GINA: That's just what I thought.

HEDVIG: But it's no use his being there if he won't come up to us.

GINA: I'll go down and speak to him at all events.

[OLD EKDAL, *in dressing gown and slippers and with a lighted pipe, appears at the door of his room.*]

EKDAL: Hialmar—isn't Hialmar at home?

GINA: No, he's gone out.

EKDAL: So early? And in such a tearing snowstorm? Well, well, just as he pleases; I can take my morning walk alone.

[*He slides the garret door aside;* HEDVIG *helps him; he goes in; she closes it after him.*]

HEDVIG: [*in an undertone*] Only think, Mother, when poor Grandfather hears that Father is going to leave us.

GINA: Oh, nonsense; Grandfather mustn't hear anything about it. It was a heaven's mercy he wasn't at home yesterday in all that hurly-burly.

HEDVIG: Yes, but—

[GREGERS *comes in by the passage door.*]

GREGERS: Well, have you any news of him?

GINA: They say he's down at Relling's.

GREGERS: At Relling's! Has he really been out with those creatures?

GINA: Yes, like enough.

GREGERS: When he ought to have been yearning for solitude, to collect and clear his thoughts—

GINA: Yes you may well say so.

[RELLING *enters from the passage.*]

HEDVIG: [*going to him*] Is Father in your room?

GINA: [*at the same time*] Is he there?

RELLING: Yes, to be sure he is.

HEDVIG: And you never let us know!

RELLING: Yes, I'm a brute. But in the first place I had to look after the other brute; I mean our demonic friend, of course; and then I fell so dead asleep that—

GINA: What does Ekdal say today?

RELLING: He says nothing whatever.

HEDVIG: Doesn't he speak?

RELLING: Not a blessed word.

GREGERS: No, no; I can understand that very well.

GINA: But what's he doing then?

RELLING: He's lying on the sofa, snoring.

GINA: Oh, is he? Yes, Ekdal's a rare one to snore.

HEDVIG: Asleep? Can he sleep?

RELLING: Well, it certainly looks like it.

GREGERS: No wonder, after the spiritual conflict that has torn him—

GINA: And then he's never been used to gadding about out of doors at night.

HEDVIG: Perhaps it's a good thing that he's getting sleep, Mother.

GINA: Of course it is, and we must take care we don't wake him up too early. Thank you, Relling. I must get the house cleaned up a bit now, and then— Come and help me, Hedvig.

[GINA *and* HEDVIG *go into the sitting room.*]

GREGERS: [*turning to* RELLING] What is your explanation of the spiritual tumult that is now going on in Hialmar Ekdal?

RELLING: A lot of spiritual tumult I've noticed in him.

GREGERS: What! Not at such a crisis, when his whole life has been placed on a new foundation? How can you think that such an individuality as Hialmar's—

RELLING: Oh, individuality—he! If he ever had any tendency to the abnormal developments you call individuality, I can assure you it was rooted out of him while he was still in his teens.

GREGERS: That would be strange indeed—considering the loving care with which he was brought up.

RELLING: By those two high-flown, hysterical maiden aunts, you mean?

GREGERS: Let me tell you that they were women who never forgot the claim of the ideal—but of course you will only jeer at me again.

RELLING: No, I'm in no humor for that. I know all about those ladies, for he has ladled out no end of rhetoric on the subject of his "two soul mothers." But I don't think he has much to thank them for. Ekdal's misfortune is that in his own circle he has always been looked upon as a shining light.

GREGERS: Not without reason, surely. Look at the depth of his mind!

RELLING: I have never discovered it. That his father believed in it I don't so much wonder; the old lieutenant has been an ass all his days.

GREGERS: He has had a childlike mind all his days; that is what you cannot understand.

RELLING: Well, so be it. But then when our dear sweet Hialmar went to college he at once passed for the great light of the future amongst his comrades too! He was handsome, the rascal—red and white—a shopgirl's dream of manly beauty; and with his superficially emotional temperament and his sympathetic voice and his talent for declaiming other people's verses and other people's thoughts—

GREGERS: [*indignantly*] Is it Hialmar Ekdal you are talking about in this strain?

RELLING: Yes, with your permission; I am simply giving you an inside view of the idol you are groveling before.

GREGERS: I should hardly have thought I was quite stone-blind.

RELLING: Yes, you are—or not far from it. You are a sick man too, you see.

GREGERS: You are right there.

RELLING: Yes. Yours is a complicated case. First of all there is that plaguy integrity fever, and then—what's worse—you are always in a delirium of hero worship; you must always have something to adore, outside yourself.

GREGERS: Yes, I must certainly seek it outside myself.

RELLING: But you make such shocking mistakes about every new phoenix you think you have discovered. Here again you have come to a cotter's cabin with your claim of the ideal, and the people of the house are insolvent.

GREGERS: If you don't think better than that of Hialmar Ekdal, what pleasure can you find in being everlastingly with him?

RELLING: Well, you see, I'm supposed to be a sort of a doctor—God help me! I have to give a hand to the poor sick folk who live under the same roof with me.

GREGERS: Oh, indeed! Hialmar Ekdal is sick too, is he?

RELLING: Most people are, worse luck.

GREGERS: And what remedy are you applying in Hialmar's case?

RELLING: My usual one. I am cultivating the life illusion in him.

GREGERS: Life—illusion? I didn't catch what you said.

RELLING: Yes, I said illusion. For illusion, you know, is the stimulating principle.

GREGERS: May I ask with what illusion Hialmar is inoculated?

RELLING: No, thank you; I don't betray professional secrets to quacks. You would probably go and muddle his case still more than you have already. But my method is infallible. I have applied it to Molvik as well. I have made him "demonic." That's the treatment for him.

GREGERS: Is he not really demonic then?

RELLING: What the devil do you mean by demonic? It's only a piece of gibberish I've invented to keep up a spark of life in him. But for that, the poor harmless creature would have succumbed to self-contempt and despair many a long year ago. And then the old lieutenant! But he has hit upon his own cure, you see.

GREGERS: Lieutenant Ekdal? What of him?

RELLING: Just think of the old bear hunter shutting himself up in that dark garret to shoot rabbits! I tell you there is not a happier sportsman in the world than that old man pottering about in there among all that rubbish. The four or five withered Christmas trees he has saved up are the same to him as the whole great fresh Höidal forest; the cock and the hens are big game birds in the fir tops, and the rabbits that flop about the garret floor are the bears he has to battle with—the mighty hunter of the mountains!

GREGERS: Poor unfortunate old man! Yes, he has indeed had to narrow the ideals of his youth.

RELLING: While I think of it, Mr. Werle junior—don't use that foreign word: ideals. We have the excellent native word: lies.

GREGERS: Do you think the two things are related?

RELLING: Yes, just about as closely as typhus and putrid fever.

GREGERS: Doctor Relling, I shall not give up the struggle until I have rescued Hialmar from your clutches!

RELLING: So much the worse for him. Rob the average man of his life illusion and you rob him of his happiness at the same stroke. [*to* HEDVIG, *who comes in from the sitting room*] Well, little wild-duck mother. I'm just going down to see whether Papa is still lying meditating upon that wonderful invention of his.

[*Goes out by passage door.*]

GREGERS: [*approaches* HEDVIG] I can see by your face that you have not yet done it.

HEDVIG: What? Oh, that about the wild duck! No.

GREGERS: I suppose your courage failed when the time came?

HEDVIG: No, that wasn't it. But when I awoke this morning and remembered what we had been talking about it seemed so strange.

GREGERS: Strange?

HEDVIG: Yes, I don't know— Yesterday evening, at the moment, I thought there was something so delightful about it; but since I have slept and thought of it again, it somehow doesn't seem worth while.

GREGERS: Ah, I thought you could not have grown up quite unharmed in this house.

HEDVIG: I don't care about that, if only Father would come up—

GREGERS: Oh, if only your eyes had been opened to that which gives life its value—if you possessed the true, joyous, fearless spirit of sacrifice you would soon see how he would come up to you. But I believe in you still, Hedvig.

[*He goes out by the passage door.* HEDVIG *wanders about the room for a time; she is on the point of going into the kitchen when a knock is heard at the garret door.* HEDVIG *goes over and opens it a little;* OLD EKDAL *comes out; she pushes the door to again.*]

EKDAL: H'm, it's not much fun to take a morning walk alone.

HEDVIG: Wouldn't you like to go shooting, Grandfather?

EKDAL: It's not the weather for it today. It's so dark there you can scarcely see where you're going.

HEDVIG: Do you never want to shoot anything besides the rabbits?

EKDAL: Do you think the rabbits aren't good enough?

HEDVIG: Yes, but what about the wild duck?

EKDAL: Ho-ho! Are you afraid I shall shoot your wild duck? Never in the world. Never!

HEDVIG: No, I suppose you couldn't; they say it's very difficult to shoot wild ducks.

EKDAL: Couldn't! Should rather think I could.

HEDVIG: How would you set about it, Grandfather? I don't mean with my wild duck, but with others.

EKDAL: I should take care to shoot them in the breast, you know; that's the surest place. And then you must shoot against the feathers, you see— not the way of the feathers.

HEDVIG: Do they die then, Grandfather?

EKDAL: Yes they die right enough—when you shoot properly. Well, I must go and brush up a bit. H'm—understand—h'm. [*Goes into his room.*]

[HEDVIG *waits a little, glances toward the sitting-room door, goes over to the bookcase, stands on tiptoe, takes the double-barreled pistol down from the shelf and looks at it.* GINA, *with brush and duster, comes from the sitting room.* HEDVIG *hastily lays down the pistol unobserved.*]

GINA: Don't stand raking amongst Father's things, Hedvig.

HEDVIG: [*goes away from the bookcase*] I was only going to tidy up a little.

GINA: You'd better go into the kitchen and see if the coffee's still hot; I'll take his breakfast on a tray when I go down to him.

[HEDVIG *goes out.* GINA *begins to sweep and clean up the studio. Presently the passage door is opened with hesitation and* HIALMAR EKDAL *looks in. He has on his overcoat but not his hat; he is unwashed, and his hair is disheveled and unkempt. His eyes are dull and heavy.*]

GINA: [*standing with the brush in her hand and looking at him*] Oh, there now, Ekdal—so you've come after all?

HIALMAR: [*comes in and answers in a toneless voice*] I come—only to depart immediately.

GINA: Yes, yes, I suppose so. But Lord help us! what a sight you are!

HIALMAR: A sight?

GINA: And your nice winter coat too! Well, that's done for.

HEDVIG: [*at the kitchen door*] Mother, hadn't I better—

[*Sees* HIALMAR, *gives a loud scream of joy and runs to him*] Oh, Father, Father!

HIALMAR: [*turns away and makes a gesture of repulsion*] Away, away, away! [*to* GINA] Keep her away from me, I say!

GINA: [*in a low tone*] Go into the sitting room, Hedvig.

[HEDVIG *does so without a word.*]

HIALMAR: [*fussily pulls out the table drawer*] I must have my books with me. Where are my books?

GINA: Which books?

HIALMAR: My scientific books, of course; the technical magazines I require for my invention.

GINA: [*searches in the bookcase*] Is it these here papercovered ones?

HIALMAR: Yes, of course.

GINA: [*lays a heap of magazines on the table*] Shan't I get Hedvig to cut them for you?

HIALMAR: I don't require to have them cut for me.

[*Short silence.*]

GINA: Then you're still set on leaving us, Ekdal?

HIALMAR: [*rummaging amongst the books*] Yes, that is a matter of course, I should think.

GINA: Well, well.

HIALMAR: [*vehemently*] How can I live here, to be stabbed to the heart every hour of the day?

GINA: God forgive you for thinking such vile things of me.

HIALMAR: Prove—

GINA: I think it's you as has got to prove.

HIALMAR: After a past like yours? There are certain claims—I may almost call them claims of the ideal—

GINA: But what about Grandfather? What's to become of him, poor dear?

HIALMAR: I know my duty; my helpless father will come with me. I am going out into the town to make arrangements—H'm [*hesitatingly*]—has anyone found my hat on the stairs?

GINA: No. Have you lost your hat?

HIALMAR: Of course I had it on when I came in last night—there's no doubt about that—but I couldn't find it this morning.

GINA: Lord help us! Where have you been to with those two ne'er-do-wells?

HIALMAR: Oh, don't bother me about trifles. Do you suppose I am in the mood to remember details?

GINA: If only you haven't caught cold, Ekdal— [*Goes out into the kitchen.*]

HIALMAR: [*talks to himself in a low tone of irritation while he empties the table drawer*] You're a scoundrel, Relling! You're a low fellow! Ah, you shameless tempter! I wish I could get someone to stick a knife into you! [*He lays some old letters on one side, finds the torn document of yesterday, takes it up and looks at the pieces, puts it down hurriedly as* GINA *enters.*]

GINA: [*sets a tray with coffee, etc., on the table*] Here's a drop of something hot, if you'd fancy it. And there's some bread and butter and a snack of meat.

HIALMAR: [*glancing at the tray*] Meat? Never under this roof! It's true I have not had a mouthful of solid food for nearly twenty-four hours, but no matter. My memoranda! The commencement of my autobiography! What has become of my diary and all my important papers? [*opens the sitting-room door but draws back*] She is there too!

GINA: Good lord! the child must be somewhere!

HIALMAR: Come out.

[*He makes room;* HEDVIG *comes, scared, into the studio.*]

HIALMAR: [*with his hand on the door handle, says to* GINA] In these, the last moments I spend in my former home, I wish to be spared from interlopers. [*Goes into the room.*]

HEDVIG: [*with a bound toward her mother, asks softly, trembling*] Does that mean me?

GINA: Stay out in the kitchen, Hedvig; or, no—you'd best go into your own room. [*speaks to* HIALMAR *as she goes in to him*] Wait a bit, Ekdal; don't rummage so in the drawers. I know where everything is.

HEDVIG: [*stands a moment immovable, in terror and perplexity, biting her lips to keep the tears; then she clenches her hands convulsively and says softly*] The wild duck! [*She steals over and takes the pistol from the shelf, opens the garret door a little way, creeps in and draws the door to after her.* HIALMAR *and* GINA *can be heard disputing in the sitting room.*]

HIALMAR: [*comes in with some manuscript books and old loose papers which he lays upon the table*] That portmanteau is of no use! There are a thousand and one things I must drag with me.

GINA: [*following with the portmanteau*] Why not leave all the rest for the present and only take a shirt and a pair of woolen drawers with you?

HIALMAR: Whew! All these exhausting preparations! [*Pulls off his overcoat and throws it upon the sofa.*]

GINA: And there's the coffee getting cold.

HIALMAR: H'm. [*Drinks a mouthful without thinking of it and then another.*]

GINA: [*dusting the backs of the chairs*] A nice job you'll have to find such another big garret for the rabbits.

HIALMAR: What! Am I to drag all those rabbits with me too?

GINA: You don't suppose Grandfather can get on without his rabbits.

HIALMAR: He must just get used to doing without them. Have not I to sacrifice very much greater things than rabbits!

GINA: [*dusting the bookcase*] Shall I put the flute in the portmanteau for you?

HIALMAR: No. No flute for me. But give me the pistol!

GINA: Do you want to take the pistol with you?

HIALMAR: Yes. My loaded pistol.

GINA: [*searching for it*] It's gone. He must have taken it in with him.

HIALMAR: Is he in the garret?

GINA: Yes, of course he's in the garret.

HIALMAR: H'm—poor lonely old man. [*He takes a piece of bread and butter, eats it and finishes his cup of coffee.*]

GINA: And if we hadn't have let that room, you could have moved in there.

HIALMAR: And continued to live under the same roof with— Never—never!

GINA: But couldn't you put up with the sitting room for a day or two? You could have it all to yourself.

HIALMAR: Never within these walls!

GINA: Well, then, down with Relling and Molvik.

HIALMAR: Don't mention those wretches' names to me! The very thought of them almost takes away my appetite. Oh no, I must go out into the storm and the snowdrift—go from house to house and seek shelter for my father and myself.

GINA: But you've got no hat, Ekdal! You've gone and lost your hat, you know.

HIALMAR: Oh, those two brutes, those slaves of all the vices! A hat must be found. [*takes another piece of bread and butter*] Some arrangements must be made. For I have no mind to throw away my life either. [*looks for something on the tray*]

GINA: What are you looking for?

HIALMAR: Butter.

GINA: I'll get some at once. [*Goes out into the kitchen.*]

HIALMAR: [*calls after her*] Oh, it doesn't matter; dry bread is good enough for me.

GINA: [*brings a dish of butter*] Look here; this is fresh churned.
  [*She pours out another cup of coffee for him; he seats himself on the sofa, spreads more butter on the already buttered bread and eats and drinks a while in silence.*]

HIALMAR: Could I, without being subject to intrusion—intrusion of any sort— could I live in the sitting room there for a day or two?

GINA: Yes, to be sure you could, if you only would.

HIALMAR: For I see no possibility of getting all Father's things out in such a hurry.

GINA: And, besides, you've surely got to tell him first as you don't mean to live with us others no more.

HIALMAR: [*pushes away his coffee cup*] Yes, there is that too; I shall have to lay bare the whole tangled story to him— I must turn matters over; I must have breathing time. I cannot take all these burdens on my shoulders in a single day.

GINA: No, especially in such horrible weather as it is outside.

HIALMAR: [*touching* WERLE's *letter*] I see that paper still lying about here.

GINA: Yes, I haven't touched it.

HIALMAR: So far as I am concerned it is mere wastepaper—

GINA: Well, *I* have certainly no notion of making any use of it.

HIALMAR: —but we had better not let it get lost all the same, in all the upset when I move it might easily—

GINA: I'll take good care of it, Ekdal.

HIALMAR: The donation is in the first instance made to Father, and it rests with him to accept or decline it.

GINA: [*sighs*] Yes, poor old Father—

HIALMAR: To make quite safe—Where shall I find some glue?

GINA: [*goes to the bookcase*] Here's the glue pot.

HIALMAR: And a brush?

GINA: The brush is here too. [*brings him the things*]

HIALMAR: [*takes a pair of scissors*] Just a strip of paper at the back— [*clips and glues*] Far be it from me to lay hands upon what is not my own—and least of all upon what belongs to a destitute old man—and to—the other as well. There now! Let it lie there for a time, and when it is dry take it away. I wish never to see that document again. Never!

[GREGERS WERLE *enters from the passage.*]

GREGERS: [*somewhat surprised*] What—are you sitting here, Hialmar?

HIALMAR: [*rises hurriedly*] I had sunk down from fatigue.

GREGERS: You have been having breakfast, I see.

HIALMAR: The body sometimes makes its claims felt too.

GREGERS: What have you decided to do?

HIALMAR: For a man like me there is only one course possible. I am just putting my most important things together. But it takes time, you know.

GINA: [*with a touch of impatience*] Am I to get the room ready for you or am I to pack your suitcase?

HIALMAR: [*after a glance of annoyance at* GREGERS] Pack—and get the room ready!

GINA: [*takes the portmanteau*] Very well; then I'll put in the shirt and the other things. [*Goes into the sitting room and draws the door to after her.*]

GREGERS: [*after a short silence*] I never dreamed that this would be the end of it. Do you really feel it a necessity to leave house and home?

HIALMAR: [*wanders about restlessly*] What would you have me do? I am not fitted to bear unhappiness, Gregers. I must feel secure and at peace in my surroundings.

GREGERS: But can you not feel that here? Just try it. I should have thought you had firm ground to build upon now—if only you start afresh. And, remember, you have your invention to live for.

HIALMAR: Oh, don't talk about my invention. It's perhaps still in the dim distance.

GREGERS: Indeed!

HIALMAR: Why, great heavens, what would you have one invent? Other people have invented almost everything already. It becomes more and more difficult every day—

GREGERS: And you have devoted so much labor to it.

HIALMAR: It was that blackguard Relling that urged me to it.

GREGERS: Relling?

HIALMAR: Yes, it was he that first made me realize my aptitude for making some notable discovery in photography.

GREGERS: Aha—it was Relling!

HIALMAR: Oh, I have been so truly happy over it! Not so much for the sake of the invention itself as because Hedvig believed in it—believed in it with a child's whole eagerness of faith. At least I have been fool enough to imagine that she believed in it.

GREGERS: Can you really think Hedvig has been false toward you?

HIALMAR: I can think anything now. It is Hedvig that stands in my way. She will blot out the sunlight from my whole life.

GREGERS: Hedvig! Is it Hedvig you are talking of? How should she blot out your sunlight?

HIALMAR: [*without answering*] How unutterably I have loved that child! How unutterably happy I have felt every time I came home to my humble room and she flew to meet me with her sweet little blinking eyes. Oh, confiding fool that I have been! I loved her unutterably—and I yielded myself up to the dream, the delusion, that she loved me unutterably in return.

GREGER: Do you call that a delusion?

HIALMAR: How should I know? I can get nothing out of Gina; and besides, she is totally blind to the ideal side of these complications. But to you I feel impelled to open my mind, Gregers. I cannot shake off this frightful doubt—perhaps Hedvig has never really and honestly loved me.

GREGERS: What would you say if she were to give you a proof of her love? [*listens*] What's that? I thought I heard the wild duck—

HIALMAR: It's the wild duck quacking. Father's in the garret.

GREGERS: Is he? [*his face lights up with joy*] I say you may yet have proof that your poor misunderstood Hedvig loves you!

HIALMAR: Oh, what proof can she give me? I dare not believe in any assurance from that quarter.

GREGERS: Hedvig does not know what deceit means.

HIALMAR: Oh, Gregers, that is just what I cannot be sure of. Who knows what Gina and that Mrs Sorby may many a time have sat here whispering and tattling about? And Hedvig usually has her ears open, I can tell you. Perhaps the deed of gift was not such a surprise to her after all. In fact, I'm not sure but that I noticed something of the sort.

GREGERS: What spirit is this that has taken possession of you?

HIALMAR: I have had my eyes opened. Just you notice—you'll see, the deed of gift is only a beginning. Mrs Sorby has always been a good deal taken up with Hedvig, and now she has the power to do whatever she likes for the child. They can take her from me whenever they please.

GREGERS: Hedvig will never, never leave you.

HIALMAR: Don't be so sure of that. If only they beckon to her and throw out a golden bait— And oh! I have loved her so unspeakably! I would have counted it my highest happiness to take her tenderly by the hand and lead her, as one leads a timid child through a great dark empty room! I am cruelly certain now that the poor photographer in his humble attic has never really and truly been anything to her. She has only cunningly contrived to keep on a good footing with him until the time came.

GREGERS: You don't believe that yourself, Hialmar.

HIALMAR: That is just the terrible part of it— I don't know what to believe—

I never can know it. But can you really doubt that it must be as I say? Ho-ho, you have far too much faith in the claim of the ideal, my good Gregers! If those others came, with the glamour of wealth about them, and called to the child: "Leave him; come to us; here life awaits you—"

GREGERS: [*quickly*] Well, what then?

HIALMAR: If I then asked her: "Hedvig, are you willing to renounce that life for me?" [*laughs scornfully*] No, thank you! You would soon hear what answer I should get.

[*A pistol shot is heard from within the garret.*]

GREGERS: [*loudly and joyfully*] Hialmar!

HIALMAR: There now; he must needs go shooting too.

GINA: [*comes in*] Oh, Ekdal, I can hear Grandfather blazing away in the garret by himself.

HIALMAR: I'll look in—

GREGERS: [*eagerly, with emotion*] Wait a moment! Do you know what that was?

HIALMAR: Yes, of course I know.

GREGERS: No, you don't know. But *I* do. That was the proof!

HIALMAR: What proof?

GREGERS: It was a child's free-will offering. She has got your father to shoot the wild duck.

HIALMAR: To shoot the wild duck!

GINA: Oh, think of that!

HIALMAR: What was that for?

GREGERS: She wanted to sacrifice to you her most cherished possession, for then she thought you would surely come to love her again.

HIALMAR: [*tenderly, with emotion*] Oh, poor child!

GINA: What things she does think of!

GREGERS: She only wanted your love again, Hialmar. She could not live without it.

GINA: [*struggling with her tears*] There, you can see for yourself, Ekdal.

HIALMAR: Gina, where is she?

GINA: [*sniffs*] Poor dear, she's sitting out in the kitchen, I daresay.

HIALMAR: [*goes over, tears open the kitchen door and says*] Hedvig, come, come in to me! [*looks around*] No, she's not here.

GINA: Then she must be in her own little room.

HIALMAR: [*without*] No, she's not here either. [*comes in*] She must have gone out.

GINA: Yes, you wouldn't have her anywheres in the house.

HIALMAR: Oh, if she would only come home quickly, so that I can tell her— Everything will come right now, Gregers; now I believe we can begin life afresh.

GREGERS: [*quietly*] I knew it; I knew the child would make amends.

[OLD EKDAL *appears at the door of his room; he is in full uniform and is busy buckling on his sword.*]

HIALMAR: [*astonished*] Father! Are you there?

GINA: Have you been firing in your room?

EKDAL: [*resentfully, approaching*] So you go shooting alone, do you, Hialmar?

HIALMAR: [*excited and confused*] Then it wasn't you that fired that shot in the garret?

EKDAL: Me that fired? H'm.

GREGERS: [*calls out to* HIALMAR] She has shot the wild duck herself!

HIALMAR: What can it mean? [*hastens to the garret door, tears it aside, looks in and calls loudly*] Hedvig!

GINA: [*runs to the door*] Good God! what's that?

HIALMAR: [*goes in*] She's lying on the floor!

GREGERS: Hedvig! Lying on the floor! [*goes in to* HIALMAR]

GINA: [*at the same time*] Hedvig! [*inside the garret*] No, no, no!

EKDAL: Ho-ho! Does she go shooting too now?

[HIALMAR, GINA *and* GREGERS *carry* HEDVIG *into the studio; in her dangling right hand she holds the pistol clasped in her fingers.*]

HIALMAR: [*distracted*] The pistol has gone off. She has wounded herself. Call for help! Help!

GINA: [*runs into the passage and calls down*] Relling! Relling! Doctor Relling, come up as quick as you can!

[HIALMAR *and* GREGERS *lay* HEDVIG *down on the sofa.*]

EKDAL: [*quietly*] The woods avenge themselves.

HIALMAR: [*on his knees beside* HEDVIG] She'll soon come to now. She's coming to; yes, yes, yes.

GINA: [*who has come in again*] Where has she hurt herself? I can't see anything.

[RELLING *comes hurriedly, and immediately after him* MOLVIK; *the latter without his waistcoat and necktie and with his coat open.*]

RELLING: What's the matter here?

GINA: They say Hedvig shot herself.

HIALMAR: Come and help us!

RELLING: Shot herself! [*He pushes the table aside and begins to examine her.*]

HIALMAR: [*kneeling and looking anxiously up at him*] It can't be dangerous? Speak, Relling! She is scarcely bleeding at all. It can't be dangerous?

RELLING: How did it happen?

HIALMAR: Oh, we don't know—

GINA: She wanted to shoot the wild duck.

RELLING: The wild duck?

HIALMAR: The pistol must have gone off.

RELLING: H'm. Indeed.

EKDAL: The woods avenge themselves. But I'm not afraid all the same. [*Goes into the garret and closes the door after him.*]

HIALMAR: Well, Relling, why don't you say something?

RELLING: The ball has entered the breast.

HIALMAR: Yes, but she's coming to!

RELLING: Surely you can see that Hedvig is dead.

GINA: [*bursts into tears*] Oh, my child, my child—

GREGERS: [*huskily*] In the depths of the sea—

HIALMAR: [*jumps up*] No, no, she must live! Oh, for God's sake, Relling—only a moment—only just till I can tell her how unspeakably I loved her all the time.

RELLING: The bullet has gone through her heart. Internal hemorrhage. Death must have been instantaneous.

HIALMAR: And I! I hunted her from me like an animal! And she crept terrified into the garret and died for love of me! [*sobbing*] I can never atone to her! I can never tell her— [*clenches his hands and cries upward*] Oh, Thou above—if Thou be indeed! Why hast Thou done this thing to me?

GINA: Hush, hush, you mustn't go on that awful way. We had no right to keep her, I suppose.

MOLVIK: The child is not dead but sleepeth.

RELLING: Bosh!

HIALMAR: [*becomes calm, goes over to the sofa, folds his arms and looks at* HEDVIG] There she lies so stiff and still.

RELLING: [*tries to loosen the pistol*] She's holding it so tight, so tight.

GINA: No, no, Relling; don't break her fingers; let the pistol be.

HIALMAR: She shall take it with her.

GINA: Yes, let her. But the child mustn't lie here for a show. She shall go to her own room, so she shall. Help me, Ekdal.

[HIALMAR *and* GINA *take* HEDVIG *between them.*]

HIALMAR: [*as they are carrying her*] Oh Gina, Gina, can you survive this?

GINA: We must help each other to bear it. For now, at least, she belongs to both of us.

MOLVIK: [*stretches out his arms and mumbles*] Blessed be the Lord; to earth thou shalt return; to earth thou shalt return—

RELLING: [*whispers*] Hold your tongue, you fool; you're drunk.

[HIALMAR *and* GINA *carry the body out through the kitchen door.* RELLING *shuts it after them.* MOLVIK *slinks out into the passage.*]

RELLING: [*goes over to* GREGERS *and says*] No one shall ever convince me that the pistol went off by accident.

GREGERS: [*who has stood terrified, with convulsive twitchings*] Who can say how the dreadful thing happened?

RELLING: The powder has burned the body of her dress. She must have pressed the pistol right against her breast and fired.

GREGERS: Hedvig has not died in vain. Did you not see how sorrow set free what is noble in him?

RELLING: Most people are ennobled by the actual presence of death. But how long do you suppose this nobility will last in him?

GREGERS: Why should it not endure and increase throughout his life?

RELLING: Before a year is over, little Hedvig will be nothing to him but a pretty theme for declamation.

GREGERS: How dare you say that of Hialmar Ekdal?

RELLING: We will talk of this again, when the grass has first withered on her grave. Then you'll hear him spouting about "the child too early torn from her father's heart"; then you'll see him steep himself in a syrup of sentiment and self-admiration and self-pity. Just you wait!

GREGERS: If you are right and I am wrong, then life is not worth living.

RELLING: Oh, life would be quite tolerable, after all, if only we could be rid of the confounded fools that keep on pestering us, in our poverty, with the claim of the ideal.

GREGERS: [*looking straight before him*] In that case I am glad that my destiny is what it is.

RELLING: May I inquire—what is your destiny?

GREGERS: [*going*] To be the thirteenth at table.

RELLING: The devil it is.

Eugene O'Neill

"The Hairy Ape"

CHARACTERS

ROBERT SMITH, "YANK"
PADDY
LONG
MILDRED DOUGLAS
HER AUNT
SECOND ENGINEER
A GUARD
A SECRETARY OF AN ORGANIZATION
STOKERS, LADIES, GENTLEMEN, ETC.

SCENES

Scene I: The firemen's forecastle of an ocean liner—an hour after sailing from New York.
Scene II: Section of promenade deck, two days out—morning.
Scene III: The stokehole. A few minutes later.
Scene IV: Same as Scene I. Half an hour later.
Scene V: Fifth Avenue, New York. Three weeks later.
Scene VI: An island near the city. The next night.
Scene VII: In the city. About a month later.
Scene VIII: In the city. Twilight of the next day.

SCENE I

The firemen's forecastle of a transatlantic liner an hour after sailing from New York for the voyage across. Tiers of narrow, steel bunks, three deep, on all sides. An entrance in rear. Benches on the floor before the bunks. The room is crowded with men, shouting, cursing, laughing, singing—a confused, inchoate uproar swelling into a sort of unity, a meaning—the bewildered, furious, baffled defiance of a beast in a cage. Nearly all the men are drunk. Many bottles are passed from hand to hand. All are dressed in dungaree pants, heavy ugly shoes. Some wear singlets, but the majority are stripped to the waist.

The treatment of this scene, or of any other scene in the play, should by no means be naturalistic. The effect sought after is a cramped space in the bowels of a ship, imprisoned by white steel. The lines of bunks, the uprights supporting them, cross each other like the steel framework of a cage. The ceiling crushes down upon the men's heads. They cannot stand upright. This accentuates the natural stooping posture which shoveling coal and the resultant over-development of back and shoulder muscles have given them. The men themselves should resemble those pictures in which the appearance of Neanderthal Man is guessed at. All are hairy-chested, with long arms of tremendous power, and low, receding brows above their small, fierce, resentful eyes. All the civilized white races are represented, but except for the slight differentiation in color of hair, skin, eyes, all these men are alike.

The curtain rises on a tumult of sound. YANK is seated in the foreground. He seems broader, fiercer, more truculent, more powerful, more sure of himself than the rest. They respect his superior strength—the grudging respect of fear. Then, too, he represents to them a self-expression, the very last word in what they are, their most highly developed individual.

VOICES: Gif me trink dere, you!
'Ave a wet!
Salute!
Gesundheit!
Skoal!
Drunk as a lord, God stiffen you!
Here's how!
Luck!
Pass back that bottle, damn you!
Pourin' it down his neck!
Ho, Froggy! Where the devil have you been?
La Touraine.
I hit him smash in yaw, py Gott!
Jenkins—the First—he's a rotten swine—
And the coppers nabbed him—and I run—
I like peer better. It don't pig head gif you.
A slut, I'm sayin'! She robbed me aslape—
To hell with 'em all!
You're a bloody liar!
Say dot again!
[Commotion. Two men about to fight are pulled apart.]
No scrappin' now!
Tonight—
See who's the best man!
Bloody Dutchman!
Tonight on the for'ard square.
I'll bet on Dutchy.
He packa da wallop, I tella you!
Shut up, Wop!

No fightin', maties. We're all chums, ain't we?

[*A voice starts bawling a song.*]

"Beer, beer, glorious beer!

Fill yourselves right up to here."

YANK: [*for the first time seeming to take notice of the uproar about him, turns around threateningly—in a tone of contemptuous authority*] Choke off dat noise! Where d'yuh get dat beer stuff? Beer, hell! Beer's for goils—and Dutchmen. Me for somep'n wit a kick to it! Gimme a drink, one of youse guys. [*Several bottles are eagerly offered. He takes a tremendous gulp at one of them; then, keeping the bottle in his hand, glares belligerently at the owner, who hastens to acquiesce in this robbery by saying*] All righto, Yank. Keep it and have another. [YANK *contemptuously turns his back on the crowd again. For a second there is an embarrassed silence. Then—*]

VOICES: We must be passing the Hook.

She's beginning to roll to it.

Six days in hell—and then Southampton.

Py Yesus, I vish somepody take my first vatch for me!

Gittin' seasick, Square-head?

Drink up and forget it!

What's in your bottle?

Gin.

Dot's nigger trink.

Absinthe? It's doped. You'll go off your chump, Froggy!

Cochon!

Whisky, that's the ticket!

Where's Paddy?

Going asleep.

Sing us that whisky song, Paddy.

[*They all turn to an old, wizened Irishman who is dozing, very drunk, on the benches forward. His face is extremely monkey-like with all the sad, patient pathos of that animal in his small eyes.*]

Singa da song, Caruso Pat!

He's gettin' old. The drink is too much for him.

He's too drunk.

PADDY: [*blinking about him, starts to his feet resentfully, swaying, holding on to the edge of a bunk*] I'm never too drunk to sing. 'Tis only when I'm dead to the world I'd be wishful to sing at all. [*with a sort of sad contempt*] "Whisky Johnny," ye want? A chanty, ye want? Now that's a queer wish from the ugly like of you, God help you. But no matther. [*He starts to sing in a thin, nasal, doleful tone.*]

Oh, whisky is the life of man!

Whisky! O Johnny! [*They all join in on this.*]

      Oh, whisky is the life of man!

        Whisky for my Johnny! [*Again chorus.*]

      Oh, whisky drove my old man mad!

        Whisky! O Johnny!

      Oh, whisky drove my old man mad!

        Whisky for my Johnny!

YANK: [*again turning around scornfully*] Aw hell! Nix on dat old sailing ship stuff! All dat bull's dead, see? And you're dead, too, yuh damned old Harp, on'y yuh don't know it. Take it easy, see. Give us a rest. Nix on de loud noise. [*with a cynical grin*] Can't youse see I'm tryin' to t'ink?

ALL: [*repeating the word after him as one with the same cynical amused mockery*] Think! [*The chorused word has a brazen metallic quality as if their throats were phonograph horns. It is followed by a general uproar of hard, barking laughter.*]

VOICES: Don't be cracking your head wit ut, Yank.

      You gat headache, py yingo!

      One thing about it—it rhymes with drink!

      Ha, ha, ha!

      Drink, don't think!

      Drink, don't think!

      Drink, don't think!

      [*A whole chorus of voices has taken up this refrain, stamping on the floor, pounding on the benches with fists.*]

YANK: [*taking a gulp from his bottle—good-naturedly*] Aw right. Can de noise. I got yuh de foist time. [*The uproar subsides. A very drunken sentimental tenor begins to sing.*]

          "Far away in Canada,

           Far across the sea,

         There's a lass who fondly waits

          Making a home for me—"

YANK: [*fiercely contemptuous*] Shut up, yuh lousy boob! Where d'yuh get dat tripe? Home? Home, hell! I'll make a home for yuh! I'll knock yuh dead. Home! T'hell wit home! Where d'yuh get dat tripe? Dis is home, see? What d'yuh want wit home? [*proudly*] I runned away from mine when I was a kid. On'y too glad to beat it, dat was me. Home was lickings for me, dat's all. But yuh can bet your shoit no one ain't never licked me since! Wanter try it, any of youse? Huh! I guess not. [*in a more placated but still contemptuous tone*] Goils waitin' for yuh, huh? Aw, hell! Dat's all tripe. Dey don't wait for no one. Dey'd double-cross yuh for a nickel. Dey're all tarts, get me? Treat 'em rough, dat's me. To hell wit 'em. Tarts, dat's what, de whole bunch of 'em.

LONG: [*very drunk, jumps on a bench excitedly, gesticulating with a bottle in his hand*] Listen 'ere, Comrades! Yank 'ere is right. 'E says this 'ere stinkin' ship is our 'ome. And 'e says as 'ome is 'ell And 'e's right! This is 'ell. We lives in 'ell, Comrades—and right enough we'll die in it. [*raging*] And who's ter blame, I arsks yer? We ain't. We wasn't born this rotten way. All men is born free and ekal. That's in the bleedin' Bible, maties. But what d'they care for the Bible—them lazy, bloated swine what travels first cabin? Them's the ones. They dragged us down 'til we're on'y wage slaves in the bowels of a bloody ship, sweatin', burnin' up, eatin' coal dust! Hit's them's ter blame— the damned Capitalist clarss!

> [*There had been a gradual murmur of contemptuous resentment rising among the men until now he is interrupted by a storm of catcalls, hisses, boos, hard laughter.*]

VOICES: Turn it off!
Shut up!
Sit down!
Closa da face!
Tamn fool! [*Etc.*]

YANK: [*standing up and glaring at* LONG] Sit down before I knock yuh down! [LONG *makes haste to efface himself.* YANK *goes on contemptuously.*] De Bible, huh? De Cap'tlist class, huh? Aw nix on dat Salvation Army-Socialist bull. Git a soapbox! Hire a hall! Come and be saved, huh? Jerk us to Jesus, huh? Aw g'wan! I've listened to lots of guys like you, see. Yuh're all wrong. Wanter know what I t'ink? Yuh ain't no good for no one. Yuh're de bunk. Yuh ain't got no noive, get me? Yuh're yellow, dat's what. Yellow, dat's you. Say! What's dem slobs in de foist cabin got to do wit us? We're better men dan dey are, ain't we? Sure! One of us guys could clean up de whole mob wit one mit. Put one of 'em down here for one watch in de stokehole, what'd happen? Dey'd carry him off on a stretcher. Dem boids don't amount to nothin'. Dey're just baggage. Who makes dis old tub run? Ain't it us guys? Well den, we belong, don't we? We belong and dey don't. Dat's all. [*A loud chorus of approval.* YANK *goes on.*] As for dis bein' hell—aw, nuts! Yuh lost your noive, dat's what. Dis is a man's job, get me? It belongs. It runs dis tub. No stiffs need apply. But yuh're a stiff, see? Yuh're yellow, dat's you.

VOICES: [*with a great hard pride in them*]
Righto!
A man's job!
Talk is cheap, Long.
He never could hold up his end.
Divil take him!
Yank's right. We make it go.
Py Gott, Yank say right ting!
We don't need no one cryin' over us.
Makin' speeches.

Throw him out!
Yellow!
Chuck him overboard!
I'll break his jaw for him!
   [*They crowd around* LONG *threateningly.*]

YANK: [*half good-natured again— contemptuously*] Aw, take it easy. Leave him alone. He ain't woith a punch. Drink up. Here's how, whoever owns dis. [*He takes a long swallow from his bottle. All drink with him. In a flash all is hilarious amiability again, back-slapping, loud talk, etc.*]

PADDY: [*who has been sitting in a blinking, melancholy daze—suddenly cries out in a voice full of old sorrow*] We belong to this, you're saying? We make the ship to go, you're saying? Yerra then, that Almighty God have pity on us! [*His voice runs into the wail of a keen, he rocks back and forth on his bench. The men stare at him, startled and impressed in spite of themselves.*] Oh, to be back in the fine days of my youth, ochone! Oh, there was fine beautiful ships them days—clippers wid tall masts touching the sky—fine strong men in them—men that was sons of the sea as if 'twas the mother that bore them. Oh, the clean skins of them, and the clear eyes, the straight backs and full chests of them! Brave men they was, and bold men surely! We'd be sailing out, bound down round the Horn maybe. We'd be making sail in the dawn, with a fair breeze, singing a chanty song wid no care to it. And astern the land would be sinking low and dying out, but we'd give it no heed but a laugh, and never a look behind. For the day that was, was enough, for we was free men—and I'm thinking 'tis only slaves do be giving heed to the day that's gone or the day to come—until they're old like me. [*with a sort of religious exaltation*] Oh, to be scudding south again wid the power of the Trade Wind driving her on steady through the nights and the days! Full sail on her! Nights and days! Nights when the foam of the wake would be flaming wid fire, when the sky'd be blazing and winking wid stars. Or the full of the moon maybe. Then you'd see her driving through the gray night, her sails stretching aloft all silver and white, not a sound on the deck, the lot of us dreaming dreams, till you'd believe 'twas no real ship at all you was on but a ghost ship like the *Flying Dutchman* they say does be roaming the seas forevermore widout touching a port. And there was the days, too. A warm sun on the clean decks. Sun warming the blood of you, and wind over the miles of shiny green ocean like strong drink to your lungs. Work—aye, hard work—but who'd mind that at all? Sure, you worked under the sky and 'twas work wid skill and daring to it. And wid the day done, in the dog watch, smoking me pipe at ease, the lookout would be raising land maybe, and we'd see the mountains of South Americy wid the red fire of the setting sun painting their white tops and the clouds floating by them! [*His tone of exaltation ceases. He goes on mournfully.*] Yerra, what's the use of talking?

'Tis a dead man's whisper. [*to* YANK *resentfully*] 'Twas them days men belonged to ships, not now. 'Twas them days a ship was part of the sea, and a man was part of a ship, and the sea joined all together and made it one. [*scornfully*] Is it one wid this you'd be, Yank—black smoke from the funnels smudging the sea, smudging the decks—the bloody engines pounding and throbbing and shaking—wid divil a sight of sun or a breath of clean air—choking our lungs wid coal dust—breaking our backs and hearts in the hell of the stokehole—feeding the bloody furnace—feeding our lives along wid the coal, I'm thinking—caged in by steel from a sight of the sky like bloody apes in the Zoo! [*with a harsh laugh*] Ho-ho, divil mend you! Is it to belong to that you're wishing? Is it a flesh and blood wheel of the engines you'd be?

YANK: [*who has been listening with a contemptuous sneer, barks out the answer*] Sure ting! Dat's me. What about it?

PADDY: [*as if to himself—with great sorrow*] Me time is past due. That a great wave wid sun in the heart of it may sweep me over the side sometime I'd be dreaming of the days that's gone!

YANK: Aw, yuh crazy Mick! [*He springs to his feet and advances on* PADDY *threateningly—then stops, fighting some queer struggle within himself—lets his hands fall to his sides—contemptuously.*] Aw, take it easy. Yuh're aw right, at dat. Yuh're bugs, dat's all—nutty as a cuckoo. All dat tripe yuh been pullin'—Aw, dat's all right. On'y it's dead, get me? Yuh don't belong no more, see. Yuh don't got de stuff. Yuh're too old. [*disgustedly*] But aw say, come up for air onct in a while, can't yuh? See what's happened since yuh croaked. [*He suddenly bursts forth vehemently, growing more and more excited.*] Say! Sure! Sure I meant it! What de hell—Say, lemme talk! Hey! Hey, you old Harp! Hey, youse guys! Say, listen to me—wait a moment—I gotter talk, see. I belong and he don't. He's dead but I'm livin'. Listen to me! Sure I'm part of de engines! Why de hell not! Dey move, don't dey? Dey're speed, ain't dey? Dey smash trou, don't dey! Twenty-five knots a hour! Dat's goin' some! Dat's new stuff! Dat belongs! But him, he's too old. He gets dizzy. Say, listen. All dat crazy tripe about nights and days; all dat crazy tripe about stars and moons; all dat crazy tripe about suns and winds, fresh air and de rest of it—Aw hell, dat's all a dope dream! Hittin' de pipe of de past, dat's what he's doin.' He's old and don't belong no more. But me, I'm young! I'm in de pink! I move wit it! It, get me! I mean de ting dat's de guts of all dis. It ploughs trou all de tripe he's been sayin'. It blows dat up! It knocks dat dead! It slams dat offen de face of de oith! It, get me! De engines and de coal and de smoke and all de rest of it! He can't breathe and swallow coal dust, but I kin, see? Dat's fresh air for me! Dat's food for me! I'm new, get me? Hell in de stokehole? Sure! It takes a man to work in hell. Hell, sure, dat's my fav'rite climate. I eat it up! I git fat on it! It's me makes it hot! It's me makes it roar! It's me makes it move! Sure, on'y for me everyting stops. It all goes dead, get me?

De noise and smoke and all de engines movin' de woild, dey stop. Dere ain't nothin' no more! Dat's what I'm sayin'. Everyting else dat makes de woild move, somep'n makes it move. It can't move witout somep'n else, see? Den yuh get down to me. I'm at de bottom, get me! Dere ain't nothin' foither. I'm de end! I'm de start! I start somep'n and de woild moves! It—dat's me!—de new dat's moiderin' de old! I'm de ting in coal dat makes it boin; I'm steam and oil for de engines; I'm de ting in noise dat makes yuh hear it; I'm smoke and express trains and steamers and factory whistles; I'm de ting in gold dat makes it money! And I'm what makes iron into steel! Steel, dat stands for de whole ting! And I'm steel—steel—steel! I'm de muscles in steel, de punch behind it! [As he says this he pounds with his fist against the steel bunks. All the men, roused to a pitch of frenzied self-glorification by his speech, do likewise. There is a deafening metallic roar, through which YANK's voice can be heard bellowing.] Slaves, hell! We run de whole woiks. All de rich guys dat tink dey're somep'n, dey ain't nothin'! Dey don't belong. But us guys, we're in de move, we're at de bottom, de whole ting is us! [PADDY from the start of YANK's speech has been taking one gulp after another from his bottle, at first frightenedly, as if he were afraid to listen, then desperately, as if to drown his senses, but finally has achieved complete indifferent, even amused, drunkenness. YANK sees his lips moving. He quells the uproar with a shout.] Hey, youse guys, take it easy! Wait a moment! De nutty Harp is sayin' somep'n.

PADDY: [is heard now—throws his head back with a mocking burst of laughter] Ho-ho-ho-ho-ho—

YANK: [drawing back his fist, with a snarl] Aw! Look out who yuh're givin' the bark!

PADDY: [begins to sing the "Miller of Dee" with enormous good nature]
"I care for nobody, no, not I,
And nobody cares for me."

YANK: [good-natured himself in a flash, interrupts PADDY with a slap on the bare back like a report] Dat's de stuff! Now yuh're gettin' wise to somep'n. Care for nobody, dat's de dope! To hell wit 'em all! And nix on nobody else carin'. I kin care for myself, get me! [Eight bells sound, muffled, vibrating through the steel walls as if some enormous brazen gong were imbedded in the heart of the ship. All the men jump up mechanically, file through the door silently close upon each other's heels in what is very like a prisoners' lockstep. YANK slaps PADDY on the back.] Our watch, yuh old Harp! [mockingly] Come on down in hell. Eat up de coal dust. Drink in de heat. It's it, see! Act like yuh liked it, yuh better—or croak yuhself.

PADDY: [with jovial defiance] To the divil wid it! I'll not report this watch. Let thim log me and be damned. I'm no slave the like of you. I'll be sittin' here at me ease, and drinking, and thinking, and dreaming dreams.

YANK: [contemptuously] Tinkin' and dreamin', what'll that get yuh? What's tinkin' got to do wit it? We move, don't we? Speed, ain't it? Fog, dat's all you stand for. But we drive trou dat, don't we? We split dat up and smash trou— twenty-five knots a hour! [*turns his back on* PADDY *scornfully*] Aw, yuh make me sick! Yuh don't belong! [*He strides out the door in rear.* PADDY *hums to himself, blinking drowsily.*]

CURTAIN

SCENE II

Two days out. A section of the promenade deck. MILDRED DOUGLAS *and her aunt are discovered reclining in deck chairs. The former is a girl of twenty, slender, delicate, with a pale, pretty face marred by a self-conscious expression of disdainful superiority. She looks fretful, nervous and discontented, bored by her own anemia. Her aunt is a pompous and proud—and fat—old lady. She is a type even to the point of a double chin and lorgnettes. She is dressed pretentiously, as if afraid her face alone would never indicate her position in life.* MILDRED *is dressed all in white.*

The impression to be conveyed by this scene is one of the beautiful, vivid life of the sea all about—sunshine on the deck in a great flood, the fresh sea wind blowing across it. In the midst of this, these two incongruous, artificial figures, inert and disharmonious, the elder like a gray lump of dough touched up with rouge, the younger looking as if the vitality of her stock had been sapped before she was conceived, so that she is the expression not of its life energy but merely of the artificialities that energy had won for itself in the spending.

MILDRED: [*looking up with affected dreaminess*] How the black smoke swirls back against the sky! Is it not beautiful?

AUNT: [*without looking up*] I dislike smoke of any kind.

MILDRED: My great-grandmother smoked a pipe—a clay pipe.

AUNT: [*ruffling*] Vulgar!

MILDRED: She was too distant a relative to be vulgar. Time mellows pipes.

AUNT: [*pretending boredom but irritated*] Did the sociology you took up at college teach you that—to play the ghoul on every possible occasion, excavating old bones? Why not let your great-grandmother rest in her grave?

MILDRED: [*dreamily*] With her pipe beside her—puffing in Paradise.

AUNT: [*with spite*] Yes, you are a natural born ghoul. You are even getting to look like one, my dear.

MILDRED: [*in a passionless tone*] I detest you, Aunt. [*looking at her critically*] Do you know what you remind me of? Of a cold pork pudding against a background of linoleum tablecloth in the kitchen of a—but the possibilities are wearisome. [*She closes her eyes.*]

AUNT: [*with a bitter laugh*] Merci for your candor. But since I am and must be your chaperon—in appearance, at least—let us patch up some sort of armed truce. For my part you are quite free to indulge any pose of eccentricity that beguiles you—as long as you observe the amenities—

MILDRED: [drawling] The inanities?

AUNT: [going on as if she hadn't heard] After exhausting the morbid thrills of social service work on New York's East Side—how they must have hated you, by the way, the poor that you made so much poorer in their own eyes!—you are now bent on making your slumming international. Well, I hope Whitechapel will provide the needed nerve tonic. Do not ask me to chaperon you there, however. I told your father I would not. I loathe deformity. We will hire an army of detectives and you may investigate everything—they allow you to see.

MILDRED: [protesting with a trace of genuine earnestness] Please do not mock at my attempts to discover how the other half lives. Give me credit for some sort of groping sincerity in that at least. I would like to help them. I would like to be some use in the world. Is it my fault I don't know how? I would like to be sincere, to touch life somewhere. [with weary bitterness] But I'm afraid I have neither the vitality nor integrity. All that was burnt out in our stock before I was born. Grandfather's blast furnaces, flaming to the sky, melting steel, making millions—then father keeping those home fires burning, making more millions—and little me at the tail-end of it all. I'm a waste product in the Bessemer process—like the millions. Or rather, I inherit the acquired trait of the by-product, wealth, but none of the energy, none of the strength of the steel that made it. I am sired by gold and damned by it, as they say at the race track—damned in more ways than one. [She laughs mirthlessly.]

AUNT: [unimpressed—superciliously] You seem to be going in for sincerity today. It isn't becoming to you, really—except as an obvious pose. Be as artificial as you are, I advise. There's a sort of sincerity in that, you know. And, after all, you must confess you like that better.

MILDRED: [again affected and bored] Yes, I suppose I do. Pardon me for my outburst. When a leopard complains of its spots, it must sound rather grotesque. [in a mocking tone] Purr, little leopard. Purr, scratch, tear, kill, gorge yourself and be happy—only stay in the jungle where your spots are camouflage. In a cage they make you conspicuous.

AUNT: I don't know what you are talking about.

MILDRED: It would be rude to talk about anything to you. Let's just talk. [She looks at her wrist watch.] Well, thank goodness, it's about time for them to come for me. That ought to give me a new thrill, Aunt.

AUNT: [affectedly troubled] You don't mean to say you're really going? The dirt—the heat must be frightful—

MILDRED: Grandfather started as a puddler. I should have inherited an immunity to heat that would make a salamander shiver. It will be fun to put it to the test.

AUNT: But don't you have to have the captain's—or someone's—permission to visit the stokehole?

MILDRED: [*with a triumphant smile*] I have it—both his and the chief engineer's. Oh, they didn't want to at first, in spite of my social service credentials. They didn't seem a bit anxious that I should investigate how the other half lives and works on a ship. So I had to tell them that my father, the president of Nazareth Steel, chairman of the board of directors of this line, had told me it would be all right.

AUNT: He didn't.

MILDRED: How naïve age makes one! But I said he did, Aunt. I even said he had given me a letter to them—which I had lost. And they were afraid to take the chance that I might be lying. [*excitedly*] So it's ho! for the stokehole. The second engineer is to escort me. [*looking at her watch again*] It's time. And here he comes, I think.

> [*The* SECOND ENGINEER *enters. He is a husky, fine-looking man of thirty-five or so. He stops before the two and tips his cap, visibly embarrassed and ill-at-ease.*]

SECOND ENGINEER: Miss Douglas?

MILDRED: Yes. [*throwing off her rugs and getting to her feet*] Are we all ready to start?

SECOND ENGINEER: In just a second, ma'am. I'm waiting for the Fourth. He's coming along.

MILDRED: [*with a scornful smile*] You don't care to shoulder this responsibility alone, is that it?

SECOND ENGINEER: [*forcing a smile*] Two are better than one. [*disturbed by her eyes, glances out to sea—blurts out*] A fine day we're having.

MILDRED: Is it?

SECOND ENGINEER: A nice warm breeze—

MILDRED: It feels cold to me.

SECOND ENGINEER: But it's hot enough in the sun—

MILDRED: Not hot enough for me. I don't like Nature. I was never athletic.

SECOND ENGINEER: [*forcing a smile*] Well, you'll find it hot enough where you're going.

MILDRED: Do you mean hell?

SECOND ENGINEER: [*flabbergasted, decides to laugh*] Ho-ho! No, I mean the stokehole.

MILDRED: My grandfather was a puddler. He played with boiling steel.

SECOND ENGINEER: [*all at sea—uneasily*] Is that so? Hum, you'll excuse me, ma'am, but are you intending to wear that dress?

MILDRED: Why not?

SECOND ENGINEER: You'll likely rub against oil and dirt. It can't be helped.

MILDRED: It doesn't matter. I have lots of white dresses.

SECOND ENGINEER: I have an old coat you might throw over—

MILDRED: I have fifty dresses like this. I will throw this one into the sea when I come back. That ought to wash it clean, don't you think?

SECOND ENGINEER: [doggedly] There's ladders to climb down that are none too clean—and dark alleyways—

MILDRED: I will wear this very dress and none other.

SECOND ENGINEER: No offense meant. It's none of my business. I was only warning you—

MILDRED: Warning? That sounds thrilling.

SECOND ENGINEER: [looking down the deck—with a sigh of relief] There's the Fourth now. He's waiting for us. If you'll come—

MILDRED: Go on. I'll follow you. [He goes. MILDRED turns a mocking smile on her aunt.] An oaf—but a handsome, virile oaf.

AUNT: [scornfully] Poser!

MILDRED: Take care. He said there were dark alleyways—

AUNT: [in the same tone] Poser!

MILDRED: [biting her lips angrily] You are right. But would that my millions were not so anemically chaste!

AUNT: Yes, for a fresh pose I have no doubt you would drag the name of Douglas in the gutter!

MILDRED: From which it sprang. Good-by, Aunt. Don't pray too hard that I may fall into the fiery furnace.

AUNT: Poser!

MILDRED: [viciously] Old hag! [She slaps her aunt insultingly across the face and walks off, laughing gaily.]

AUNT: [screams after her] I said poser!

CURTAIN

SCENE III

The stokehole. In the rear, the dimly-outlined bulks of the furnaces and boilers. High overhead one hanging electric bulb sheds just enough light through the murky air laden with coal dust to pile up masses of shadows everywhere. A line of men, stripped to the waist, is before the furnace doors. They bend over, looking neither to right nor left, handling their shovels as if they were part of their bodies, with a strange, awkward, swinging rhythm. They use the shovels to throw open the furnace doors. Then from these fiery round holes in the black a flood of terrific light and heat pours full upon the men who are outlined in silhouette in the crouching, inhuman attitudes of chained gorillas. The men shovel with a rhythmic motion, swinging as on a pivot from the coal which lies in heaps on the floor behind to hurl it into the flaming mouths before them. There is a tumult of noise—the brazen clang of the furnace doors as they are flung open or slammed shut, the grating, teeth-gritting grind of steel against steel, of crunching coal. This clash of sounds stuns one's ears with its rending dissonance. But there is order in it, rhythm, a mechanical regulated recurrence, a tempo. And rising above all, making the air hum with the quiver of liberated energy, the roar of leaping flames in the furnaces, the monotonous throbbing beat of the engines.

As the curtain rises, the furnace doors are shut. The men are taking a breathing spell. One or two are arranging the coal behind them, pulling it into more accessible heaps. The others can be dimly made out leaning on their shovels in relaxed attitudes of exhaustion.

PADDY: [*from somewhere in the line—plaintively*] Yerra, will this divil's own watch nivir end? Me back is broke. I'm destroyed entirely.

YANK: [*from the center of the line—with exuberant scorn*] Aw, yuh make me sick! Lie down and croak, why don't yuh? Always beefin', dat's you! Say, dis is a cinch! Dis was made for me! It's my meat, get me! [*A whistle is blown—a thin, shrill note from somewhere overhead in the darkness.* YANK *curses without resentment.*] Dere's de damn engineer crackin' de whip. He tinks we're loafin'.

PADDY: [*vindictively*] God stiffen him!

YANK: [*in an exultant tone of command*] Come on, youse guys! Git into de game! She's gittin' hungry! Pile some grub in her. Trow it into her belly! Come on now, all of youse! Open her up!

[*At this last all the men, who have followed his movements of getting into position, throw open their furnace doors with a deafening clang. The fiery light floods over their shoulders as they bend round for the coal. Rivulets of sooty sweat have traced maps on their backs. The enlarged muscles form bunches of high light and shadow.*]

YANK: [*chanting a count as he shovels without seeming effort*] One—two—tree— [*his voice rising exultantly in the joy of battle*] Dat's de stuff! Let her have it! All togedder now! Sling it into her! Let her ride! Shoot de piece now! Call de toin on her! Drive her into it! Feel her move! Watch her smoke! Speed, dat's her middle name! Give her coal, youse guys! Coal, dat's her booze! Drink it up, baby! Let's see yuh sprint! Dig in and gain a lap! Dere she go-o-es.

[*This last in the chanting formula of the gallery gods at the six-day bike race. He slams his furnace door shut. The others do likewise with as much unison as their wearied bodies will permit. The effect is of one fiery eye after another being blotted out with a series of accompanying bangs.*]

PADDY: [*groaning*] Me back is broke. I'm bate out—bate—

[*There is a pause. Then the inexorable whistle sounds again from the dim regions above the electric light. There is a growl of cursing rage from all sides.*]

YANK: [*shaking his fist upward—contemptuously*] Take it easy dere, you! Who
d'yuh tink's runnin' dis game, me or you? When I git ready, we move. Not
before! When I git ready, get me!

VOICES: [*approvingly*] That's the stuff!

                    Yank tal him, py golly!

                    Yank ain't affeerd.

                    Goot poy, Yank!

                    Give 'im hell!

                    Tell 'im 'e's a bloody swine! ·

                    Bloody slave-driver!

YANK: [*contemptuously*] He ain't got no noive. He's yellow, get me? All de
engineers is yellow. Dey got streaks a mile wide. Aw, to hell wit him! Let's
move, youse guys. We had a rest. Come on, she needs it! Give her pep! It
ain't for him. Him and his whistle, dey don't belong. But we belong, see! We
gotter feed de baby! Come on!

    [*He turns and flings his furnace door open. They all follow his lead. At
this instant the* SECOND *and* FOURTH ENGINEERS *enter from the darkness
on the left with* MILDRED *between them. She starts, turns paler, her pose
is crumbling, she shivers with fright in spite of the blazing heat, but
forces herself to leave the* ENGINEERS *and take a few steps nearer the men.
She is right behind* YANK. *All this happens quickly while the men have
their backs turned.*]

YANK: Come on, youse guys! [*He is turning to get coal when the whistle sounds
again in a peremptory, irritating note. This drives* YANK *into a sudden fury.
While the other men have turned full around and stopped dumbfounded by
the spectacle of* MILDRED *standing there in her white dress,* YANK *does not turn
far enough to see her. Besides, his head is thrown back, he blinks upward
through the murk trying to find the owner of the whistle, he brandishes his
shovel murderously over his head in one hand, pounding on his chest, gorilla-
like, with the other, shouting.*] Toin off dat whistle! Come down outa dere,
yuh yellow, brass-buttoned, Belfast bum, yuh! Come down and I'll knock
yer brains out! Yuh lousy, stinkin', yellow mut of a Catholic-moiderin'
bastard! Come down and I'll moider yuh! Pullin' dat whistle on me, huh? I'll
show yuh! I'll crash yer skull in! I'll drive yer teet' down yer troat! I'll slam yer
nose trou de back of yer head! I'll cut yer guts out for a nickel, yuh lousy
boob, yuh dirty, crummy, muck-eatin' son of a— [*Suddenly he becomes
conscious of all the other men staring at something directly behind his back.
He whirls defensively with a snarling, murderous growl, crouching to spring,
his lips drawn back over his teeth, his small eyes gleaming ferociously. He sees*
MILDRED, *like a white apparition in the full light from the open furnace doors.
He glares into her eyes, turned to stone. As for her, during his speech she has
listened, paralyzed with horror, terror, her whole personality crushed, beaten*

in, collapsed, by the terrific impact of this unknown, abysmal brutality, naked and shameless. As she looks at his gorilla face, as his eyes bore into hers, she utters a low, choking cry and shrinks away from him, putting both hands up before her eyes to shut out the sight of his face, to protect her own. This startles YANK *to a reaction. His mouth falls open, his eyes grow bewildered.*]

MILDRED: [*about to faint—to the* ENGINEERS, *who now have her one by each arm— whimperingly*] Take me away! Oh, the filthy beast!

> [*She faints. They carry her quickly back, disappearing in the darkness at the left, rear. An iron door clangs shut. Rage and bewildered fury rush back on* YANK. *He feels himself insulted in some unknown fashion in the very heart of his pride. He roars*]

God damn yuh! [*and hurls his shovel after them at the door which has just closed. It hits the steel bulkhead with a clang and falls clattering on the steel floor. From overhead the whistle sounds again in a long, angry, insistent command.*]

CURTAIN

SCENE IV

The firemen's forecastle. YANK's *watch has just come off duty and had dinner. Their faces and bodies shine from a soap and water scrubbing but around their eyes, where a hasty dousing does not touch, the coal dust sticks like black make-up, giving them a queer, sinister expression.* YANK *has not washed either face or body. He stands out in contrast to them, a blackened, brooding figure. He is seated forward on a bench in the exact attitude of Rodin's "The Thinker." The others, most of them smoking pipes, are staring at* YANK *half-apprehensively, as if fearing an outburst; half-amusedly as if they saw a joke somewhere that tickled them.*

VOICES: He ain't ate nothin'.
> Py golly, a fallar gat to gat grub in him.
> Divil a lie.
> Yank feeda da fire, no feeda da face.
> Ha-ha.
> He ain't even washed hisself.
> He's forgot.
> Hey, Yank, you forgot to wash.

YANK: [*sullenly*] Forgot nothin'! To hell wit washin'.

VOICES: It'll stick to you.
> It'll get under your skin.
> Give yer the bleedin' itch, that's wot.
> It makes spots on you—like a leopard.
> Like a piebald nigger, you mean.
> Better wash up, Yank.

You sleep better.
Wash up, Yank.
Wash up! Wash up!

YANK: [*resentfully*] Aw say, youse guys. Lemme alone. Can't youse see I'm tryin' to tink?

ALL: [*repeating the word after him as one with cynical mockery*] Think! [*The word has a brazen, metallic quality as if their throats where phonograph horns. It is followed by a chorus of hard, barking laughter.*]

YANK: [*springing to his feet and glaring at them belligerently*] Yes, tink! Tink, dat's what I said! What about it?

[*They are silent, puzzled by his sudden resentment at what used to be one of his jokes.* YANK *sits down again in the same attitude of "The Thinker."*]

VOICES: Leave him alone.
He's got a grouch on.
Why wouldn't he?

PADDY: [*with a wink at the others*] Sure I know what's the matther. 'Tis aisy to see. He's fallen in love, I'm telling you.

ALL: [*repeating the word after him as one with cynical mockery*] Love! [*The word has a brazen, metallic quality as if their throats were phonograph horns. It is followed by a chorus of hard, barking laughter.*]

YANK: [*with a contemptuous snort*] Love, hell! Hate, dat's what. I've fallen in hate, get me?

PADDY: [*philosophically*] 'Twould take a wise man to tell one from the other. [*with a bitter, ironical scorn, increasing as he goes on*] But I'm telling you it's love that's in it. Sure what else but love for us poor bastes in the stokehole would be bringing a fine lady, dressed like a white quane, down a mile of ladders and steps to be havin' a look at us? [*A growl of anger goes up from all sides.*]

LONG: [*jumping on a bench—hectically*] Hinsultin' us! Hinsultin' us, the bloody cow! And them bloody engineers! What right 'as they got to be exhibitin' us 's if we was bleedin' monkeys in a menagerie? Did we sign for hinsults to our dignity as 'onest workers? Is that in the ship's articles? You kin bloody well bet it ain't! But I knows why they done it. I arsked a deck steward 'o she was and 'e told me. 'Er old man's a bleedin' millionaire, a bloody Capitalist! 'E's got enuf bloody gold to sink this bleedin' ship! 'E makes arf the bloody steel in the world! 'E owns this bloody boat! And you and me, Comrades, we're 'is slaves! And the skipper and mates and engineers, they're 'is slaves! And she's 'is bloody daughter and we're all 'er slaves, too! And she gives 'er orders as 'ow she wants to see the bloody animals below decks and down they takes 'er! [*There is a roar of rage from all sides.*]

YANK: [*blinking at him bewilderedly*] Say! Wait a moment! Is all dat straight goods?

LONG: Straight as string! The bleedin' steward as waits on 'em, 'e told me about 'er. And what're we goin' ter do, I arsks yer? 'Ave we got ter swaller 'er hinsults like dogs? It ain't in the ship's articles. I tell yer we got a case. We kin go to law—

YANK: [*with abysmal contempt*] Hell! Law!

ALL: [*repeating the word after him as one with cynical mockery*] Law! [*The word has a brazen metallic quality as if their throats were phonograph horns. It is followed by a chorus of hard, barking laughter.*]

LONG: [*feeling the ground slipping from under his feet—desperately*] As voters and citizens we kin force the bloody governments—

YANK: [*with abysmal contempt*] Hell! Governments!

ALL: [*repeating the word after him as one with cynical mockery*] Governments! [*The word has a brazen metallic quality as if their throats were phonograph horns. It is followed by a chorus of hard, barking laughter.*]

LONG: [*hysterically*] We're free and equal in the sight of God—

YANK: [*with abysmal contempt*] Hell! God!

ALL: [*repeating the word after him as one with cynical mockery*] God! [*The word has a brazen metallic quality as if their throats were phonograph horns. It is followed by a chorus of hard, barking laughter.*]

YANK: [*witheringly*] Aw, join de Salvation Army!

ALL: Sit down! Shut up! Damn fool! Sea-lawyer!

[LONG *slinks back out of sight.*]

PADDY: [*continuing the trend of his thoughts as if he had never been interrupted— bitterly*] And there she was standing behind us, and the Second pointing at us like a man you'd hear in a circus would be saying: In this cage is a queerer kind of baboon than ever you'd find in darkest Africy. We roast them in their own sweat—and be damned if you won't hear some of thim saying they like it! [*He glances scornfully at* YANK.]

YANK: [*with a bewildered uncertain growl*] Aw!

PADDY: And there was Yank roarin' curses and turning round wid his shovel to brain her—and she looked at him, and him at her—

YANK: [*slowly*] She was all white. I tought she was a ghost. Sure.

PADDY: [*with heavy, biting sarcasm*] 'Twas love at first sight, divil a doubt of it! If you'd seen the endearin' look on her pale mug when she shriveled away with her hands over her eyes to shut out the sight of him! Sure, 'twas as if she'd seen a great hairy ape escaped from the Zoo!

YANK: [*stung—with a growl of rage*] Aw!

PADDY: And the loving way Yank heaved his shovel at the skull of her, only she was out the door! [*a grin breaking over his face*] 'Twas touching, I'm telling you! It put the touch of home, swate home in the stokehole. [*There is a roar of laughter from all.*]

YANK: [*glaring at* PADDY *menacingly*] Aw, choke dat off, see!

PADDY: [*not heeding him—to the others*] And her grabbin' at the Second's arm for protection. [*with a grotesque imitation of a woman's voice*] Kiss me, Engineer dear, for it's dark down here and me old man's in Wall Street making money! Hug me tight, darlin', for I'm afeerd in the dark and me mother's on deck makin' eyes at the skipper! [*Another roar of laughter.*]

YANK: [*threateningly*] Say! What yuh tryin' to do, kid me, yuh old Harp?

PADDY: Divil a bit! Ain't I wishin' myself you'd brained her?

YANK: [*fiercely*] I'll brain her! I'll brain her yet, wait 'n' see! [*coming over to* PADDY—*slowly*] Say, is dat what she called me—a hairy ape?

PADDY: She looked it at you if she didn't say the word itself.

YANK: [*grinning horribly*] Hairy ape, huh? Sure! Dat's de way she looked at me, aw right. Hairy ape! So dat's me, huh? [*bursting into rage—as if she were still in front of him*] Yuh skinny tart! Yuh white-faced bum, yuh! I'll show yuh who's a ape! [*turning to the others, bewilderment seizing him again*] Say, youse guys. I was bawlin' him out for pullin' de whistle on us. You heard me. And den I seen youse lookin' at somep'n and I tought he'd sneaked down to come up in back of me, and I hopped round to knock him dead wit de shovel. And dere she was wit de light on her! Christ, yuh coulda pushed me over with a finger! I was scared, get me? Sure! I tought she was a ghost, see? She was all in white like dey wrap around stiffs. You seen her. Kin yuh blame me? She didn't belong, dat's what. And den when I come to and seen it was a real skoit and seen de way she was lookin' at me—like Paddy said— Christ, I was sore, get me? I don't stand for dat stuff from nobody. And I flung de shovel—on'y she'd beat it. [*furiously*] I wished it'd banged her! I wished it'd knocked her block off!

LONG: And be 'anged for murder or 'lectrocuted? She ain't bleedin' well worth it.

YANK: I don't give a damn what! I'd be square wit her, wouldn't I? Tink I wanter let her put somep'n over on me? Tink I'm goin' to let her git away wit dat stuff? Yuh don't know me! No one ain't never put nothin' over on me and got away wit it, see!—not dat kind of stuff—no guy and no skoit neither! I'll fix her! Maybe she'll come down again—

VOICE: No chance, Yank. You scared her out of a year's growth.

YANK: I scared her? Why de hell should I scare her? Who de hell is she? Ain't she de same as me? Hairy ape, huh? [*with his old confident bravado*] I'll show her I'm better'n her, if she on'y knew it. I belong and she don't, see! I move and she's dead! Twenty-five knots a hour, dat's me! Dat carries her but I make dat. She's on'y baggage. Sure! [*again bewilderedly*] But, Christ, she was funny lookin'! Did yuh pipe her hands? White and skinny. Yuh could see de bones through 'em. And her mush, dat was dead white, too. And her eyes, dey was like dey'd seen a ghost. Me, dat was! Sure! Hairy ape! Ghost, huh? Look at dat arm! [*He extends his right arm, swelling out the great muscles.*] I coulda took her wit dat, wit just my little finger even, and broke her in two. [*again bewilderedly*] Say, who is dat skoit, huh? What is she? What's she come from? Who made her? Who give her de noive to look at me like dat? Dis ting's got my goat right. I don't get her. She's new to me. What does a skoit like her mean, huh? She don't belong, get me! I can't see her.

[*with growing anger*] But one ting I'm wise to, aw right, aw right! Youse all kin bet your shoits I'll git even wit her. I'll show her if she tinks she— She grinds de organ and I'm on de string, huh? I'll fix her! Let her come down again and I'll fling her in de furnace! She'll move den! She won't shiver at nothin', den! Speed, dat'll be her! She'll belong den! [*He grins horribly.*]

PADDY: She'll never come. She's had her belly-full, I'm telling you. She'll be in bed now, I'm thinking, wid ten doctors and nurses feedin' her salts to clean the fear out of her.

YANK: [*enraged*] Yuh tink I made her sick, too, do yuh? Just lookin' at me, huh? Hairy ape, huh? [*in a frenzy of rage*] I'll fix her! I'll tell her where to git off! She'll git down on her knees and take it back or I'll bust de face offen her! [*shaking one fist upward and beating on his chest with the other*] I'll find yuh! I'm comin', d'yuh hear? I'll fix yuh, God damn yuh! [*He makes a rush for the door.*]

VOICES: Stop him!
          He'll get shot!
          He'll murder her!
          Trip him up!
          Hold him!
          He's gone crazy!
          Gott, he's strong!
          Hold him down!
          Look out for a kick!
          Pin his arms!
          [*They have all piled on him and, after a fierce struggle, by sheer weight of numbers have borne him to the floor just inside the door.*]

PADDY: [*who has remained detached*] Kape him down till he's cooled off. [*scornfully*] Yerra, Yank, you're a great fool. Is it payin' attention at all you are to the like of that skinny sow widout one drop of rale blood in her?

YANK: [*frenziedly, from the bottom of the heap*] She done me doit! She done me doit, didn't she? I'll get square wit her! I'll get her some way! Git offen me, youse guys! Lemme up! I'll show her who's a ape!

CURTAIN

SCENE V

Three weeks later. A corner of Fifth Avenue in the Fifties on a fine Sunday morning. A general atmosphere of clean, well-tidied, wide street; a flood of mellow, tempered sunshine; gentle, genteel breezes. In the rear, the show windows of two shops, a jewelry establishment on the corner, a furrier's next to it. Here the adornments of extreme wealth are tantalizingly displayed. The jeweler's window is gaudy with glittering diamonds, emeralds, rubies, pearls, etc., fashioned in ornate tiaras, crowns, necklaces, collars, etc. From each piece hangs an enormous tag from which a dollar sign and numerals in intermittent electric lights wink out the incredible prices. The same in the furrier's. Rich furs of all varieties hang there bathed in a downpour of artificial light. The general effect is of a background of magnificence cheapened and made grotesque by commercialism, a background in tawdry disharmony with the clear light and sunshine on the street itself.

Up the side street YANK *and* LONG *come swaggering.* LONG *is dressed in shore clothes, wears a black Windsor tie, cloth cap.* YANK *is in his dirty dungarees. A fireman's cap with black peak is cocked defiantly on the side of his head. He has not shaved for days and around his fierce, resentful eyes—as around those of* LONG *to a lesser degree—the black smudge of coal dust still sticks like make-up. They hesitate and stand together at the corner, swaggering, looking about them with a forced, defiant contempt.*

LONG: [*indicating it all with an oratorical gesture*] Well, 'ere we are. Fif' Avenoo. This 'ere's their bleedin' private lane, as yer might say. [*bitterly*] We're trespassers 'ere. Proletarians keep orf the grass!

YANK: [*dully*] I don't see no grass, yuh boob. [*staring at the sidewalk*] Clean, ain't it? Yuh could eat a fried egg offen it. The white wings got some job sweepin' dis up. [*looking up and down the avenue–surlily*] Where's all de white-collar stiffs yuh said was here—and de skoits—*her* kind?

LONG: In church, blarst 'em! Arskin' Jesus to give 'em more money.

YANK: Choich, huh? I useter go to choich onct—sure—when I was a kid. Me old man and woman, dey made me. Dey never went demselves, dough. Always got too big a head on Sunday mornin', dat was dem. [*with a grin*] Dey was scrappers for fair, bot' of dem. On Satiday nights when dey bot' got a skinful dey could put up a bout oughter been staged at de Garden. When dey got trough dere wasn't a chair or table wit a leg under it. Or else dey bot' jumped on me for somep'n. Dat was where I loined to take punishment. [*with a grin and a swagger*] I'm a chip offen de old block, get me?

LONG: Did yer old man follow the sea?

YANK: Naw. Worked along shore. I runned away when me old lady croaked wit de tremens. I helped at truckin' and in de market. Den I shipped in de stokehole. Sure. Dat belongs. De rest was nothin'. [*looking around him*] I ain't never seen dis before. De Brooklyn waterfront, dat was where I was dragged up. [*taking a deep breath*] Dis ain't so bad at dat, huh?

LONG: Not bad? Well, we pays for it wiv our bloody sweat, if yer wants to know!

YANK: [*with sudden angry disgust*] Aw, hell! I don't see no one, see—like her. All dis gives me a pain. It don't belong. Say, ain't dere a back room around dis dump? Let's go shoot a ball. All dis is too clean and quiet and dolled-up, get me! It gives me a pain.

LONG: Wait and yer'll bloody well see—

YANK: I don't wait for no one. I keep on de move. Say, what yuh drag me up here for, anyway? Tryin' to kid me, yuh simp, yuh?

LONG: Yer wants to get back at 'er, don't yer? That's what yer been sayin' every bloomin' hour since she hinsulted yer.

YANK: [*vehemently*] Sure ting I do! Didn't I try to get even wit her in Southampton? Didn't I sneak on de dock and wait for her by de gangplank? I was goin' to spit in her pale mug, see! Sure, right in her pop-eyes! Dat woulda made me even, see? But no chanct. Dere was a whole army of plainclothes bulls around. Dey spotted me and gimme de bum's rush. I never seen her. But I'll git square wit her yet, you watch! [*furiously*] De lousy tart! She tinks she kin get away wit moider—but not wit me! I'll fix her! I'll tink of a way!

LONG: [*as disgusted as he dares to be*] Ain't that why I brought yer up 'ere—to show yer? Yer been lookin' at this 'ere 'ole affair wrong. Yer been actin' an' talkin' 's if it was all a bleedin' personal matter between yer and that bloody cow. I wants to convince yer she was on'y a representative of 'er clarss. I wants to awaken yer bloody clarss consciousness. Then yer'll see it's 'er clarss yer've got to fight, not 'er alone. There's a 'ole mob of 'em like 'er, Gawd blind 'em!

YANK: [*spitting on his hands–belligerently*] De more de merrier when I gits started. Bring on de gang!

LONG: Yer'll see 'em in arf a mo', when that church lets out. [*He turns and sees the window display in the two stores for the first time.*] Blimey! Look at that, will yer? [*They both walk back and stand looking in the jeweler's.* LONG *flies into a fury.*] Just look at this 'ere bloomin' mess! Just look at it! Look at the bleedin' prices on 'em—more'n our 'ole bloody stokehole makes in ten voyages sweatin' in 'ell! And they—'er and 'er bloody clarss—buys 'em for toys to dangle on 'em! One of these 'ere would buy scoff for a starvin' family for a year!

YANK: Aw, cut de sob stuff! T' hell wit de starvin' family. Yuh'll be passin' de hat to me next. [*with naïve admiration*] Say, dem tings is pretty, huh? Bet yuh dey'd hock for a piece of change aw right. [*then turning away, bored*] But, aw hell, what good are dey? Let her have 'em. Dey don't belong no more'n she does. [*with a gesture of sweeping the jewelers into oblivion*] All dat don't count, get me?

LONG: [*who has moved to the furrier's—indignantly*] And I s'pose this 'ere don't neither—skins of poor, 'armless animals slaughtered so as 'er and 'ers can keep their bleedin' noses warm!

YANK: [*who has been staring at something inside–with queer excitement*] Take a slant at dat! Give it de once-over! Monkey fur—two t'ousand bucks! [*bewilderedly*] Is dat straight goods—monkey fur? What de hell—?

LONG: [*bitterly*] It's straight enuf. [*with grim humor*] They wouldn't bloody well pay that for a 'airy ape's skin—no, nor for the 'ole livin' ape with all 'is 'ead, and body, and soul thrown in!

YANK: [*clenching his fists, his face growing pale with rage as if the skin in the window were a personal insult*] Trowin' it up in my face! Christ! I'll fix her!

LONG: [*excitedly*] Church is out. 'Ere they come, the bleedin' swine. [*after a glance at* YANK's *lowering face—uneasily*] Easy goes, Comrade. Keep yer bloomin' temper. Remember force defeats itself. It ain't our weapon. We must impress our demands through peaceful means—the votes of the on-marching proletarians of the bloody world!

YANK: [*with abysmal contempt*] Votes, hell! Votes is a joke, see. Votes for women! Let dem do it!

LONG: [*still more uneasily*] Calm, now. Treat 'em wiv the proper contempt. Observe the bleedin' parasites but 'old yer 'orses.

YANK: [*angrily*] Git away from me! Yuh're yellow, dat's what. Force, dat's me! De punch, dat's me every time, see!

   [*The crowd from church enter from the right, sauntering slowly and affectedly, their heads held stiffly up, looking neither to right nor left, talking in toneless, simpering voices. The women are rouged, cal-cimined, dyed, overdressed to the nth degree. The men are in Prince Alberts, high hats, spats, canes, etc. A procession of gaudy marionettes, yet with something of the relentless horror of Frankensteins in their detached, mechanical unawareness.*]

VOICES: Dear Doctor Caiaphas! He is so sincere!
   What was the sermon? I dozed off.
   About the radicals, my dear—and the false doctrines that are being preached.
   We must organize a hundred per cent American bazaar.
   And let everyone contribute one one-hundredth per cent of their income tax.
   What an original idea!
   We can devote the proceeds to rehabilitating the veil of the temple.
   But that has been done so many times.

YANK: [*glaring from one to the other of them—with an insulting snort of scorn*] Huh! Huh! [*Without seeming to see him, they make wide detours to avoid the spot where he stands in the middle of the sidewalk.*]

LONG: [*frightenedly*] Keep yer bloomin' mouth shut, I tells yer.

YANK: [*viciously*] G'wan! Tell it to Sweeney! [*He swaggers away and deliberately lurches into a top-hatted gentleman, then glares at him pugnaciously.*] Say, who d'yuh tink yuh're bumpin'? Tink yuh own de oith?

GENTLEMAN: [*coldly and affectedly*] I beg your pardon. [*He has not looked at* YANK *and passes on without a glance, leaving him bewildered.*]

LONG: [*rushing up and grabbing* YANK's *arm*] 'Ere! Come away! This wasn't what I meant. Yer'll 'ave the bloody coppers down on us.

YANK: [*savagely—giving him a push that sends him sprawling*] G'wan!

LONG: [*picks himself up—hysterically*] I'll pop orf then. This ain't what I meant. And whatever 'appens, yer can't blame me. [*He slinks off left.*]

YANK: T' hell wit youse! [*He approaches a lady—with a vicious grin and a smirking wink.*] Hello, Kiddo. How's every little ting? Got anyting on for tonight? I know an old boiler down to de docks we kin crawl into. [*The lady stalks by without a look, without a change of pace.* YANK *turns to others—insultingly.*] Holy smokes, what a mug! Go hide yuhself before de horses shy at yuh. Gee, pipe de heine on dat one! Say, youse, yuh look like de stoin of a ferryboat. Paint and powder! All dolled up to kill! Yuh look like stiffs laid out for de boneyard! Aw, g'wan, de lot of youse! Yuh give me de eye-ache. Yuh don't belong, get me! Look at me, why don't youse dare? I belong, dat's me! [*pointing to a skyscraper across the street which is in process of construction—with bravado*] See dat building goin' up dere? See de steel work? Steel, dat's me! Youse guys live on it and tink yuh're somep'n. But I'm *in* it, see! I'm de hoistin' engine dat makes it go up! I'm it—de inside and bottom of it! Sure! I'm steel and steam and smoke and de rest of it! It moves—speed—twenty-five stories up—and me at de top and bottom—movin'! Youse simps don't move. Yuh're on'y dolls I winds up to see 'm spin. Yuh're de garbage, get me—de leavins—de ashes we dump over de side! Now, what 'a' yuh gotta say? [*But as they seem neither to see nor hear him, he flies into a fury.*] Bums! Pigs! Tarts! Bitches! [*He turns in a rage on the men, bumping viciously into them but not jarring them the least bit. Rather it is he who recoils after each collision. He keeps growling.*] Git off de oith! G'wan, yuh bum! Look where yuh're goin', can't yuh? Git outa here! Fight, why don't yuh? Put up yer mits! Don't be a dog! Fight or I'll knock yuh dead!

> [*But, without seeming to see him, they all answer with mechanical affected politeness*]:

I beg your pardon. [*Then at a cry from one of the women, they all scurry to the furrier's window.*]

THE WOMAN: [*ecstatically, with a gasp of delight*] Monkey fur! [*The whole crowd of men and women chorus after her in the same tone of affected delight.*] Monkey fur!

YANK: [*with a jerk of his head back on his shoulders, as if he had received a punch full in the face—raging*] I see yuh, all in white! I see yuh, yuh white-faced tart, yuh! Hairy ape, huh? I'll hairy ape yuh!

> [*He bends down and grips at the street curbing as if to pluck it out and hurl it. Foiled in this, snarling with passion, he leaps to the lamp-post on the corner and tries to pull it up for a club. Just at that moment a bus is heard rumbling up. A fat, high-hatted, spatted gentleman runs out from the side street. He calls out plaintively*]: Bus! Bus! Stop there! [*and runs full tilt into the bending, straining* YANK, *who is bowled off his balance.*]

YANK: [*seeing a fight—with a roar of joy as he springs to his feet*] At last! Bus, huh? I'll bust yuh! [*He lets drive a terrific swing, his fist landing full on the fat gentleman's face. But the gentleman stands unmoved as if nothing had happened.*]

GENTLEMAN: I beg your pardon. [*then irritably*] You have made me lose my bus. [*He claps his hands and begins to scream*]: Officer! Officer!

[*Many police whistles shrill out on the instant and a whole platoon of policemen rush in on* YANK *from all sides. He tries to fight but is clubbed to the pavement and fallen upon. The crowd at the window have not moved or noticed this disturbance. The clanging gong of the patrol wagon approaches with a clamoring din.*]

CURTAIN

SCENE VI

Night of the following day. A row of cells in the prison on Blackwells Island. The cells extend back diagonally from right front to left rear. They do not stop, but disappear in the dark background as if they ran on, numberless, into infinity. One electric bulb from the low ceiling of the narrow corridor sheds its light through the heavy steel bars of the cell at the extreme front and reveals part of the interior. YANK *can be seen within, crouched on the edge of his cot in the attitude of Rodin's "The Thinker." His face is spotted with black and blue bruises. A blood-stained bandage is wrapped around his head.*

YANK: [*suddenly starting as if awakening from a dream, reaches out and shakes the bars—aloud to himself, wonderingly*] Steel. Dis is de Zoo, huh? [*A burst of hard, barking laughter comes from the unseen occupants of the cells, runs back down the tier, and abruptly ceases.*]

VOICES: [*mockingly*] The Zoo? That's a new name for this coop—a damn good name!
Steel, eh? You said a mouthful. This is the old iron house.
Who is that boob talkin'?
He's the bloke they brung in out of his head. The bulls had beat him up fierce.

YANK: [*dully*] I musta been dreamin'. I tought I was in a cage at de Zoo—but de apes don't talk, do dey?

VOICES: [*with mocking laughter*] You're in a cage aw right.
A coop!
A pen!
A sty!
A kennel! [*Hard laughter—a pause.*]
Say, guy! Who are you? No, never mind lying. What are you?
Yes, tell us your sad story. What's your game?
What did they jug yuh for?

YANK: [*dully*] I was a fireman—stokin' on de liners. [*then with sudden rage, rattling his cell bars*] I'm a hairy ape, get me? And I'll bust youse all in de jaw if yuh don't lay off kiddin' me.

VOICES: Huh! You're a hard boiled duck, ain't you!
When you spit, it bounces! [*Laughter.*]

Aw, can it. He's a regular guy. Ain't you?

What did he say he was—a ape?

YANK: [*defiantly*] Sure ting! Ain't dat what youse all are—apes?

[*A silence. Then a furious rattling of bars from down the corridor.*]

A VOICE: [*thick with rage*] I'll show yuh who's a ape, yuh bum!

VOICES: Ssshh! Nix!

Can de noise!

Piano!

You'll have the guard down on us!

YANK: [*scornfully*] De guard? Yuh mean de keeper, don't yuh?

[*Angry exclamations from all the cells.*]

VOICE: [*placatingly*] Aw, don't pay no attention to him. He's off his nut from the beatin'-up he got. Say, you guy! We're waitin' to hear what they landed you for—or ain't yuh tellin'?

YANK: Sure, I'll tell youse. Sure! Why de hell not? On'y—youse won't get me. Nobody gets me but me, see? I started to tell de Judge and all he says was: "Toity days to tink it over." Tink it over! Christ, dat's all I been doin' for weeks! [*after a pause*] I was tryin' to git even wit someone, see?—someone dat done me doit.

VOICES: [*cynically*] De old stuff, I bet. Your goil, huh?

Give yuh the double-cross, huh?

That's them every time!

Did yuh beat up de odder guy?

YANK: [*disgustedly*] Aw, yuh're all wrong! Sure dere was a skoit in it—but not what youse mean, not dat old tripe. Dis was a new kind of skoit. She was dolled up all in white—in de stokehole. I tought she was a ghost. Sure. [*A pause.*]

VOICES: [*whispering*] Gee, he's still nutty.

Let him rave. It's fun listenin'.

YANK: [*unheeding—groping in his thoughts*] Her hands—dey was skinny and white like dey wasn't real but painted on somep'n. Dere was a million miles from me to her—twenty-five knots a hour. She was like some dead ting de cat brung in. Sure, dat's what. She didn't belong. She belonged in de window of a toy store, or on de top of a garbage can, see! Sure! [*He breaks out angrily.*] But would yuh believe it, she had de noive to do me doit. She lamped me like she was seein' somep'n broke loose from de menagerie. Christ, yuh'd oughter seen her eyes! [*He rattles the bars of his cell furiously.*] But I'll get back at her yet, you watch! And if I can't find her I'll take it out on de gang she runs wit. I'm wise to where dey hangs out now. I'll show her who belongs! I'll show her who's in de move and who ain't. You watch my smoke!

VOICES: [*serious and joking*] Dat's de talkin'!

Take her for all she's got!

What was this dame, anyway? Who was she, eh?

YANK: I dunno. First cabin stiff. Her old man's a millionaire, dey says—name of Douglas.

VOICES: Douglas? That's the president of the Steel Trust, I bet.

Sure. I seen his mug in de papers.

He's filthy with dough.

VOICE: Hey, feller, take a tip from me. If you want to get back at that dame, you better join the Wobblies. You'll get some action then.

YANK: Wobblies? What de hell's dat?

VOICE: A gang of blokes—a tough gang. I been readin' about 'em today in the paper. The guard give me the *Sunday Times*. There's a long spiel about 'em. It's from a speech made in the Senate by a guy named Senator Queen. [*He is in the cell next to* YANK's. *There is a rustling of paper.*] Wait'll I see if I got light enough and I'll read you. Listen. [*He reads.*] "There is a menace existing in this country today which threatens the vitals of our fair Republic—as foul a menace against the very life-blood of the American Eagle as was the foul conspiracy of Catiline against the eagles of ancient Rome!"

VOICE: [*disgustedly*] Aw, hell! Tell him to salt de tail of dat eagle!

VOICE: [*reading*] "I refer to that devil's brew of rascals, jailbirds, murderers and cutthroats who libel all honest working men by calling themselves the Industrial Workers of the World; but in the light of their nefarious plots, I call them the Industrious *Wreckers* of the World!"

YANK: [*with vengeful satisfaction*] Wreckers, dat's de right dope! Dat belongs! Me for dem!

VOICE: Ssshh! [*reading*] "This fiendish organization is a foul ulcer on the fair body of our Democracy—"

VOICE: Democracy, hell! Give him the boid, fellers—the raspberry! [*They do.*]

VOICE: Ssshh! [*reading*] "Like Cato I say to this Senate, the I. W. W. must be destroyed! For they represent an ever-present dagger pointed at the heart of the greatest nation the world has ever known, where all men are born free and equal, with equal opportunities to all, where the Founding Fathers have guaranteed to each one happiness, where Truth, Honor, Liberty, Justice, and the Brotherhood of Man are a religion absorbed with one's mother's milk, taught at our father's knee, sealed, signed, and stamped upon in the glorious Constitution of these United States!" [*A perfect storm of hisses, catcalls, boos, and hard laughter.*]

VOICES: [*scornfully*] Hurrah for de Fort' of July!

Pass de hat!

Liberty!

Justice!

Honor!

Opportunity!

Brotherhood!

ALL: [with abysmal scorn] Aw, hell!

VOICE: Give that Queen Senator guy the bark! All togedder now—one—two—tree— [A terrific chorus of barking and yapping.]

GUARD: [from a distance] Quiet there, youse—or I'll git the hose.
          [The noise subsides.]

YANK: [with growling rage] I'd like to catch dat senator guy alone for a second. I'd loin him some trute!

VOICE: Ssshh! Here's where he gits down to cases on the Wobblies. [reads] "They plot with fire in one hand and dynamite in the other. They stop not before murder to gain their ends, nor at the outraging of defenseless womanhood. They would tear down society, put the lowest scum in the seats of the mighty, turn Almighty God's revealed plan for the world topsy-turvy, and make of our sweet and lovely civilization a shambles, a desolation where man, God's masterpiece, would soon degenerate back to the ape!"

VOICE: [to YANK] Hey, you guy. There's your ape stuff again.

YANK: [with a growl of fury] I got him. So dey blow up tings, do dey? Dey turn tings round, do dey? Hey, lend me dat paper, will yuh?

VOICE: Sure. Give it to him. On'y keep it to yourself, see. We don't wanter listen to no more of that slop.

VOICE: Here you are. Hide it under your mattress.

YANK: [reaching out] Tanks. I can't read much but I kin manage. [He sits, the paper in the hand at his side, in the attitude of Rodin's "The Thinker." A pause. Several snores from down the corridor. Suddenly YANK jumps to his feet with a furious groan as if some appalling thought had crashed on him—bewilderedly.] Sure—her old man—president of de Steel Trust—makes half de steel in de world—steel—where I tought I belonged—drivin' trou—movin'—in dat—to make her—and cage me in for her to spit on! Christ! [He shakes the bars of his cell door till the whole tier trembles. Irritated, protesting exclamations from those awakened or trying to get to sleep.] He made dis—dis cage! Steel! It don't belong, dat's what! Cages, cells, locks, bolts, bars—dat's what it means!—holdin' me down wit him at de top! But I'll drive trou! Fire, dat melts it! I'll be fire—under de heap—fire dat never goes out—hot as hell—breakin' out in de night—[While he has been saying this last he has shaken his cell door to a clanging accompaniment. As he comes to the "breakin' out" he seizes one bar with both hands and, putting his two feet up against the others so that his position is parallel to the floor like a monkey's, he gives a great wrench backwards. The bar bends like a licorice stick under his tremendous strength. Just at this moment the PRISON GUARD rushes in, dragging a hose behind him.]

GUARD: [angrily] I'll loin youse bums to wake me up! [sees YANK] Hello, it's you, huh? Got the D. Ts., hey? Well, I'll cure 'em. I'll drown your snakes for yuh! [noticing the bar] Hell, look at dat bar bended! On'y a bug is strong enough for dat!

YANK: [*glaring at him*] Or a hairy ape, yuh big yellow bum! Look out! Here I
come! [*He grabs another bar.*]

GUARD: [*scared now—yelling off left*] Toin de hose on, Ben!—full pressure! And
call de others—and a straitjacket!

> [*The curtain is falling. As it hides* YANK *from view, there is a splattering
> smash as the stream of water hits the steel of* YANK'S *cell.*]

CURTAIN

SCENE VII

*Nearly a month later. An I. W. W. local near the waterfront, showing the interior
of a front room on the ground floor, and the street outside. Moonlight on the narrow
street, buildings massed in black shadow. The interior of the room, which is general
assembly room, office, and reading room, resembles some dingy settlement boys'
club. A desk and high stool are in one corner. A table with papers, stacks of
pamphlets, chairs about it, is at center. The whole is decidedly cheap, banal,
commonplace and unmysterious as a room could well be. The secretary is perched on
the stool making entries in a large ledger. An eye shade casts his face into shadows.
Eight or ten men, longshoremen, iron workers, and the like, are grouped about the
table. Two are playing checkers. One is writing a letter. Most of them are smoking
pipes. A big signboard is on the wall at the rear, "Industrial Workers of the World—
Local No. 57."*

> [YANK *comes down the street outside. He is dressed as in Scene Five. He
> moves cautiously, mysteriously. He comes to a point opposite the door;
> tiptoes softly up to it, listens, is impressed by the silence within, knocks
> carefully, as if he were guessing at the password to some secret rite.
> Listens. No answer. Knocks again a bit louder. No answer. Knocks
> impatiently, much louder.*]

SECRETARY: [*turning around on his stool*] What the hell is that—someone knocking? [*shouts*] Come in, why don't you?

> [*All the men in the room look up.* YANK *opens the door slowly, gingerly, as
> if afraid of an ambush. He looks around for secret doors, mystery, is
> taken aback by the commonplaceness of the room and the men in it,
> thinks he may have gotten in the wrong place, then sees the signboard on
> the wall and is reassured.*]

YANK: [*blurts out*] Hello.

MEN: [*reservedly*] Hello.

YANK: [*more easily*] I tought I'd bumped into de wrong dump.

SECRETARY: [*scrutinizing him carefully*] Maybe you have. Are you a member?

YANK: Naw, not yet. Dat's what I come for—to join.

SECRETARY: That's easy. What's your job—longshore?

YANK: Naw. Fireman—stoker on de liners.

SECRETARY: [*with satisfaction*] Welcome to our city. Glad to know you people are waking up at last. We haven't got many members in your line.

YANK: Naw. Dey're all dead to de woild.

SECRETARY: Well, you can help to wake 'em. What's your name? I'll make out your card.

YANK: [*confused*] Name? Lemme tink.

SECRETARY: [*sharply*] Don't you know your own name?

YANK: Sure; but I been just Yank for so long—Bob, dat's it—Bob Smith.

SECRETARY: [*writing*] Robert Smith. [*fills out the rest of card*] Here you are. Cost you half a dollar.

YANK: Is dat all—four bits? Dat's easy. [*gives the Secretary the money*]

SECRETARY: [*throwing it in drawer*] Thanks. Well, make yourself at home. No introductions needed. There's literature on the table. Take some of those pamphlets with you to distribute aboard ship. They may bring results. Sow the seed, only go about it right. Don't get caught and fired. We got plenty out of work. What we need is men who can hold their jobs—and work for us at the same time.

YANK: Sure. [*But he still stands, embarrassed and uneasy.*]

SECRETARY: [*looking at him—curiously*] What did you knock for? Think we had a coon in uniform to open doors?

YANK: Naw. I tought it was locked—and dat yuh'd wanter give me the once-over trou a peep-hole or somep'n to see if I was right.

SECRETARY: [*alert and suspicious but with an easy laugh*] Think we were running a crap game? That door is never locked. What put that in your nut?

YANK: [*with a knowing grin, convinced that this is all camouflage, a part of the secrecy*] Dis burg is full of bulls, ain't it?

SECRETARY: [*sharply*] What have the cops got to do with us? We're breaking no laws.

YANK: [*with a knowing wink*] Sure. Youse wouldn't for woilds. Sure. I'm wise to dat.

SECRETARY: You seem to be wise to a lot of stuff none of us knows about.

YANK: [*with another wink*] Aw, dat's aw right, see. [*then made a bit resentful by the suspicious glances from all sides*] Aw, can it! Youse needn't put me trou de toid degree. Can't youse see I belong? Sure! I'm reg'lar. I'll stick, get me? I'll shoot de woiks for youse. Dat's why I wanted to join in.

SECRETARY: [*breezily, feeling him out*] That's the right spirit. Only are you sure you understand what you've joined? It's all plain and above board; still, some guys get a wrong slant on us. [*sharply*] What's your notion of the purpose of the I. W. W.?

YANK: Aw, I know all about it.

SECRETARY: [*sarcastically*] Well, give us some of your valuable information.

YANK: [*cunningly*] I know enough not to speak outa my toin. [*then resentfully again*] Aw, say! I'm reg'lar. I'm wise to de game. I know yuh got to watch your step wit a stranger. For all youse know, I might be a plain-clothes dick, or somep'n, dat's what yuh're tinkin', huh? Aw, forget it! I belong, see? Ask any guy down to de docks if I don't.

SECRETARY: Who said you didn't?

YANK: After I'm 'nitiated, I'll show yuh.

SECRETARY: [*astounded*] Initiated? There's no initiation.

YANK: [*disappointed*] Ain't there no password—no grip nor nothin'?

SECRETARY: What'd you think this is—the Elks—or the Black Hand?

YANK: De Elks, hell! De Black Hand, dey're a lot of yellow back-stickin' Ginees. Naw. Dis is a man's gang, ain't it?

SECRETARY: You said it! That's why we stand on our two feet in the open. We got no secrets.

YANK: [*surprised but admiringly*] Yuh mean to say yuh always run wide open—like dis?

SECRETARY: Exactly.

YANK: Den yuh sure got your noive wit youse!

SECRETARY: [*sharply*] Just what was it made you want to join us? Come out with that straight.

YANK: Yuh call me? Well, I got noive, too! Here's my hand. Yuh wanter blow tings up, don't yuh? Well, dat's me! I belong!

SECRETARY: [*with pretended carelessness*] You mean change the unequal conditions of society by legitimate direct action—or with dynamite?

YANK: Dynamite! Blow if offen de oith—steel—all de cages—all de factories, steamers, buildings, jails—de Steel Trust and all dat makes it go.

SECRETARY: So—that's your idea, eh? And did you have any special job in that line you wanted to propose to us? [*He makes a sign to the men, who get up cautiously one by one and group behind* YANK.]

YANK: [*boldy*] Sure, I'll come out wit it. I'll show youse I'm one of de gang. Dere's dat millionaire guy, Douglas—

SECRETARY: President of the Steel Trust, you mean? Do you want to assassinate him?

YANK: Naw, dat don't get yuh nothin'. I mean blow up de factory, de woiks, where he makes de steel. Dat's what I'm after—to blow up de steel, knock all de steel in de woild up to de moon. Dat'll fix tings! [*eagerly, with a touch of bravado*] I'll do it by me lonesome! I'll show yuh! Tell me where his woiks is, how to get there, all de dope. Gimme de stuff, de old butter—and watch me do de rest! Watch de smoke and see it move! I don't give a damn if dey nab me—long as it's done! I'll soive life for it—and give 'em de laugh! [*half to himself*] And I'll write her a letter and tell her de hairy ape done it. Dat'll square tings.

SECRETARY: [*stepping away from* YANK] Very interesting. [*He gives a signal. The men, huskies all, throw themselves on* YANK *and before he knows it they have his legs and arms pinioned. But he is too flabbergasted to make a struggle, anyway. They feel him over for weapons.*]

MAN: No gat, no knife. Shall we give him what's what and put the boots to him?

SECRETARY: No. He isn't worth the trouble we'd get into. He's too stupid. [*He comes closer and laughs mockingly in* YANK's *face.*] Ho-ho! By God, this is the biggest joke they've put up on us yet. Hey, you Joke! Who sent you—Burns or Pinkerton? No, by God, you're such a bonehead I'll bet you're in the Secret Service! Well, you dirty spy, you rotten agent provocator, you can go back and tell whatever skunk is paying you blood-money for betraying your brothers that he's wasting his coin. You couldn't catch a cold. And tell him that all he'll ever get on us, or ever has got, is just his own sneaking plots that he's framed up to put us in jail. We are what our manifesto says we are, neither more nor less—and we'll give him a copy of that any time he calls. And as for you— [*He glares scornfully at* YANK, *who is sunk in an oblivious stupor.*] Oh, hell, what's the use of talking? You're a brainless ape.

YANK: [*aroused by the word to fierce but futile struggles*] What's dat, yuh Sheeny bum, yuh!

SECRETARY: Throw him out, boys.

> [*In spite of his struggles, this is done with gusto and éclat. Propelled by several parting kicks,* YANK *lands sprawling in the middle of the narrow cobbled street. With a growl he starts to get up and storm the closed door, but stops bewildered by the confusions in his brain, pathetically impotent. He sits there brooding, in as near to the attitude of Rodin's "Thinker" as he can get in his position.*]

YANK: [*bitterly*] So dem boids don't tink I belong, neider. Aw, to hell wit 'em! Dey're in de wrong pew—de same old bull—soap-boxes and Salvation Army—no guts! Cut out an hour offen de job a day and make me happy! Gimme a dollar more a day and make me happy! Tree square a day, and cauliflowers in de front yard—ekal rights—a woman and kids—a lousy vote—and I'm all fixed for Jesus, huh? Aw, hell! What does dat get yuh? Dis ting's in your inside, but it ain't your belly. Feedin' your face—sinkers and coffee—dat don't touch it. It's way down—at de bottom. Yuh can't grab it, and yuh can't stop it. It moves, and everything moves. It stops and de whole woild stops. Dat's me now—I don't tick, see?—I'm a busted Ingersoll, dat's what. Steel was me, and I owned de woild. Now I ain't steel, and de woild owns me. Aw, hell! I can't see—it's all dark, get me? It's all wrong! [*He turns a bitter mocking face up like an ape gibbering at the moon.*] Say, youse up dere, Man in de Moon, yuh look so wise, gimme de answer, huh? Slip me de inside dope, de information right from de stable—where do I get off at, huh?

A POLICEMAN: [*who has come up the street in time to hear this last—with grim humor*] You'll get off at the station, you boob, if you don't get up out of that and keep movin'.

YANK: [*looking up at him—with a hard, bitter laugh*] Sure! Lock me up! Put me in a cage! Dat's de on'y answer yuh know. G'wan, lock me up!

POLICEMAN: What you been doin'?

YANK: Enuf to gimme life for! I was born, see? Sure, dat's de charge. Write it in de blotter. I was born, get me!

POLICEMAN: [*jocosely*] God pity your old woman! [*then matter-of-fact*] But I've no time for kidding. You're soused. I'd run you in but it's too long a walk to the station. Come on now, get up, or I'll fan your ears with this club. Beat it now! [*He hauls* YANK *to his feet.*]

YANK: [*in a vague mocking tone*] Say, where do I go from here?

POLICEMAN: [*giving him a push—with a grin, indifferently*] Go to hell.

CURTAIN

SCENE VIII

Twilight of the next day. the monkey house at the Zoo. One spot of clear gray light falls on the front of one cage so that the interior can be seen. The other cages are vague, shrouded in shadow from which chatterings pitched in a conversational tone can be heard. On the one cage a sign from which the word "gorilla" stands out. The gigantic animal himself is seen squatting on his haunches on a bench in much the same attitude as Rodin's "Thinker." YANK enters from the left. Immediately a chorus of angry chattering and screeching breaks out. The gorilla turns his eyes but makes no sound or move.

YANK: [*with a hard, bitter laugh*] Welcome to your city, huh? Hail, hail, de gang's all here! [*At the sound of his voice the chattering dies away into an attentive silence.* YANK *walks up to the gorilla's cage and, leaning over the railing, stares in at its occupant, who stares back at him, silent and motionless. There is a pause of dead stillness. Then* YANK *begins to talk in a friendly confidential tone, half-mockingly, but with a deep undercurrent of sympathy.*] Say, yuh're some hard-lookin' guy, ain't yuh? I seen lots of tough nuts dat de gang called gorillas, but yuh're de foist real one I ever seen. Some chest yuh got, and shoulders, and dem arms and mits! I bet yuh got a punch in eider fist dat'd knock 'em all silly! [*This with genuine admiration. The gorilla, as if he understood, stands upright, swelling out his chest and pounding on it with his fist.* YANK *grins sympathetically.*] Sure, I get yuh. Yuh challenge de whole woild, huh? Yuh got what I was sayin' even if yuh muffed de woids. [*then bitterness creeping in*] And why wouldn't yuh get me? Ain't we both members of de same club—de Hairy Apes? [*They stare at each other—a pause—then* YANK *goes on slowly and bitterly.*] So yuh're what she seen when she looked at me, de white-faced tart! I was you to her, get me? On'y outa de cage—broke out—free to moider her, see? Sure! Dat's what she tought. She wasn't wise dat I was in a cage, too—worser'n yours—sure—a damn sight—'cause you got some chanct to bust loose—but me— [*He grows confused.*] Aw, hell! It's all wrong, ain't it? [*A pause.*] I s'pose yuh wanter know what I'm doin' here, huh? I been warmin' a bench down to de

Battery—ever since last night. Sure. I seen de sun come up. Dat was pretty,
too—all red and pink and green. I was lookin' at de skyscrapers—steel—and
all de ships comin' in, sailin' out, all over de oith—and dey was steel, too.
De sun was warm, dey wasn't no clouds, and dere was a breeze blowin'.
Sure, it was great stuff. I got it aw right—what Paddy said about dat bein' de
right dope—on'y I couldn't get *in* it, see? I couldn't belong in dat. It was over
my head. And I kept tinkin'—and den I beat it up here to see what youse was
like. And I waited till dey was all gone to git yuh alone. Say, how d'yuh feel
sittin' in dat pen all de time, havin' to stand for 'em comin' and starin' at
yuh—de white-faced, skinny tarts and de boobs what marry 'em—makin'
fun of yuh, laughin' at yuh, gittin' scared of you—damn 'em! [*He pounds on
the rail with his fist. The gorilla rattles the bars of his cage and snarls. All the
other monkeys set up an angry chattering in the darkness.* YANK *goes on
excitedly.*] Sure! Dat's de way it hits me, too. On'y yuh're lucky, see? Yuh
don't belong wit 'em and yuh know it. But me, I belong wit 'em—but I don't,
see? Dey don't belong wit me, dat's what. Get me? Tinkin' is hard— [*He
passes one hand across his forehead with a painful gesture. The gorilla growls
impatiently.* YANK *goes on gropingly.*] It's dis way, what I'm drivin' at. Youse
can sit and dope dream in de past, green woods, de jungle and de rest of it.
Den yuh belong and dey don't. Den yuh kin laugh at 'em, see? Yuh're de
champ of de woild. But me—I ain't got no past to tink in, nor nothin' dat's
comin', on'y what's now—and dat don't belong. Sure, you're de best off!
Yuh can't tink, can yuh? Yuh can't talk neider. But I kin make a bluff at
talkin' and tinkin'—a'most git away wit it—a'most!—and dat's where de
joker comes in. [*He laughs.*] I ain't on oith and I ain't in heaven, get me? I'm
in de middle tryin' to separate 'em, takin' all de woist punches from bot' of
'em. Maybe dat's what dey call hell, huh? But you, yuh're at de bottom. You
belong! Sure! Yuh're de on'y one in de woild dat does, yuh lucky stiff! [*The
gorilla growls proudly.*] And dat's why dey gotter put yuh in a cage, see? [*The
gorilla roars angrily.*] Sure! Yuh get me. It beats it when you try to tink it or
talk it—it's way down—deep—behind—you 'n' me we feel it. Sure! Bot'
members of dis club! [*He laughs—then in a savage tone*] What de hell! T'
hell wit it! A little action, dat's our meat! Dat belongs! Knock 'em down and
keep bustin' 'em till dey croak yuh wit a gat—wit steel! Sure! Are yuh game?
Dey've looked at youse, ain't dey—in a cage? Wanter git even? Wanter wind
up like a sport 'stead of croakin' slow in dere? [*The gorilla roars an emphatic
affirmative.* YANK *goes on with a sort of furious exaltation.*] Sure! Yuh're
reg'lar! Yuh'll stick to de finish! Me 'n' you, huh?—bot' members of this
club! We'll put up one last star bout dat'll knock 'em offen deir seats! Dey'll
have to make de cages stronger after we're trou! [*The gorilla is straining at his
bars, growling, hopping from one foot to the other.* YANK *takes a jimmy from
under his coat and forces the lock on the cage door. He throws this open.*]
Pardon from de governor! Step out and shake hands. I'll take yuh for a walk

down Fif' Avenoo. We'll knock 'em offen de oith and croak wit de band playin'. Come on, Brother. [*The gorilla scrambles gingerly out of his cage. Goes to* YANK *and stands looking at him.* YANK *keeps his mocking tone—holds out his hand.*] Shake—de secret grip of our order. [*Something, the tone of mockery, perhaps, suddenly enrages the animal. With a spring he wraps his huge arms around* YANK *in a murderous hug. There is a crackling snap of crushed ribs—a gasping cry, still mocking, from* YANK.] Hey, I didn't say kiss me! [*The gorilla lets the crushed body slip to the floor; stands over it uncertainly, considering; then picks it up, throws it in the cage, shuts the door, and shuffles off menacingly into the darkness at left. A great uproar of frightened chattering and whimpering comes from the other cages. Then* YANK *moves, groaning, opening his eyes, and there is silence. He mutters painfully*] Say—dey oughter match him—wit Zybszko. He got me, aw right. I'm trou. Even him didn't tink I belonged. [*then, with sudden passionate despair*] Christ, where do I get off at? Where do I fit in? [*checking himself as suddenly*] Aw, what de hell! No squawkin', see! No quittin', get me! Croak wit your boots on! [*He grabs hold of the bars of the cage and hauls himself painfully to his feet—looks around him bewilderedly—forces a mocking laugh.*] In de cage, huh? [*in the strident tones of a circus barker*] Ladies and gents, step forward and take a slant at de one and only—[*his voice weakening*]—one and original—Hairy Ape from de wilds of—

> [*He slips in a heap on the floor and dies. The monkeys set up a chattering, whimpering wail. And, perhaps, the Hairy Ape at last belongs.*]

CURTAIN

Bertolt Brecht

Mother Courage and Her Children

Translated by Ralph Manheim

CHARACTERS

MOTHER COURAGE
KATTRIN, *her mute daughter*
EILIF, *her elder son*
SWISS CHEESE, *her younger son*
THE RECRUITER
THE SERGEANT
THE COOK
THE GENERAL
THE CHAPLAIN
THE ORDNANCE OFFICER
YVETTE POTTIER
THE MAN WITH THE PATCH
    OVER HIS EYE
THE OTHER SERGEANT

THE OLD COLONEL
A CLERK
A YOUNG SOLDIER
AN OLDER SOLDIER
A PEASANT
THE PEASANT'S WIFE
THE YOUNG MAN
THE OLD WOMAN
ANOTHER PEASANT
THE PEASANT WOMAN
A YOUNG PEASANT
THE LIEUTENANT
SOLDIERS
A VOICE

SCENE I

Spring, 1624. General Oxenstjerna recruits troops in Dalarna for the Polish campaign. The canteen woman, Anna Fierling, known as Mother Courage, loses a son.

Highway near a city.
    A SERGEANT *and a* RECRUITER *stand shivering.*
THE RECRUITER: How can anybody get a company together in a place like this? Sergeant, sometimes I feel like committing suicide. The general wants me to recruit four platoons by the twelfth, and the people around here are so depraved I can't sleep at night. I finally get hold of a man, I close my eyes and pretend not to see that he's chicken-breasted and he's got varicose veins, I get him good and drunk and he signs up. While I'm paying for the drinks, he

steps out, I follow him to the door because I smell a rat: Sure enough, he's gone, like a fart out of a goose. A man's word doesn't mean a thing, there's no honor, no loyalty. This place has undermined my faith in humanity, sergeant.

THE SERGEANT: It's easy to see these people have gone too long without a war. How can you have morality without a war, I ask you? Peace is a mess, it takes a war to put things in order. In peacetime the human race goes to the dogs. Man and beast are treated like so much dirt. Everybody eats what they like, a big piece of cheese on white bread, with a slice of meat on top of the cheese. Nobody knows how many young men or good horses there are in that town up ahead, they've never been counted. I've been in places where they hadn't had a war in as much as seventy years, the people had no names, they didn't even know who they were. It takes a war before you get decent lists and records; then your boots are done up in bales and your grain in sacks, man and beast are properly counted and marched away, because people realize that without order they can't have a war.

THE RECRUITER: How right you are!

THE SERGEANT: Like all good things, a war is hard to get started. But once it takes root, it's vigorous; then people are as scared of peace as dice players are of laying off, because they'll have to reckon up their losses. But at first they're scared of war. It's the novelty.

THE RECRUITER: Say, there comes a wagon. Two women and two young fellows. Keep the old woman busy, sergeant. If this is another flop, you won't catch me standing out in this April wind any more.

[*A Jew's harp is heard. Drawn by two young men, a covered wagon approaches. In the wagon sit* MOTHER COURAGE *and her mute daughter* KATTRIN.]

MOTHER COURAGE: Good morning, sergeant.

THE SERGEANT: [*barring the way*] Good morning, friends. Who are you?

MOTHER COURAGE: Business people. [*sings*]

> Hey, Captains, make the drum stop drumming
> And let your soldiers take a seat.
> Here's Mother Courage, with boots she's coming
> To help along their aching feet.
> How can they march off to the slaughter
> With baggage, cannon, lice and fleas
> Across the rocks and through the water
> Unless their boots are in one piece?
>   The spring is come. Christian, revive!
>   The snowdrifts melt. The dead lie dead.
>   And if by chance you're still alive
>   It's time to rise and shake a leg.

O Captains, don't expect to send them
To death with nothing in their crops.
First you must let Mother Courage mend them
In mind and body with her schnapps.
On empty bellies it's distressing
To stand up under shot and shell.
But once they're full, you have my blessing
To lead them to the jaws of hell.
    The spring is come. Christian, revive!
    The snowdrifts melt, the dead lie dead.
    And if by chance you're still alive
    It's time to rise and shake a leg.

THE SERGEANT: Halt, you scum. Where do you belong?

THE ELDER SON: Second Finnish Regiment.

THE SERGEANT: Where are your papers?

MOTHER COURAGE: Papers?

THE YOUNGER SON: But she's Mother Courage!

THE SERGEANT: Never heard of her. Why Courage?

MOTHER COURAGE: They call me Courage, sergeant, because when I saw ruin staring me in the face I drove out of Riga through cannon fire with fifty loaves of bread in my wagon. They were getting moldy, it was high time, I had no choice.

THE SERGEANT: No wisecracks. Where are your papers?

MOTHER COURAGE: [*fishing a pile of papers out of a tin box and climbing down*] Here are my papers, sergeant. There's a whole missal, picked it up in Alt-Ötting to wrap cucumbers in, and a map of Moravia, God knows if I'll ever get there, if I don't it's a total loss. And this here certifies that my horse hasn't got foot-and-mouth disease, too bad, he croaked on us, he cost fifteen guilders, but not out of my pocket, glory be. Is that enough paper?

THE SERGEANT: Are you trying to pull my leg? I'll teach you to get smart. You know you need a license.

MOTHER COURAGE: You mind your manners and don't go telling my innocent children that I'd go anywhere near your leg, it's indecent. I want no truck with you. My license in the Second Regiment is my honest face, and if you can't read it, that's not my fault. I'm not letting anybody put his seal on it.

THE RECRUITER: Sergeant, I detect a spirit of insubordination in this woman. In our camp we need respect for authority.

MOTHER COURAGE: Wouldn't sausage be better?

THE SERGEANT: Name.

MOTHER COURAGE: Anna Fierling.

THE SERGEANT: Then you're all Fierlings?

MOTHER COURAGE: What do you mean? Fierling is my name. Not theirs.

THE SERGEANT: Aren't they all your children?

MOTHER COURAGE: That they are, but why should they all have the same name? [*pointing at the elder son*] This one, for instance. His name is Eilif Nojocki. How come? Because his father always claimed to be called Kojocki or Mojocki. The boy remembers him well, except the one he remembers was somebody else, a Frenchman with a goatee. But aside from that, he inherited his father's intelligence; that man could strip the pants off a peasant's ass without his knowing it. So, you see, we've each got our own name.

THE SERGEANT: Each different, you mean?

MOTHER COURAGE: Don't act so innocent.

THE SERGEANT: I suppose that one's a Chinaman? [*indicating the younger son*]

MOTHER COURAGE: Wrong. He's Swiss.

THE SERGEANT: After the Frenchman?

MOTHER COURAGE: What Frenchman? I never heard of any Frenchman. Don't get everything balled up or we'll be here all day. He's Swiss, but his name is Fejos, the name has nothing to do with his father. He had an entirely different name, he was an engineer, built fortifications, but he drank.

[SWISS CHEESE *nods, beaming; the mute* KATTRIN *is also tickled.*]

THE SERGEANT: Then how can his name be Fejos?

MOTHER COURAGE: I wouldn't want to offend you, but you haven't got much imagination. Naturally his name is Fejos because when he came I was with a Hungarian, it was all the same to him, he was dying of kidney trouble though he never touched a drop, a very decent man. The boy takes after him.

THE SERGEANT: But you said he wasn't his father?

MOTHER COURAGE: He takes after him all the same. I call him Swiss Cheese, how come, because he's good at pulling the wagon. [*pointing at her daughter*] Her name is Kattrin Haupt, she's half German.

THE SERGEANT: A fine family, I must say.

MOTHER COURAGE: Yes, I've been all over the world with my wagon.

THE SERGEANT: It's all being taken down. [*He takes it down.*] You're from Bamberg, Bavaria. What brings you here?

MOTHER COURAGE: I couldn't wait for the war to kindly come to Bamberg.

THE RECRUITER: You wagon pullers ought to be called Jacob Ox and Esau Ox. Do you ever get out of harness?

EILIF: Mother, can I clout him one on the kisser? I'd like to.

MOTHER COURAGE: And I forbid you. You stay put. And now, gentlemen, wouldn't you need a nice pistol, or a belt buckle, yours is all worn out, sergeant.

THE SERGEANT: I need something else. I'm not blind. Those young fellows are built like tree trunks, big broad chests, sturdy legs. Why aren't they in the army? That's what I'd like to know.

MOTHER COURAGE: [*quickly*] Nothing doing, sergeant. My children aren't cut out for soldiers.

THE RECRUITER: Why not? There's profit in it, and glory. Peddling shoes is woman's work. [*to* EILIF] Step up; let's feel if you've got muscles or if you're a sissy.

MOTHER COURAGE: He's a sissy. Give him a mean look and he'll fall flat on his face.

THE RECRUITER: And kill a calf if it happens to be standing in the way. [*tries to lead him away*]

MOTHER COURAGE: Leave him alone. He's not for you.

THE RECRUITER: He insulted me. He referred to my face as a kisser. Him and me will now step out in the field and discuss this thing as man to man.

EILIF: Don't worry, mother. I'll take care of him.

MOTHER COURAGE: You stay put. You no-good! I know you, always fighting. He's got a knife in his boot, he's a knifer.

THE RECRUITER: I'll pull it out of him like a milk tooth. Come on, boy.

MOTHER COURAGE: Sergeant, I'll report you to the colonel. He'll throw you in the lock-up. The lieutenant is courting my daughter.

THE SERGEANT: No rough stuff, brother. [*to* MOTHER COURAGE] What have you got against the army? Wasn't his father a soldier? Didn't he die fair and square? You said so yourself.

MOTHER COURAGE: He's only a child. You want to lead him off to slaughter, I know you. You'll get five guilders for him.

THE RECRUITER: He'll get a beautiful cap and top boots.

EILIF: Not from you.

MOTHER COURAGE: Oh, won't you come fishing with me? said the fisherman to the worm. [*to* SWISS CHEESE] Run and yell that they're trying to steal your brother. [*She pulls a knife.*] Just try and steal him. I'll cut you down, you dogs. I'll teach you to put him in your war! We do an honest business in ham and shirts, we're peaceful folk.

THE SERGEANT: I can see by the knife how peaceful you are. You ought to be ashamed of yourself, put that knife away, you bitch. A minute ago you admitted you lived off war, how else would you live, on what? How can you have a war without soldiers?

MOTHER COURAGE: It doesn't have to be my children.

THE SERGEANT: I see. You'd like the war to eat the core and spit out the apple. You want your brood to batten on war, tax-free. The war can look out for itself, is that it? You call yourself Courage, eh? And you're afraid of the war that feeds you. Your sons aren't afraid of it, I can see that.

EILIF: I'm not afraid of any war.

THE SERGEANT: Why should you be? Look at me: Has the soldier's life disagreed with me? I was seventeen when I joined up.

MOTHER COURAGE: You're not seventy yet.

THE SERGEANT: I can wait.

MOTHER COURAGE: Sure. Under ground.

THE SERGEANT: Are you trying to insult me? Telling me I'm going to die?

MOTHER COURAGE: But suppose it's the truth? I can see the mark on you. You look like a corpse on leave.

SWISS CHEESE: She's got second sight. Everybody says so. She can tell the future.

THE RECRUITER: Then tell the sergeant his future. It might amuse him.

THE SERGEANT: I don't believe in that stuff.

MOTHER COURAGE: Give me your helmet. [*He gives it to her.*]

THE SERGEANT: It doesn't mean any more than taking a shit in the grass. But go ahead for the laugh.

MOTHER COURAGE: [*takes a sheet of parchment and tears it in two*] Eilif, Swiss Cheese, Kattrin: That's how we'd all be torn apart if we got mixed up too deep in the war. [*to the* SERGEANT] Seeing it's you, I'll do it for nothing. I make a black cross on this piece. Black is death.

SWISS CHEESE: She leaves the other one blank. Get it?

MOTHER COURAGE: Now I fold them, and now I shake them up together. Same as we're all mixed up together from the cradle to the grave. And now you draw, and you'll know the answer.

[*The* SERGEANT *hesitates.*]

THE RECRUITER: [*to* EILIF] I don't take everybody, I'm known to be picky and choosy, but you've got spirit, I like that.

THE SERGEANT: [*fishing in the helmet*] Damn foolishness! Hocus-pocus!

SWISS CHEESE: He's pulled a black cross. He's through.

THE RECRUITER: Don't let them scare you, there's not enough bullets for everybody.

THE SERGEANT: [*hoarsely*] You've fouled me up.

MOTHER COURAGE: You fouled yourself up the day you joined the army. And now we'll be going, there isn't a war every day, I've got to take advantage.

THE SERGEANT: Hell and damnation! Don't try to hornswoggle me. We're taking your bastard to be a soldier.

EILIF: I'd like to be a soldier, mother.

MOTHER COURAGE: You shut your trap, you Finnish devil.

EILIF: Swiss Cheese wants to be a soldier too.

MOTHER COURAGE: That's news to me. I'd better let you draw too, all three of you. [*She goes to the rear to mark crosses on slips of parchment.*]

THE RECRUITER: [*to* EILIF] It's been said to our discredit that a lot of religion goes on in the Swedish camp, but that's slander to blacken our reputation. Hymn singing only on Sunday, one verse! And only if you've got a voice.

MOTHER COURAGE: [*comes back with the slips in the* SERGEANT's *helmet*] Want to sneak away from their mother, the devils, and run off to war like calves to a salt lick. But we'll draw lots on it, then they'll see that the world is no vale of smiles with a "Come along, son, we're short on generals." Sergeant, I'm very much afraid they won't come through the war. They've got terrible characters, all three of them. [*She holds out the helmet to* EILIF] There. Pick a slip. [*He picks one and unfolds it. She snatches it away from him.*] There you have it. A cross! Oh, unhappy mother that I am, oh, mother of sorrows. Has he got to die? Doomed to perish in the springtime of his life? If he joins the army, he'll bite the dust, that's sure. He's too brave, just like his father. If he's not smart, he'll go the way of all flesh, the slip proves it. [*She roars at him.*] Are you going to be smart?

EILIF: Why not?

MOTHER COURAGE: The smart thing to do is to stay with your mother, and if they make fun of you and call you a sissy, just laugh.

THE RECRUITER: If you're shitting in your pants, we'll take your brother.

MOTHER COURAGE: I told you to laugh. Laugh! And now you pick, Swiss Cheese. I'm not so worried about you, you're honest. [*He picks a slip.*] Oh! Why, have you got that strange look? It's got to be blank. There can't be a cross on it. No, I can't lose you. [*She takes the slip.*] A cross? Him too? Maybe it's because he's so stupid. Oh, Swiss Cheese, you'll die too, unless you're very honest the whole time, the way I've taught you since you were a baby, always bringing back the change when I sent you to buy bread. That's the only way you can save yourself. Look, sergeant, isn't that a black cross?

THE SERGEANT: It's a cross all right. I don't see how I could have pulled one. I always stay in the rear. [*to the* RECRUITER] It's on the up and up. Her own get it too.

SWISS CHEESE: I get it too. But I can take a hint.

MOTHER COURAGE: [*to* KATTRIN] Now you're the only one I'm sure of, you're a cross yourself because you've got a good heart. [*She holds up the helmet to* KATTRIN *in the wagon, but she herself takes out the slip.*] It's driving me to despair. It can't be right, maybe I mixed them wrong. Don't be too good-natured, Kattrin, don't, there's a cross on your path too. Always keep very quiet, that ought to be easy seeing you're dumb. Well, now you know. Be careful, all of you, you'll need to be. And now we'll climb up and drive on. [*She returns the* SERGEANT's *helmet and climbs up into the wagon.*]

THE RECRUITER: [*to the* SERGEANT] Do something!

THE SERGEANT: I'm not feeling so good.

THE RECRUITER: Maybe you caught cold when you took your helmet off in the wind. Tell her you want to buy something. Keep her busy. [*aloud*] You could at least take a look at that buckle, sergeant. After all, selling things is these good people's living. Hey, you, the sergeant wants to buy that belt buckle.

MOTHER COURAGE: Half a guilder. A buckle like that is worth two guilders. [*She climbs down.*]

THE SERGEANT: It's not new. This wind! I can't examine it here. Let's go where it's quiet. [*He goes behind the wagon with the buckle.*]

MOTHER COURAGE: I haven't noticed any wind.

THE SERGEANT: Maybe it is worth half a guilder. It's silver.

MOTHER COURAGE: [*joins him behind the wagon*] Six solid ounces.

THE RECRUITER: [*to* EILIF] And then we'll have a drink, just you and me. I've got your enlistment bonus right here. Come on.

[EILIF *stands undecided.*]

MOTHER COURAGE: All right. Half a guilder.

THE SERGEANT: I don't get it. I always stay in the rear. There's no safer place for a sergeant. You can send the men up forward to win glory. You've spoiled my dinner. It won't go down, I know it, not a bite.

MOTHER COURAGE: Don't take it to heart. Don't let it spoil your appetite. Just keep behind the lines. Here, take a drink of schnapps, man. [*She hands him the bottle.*]

THE RECRUITER: [*has taken* EILIF's *arm and is pulling him away toward the rear*] A bonus of ten guilders, and you'll be a brave man and you'll fight for the king, and the women will tear each other's hair out over you. And you can clout me one on the kisser for insulting you. [*Both go out.*]

    [*Mute* KATTRIN *jumps down from the wagon and emits raucous sounds.*]

MOTHER COURAGE: Just a minute, Kattrin, just a minute. The sergeant's paying up. [*bites the half guilder*] I'm always suspicious of money. I'm a burnt child, sergeant. But your coin is good. And now we'll be going. Where's Eilif?

SWISS CHEESE: He's gone with the recruiter.

MOTHER COURAGE: [*stands motionless, then*] You simple soul. [*to* KATTRIN] I know. You can't talk, you couldn't help it.

THE SERGEANT: You could do with a drink yourself, mother. That's the way it goes. Soldiering isn't the worst thing in the world. You want to live off the war, but you want to keep you and yours out of it. Is that it?

MOTHER COURAGE: Now you'll have to pull with your brother, Kattrin.

    [*Brother and sister harness themselves to the wagon and start pulling.* MOTHER COURAGE *walks beside them. The wagon rolls off.*]

THE SERGEANT: [*looking after them*]

    If you want the war to work for you
    You've got to give the war its due.

SCENE II

In 1625 and 1626 Mother Courage crosses Poland in the train of the Swedish armies. Outside the fortress of Wallhof she meets her son again.— A capon is successfully sold, the brave son's fortunes are at their zenith.

The GENERAL's *tent.*

    Beside it the kitchen. The thunder of cannon. The COOK *is arguing with* MOTHER COURAGE, *who is trying to sell him a capon.*

THE COOK: Sixty hellers for that pathetic bird?

MOTHER COURAGE: Pathetic bird? You mean this plump beauty? Are you trying to tell me that a general who's the biggest eater for miles around—God help you if you haven't got anything for his dinner—can't afford a measly sixty hellers?

THE COOK: I can get a dozen like it for ten hellers right around the corner.

MOTHER COURAGE: What, you'll find a capon like this right around the corner? With a siege on and everybody so starved you can see right through them. Maybe you'll scare up a rat, maybe, I say, 'cause they've all been eaten, I've seen five men chasing a starved rat for hours. Fifty hellers for a giant capon in the middle of a siege.

THE COOK: We're not besieged; they are. We're the besiegers, can't you get that through your head?

MOTHER COURAGE: But we haven't got anything to eat either, in fact we've got less than the people in the city. They've hauled it all inside. I hear their life is one big orgy. And look at us. I've been around to the peasants, they haven't got a thing.

THE COOK: They've got plenty. They hide it.

MOTHER COURAGE: [*triumphantly*] Oh, no! They're ruined, that's what they are. They're starving. I've seen them. They're so hungry they're digging up roots. They lick their fingers when they've eaten a boiled strap. That's the situation. And here I've got a capon and I'm supposed to let it go for forty hellers.

THE COOK: Thirty, not forty. Thirty, I said.

MOTHER COURAGE: It's no common capon. They tell me this bird was so talented that he wouldn't eat unless they played music, he had his own favorite march. He could add and subtract, that's how intelligent he was. And you're trying to tell me forty hellers is too much. The general will bite your head off if there's nothing to eat.

THE COOK: You know what I'm going to do? [*He takes a piece of beef and sets his knife to it.*] Here I've got a piece of beef. I'll roast it. Think it over. This is your last chance.

MOTHER COURAGE: Roast and be damned. It's a year old.

THE COOK: A day old. That ox was running around only yesterday afternoon, I saw him with my own eyes.

MOTHER COURAGE: Then he must have stunk on the hoof.

THE COOK: I'll cook it five hours if I have to. We'll see if it's still tough. [*He cuts into it.*]

MOTHER COURAGE: Use plenty of pepper, maybe the general won't notice the stink.
    [*The* GENERAL, *a* CHAPLAIN *and* EILIF *enter the tent.*]

THE GENERAL: [*slapping* EILIF *on the back*] All right, son, into your general's tent you go, you'll sit at my right hand. You've done a heroic deed and you're a pious trooper, because this is a war of religion and what you did was done for God, that's what counts with me. I'll reward you with a gold bracelet when I take the city. We come here to save their souls and what do those filthy, shameless peasants do? They drive their cattle away. And they stuff their priests with meat, front and back. But you taught them a lesson. Here's a tankard of red wine for you. [*He pours.*] We'll down it in one gulp. [*They do so.*] None for the chaplain, he's got his religion. What would you like for dinner, sweetheart?

EILIF: A scrap of meat. Why not?

THE GENERAL: Cook! Meat!

THE COOK: And now he brings company when there's nothing to eat.

    [*Wanting to listen,* MOTHER COURAGE *makes him stop talking.*]

EILIF: Cutting down peasants whets the appetite.

MOTHER COURAGE: God, it's my Eilif.

THE COOK: Who?

MOTHER COURAGE: My eldest. I haven't seen hide nor hair of him in two years, he was stolen from me on the highway. He must be in good if the general invites him to dinner, and what have you got to offer? Nothing. Did you hear what the general's guest wants for dinner? Meat! Take my advice, snap up this capon. The price is one guilder.

THE GENERAL: [*has sat down with* EILIF, *bellows*] Food, Lamb, you lousy, no-good cook, or I'll kill you.

THE COOK: All right, hand it over. This is extortion.

MOTHER COURAGE: I thought it was a pathetic bird.

THE COOK: Pathetic is the word. Hand it over. Fifty hellers! It's highway robbery.

MOTHER COURAGE: One guilder, I say. For my eldest son, the general's honored guest, I spare no expense.

THE COOK: [*gives her the money*] Then pluck it at least while I make the fire.

MOTHER COURAGE: [*sits down to pluck the capon*] Won't he be glad to see me! He's my brave, intelligent son. I've got a stupid one too, but he's honest. The girl's a total loss. But at least she doesn't talk, that's something.

THE GENERAL: Take another drink, son, it's my best Falerno, I've only got another barrel or two at the most, but it's worth it to see that there's still some true faith in my army. The good shepherd here just looks on, all he knows how to do is preach. Can he do anything? No. And now, Eilif my son, tell us all about it, how cleverly you hoodwinked those peasants and captured those twenty head of cattle. I hope they'll be here soon.

EILIF: Tomorrow. Maybe the day after.

MOTHER COURAGE: Isn't my Eilif considerate, not bringing those oxen in until tomorrow, or you wouldn't have even said hello to my capon.

EILIF: Well, it was like this: I heard the peasants were secretly—mostly at night— rounding up the oxen they'd hidden in a certain forest. The city people had arranged to come and get them. I let them round the oxen up, I figured they'd find them easier than I would. I made my men ravenous for meat, put them on short rations for two days until their mouths watered if they even heard a word beginning with *me* . . . like measles.

THE GENERAL: That was clever of you.

EILIF: Maybe. The rest was a pushover. Except the peasants had clubs and there were three times more of them and they fell on us like bloody murder. Four of them drove me into a clump of bushes, they knocked my sword out of my hand and yelled: Surrender! Now what'll I do, I says to myself, they'll make hash out of me.

THE GENERAL: What did you do?

EILIF: I laughed.

THE GENERAL: You laughed?

EILIF: I laughed. Which led to a conversation. The first thing you know, I'm bargaining. Twenty guilders is too much for that ox, I say, how about fifteen? Like I'm meaning to pay. They're flummoxed, they scratch their heads. Quick, I reach for my sword and mow them down. Necessity knows no law. See what I mean?

THE GENERAL: What do you say to that, shepherd?

CHAPLAIN: Strictly speaking, that maxim is not in the Bible. But our Lord was able to turn five loaves into five hundred. So there was no question of poverty; he could tell people to love their neighbors because their bellies were full. Nowadays it's different.

THE GENERAL: [*laughs*] Very different. All right, you Pharisee, take a swig. [*to* EILIF] You mowed them down, splendid, so my fine troops could have a decent bite to eat. Doesn't the Good Book say: "Whatsoever thou doest for the least of my brethren, thou doest for me"? And what have you done for them? You've got them a good chunk of beef for their dinner. They're not used to moldy crusts; in the old days they had a helmetful of white bread and wine before they went out to fight for God.

EILIF: Yes, I reached for my sword and I mowed them down.

THE GENERAL: You're a young Caesar. You deserve to see the king.

EILIF: I have, in the distance. He shines like a light. He's my ideal.

THE GENERAL: You're something like him already, Eilif. I know the worth of a brave soldier like you. When I find one, I treat him like my own son. [*He leads him to the map.*] Take a look at the situation, Eilif; we've still got a long way to go.

MOTHER COURAGE: [*who has been listening starts plucking her capon furiously*] He must be a rotten general.

THE COOK: Eats like a pig, but why rotten?

MOTHER COURAGE: Because he needs brave soldiers, that's why. If he planned his campaigns right, what would he need brave soldiers for? The run-of-the-mill would do. Take it from me, whenever you find a lot of virtues, it shows that something's wrong.

THE COOK: I'd say it proves that something is all right.

MOTHER COURAGE: No, that something's wrong. See, when a general or a king is real stupid and leads his men up shit creek, his troops need courage, that's a virtue. If he's stingy and doesn't hire enough soldiers, they've all got to be Herculeses. And if he's a slob and lets everything go to pot, they've got to be as sly as serpents or they're done for. And if he's always expecting too much of them, they need an extra dose of loyalty. A country that's run right, or a good king or a good general, doesn't need any of these virtues. You don't need virtues in a decent country, the people can all be perfectly ordinary, medium-bright, and cowards too for my money.

THE GENERAL: I bet your father was a soldier.
EILIF: A great soldier, I'm told. My mother warned me about it. Makes me think of
a song.
THE GENERAL: Sing it! [*bellowing*] Where's that food!
EILIF: It's called: The Song of the Old Wife and the Soldier.
[*He sings, doing a war dance with his saber.*]

A gun or a pike, they can kill who they like
And the torrent will swallow a wader
You had better think twice before battling with ice
Said the old wife to the soldier.
Cocking his rifle he leapt to his feet
Laughing for joy as he heard the drum beat
The wars cannot hurt me, he told her.
He shouldered his gun and he picked up his knife
To see the wide world. That's the soldier's life.
Those were the words of the soldier.

Ah, deep will they lie who wise counsel defy
Learn wisdom from those that are older
Oh, don't venture too high or you'll fall from the sky
Said the old wife to the soldier.
But the young soldier with knife and with gun
Only laughed a cold laugh and stepped into the run.
The water can't hurt me, he told her.
And when the moon on the rooftop shines white
We'll be coming back. You can pray for that night.
Those were the words of the soldier.

MOTHER COURAGE: [*in the kitchen, continues the song, beating a pot with a spoon*]

Like the smoke you'll be gone and no warmth linger on
And your deeds only leave me the colder!
Oh, see the smoke race. Oh, dear God keep him safe!
That's what she said of the soldier.

EILIF: What's that?
MOTHER COURAGE: [*goes on singing*]

And the young soldier with knife and with gun
Was swept from his feet till he sank in the run
And the torrent swallowed the waders.
Cold shone the moon on the rooftop white
But the soldier was carried away with the ice
And what was it she heard from the soldiers?

Like the smoke he was gone and no warmth lingered on
And his deeds only left her the colder.
Ah, deep will they lie who wise counsel defy!
That's what she said to the soldiers.

THE GENERAL: What do they think they're doing in my kitchen?

EILIF: [*has gone into the kitchen. He embraces his mother.*] Mother! It's you! Where are the others?

MOTHER COURAGE: [*in his arms*] Snug as a bug in a rug. Swiss Cheese is paymaster of the Second Regiment; at least he won't be fighting, I couldn't keep him out altogether.

EILIF: And how about your feet?

MOTHER COURAGE: Well, it's hard getting my shoes on in the morning.

THE GENERAL: [*has joined them*] Ah, so you're his mother. I hope you've got more sons for me like this fellow here.

EILIF: Am I lucky! There you're sitting in the kitchen hearing your son being praised.

MOTHER COURAGE: I heard it all right! [*She gives him a slap in the face.*]

EILIF: [*holding his cheek*] For capturing the oxen?

MOTHER COURAGE: No. For not surrendering when the four of them were threatening to make hash out of you? Didn't I teach you to take care of yourself? You Finnish devil!

[*The* GENERAL *and the* CHAPLAIN *laugh.*]

SCENE III

Three years later Mother Courage and parts of a Finnish regiment are taken prisoner. She is able to save her daughter and her wagon, but her honest son dies.

Army camp.

Afternoon. On a pole the regimental flag. MOTHER COURAGE *has stretched a clothesline between her wagon, on which all sorts of merchandise is hung in display, and a large cannon. She and* KATTRIN *are folding washing and piling it on the cannon. At the same time she is negotiating with an* ORDNANCE OFFICER *over a sack of bullets.* SWISS CHEESE, *now in the uniform of a paymaster, is looking on. A pretty woman,* YVETTE POTTIER, *is sitting with a glass of brandy in front of her, sewing a gaudy-colored hat. She is in her stocking feet, her red high-heeled shoes are on the ground beside her.*

THE ORDNANCE OFFICER: I'll let you have these bullets for two guilders. It's cheap, I need the money, because the colonel's been drinking with the officers for two days and we're out of liquor.

MOTHER COURAGE: That's ammunition for the troops.If it's found here, I'll be court-martialed. You punks sell their bullets and the men have nothing to shoot at the enemy.

THE ORDNANCE OFFICER: Don't be hard-hearted, you scratch my back, I'll scratch yours.

MOTHER COURAGE: I'm not taking any army property. Not at that price.

THE ORDNANCE OFFICER: You can sell it for five guilders, maybe eight, to the ordnance officer of the Fourth before the day is out, if you're quiet about it and give him a receipt for twelve. He hasn't an ounce of ammunition left.

MOTHER COURAGE: Why don't you do it yourself?

THE ORDNANCE OFFICER: Because I don't trust him, he's a friend of mine.

MOTHER COURAGE: [*takes the sack*] Hand it over. [*To* KATTRIN] Take it back there and pay him one and a half guilders. [*in response to the* ORDNANCE OFFICER'*s protest*] One and a half guilders, I say. [KATTRIN *drags the sack behind the wagon, the* ORDNANCE OFFICER *follows her.* MOTHER COURAGE *to* SWISS CHEESE] Here's your underdrawers, take good care of them, this is October, might be coming on fall, I don't say it will be, because I've learned that nothing is sure to happen the way we think, not even the seasons. But whatever happens, your regimental funds have to be in order. Are your funds in order?

SWISS CHEESE: Yes, mother.

MOTHER COURAGE: Never forget that they made you paymaster because you're honest and not brave like your brother, and especially because you're too simple-minded to get the idea of making off with the money. That's a comfort to me. And don't go mislaying your drawers.

SWISS CHEESE: No, mother. I'll put them under my mattress. [*starts to go*]

THE ORDNANCE OFFICER: I'll go with you, paymaster.

MOTHER COURAGE: Just don't teach him any of your tricks.

[*Without saying good-bye the* ORDNANCE OFFICER *goes out with* SWISS CHEESE.]

YVETTE: [*waves her hand after the* ORDNANCE OFFICER] You might say good-bye, officer.

MOTHER COURAGE: [*to* YVETTE] I don't like to see those two together. He's not the right kind of company for my Swiss Cheese. But the war's getting along pretty well. More countries are joining in all the time, it can go on for another four, five years, easy. With a little planning ahead, I can do good business if I'm careful. Don't you know you shouldn't drink in the morning with your sickness?

YVETTE: Who says I'm sick, it's slander.

MOTHER COURAGE: Everybody says so.

YVETTE: Because they're all liars. Mother Courage, I'm desperate. They all keep out of my way like I'm a rotten fish on account of those lies. What's the good of fixing my hat? [*She throws it down.*] That's why I drink in the morning, I never used to, I'm getting crow's-feet, but it doesn't matter now. In the Second Finnish Regiment they all know me. I should have stayed home when my first love walked out on me. Pride isn't for the likes of us. If we can't put up with shit, we're through.

MOTHER COURAGE: Just don't start in on your Pieter and how it all happened in front of my innocent daughter.

YVETTE: She's just the one to hear it, it'll harden her against love.

MOTHER COURAGE: Nothing can harden them.

YVETTE: Then I'll talk about it because it makes me feel better. It begins with my growing up in fair Flanders, because if I hadn't I'd never have laid eyes on him and I wouldn't be here in Poland now, because he was an army cook, blond, a Dutchman, but skinny. Kattrin, watch out for the skinny ones, but I didn't know that then, and another thing I didn't know is that he had another girl even then, and they all called him Pete the Pipe, because he didn't even take his pipe out of his mouth when he was doing it, that's all it meant to him. [*She sings the "Song of Fraternization."*]

> When I was only sixteen
> The foe came into our land.
> He laid aside his sabre
> And with a smile he took my hand.
>   After the May parade
>   The May light starts to fade.
>   The regiment dressed by the right
>   Then drums were beaten, that's the drill.
>   The foe took us behind the hill
>   And fraternized all night.
>
> There were so many foes came
> And mine worked in the mess.
> I loathed him in the daytime.
> At night I loved him none the less.
>   After the May parade
>   The May light starts to fade.
>   The regiment dressed by the right
>   Then drums were beaten, that's the drill.
>   The foe took us behind the hill
>   And fraternized all night.
>
> The love which came upon me
> Was wished on me by fate.
> My friends could never grasp why
> I found it hard to share their hate.
>   The fields were wet with dew
>   When sorrow first I knew.
>   The regiment dressed by the right

Then drums were beaten, that's the drill
And then the foe, my lover still
Went marching from our sight.

Well, I followed him, but I never found him. That was five years ago. [*She goes behind the wagon with an unsteady gait.*]

MOTHER COURAGE: You've left your hat.

YVETTE: Anybody that wants it can have it.

MOTHER COURAGE: Let that be a lesson to you, Kattrin. Have no truck with soldiers. It's love that makes the world go round, so you'd better watch out. Even with a civilian it's no picnic. He says he'd kiss the ground you put your little feet on, talking of feet, did you wash yours yesterday, and then you're his slave. Be glad you're dumb, that way you'll never contradict yourself or want to bite your tongue off because you've told the truth, it's a gift of God to be dumb. Here comes the general's cook, I wonder what he wants.

[*The* COOK *and the* CHAPLAIN *enter.*]

THE CHAPLAIN: I've got a message for you from your son Eilif. The cook here thought he'd come along, he's taken a shine to you.

THE COOK: I only came to get a breath of air.

MOTHER COURAGE: You can always do that here if you behave, and if you don't, I can handle you. Well, what does he want? I've got no money to spare.

THE CHAPLAIN: Actually he wanted me to see his brother, the paymaster.

MOTHER COURAGE: He's not here any more, or anywhere else either. He's not his brother's paymaster. I don't want him leading him into temptation and being smart at his expense. [*gives him money from the bag slung around her waist*] Give him this, it's a sin, he's speculating on mother love and he ought to be ashamed.

THE COOK: He won't do it much longer, then he'll be marching off with his regiment, maybe to his death, you never can tell. Better make it a little more, you'll be sorry later. You women are hard-hearted, but afterwards you're sorry. A drop of brandy wouldn't have cost much when it was wanted, but it wasn't given, and later, for all you know, he'll be lying in the cold ground and you can't dig him up again.

THE CHAPLAIN: Don't be sentimental, cook. There's nothing wrong with dying in battle, it's a blessing, and I'll tell you why. This is a war of religion. Not a common war, but a war for the faith, and therefore pleasing to God.

THE COOK: That's a fact. In a way you could call it a war, because of the extortion and killing and looting, not to mention a bit of rape, but it's a war of religion, which makes it different from all other wars, that's obvious. But it makes a man thirsty all the same, you've got to admit that.

THE CHAPLAIN: [*to* MOTHER COURAGE, *pointing at the* COOK] I tried to discourage him, but he says you've turned his head, he sees you in his dreams.

THE COOK: [*lights a short-stemmed pipe*] All I want is a glass of brandy from your fair hand, nothing more sinful. I'm already so shocked by the jokes the chaplain's been telling me, I bet I'm still red in the face.

MOTHER COURAGE: And him a clergyman! I'd better give you fellows something to drink or you'll be making me immoral propositions just to pass the time.

THE CHAPLAIN: This is temptation, said the deacon, and succumbed to it. [*turning toward* KATTRIN *as he leaves*] And who is this delightful young lady?

MOTHER COURAGE: She's not delightful, she's a respectable young lady.

[*The* CHAPLAIN *and the* COOK *go behind the wagon with* MOTHER COURAGE. KATTRIN *looks after them, then she walks away from the washing and approaches the hat. She picks it up, sits down and puts on the red shoes. From the rear* MOTHER COURAGE *is heard talking politics with the* CHAPLAIN *and the* COOK.]

MOTHER COURAGE: The Poles here in Poland shouldn't have butted in. All right, our king marched his army into their country. But instead of keeping the peace, the Poles start butting into their own affairs and attack the king while he's marching quietly through the landscape. That was a breach of the peace and the blood is on their head.

THE CHAPLAIN: Our king had only one thing in mind: freedom. The emperor had everybody under his yoke, the Poles as much as the Germans; the king had to set them free.

THE COOK: I see it this way, your brandy's first-rate, I can see why I liked your face, but we were talking about the king. This freedom he was trying to introduce into Germany cost him a fortune, he had to levy a salt tax in Sweden, which, as I said, cost the poor people a fortune. Then he had to put the Germans in jail and break them on the rack because they liked being the emperor's slaves. Oh yes, the king made short shrift of anybody that didn't want to be free. In the beginning he only wanted to protect Poland against wicked people, especially the emperor, but the more he ate the more he wanted, and pretty soon he was protecting all of Germany. But the Germans didn't take it lying down and the king got nothing but trouble for all his kindness and expense, which he naturally had to defray from taxes, which made for bad blood, but that didn't discourage him. He had one thing in his favor, the word of God, which was lucky, because otherwise people would have said he was doing it all for himself and what he hoped to get out of it. As it was, he always had a clear conscience and that was all he really cared about.

MOTHER COURAGE: It's easy to see you're not a Swede, or you wouldn't talk like that about the Hero-King.

THE CHAPLAIN: You're eating his bread, aren't you?

THE COOK: I don't eat his bread, I bake it.

MOTHER COURAGE: He can't be defeated because his men believe in him. [*earnestly*] When you listen to the big wheels talk, they're making war for reasons of piety, in the name of everything that's fine and noble. But when you take another look, you see that they're not so dumb; they're making war for profit. If they weren't, the small fry like me wouldn't have anything to do with it.

THE COOK: That's a fact.

THE CHAPLAIN: And it wouldn't hurt you as a Dutchman to take a look at that flag up there before you express opinions in Poland.

MOTHER COURAGE: We're all good Protestants here! Prosit! [KATTRIN *has started strutting about with* YVETTE's *hat on, imitating* YVETTE's *gait.*]

[*Suddenly cannon fire and shots are heard. Drums.* MOTHER COURAGE, *the* COOK *and the* CHAPLAIN *run out from behind the wagon, the two men still with glasses in hand. The* ORDNANCE OFFICER *and a* SOLDIER *rush up to the cannon and try to push it away.*]

MOTHER COURAGE: What's going on? Let me get my washing first, you lugs. [*She tries to rescue her washing.*]

THE ORDNANCE OFFICER: The Catholics. They're attacking. I don't know as we'll get away. [*to the* SOLDIER] Get rid of the gun! [*runs off*]

THE COOK: Christ, I've got to find the general. Courage, I'll be back for a little chat in a day or two. [*rushes out*]

MOTHER COURAGE: Stop, you've forgotten your pipe.

THE COOK: [*from the distance*] Keep it for me! I'll need it.

MOTHER COURAGE: Just when we were making a little money!

THE CHAPLAIN: Well, I guess I'll be going too. It might be dangerous though, with the enemy so close. Blessed are the peaceful is the best motto in wartime. If only I had a cloak to cover up with.

MOTHER COURAGE: I'm not lending any cloaks, not on your life. I've had bitter experience in that line.

THE CHAPLAIN: But my religion puts me in special danger.

MOTHER COURAGE: [*bringing him a cloak*] It's against my better conscience. And now run along.

THE CHAPLAIN: Thank you kindly, you've got a good heart. But maybe I'd better sit here a while. The enemy might get suspicious if they see me running.

MOTHER COURAGE: [*to the* SOLDIER] Leave it lay, you fool, you won't get paid extra. I'll take care of it for you, you'd only get killed.

THE SOLDIER: [*running away*] I tried. You're my witness.

MOTHER COURAGE: I'll swear it on the Bible. [*sees her daughter with the hat*] What are you doing with that floozy hat? Take it off, have you gone out of your mind? Now of all times, with the enemy on top of us? [*She tears the hat off* KATTRIN's *head.*] You want them to find you and make a whore out of you? And those shoes! Take them off, you woman of Babylon! [*She tries to pull them off.*] Jesus Christ, chaplain, make her take those shoes off! I'll be right back. [*She runs to the wagon.*]

YVETTE: [*enters, powdering her face*] What's this I hear? The Catholics are coming? Where's my hat? Who's been stamping on it? I can't be seen like this if the Catholics are coming. What'll they think of me? I haven't even got a mirror. [*to the chaplain*] How do I look? Too much powder?

THE CHAPLAIN: Just right.

YVETTE: And where are my red shoes? [*She doesn't see them because* KATTRIN *hides her feet under her skirt.*] I left them here. I've got to get back to my tent. In my bare feet. It's disgraceful! [*goes out*]

[SWISS CHEESE *runs in carrying a small box.*]

MOTHER COURAGE: [*comes out with her hands full of ashes, to* KATTRIN] Ashes. [*to* SWISS CHEESE] What you got there?

SWISS CHEESE: The regimental funds.

MOTHER COURAGE: Throw it away! No more paymastering for you.

SWISS CHEESE: I'm responsible for it. [*He goes rear.*]

MOTHER COURAGE: [*to the* CHAPLAIN] Take your clergyman's coat off, chaplain, or they'll recognize you, cloak or no cloak. [*She rubs* KATTRIN's *face with ashes.*] Hold still! There. With a little dirt you'll be safe. What a mess! The sentries were drunk. Hide your light under a bushel, as the Good Book says. When a soldier, especially a Catholic, sees a clean face, she's a whore before she knows it. Nobody feeds them for weeks. When they finally loot some provisions, the next thing they want is women. That'll do it. Let me look at you. Not bad. Like you'd been wallowing in a pigsty. Stop shaking. You're safe now. [*to* SWISS CHEESE] What did you do with the cashbox?

SWISS CHEESE: I thought I'd put it in the wagon.

MOTHER COURAGE: [*horrified*] What! In my wagon? Of all the sinful stupidity! If my back is turned for half a second! They'll hang us all!

SWISS CHEESE: Then I'll put it somewhere else, or I'll run away with it.

MOTHER COURAGE: You'll stay right here. It's too late.

THE CHAPLAIN: [*still changing, comes forward*] Heavens, the flag!

MOTHER COURAGE: [*takes down the regimental flag*] Bozhe moi! I'm so used to it I don't see it. Twenty-five years I've had it. [*The cannon fire grows louder.*]

[*Morning, three days later. The cannon is gone.* MOTHER COURAGE, KATTRIN, *the* CHAPLAIN, *and* SWISS CHEESE *are sitting dejectedly over a meal.*]

SWISS CHEESE: This is the third day I've been sitting here doing nothing; the sergeant has always been easy on me, but now he must be starting to wonder: where can Swiss Cheese be with the cashbox?

MOTHER COURAGE: Be glad they haven't tracked you down.

THE CHAPLAIN: What about me? I can't hold a service here either. The Good Book says: "Whosoever hath a full heart, his tongue runneth over." Heaven help me if mine runneth over.

MOTHER COURAGE: That's the way it is. Look what I've got on my hands: one with a religion and one with a cashbox. I don't know which is worse.

THE CHAPLAIN: Tell yourself that we're in the hands of God.

MOTHER COURAGE: I don't think we're that bad off, but all the same I can't sleep at night. If it weren't for you, Swiss Cheese, it'd be easier. I think I've put myself in the clear. I told them I was against the antichrist; he's a Swede with horns, I told them, and I'd noticed the left horn was kind of worn down. I interrupted the questioning to ask where I could buy holy candles cheap. I knew what to say because Swiss Cheese's father was a Catholic and he used to make jokes about it. They didn't really believe me, but their regiment had no provisioner, so they looked the other way. Maybe we stand to gain. We're prisoners, but so are lice on a dog.

THE CHAPLAIN: This milk is good. Though there's not very much of it or of anything else. Maybe we'll have to cut down on our Swedish appetites. But such is the lot of the vanquished.

MOTHER COURAGE: Who's vanquished? Victory and defeat don't always mean the same thing to the big wheels up top and the small fry underneath. Not by a long shot. In some cases defeat is a blessing to the small fry. Honor's lost, but nothing else. One time in Livonia our general got such a shellacking from the enemy that in the confusion I laid hands on a beautiful white horse from the baggage train. That horse pulled my wagon for seven months, until we had a victory and they checked up. On the whole, you can say that victory and defeat cost us plain people plenty. The best thing for us is when politics gets bogged down. [*to* SWISS CHEESE] Eat!

SWISS CHEESE: I've lost my appetite. How's the sergeant going to pay the men?

MOTHER COURAGE: Troops never get paid when they're running away.

SWISS CHEESE: But they've got it coming to them. If they're not paid, they don't need to run. Not a step.

MOTHER COURAGE: Swiss Cheese, you're too conscientious, it almost frightens me. I brought you up to be honest, because you're not bright, but somewhere it's got to stop. And now me and the chaplain are going to buy a Catholic flag and some meat. Nobody can buy meat like the chaplain, he goes into a trance and heads straight for the best piece, I guess it makes his mouth water and that shows him the way. At least they let me carry on my business. Nobody cares about a shopkeeper's religion, all they want to know is the price. Protestant pants are as warm as any other kind.

THE CHAPLAIN: Like the friar said when somebody told him the Lutherans were going to stand the whole country on its head. They'll always need beggars, he says. [MOTHER COURAGE *disappears into the wagon.*] But she's worried about that cashbox. They've taken no notice of us so far, they think we're all part of the wagon, but how long can that go on?

SWISS CHEESE: I can take it away.

THE CHAPLAIN: That would be almost more dangerous. What if somebody sees you? They've got spies. Yesterday morning, just as I'm relieving myself, one of them jumps out of the ditch. I was so scared I almost let out a prayer. That would have given me away. I suppose they think they can tell a Protestant by the smell of his shit. He was a little runt with a patch over one eye.

MOTHER COURAGE: [*climbing down from the wagon with a basket*] Look what I've found. You shameless slut! [*She holds up the red shoes triumphantly.*] Yvette's red shoes! She's swiped them in cold blood. It's your fault. Who told her she was a delightful young lady? [*She puts them into the basket.*] I'm giving them back. Stealing Yvette's shoes! She ruins herself for money, that I can understand. But you'd like to do it free of charge, for pleasure. I've told you, you'll have to wait for peace. No soldiers! Just wait for peace with your worldly ways.

THE CHAPLAIN: She doesn't seem very worldly to me.

MOTHER COURAGE: Too worldly for me. In Dalarna she was like a stone, which is all they've got around there. The people used to say: We don't see the cripple. That's the way I like it. That way she's safe. [*to* SWISS CHEESE] You leave that box where it is, hear? And keep an eye on your sister, she needs it. The two of you will be the death of me. I'd sooner take care of a bag of fleas. [*She goes off with the* CHAPLAIN. KATTRIN *starts clearing away the dishes.*]

SWISS CHEESE: Won't be many more days when I can sit in the sun in my shirtsleeves. [KATTRIN *points to a tree.*] Yes, the leaves are all yellow. [KATTRIN *asks him, by means of gestures, whether he wants a drink.*] Not now. I'm thinking. [*Pause.*] She says she can't sleep. I'd better get the cashbox out of here, I've found a hiding place. All right, get me a drink. [KATTRIN *goes behind the wagon.*] I'll hide it in the rabbit hole down by the river until I can take it away. Maybe late tonight. I'll go get it and take it to the regiment. I wonder how far they've run in three days? Won't the sergeant be surprised! Well, Swiss Cheese, this is a pleasant disappointment, that's what he'll say. I trust you with the regimental cashbox and you bring it back.

[*As* KATTRIN *comes out from behind the wagon with a glass of brandy, she comes face to face with two men. One is a* SERGEANT. *The other removes his hat and swings it through the air in a ceremonious greeting. He has a patch over one eye.*]

THE MAN WITH THE PATCH: Good morning, my dear. Have you by any chance seen a man from the headquarters of the Second Finnish Regiment?

[*Scared out of her wits,* KATTRIN *runs front, spilling the brandy. The two exchange looks and withdraw after seeing* SWISS CHEESE *sitting there.*]

SWISS CHEESE: [*starting up from his thoughts*] You've spilled half of it. What's the fuss about? Poke yourself in the eye? I don't understand you. I'm getting out of here, I've made up my mind, it's best. [*He stands up. She does everything she can think of to call his attention to the danger. He only evades her.*] I wish I could understand you. Poor thing, I know you're trying to tell me something, you just can't say it. Don't worry about spilling the brandy, I'll be drinking plenty more. What's one glass? [*He takes the cashbox out of the wagon and hides it under his jacket.*] I'll be right back. Let me go, you're making me angry. I know you mean well. If only you could talk.

[*When she tries to hold him back, he kisses her and tears himself away. He goes out. She is desperate, she races back and forth, uttering short inarticulate sounds. The* CHAPLAIN *and* MOTHER COURAGE *come back.* KATTRIN *gesticulates wildly at her mother.*]

MOTHER COURAGE: What's the matter? You're all upset. Has somebody hurt you?

Where's Swiss Cheese? Tell it to me in order, Kattrin. Your mother understands you. What, the no-good's taken the cashbox? I'll hit him over the head with it, the sneak. Take your time, don't talk nonsense, use your hands, I don't like it when you howl like a dog, what will the chaplain think? It gives him the creeps. A one-eyed man?

THE CHAPLAIN: The one-eyed man is a spy. Did they arrest Swiss Cheese? [KATTRIN *shakes her head and shrugs her shoulders.*] We're done for.

MOTHER COURAGE: [*takes a Catholic flag out of her basket. The* CHAPLAIN *fastens it to the flagpole.*] Hoist the new flag!

THE CHAPLAIN: [*bitterly*] All good Catholics here.

[*Voices are heard from the rear. The two men bring in* SWISS CHEESE.]

SWISS CHEESE: Let me go, I haven't got anything. Stop twisting my shoulder, I'm innocent.

THE SERGEANT: He belongs here. You know each other.

MOTHER COURAGE: What makes you think that?

SWISS CHEESE: I don't know them. I don't even know who they are. I had a meal here, it cost me ten hellers. Maybe you saw me sitting here, it was too salty.

THE SERGEANT: Who are you anyway?

MOTHER COURAGE: We're respectable people. And it's true. He had a meal here. He said it was too salty.

THE SERGEANT: Are you trying to tell me you don't know each other?

MOTHER COURAGE: Why should I know him? I don't know everybody. I don't ask people what their name is or if they're heathens; if they pay, they're not heathens. Are you a heathen?

SWISS CHEESE: Of course not.

THE CHAPLAIN: He ate his meal and he behaved himself. He didn't open his mouth except when he was eating. Then you have to.

THE SERGEANT: And who are you?

MOTHER COURAGE: He's only my bartender. You gentlemen must be thirsty, I'll get you a drink of brandy, you must be hot and tired.

THE SERGEANT: We don't drink on duty. [*to* SWISS CHEESE] You were carrying something. You must have hidden it by the river. You had something under your jacket when you left here.

MOTHER COURAGE: Was it really him?

SWISS CHEESE: I think you must have seen somebody else. I saw a man running with something under his jacket. You've got the wrong man.

MOTHER COURAGE: That's what I think too, it's a misunderstanding. These things happen. I'm a good judge of people, I'm Mother Courage, you've heard of me, everybody knows me. Take it from me, this man has an honest face.

THE SERGEANT: We're looking for the cashbox of the Second Finnish Regiment. We know what the man in charge of it looks like. We've been after him for two days. You're him.

SWISS CHEESE: I'm not.

THE SERGEANT: Hand it over. If you don't you're a goner, you know that. Where is it?

MOTHER COURAGE: [*with urgency*] He'd hand it over, wouldn't he, knowing he was a goner if he didn't? I've got it, he'd say, take it, you're stronger. He's not that stupid. Speak up, you stupid idiot, the sergeant's giving you a chance.

SWISS CHEESE: But I haven't got it.

THE SERGEANT: In that case come along. We'll get it out of you.

[*They lead him away.*]

MOTHER COURAGE: [*shouts after them*] He'd tell you. He's not that stupid. And don't twist his shoulder off! [*runs after them*]

[*The same evening. The* CHAPLAIN *and mute* KATTRIN *are washing dishes and scouring knives.*]

THE CHAPLAIN: That boy's in trouble. There are cases like that in the Bible. Take the Passion of our Lord and Saviour. There's an old song about it. [*He sings the "Song of the Hours."*]

In the first hour Jesus mild
Who had prayed since even
Was betrayed and led before
Pontius the heathen.

Pilate found him innocent
Free from fault and error.
Therefore, having washed his hands
Send him to King Herod.

In the third hour he was scourged
Stripped and clad in scarlet
And a plaited crown of thorns
Set upon his forehead.

On the Son of Man they spat
Mocked him and made merry.
Then the cross of death was brought
Given him to carry.

At the sixth hour with two thieves
To the cross they nailed him
And the people and the thieves
Mocked him and reviled him.

This is Jesus King of Jews
Cried they in derision
Till the sun withdrew its light
From that awful vision.

At the ninth hour Jesus wailed
Why hast thou me forsaken?
Soldiers brought him vinegar
Which he left untaken.

Then he yielded up the ghost
And the earth was shaken.
Rended was the temple's veil
And the saints were wakened.

Soldiers broke the two thieves' legs
As the night descended
Thrust a spear in Jesus' side
When his life had ended.

Still they mocked, as from his wound
Flowed the blood and water
Thus blasphemed the Son of Man
With their cruel laughter.

MOTHER COURAGE: [*enters in a state of agitation*] His life's at stake. But they say the sergeant will listen to reason. Only it mustn't come out that he's our Swiss Cheese, or they'll say we've been giving him aid and comfort. All they want is money. But where will we get the money? Hasn't Yvette been here? I met her just now, she's latched onto a colonel, he's thinking of buying her a provisioner's business.

THE CHAPLAIN: Are you really thinking of selling?

MOTHER COURAGE: How else can I get the money for the sergeant?

THE CHAPLAIN: But what will you live on?

MOTHER COURAGE: That's the hitch.

[YVETTE POTTIER *comes in with a doddering* COLONEL.]

YVETTE: [*embracing* MOTHER COURAGE] My dear Mother Courage. Here we are again! [*whispering*] He's willing. [*aloud*] This is my dear friend who advises me on business matters. I just chanced to hear that you wish to sell your wagon, due to circumstances. I might be interested.

MOTHER COURAGE: Mortgage it, not sell it, let's not be hasty. It's not so easy to buy a wagon like this in wartime.

YVETTE: [*disappointed*] Only mortgage it? I thought you wanted to sell it. In that case, I don't know if I'm interested. [*to the* COLONEL] What do you think?

THE COLONEL: Just as you say, my dear.

MOTHER COURAGE: It's only being mortgaged.

YVETTE: I thought you needed money.

MOTHER COURAGE: [*firmly*] I need the money, but I'd rather run myself ragged looking for an offer than sell now. The wagon is our livelihood. It's an opportunity for you, Yvette, God knows when you'll find another like it and have such a good friend to advise you. See what I mean?

YVETTE: My friend thinks I should snap it up, but I don't know. If it's only being mortgaged . . . Don't you agree that we ought to buy?

THE COLONEL: Yes, my dear.

MOTHER COURAGE: Then you'll have to look for something that's for sale, maybe you'll find something if you take your time and your friend goes around with you. Maybe in a week or two you'll find the right thing.

YVETTE: Then we'll go looking, I love to go looking for things, and I love to go around with you, Poldi, it's a real pleasure. Even if it takes two weeks. When would you pay the money back if you get it?

MOTHER COURAGE: I can pay it back in two weeks, maybe one.

YVETTE: I can't make up my mind, Poldi, chéri, tell me what to do. [*She takes the* COLONEL *aside.*] I know she's got to sell, that's definite. The lieutenant, you know who I mean, the blond one, he'd be glad to lend me the money. He's mad about me, he says I remind him of somebody. What do you think?

THE COLONEL: Keep away from that lieutenant. He's no good. He'll take advantage. Haven't I told you I'd buy you something, pussykins?

YVETTE: I can't accept it from you. But then if you think the lieutenant might take advantage . . . Poldi, I'll accept it from you.

THE COLONEL: I hope so.

YVETTE: Your advice is to take it?

THE COLONEL: That's my advice.

YVETTE: [*goes back to* MOTHER COURAGE] My friend advises me to do it. Write me out a receipt, say the wagon belongs to me complete with stock and furnishings when the two weeks are up. We'll take inventory right now, then I'll bring you the two hundred guilders. [*to the* COLONEL] You go back to camp, I'll join you in a little while, I've got to take inventory, I don't want anything missing from my wagon. [*She kisses him. He leaves. She climbs up in the wagon.*] I don't see very many boots.

MOTHER COURAGE: Yvette. This is no time to inspect your wagon if it is yours. You promised to see the sergeant about my Swiss Cheese, you've got to hurry. They say he's to be court-martialed in an hour.

YVETTE: Just let me count the shirts.

MOTHER COURAGE: [*pulls her down by the skirt*] You hyena, it's Swiss Cheese, his life's at stake. And don't tell anybody where the offer comes from, in heaven's name say it's your gentleman friend, or we'll all get it, they'll say we helped him.

YVETTE: I've arranged to meet One-Eye in the woods, he must be there already.

THE CHAPLAIN: And there's no need to start out with the whole two hundred, offer a hundred and fifty, that's plenty.

MOTHER COURAGE: Is it your money? You just keep out of this. Don't worry, you'll get your bread and soup. Go on now and don't haggle. It's his life. [*She gives* YVETTE *a push to start her on her way.*]

THE CHAPLAIN: I didn't meant to butt in, but what are we going to live on? You've got an unemployable daughter on your hands.

MOTHER COURAGE: You muddlehead, I'm counting on the regimental cashbox. They'll allow for his expenses, won't they?

THE CHAPLAIN: But will she handle it right?

MOTHER COURAGE: It's in her own interest. If I spend her two hundred, she gets the wagon. She's mighty keen on it, how long can she expect to hold on to her colonel? Kattrin, you scour the knives, use pumice. And you, don't stand around like Jesus on the Mount of Olives, bestir yourself, wash those glasses, we're expecting at least fifty for dinner, and then it'll be the same old story: "Oh my feet, I'm not used to running around, I don't run around in the pulpit." I think they'll set him free. Thank God they're open to bribery. They're not wolves, they're human and out for money. Bribe-taking in humans is the same as mercy in God. It's our only hope. As long as people take bribes, you'll have mild sentences and even the innocent will get off once in a while.

YVETTE: [*comes in panting*] They want two hundred. And we've got to be quick. Or it'll be out of their hands. I'd better take One-Eye to see my colonel right away. He confessed that he'd had the cashbox, they put the thumb screws on him. But he threw it in the river when he saw they were after him. The box is gone. Should I run and get the money from my colonel?

MOTHER COURAGE: The box is gone? How will I get my two hundred back?

YVETTE: Ah, so you thought you could take it out of the cashbox? You thought you'd put one over on me. Forget it. If you want to save Swiss Cheese, you'll just have to pay, or maybe you'd like me to drop the whole thing and let you keep your wagon?

MOTHER COURAGE: This is something I hadn't reckoned with. But don't rush me, you'll get the wagon, I know it's down the drain, I've had it for seventeen years. Just let me think a second, it's all so sudden. What'll I do, I can't give them two hundred, I guess you should have bargained. If I haven't got a few guilders to fall back on, I'll be at the mercy of the first Tom, Dick, or Harry. Say I'll give them a hundred and twenty, I'll lose my wagon anyway.

YVETTE: They won't go along. One-Eye's in a hurry, he's so keyed-up he keeps looking behind him. Hadn't I better give them the whole two hundred?

MOTHER COURAGE: [*in despair*] I can't do it. Thirty years I've worked. She's twenty-five and no husband. I've got her to keep too. Don't needle me, I know what I'm doing. Say a hundred and twenty or nothing doing.

YVETTE: It's up to you. [*goes out quickly*]

[MOTHER COURAGE *looks neither at the* CHAPLAIN *nor at her daughter. She sits down to help* KATTRIN *scour the knives*.]

MOTHER COURAGE: Don't break the glasses. They're not ours any more. Watch what you're doing, you'll cut yourself. Swiss Cheese will be back, I'll pay two hundred if I have to. You'll have your brother. With eighty guilders we can buy a peddler's pack and start all over. Worse things have happened.

THE CHAPLAIN: The Lord will provide.

MOTHER COURAGE: Rub them dry. [*They scour the knives in silence. Suddenly* KATTRIN *runs sobbing behind the wagon.*]

YVETTE: [*comes running*] They won't go along. I warned you. One-Eye wanted to run out on me, he said it was no use. He said we'd hear the drums any minute, meaning he'd been sentenced. I offered a hundred and fifty. He didn't even bother to shrug his shoulders. When I begged and pleaded, he promised to wait till I'd spoken to you again.

MOTHER COURAGE: Say I'll give him the two hundred. Run.

[YVETTE *runs off. They sit in silence. The* CHAPLAIN *has stopped washing the glasses.*] Maybe I bargained too long. [*Drums are heard in the distance. The* CHAPLAIN *stands up and goes to the rear.* MOTHER COURAGE *remains seated. It grows dark. The drums stop. It grows light again.* MOTHER COURAGE *has not moved.*]

YVETTE: [*enters, very pale*] Now you've done it with your haggling and wanting to keep your wagon. Eleven bullets he got, that's all. I don't know why I bother with you any more, you don't deserve it. But I've picked up a little information. They don't believe the cashbox is really in the river. They suspect it's here and they think you were connected with him. They're going to bring him here, they think maybe you'll give yourself away when you see him. I'm warning you: You don't know him, or you're all dead ducks. I may as well tell you, they're right behind me. Should I keep Kattrin out of the way? [MOTHER COURAGE *shakes her head.*] Does she know? Maybe she didn't hear the drums or maybe she didn't understand.

MOTHER COURAGE: She knows. Get her.

[YVETTE *brings* KATTRIN, *who goes to her mother and stands beside her.* MOTHER COURAGE *takes her by the hand. Two soldiers come in with a stretcher on which something is lying under a sheet. The* SERGEANT *walks beside them. They set the stretcher down.*]

THE SERGEANT: We've got a man here and we don't know his name. We need it for the records. He had a meal with you. Take a look, see if you know him. [*He removes the sheet.*] Do you know him? [MOTHER COURAGE *shakes her head.*] What? You'd never seen him before he came here for a meal? [MOTHER COURAGE *shakes her head.*] Pick him up. Throw him on the dump. Nobody knows him. [*They carry him away.*]

SCENE IV

Mother Courage sings the "Song of the Great Capitulation."

Outside an officer's tent.

MOTHER COURAGE *is waiting. A* CLERK *looks out of the tent.*

THE CLERK: I know you. You had a Protestant paymaster at your place, he was hiding. I wouldn't put in any complaints if I were you.

MOTHER COURAGE: I'm putting in a complaint. I'm innocent. If I take this lying down, it'll look as if I had a guilty conscience. First they ripped up my whole wagon with their sabers, then they wanted me to pay a fine of five talers for no reason at all.

THE CLERK: I'm advising you for your own good: Keep your trap shut. We haven't got many provisioners and we'll let you keep on with your business, especially if you've got a guilty conscience and pay a fine now and then.

MOTHER COURAGE: I'm putting in a complaint.

THE CLERK: Have it your way. But you'll have to wait till the captain can see you. [*disappears into the tent*]

A YOUNG SOLDIER: [*enters in a rage*] Bouque la Madonne! Where's that stinking captain? He embezzled my reward and now he's drinking it up with his whores. I'm going to get him!

AN OLDER SOLDIER: [*comes running after him*] Shut up. They'll put you in the stocks!

THE YOUNG SOLDIER: Come on out, you crook! I'll make chops out of you. Embezzling my reward! Who jumps in the river? Not another man in the whole squad, only me. And I can't even buy myself a beer. I won't stand for it. Come on out and let me cut you to pieces!

THE OLDER SOLDIER: Holy Mary! He'll ruin himself.

MOTHER COURAGE: They didn't give him a reward?

THE YOUNG SOLDIER: Let me go. I'll run you through too, the more the merrier.

THE OLDER SOLDIER: He saved the colonel's horse and they didn't give him a reward. He's young, he hasn't been around long.

MOTHER COURAGE: Let him go, he's not a dog, you don't have to tie him up. Wanting a reward is perfectly reasonable. Why else would he distinguish himself?

THE YOUNG SOLDIER: And him drinking in there! You're all a lot of yellowbellies. I distinguished myself and I want my reward.

MOTHER COURAGE: Young man, don't shout at me. I've got my own worries and besides, go easy on your voice, you may need it. You'll be hoarse when the captain comes out, you won't be able to say boo and he won't be able to put you in the stocks till you're blue in the face. People that yell like that don't last long, maybe half an hour, then they're so exhausted you have to sing them to sleep.

THE YOUNG SOLDIER: I'm not exhausted and who wants to sleep? I'm hungry. They make our bread out of acorns and hemp seed, and they skimp on that. He's whoring away my reward and I'm hungry. I'll murder him.

MOTHER COURAGE: I see. You're hungry. Last year your general made you cut across the fields to trample down the grain. I could have sold a pair of boots for ten guilders if anybody'd had ten guilders and if I'd had any boots. He thought he'd be someplace else this year, but now he's still here and everybody's starving. I can see that you might be good and mad.

THE YOUNG SOLDIER: He can't do this to me, save your breath, I won't put up with injustice.

MOTHER COURAGE: You're right, but for how long? How long won't you put up with injustice? An hour? Two hours? You see, you never thought of that, though it's very important, because it's miserable in the stocks when it suddenly dawns on you that you *can* put up with injustice.

THE YOUNG SOLDIER: I don't know why I listen to you. Bouque la Madonne! Where's the captain?

MOTHER COURAGE: You listen to me because I'm not telling you anything new. You know your temper has gone up in smoke, it was a short temper and you need a long one, but that's a hard thing to come by.

THE YOUNG SOLDIER: Are you trying to say I've no right to claim my reward?

MOTHER COURAGE: Not at all. I'm only saying your temper isn't long enough, it won't get you anywhere. Too bad. If you had a long temper, I'd even egg you on. Chop the bastard up, that's what I'd say, but suppose you don't chop him up, because your tail's drooping and you know it. I'm left standing there like a fool and the captain takes it out on me.

THE OLDER SOLDIER: You're right. He's only blowing off steam.

THE YOUNG SOLDIER: We'll see about that. I'll cut him to pieces. [*He draws his sword.*] When he comes out, I'll cut him to pieces.

THE CLERK: [*looks out*] The captain will be here in a moment. Sit down.

[*The* YOUNG SOLDIER *sits down.*]

MOTHER COURAGE: There he sits. What did I tell you? Sitting, aren't you? Oh, they know us like a book, they know how to handle us. Sit down! And down we sit. You can't start a riot sitting down. Better not stand up again, you won't be able to stand the way you were standing before. Don't be embarrassed on my account, I'm no better, not a bit of it. We were full of piss and vinegar, but they've bought it off. Look at me. No back talk, it's bad for business. Let me tell you about the great capitulation. [*She sings the "Song of the Great Capitulation."*]

> When I was young, no more than a spring chicken
> I too thought that I was really quite the cheese
> (No common peddler's daughter, not I with my looks
>   and my talent and striving for higher things!)
> One little hair in the soup would make me sicken
> And at me no man would dare to sneeze.
> (It's all or nothing, no second best for me. I've got
>   what it takes, the rules are for somebody else!)
> But a chickadee
> Sang wait and see!
>   And you go marching with the show

In step, however fast or slow
And rattle off your little song:
It won't be long.
And then the whole thing slides.
You think God provides—
But you've got it wrong.

And before one single year had wasted
I had learned to swallow down the bitter brew
(Two kids on my hands and the price of bread and
     who do they take me for anyway!)
Man, the double-edged shellacking that I tasted
On my ass and knees I was when they were through.
(You've got to get along with people, one good turn deserves
     another, no use trying to ram your head through the wall!)
And the chickadee
Sang wait and see!
     And she goes marching with the show
     In step, however fast or slow
     And rattles off her little song:
     And then the whole thing slides
     You think God provides—
     But you've got it wrong.

I've seen many fired by high ambition
No star's big or high enough to reach out for.
(It's ability that counts, where there's a will there's a way,
     one way or another we'll swing it!)
Then while moving mountains they get a suspicion
That to wear a straw hat is too big a chore.
(No use being too big for your britches!)
And the chickadee
Sings wait and see!
     And they go marching with the show
     In step, however fast or slow
     And rattle off their little song:
     It won't be long.
     And then the whole thing slides!
     You think God provides—
     But you've got it wrong!

MOTHER COURAGE: [*to the* YOUNG SOLDIER] So here's what I think: Stay here with
     your sword if your anger's big enough, I know you have good reason, but if
     it's a short quick anger, better make tracks!
THE YOUNG SOLDIER: Kiss my ass! [*He staggers off, the* OLDER SOLDIER *after him.*]

THE CLERK: [*sticking his head out*] The captain is here. You can put in your complaint now.

MOTHER COURAGE: I've changed my mind. No complaint. [*She goes out.*]

SCENE V

Two years have passed. The war has spread far and wide. With scarcely a pause Mother Courage's little wagon rolls through Poland, Moravia, Bavaria, Italy, and back again to Bavaria. 1631. Tilly's victory at Magdeburg costs Mother Courage four officers' shirts.

MOTHER COURAGE'*s wagon has stopped in a devastated village.*

Thin military music is heard from the distance. Two soldiers at the bar are being waited on by KATTRIN *and* MOTHER COURAGE. *One of them is wearing a lady's fur coat over his shoulders.*

MOTHER COURAGE: What's that? You can't pay? No money, no schnapps. Plenty of victory marches for the Lord but no pay for the men.

THE SOLDIER: I want my schnapps. I came too late for the looting. The general skunked us: permission to loot the city for exactly one hour. Says he's not a monster; the mayor must have paid him.

THE CHAPLAIN: [*staggers in*] There's still some wounded in the house. The peasant and his family. Help me, somebody, I need linen.

[*The* SECOND SOLDIER *goes out with him.* KATTRIN *gets very excited and tries to persuade her mother to hand out linen.*]

MOTHER COURAGE: I haven't got any. The regiment's bought up all my bandages. You think I'm going to rip up my officers' shirts for the likes of them?

THE CHAPLAIN: [*calling back*] I need linen, I tell you.

MOTHER COURAGE: [*sitting down on the wagon steps to keep* KATTRIN *out*] Nothing doing. They don't pay, they got nothing to pay with.

THE CHAPLAIN: [*bending over a woman whom he has carried out*] Why did you stay here in all that gunfire?

THE PEASANT WOMAN: [*feebly*] Farm.

MOTHER COURAGE: You won't catch them leaving their property. And I'm expected to foot the bill. I won't do it.

THE FIRST SOLDIER: They're Protestants. Why do they have to be Protestants?

MOTHER COURAGE: Religion is the least of their worries. They've lost their farm.

THE SECOND SOLDIER: They're no Protestants. They're Catholics like us.

THE FIRST SOLDIER: How do we know who we're shooting at?

A PEASANT: [*whom the* CHAPLAIN *brings in*] They got my arm.

THE CHAPLAIN: Where's the linen?

[*All look at* MOTHER COURAGE, *who does not move.*]

MOTHER COURAGE: I can't give you a thing. What with all my taxes, duties, fees and

bribes! [*Making guttural sounds,* KATTRIN *picks up a board and threatens her mother with it.*] Are you crazy? Put that board down, you slut, or I'll smack you. I'm not giving anything, you can't make me, I've got to think of myself. [*The* CHAPLAIN *picks her up from the step and puts her down on the ground. Then he fishes out some shirts and tears them into strips.*]
My shirts! Half a guilder apiece! I'm ruined!
[*The anguished cry of a baby is heard from the house.*]

THE PEASANT: The baby's still in there!
[KATTRIN *runs in.*]

THE CHAPLAIN: [*to the woman*] Don't move. They're bringing him out.

MOTHER COURAGE: Get her out of there. The roof'll cave in.

THE CHAPLAIN: I'm not going in there again.

MOTHER COURAGE: [*torn*] Don't run hog-wild with my expensive linen.
[KATTRIN *emerges from the ruins carrying an infant.*]

MOTHER COURAGE: Oh, so you've found another baby to carry around with you? Give that baby back to its mother this minute, or it'll take me all day to get it away from you. Do you hear me? [*to the* SECOND SOLDIER] Don't stand there gaping, go back and tell them to stop that music, I can see right here that they've won a victory. Your victory's costing me a pretty penny.
[KATTRIN *rocks the baby in her arms, humming a lullaby.*]

MOTHER COURAGE: There she sits, happy in all this misery; give it back this minute, the mother's coming to. [*She pounces on the* FIRST SOLDIER *who has been helping himself to the drinks and is now making off with the bottle.*]
Pshagreff! Beast! Haven't you had enough victories for today? Pay up.

FIRST SOLDIER: I'm broke.

MOTHER COURAGE: [*tears the fur coat off him*] Then leave the coat here, it's stolen anyway.

THE CHAPLAIN: There's still somebody in there.

SCENE VI

Outside Ingolstadt in Bavaria Mother Courage attends the funeral of Tilly, the imperial field marshal. Conversations about heroes and the longevity of the war. The chaplain deplores the waste of his talents. Mute Kattrin gets the red shoes. 1632.

Inside MOTHER COURAGE'*s tent.*
A bar open to the rear. Rain. In the distance drum rolls and funeral music. The CHAPLAIN *and the regimental* CLERK *are playing a board game.* MOTHER COURAGE *and her daughter are taking inventory.*

THE CHAPLAIN: The procession's starting.

MOTHER COURAGE: It's a shame about the general—socks: twenty-two pairs—I hear he was killed by accident. On account of the fog in the fields. He's up front encouraging the troops. "Fight to the death, boys," he sings out. Then he rides back, but he gets lost in the fog and rides back forward. Before you know it he's in the middle of the battle and stops a bullet—lanterns: we're down to four. [*A whistle from the rear. She goes to the bar.*] You men ought to be ashamed, running out on your late general's funeral! [*She pours drinks.*]

THE CLERK: They shouldn't have been paid before the funeral. Now they're getting drunk instead.

THE CHAPLAIN: [*to the* CLERK] Shouldn't you be at the funeral?

THE CLERK: In this rain?

MOTHER COURAGE: With you it's different, the rain might spoil your uniform. It seems they wanted to ring the bells, naturally, but it turned out the churches had all been shot to pieces by his orders, so the poor general won't hear any bells when they lower him into his grave. They're going to fire a three-gun salute instead, so it won't be too dull—seventeen sword belts.

CRIES: [*from the bar*] Hey! Brandy!

MOTHER COURAGE: Money first! No, you can't come into my tent with your muddy boots! You can drink outside, rain or no rain. [*to the* CLERK] I'm only letting officers in. It seems the general had been having his troubles. Mutiny in the Second Regiment because he hadn't paid them. It's a war of religion, he says, should they profit by their faith?

    [*Funeral march. All look to the rear.*]

THE CHAPLAIN: Now they're marching past the body.

MOTHER COURAGE: I feel sorry when a general or an emperor passes away like this, maybe he thought he'd do something big, that posterity would still be talking about and maybe put up a statue in his honor, conquer the world, for instance, that's a nice ambition for a general, he doesn't know any better. So he knocks himself out, and then the common people come and spoil it all, because what do they care about greatness, all they care about is a mug of beer and maybe a little company. The most beautiful plans have been wrecked by the smallness of the people that are supposed to carry them out. Even an emperor can't do anything by himself, he needs the support of his soldiers and his people. Am I right?

THE CHAPLAIN: [*laughing*] Courage, you're right, except about the soldiers. They do their best. With those fellows out there, for instance, drinking their brandy in the rain, I'll undertake to carry on one war after another for a hundred years, two at once if I have to, and I'm not a general by trade.

MOTHER COURAGE: Then you don't think the war might stop?

THE CHAPLAIN: Because the general's dead? Don't be childish. They grow by the dozen, there'll always be plenty of heroes.

MOTHER COURAGE: Look here, I'm not asking you for the hell of it. I've been wondering whether to lay in supplies while they're cheap, but if the war stops, I can throw them out the window.

THE CHAPLAIN: I understand. You want a serious answer. There have always been people who say: "The war will be over some day." I say there's no guarantee the war will ever be over. Naturally a brief intermission is conceivable. Maybe the war needs a breather, a war can even break its neck, so to speak. There's always a chance of that, nothing is perfect here below. Maybe there never will be a perfect war, one that lives up to all our expectations. Suddenly, for some unforeseen reason, a war can bog down, you can't think of everything. Some little oversight and your war's in trouble. And then you've got to pull it out of the mud. But the kings and emperors, not to mention the pope, will always come to its help in adversity. On the whole, I'd say this war has very little to worry about, it'll live to a ripe old age.

A SOLDIER: [*sings at the bar*]

> A drink, and don't be slow!
> A soldier's got to go
> And fight for his religion.

Make it double, this is a holiday.

MOTHER COURAGE: If I could only be sure . . .

THE CHAPLAIN: Figure it out for yourself. What's to stop the war?

THE SOLDIER: [*sings*]

> Your breasts, girl, don't be slow!
> A soldier's got to go
> And ride away to Pilsen.

THE CLERK: [*suddenly*] But why can't we have peace? I'm from Bohemia, I'd like to go home when the time comes.

THE CHAPLAIN: Oh, you'd like to go home? Ah, peace! What becomes of the hole when the cheese has been eaten?

THE SOLDIER: [*sings*]

> Play cards, friends, don't be slow!
> A soldier's got to go
> No matter if it's Sunday.
>
> A prayer, priest, don't be slow!
> A soldier's got to go
> And die for king and country.

THE CLERK: In the long run nobody can live without peace.

THE CHAPLAIN: The way I see it, war gives you plenty of peace. It has its peaceful moments. War meets every need, including the peaceful ones, everything's taken care of, or your war couldn't hold its own. In a war you can shit the same as in the dead of peace, you can stop for a beer between battles, and even on the march you can always lie down on your elbows and take a little nap by the roadside. You can't play cards when you're fighting; but then you can't when you're plowing in the dead of peace either, but after a victory the sky's the limit. Maybe you've had a leg shot off, at first you raise a howl, you make a big thing of it. But then you calm down or they give you schnapps, and in the end you're hopping around again and the war's no worse off than before. And what's to prevent you from multiplying in the thick of the slaughter, behind a barn or someplace, in the long run how can they stop you, and then the war has your progeny to help it along. Take it from me, the war will always find an answer. Why would it have to stop?

[KATTRIN *has stopped working and is staring at the* CHAPLAIN.]

MOTHER COURAGE: Then I'll buy the merchandise. You've convinced me. [KATTRIN *suddenly throws down a basket full of bottles and runs out.*] Kattrin! [*laughs*] My goodness, the poor thing's been hoping for peace. I promised her she'd get a husband when peace comes. [*She runs after her.*]

THE CLERK: [*getting up*] I win, you've been too busy talking. Pay up.

MOTHER COURAGE: [*comes back with* KATTRIN.] Be reasonable, the war'll go on a little longer and we'll make a little more money, then peace will be even better. Run along to town now, it won't take you ten minutes, and get the stuff from the Golden Lion, only the expensive things, we'll pick up the rest in the wagon later, it's all arranged, the regimental clerk here will go with you. They've almost all gone to the general's funeral, nothing can happen to you. Look sharp, don't let them take anything away from you, think of your dowry.

[KATTRIN *puts a kerchief over her head and goes with the* CLERK.]

THE CHAPLAIN: Is it all right letting her go with the clerk?

MOTHER COURAGE: Who'd want to ruin her? She's not pretty enough.

THE CHAPLAIN: I've come to admire the way you handle your business and pull through every time. I can see why they call you Mother Courage.

MOTHER COURAGE: Poor people need courage. Why? Because they're sunk. In their situation it takes gumption just to get up in the morning. Or to plow a field in the middle of a war. They even show courage by bringing children into the world, because look at the prospects. The way they butcher and execute each other, think of the courage they need to look each other in the face. And putting up with an emperor and a pope takes a whale of a lot of courage, because those two are the death of the poor. [*She sits down, takes a small pipe from her pocket and smokes.*]

You could be making some kindling.

THE CHAPLAIN: [*reluctantly takes his jacket off and prepares to chop*] Chopping wood isn't really my trade, you know, I'm a shepherd of souls.

MOTHER COURAGE: Sure. But I have no soul and I need firewood.

THE CHAPLAIN: What's that pipe.

MOTHER COURAGE: Just a pipe.

THE CHAPLAIN: No, it's not "just a pipe," it's a very particular pipe.

MOTHER COURAGE: Really?

THE CHAPLAIN: It's the cook's pipe from the Oxenstjerna regiment.

MOTHER COURAGE: If you know it all, why the mealy-mouthed questions?

THE CHAPLAIN: I didn't know if *you* knew. You could have been rummaging through your belongings and laid hands on some pipe and picked it up without thinking.

MOTHER COURAGE: Yes. Maybe that's how it was.

THE CHAPLAIN: Except it wasn't. You knew who that pipe belongs to.

MOTHER COURAGE: What of it?

THE CHAPLAIN: Courage, I'm warning you. It's my duty. I doubt if you ever lay eyes on the man again, but that's no calamity, in fact you're lucky. If you ask me, he wasn't steady. Not at all.

MOTHER COURAGE: What makes you say that? He was a nice man.

THE CHAPLAIN: Oh, you think he was nice? I differ. Far be it from me to wish him any harm, but I can't say he was nice. I'd say he was a scheming Don Juan. If you don't believe me, take a look at his pipe. You'll have to admit that it shows up his character.

MOTHER COURAGE: I don't see anything. It's beat up.

THE CHAPLAIN: It's half bitten through. A violent man. That is the pipe of a ruthless, violent man, you must see that if you've still got an ounce of good sense.

MOTHER COURAGE: Don't wreck my chopping block.

THE CHAPLAIN: I've told you I wasn't trained to chop wood. I studied theology. My gifts and abilities are being wasted on muscular effort. The talents that God gave me are lying fallow. That's a sin. You've never heard me preach. With one sermon I can whip a regiment into such a state that they take the enemy for a flock of sheep. Then men care no more about their lives than they would about a smelly old sock that they're ready to throw away in hopes of final victory. God has made me eloquent. You'll swoon when you hear me preach.

MOTHER COURAGE: I don't want to swoon. What good would that do me?

THE CHAPLAIN: Courage, I've often wondered if maybe you didn't conceal a warm heart under that hard-bitten talk of yours. You too are human, you need warmth.

MOTHER COURAGE: The best way to keep this tent warm is with plenty of firewood.

THE CHAPLAIN: Don't try to put me off. Seriously, Courage, I sometimes wonder if we couldn't make our relationship a little closer. I mean, seeing that the whirlwind of war has whirled us so strangely together.

MOTHER COURAGE: Seems to me it's close enough. I cook your meals and you do chores, such as chopping wood, for instance.

THE CHAPLAIN: [*goes toward her*] You know what I mean by "closer"; it has nothing to do with meals and chopping wood and such mundane needs. Don't harden your heart, let it speak.

MOTHER COURAGE: Don't come at me with that ax. That's too close a relationship.

THE CHAPLAIN: Don't turn it to ridicule. I'm serious, I've given it careful thought.

MOTHER COURAGE: Chaplain, don't be silly. I like you, I don't want to have to scold you. My aim in life is to get through, me and my children and my wagon. I don't think of it as mine and besides I'm not in the mood for private affairs. Right now I'm taking a big risk, buying up merchandise with the general dead and everybody talking peace. What'll you do if I'm ruined? See? You don't know. Chop that wood, then we'll be warm in the evening, which is a good thing in times like these. Now what? [*She stands up.*]

> [*Enter* KATTRIN *out of breath, with a wound across her forehead and over one eye. She is carrying all sorts of things, packages, leather goods, a drum, etc.*]

MOTHER COURAGE: What's that? Assaulted? On the way back? She was assaulted on the way back. Must have been that soldier that got drunk here! I shouldn't have let you go! Throw the stuff down! It's not bad, only a flesh wound. I'll bandage it, it'll heal in a week. They're worse than wild beasts. [*She bandages the wound.*]

THE CHAPLAIN: I can't find fault with them. At home they never raped anybody. I blame the people that start wars, they're the ones that dredge up man's lowest instincts.

MOTHER COURAGE: Didn't the clerk bring you back? That's because you're respectable, they don't give a damn. It's not a deep wound, it won't leave a mark. There, all bandaged. Don't fret, I've got something for you. I've been keeping it for you on the sly, it'll be a surprise. [*She fishes* YVETTE's *red shoes out of a sack.*] See? You've always wanted them. Now you've got them. Put then on quick before I regret it. It won't leave a mark, though I wouldn't mind if it did. The girls that attract them get the worst of it. They drag them around till there's nothing left of them. If you don't appeal to them, they won't harm you. I've seen girls with pretty faces, a few years later they'd have given a wolf the creeps. They can't step behind a bush without fearing the worst. It's like trees. The straight tall ones get chopped down for ridgepoles, the crooked ones enjoy life. In other words, it's a lucky break. The shoes are still in good condition, I've kept them nicely polished.

> [KATTRIN *leaves the shoes where they are and crawls into the wagon.*]

THE CHAPLAIN: I hope she won't be disfigured.

MOTHER COURAGE: There'll be a scar. She can stop waiting for peace.

THE CHAPLAIN: She didn't let them take anything.

MOTHER COURAGE: Maybe I shouldn't have drummed it into her. If I only knew what went on in her head. One night she stayed out, the only time in all these years. Afterwards she traipsed around as usual, except she worked harder. I never could find out what happened. I racked my brains for quite some time. [*She picks up the articles brought by* KATTRIN *and sorts them angrily.*] That's war for you! A fine way to make a living!

[*Cannon salutes are heard.*]

THE CHAPLAIN: Now they're burying the general. This is a historic moment.

MOTHER COURAGE: To me it's a historic moment when they hit my daughter over the eye. She's a wreck, she'll never get a husband now, and she's so crazy about children. It's the war that made her dumb too, a soldier stuffed something in her mouth when she was little. I'll never see Swiss Cheese again and where Eilif is, God knows. God damn the war.

SCENE VII

Mother Courage at the height of her business career.

Highway.

The CHAPLAIN, MOTHER COURAGE *and her daughter* KATTRIN *are pulling the wagon. New wares are hanging on it.* MOTHER COURAGE *is wearing a necklace of silver talers.*

MOTHER COURAGE: Stop running down the war. I won't have it. I know it destroys the weak, but the weak haven't a chance in peacetime either. And war is a better provider. [*sings*]

> If you're not strong enough to take it
> The victory will find you dead.
> A war is only what you make it.
> It's business, not with cheese but lead.

And what good is it staying in one place? The stay-at-homes are the first to get it. [*sings*]

> Some people think they'd like to ride out
> The war, leave danger to the brave
> And dig themselves a cozy hideout—
> They'll dig themselves an early grave.
> I've seen them running from the thunder
> To find a refuge from the war
> But once they're resting six feet under
> They wonder what they hurried for.
> [*They plod on.*]

SCENE VIII

In the same year Gustavus Adolphus, King of Sweden, is killed at the battle
of Lützen. Peace threatens to ruin Mother Courage's business. Her brave
son performs one heroic deed too many and dies an ignominious death.

A *camp.*

> A *summer morning. An* OLD WOMAN *and her son are standing by the wagon.*
> *The son is carrying a large sack of bedding.*

MOTHER COURAGE'S VOICE: [*from the wagon*] Does it have to be at this unearthly
   hour?

THE YOUNG MAN: We've walked all night, twenty miles, and we've got to go back
   today.

MOTHER COURAGE'S VOICE: What can I do with bedding? The people haven't any
   houses.

THE YOUNG MAN: Wait till you've seen it.

THE OLD WOMAN: She won't take it either. Come on.

THE YOUNG MAN: They'll sell the roof from over our heads for taxes. Maybe she'll
   give us three guilders if you throw in the cross. [*Bells start ringing.*] Listen,
   mother!

VOICES: [*from the rear*] Peace! The king of Sweden is dead!

MOTHER COURAGE: [*sticks her head out of the wagon. She has not yet done her hair.*]
   Why are the bells ringing in the middle of the week?

THE CHAPLAIN: [*crawls out from under the wagon*] What are they shouting?

MOTHER COURAGE: Don't tell me peace has broken out when I've just taken in more
   supplies.

THE CHAPLAIN: [*shouting toward the rear*] Is it true? Peace?

VOICE: Three weeks ago, they say. But we just found out.

THE CHAPLAIN: [*to* MOTHER COURAGE] What else would they ring the bells for?

VOICE: There's a whole crowd of Lutherans, they've driven their carts into town.
   They brought the news.

THE YOUNG MAN: Mother, it's peace. What's the matter?

> [*The* OLD WOMAN *has collapsed.*]

MOTHER COURAGE: [*going back into the wagon*] Heavenly saints! Kattrin, peace!
   Put your black dress on! We're going to church. We owe it to Swiss Cheese.
   Can it be true?

THE YOUNG MAN: The people here say the same thing. They've made peace. Can
   you get up? [*The* OLD WOMAN *stands up, still stunned.*] I'll get the saddle shop
   started again. I promise. Everything will be all right. Father will get his bed
   back. Can you walk? [*to the* CHAPLAIN] She fainted. It was the news. She
   thought peace would never come again. Father said it would. We'll go
   straight home. [*Both go out.*]

MOTHER COURAGE'S VOICE: Give her some brandy.

THE CHAPLAIN: They're gone.

MOTHER COURAGE'S VOICE: What's going on in camp?

THE CHAPLAIN: A big crowd. I'll go see. Shouldn't I put on my clericals?

MOTHER COURAGE'S VOICE: Better make sure before you step out in your antichrist costume. I'm glad to see peace, even if I'm ruined. At least I've brought two of my children through the war. Now I'll see my Eilif again.

THE CHAPLAIN: Look who's coming down the road. If it isn't the general's cook!

THE COOK: [*rather bedraggled, carrying a bundle*] Can I believe my eyes? The chaplain!

THE CHAPLAIN: Courage! A visitor!

[MOTHER COURAGE *climbs down*.]

THE COOK: Didn't I promise to come over for a little chat as soon as I had time? I've never forgotten your brandy, Mrs. Fierling.

MOTHER COURAGE: Mercy, the general's cook! After all these years! Where's Eilif, my eldest?

THE COOK: Isn't he here yet? He left ahead of me, he was coming to see you too.

THE CHAPLAIN: I'll put on my clericals, wait for me. [*goes out behind the wagon*]

MOTHER COURAGE: Then he'll be here any minute. [*calls into the wagon*] Kattrin, Eilif's coming! Bring the cook a glass of brandy! [KATTRIN *does not appear*] Put a lock of hair over it, and forget it! Mr. Lamb is no stranger. [*gets the brandy herself*] She won't come out. Peace doesn't mean a thing to her, it's come too late. They hit her over the eye, there's hardly any mark, but she thinks people are staring at her.

THE COOK: Ech, war! [*He and* MOTHER COURAGE *sit down*.]

MOTHER COURAGE: Cook, you find me in trouble. I'm ruined.

THE COOK: What? Say, that's a shame.

MOTHER COURAGE: Peace has done me in. Only the other day I stocked up. The chaplain's advice. And now they'll all demobilize and leave me sitting on my merchandise.

THE COOK: How could you listen to the chaplain? If I'd had time, I'd have warned you against him, but the Catholics came too soon. He's a fly-by-night. So now he's the boss here?

MOTHER COURAGE: He washed my dishes and helped me pull the wagon.

THE COOK: Him? Pulling? I guess he's told you a few of his jokes too, I wouldn't put it past him, he has a unsavory attitude toward women, I tried to reform him, it was hopeless. He's not steady.

MOTHER COURAGE: Are you steady?

THE COOK: If nothing else, I'm steady. Prosit!

MOTHER COURAGE: Steady is no good. I've only lived with one steady man, thank the Lord. I never had to work so hard, he sold the children's blankets when spring came, and he thought my harmonica was unchristian. In my opinion you're not doing yourself any good by admitting you're steady.

THE COOK: You've still got your old bite, but I respect you for it.

MOTHER COURAGE: Don't tell me you've been dreaming about my old bite.

THE COOK: Well, here we sit, with the bells of peace and your world-famous brandy, that hasn't its equal.

MOTHER COURAGE: The bells of peace don't strike my fancy right now. I don't see them paying the men, they're behind-hand already. Where does that leave me with my famous brandy? Have you been paid?

THE COOK: [*hesitantly*] Not really. That's why we demobilized ourselves. Under the circumstances, I says to myself, why should I stay on? I'll go see my friends in the meantime. So here we are.

MOTHER COURAGE: You mean you're out of funds?

THE COOK: If only they'd stop those damn bells! I'd be glad to go into some kind of business. I'm sick of being a cook. They give me roots and shoe leather to work with, and then they throw the hot soup in my face. A cook's got a dog's life these days. I'd rather be in combat, but now we've got peace. [*The* CHAPLAIN *appears in his original dress.*] We'll discuss it later.

THE CHAPLAIN: It's still in good condition. There were only a few moths in it.

THE COOK: I don't see why you bother. They won't take you back. Who are you going to inspire now to be an honest soldier and earn his pay at the risk of his life? Besides, I've got a bone to pick with you. Advising this lady to buy useless merchandise on the ground that the war would last forever.

THE CHAPLAIN: [*heatedly*] And why, I'd like to know, is it any of your business?

THE COOK: Because it's unscrupulous. How can you meddle in other people's business and give unsolicited advice?

THE CHAPLAIN: Who's meddling? [*to* MOTHER COURAGE] I didn't know you were accountable to this gentleman, I didn't know you were so intimate with him.

MOTHER COURAGE: Don't get excited, the cook is only giving his private opinion. And you can't deny that your war was a dud.

THE CHAPLAIN: Courage, don't blaspheme against peace. You're a battlefield hyena.

MOTHER COURAGE: What am I?

THE COOK: If you insult this lady, you'll hear from me.

THE CHAPLAIN: I'm not talking to you. Your intentions are too obvious. [*to* MOTHER COURAGE] But when I see you picking up peace with thumb and forefinger like a snotty handkerchief, it revolts my humanity; you don't want peace, you want war, because you profit by it, but don't forget the old saying: "He hath need of a long spoon that eateth with the devil."

MOTHER COURAGE: I've no use for war and war hasn't much use for me. Anyway, I'm not letting anybody call me a hyena, you and me are through.

THE CHAPLAIN: How can you complain about peace when it's such a relief to everybody else? On account of the old rags in your wagon?

MOTHER COURAGE: My merchandise isn't old rags, it's what I live off, and so did you.

THE CHAPLAIN: Off war, you mean. Aha!

THE COOK: [*to the* CHAPLAIN] You're a grown man, you ought to know there's no sense in giving advice. [*to* MOTHER COURAGE] The best thing you can do now is to sell off certain articles quick, before the prices hit the floor. Dress yourself and get started, there's no time to lose.

MOTHER COURAGE: That's very sensible advice. I think I'll do it.

THE CHAPLAIN: Because the cook says so!

MOTHER COURAGE: Why didn't *you* say so? He's right, I'd better run over to the market. [*She goes into the wagon.*]

THE COOK: My round, chaplain. No presence of mind. Here's what you should have said: me give you advice? All I ever did was talk politics! Don't try to take me on. Cockfighting is undignified in a clergyman.

THE CHAPLAIN: If you don't shut up, I'll murder you, undignified or not.

THE COOK: [*taking off his shoe and unwinding the wrappings from his feet*] If the war hadn't made a godless bum out of you, you could easily come by a parsonage now that peace is here. They won't need cooks, there's nothing to cook, but people still do a lot of believing, that hasn't changed.

THE CHAPLAIN: See here, Mr. Lamb. Don't try to squeeze me out. Being a bum has made me a better man. I couldn't preach to them any more.

[YVETTE POTTIER *enters, elaborately dressed in black, with a cane. She is much older and fatter and heavily powdered. Behind her a servant.*]

YVETTE: Hello there! Is this the residence of Mother Courage?

THE CHAPLAIN: Right you are. With whom have we the pleasure?

YVETTE: The Countess Starhemberg, my good people. Where is Mother Courage?

THE CHAPLAIN: [*calls into the wagon*] Countess Starhemberg wishes to speak to you!

MOTHER COURAGE: I'm coming.

YVETTE: It's Yvette!

MOTHER COURAGE'S VOICE: My goodness! It's Yvette!

YVETTE: Just dropped in to see how you're doing. [*The* COOK *has turned around in horror.*] Pieter!

THE COOK: Yvette!

YVETTE: Blow me down! How did you get here?

THE COOK: In a cart.

THE CHAPLAIN: Oh, you know each other? Intimately?

YVETTE: I should think so. [*She looks the* COOK *over.*] Fat!

THE COOK: You're not exactly willowy yourself.

YVETTE: All the same I'm glad I ran into you, you bum. Now I can tell you what I think of you.

THE CHAPLAIN: Go right ahead, spare no details, but wait until Courage comes out.

MOTHER COURAGE: [*comes out with all sorts of merchandise*] Yvette! [*They embrace.*] But what are you in mourning for?

YVETTE: Isn't it becoming? My husband the colonel died a few years ago.

MOTHER COURAGE: The old geezer that almost bought my wagon?

YVETTE: His elder brother.

MOTHER COURAGE: You must be pretty well fixed. It's nice to find somebody that's made a good thing out of the war.

YVETTE: Oh well, it's been up and down and back up again.

MOTHER COURAGE: Let's not say anything bad about colonels. They make money by the bushel.

THE CHAPLAIN: If I were you, I'd put my shoes back on again. [*to* YVETTE] Countess Starhemberg, you promised to tell us what you think of this gentleman.

THE COOK: Don't make a scene here.

MOTHER COURAGE: He's a friend of mine, Yvette.

YVETTE: He's Pete the Pipe, that's who he is.

THE COOK: Forget the nicknames, my name is Lamb.

MOTHER COURAGE: [*laughs*] Pete the Pipe! That drove the women crazy! Say, I've saved your pipe.

THE CHAPLAIN: And smoked it.

YVETTE: It's lucky I'm here to warn you. He's the worst rotter that ever infested the coast of Flanders. He ruined more girls than he's got fingers.

THE COOK: That was a long time ago. I've changed.

YVETTE: Stand up when a lady draws you into a conversation! How I loved this man! And all the while he was seeing a little bandylegged brunette, ruined her too, naturally.

THE COOK: Seems to me I started you off on a prosperous career.

YVETTE: Shut up, you depressing wreck! Watch your step with him, his kind are dangerous even when they've gone to seed.

MOTHER COURAGE: [*to* YVETTE] Come along, I've got to sell my stuff before the prices drop. Maybe you can help me, with your army connections. [*calls into the wagon*] Kattrin, forget about church, I'm running over to the market. When Eilif comes, gives him a drink. [*goes out with* YVETTE]

YVETTE: [*in leaving*] To think that such a man could lead me astray! I can thank my lucky stars that I was able to rise in the world after that. I've put a spoke in your wheel, Pete the Pipe, and they'll give me credit for it in heaven when my time comes.

THE CHAPLAIN: Our conversation seems to illustrate the old adage: The mills of God grind slowly. What do you think of my jokes now?

THE COOK: I'm just unlucky. I'll come clean: I was hoping for a hot meal. I'm starving. And now they're talking about me, and she'll get the wrong idea. I think I'll beat it before she comes back.

THE CHAPLAIN: I think so too.

THE COOK: Chaplain, I'm fed up on peace already. Men are sinners from the cradle, fire and sword are their natural lot. I wish I were cooking for the general again, God knows where he is, I'd roast a fine fat capon, with mustard sauce and a few carrots.

THE CHAPLAIN: Red cabbage. Red cabbage with capon.

THE COOK: That's right, but he wanted carrots.

THE CHAPLAIN: He was ignorant.

THE COOK: That didn't prevent you from gorging yourself.

THE CHAPLAIN: With repugnance.

THE COOK: Anyway you'll have to admit those were good times.

THE CHAPLAIN: I might admit that.

THE COOK: Now you've called her a hyena, your good times here are over. What are you staring at?

THE CHAPLAIN: Eilif! [EILIF *enters, followed by soldiers with pikes. His hands are fettered. He is deathly pale.*] What's wrong?

EILIF: Where's mother?

THE CHAPLAIN: Gone to town.

EILIF: I heard she was here. They let me come and see her.

THE COOK: [*to the soldiers*] Where are you taking him?

A SOLDIER: No good place.

THE CHAPLAIN: What has he done?

THE SOLDIER: Broke into a farm. The peasant's wife is dead.

THE CHAPLAIN: How could you do such a thing?

EILIF: It's what I've been doing all along.

THE COOK: But in peacetime!

EILIF: Shut your trap. Can I sit down till she comes?

THE SOLDIER: We haven't time.

THE CHAPLAIN: During the war they honored him for it, he sat at the general's right hand. Then it was bravery. Couldn't we speak to the officer?

THE SOLDIER: No use. What's brave about taking a peasant's cattle?

THE COOK: It was stupid.

EILIF: If I'd been stupid, I'd have starved, wise guy.

THE COOK: And for being smart your head comes off.

THE CHAPLAIN: Let's get Kattrin at least.

EILIF: Leave her be. Get me a drink of schnapps.

THE SOLDIER: No time. Let's go!

THE CHAPLAIN: And what should we tell your mother?

EILIF: Tell her it wasn't any different, tell her it was the same. Or don't tell her anything.

    [*The soldiers drive him away.*]

THE CHAPLAIN: I'll go with you on your hard journey.

EILIF: I don't need any sky pilot.

THE CHAPLAIN: You don't know yet. [*He follows him.*]

THE COOK: [*calls after them*] I'll have to tell her, she'll want to see him.

THE CHAPLAIN: Better not tell her anything. Or say he was here and he'll come again, maybe tomorrow. I'll break it to her when I get back. [*hurries out*]

    [*The* COOK *looks after them, shaking his head, then he walks anxiously about. Finally he approaches the wagon.*]

THE COOK: Hey! Come on out! I can see why you'd hide from peace. I wish I could do it myself. I'm the general's cook, remember? Wouldn't you have a bite to eat, to do me till your mother gets back? A slice of ham or just a piece of bread while I'm waiting. [*He looks in.*] She's buried her head in a blanket. [*The sound of gunfire in the rear.*]

MOTHER COURAGE: [*runs in.· She is out of breath and still has her merchandise.*] Cook, the peace is over, the war started up again three days ago. I hadn't sold my stuff yet when I found out. Heaven be praised! They're shooting each other up in town, the Catholics and Lutherans. We've got to get out of here. Kattrin, start packing. What have *you* got such a long face about? What's wrong?

THE COOK: Nothing.

MOTHER COURAGE: Something's wrong, I can tell by your expression.

THE COOK: Maybe it's the war starting up again. Now I probably won't get anything hot to eat before tomorrow night.

MOTHER COURAGE: That's a lie, cook.

THE COOK: Eilif was here. He couldn't stay.

MOTHER COURAGE: He was here? Then we'll see him on the march. I'm going with the troops this time. How does he look?

THE COOK: The same.

MOTHER COURAGE: He'll never change. The war couldn't take him away from me. He's smart. Could you help me pack? [*She starts packing.*] Did he tell you anything? Is he in good with the general? Did he say anything about his heroic deeds?

THE COOK: [*gloomily*] They say he's been at one of them again.

MOTHER COURAGE: Tell me later, we've got to be going. [KATTRIN *emerges.*]Kattrin, peace is over. We're moving. [*to the* COOK] What's the matter with you?

THE COOK: I'm going to enlist.

MOTHER COURAGE: I've got a suggestion. Why don't . . . ? Where's the chaplain?

THE COOK: Gone to town with Eilif.

MOTHER COURAGE: Then come a little way with me, Lamb. I need help.

THE COOK: That incident with Yvette . . .

MOTHER COURAGE: It hasn't lowered you in my estimation. Far from it. Where there's smoke there's fire. Coming?

THE COOK: I won't say no.

MOTHER COURAGE: The Twelfth Regiment has shoved off. Take the shaft. Here's a chunk of bread. We'll have to circle around to meet the Lutherans. Maybe I'll see Eilif tonight. He's my favorite. It's been a short peace. And we're on the move again. [*She sings, while the* COOK *and* KATTRIN *harness themselves to the wagon.*]

> From Ulm to Metz, from Metz to Pilsen
> Courage is right there in the van.

The war both in and out of season
With shot and shell will feed its man.
But lead alone is not sufficient
The war needs soldiers to subsist!
Its diet elseways is deficient.
The war is hungry! So enlist!

SCENE IX

The great war of religion has been going on for sixteen years. Germany has lost more than half its population. Those whom the slaughter has spared have been laid low by epidemics. Once-flourishing countrysides are ravaged by famine. Wolves prowl through the charred ruins of the cities. In the fall of 1634 we find Mother Courage in Germany, in the Fichtelgebirge, at some distance from the road followed by the Swedish armies. Winter comes early and is exceptionally severe. Business is bad, begging is the only resort. The cook receives a letter from Utrecht and is dismissed.

Outside a half-demolished presbytery.
Gray morning in early winter. Gusts of wind. MOTHER COURAGE *and the* COOK *in shabby sheepskins by the wagon.*

THE COOK: No light. Nobody's up yet.

MOTHER COURAGE: But it's a priest. He'll have to crawl out of bed to ring the bells. Then he'll get himself a nice bowl of hot soup.

THE COOK: Go on, you saw the village, everything's been burned to a crisp.

MOTHER COURAGE: But somebody's here, I heard a dog bark.

THE COOK: If the priest's got anything, he won't give it away.

MOTHER COURAGE: Maybe if we sing . . .

THE COOK: I've had it up to here. [*suddenly*] I got a letter from Utrecht. My mother's died of cholera and the tavern belongs to me. Here's the letter if you don't believe me. It's no business of yours what my aunt says about my evil ways, but never mind, read it.

MOTHER COURAGE: [*reads the letter*] Lamb, I'm sick of roaming around, myself. I feel like a butcher's dog that pulls the meat cart but doesn't get any for himself. I've nothing left to sell and the people have no money to pay for it. In Saxony a man in rags tried to foist a cord of books on me for two eggs, and in Württemberg they'd have let their plow go for a little bag of salt. What's the good of plowing? Nothing grows but brambles. In Pomerania they say the villagers have eaten up all the babies, and that nuns have been caught at highway robbery.

THE COOK: It's the end of the world.

MOTHER COURAGE: Sometimes I have visions of myself driving through hell, selling sulphur and brimstone, or through heaven peddling refreshments to the roaming souls. If me and the children I've got left could find a place where there's no shooting, I wouldn't mind a few years of peace and quiet.

THE COOK: We could open up the tavern again. Think it over, Anna. I made up my mind last night; with or without you, I'm going back to Utrecht. In fact I'm leaving today.

MOTHER COURAGE: I'll have to talk to Kattrin. It's kind of sudden, and I don't like to make decisions in the cold with nothing in my stomach. Kattrin! [KATTRIN *climbs out of the wagon.*] Kattrin, I've got something to tell you. The cook and me are thinking of going to Utrecht. They've left him a tavern there. You'd be living in one place, you'd meet people. A lot of men would be glad to get a nice, well-behaved girl, looks aren't everything. I'm all for it. I get along fine with the cook. I've got to hand it to him: He's got a head for business. We'd eat regular meals, wouldn't that be nice? And you'd have your own bed, wouldn't you like that? It's no life on the road, year in year out. You'll go to rack and ruin. You're crawling with lice already. We've got to decide, you see, we could go north with the Swedes, they must be over there. [*She points to the left.*] I think we'll do it, Kattrin.

THE COOK: Anna, could I have a word with you alone?

MOTHER COURAGE: Get back in the wagon, Kattrin.

[KATTRIN *climbs back in.*]

THE COOK: I interrupted you because I see there's been a misunderstanding. I thought it was too obvious to need saying. But if it isn't, I'll just have to say it. You can't take her, it's out of the question. Is that plain enough for you?

[KATTRIN *sticks her head out of the wagon and listens.*]

MOTHER COURAGE: You want me to leave Kattrin?

THE COOK: Look at it this way. There's no room in the tavern. It's not one of those places with three taprooms. If the two of us put our shoulder to the wheel, we can make a living, but not three, it can't be done. Kattrin can keep the wagon.

MOTHER COURAGE: I'd been thinking she could find a husband in Utrecht.

THE COOK: Don't make me laugh! How's she going to find a husband? At her age? And dumb! And with that scar!

MOTHER COURAGE: Not so loud.

THE COOK: Shout or whisper, the truth's the truth. And that's another reason why I can't have her in the tavern. The customers won't want a sight like that staring them in the face. Can you blame them?

MOTHER COURAGE: Shut up. Not so loud, I say.

THE COOK: There's a light in the presbytery. Let's sing.

MOTHER COURAGE: How could she pull the wagon by herself? She's afraid of the war. She couldn't stand it. The dreams she must have! I hear her groaning at night. Especially after battles. What she sees in her dreams, God knows. It's pity that makes her suffer so. The other day the wagon hit a hedgehog, I found it hidden in her blanket.

THE COOK: The tavern's too small. [*He calls.*] Worthy gentleman and members of the household! We shall now sing the Song of Solomon, Julius Caesar, and other great men, whose greatness didn't help them any. Just to show you that we're God-fearing people ourselves, which makes it hard for us, especially in the winter. [*They sing.*]

>You saw the wise King Solomon
>You know what came of him.
>To him all hidden things were plain.
>He cursed the hour gave birth to him.
>And saw that everything was vain.
>How great and wise was Solomon!
>Now think about his case. Alas
>A useful lesson can be won.
>It's wisdom that had brought him to that pass!
>How happy is the man with none!

Our beautiful song proves that virtues are dangerous things, better steer clear of them, enjoy life, eat a good breakfast, a bowl of hot soup, for instance. Take me, I haven't got any soup and wish I had, I'm a soldier, but what has my bravery in all those battles got me, nothing, I'm starving, I'd be better off if I'd stayed home like a yellowbelly. And I'll tell you why.

>You saw the daring Caesar next
>You know what he became.
>They deified him in his life
>But then they killed him just the same.
>And as they raised the fatal knife
>How loud he cried: "You too, my son!"
>Now think about his case. Alas
>A useful lesson can be won.
>It's daring that had brought him to that pass!
>How happy is the man with none!

[*in an undertone*] They're not even looking out. Worthy gentleman and members of the household! Maybe you'll say, all right, if bravery won't keep body and soul together, try honesty. That may fill your belly or at least get you a drop to drink. Let's look into it.

>You've heard of honest Socrates
>Who never told a lie.

They weren't so grateful as you'd think
Instead they sentenced him to die
And handed him the poisoned drink.
How honest was the people's noble son!
Now think about his case. Alas
A useful lesson can be won.
His honesty had brought him to that pass.
How happy is the man with none!

Yes, they tell us to be charitable and to share what we have, but what if we haven't got anything? Maybe philanthropists have a rough time of it too, it stands to reason, they need a little something for themselves. Yes, charity is a rare virtue, because it doesn't pay.

St. Martin couldn't bear to see
His fellows in distress.
He saw a poor man in the snow.
"Take half my cloak!" He did, and lo!
They both of them froze none the less.
He thought his heavenly reward was won.
Now think about his case. Alas
A useful lesson can be won.
Unselfishness had brought him to that pass
How happy is the man with none!

That's our situation. We're God-fearing folk, we stick together, we don't steal, we don't murder, we don't set fire to anything! You could say that we set an example which bears out the song, we sink lower and lower, we seldom see any soup, but if we were different, if we were thieves and murderers, maybe our bellies would be full. Because virtue isn't rewarded, only wickedness, the world needn't be like this, but it is.

And here you see God-fearing folk
Observing God's ten laws.
So far He hasn't taken heed.
You people sitting warm indoors
Help to relieve our bitter need!
Our virtue can be counted on.
Now think about our case. Alas
A useful lesson can be won.
The fear of God has brought us to this pass.
How happy is the man with none!

VOICE: [*from above*] Hey, down there! Come on up! We've got some good thick soup.

MOTHER COURAGE: Lamb, I couldn't get anything down. I know what you say makes sense, but is it your last word? We've always been good friends.

THE COOK: My last word. Think it over.

MOTHER COURAGE: I don't need to think it over. I won't leave her.

THE COOK: It wouldn't be wise, but there's nothing I can do. I'm not inhuman, but it's a small tavern. We'd better go in now, or there won't be anything left, we'll have been singing in the cold for nothing.

MOTHER COURAGE: I'll get Kattrin.

THE COOK: Better bring it down for her. They'll get a fright if the three of us barge in. [*They go out.*]

> [KATTRIN *climbs out of the wagon. She is carrying a bundle. She looks around to make sure the others are gone. Then she spreads out an old pair of the* COOK's *trousers and a skirt belonging to her mother side by side on a wheel of the wagon so they can easily be seen. She is about to leave with her bundle when* MOTHER COURAGE *comes out of the house.*]

MOTHER COURAGE: [*with a dish of soup*] Kattrin! Stop! Kattrin! Where do you think you're going with that bundle? Have you taken leave of your wits? [*She examines the bundle.*] She's packed her things. Were you listening? I've told him it's no go with Utrecht and his lousy tavern, what would we do there? A tavern's no place for you and me. The war still has a thing or two up its sleeve for us. [*She sees the trousers and skirt.*] You're stupid. Suppose I'd seen that and you'd been gone? [KATTRIN *tries to leave,* MOTHER COURAGE *holds her back.*] And don't go thinking I've given him the gate on your account. It's the wagon. I won't part with the wagon, I'm used to it, it's not you, it's the wagon. We'll go in the other direction, we'll put the cook's stuff out here where he'll find it, the fool. [*She climbs up and throws down a few odds and ends to join the trousers.*] There. Now we're shut of him, you won't see me taking anyone else into the business. From now on it's you and me. This winter will go by like all the rest. Harness up, it looks like snow.

> [*They harness themselves to the wagon, turn it around and pull it away. When the* COOK *comes out he sees his things and stands dumbfounded.*]

SCENE X

Throughout 1635 Mother Courage and her daughter Kattrin pull the wagon over the roads of central Germany in the wake of the increasingly bedraggled armies.

Highway.

> MOTHER COURAGE *and* KATTRIN *are pulling the wagon. They come to a peasant's house. A voice is heard singing from within.*

THE VOICE: The rose bush in our garden
                          Rejoiced our hearts in spring
                          It bore such lovely flowers.
                          We planted it last season
                          Before the April showers.
                          A garden is a blessèd thing
                          It bore such lovely flowers.

                          When winter comes a-stalking
                          and gales great snow storms bring
                          They trouble us but little.
                          We've lately finished caulking
                          The roof with moss and wattle.
                          A sheltering roof's a blessèd thing
                          When winter comes a-stalking.

[MOTHER COURAGE *and* KATTRIN *have stopped to listen. Then they move on.*]

SCENE XI

January 1636. The imperial troops threaten the Protestant city of Halle. The stone speaks. Mother Courage loses her daughter and goes on alone. The end of the war is not in sight.

The wagon, much the worse for wear, is standing beside a peasant house with an enormous thatch roof. The house is built against the side of a stony hill. Night.
     A LIEUTENANT *and three* SOLDIERS *in heavy armor step out of the woods.*

THE LIEUTENANT: I don't want any noise. If anybody yells, run him through with your pikes.

THE FIRST SOLDIER: But we need a guide. We'll have to knock if we want them to come out.

THE LIEUTENANT: Knocking sounds natural. It could be a cow bumping against the barn wall.
     [*The* SOLDIERS *knock on the door. A* PEASANT WOMAN *opens. They hold their hands over her mouth. Two* SOLDIERS *go in.*]

A MAN'S VOICE [*inside*] Who's there?
     [*The* SOLDIERS *bring out a* PEASANT *and his son.*]

THE LIEUTENANT: [*points to the wagon, in which* KATTRIN *has appeared*] There's another one. [*A* SOLDIER *pulls her out.*] Anybody else live here?

THE PEASANT COUPLE: This is our son.—That's a dumb girl.—Her mother's gone into the town on business.—Buying up people's belongings, they're selling cheap because they're getting out.—They're provisioners.

THE LIEUTENANT: I'm warning you to keep quiet, one squawk and you'll get a pike over the head. All right. I need somebody who can show us the path into the city. [*points to the* YOUNG PEASANT] You. Come here!

THE YOUNG PEASANT: I don't know no path.

THE SECOND SOLDIER: [*grinning*] He don't know no path.

THE YOUNG PEASANT: I'm not helping the Catholics.

THE LIEUTENANT: [*to the* SECOND SOLDIER] Give him a feel of your pike!

THE YOUNG PEASANT: [*forced down on his knees and threatened with the pike*] You can kill me. I won't do it.

THE FIRST SOLDIER: I know what'll make him think twice. [*He goes over to the barn.*] Two cows and an ox. Get this: If you don't help us, I'll cut them down.

THE YOUNG PEASANT: Not the animals!

THE PEASANT WOMAN: [*in tears*] Captain, spare our animals or we'll starve.

THE LIEUTENANT: If he insists on being stubborn, they're done for.

THE FIRST SOLDIER: I'll start with the ox.

THE YOUNG PEASANT: [*to the old man*] Do I have to? [*The old woman nods.*] I'll do it.

THE PEASANT WOMAN: And thank you kindly for your forbearance, Captain, for ever and ever, amen.

  [*The* PEASANT *stops her from giving further thanks.*]

THE FIRST SOLDIER: Didn't I tell you? With them it's the animals that come first.

  [*Led by the* YOUNG PEASANT, *the* LIEUTENANT *and the* SOLDIERS *continue on their way.*]

THE PEASANT: I wish I knew what they're up to. Nothing good.

THE PEASANT WOMAN: Maybe they're only scouts.—What are you doing?

THE PEASANT: [*putting a ladder against the roof and climbing up*] See if they're alone. [*on the roof*] Men moving in the woods. All the way to the quarry. Armor in the clearing. And a cannon. It's more than a regiment. God have mercy on the city and everybody in it.

THE PEASANT WOMAN: See any light in the city?

THE PEASANT: No. They're all asleep. [*He climbs down.*] If they get in, they'll kill everybody.

THE PEASANT WOMAN: The sentry will see them in time.

THE PEASANT: They must have killed the sentry in the tower on the hill, or he'd have blown his horn.

THE PEASANT WOMAN: If there were more of us . . .

THE PEASANT: All by ourselves up here with a cripple . . .

THE PEASANT WOMAN: We can't do a thing. Do you think . . .

THE PEASANT: Not a thing.

THE PEASANT WOMAN: We couldn't get down there in the dark.

THE PEASANT: The whole hillside is full of them. We can't even give a signal.

THE PEASANT WOMAN: They'd kill us.

THE PEASANT: No, we can't do a thing.

THE PEASANT WOMAN: [*to* KATTRIN] Pray, poor thing, pray! We can't stop the bloodshed. If you can't talk, at least you can pray. He'll hear you if nobody else does. I'll help you. [*All kneel,* KATTRIN *behind the* PEASANTS.] Our Father which art in heaven, hear our prayer. Don't let the town perish with everybody in it, all asleep and unsuspecting. Wake them, make them get up and climb the walls and see the enemy coming through the night with cannon and pikes, through the fields and down the hillside. [*back to* KATTRIN] Protect our mother and don't let the watchman sleep, wake him before it's too late. And succor our brother-in-law, he's in there with his four children, let them not perish, they're innocent and don't know a thing. [*to* KATTRIN, *who groans*] The littlest is less than two, the oldest is seven. [*Horrified,* KATTRIN *stands up.*] Our Father, hear us, for Thou alone canst help, we'll all be killed, we're weak, we haven't any pikes or anything, we are powerless and in Thine hands, we and our animals and the whole farm, and the city too, it's in Thine hands, and the enemy is under the walls with great might.

> [KATTRIN *has crept unnoticed to the wagon, taken something out of it, put it under her apron and climbed up the ladder to the roof of the barn.*]

THE PEASANT WOMAN: Think upon the children in peril, especially the babes in arms and the old people that can't help themselves and all God's creatures.

THE PEASANT: And forgive us our trespasses as we forgive them that trespass against us. Amen.

> [KATTRIN, *sitting on the roof, starts beating the drum that she has taken out from under her apron.*]

THE PEASANT WOMAN: Jesus! What's she doing?

THE PEASANT: She's gone crazy.

THE PEASANT WOMAN: Get her down, quick!

> [*The* PEASANT *runs toward the ladder, but* KATTRIN *pulls it up on the roof.*]

THE PEASANT WOMAN: She'll be the death of us all.

THE PEASANT: Stop that, you cripple!

THE PEASANT WOMAN: She'll have the Catholics down on us.

THE PEASANT: [*looking around for stones*] I'll throw rocks at you.

THE PEASANT WOMAN: Have you no pity? Have you no heart? We're dead if they find out it's us! They'll run us through!

> [KATTRIN *stares in the direction of the city, and goes on drumming.*]

THE PEASANT WOMAN: [*to the* PEASANT] I told you not to let those tramps stop here. What do they care if the soldiers drive our last animals away?

THE LIEUTENANT: [*rushes in with his* SOLDIERS *and the* YOUNG PEASANT] I'll cut you to pieces!

THE PEASANT WOMAN: We're innocent, captain. We couldn't help it. She sneaked up there. We don't know her.

THE LIEUTENANT: Where's the ladder?

THE PEASANT: Up top.

THE LIEUTENANT: [*to* KATTRIN] Throw down that drum. It's an order!

   [KATTRIN *goes on drumming*.]

THE LIEUTENANT: You're all in this together! This'll be the end of you!

THE PEASANT: They've felled some pine trees in the woods over there. We could get one and knock her down . . .

THE FIRST SOLDIER: [*to the* LIEUTENANT] Request permission to make a suggestion. [*He whispers something in the* LIEUTENANT's *ear. He nods*.] Listen. We've got a friendly proposition. Come down, we'll take you into town with us. Show us your mother and we won't touch a hair of her head.

   [KATTRIN *goes on drumming*.]

THE LIEUTENANT: [*pushes him roughly aside*] She doesn't trust you. No wonder with your mug. [*he calls up*] If I give you my word? I'm an officer, you can trust my word of honor.

   [*She drums still louder*.]

THE LIEUTENANT: Nothing is sacred to her.

THE YOUNG PEASANT: It's not just her mother, lieutenant!

THE FIRST SOLDIER: We can't let this go on. They'll hear it in the city.

THE LIEUTENANT: We'll have to make some kind of noise that's louder than the drums. What could we make noise with?

THE FIRST SOLDIER: But we're not supposed to make noise.

THE LIEUTENANT: An innocent noise, stupid. A peaceable noise.

THE PEASANT: I could chop wood.

THE LIEUTENANT: That's it, chop! [*The* PEASANT *gets an ax and chops at a log*.] Harder! Harder! You're chopping for your life.

   [*Listening,* KATTRIN *has been drumming more softly. Now she looks anxiously around and goes on drumming as before*.]

THE LIEUTENANT: [*to the* PEASANT] Not loud enough. [*to the* FIRST SOLDIER] You chop too.

THE PEASANT: There's only one ax. [*stops chopping*]

THE LIEUTENANT: We'll have to set the house on fire. Smoke her out.

THE PEASANT: That won't do any good, captain. If the city people see fire up here, they'll know what's afoot.

   [*Still drumming,* KATTRIN *has been listening again. Now she laughs*.]

THE LIEUTENANT: Look, she's laughing at us. I'll shoot her down, regardless. Get the musket!

   [*Two* SOLDIERS *run out.* KATTRIN *goes on drumming*.]

THE PEASANT WOMAN: I've got it, captain. That's their wagon over there. If we start smashing it up, she'll stop. The wagon's all they've got.

THE LIEUTENANT: [*to the* YOUNG PEASANT] Smash away. [*to* KATTRIN] We'll smash your wagon if you don't stop.

   [*The* YOUNG PEASANT *strikes a few feeble blows at the wagon*.]

THE PEASANT WOMAN: Stop it, you beast!

> [KATTRIN *stares despairingly at the wagon and emits pitiful sounds. But she goes on drumming.*]

THE LIEUTENANT: Where are those stinkers with the musket?

THE FIRST SOLDIER: They haven't heard anything in the city yet, or we'd hear their guns.

THE LIEUTENANT: [*to* KATTRIN] They don't hear you. And now we're going to shoot you down. For the last time: Drop that drum!

THE YOUNG PEASANT: [*suddenly throws the plank away*] Keep on drumming! Or they'll all be killed! Keep on drumming, keep on drumming . . .

> [*The* SOLDIER *throws him down and hits him with his pike.* KATTRIN *starts crying, but goes on drumming.*]

THE PEASANT WOMAN: Don't hit him in the back! My God, you're killing him.

> [*The* SOLDIERS *run in with the musket.*]

THE SECOND SOLDIER: The colonel's foaming at the mouth. We'll be court-martialed.

THE LIEUTENANT: Set it up! Set it up! [*to* KATTRIN, *while the musket is being set up on its stand*] For the last time: Stop that drumming! [KATTRIN *in tears drums as loud as she can.*] Fire!

> [*The* SOLDIERS *fire.* KATTRIN *is hit. She beats the drum a few times more and then slowly collapses.*]

THE LIEUTENANT: Now we'll have some quiet.

> [*But* KATTRIN's last drumbeats are answered by the city's cannon. A confused hubbub of alarm bells and cannon is heard in the distance.]

THE FIRST SOLDIER: She's done it.

SCENE XII

Night, toward morning. The fifes and drums of troops marching away.

Outside the wagon MOTHER COURAGE *sits huddled over her daughter. The peasant couple are standing beside them.*

THE PEASANT: [*hostile*] You'll have to be going, woman. There's only one more regiment to come. You can't go alone.

MOTHER COURAGE: Maybe I can get her to sleep. [*She sings.*]

> Lullaby baby
> What stirs in the hay?
> The neighbor brats whimper
> Mine are happy and gay.
> They go in tatters

> And you in silk down
> Cut from an angel's
> Best party gown.
>
> They've nothing to munch on
> And you will have pie
> Just tell your mother
> In case it's too dry.
> Lullaby baby
> What stirs in the hay?
> The one lies in Poland
> The other—who can say?

Now she's asleep. You shouldn't have told her about your brother-in-law's children.

THE PEASANT: Maybe it wouldn't have happened if you hadn't gone to town to swindle people.

MOTHER COURAGE: I'm glad she's sleeping now.

THE PEASANT WOMAN: She's not sleeping, you'll have to face it, she's dead.

THE PEASANT: And it's time you got started. There are wolves around here, and what's worse, marauders.

MOTHER COURAGE: Yes. [*She goes to the wagon and takes out a sheet of canvas to cover the body with.*]

THE PEASANT WOMAN: Haven't you anybody else? Somebody you can go to?

MOTHER COURAGE: Yes, there's one of them left. Eilif.

THE PEASANT: [*while* MOTHER COURAGE *covers the body*] Go find him. We'll attend to this one, give her a decent burial. Set your mind at rest.

MOTHER COURAGE: Here's money for your expenses. [*She gives the peasant money.*]
[*The* PEASANT *and his son shake hands with her and carry* KATTRIN *away.*]

THE PEASANT WOMAN: [*on the way out*] Hurry up!

MOTHER COURAGE: [*harnesses herself to the wagon*] I hope I can pull the wagon alone. I'll manage, there isn't much in it. I've got to get back in business.
[*Another regiment marches by with fifes and drums in the rear.*]

MOTHER COURAGE: Hey, take me with you! [*She starts to pull.*]
[*Singing is heard in the rear.*]

> With all the killing and recruiting
> The war will worry on a while.
> In ninety years they'll still be shooting.
> It's hardest on the rank-and-file.
> Our food is swill, our pants all patches
> The higher-ups steal half our pay

And still we dream of God-sent riches.
Tomorrow is another day!
   The spring is come! Christian, revive!
   The snowdrifts melt, the dead lie dead!
   And if by chance you're still alive
   It's time to rise and shake a leg.

Arthur Miller

Death of a Salesman

CHARACTERS

WILLY LOMAN

LINDA, *his wife*

BIFF
HAPPY } *his sons*

UNCLE BEN

CHARLEY

BERNARD

THE WOMAN

HOWARD WAGNER

JENNY

STANLEY

MISS FORSYTHE

LETTA

The action takes place in WILLY LOMAN'S *house and yard and in various places he visits in the New York and Boston of today.*

ACT I

A melody is heard, played upon a flute. It is small and fine, telling of grass and trees and the horizon. The curtain rises.

Before us is the Salesman's house. We are aware of towering, angular shapes behind it, surrounding it on all sides. Only the blue light of the sky falls upon the house and forestage; the surrounding area shows an angry glow of orange. As more light appears, we see a solid vault of apartment houses around the small, fragile-seeming home. An air of the dream clings to the place, a dream rising out of reality. The kitchen at center seems actual enough, for there is a kitchen table with three chairs, and a refrigerator. But no other fixtures are seen. At the back of the kitchen there is a draped entrance, which leads to the living-room. To the right of the kitchen, on a level raised two feet, is a bedroom furnished only with a brass bedstead and a straight chair. On a shelf over the bed a silver athletic trophy stands. A window opens onto the apartment house at the side.

Behind the kitchen, on a level raised six and a half feet, is the boys' bedroom, at present barely visible. Two beds are dimly seen, and at the back of

*the room a dormer window. (This bedroom is above the unseen living-room.)
At the left a stairway curves up to it from the kitchen.*

*The entire setting is wholly or, in some places, partially transparent. The
roof-line of the house is one-dimensional; under and over it we see the apartment buildings. Before the house lies an apron, curving beyond the forestage
into the orchestra. This forward area serves as the back yard as well as the
locale of all Willy's imaginings and of his city scenes. Whenever the action
is in the present the actors observe the imaginary wall-lines, entering the
house only through its door at the left. But in the scenes of the past these
boundaries are broken, and characters enter or leave a room by stepping
"through" a wall onto the forestage.*

> [*From the right,* WILLY LOMAN, *the Salesman, enters, carrying two
> large sample cases. The flute plays on. He hears but is not aware of it.
> He is past sixty years of age, dressed quietly. Even as he crosses the
> stage to the doorway of the house, his exhaustion is apparent. He
> unlocks the door, comes into the kitchen, and thankfully lets his
> burden down, feeling the soreness of his palms. A word-sigh escapes
> his lips—it might be "Oh, boy, oh, boy." He closes the door, then
> carries his cases out into the living-room, through the draped kitchen
> doorway.*]

> LINDA, *his wife, has stirred in her bed at the right. She gets out and
> puts on a robe, listening. Most often jovial, she has developed an
> iron repression of her exceptions to Willy's behavior—she more than
> loves him, she admires him, as though his mercurial nature, his
> temper, his massive dreams and little cruelties, served her only as
> sharp reminders of the turbulent longings within him, longings which
> she shares but lacks the temperament to utter and follow to their end.*]

LINDA: [*hearing* WILLY *outside the bedroom, calls with some trepidation*] Willy!

WILLY: It's all right. I came back.

LINDA: Why? What happened? [*slight pause*] Did something happen, Willy?

WILLY: No, nothing happened.

LINDA: You didn't smash the car, did you?

WILLY: [*with casual irritation*] I said nothing happened. Didn't you hear me?

LINDA: Don't you feel well?

WILLY: I'm tired to the death. [*The flute has faded away. He sits on the bed
beside her, a little numb.*] I couldn't make it. I just couldn't make it,
Linda.

LINDA: [*very carefully, delicately*] Where were you all day? You look terrible.

WILLY: I got as far as a little above Yonkers. I stopped for a cup of coffee.
Maybe it was the coffee.

LINDA: What?

WILLY: [*after a pause*] I suddenly couldn't drive any more. The car kept going
off onto the shoulder, y'know?

LINDA: [*helpfully*] Oh. Maybe it was the steering again. I don't think Angelo
knows the Studebaker.

WILLY: No, it's me, it's me. Suddenly I realize I'm goin' sixty miles an hour
and I don't remember the last five minutes. I'm—I can't seem to—keep
my mind to it.

LINDA: Maybe it's your glasses. You never went for your new glasses.

WILLY: No, I see everything. I came back ten miles an hour. It took me nearly four hours from Yonkers.

LINDA: [*resigned*] Well, you'll just have to take a rest, Willy, you can't continue this way.

WILLY: I just got back from Florida.

LINDA: But you didn't rest your mind. Your mind is overactive, and the mind is what counts, dear.

WILLY: I'll start out in the morning. Maybe I'll feel better in the morning. [*She is taking off his shoes.*] These goddam arch supports are killing me.

LINDA: Take an aspirin. Should I get you an aspirin? It'll soothe you.

WILLY: [*with wonder*] I was driving along, you understand? And I was fine. I was even observing the scenery. You can imagine, me looking at scenery, on the road every week of my life. But it's so beautiful up there, Linda, the trees are so thick, and the sun is warm. I opened the windshield and just let the warm air bathe over me. And then all of a sudden I'm goin' off the road! I'm tellin' ya, I absolutely forgot I was driving. If I'd've gone the other way over the white line I might've killed somebody. So I went on again—and five minutes later I'm dreamin' again, and I nearly— [*He presses two fingers against his eyes.*] I have such thoughts, I have such strange thoughts.

LINDA: Willy, dear. Talk to them again. There's no reason why you can't work in New York.

WILLY: They don't need me in New York. I'm the New England man. I'm vital in New England.

LINDA: But you're sixty years old. They can't expect you to keep traveling every week.

WILLY: I'll have to send a wire to Portland. I'm supposed to see Brown and Morrison tomorrow morning at ten o'clock to show the line. Goddammit, I could sell them! [*He starts putting on his jacket.*]

LINDA: [*taking the jacket from him*] Why don't you go down to the place tomorrow and tell Howard you've simply got to work in New York? You're too accommodating, dear.

WILLY: If old man Wagner was alive I'd a been in charge of New York now! That man was a prince, he was a masterful man. But that boy of his, that Howard, he don't appreciate. When I went north the first time, the Wagner Company didn't know where New England was!

LINDA: Why don't you tell those things to Howard, dear?

WILLY: [*encouraged*] I will, I definitely will. Is there any cheese?

LINDA: I'll make you a sandwich.

WILLY: No, go to sleep. I'll take some milk. I'll be up right away. The boys in?

LINDA: They're sleeping. Happy took Biff on a date tonight.

WILLY: [*interested*] That so?

LINDA: It was so nice to see them shaving together, one behind the other, in the bathroom. And going out together. You notice? The whole house smells of shaving lotion.

WILLY: Figure it out. Work a lifetime to pay off a house. You finally own it, and there's nobody to live in it.

LINDA: Well, dear, life is a casting off. It's always that way.

WILLY: No, no, some people—some people accomplish something. Did Biff say anything after I went this morning?

LINDA: You shouldn't have criticized him, Willy, especially after he just got off the train. You mustn't lose your temper with him.

WILLY: When the hell did I lose my temper? I simply asked him if he was making any money. Is that a criticism?

LINDA: But, dear, how could he make any money?

WILLY: [*worried and angered*] There's such an undercurrent in him. He became a moody man. Did he apologize when I left this morning?

LINDA: He was crestfallen, Willy. You know how he admires you. I think if he finds himself, then you'll both be happier and not fight any more.

WILLY: How can he find himself on a farm? Is that a life? A farmhand? In the beginning, when he was young, I thought, well, a young man, it's good for him to tramp around, take a lot of different jobs. But it's more than ten years now and he has yet to make thirty-five dollars a week!

LINDA: He's finding himself, Willy.

WILLY: Not finding yourself at the age of thirty-four is a disgrace!

LINDA: Shh!

WILLY: The trouble is he's lazy, goddammit!

LINDA: Willy, please!

WILLY: Biff is a lazy bum!

LINDA: They're sleeping. Get something to eat. Go on down.

WILLY: Why did he come home? I would like to know what brought him home.

LINDA: I don't know. I think he's still lost, Willy. I think he's very lost.

WILLY: Biff Loman is lost. In the greatest country in the world a young man with such—personal attractiveness, gets lost. And such a hard worker. There's one thing about Biff—he's not lazy.

LINDA: Never.

WILLY: [*with pity and resolve*] I'll see him in the morning; I'll have a nice talk with him. I'll get him a job selling. He could be big in no time. My God! Remember how they used to follow him around in high school? When he smiled at one of them their faces lit up. When he walked down the street . . . [*He loses himself in reminiscences.*]

LINDA: [*trying to bring him out of it*] Willy, dear, I got a new kind of American-type cheese today. It's whipped.

WILLY: Why do you get American when I like Swiss?

LINDA: I just thought you'd like a change—

WILLY: I don't want a change! I want Swiss cheese. Why am I always being contradicted?

LINDA: [*with a covering laugh*] I thought it would be a surprise.

WILLY: Why don't you open a window in here, for God's sake?

LINDA: [*with infinite patience*] They're all open, dear.

WILLY: The way they boxed us in here. Bricks and windows, windows and bricks.

LINDA: We should've bought the land next door.

WILLY: The street is lined with cars. There's not a breath of fresh air in the neighborhood. The grass don't grow any more, you can't raise a carrot in the back yard. They should've had a law against apartment houses. Remember those two beautiful elm trees out there? When I and Biff hung the swing between them?

LINDA: Yeah, like being a million miles from the city.

WILLY: They should've arrested the builder for cutting those down. They massacred the neighborhood. [*lost*] More and more I think of those days, Linda. This time of year it was lilac and wisteria. And then the peonies would come out, and the daffodils. What fragrance in this room!

LINDA: Well, after all, people had to move somewhere.

WILLY: No, there's more people now.

LINDA: I don't think there's more people. I think—

WILLY: There's more people! That's what's ruining this country! Population is getting out of control. The competition is maddening! Smell the stink from that apartment house! And another one on the other side . . . How can they whip cheese?

[*On Willy's last line,* BIFF *and* HAPPY *raise themselves up in their beds, listening.*]

LINDA: Go down, try it. And be quiet.

WILLY: [*turning to* LINDA, *guiltily*] You're not worried about me, are you, sweetheart?

BIFF: What's the matter?

HAPPY: Listen!

LINDA: You've got too much on the ball to worry about.

WILLY: You're my foundation and my support, Linda.

LINDA: Just try to relax, dear. You make mountains out of molehills.

WILLY: I won't fight with him any more. If he wants to go back to Texas, let him go.

LINDA: He'll find his way.

WILLY: Sure. Certain men just don't get started till later in life. Like Thomas Edison, I think. Or B. F. Goodrich. One of them was deaf. [*He starts for the bedroom doorway.*] I'll put my money on Biff.

LINDA: And Willy—if it's warm Sunday we'll drive in the country. And we'll open the windshield, and take lunch.

WILLY: No, the windshields don't open on the new cars.

LINDA: But you opened it today.

WILLY: Me? I didn't. [*He stops.*] Now isn't that peculiar! Isn't that a remarkable— [*He breaks off in amazement and fright as the flute is heard distantly.*]

LINDA: What, darling?

WILLY: That is the most remarkable thing.

LINDA: What, dear?

WILLY: I was thinking of the Chevvy. [*slight pause*] Nineteen twenty-eight . . . when I had that red Chevvy— [*breaks off*] That funny? I coulda sworn I was driving that Chevvy today.

LINDA: Well, that's nothing. Something must've reminded you.

WILLY: Remarkable. Ts. Remember those days? The way Biff used to simonize that car? The dealer refused to believe there was eighty thousand miles on it. [*He shakes his head.*] Heh! [*to* LINDA] Close your eyes, I'll be right up. [*He walks out of the bedroom.*]

HAPPY: [*to* BIFF] Jesus, maybe he smashed up the car again!

LINDA: [*calling after* WILLY] Be careful on the stairs, dear! The cheese is on the middle shelf! [*She turns, goes over to the bed, takes his jacket, and goes out of the bedroom.*]

[*Light has risen on the boys' room. Unseen,* WILLY *is heard talking to himself, "Eighty thousand miles," and a little laugh.* BIFF *gets out of bed, comes downstage a bit, and stands attentively.* BIFF *is two years older than his brother* HAPPY, *well built, but in these days bears a worn air and seems less self-assured. He has succeeded less, and his dreams are stronger and less acceptable than Happy's.* HAPPY *is tall, powerfully made. Sexuality is like a visible color on him, or a scent that many women have discovered. He, like his brother, is lost, but in a different way, for he has never allowed himself to turn his face toward defeat and is thus more confused and hard-skinned, although seemingly more content.*]

HAPPY: [*getting out of bed*] He's going to get his license taken away if he keeps that up. I'm getting nervous about him, y'know, Biff?

BIFF: His eyes are going.

HAPPY: No, I've driven with him. He sees all right. He just doesn't keep his mind on it. I drove into the city with him last week. He stops at a green light and then it turns red and he goes. [*He laughs.*]

BIFF: Maybe he's color-blind.

HAPPY: Pop? Why he's got the finest eye for color in the business. You know that.

BIFF: [*sitting down on his bed*] I'm going to sleep.

HAPPY: You're not still sour on Dad, are you, Biff?

BIFF: He's all right, I guess.

WILLY: [*underneath them, in the living-room*] Yes, sir, eighty thousand miles—eighty-two thousand!

BIFF: You smoking?

HAPPY: [*holding out a pack of cigarettes*] Want one?

BIFF: [*taking a cigarette*] I can never sleep when I smell it.

WILLY: What a simonizing job, heh!

HAPPY: [*with deep sentiment*] Funny, Biff, y'know? Us sleeping in here again? The old beds. [*He pats his bed affectionately*] All the talk that went across those two beds, huh? Our whole lives.

BIFF: Yeah. Lotta dreams and plans.

HAPPY: [*with a deep and masculine laugh*] About five hundred women would like to know what was said in this room.

[*They share a soft laugh.*]

BIFF: Remember that big Betsy something—what the hell was her name—over on Bushwick Avenue?

HAPPY: [*combing his hair*] With the collie dog!

BIFF: That's the one. I got you in there, remember?

HAPPY: Yeah, that was my first time—I think. Boy, there was a pig! [They *laugh, almost crudely.*] You taught me everything I know about women. Don't forget that.

BIFF: I bet you forgot how bashful you used to be. Especially with girls.

HAPPY: Oh, I still am, Biff.

BIFF: Oh, go on.

HAPPY: I just control it, that's all. I think I got less bashful and you got more so. What happened, Biff? Where's the old humor, the old confidence? [*He shakes Biff's knee.* BIFF *gets up and moves restlessly about the room.*] What's the matter?

BIFF: Why does Dad mock me all the time?

HAPPY: He's not mocking you, he—

BIFF: Everything I say there's a twist of mockery on his face. I can't get near him.

HAPPY: He just wants you to make good, that's all. I wanted to talk to you about Dad for a long time, Biff. Something's— happening to him. He— talks to himself.

BIFF: I noticed that this morning. But he always mumbled.

HAPPY: But not so noticeable. It got so embarrassing I sent him to Florida. And you know something? Most of the time he's talking to you.

BIFF: What's he say about me?

HAPPY: I can't make it out.

BIFF: What's he say about me?

HAPPY: I think the fact that you're not settled, that you're still kind of up in the air . . .

BIFF: There's one or two other things depressing him, Happy.

HAPPY: What do you mean?

BIFF: Never mind. Just don't lay it all to me.

HAPPY: But I think if you just got started—I mean—is there any future for you out there?

BIFF: I tell ya, Hap, I don't know what the future is. I don't know—what I'm supposed to want.

HAPPY: What do you mean?

BIFF: Well, I spent six or seven years after high school trying to work myself up. Shipping clerk, salesman, business of one kind or another. And it's a measly manner of existence. To get on that subway on the hot mornings in summer. To devote your whole life to keeping stock, or making phone calls, or selling or buying. To suffer fifty weeks of the year for the sake of a two-week vacation, when all you really desire is to be outdoors, with your shirt off. And always to have to get ahead of the next fella. And still— that's how you build a future.

HAPPY: Well, you really enjoy it on a farm? Are you content out there?

BIFF: [*with rising agitation*] Hap, I've had twenty or thirty different kinds of jobs since I left home before the war, and it always turns out the same. I just realized it lately. In Nebraska when I herded cattle, and the Dakotas, and Arizona, and now in Texas. It's why I came home now, I guess, because I realized it. This farm I work on, it's spring there now, see? And they've got about fifteen new colts. There's nothing more inspiring or—beautiful than the sight of a mare and a new colt. And it's cool there now, see? Texas is cool now, and it's spring. And whenever spring comes to where I am, I suddenly get the feeling, my God, I'm not gettin' anywhere! What the hell am I doing, playing around with horses, twenty-eight dollars a week! I'm thirty-four years old, I oughta be makin' my future. That's when I come running home. And now, I get here, and I don't know what to do with myself. [*after a pause*] I've always made a point of not wasting my life, and everytime I come back here I know that all I've done is to waste my life.

HAPPY: You're a poet, you know that, Biff? You're a—you're an idealist!

BIFF: No, I'm mixed up very bad. Maybe I oughta get married. Maybe I oughta get stuck into something. Maybe that's my trouble. I'm like a boy. I'm not married, I'm not in business, I just—I'm like a boy. Are you content, Hap? You're a success, aren't you? Are you content?

HAPPY: Hell, no!

BIFF: Why? You're making money, aren't you?

HAPPY: [*moving about with energy, expressiveness*] All I can do now is wait for the merchandise manager to die. And suppose I get to be merchandise manager? He's a good friend of mine, and he just built a terrific estate on Long Island. And he lived there about two months and sold it, and now he's building another one. He can't enjoy it once it's finished. And I know that's just what I would do. I don't know what the hell I'm workin' for. Sometimes I sit in my apartment—all alone. And I think of the rent I'm paying. And it's crazy. But then, it's what I always wanted. My own apartment, a car, and plenty of women. And still, goddammit, I'm lonely.

BIFF: [*with enthusiasm*] Listen, why don't you come out West with me?

HAPPY: You and I, heh?

BIFF: Sure, maybe we could buy a ranch. Raise cattle, use our muscles. Men built like we are should be working out in the open.

HAPPY: [*avidly*] The Loman Brothers, heh?

BIFF: [*with vast affection*] Sure, we'd be known all over the counties!

HAPPY: [*enthralled*] That's what I dream about, Biff. Sometimes I want to just rip my clothes off in the middle of the store and outbox that goddam merchandise manager. I mean I can outbox, outrun, and outlift anybody in that store, and I have to take orders from those common, petty sons-of-bitches till I can't stand it any more.

BIFF: I'm tellin' you, kid, if you were with me I'd be happy out there.

HAPPY: [*enthused*] See, Biff, everybody around me is so false that I'm constantly lowering my ideals . . .

BIFF: Baby, together we'd stand up for one another, we'd have someone to trust.

HAPPY: If I were around you—

BIFF: Hap, the trouble is we weren't brought up to grub for money. I don't know how to do it.

HAPPY: Neither can I!

BIFF: Then let's go!

HAPPY: The only thing is—what can you make out there?

BIFF: But look at your friend. Builds an estate and then hasn't the peace of mind to live in it.

HAPPY: Yeah, but when he walks into the store the waves part in front of him. That's fifty-two thousand dollars a year coming through the revolving door, and I got more in my pinky finger than he's got in his head.

BIFF: Yeah, but you just said—

HAPPY: I gotta show some of those pompous, self-important executives over there that Hap Loman can make the grade. I want to walk into the store the way he walks in. Then I'll go with you, Biff. We'll be together yet, I swear. But take those two we had tonight. Now weren't they gorgeous creatures?

BIFF: Yeah, yeah, most gorgeous I've had in years.

HAPPY: I get that any time I want, Biff. Whenever I feel disgusted. The only trouble is, it gets like bowling or something. I just keep knockin' them over and it doesn't mean anything. You still run around a lot?

BIFF: Naa. I'd like to find a girl—steady, somebody with substance.

HAPPY: That's what I long for.

BIFF: Go on! You'd never come home.

HAPPY: I would! Somebody with character, with resistance! Like Mom, y'know? You're gonna call me a bastard when I tell you this. That girl Charlotte I was with tonight is engaged to be married in five weeks. [*He tries on his new hat.*]

BIFF: No kiddin'!

HAPPY: Sure, the guy's in line for the vice-presidency of the store. I don't know what gets into me, maybe I just have an overdeveloped sense of competition or something, but I went and ruined her, and furthermore I can't get rid of her. And he's the third executive I've done that to. Isn't that a crummy characteristic? And to top it all, I go to their weddings! [*indignantly, but laughing*] Like I'm not supposed to take bribes. Manufacturers offer me a hundred-dollar bill now and then to throw an order their way. You know how honest I am, but it's like this girl, see. I hate myself for it. Because I don't want the girl, and, still, I take it and—I love it!

BIFF: Let's go to sleep.

HAPPY: I guess we didn't settle anything, heh?

BIFF: I just got one idea that I think I'm going to try.

HAPPY: What's that?

BIFF: Remember Bill Oliver?

HAPPY: Sure, Oliver is very big now. You want to work for him again?

BIFF: No, but when I quit he said something to me. He put his arm on my shoulder, and he said, "Biff, if you ever need anything, come to me."

HAPPY: I remember that. That sounds good.

BIFF: I think I'll go to see him. If I could get ten thousand or even seven or eight thousand dollars I could buy a beautiful ranch.

HAPPY: I bet he'd back you. 'Cause he thought highly of you, Biff. I mean, they all do. You're well liked, Biff. That's why I say to come back here, and

we both have the apartment. And I'm tellin' you, Biff, any babe you
want . . .

BIFF: No, with a ranch I could do the work I like and still be something. I just
wonder though. I wonder if Oliver still thinks I stole that carton of
basketballs.

HAPPY: Oh, he probably forgot that long ago. It's almost ten years. You're too
sensitive. Anyway, he didn't really fire you.

BIFF: Well, I think he was going to. I think that's why I quit. I was never sure
whether he knew or not. I know he thought the world of me, though. I was
the only one he'd let lock up the place.

WILLY: [below] You gonna wash the engine, Biff?

HAPPY: Shh!

[BIFF looks at HAPPY, who is gazing down, listening. WILLY is mumbling in the parlor.]

HAPPY: You hear that?

[They listen. WILLY laughs warmly.]

BIFF: [growing angry] Doesn't he know Mom can hear that?

WILLY: Don't get your sweater dirty, Biff!

[A look of pain crosses BIFF's face.]

HAPPY: Isn't that terrible? Don't leave again, will you? You'll find a job here.
You gotta stick around. I don't know what to do about him, it's getting
embarrassing.

WILLY: What a simonizing job!

BIFF: Mom's hearing that!

WILLY: No kiddin', Biff, you got a date? Wonderful!

HAPPY: Go on to sleep. But talk to him in the morning, will you?

BIFF: [reluctantly getting into bed] With her in the house. Brother!

HAPPY: [getting into bed] I wish you'd have a good talk with him.

[The light on their room begins to fade.]

BIFF: [to himself in bed] That selfish, stupid . . .

HAPPY: Sh . . . Sleep, Biff.

[Their light is out. Well before they have finished speaking, WILLY's
form is dimly seen below in the darkened kitchen. He opens the
refrigerator, searches in there, and takes out a bottle of milk. The
apartment houses are fading out, and the entire house and surroundings become covered with leaves. Music insinuates itself as the leaves
appear.]

WILLY: Just wanna be careful with those girls, Biff, that's all. Don't make any
promises. No promises of any kind. Because a girl, y'know, they always
believe what you tell 'em, and you're very young, Biff, you're too young
to be talking seriously to girls.

[Light rises on the kitchen. WILLY, talking, shuts the refrigerator
door and comes downstage to the kitchen table. He pours milk into
a glass. He is totally immersed in himself, smiling faintly.]

WILLY: Too young entirely, Biff. You want to watch your schooling first. Then
when you're all set, there'll be plenty of girls for a boy like you. [He
smiles broadly at a kitchen chair.] That so? The girls pay for you? [He
laughs.] Boy, you must really be makin' a hit.

[WILLY *is gradually addressing—physically—a point offstage, speaking through the wall of the kitchen, and his voice has been rising in volume to that of a normal conversation.*]

WILLY: I been wondering why you polish the car so careful. Ha! Don't leave the hubcaps, boys. Get the chamois to the hubcaps. Happy, use newspaper on the windows, it's the easiest thing. Show him how to do it, Biff! You see, Happy? Pad it up, use it like a pad. That's it, that's it, good work. You're doin' all right, Hap. [*he pauses, then nods in approbation for a few seconds, then looks upward*] Biff, first thing we gotta do when we get time is clip that big branch over the house. Afraid it's gonna fall in a storm and hit the roof. Tell you what. We get a rope and sling her around, and then we climb up there with a couple of saws and take her down. Soon as you finish the car, boys, I wanna see ya. I got a surprise for you, boys.

BIFF: [*offstage*] Whatta ya got, Dad?

WILLY: No, you finish first. Never leave a job till you're finished—remember that. [*looking toward the "big trees"*] Biff, up in Albany I saw a beautiful hammock. I think I'll buy it next trip, and we'll hang it right between those two elms. Wouldn't that be something? Just swingin' there under those branches. Boy, that would be . . .

[YOUNG BIFF *and* YOUNG HAPPY *appear from the direction* WILLY *was addressing.* HAPPY *carries rags and a pail of water.* BIFF, *wearing a sweater with a block "S," carries a football.*]

BIFF: [*pointing in the direction of the car offstage*] How's that, Pop, professional?

WILLY: Terrific. Terrific job, boys. Good work, Biff.

HAPPY: Where's the surprise, Pop?

WILLY: In the back seat of the car.

HAPPY: Boy! [*He runs off.*]

BIFF: What is it, Dad? Tell me, what'd you buy?

WILLY: [*laughing, cuffs him*] Never mind, something I want you to have.

BIFF: [*turns and starts off*] What is it, Hap?

HAPPY: [*offstage*] It's a punching bag!

BIFF: Oh, Pop!

WILLY: It's got Gene Tunney's signature on it!

[HAPPY *runs onstage with a punching bag.*]

BIFF: Gee, how'd you know we wanted a punching bag?

WILLY: Well, it's the finest thing for the timing.

HAPPY: [*lies down on his back and pedals with his feet*] I'm losing weight, you notice, Pop?

WILLY: [*to* HAPPY] Jumping rope is good too.

BIFF: Did you see the new football I got?

WILLY: [*examining the ball*] Where'd you get a new ball?

BIFF: The coach told me to practice my passing.

WILLY: That so? And he gave you the ball, heh?

BIFF: Well, I borrowed it from the locker room. [*He laughs confidentially.*]

WILLY: [*laughing with him at the theft*] I want you to return that.

HAPPY: I told you he wouldn't like it!

BIFF: [*angrily*] Well, I'm bringing it back!

WILLY: [*stopping the incipient argument, to* HAPPY] Sure, he's gotta practice with a regulation ball, doesn't he? [*to* BIFF] Coach'll probably congratulate you on your initiative!

BIFF: Oh, he keeps congratulating my initiative all the time, Pop.

WILLY: That's because he likes you. If somebody else took that ball there'd be an uproar. So what's the report, boys, what's the report?

BIFF: Where'd you go this time, Dad? Gee we were lonesome for you.

WILLY: [*pleased, puts an arm around each boy and they come down to the apron*] Lonesome, heh?

BIFF: Missed you every minute.

WILLY: Don't say? Tell you a secret, boys. Don't breathe it to a soul. Someday I'll have my own business, and I'll never have to leave home any more.

HAPPY: Like Uncle Charley, heh?

WILLY: Bigger than Uncle Charley! Because Charley is not—liked. He's liked, but he's not—well liked.

BIFF: Where'd you go this time, Dad?

WILLY: Well, I got on the road, and I went north to Providence. Met the Mayor.

BIFF: The Mayor of Providence!

WILLY: He was sitting in the hotel lobby.

BIFF: What'd he say?

WILLY: He said, "Morning!" And I said, "You got a fine city here, Mayor." And then he had coffee with me. And then I went to Waterbury. Waterbury is a fine city. Big clock city, the famous Waterbury clock. Sold a nice bill there. And then Boston—Boston is the cradle of the Revolution. A fine city. And a couple of other towns in Mass., and on to Portland and Bangor and straight home!

BIFF: Gee, I'd love to go with you sometime, Dad.

WILLY: Soon as summer comes.

HAPPY: Promise?

WILLY: You and Hap and I, and I'll show you all the towns. America is full of beautiful towns and fine, upstanding people. And they know me, boys, they know me up and down New England. The finest people. And when I bring you fellas up, there'll be open sesame for all of us, 'cause one thing, boys: I have friends. I can park my car in any street in New England, and the cops protect it like their own. This summer, heh?

BIFF and HAPPY: [*together*] Yeah! You bet!

WILLY: We'll take our bathing suits.

HAPPY: We'll carry your bags, Pop!

WILLY: Oh, won't that be something! Me comin' into the Boston stores with you boys carryin' my bags. What a sensation!

[BIFF *is prancing around, practicing passing the ball.*]

WILLY: You nervous, Biff, about the game?

BIFF: Not if you're gonna be there.

WILLY: What do they say about you in school, now that they made you captain?

HAPPY: There's a crowd of girls behind him everytime the classes change.

BIFF: [*taking* WILLY's *hand*] This Saturday, Pop, this Saturday—just for you, I'm going to break through for a touchdown.

HAPPY: You're supposed to pass.

BIFF: I'm takin' one play for Pop. You watch me, Pop, and when I take off my helmet, that means I'm breakin' out. Then you watch me crash through that line!

WILLY: [*kisses* BIFF] Oh, wait'll I tell this in Boston!

> [BERNARD *enters in knickers. He is younger than* BIFF, *earnest and loyal, a worried boy.*]

BERNARD: Biff, where are you? You're supposed to study with me today.

WILLY: Hey, looka Bernard. What're you lookin' so anemic about, Bernard?

BERNARD: He's gotta study, Uncle Willy. He's got Regents next week.

HAPPY: [*tauntingly, spinning* BERNARD *around*] Let's box, Bernard!

BERNARD: Biff! [*He gets away from* HAPPY.] Listen, Biff, I heard Mr. Birnbaum say that if you don't start studyin' math he's gonna flunk you, and you won't graduate. I heard him!

WILLY: You better study with him, Biff. Go ahead now.

BERNARD: I heard him!

BIFF: Oh, Pop, you didn't see my sneakers! [*He holds up a foot for* WILLY *to look at.*]

WILLY: Hey, that's a beautiful job of printing!

BERNARD: [*wiping his glasses*] Just because he printed University of Virginia on his sneakers doesn't mean they've got to graduate him, Uncle Willy!

WILLY: [*angrily*] What're you talking about? With scholarships to three universities they're gonna flunk him?

BERNARD: But I heard Mr. Birnbaum say—

WILLY: Don't be a pest, Bernard! [*to his boys*] What an anemic!

BERNARD: Okay, I'm waiting for you in my house, Biff.

> [BERNARD *goes off. The* LOMANS *laugh.*]

WILLY: Bernard is not well liked, is he?

BIFF: He's liked, but he's not well liked.

HAPPY: That's right, Pop.

WILLY: That's just what I mean. Bernard can get the best marks in school, y'understand, but when he gets out in the business world, y'understand, you are going to be five times ahead of him. That's why I thank Almighty God you're both built like Adonises. Because the man who makes an appearance in the business world, the man who creates personal interest, is the man who gets ahead. Be liked and you will never want. You take me, for instance. I never have to wait in line to see a buyer. "Willy Loman is here!" That's all they have to know, and I go right through.

BIFF: Did you knock them dead, Pop?

WILLY: Knocked 'em cold in Providence, slaughtered 'em in Boston.

HAPPY: [*on his back, pedaling again*] I'm losing weight, you notice, Pop?

> [LINDA *enters, as of old, a ribbon in her hair, carrying a basket of washing.*]

LINDA: [*with youthful energy*] Hello, dear!

WILLY: Sweetheart!

LINDA: How'd the Chevvy run?

WILLY: Chevrolet, Linda, is the greatest car ever built. [*to the boys*] Since when do you let your mother carry wash up the stairs?

BIFF: Grab hold there, boy!

HAPPY: Where to, Mom?

LINDA: Hang them up on the line. And you better go down to your friends, Biff. The cellar is full of boys. They don't know what to do with themselves.

BIFF: Ah, when Pop comes home they can wait!

WILLY: [*laughs appreciatively*] You better go down and tell them what to do, Biff.

BIFF: I think I'll have them sweep out the furnace room.

WILLY: Good work, Biff.

BIFF: [*goes through wall-line of kitchen to doorway at back and calls down*] Fellas! Everybody sweep out the furnace room! I'll be right down!

VOICES: All right! Okay, Biff.

BIFF: George and Sam and Frank, come out back! We're hangin' up the wash! Come on, Hap, on the double! [*He and* HAPPY *carry out the basket.*]

LINDA: The way they obey him!

WILLY: Well, that's training, the training. I'm tellin' you, I was sellin' thousands and thousands, but I had to come home.

LINDA: Oh, the whole block'll be at that game. Did you sell anything?

WILLY: I did five hundred gross in Providence and seven hundred gross in Boston.

LINDA: No! Wait a minute, I've got a pencil. [*She pulls pencil and paper out of her apron pocket.*] That makes your commission . . . Two hundred— my God! Two hundred and twelve dollars!

WILLY: Well, I didn't figure it yet, but . . .

LINDA: How much did you do?

WILLY: Well, I—I did—about a hundred and eighty gross in Providence. Well, no—it came to—roughly two hundred gross on the whole trip.

LINDA: [*without hesitation*] Two hundred gross. That's . . . [*She figures.*]

WILLY: The trouble was that three of the stores were half closed for inventory in Boston. Otherwise I woulda broke records.

LINDA: Well, it makes seventy dollars and some pennies. That's very good.

WILLY: What do we owe?

LINDA: Well, on the first there's sixteen dollars on the refrigerator—

WILLY: Why sixteen?

LINDA: Well, the fan belt broke, so it was a dollar eighty.

WILLY: But it's brand new.

LINDA: Well, the man said that's the way it is. Till they work themselves in, y'know.

[*They move through the wall-line into the kitchen.*]

WILLY: I hope we didn't get stuck on that machine.

LINDA: They got the biggest ads of any of them!

WILLY: I know, it's a fine machine. What else?

LINDA: Well, there's nine-sixty for the washing machine. And for the vacuum cleaner there's three and a half due on the fifteenth. Then the roof, you got twenty-one dollars remaining.

WILLY: It don't leak, does it?

LINDA: No, they did a wonderful job. Then you owe Frank for the carburetor.

WILLY: I'm not going to pay that man! That goddam Chevrolet, they ought to prohibit the manufacture of that car!

LINDA: Well, you owe him three and a half. And odds and ends, comes to around a hundred and twenty dollars by the fifteenth.

WILLY: A hundred and twenty dollars! My God, if business don't pick up I don't know what I'm gonna do!

LINDA: Well, next week you'll do better.

WILLY: Oh, I'll knock 'em dead next week. I'll go to Hartford. I'm very well liked in Hartford. You know, the trouble is, Linda, people don't seem to take to me.

[*They move onto the forestage.*]

LINDA: Oh, don't be foolish.

WILLY: I know it when I walk in. They seem to laugh at me.

LINDA: Why? Why would they laugh at you? Don't talk that way, Willy.

[WILLY *moves to the edge of the stage.* LINDA *goes into the kitchen and starts to darn stockings.*]

WILLY: I don't know the reason for it, but they just pass me by. I'm not noticed.

LINDA: But you're doing wonderful, dear. You're making seventy to a hundred dollars a week.

WILLY: But I gotta be at it ten, twelve hours a day. Other men—I don't know —they do it easier. I don't know why—I can't stop myself—I talk too much. A man oughta come in with a few words. One thing about Charley. He's a man of few words, and they respect him.

LINDA: You don't talk too much, you're just lively.

WILLY: [*smiling*] Well, I figure, what the hell, life is short, a couple of jokes. [*to himself*] I joke too much! [*The smile goes.*]

LINDA: Why? You're—

WILLY: I'm fat. I'm very—foolish to look at, Linda. I didn't tell you, but Christmas time I happened to be calling on F. H. Stewarts, and a salesman I know, as I was going in to see the buyer I heard him say something about —walrus. And I—I cracked him right across the face. I won't take that. I simply will not take that. But they do laugh at me. I know that.

LINDA: Darling . . .

WILLY: I gotta overcome it. I know I gotta overcome it. I'm not dressing to advantage, maybe.

LINDA: Willy, darling, you're the handsomest man in the world—

WILLY: Oh, no, Linda.

LINDA: To me you are. [*slight pause*] The handsomest.

[*From the darkness is heard the laughter of a woman.* WILLY *doesn't turn to it, but it continues through* LINDA's *lines.*]

LINDA: And the boys, Willy. Few men are idolized by their children the way you are.

[*Music is heard as behind a scrim, to the left of the house,* THE WOMAN, *dimly seen, is dressing.*]

WILLY: [*with great feeling*] You're the best there is, Linda, you're a pal, you know that? On the road—on the road I want to grab you sometimes and just kiss the life outa you.

[*The laughter is loud now, and he moves into a brightening area at the left, where* THE WOMAN *has come from behind the scrim and is standing, putting on her hat, looking into a "mirror" and laughing.*]

WILLY: 'Cause I get so lonely—especially when business is bad and there's nobody to talk to. I get the feeling that I'll never sell anything again, that I won't make a living for you, or a business, a business for the boys. [*He talks through* THE WOMAN's *subsiding laughter;* THE WOMAN *primps at the "mirror."*] There's so such I want to make for—

THE WOMAN: Me? You didn't make me, Willy. I picked you.

WILLY: [*pleased*] You picked me?

THE WOMAN: [*who is quite proper-looking,* Willy's *age*] I did. I've been sitting at that desk watching all the salesmen go by, day in, day out. But you've got such a sense of humor, and we do have such a good time together, don't we?

WILLY: Sure, sure. [*He takes her in his arms.*] Why do you have to go now?

THE WOMAN: It's two o'clock . . .

WILLY: No, come on in! [*He pulls her.*]

THE WOMAN: . . . my sisters'll be scandalized. When'll you be back?

WILLY: Oh, two weeks about. Will you come up again?

THE WOMAN: Sure thing. You do make me laugh. It's good for me. [*She squeezes his arm, kisses him.*] And I think you're a wonderful man.

WILLY: You picked me, heh?

THE WOMAN: Sure. Because you're so sweet. And such a kidder.

WILLY: Well, I'll see you next time I'm in Boston.

THE WOMAN: I'll put you right through to the buyers.

WILLY: [*slapping her bottom*] Right. Well, bottoms up!

THE WOMAN: [*slaps him gently and laughs*] You just kill me, Willy. [*He suddenly grabs her and kisses her roughly.*] You kill me. And thanks for the stockings. I love a lot of stockings. Well, good night.

WILLY: Good night. And keep your pores open!

THE WOMAN: Oh, Willy!

[THE WOMAN *bursts out laughing, and* LINDA's *laughter blends in.* THE WOMAN *disappears into the dark. Now the area at the kitchen table brightens.* LINDA *is sitting where she was at the kitchen table, but now is mending a pair of her silk stockings.*]

LINDA: You are, Willy. The handsomest man. You've got no reason to feel that—

WILLY: [*coming out of* THE WOMAN's *dimming area and going over to* LINDA] I'll make it all up to you, Linda, I'll—

LINDA: There's nothing to make up, dear. You're doing fine, better than—

WILLY: [*noticing her mending*] What's that?

LINDA: Just mending my stockings. They're so expensive—

WILLY: [*angrily, taking them from her*] I won't have you mending stockings in this house! Now throw them out!

[LINDA *puts the stockings in her pocket.*]

BERNARD: [*entering on the run*] Where is he? If he doesn't study!

WILLY: [*moving to the forestage, with great agitation*] You'll give him the answers!

BERNARD: I do, but I can't on a Regents! That's a state exam! They're liable to arrest me!

WILLY: Where is he? I'll whip him, I'll whip him!

LINDA: And he'd better give back that football, Willy, it's not nice.

WILLY: Biff! Where is he? Why is he taking everything?

LINDA: He's too rough with the girls, Willy. All the mothers are afraid of him!

WILLY: I'll whip him!

BERNARD: He's driving the car without a license!

[THE WOMAN'S *laugh is heard.*]

WILLY: Shut up!

LINDA: All the mothers—

WILLY: Shut up!

BERNARD: [*backing quietly away and out*] Mr. Birnbaum says he's stuck up.

WILLY: Get outa here!

BERNARD: If he doesn't buckle down he'll flunk math! [*He goes off.*]

LINDA: He's right, Willy, you've gotta—

WILLY: [*exploding at her*] There's nothing the matter with him! You want him to be a worm like Bernard? He's got spirit, personality . . .

[*As he speaks,* LINDA, *almost in tears, exits into the living-room.* WILLY *is alone in the kitchen, wilting and staring. The leaves are gone. It is night again, and the apartment houses look down from behind.*]

WILLY: Loaded with it. Loaded! What is he stealing? He's giving it back, isn't he? Why is he stealing? What did I tell him? I never in my life told him anything but decent things.

[HAPPY *in pajamas has come down the stairs;* WILLY *suddenly becomes aware of* HAPPY'S *presence.*]

HAPPY: Let's go now, come on.

WILLY: [*sitting down at the kitchen table*] Huh! Why did she have to wax the floors herself? Everytime she waxes the floors she keels over. She knows that!

HAPPY: Shh! Take it easy. What brought you back tonight?

WILLY: I got an awful scare. Nearly hit a kid in Yonkers. God! Why didn't I go to Alaska with my brother Ben that time! Ben! That man was a genius, that man was success incarnate! What a mistake! He begged me to go.

HAPPY: Well, there's no use in—

WILLY: You guys! There was a man started with the clothes on his back and ended up with diamond mines!

HAPPY: Boy, someday I'd like to know how he did it.

WILLY: What's the mystery? The man knew what he wanted and went out and got it! Walked into a jungle, and comes out, the age of twenty-one, and he's rich! The world is an oyster, but you don't crack it open on a mattress!

HAPPY: Pop, I told you I'm gonna retire you for life.

WILLY: You'll retire me for life on seventy goddam dollars a week? And your women and your car and your apartment, and you'll retire me for life! Christ's sake, I couldn't get past Yonkers' today! Where are you guys, where are you? The woods are burning! I can't drive a car!

[CHARLEY *has appeared in the doorway. He is a large man, slow of speech, laconic, immovable. In all he says, despite what he says, there is pity, and, now, trepidation. He has a robe over pajamas, slippers on his feet. He enters the kitchen.*]

CHARLEY: Everything all right?

HAPPY: Yeah, Charley, everything's . . .

WILLY: What's the matter?

CHARLEY: I heard some noise. I thought something happened. Can't we do something about the walls? You sneeze in here, and in my house hats blow off.

HAPPY: Let's go to bed, Dad. Come on.

[CHARLEY *signals to* HAPPY *to go.*]

WILLY: You go ahead, I'm not tired at the moment.

HAPPY: [*to* WILLY] Take it easy, huh? [*He exits.*]

WILLY: What're you doin' up?

CHARLEY: [*sitting down at the kitchen table opposite* WILLY] Couldn't sleep good. I had a heartburn.

WILLY: Well, you don't know how to eat.

CHARLEY: I eat with my mouth.

WILLY: No, you're ignorant. You gotta know about vitamins and things like that.

CHARLEY: Come on, let's shoot. Tire you out a little.

WILLY: [*hesitantly*] All right. You got cards?

CHARLEY: [*taking a deck from his pocket*] Yeah, I got them. Someplace. What is it with those vitamins?

WILLY: [*dealing*] They build up your bones. Chemistry.

CHARLEY: Yeah, but there's no bones in a heartburn.

WILLY: What are you talkin' about? Do you know the first thing about it?

CHARLEY: Don't get insulted.

WILLY: Don't talk about something you don't know anything about.

[*They are playing. Pause.*]

CHARLEY: What're you doin' home?

WILLY: A little trouble with the car.

CHARLEY: Oh. [*pause*] I'd like to take a trip to California.

WILLY: Don't say.

CHARLEY: You want a job?

WILLY: I got a job, I told you that. [*after a slight pause*] What the hell are you offering me a job for?

CHARLEY: Don't get insulted.

WILLY: Don't insult me.

CHARLEY: I don't see no sense in it. You don't have to go on this way.

WILLY: I got a good job. [*slight pause*] What do you keep comin' in here for?

CHARLEY: You want me to go?

WILLY: [*after a pause, withering*] I can't understand it. He's going back to Texas again. What the hell is that?

CHARLEY: Let him go.

WILLY: I got nothin' to give him, Charley, I'm clean, I'm clean.

CHARLEY: He won't starve. None a them starve. Forget about him.

WILLY: Then what have I got to remember?

CHARLEY: You take it too hard. To hell with it. When a deposit bottle is broken you don't get your nickel back.

WILLY: That's easy enough for you to say.

CHARLEY: That ain't easy for me to say.

WILLY: Did you see the ceiling I put up in the living-room?

CHARLEY: Yeah, that's a piece of work. To put up a ceiling is a mystery to me. How do you do it?

WILLY: What's the difference?

CHARLEY: Well, talk about it.

WILLY: You gonna put up a ceiling?

CHARLEY: How could I put up a ceiling?

WILLY: Then what the hell are you bothering me for?

CHARLEY: You're insulted again.

WILLY: A man who can't handle tools is not a man. You're disgusting.

CHARLEY: Don't call me disgusting, Willy.

> [UNCLE BEN, *carrying a valise and an umbrella, enters the forestage from around the right corner of the house. He is a stolid man, in his sixties, with a mustache and an authoritative air. He is utterly certain of his destiny, and there is an aura of far places about him. He enters exactly as* WILLY *speaks.*]

WILLY: I'm getting awfully tired, Ben.

> [*Ben's music is heard.* BEN *looks around at everything.*]

CHARLEY: Good, keep playing; you'll sleep better. Did you call me Ben?

> [BEN *looks at his watch.*]

WILLY: That's funny. For a second there you reminded me of my brother Ben.

BEN: I only have a few minutes. [*He strolls, inspecting the place.* WILLY *and* CHARLEY *continue playing.*]

CHARLEY: You never heard from him again, heh? Since that time?

WILLY: Didn't Linda tell you? Couple of weeks ago we got a letter from his wife in Africa. He died.

CHARLEY: That so.

BEN: [*chuckling*] So this is Brooklyn, eh?

CHARLEY: Maybe you're in for some of his money.

WILLY: Naa, he had seven sons. There's just one opportunity I had with that man . . .

BEN: I must make a train, William. There are several properties I'm looking at in Alaska.

WILLY: Sure, sure! If I'd gone with him to Alaska that time, everything would've been totally different.

CHARLEY: Go on, you'd froze to death up there.

WILLY: What're you talking about?

BEN: Opportunity is tremendous in Alaska, William. Surprised you're not up there.

WILLY: Sure, tremendous.

CHARLEY: Heh?

WILLY: There was the only man I ever met who knew the answers.

CHARLEY: Who?

BEN: How are you all?

WILLY: [*taking a pot, smiling*] Fine, fine.

CHARLEY: Pretty sharp tonight.

BEN: Is Mother living with you?

WILLY: No, she died a long time ago.

CHARLEY: Who?

BEN: That's too bad. Fine specimen of a lady, Mother.

WILLY: [*to* CHARLEY] Heh?

BEN: I'd hoped to see the old girl.

CHARLEY: Who died?

BEN: Heard anything from Father, have you?

WILLY: [*unnerved*] What do you mean, who died?

CHARLEY: [*taking a pot*] What're you talkin' about?

BEN: [*looking at his watch*] William, it's half-past eight!

WILLY: [*as though to dispel his confusion he angrily stops* CHARLEY'S *hand*] That's my build!

CHARLEY: I put the ace—

WILLY: If you don't know how to play the game I'm not gonna throw my money away on you!

CHARLEY: [*rising*] It was my ace, for God's sake!

WILLY: I'm through, I'm through!

BEN: When did Mother die?

WILLY: Long ago. Since the beginning you never knew how to play cards.

CHARLEY: [*picks up the cards and goes to the door*] All right! Next time I'll bring a deck with five aces.

WILLY: I don't play that kind of game!

CHARLEY: [*turning to him*] You ought to be ashamed of yourself!

WILLY: Yeah?

CHARLEY: Yeah! [*He goes out.*]

WILLY: [*slamming the door after him*] Ignoramus!

BEN: [*as* WILLY *comes toward him through the wall-line of the kitchen*] So you're William.

WILLY: [*shaking* BEN'S *hand*] Ben! I've been waiting for you so long! What's the answer? How did you do it?

BEN: Oh, there's a story in that.

[LINDA *enters the forestage, as of old, carrying the wash basket.*]

LINDA: Is this Ben?

BEN: [*gallantly*] How do you do, my dear.

LINDA: Where've you been all these years? Willy's always wondered why you—

WILLY: [*pulling* BEN *away from her impatiently*] Where is Dad? Didn't you follow him? How did you get started?

BEN: Well, I don't know how much you remember.

WILLY: Well, I was just a baby, of course, only three or four years old—

BEN: Three years and eleven months.

WILLY: What a memory, Ben!

BEN: I have many enterprises, William, and I have never kept books.

WILLY: I remember I was sitting under the wagon in—was it Nebraska?

BEN: It was South Dakota, and I gave you a bunch of wild flowers.

WILLY: I remember you walking away down some open road.

BEN: [*laughing*] I was going to find Father in Alaska.

WILLY: Where is he?

BEN: At that age I had a very faulty view of geography, William. I discovered after a few days that I was heading due south, so instead of Alaska, I ended up in Africa.

LINDA: Africa!

WILLY: The Gold Coast!

BEN: Principally diamond mines.

LINDA: Diamond mines!

BEN: Yes, my dear. But I've only a few minutes—

WILLY: No! Boys! Boys! [YOUNG BIFF *and* HAPPY *appear.*] Listen to this. This is your Uncle Ben, a great man! Tell my boys, Ben!

BEN: Why, boys, when I was seventeen I walked into the jungle, and when I was twenty-one I walked out. [*he laughs*] And by God I was rich.

WILLY: [*to the boys*] You see what I been talking about? The greatest things can happen!

BEN: [*glancing at his watch*] I have an appointment in Ketchikan Tuesday week.

WILLY: No, Ben! Please tell about Dad. I want my boys to hear. I want them to know the kind of stock they spring from. All I remember is a man with a big beard, and I was in Mamma's lap, sitting around a fire, and some kind of high music.

BEN: His flute. He played the flute.

WILLY: Sure, the flute, that's right!

[*New music is heard, a high, rollicking tune.*]

BEN: Father was a very great and a very wild-hearted man. We would start in Boston, and he'd toss the whole family into the wagon, and then he'd drive the team right across the country; through Ohio, and Indiana, Michigan, Illinois, and all the Western states. And we'd stop in the towns and sell the flutes that he'd made on the way. Great inventor, Father. With one gadget he made more in a week than a man like you could make in a lifetime.

WILLY: That's just the way I'm bringing them up, Ben—rugged, well liked, all-around.

BEN: Yeah? [*to* BIFF] Hit that, boy—hard as you can. [*he pounds his stomach*]
BIFF: Oh, no, sir!
BEN: [*taking boxing stance*] Come on, get to me! [*He laughs.*]
BIFF: Okay! [*He cocks his fists and starts in.*]
LINDA: [*to* WILLY] Why must he fight, dear?
BEN: [*sparring with* BIFF] Good boy! Good boy!
WILLY: How's that, Ben, heh?
HAPPY: Give him the left, Biff!
LINDA: Why are you fighting?
BEN: Good boy! [*Suddenly comes in, trips* BIFF, *and stands over him, the point of his umbrella poised over* BIFF's *eye.*]
LINDA: Look out, Biff!
BIFF: Gee!
BEN: [*patting* BIFF's *knee*] Never fight fair with a stranger, boy. You'll never get out of the jungle that way. [*taking* LINDA's *hand and bowing*] It was an honor and a pleasure to meet you, Linda.
LINDA: [*withdrawing her hand coldly, frightened*] Have a nice—trip.
BEN: [*to* WILLY] And good luck with your—what do you do?
WILLY: Selling.
BEN: Yes. Well . . . [*He raises his hand in farewell to all.*]
WILLY: No, Ben, I don't want you to think . . . [*He takes* BEN's *arm to show him.*] It's Brooklyn, I know, but we hunt too.
BEN: Really, now.
WILLY: Oh, sure, there's snakes and rabbits and—that's why I moved out here. Why, Biff can fell any one of these trees in no time! Boys! Go right over to where they're building the apartment house and get some sand. We're gonna rebuild the entire front stoop right now! Watch this, Ben!
BIFF: Yes, sir! On the double, Hap!
HAPPY: [*as he and* BIFF *run off*] I lost weight, Pop, you notice?
[CHARLEY *enters in knickers, even before the boys are gone.*]
CHARLEY: Listen, if they steal any more from that building the watchman'll put the cops on them!
LINDA: [*to* WILLY] Don't let Biff . . .
[BEN *laughs lustily.*]
WILLY: You shoulda seen the lumber they brought home last week. At least a dozen six-by-tens worth all kinds a money.
CHARLEY: Listen, if that watchman—
WILLY: I gave them hell, understand. But I got a couple of fearless characters there.
CHARLEY: Willy, the jails are full of fearless characters.
BEN: [*clapping* WILLY *on the back, with a laugh at* CHARLEY] And the stock exchange, friend!
WILLY: [*joining in* BEN's *laughter*] Where are the rest of your pants?
CHARLEY: My wife bought them.
WILLY: Now all you need is a golf club and you can go upstairs and go to sleep. [*to* BEN] Great athlete! Between him and his son Bernard they can't hammer a nail!

BERNARD: [*rushing in*] The watchman's chasing Biff!

WILLY: [*angrily*] Shut up! He's not stealing anything!

LINDA: [*alarmed, hurrying off left*] Where is he? Biff, dear! [*She exits.*]

WILLY: [*moving toward the left, away from* BEN] There's nothing wrong. What's the matter with you?

BEN: Nervy boy. Good!

WILLY: [*laughing*] Oh, nerves of iron, that Biff!

CHARLEY: Don't know what it is. My New England man comes back and he's bleedin', they murdered him up there.

WILLY: It's contacts, Charley, I got important contacts!

CHARLEY: [*sarcastically*] Glad to hear it, Willy. Come in later, we'll shoot a little casino. I'll take some of your Portland money. [*He laughs at* WILLY *and exits.*]

WILLY: [*turning to* BEN] Business is bad, it's murderous. But not for me, of course.

BEN: I'll stop by on my way back to Africa.

WILLY: [*longingly*] Can't you stay a few days? You're just what I need, Ben, because I—I have a fine position here, but I—well, Dad left when I was such a baby and I never had a chance to talk to him and I still feel—kind of temporary about myself.

BEN: I'll be late for my train.

> [*They are at opposite ends of the stage.*]

WILLY: Ben, my boys—can't we talk? They'd go into the jaws of hell for me, see, but I—

BEN: William, you're being first-rate with your boys. Outstanding, manly chaps!

WILLY: [*hanging on to his words*] Oh, Ben, that's good to hear! Because sometimes I'm afraid that I'm not teaching them the right kind of— Ben, how should I teach them?

BEN: [*giving great weight to each word, and with a certain vicious audacity*] William, when I walked into the jungle, I was seventeen. When I walked out I was twenty-one. And, by God, I was rich! [*He goes off into darkness around the right corner of the house.*]

WILLY: . . . was rich! That's just the spirit I want to imbue them with! To walk into a jungle! I was right! I was right! I was right!

> [BEN *is gone, but* WILLY *is still speaking to him as* LINDA, *in nightgown and robe, enters the kitchen, glances around for* WILLY, *then goes to the door of the house, looks out and sees him. Comes down to his left. He looks at her.*]

LINDA: Willy, dear? Willy?

WILLY: I was right!

LINDA: Did you have some cheese? [*He can't answer.*] It's very late, darling. Come to bed, heh?

WILLY: [*looking straight up*] Gotta break your neck to see a star in this yard.

LINDA: You coming in?

WILLY: Whatever happened to that diamond watch fob? Remember? When Ben came from Africa that time? Didn't he give me a watch fob with a diamond in it?

LINDA: You pawned it, dear. Twelve, thirteen years ago. For Biff's radio correspondence course.

WILLY: Gee, that was a beautiful thing. I'll take a walk.

LINDA: But you're in your slippers.

WILLY: [*starting to go around the house at the left*] I was right! I was! [*half to* LINDA, *as he goes, shaking his head*] What a man! There was a man worth talking to. I was right!

LINDA: [*calling after* WILLY] But in your slippers, Willy!

[WILLY *is almost gone when* BIFF, *in his pajamas, comes down the stairs and enters the kitchen.*]

BIFF: What is he doing out there?

LINDA: Sh!

BIFF: God Almighty, Mom, how long has he been doing this?

LINDA: Don't, he'll hear you.

BIFF: What the hell is the matter with him?

LINDA: It'll pass by morning.

BIFF: Shouldn't we do anything?

LINDA: Oh, my dear, you should do a lot of things, but there's nothing to do, so go to sleep.

[HAPPY *comes down the stairs and sits on the steps.*]

HAPPY: I never heard him so loud, Mom.

LINDA: Well, come around more often; you'll hear him. [*She sits down at the table and mends the lining of* WILLY's *jacket.*]

BIFF: Why didn't you ever write me about this, Mom?

LINDA: How would I write to you? For over three months you had no address.

BIFF: I was on the move. But you know I thought of you all the time. You know that, don't you, pal?

LINDA: I know, dear, I know. But he likes to have a letter. Just to know that there's still a possibility for better things.

BIFF: He's not like this all the time, is he?

LINDA: It's when you come home he's always the worst.

BIFF: When I come home?

LINDA: When you write you're coming, he's all smiles, and talks about the future, and—he's just wonderful. And then the closer you seem to come, the more shaky he gets, and then, by the time you get here, he's arguing, and he seems angry at you. I think it's just that maybe he can't bring himself to—to open up to you. Why are you so hateful to each other? Why is that?

BIFF: [*evasively*] I'm not hateful, Mom.

LINDA: But you no sooner come in the door than you're fighting!

BIFF: I don't know why. I mean to change. I'm tryin', Mom, you understand?

LINDA: Are you home to stay now?

BIFF: I don't know. I want to look around see what's doin'.

LINDA: Biff, you can't look around all your life, can you?

BIFF: I just can't take hold, Mom. I can't take hold of some kind of a life.

LINDA: Biff, a man is not a bird, to come and go with the springtime.

BIFF: Your hair . . . [*He touches her hair.*] Your hair got so gray.

LINDA: Oh, it's been gray since you were in high school. I just stopped dyeing it, that's all.

BIFF: Dye it again, will ya? I don't want my pal looking old. [*He smiles.*]

LINDA: You're such a boy! You think you can go away for a year and . . . You've got to get it into your head now that one day you'll knock on this door and there'll be strange people here—

BIFF: What are you talking about? You're not even sixty, Mom.

LINDA: But what about your father?

BIFF: [*lamely*] Well, I meant him too.

HAPPY: He admires Pop.

LINDA: Biff, dear, if you don't have any feeling for him, then you can't have any feeling for me.

BIFF: Sure I can, Mom.

LINDA: No. You can't just come to see me, because I love him. [*with a threat, but only a threat, of tears*] He's the dearest man in the world to me, and I won't have anyone making him feel unwanted and low and blue. You've got to make up your mind now, darling, there's no leeway any more. Either he's your father and you pay him that respect, or else you're not to come here. I know he's not easy to get along with—nobody knows that better than me—but . . .

WILLY: [*from the left, with a laugh*] Hey, hey, Biffo!

BIFF: [*starting to go out after* WILLY] What the hell is the matter with him? [HAPPY *stops him.*]

LINDA: Don't—don't go near him!

BIFF: Stop making excuses for him! He always, always wiped the floor with you. Never had an ounce of respect for you.

HAPPY: He's always had respect for—

BIFF: What the hell do you know about it?

HAPPY: [*surlily*] Just don't call him crazy!

BIFF: He's got no character— Charley wouldn't do this. Not in his own house —spewing out that vomit from his mind.

HAPPY: Charley never had to cope with what he's got to.

BIFF: People are worse off than Willy Loman. Believe me, I've seen them!

LINDA: Then make Charley your father, Biff. You can't do that, can you? I don't say he's a great man. Willy Loman never made a lot of money. His name was never in the paper. He's not the finest character that ever lived. But he's a human being, and a terrible thing is happening to him. So attention must be paid. He's not to be allowed to fall into his grave like an old dog. Attention, attention must be finally paid to such a person. You called him crazy—

BIFF: I didn't mean—

LINDA: No, a lot of people think he's lost his—balance. But you don't have to be very smart to know what his trouble is. The man is exhausted.

HAPPY: Sure!

LINDA: A small man can be just as exhausted as a great man. He works for a company thirty-six years this March, opens up unheard-of territories to their trademark, and now in his old age they take his salary away.

HAPPY: [*indignantly*] I didn't know that, Mom.

LINDA: You never asked, my dear! Now that you get your spending money someplace else you don't trouble your mind with him.

HAPPY: But I gave you money last—

LINDA: Christmas time, fifty dollars! To fix the hot water it cost ninety-seven fifty! For five weeks he's been on straight commission, like a beginner, an unknown!

BIFF: Those ungrateful bastards!

LINDA: Are they any worse than his sons? When he brought them business, when he was young, they were glad to see him. But now his old friends, the old buyers that loved him so and always found some order to hand him in a pinch—they're all dead, retired. He used to be able to make six, seven calls a day in Boston. Now he takes his valises out of the car and puts them back and takes them out again and he's exhausted. Instead of walking he talks now. He drives seven hundred miles, and when he gets there no one knows him any more, no one welcomes him. And what goes through a man's mind, driving seven hundred miles home without having earned a cent? Why shouldn't he talk to himself? Why? When he has to go to Charley and borrow fifty dollars a week and pretend to me that it's his pay? How long can that go on? How long? You see what I'm sitting here and waiting for? And you tell me he has no character? The man who never worked a day but for your benefit? When does he get the medal for that? Is this his reward—to turn around at the age of sixty-three and find his sons, who he loved better than his life, one a philandering bum—

HAPPY: Mom!

LINDA: That's all you are, my baby! [*to* BIFF] And you! What happened to the love you had for him? You were such pals! How you used to talk to him on the phone every night! How lonely he was till he could come home to you!

BIFF: All right, Mom. I'll live here in my room, and I'll get a job. I'll keep away from him, that's all.

LINDA: No, Biff. You can't stay here and fight all the time.

BIFF: He threw me out of this house, remember that.

LINDA: Why did he do that? I never knew why.

BIFF: Because I know he's a fake and he doesn't like anybody around who knows!

LINDA: Why a fake? In what way? What do you mean?

BIFF: Just don't lay it all at my feet. It's between me and him—that's all I have to say. I'll chip in from now on. He'll settle for half my pay check. He'll be all right. I'm going to bed. [*he starts for the stairs*]

LINDA: He won't be all right.

BIFF: [*turning on the stairs, furiously*] I hate this city and I'll stay here. Now what do you want?

LINDA: He's dying, Biff.

[HAPPY *turns quickly to her, shocked.*]

BIFF: [*after a pause*] Why is he dying?

LINDA: He's been trying to kill himself.

BIFF: [*with great horror*] How?

LINDA: I live from day to day.

BIFF: What're you talking about?

LINDA: Remember I wrote you that he smashed up the car again? In February?

BIFF: Well?

LINDA: The insurance inspector came. He said that they have evidence. That all these accidents in the last year—weren't—weren't—accidents.

HAPPY: How can they tell that? That's a lie.

LINDA: It seems there's a woman . . . [*she takes a breath as*]

⌠BIFF: [*sharply but contained*] What woman?

⌡LINDA: [*simultaneously*] . . . and this woman . . .

LINDA: What?

BIFF: Nothing. Go ahead.

LINDA: What did you say?

BIFF: Nothing. I just said what woman?

HAPPY: What about her?

LINDA: Well, it seems she was walking down the road and saw his car. She says that he wasn't driving fast at all, and that he didn't skid. She says he came to that little bridge, and then deliberately smashed into the railing, and it was only the shallowness of the water that saved him.

BIFF: Oh, no, he probably just fell asleep again.

LINDA: I don't think he fell asleep.

BIFF: Why not?

LINDA: Last month . . . [*with great difficulty*] Oh, boys, it's so hard to say a thing like this! He's just a big stupid man to you, but I tell you there's more good in him than in many other people. [*she chokes, wipes her eyes*] I was looking for a fuse. The lights blew out, and I went down the cellar. And behind the fuse box—it happened to fall out—was a length of rubber pipe—just short.

HAPPY: No kidding?

LINDA: There's a little attachment on the end of it. I knew right away. And sure enough, on the bottom of the water heater there's a new little nipple on the gas pipe.

HAPPY: [*angrily*] That—jerk.

BIFF: Did you have it taken off?

LINDA: I'm—I'm ashamed to. How can I mention it to him? Every day I go down and take away that little rubber pipe. But, when he comes home, I put it back where it was. How can I insult him that way? I don't know what to do. I live from day to day, boys. I tell you, I know every thought in his mind. It sounds so old-fashioned and silly, but I tell you he put his whole life into you and you've turned your backs on him. [*she is bent over in the chair, weeping, her face in her hands*] Biff, I swear to God! Biff, his life is in your hands!

HAPPY: [*to* BIFF] How do you like that damned fool!

BIFF: [*kissing her*] All right, pal, all right. It's all settled now. I've been remiss. I know that, Mom. But now I'll stay, and I swear to you, I'll apply myself. [*kneeling in front of her, in a fever of self-reproach*] It's just—you see, Mom, I don't fit in business. Not that I won't try. I'll try, and I'll make good.

HAPPY: Sure you will. The trouble with you in business was you never tried to please people.

BIFF: I know, I—

HAPPY: Like when you worked for Harrison's. Bob Harrison said you were tops, and then you go and do some damn fool thing like whistling whole songs in the elevator like a comedian.

BIFF: [*against* HAPPY] So what? I like to whistle sometimes.

HAPPY: You don't raise a guy to a responsible job who whistles in the elevator!

LINDA: Well, don't argue about it now.

HAPPY: Like when you'd go off and swim in the middle of the day instead of taking the line around.

BIFF: [*his resentment rising*] Well, don't you run off? You take off sometimes, don't you? On a nice summer day?

HAPPY: Yeah, but I cover myself!

LINDA: Boys!

HAPPY: If I'm going to take a fade the boss can call any number where I'm supposed to be and they'll swear to him that I just left. I'll tell you something that I hate to say, Biff, but in the business world some of them think you're crazy.

BIFF [*angered*] Screw the business world!

HAPPY: All right, screw it! Great, but cover yourself!

LINDA: Hap, Hap!

BIFF: I don't care what they think! They've laughed at Dad for years, and you know why? Because we don't belong in this nuthouse of a city! We should be mixing cement on some open plain, or—or carpenters. A carpenter is allowed to whistle!

[WILLY *walks in from the entrance of the house, at left.*]

WILLY: Even your grandfather was better than a carpenter. [*Pause. They watch him.*] You never grew up. Bernard does not whistle in the elevator, I assure you.

BIFF: [*as though to laugh* WILLY *out of it*] Yeah, but you do, Pop.

WILLY: I never in my life whistled in an elevator! And who in the business world thinks I'm crazy?

BIFF: I didn't mean it like that, Pop. Now don't make a whole thing out of it, will ya?

WILLY: Go back to the West! Be a carpenter, a cowboy, enjoy yourself!

LINDA: Willy, he was just saying—

WILLY: I heard what he said!

HAPPY: [*trying to quiet* WILLY] Hey, Pop, come on now . . .

WILLY: [*continuing over Happy's line*] They laugh at me, heh? Go to Filene's, go to the Hub, go to Slattery's, Boston. Call out the name Willy Loman and see what happens! Big shot!

BIFF: All right, Pop.

WILLY: Big!

BIFF: All right!

WILLY: Why do you always insult me?

BIFF: I didn't say a word. [*to* LINDA] Did I say a word?

LINDA: He didn't say anything, Willy.

WILLY: [*going to the doorway of the living-room*] All right, good night, good night.

LINDA: Willy, dear, he just decided . . .

WILLY: [*to* BIFF] If you get tired hanging around tomorrow, paint the ceiling I put up in the living-room.

BIFF: I'm leaving early tomorrow.

HAPPY: He's going to see Bill Oliver, Pop.

WILLY: [*interestedly*] Oliver? For what?

BIFF: [*with reserve, but trying, trying*] He always said he'd stake me. I'd like to go into business, so maybe I can take him up on it.

LINDA: Isn't that wonderful?

WILLY: Don't interrupt. What's wonderful about it? There's fifty men in the City of New York who'd stake him. [*to* BIFF] Sporting goods?

BIFF: I guess so. I know something about it and—

WILLY: He knows something about it! You know sporting goods better than Spalding, for God's sake! How much is he giving you?

BIFF: I don't know, I didn't even see him yet, but—

WILLY: Then what're you talkin' about?

BIFF: [*getting angry*] Well, all I said was I'm gonna see him, that's all!

WILLY: [*turning away*] Ah, you're counting your chickens again.

BIFF: [*starting left for the stairs*] Oh, Jesus, I'm going to sleep!

WILLY: [*calling after him*] Don't curse in this house!

BIFF: [*turning*] Since when did you get so clean?

HAPPY: [*trying to stop them*] Wait a . . .

WILLY: Don't use that language to me! I won't have it!

HAPPY: [*grabbing* BIFF, *shouts*] Wait a minute! I got an idea. I got a feasible idea. Come here, Biff, let's talk this over now, let's talk some sense here. When I was down in Florida last time, I thought of a great idea to sell sporting goods. It just came back to me. You and I, Biff—we have a line, the Loman Line. We train a couple of weeks, and put on a couple of exhibitions, see?

WILLY: That's an idea!

HAPPY: Wait! We form two basketball teams, see? Two waterpolo teams. We play each other. It's a million dollars' worth of publicity. Two brothers, see? The Loman Brothers. Displays in the Royal Palms—all the hotels. And banners over the ring and the basketball court: "Loman Brothers." Baby, we could sell sporting goods!

WILLY: That is a one-million-dollar idea!

LINDA: Marvelous!

BIFF: I'm in great shape as far as that's concerned.

HAPPY: And the beauty of it is, Biff, it wouldn't be like a business. We'd be out playin' ball again . . .

BIFF: [*enthused*] Yeah, that's . . .

WILLY: Million-dollar . . .

HAPPY: And you wouldn't get fed up with it, Biff. It'd be the family again. There'd be the old honor, and comradeship, and if you wanted to go off for a swim or somethin'—well, you'd do it! Without some smart cooky gettin' up ahead of you!

WILLY: Lick the world! You guys together could absolutely lick the civilized world.

BIFF: I'll see Oliver tomorrow. Hap, if we could work that out . . .

LINDA: Maybe things are beginning to—

WILLY: [*wildly enthused, to* LINDA] Stop interrupting! [*to* BIFF] But don't wear sport jacket and slacks when you see Oliver.

BIFF: No, I'll—

WILLY: A business suit, and talk as little as possible, and don't crack any jokes.

BIFF: He did like me. Always liked me.

LINDA: He loved you!

WILLY: [*to* LINDA] Will you stop! [*to* BIFF] Walk in very serious. You are not applying for a boy's job. Money is to pass. Be quiet, fine, and serious. Everybody likes a kidder, but nobody lends him money.

HAPPY: I'll try to get some myself, Biff. I'm sure I can.

WILLY: I see great things for you kids, I think your troubles are over. But remember, start big and you'll end big. Ask for fifteen. How much you gonna ask for?

BIFF: Gee, I don't know—

WILLY: And don't say "Gee." "Gee" is a boy's word. A man walking in for fifteen thousand dollars does not say "Gee!"

BIFF: Ten, I think, would be top though.

WILLY: Don't be so modest. You always started too low. Walk in with a big laugh. Don't look worried. Start off with a couple of your good stories to lighten things up. It's not what you say, it's how you say it—because personality always wins the day.

LINDA: Oliver always thought the highest of him—

WILLY: Will you let me talk?

BIFF: Don't yell at her, Pop, will ya?

WILLY: [*angrily*] I was talking, wasn't I?

BIFF: I don't like you yelling at her all the time, and I'm tellin' you, that's all.

WILLY: What're you, takin' over this house?

LINDA: Willy—

WILLY: [*turning on her*] Don't take his side all the time, goddammit!

BIFF: [*furiously*] Stop yelling at her!

WILLY: [*suddenly pulling on his cheek, beaten down, guilt ridden*] Give my best to Bill Oliver—he may remember me.
        [*He exits through the living-room doorway.*]

LINDA: [*her voice subdued*] What'd you have to start that for? [BIFF *turns away.*] You see how sweet he was as soon as you talked hopefully? [*She goes over to* BIFF] Come up and say good night to him. Don't let him go to bed that way.

HAPPY: Come on, Biff, let's buck him up.

LINDA: Please, dear. Just say good night. It takes so little to make him happy. Come. [*She goes through the living-room doorway, calling upstairs from within the living-room:*] Your pajamas are hanging in the bathroom, Willy!

HAPPY: [*looking toward where* LINDA *went out*] What a woman! They broke the mold when they made her. You know that, Biff?

BIFF: He's off salary. My God, working on commission!

HAPPY: Well, let's face it: he's no hot-shot selling man. Except that sometimes, you have to admit, he's a sweet personality.

BIFF: [*deciding*] Lend me ten bucks, will ya? I want to buy some new ties.

HAPPY: I'll take you to a place I know. Beautiful stuff. Wear one of my striped shirts tomorrow.

BIFF: She got gray. Mom got awful old. Gee, I'm gonna go in to Oliver tomorrow and knock him for a—

HAPPY: Come on up. Tell that to Dad. Let's give him a whirl. Come on.

BIFF: [*steamed up*] You know, with ten thousand bucks, boy!

HAPPY: [*as they go into the living-room*] That's the talk, Biff, that's the first time I've heard the old confidence out of you! [*from within the living-room, fading off*] You're gonna live with me, kid, and any babe you want just say the word . . . [*The last lines are hardly heard. They are mounting the stairs to their parents' bedroom.*]

LINDA: [*entering her bedroom and addressing* WILLY, *who is in the bathroom. She is straightening the bed for him*] Can you do anything about the shower? It drips.

WILLY: [*from the bathroom*] All of a sudden everything falls to pieces! Goddam plumbing, oughta be sued, those people. I hardly finished putting it in and the thing . . . [*his words rumble off.*]

LINDA: I'm just wondering if Oliver will remember him. You think he might?

WILLY: [*coming out of the bathroom in his pajamas*] Remember him? What's the matter with you, you crazy? If he'd've stayed with Oliver he'd be on top by now! Wait'll Oliver gets a look at him. You don't know the average caliber any more. The average young man today—[*he is getting into bed*]—is got a caliber of zero. Greatest thing in the world for him was to bum around.

[BIFF *and* HAPPY *enter the bedroom. Slight pause.*]

WILLY: [*stops short, looking at* BIFF] Glad to hear it, boy.

HAPPY: He wanted to say good night to you, sport.

WILLY: [*to* BIFF] Yeah. Knock him dead, boy. What'd you want to tell me?

BIFF: Just take it easy, Pop. Good night. [*He turns to go.*]

WILLY: [*unable to resist*] And if anything falls off the desk while you're talking to him—like a package or something—don't you pick it up. They have office boys for that.

LINDA: I'll make a big breakfast—

WILLY: Will you let me finish? [*to* BIFF] Tell him you were in the business in the West. Not farm work.

BIFF: All right, Dad.

LINDA: I think everything—

WILLY: [*going right through her speech*] And don't undersell yourself. No less than fifteen thousand dollars.

BIFF: [*unable to bear him*] Okay. Good night, Mom. [*He starts moving.*]

WILLY: Because you got a greatness in you, Biff, remember that. You got all kinds a greatness . . . [*He lies back, exhausted.*]
[BIFF *walks out.*]

LINDA: [*calling after* BIFF] Sleep well, darling!

HAPPY: I'm gonna get married, Mom. I wanted to tell you.

LINDA: Go to sleep, dear.

HAPPY: [*going*] I just wanted to tell you.

WILLY: Keep up the good work. [HAPPY *exits.*] God . . . remember that Ebbets Field game? The championship of the city?

LINDA: Just rest. Should I sing to you?

WILLY: Yeah. Sing to me. [LINDA *hums a soft lullaby.*] When that team came out—he was the tallest, remember?

LINDA: Oh, yes. And in gold.
[BIFF *enters the darkened kitchen, takes a cigarette, and leaves the house. He comes downstage into a golden pool of light. He smokes, staring at the night.*]

WILLY: Like a young god. Hercules—something like that. And the sun, the sun all around him. Remember how he waved to me? Right up from the field, with the representatives of three colleges standing by? And the buyers I brought, and the cheers when he came out—Loman, Loman, Loman! God Almighty, he'll be great yet. A star like that, magnificent, can never really fade away!
[*The light on* WILLY *is fading. The gas heater begins to glow through the kitchen wall, near the stairs, a blue flame beneath red coils.*]

LINDA: [*timidly*] Willy dear, what has he got against you?

WILLY: I'm so tired. Don't talk any more.
[BIFF *slowly returns to the kitchen. He stops, stares toward the heater.*]

LINDA: Will you ask Howard to let you work in New York?

WILLY: First thing in the morning. Everything'll be all right.
[BIFF *reaches behind the heater and draws out a length of rubber tubing. He is horrified and turns his head toward Willy's room, still dimly lit, from which the strains of* LINDA's *desperate but monotonous humming rise.*]

WILLY: [*staring through the window into the moonlight*] Gee, look at the moon moving between the buildings!
[BIFF *wraps the tubing around his hand and quickly goes up the stairs.*]

ACT II

[*Music is heard, gay and bright. The curtain rises as the music fades away.* WILLY, *in shirt sleeves, is sitting at the kitchen table, sipping coffee, his hat in his lap.* LINDA *is filling his cup when she can.*]

WILLY: Wonderful coffee. Meal in itself.

LINDA: Can I make you some eggs?

WILLY: No. Take a breath.

LINDA: You look so rested, dear.

WILLY: I slept like a dead one. First time in months. Imagine, sleeping till ten on a Tuesday morning. Boys left nice and early, heh?

LINDA: They were out of here by eight o'clock.

WILLY: Good work!

LINDA: It was so thrilling to see them leaving together. I can't get over the shaving lotion in this house!

WILLY: [*smiling*] Mmm—

LINDA: Biff was very changed this morning. His whole attitude seemed to be hopeful. He couldn't wait to get downtown to see Oliver.

WILLY: He's heading for a change. There's no question, there simply are certain men that take longer to get—solidified. How did he dress?

LINDA: His blue suit. He's so handsome in that suit. He could be a—anything in that suit!

[WILLY *gets up from the table.* LINDA *holds his jacket for him.*]

WILLY: There's no question, no question at all. Gee, on the way home tonight I'd like to buy some seeds.

LINDA: [*laughing*] That'd be wonderful. But not enough sun gets back there. Nothing'll grow any more.

WILLY: You wait, kid, before it's all over we're gonna get a little place out in the country, and I'll raise some vegetables, a couple of chickens . . .

LINDA: You'll do it yet, dear.

[WILLY *walks out of his jacket.* LINDA *follows him.*]

WILLY: And they'll get married, and come for a weekend. I'd built a little guest house. 'Cause I got so many fine tools, all I'd need would be a little lumber and some peace of mind.

LINDA: [*joyfully*] I sewed the lining . . .

WILLY: I could build two guest houses, so they'd both come. Did he decide how much he's going to ask Oliver for?

LINDA: [*getting him into the jacket*] He didn't mention it, but I imagine ten or fifteen thousand. You going to talk to Howard today?

WILLY: Yeah. I'll put it to him straight and simple. He'll just have to take me off the road.

LINDA: And Willy, don't forget to ask for a little advance, because we've got the insurance premium. It's the grace period now.

WILLY: That's a hundred . . . ?

LINDA: A hundred and eight, sixty-eight. Because we're a little short again.

WILLY: Why are we short?

LINDA: Well, you had the motor job on the car . . .

WILLY: That goddam Studebaker!

LINDA: And you got one more payment on the refrigerator . . .

WILLY: But it just broke again!

LINDA: Well, it's old, dear.

WILLY: I told you we should've bought a well-advertised machine. Charley bought a General Electric and it's twenty years old and it's still good, that son-of-a-bitch.

LINDA: But, Willy—

WILLY: Whoever heard of a Hastings refrigerator? Once in my life I would like to own something outright before it's broken! I'm always in a race with the junkyard! I just finished paying for the car and it's on its last legs. The refrigerator consumes belts like a goddam maniac. They time those things. They time them so when you finally paid for them, they're used up.

LINDA: [*buttoning up his jacket as he unbuttons it*] All told, about two hundred dollars would carry us, dear. But that includes the last payment on the mortgage. After this payment, Willy, the house belongs to us.

WILLY: It's twenty-five years!

LINDA: Biff was nine years old when we bought it.

WILLY: Well, that's a great thing. To weather a twenty-five year mortgage is—

LINDA: It's an accomplishment.

WILLY: All the cement, the lumber, the reconstruction I put in this house! There ain't a crack to be found in it any more.

LINDA: Well, it served its purpose.

WILLY: What purpose? Some stranger'll come along, move in, and that's that. If only Biff would take this house, and raise a family . . . [*he starts to go*] Good-by, I'm late.

LINDA: [*suddenly remembering*] Oh, I forgot! You're supposed to meet them for dinner.

WILLY: Me?

LINDA: At Frank's Chop House on Forty-eighth near Sixth Avenue.

WILLY: Is that so! How about you?

LINDA: No, just the three of you. They're gonna blow you to a big meal!

WILLY: Don't say! Who thought of that?

LINDA: Biff came to me this morning, Willy, and he said, "Tell Dad, we want to blow him to a big meal." Be there six o'clock. You and your two boys are going to have dinner.

WILLY: Gee whiz! That's really somethin'. I'm gonna knock Howard for a loop, kid. I'll get an advance, and I'll come home with a New York job. Goddammit, now I'm gonna do it!

LINDA: Oh, that's the spirit, Willy!

WILLY: I will never get behind a wheel the rest of my life!

LINDA: It's changing, Willy, I can feel it changing!

WILLY: Beyond a question. G'by, I'm late. [*He starts to go again.*]

LINDA: [*calling after him as she runs to the kitchen table for a handkerchief*] You got your glasses?

WILLY: [*feels for them, then comes back in*] Yeah, yeah, got my glasses.

LINDA: [*giving him the handkerchief*] And a handkerchief.

WILLY: Yeah, handkerchief.

LINDA: And your saccharine?

WILLY: Yeah, my saccharine.

LINDA: Be careful on the subway stairs.

[*She kisses him, and a silk stocking is seen hanging from her hand.* WILLY *notices it.*]

WILLY: Will you stop mending stockings? At least while I'm in the house. It gets me nervous. I can't tell you. Please.

[LINDA *hides the stocking in her hand as she follows* WILLY *across the forestage in front of the house.*]

LINDA: Remember, Frank's Chop House.

WILLY: [*passing the apron*] Maybe beets would grow out there.

LINDA: [*laughing*] But you tried so many times.

WILLY: Yeah. Well, don't work hard today. [*He disappears around the right corner of the house.*]

LINDA: Be careful!

[*As* WILLY *vanishes,* LINDA *waves to him. Suddenly the phone rings. She runs across the stage and into the kitchen and lifts it.*]

LINDA: Hello? Oh, Biff! I'm so glad you called, I just . . . Yes, sure, I just told him. Yes, he'll be there for dinner at six o'clock, I didn't forget. Listen, I was just dying to tell you. You know that little rubber pipe I told you about? That he connected to the gas heater? I finally decided to go down the cellar this morning and take it away and destroy it. But it's gone! Imagine? He took it away himself, it isn't there! [*She listens.*] When? Oh, then you took it. Oh—nothing, it's just that I'd hoped he'd taken it away himself. Oh, I'm not worried, darling, because this morning he left in such high spirits, it was like the old days! I'm not afraid any more. Did Mr. Oliver see you? . . . Well, you wait there then. And make a nice impression on him, darling. Just don't perspire too much before you see him. And have a nice time with Dad. He may have big news too! . . . That's right, a New York job. And be sweet to him tonight, dear. Be loving to him. Because he's only a little boat looking for a harbor. [*she is trembling with sorrow and joy*] Oh, that's wonderful, Biff, you'll save his life. Thanks, darling. Just put your arm around him when he comes into the restaurant. Give him a smile. That's the boy . . . Good-by, dear. . . . You got your comb? . . . That's fine Good-by, Biff dear.

[*In the middle of her speech,* HOWARD WAGNER, *thirty-six, wheels on a small typewriter table on which is a wire-recording machine and proceeds to plug it in. This is on the left forestage. Light slowly fades on* LINDA *as it rises on* HOWARD. HOWARD *is intent on threading the machine and only glances over his shoulder as* WILLY *appears.*]

WILLY: Pst! Pst!

HOWARD: Hello, Willy, come in.

WILLY: Like to have a little talk with you, Howard.

HOWARD: Sorry to keep you waiting. I'll be with you in a minute.

WILLY: What's that, Howard?

HOWARD: Didn't you ever see one of these? Wire recorder.

WILLY: Oh. Can we talk a minute?

HOWARD: Records things. Just got delivery yesterday. Been driving me crazy, the most terrific machine I ever saw in my life. I was up all night with it.

WILLY: What do you do with it?

HOWARD: I bought it for dictation, but you can do anything with it. Listen to this. I had it home last night. Listen to what I picked up. The first one is my daughter. Get this. [*he flicks the switch and "Roll out the Barrel" is heard being whistled*] Listen to that kid whistle.

WILLY: That is lifelike, isn't it?

HOWARD: Seven years old. Get that tone.

WILLY: Ts, ts. Like to ask a little favor if you . . .

[*The whistling breaks off, and the voice of* HOWARD'S DAUGHTER *is heard.*]

HIS DAUGHTER: "Now you, Daddy."

HOWARD: She's crazy for me! [*Again the same song is whistled.*] That's me! Ha! [*He winks.*]

WILLY: You're very good!

[*The whistling breaks off again. The machine runs silent for a moment.*]

HOWARD: Sh! Get this now, this is my son.

HIS SON: "The capital of Alabama is Montgomery; the capital of Arizona is Phoenix; the capital of Arkansas is Little Rock; the capital of California is Sacramento . . ." [*and on, and on*]

HOWARD: [*holding up five fingers*] Five years old, Willy!

WILLY: He'll make an announcer some day!

HIS SON: [*continuing*] "The capital . . ."

HOWARD: Get that—alphabetical order! [*The machine breaks off suddenly.*] Wait a minute. The maid kicked the plug out.

WILLY: It certainly is a—

HOWARD: Sh, for God's sake!

HIS SON: "It's nine o'clock, Bulova watch time. So I have to go to sleep."

WILLY: That really is—

HOWARD: Wait a minute! The next is my wife.

[*They wait.*]

HOWARD'S VOICE: "Go on, say something." [*pause*] "Well, you gonna talk?"

HIS WIFE: "I can't think of anything."

HOWARD'S VOICE: "Well, talk—it's turning."

HIS WIFE: [*shyly, beaten*] "Hello." [*silence*] "Oh, Howard, I can't talk into this . . ."

HOWARD: [*snapping the machine off*] That was my wife.

WILLY: That is a wonderful machine. Can we—

HOWARD: I tell you, Willy, I'm gonna take my camera, and my bandsaw, and all my hobbies, and out they go. This is the most fascinating relaxation I ever found.

WILLY: I think I'll get one myself.

HOWARD: Sure, they're only a hundred and a half. You can't do without it. Supposing you wanna hear Jack Benny, see? But you can't be at home at that hour. So you tell the maid to turn the radio on when Jack Benny comes on, and this automatically goes on with the radio . . .

WILLY: And when you come home you . . .

HOWARD: You can come home twelve o'clock, one o'clock, any time you like, and you get yourself a Coke and sit yourself down, throw the switch, and there's Jack Benny's program in the middle of the night!

WILLY: I'm definitely going to get one. Because lots of time I'm on the road, and I think to myself, what I must be missing on the radio!

HOWARD: Don't you have a radio in the car?

WILLY: Yeah, but who ever thinks of turning it on?

HOWARD: Say, aren't you supposed to be in Boston?

WILLY: That's what I want to talk to you about, Howard. You got a minute?
    [*He draws a chair in from the wing.*]

HOWARD: What happened? What're you doing here?

WILLY: Well . . .

HOWARD: You didn't crack up again, did you?

WILLY: Oh, no. No . . .

HOWARD: Geez, you had me worried there for a minute. What's the trouble?

WILLY: Well, tell you the truth, Howard. I've come to the conclusion that I'd rather not travel any more.

HOWARD: Not travel! Well, what'll you do?

WILLY: Remember, Christmas time, when you had the party here? You said you'd try to think of some spot for me here in town.

HOWARD: With us?

WILLY: Well, sure.

HOWARD: Oh, yeah, yeah. I remember. Well, I couldn't think of anything for you, Willy.

WILLY: I tell ya, Howard. The kids are all grown up, y'know. I don't need much any more. If I could take home—well, sixty-five dollars a week, I could swing it.

HOWARD: Yeah, but Willy, see I—

WILLY: I tell ya why, Howard. Speaking frankly and between the two of us, y'know—I'm just a little tired.

HOWARD: Oh, I could understand that, Willy. But you're a road man, Willy, and we do a road business. We've only got a half-dozen salesmen on the floor here.

WILLY: God knows, Howard, I never asked a favor of any man. But I was with the firm when your father used to carry you up here in his arms.

HOWARD: I know that, Willy, but—

WILLY: Your father came to me the day you were born and asked me what I thought of the name of Howard, may he rest in peace.

HOWARD: I appreciate that, Willy, but there just is no spot here for you. If I had a spot I'd slam you right in, but I just don't have a single solitary spot.
    [*He looks for his lighter.* WILLY *has picked it up and gives it to him. Pause.*]

WILLY: [*with increasing anger*] Howard, all I need to set my table is fifty dollars a week.

HOWARD: But where am I going to put you, kid?

WILLY: Look, it isn't a question of whether I can sell merchandise, is it?

HOWARD: No, but it's a business, kid, and everybody's gotta pull his own weight.

WILLY: [*desperately*] Just let me tell you a story, Howard—

HOWARD: 'Cause you gotta admit, business is business.

WILLY: [*angrily*] Business is definitely business, but just listen for a minute. You don't understand this. When I was a boy—eighteen, nineteen—I was already on the road. And there was a question in my mind as to whether selling had a future for me. Because in those days I had a yearning to go to Alaska. See, there were three gold strikes in one month in Alaska, and I felt like going out. Just for the ride, you might say.

HOWARD: [*barely interested*] Don't say.

WILLY: Oh, yeah, my father lived many years in Alaska. He was an adventurous man. We've got quite a little streak of self-reliance in our family. I thought I'd go out with my older brother and try to locate him, and maybe settle in the North with the old man. And I was almost decided to go, when I met a salesman in the Parker House. His name was Dave Singleman. And he was eighty-four years old, and he'd drummed merchandise in thirty-one states. And old Dave, he'd go up to his room, y'understand, put on his green velvet slippers—I'll never forget—and pick up his phone and call the buyers, and without ever leaving his room, at the age of eighty-four, he made his living. And when I saw that, I realized that selling was the greatest career a man could want. 'Cause what could be more satisfying than to be able to go, at the age of eighty-four, into twenty or thirty different cities, and pick up a phone, and be remembered and loved and helped by so many different people? Do you know? when he died—and by the way he died the death of a salesman, in his green velvet slippers in the smoker of the New York, New Haven and Hartford, going into Boston—when he died, hundreds of salesmen and buyers were at his funeral. Things were sad on a lotta trains for months after that. [*He stands up.* HOWARD *has not looked at him.*] In those days there was personality in it, Howard. There was respect, and comradeship, and gratitude in it. Today, it's all cut and dried, and there's no chance for bringing friendship to bear—or personality. You see what I mean? They don't know me any more.

HOWARD: [*moving away, to the right*] That's just the thing, Willy.

WILLY: If I had forty dollars a week—that's all I'd need. Forty dollars, Howard.

HOWARD: Kid, I can't take blood from a stone, I—

WILLY: [*desperation is on him now*] Howard, the year Al Smith was nominated, your father came to me and—

HOWARD: [*starting to go off*] I've got to see some people, kid.

WILLY: [*stopping him*] I'm talking about your father! There were promises made across this desk! You mustn't tell me you've got people to see—I put thirty-four years into this firm, Howard, and now I can't pay my insurance! You can't eat the orange and throw the peel away—a man is not a piece of fruit! [*after a pause*] Now pay attention. Your father—in 1928 I had a big year. I averaged a hundred and seventy dollars a week in commissions.

HOWARD: [*impatiently*] Now, Willy, you never averaged—

WILLY: [*banging his hand on the desk*] I averaged a hundred and seventy dollars a week in the year of 1928! And your father came to me—or rather, I was in the office here—it was right over this desk—and he put his hand on my shoulder—

HOWARD: [*getting up*] You'll have to excuse me, Willy, I gotta see some people. Pull yourself together. [*going out*] I'll be back in a little while.

[*On* HOWARD's *exit, the light on his chair grows very bright and strange.*]

WILLY: Pull myself together! What the hell did I say to him? My God, I was yelling at him! How could I! [WILLY *breaks off, staring at the light, which occupies the chair, animating it.*] Frank, Frank, don't you remember what you told me that time? How you put your hand on my shoulder, and Frank . . . [*He leans on the desk and as he speaks the dead man's name he accidentally switches on the recorder, and instantly*]

HOWARD'S SON: ". . . of New York is Albany. The capital of Ohio is Cincinnati, the capital of Rhode Island is . . ." [*The recitation continues.*]

WILLY: [*leaping way with fright, shouting*] Ha! Howard! Howard! Howard!

HOWARD: [*rushing in*] What happened?

WILLY: [*pointing at the machine, which continues nasally, childishly, with the capital cities*] Shut it off! Shut it off!

HOWARD: [*pulling the plug out*] Look, Willy . . .

WILLY: [*pressing his hands to his eyes*] I gotta get myself some coffee. I'll get some coffee . . .

[WILLY *starts to walk out.* HOWARD *stops him.*]

HOWARD: [*rolling up the cord*] Willy, look . . .

WILLY: I'll go to Boston.

HOWARD: Willy, you can't go to Boston for us.

WILLY: Why can't I go?

HOWARD: I don't want you to represent us. I've been meaning to tell you for a long time now.

WILLY: Howard, are you firing me?

HOWARD: I think you need a good long rest, Willy.

WILLY: Howard—

HOWARD: And when you feel better, come back, and we'll see if we can work something out.

WILLY: But I gotta earn money, Howard. I'm in no position to—

HOWARD: Where are your sons? Why don't your sons give you a hand?

WILLY: They're working on a very big deal.

HOWARD: This is no time for false pride, Willy. You go to your sons and you tell them that you're tired. You've got two great boys, haven't you?

WILLY: Oh, no question, no question, but in the meantime . . .

HOWARD: Then that's that, heh?

WILLY: All right, I'll go to Boston tomorrow.

HOWARD: No, no.

WILLY: I can't throw myself on my sons. I'm not a cripple!

HOWARD: Look, kid, I'm busy this morning.

WILLY: [*grasping* HOWARD's *arm*] Howard, you've got to let me go to Boston!
HOWARD: [*hard, keeping himself under control*] I've got a line of people to see
this morning. Sit down, take five minutes, and pull yourself together, and
then go home, will ya? I need the office, Willy. [*He starts to go, turns,
remembering the recorder, starts to push off the table holding the recorder.*] Oh, yeah. Whenever you can this week, stop by and drop off the
samples. You'll feel better, Willy, and then come back and we'll talk. Pull
yourself together, kid, there's people outside.

> [HOWARD *exits, pushing the table off left.* WILLY *stares into space,
> exhausted. Now the music is heard*—BEN's *music*—*first distantly,
> then closer. As* WILLY *speaks,* BEN *enters from the right. He carries
> valise and umbrella.*]

WILLY: Oh, Ben, how did you do it? What is the answer? Did you wind up
the Alaska deal already?
BEN: Doesn't take much time if you know what you're doing. Just a short
business trip. Boarding ship in an hour. Wanted to say good-by.
WILLY: Ben, I've got to talk to you.
BEN: [*glancing at his watch*] Haven't much time, William.
WILLY: [*crossing the apron to* BEN] Ben, nothing's working out. I don't know
what to do.
BEN: Now, look here, William. I've bought timberland in Alaska and I need a
man to look after things for me.
WILLY: God, timberland! Me and my boys in those grand outdoors!
BEN: You've a new continent at your doorstep, William. Get out of these
cities, they're full of talk and time payments and courts of law. Screw on
your fists and you can fight for a fortune up there.
WILLY: Yes, yes! Linda, Linda!

> [LINDA *enters as of old, with the wash.*]

LINDA: Oh, you're back?
BEN: I haven't much time.
WILLY: No, wait! Linda, he's got a proposition for me in Alaska.
LINDA: But you've got—[*to* BEN] He's got a beautiful job here.
WILLY: But in Alaska, kid, I could—
LINDA: You're doing well enough, Willy!
BEN: [*to* LINDA] Enough for what, my dear?
LINDA: [*frightened of* BEN *and angry at him*] Don't say those things to him!
Enough to be happy right here, right now. [*to* WILLY, *while* BEN *laughs*]
Why must everybody conquer the world? You're well liked, and the boys
love you, and someday—[*to* BEN]—why old man Wagner told him just
the other day that if he keeps it up he'll be a member of the firm, didn't
he, Willy?
WILLY: Sure, sure. I am building something with this firm, Ben, and if a man
is building something he must be on the right track, mustn't he?
BEN: What are you building? Lay your hand on it. Where is it?
WILLY: [*hesitantly*] That's true, Linda, there's nothing.
LINDA: Why? [*to* BEN] There's a man eighty-four years old—
WILLY: That's right, Ben, that's right. When I look at that man I say, what
is there to worry about?

BEN: Bah!

WILLY: It's true, Ben. All he has to do is go into any city, pick up the phone, and he's making his living and you know why?

BEN: [*picking up his valise*] I've got to go.

WILLY: [*holding BEN back*] Look at this boy!

> [BIFF, *in his high school sweater, enters carrying suitcase.* HAPPY *carries* BIFF'S *shoulder guards, gold helmet, and football pants.*]

WILLY: Without a penny to his name, three great universities are begging for him, and from there the sky's the limit, because it's not what you do, Ben. It's who you know and the smile on your face! It's contacts, Ben, contacts! The whole wealth of Alaska passes over the lunch table at the Commodore Hotel, and that's the wonder, the wonder of this country, that a man can end with diamonds here on the basis of being liked! [*he turns to* BIFF] And that's why when you get out on that field today it's important. Because thousands of people will be rooting for you and loving you. [*to* BEN, *who has again begun to leave*] And Ben! when he walks into a business office his name will sound out like a bell and all the doors will open to him! I've seen it, Ben, I've seen it a thousand times! You can't feel it with your hand like timber, but it's there!

BEN: Good-by, William.

WILLY: Ben, am I right? Don't you think I'm right? I value your advice.

BEN: There's a new continent at your doorstep, William. You could walk out rich. Rich! [*He is gone.*]

WILLY: We'll do it here, Ben! You hear me? We're gonna do it here!

> [YOUNG BERNARD *rushes. The gay music of the Boys is heard.*]

BERNARD: Oh, gee, I was afraid you left already!

WILLY: Why? What time is it?

BERNARD: It's half-past one!

WILLY: Well, come on, everybody! Ebbets Field next stop! Where's the pennants? [*He rushes through the wall-line of the kitchen and out into the living-room.*]

LINDA: [*to* BIFF] Did you pack fresh underwear?

BIFF: [*who has been limbering up*] I want to go!

BERNARD: Biff, I'm carrying your helmet, ain't I?

HAPPY: No, I'm carrying the helmet.

BERNARD: Oh, Biff, you promised me.

HAPPY: I'm carrying the helmet.

BERNARD: How am I going to get in the locker room?

LINDA: Let him carry the shoulder guards. [*She puts her coat and hat on in the kitchen.*]

BERNARD: Can I, Biff? 'Cause I told everybody I'm going to be in the locker room.

HAPPY: In Ebbets Field it's the clubhouse.

BERNARD: I meant the clubhouse. Biff!

HAPPY: Biff!

BIFF: [*grandly, after a slight pause*] Let him carry the shoulder guards.

HAPPY: [*as he gives* BERNARD *the shoulder guards*] Stay close to us now.

> [WILLY *rushes in with the pennants.*]

WILLY: [*handing them out*] Everybody wave when Biff comes out on the field. [HAPPY *and* BERNARD *run off.*] You set now, boy?

    [*The music has died away.*]

BIFF: Ready to go, Pop. Every muscle is ready.

WILLY: [*at the edge of the apron*] You realize what this means?

BIFF: That's right, Pop.

WILLY: [*feeling* BIFF's *muscles*] You're comin' home this afternoon captain of the All-Scholastic Championship Team of the City of New York.

BIFF: I got it, Pop. And remember, pal, when I take off my helmet, that touchdown is for you.

WILLY: Let's go! [*He is starting out, with his arm around* BIFF, *when* CHARLEY *enters, as of old, in knickers.*] I got no room for you, Charley.

CHARLEY: Room? For what?

WILLY: In the car.

CHARLEY: You goin' for a ride? I wanted to shoot some casino.

WILLY: [*furiously*] Casino! [*incredulously*] Don't you realize what today is?

LINDA: Oh, he knows, Willy. He's just kidding you.

WILLY: That's nothing to kid about!

CHARLEY: No, Linda, what's goin' on?

LINDA: He's playing in Ebbets Field.

CHARLEY: Baseball in this weather?

WILLY: Don't talk to him. Come on, come on! [*He is pushing them out.*]

CHARLEY: Wait a minute, didn't you hear the news?

WILLY: What?

CHARLEY: Don't you listen to the radio? Ebbets Field just blew up.

WILLY: You go to hell! [CHARLEY *laughs. Pushing them out.*] Come on, come on! We're late.

CHARLEY: [*as they go*] Knock a homer, Biff, knock a homer!

WILLY: [*the last to leave, turning to* CHARLEY] I don't think that was funny, Charley. This is the greatest day of his life.

CHARLEY: Willy, when are you going to grow up?

WILLY: Yeah, heh? When this game is over, Charley, you'll be laughing out the other side of your face. They'll be calling him another Red Grange. Twenty-five thousand a year.

CHARLEY: [*kidding*] Is that so?

WILLY: Yeah, that's so.

CHARLEY: Well, then, I'm sorry, Willy. But tell me something.

WILLY: What?

CHARLEY: Who is Red Grange?

WILLY: Put up your hands. Goddam you, put up your hands!

    [CHARLEY, *chuckling, shakes his head and walks away, around the left corner of the stage.* WILLY *follows him. The music rises to a mocking frenzy.*]

WILLY: Who the hell do you think you are, better than everybody else? You don't know everything, you big, ignorant, stupid. . . . Put up your hands!

    [*Light rises, on the right side of the forestage, on a small table in the reception room of* CHARLEY's *office Traffic sounds are heard.*

BERNARD, *now mature, sits whistling to himself. A pair of tennis rackets and an overnight bag are on the floor beside him.*]

WILLY: [*offstage*] What are you walking away for? Don't walk away! If you're going to say something say it to my face! I know you laugh at me behind my back. You'll laugh out of the other side of your goddam face after this game. Touchdown! Touchdown! Eighty thousand people! Touchdown Right between the goal posts.

[BERNARD *is a quiet, earnest, but self-assured young man.* WILLY's *voice is coming from right upstage now.* BERNARD *lowers his feet off the table and listens.* JENNY, *his father's secretary, enters.*]

JENNY: [*distressed*] Say, Bernard, will you go out in the hall?

BERNARD: What is that noise? Who is it?

JENNY: Mr. Loman. He just got off the elevator.

BERNARD: [*getting up*] Who's he arguing with?

JENNY: Nobody. There's nobody with him. I can't deal with him any more, and your father gets all upset everytime he comes. I've got a lot of typing to do, and your father's waiting to sign it. Will you see him?

WILLY: [*entering*] Touchdown! Touch—[*he sees* JENNY.] Jenny, Jenny, good to see you. How're ya? Workin'? Or still honest?

JENNY: Fine. How've you been feeling?

WILLY: Not much any more, Jenny. Ha, ha! [*He is surprised to see the rackets.*]

BERNARD: Hello, Uncle Willy.

WILLY: [*almost shocked*] Bernard! Well, look who's here! [*He comes quickly, guiltily, to* BERNARD *and warmly shakes his hand.*]

BERNARD: How are you? Good to see you.

WILLY: What are you doing here?

BERNARD: Oh, just stopped off to see Pop. Get off my feet till my train leaves. I'm going to Washington in a few minutes.

WILLY: Is he in?

BERNARD: Yes, he's in his office with the accountants. Sit down.

WILLY: [*sitting down*] What're you going to do in Washington?

BERNARD: Oh, just a case I've got there, Willy.

WILLY: That so? [*indicating the rackets*] You going to play tennis there?

BERNARD: I'm staying with a friend who's got a court.

WILLY: Don't say. His own tennis court. Must be fine people, I bet.

BERNARD: They are, very nice. Dad tells me Biff's in town.

WILLY: [*with a big smile*] Yeah, Biff's in. Working on a very big deal, Bernard.

BERNARD: What's Biff doing?

WILLY: Well, he's been doing very big things in the West. But he decided to establish himself here. Very big. We're having dinner. Did I hear your wife had a boy?

BERNARD: That's right. Our second.

WILLY: Two boys! What do you know!

BERNARD: What kind of a deal has Biff got?

WILLY: Well, Bill Oliver—very big sporting-goods man—he wants Biff very badly. Called him in from the West. Long distance, carte blanche, special deliveries. Your friends have their own private tennis court?

BERNARD: You still with the old firm, Willy?

WILLY: [*after a pause*] I'm—I'm overjoyed to see how you made the grade, Bernard, overjoyed. It's an encouraging thing to see a young man really— really— Looks very good for Biff—very—[*He breaks off, then:*] Bernard— [*He is so full of emotion, he breaks off again.*]

BERNARD: What is it, Willy?

WILLY: [*small and alone*] What—what's the secret?

BERNARD: What secret?

WILLY: How—how did you? Why didn't he ever catch on?

BERNARD: I wouldn't know that, Willy.

WILLY: [*confidentially, desperately*] You were his friend, his boyhood friend. There's something I don't understand about it. His life ended after that Ebbets Field game. From the age of seventeen nothing good ever happened to him.

BERNARD: He never trained himself for anything.

WILLY: But he did, he did. After high school he took so many correspondence courses. Radio mechanics; television; God knows what, and never made the slightest mark.

BERNARD: [*taking off his glasses*] Willy, do you want to talk candidly?

WILLY: [*rising, faces* BERNARD] I regard you as a very brilliant man, Bernard. I value your advice.

BERNARD: Oh, the hell with the advice, Willy. I couldn't advise you. There's just one thing I've always wanted to ask you. When he was supposed to graduate, and the math teacher flunked him—

WILLY: Oh, that son-of-a-bitch ruined his life.

BERNARD: Yeah, but, Willy, all he had to do was go to summer school and make up that subject.

WILLY: That's right, that's right.

BERNARD: Did you tell him not to go to summer school?

WILLY: Me? I begged him to go. I ordered him to go!

BERNARD: Then why wouldn't he go?

WILLY: Why? Why! Bernard, that question has been trailing me like a ghost for the last fifteen years. He flunked the subject, and laid down and died like a hammer hit him!

BERNARD: Take it easy, kid.

WILLY: Let me talk to you—I got nobody to talk to. Bernard, Bernard, was it my fault? Y'see? It keeps going around in my mind, maybe I did something to him. I got nothing to give him.

BERNARD: Don't take it so hard.

WILLY: Why did he lay down? What is the story there? You were his friend!

BERNARD: Willy, I remember, it was June, and our grades came out. And he'd flunked math.

WILLY: That son-of-a-bitch!

BERNARD: No, it wasn't right then. Biff just got very angry, I remember, and he was ready to enroll in summer school.

WILLY: [*surprised*] He was?

BERNARD: He wasn't beaten by it at all. But then, Willy, he disappeared from the block for almost a month. And I got the idea that he'd gone up to New England to see you. Did he have a talk with you then?

[WILLY *stares in silence.*]

BERNARD: Willy?

WILLY: [*with a strong edge of resentment in his voice*] Yeah, he came to Boston. What about it?

BERNARD: Well, just that when he came back—I'll never forget this, it always mystifies me. Because I'd thought so well of Biff, even though he'd always taken advantage of me. I loved him, Willy, y'know? And he came back after that month and took his sneakers—remember the sneakers with "University of Virginia" printed on them? He was so proud of those, wore them every day. And he took them down in the cellar, and burned them up in the furnace. We had a fist fight. It lasted at least half an hour. Just the two of us, punching each other down the cellar, and crying right through it. I've often thought of how strange it was that I knew he'd given up his life. What happened in Boston, Willy?

[WILLY *looks at him as at an intruder.*]

BERNARD: I just bring it up because you asked me.

WILLY: [*angrily*] Nothing. What do you mean, "What happened?" What's that got to do with anything?

BERNARD: Well don't get sore.

WILLY: What are you trying to do, blame it on me? If a boy lays down is that my fault?

BERNARD: Now, Willy, don't get—

WILLY: Well, don't—don't talk to me that way! What does that mean, "What happened?"

[CHARLEY *enters. He is in his vest, and he carries a bottle of bourbon.*]

CHARLEY: Hey, you're going to miss that train. [*He waves the bottle.*]

BERNARD: Yeah, I'm going. [*He takes the bottle.*] Thanks, Pop. [*He picks up his rackets and bag.*] Good-by, Willy, and don't worry about it. You know, "If at first you don't succeed . . ."

WILLY: Yes, I believe in that.

BERNARD: But sometimes, Willy, it's better for a man just to walk away.

WILLY: Walk away?

BERNARD: That's right.

WILLY: But if you can't walk away?

BERNARD: [*after a slight pause*] I guess that's when it's tough. [*Extending his hand*] Good-by, Willy.

WILLY: [*shaking* BERNARD'*s hand*] Good-by, boy.

CHARLEY: [*an arm on* BERNARD'*s shoulder*] How do you like this kid? Gonna argue a case in front of the Supreme Court.

BERNARD: [*protesting*] Pop!

WILLY: [*genuinely shocked, pained, and happy*] No! The Supreme Court!

BERNARD: I gotta run. 'By, Dad!

CHARLEY: Knock 'em dead, Bernard!

[BERNARD *goes off.*]

WILLY: [*as* CHARLEY *takes out his wallet*] The Supreme Court! And he didn't even mention it!

CHARLEY: [*counting out money on the desk*] He don't have to—he's gonna do it.

WILLY: And you never told him what to do, did you? You never took any interest in him.

CHARLEY: My salvation is that I never took any interest in anything. There's some money—fifty dollars. I got an accountant inside.

WILLY: Charley, look . . . [*with difficulty*] I got my insurance to pay. If you can manage it—I need a hundred and ten dollars.

[CHARLEY *doesn't reply for a moment; merely stops moving.*]

WILLY: I'd draw it from my bank but Linda would know, and I . . .

CHARLEY: Sit down, Willy.

WILLY: [*moving toward the chair*] I'm keeping an account of everything, remember. I'll pay every penny back. [*He sits.*]

CHARLEY: Now listen to me, Willy.

WILLY: I want you to know I appreciate . . .

CHARLEY: [*sitting down on the table*] Willy, what're you doin'? What the hell is goin' on in your head?

WILLY: Why? I'm simply . . .

CHARLEY: I offered you a job. You can make fifty dollars a week. And I won't send you on the road.

WILLY: I've got a job.

CHARLEY: Without pay? What kind of a job is a job without pay? [*He rises.*] Now, look, kid, enough is enough. I'm no genius but I know when I'm being insulted.

WILLY: Insulted!

CHARLEY: Why don't you want to work for me?

WILLY: What's the matter with you? I've got a job.

CHARLEY: Then what're you walkin' in here every week for?

WILLY: [*getting up*] Well, if you don't want me to walk in here—

CHARLEY: I am offering you a job.

WILLY: I don't want your goddam job!

CHARLEY: When the hell are you going to grow up?

WILLY: [*furiously*] You big ignoramus, if you say that to me again I'll rap you one! I don't care how big you are! [*He's ready to fight.*]

[*Pause.*]

CHARLEY: [*kindly, going to him*] How much do you need, Willy?

WILLY: Charley, I'm strapped. I'm strapped. I don't know what to do. I was just fired.

CHARLEY: Howard fired you?

WILLY: That snotnose. Imagine that? I named him. I named him Howard.

CHARLEY: Willy, when're you gonna realize that them things don't mean anything? You named him Howard, but you can't sell that. The only thing you got in this world is what you can sell. And the funny thing is that you're a salesman, and you don't know that.

WILLY: I've tried to think otherwise, I guess. I always felt that if a man was impressive, and well liked, that nothing—

CHARLEY: Why must everybody like you? Who liked J. P. Morgan? Was he impressive? In a Turkish bath he'd look like a butcher. But with his pockets on he was very well liked. Now listen, Willy, I know you don't like me, and nobody can say I'm in love with you, but I'll give you a job because—just for the hell of it, put it that way. Now what do you say?

WILLY: I—I just can't work for you, Charley.

CHARLEY: What're you, jealous of me?

WILLY: I can't work for you, that's all, don't ask me why.

CHARLEY: [*angered, takes out more bills*] You been jealous of me all your life, you damned fool! Here, pay your insurance. [*He puts the money in* WILLY's *hand.*]

WILLY: I'm keeping strict accounts.

CHARLEY: I've got some work to do. Take care of yourself. And pay your insurance.

WILLY: [*moving to the right*] Funny, y'know? After all the highways, and the trains, and the appointments, and the years, you end up worth more dead than alive.

CHARLEY: Willy, nobody's worth nothin' dead. [*after a slight pause*] Did you hear what I said?

[WILLY *stands still, dreaming.*]

CHARLEY: Willy!

WILLY: Apologize to Bernard for me when you see him. I didn't mean to argue with him. He's a fine boy. They're all fine boys, and they'll end up big— all of them. Someday they'll all play tennis together. Wish me luck, Charley. He saw Bill Oliver today.

CHARLEY: Good luck.

WILLY: [*on the verge of tears*] Charley, you're the only friend I got. Isn't that a remarkable thing? [*He goes out.*]

CHARLEY: Jesus!

[CHARLEY *stares after him a moment and follows. All light blacks out. Suddenly raucous music is heard, and a red glow rises behind the screen at right.* STANLEY, *a young waiter, appears, carrying a table, followed by* HAPPY, *who is carrying two chairs.*]

STANLEY: [*putting the table down*] That's all right, Mr. Loman, I can handle it myself. [*he turns and takes the chairs from* HAPPY *and places them at the table*]

HAPPY: [*glancing around*] Oh, this is better.

STANLEY: Sure, in the front there you're in the middle of all kinds of noise. Whenever you got a party, Mr. Loman, you just tell me and I'll put you back here. Y'know, there's a lotta people they don't like it private, because when they go out they like to see a lotta action around them because they're sick and tired to stay in the house by theirself. But I know you, you ain't from Hackensack. You know what I mean?

HAPPY: [*sitting down*] So how's it coming, Stanley?

STANLEY: Ah, it's a dog's life. I only wish during the war they'd a took me in the Army. I coulda been dead by now.

HAPPY: My brother's back, Stanley.

STANLEY: Oh, he come back, heh? From the Far West.

HAPPY: Yeah, big cattle man, my brother, so treat him right. And my father's coming too.

STANLEY: Oh, your father too!

HAPPY: You got a couple of nice lobsters?

STANLEY: Hundred per cent, big.

HAPPY: I want them with claws.

STANLEY: Don't worry, I don't give you no mice. [HAPPY *laughs.*] How about some wine? It'll put a head on the meal.

HAPPY: No. You remember, Stanley, that recipe I brought you from overseas? With the champagne in it?

STANLEY: Oh, yeah, sure. I still got it tacked up yet in the kitchen. But that'll have to cost a buck apiece anyways.

HAPPY: That's all right.

STANLEY: What'd you, hit a number or somethin'?

HAPPY: No, it's a little celebration. My brother is—I think he pulled off a big deal today. I think we're going into business together.

STANLEY: Great! That's the best for you. Because a family business, you know what I mean?—that's the best.

HAPPY: That's what I think.

STANLEY: 'Cause what's the difference? Somebody steals? It's in the family. Know what I mean? [*sotto voce*] Like this bartender here. The boss is goin' crazy what kinda leak he's got in the cash register. You put it in but it don't come out.

HAPPY: [*raising his head*] Sh!

STANLEY: What?

HAPPY: You notice I wasn't lookin' right or left, was I?

STANLEY: No.

HAPPY: And my eyes are closed.

STANLEY: So what's the—?

HAPPY: Strudel's comin'.

STANLEY: [*catching on, looks around*] Ah, no, there's no—
[*He breaks off as a furred, lavishly dressed* GIRL *enters and sits at the next table. Both follow her with their eyes.*]

STANLEY: Geez, how'd ya know?

HAPPY: I got radar or something. [*staring directly at her profile*] Oooooooo . . . Stanley.

STANLEY: I think that's for you, Mr. Loman.

HAPPY: Look at that mouth. Oh God. And the binoculars.

STANLEY: Geez, you got a life, Mr. Loman.

HAPPY: Wait on her.

STANLEY: [*going to the* GIRL's *table*] Would you like a menu, ma'am?

GIRL: I'm expecting someone, but I'd like a—

HAPPY: Why don't you bring her—excuse me, miss, do you mind? I sell champagne, and I'd like you to try my brand. Bring her a champagne, Stanley.

GIRL: That's awfully nice of you.

HAPPY: Don't mention it. It's all company money. [*He laughs.*]

GIRL: That's a charming product to be selling, isn't it?

HAPPY: Oh, gets to be like everything else. Selling is selling, y'know.

GIRL: I suppose.

HAPPY: You don't happen to sell, do you?

GIRL: No, I don't sell.

HAPPY: Would you object to a compliment from a stranger? You ought to be on a magazine cover.

GIRL: [*looking at him a little archly*] I have been.

[STANLEY *comes in with a glass of champagne.*]

HAPPY: What'd I say before, Stanley? You see? She's a cover girl.

STANLEY: Oh, I could see, I could see.

HAPPY: [*to the* GIRL] What magazine?

GIRL: Oh, a lot of them. [*she takes the drink*] Thank you.

HAPPY: You know what they say in France, don't you? "Champagne is the drink of the complexion"—Hya, Biff!

[BIFF *has entered and sits with* HAPPY.]

BIFF: Hello, kid. Sorry I'm late.

HAPPY: I just got here. Uh, Miss—?

GIRL: Forsythe.

HAPPY: Miss Forsythe, this is my brother.

BIFF: Is Dad here?

HAPPY: His name is Biff. You might've heard of him. Great football player.

GIRL: Really? What team?

HAPPY: Are you familiar with football?

GIRL: No, I'm afraid I'm not.

HAPPY: Biff is quarterback with the New York Giants.

GIRL: Well, that is nice, isn't it? [*She drinks.*]

HAPPY: Good health.

GIRL: I'm happy to meet you.

HAPPY: That's my name. Hap. It's really Harold, but at West Point they called me Happy.

GIRL: [*now really impressed*] Oh, I see. How do you do? [*She turns her profile.*]

BIFF: Isn't Dad coming?

HAPPY: You want her?

BIFF: Oh, I could never make that.

HAPPY: I remember the time that idea would never come into your head. Where's the old confidence, Biff?

BIFF: I just saw Oliver—

HAPPY: Wait a minute. I've got to see that old confidence again. Do you want her? She's on call.

BIFF: Oh, no. [*He turns to look at the* GIRL.]

HAPPY: I'm telling you. Watch this. [*turning to the* GIRL] Honey? [*she turns to him*] Are you busy?

GIRL: Well, I am . . . but I could make a phone call.

HAPPY: Do that, will you, honey? And see if you can get a friend. We'll be here for a while. Biff is one of the greatest football players in the country.

GIRL: [*standing up*] Well, I'm certainly happy to meet you.

HAPPY: Come back soon.

GIRL: I'll try.

HAPPY: Don't try, honey, try hard.

[*The* GIRL *exits.* STANLEY *follows, shaking his head in bewildered admiration.*]

HAPPY: Isn't that a shame now? A beautiful girl like that? That's why I can't get married. There's not a good woman in a thousand. New York is loaded with them, kid!

BIFF: Hap, look—

HAPPY: I told you she was on call!

BIFF: [*strangely unnerved*] Cut it out, will ya? I want to say something to you.

HAPPY: Did you see Oliver?

BIFF: I saw him all right. Now look, I want to tell Dad a couple of things and I want you to help me.

HAPPY: What? Is he going to back you?

BIFF: Are you crazy? You're out of your goddam head, you know that?

HAPPY: Why? What happened?

BIFF: [*breathlessly*] I did a terrible thing today, Hap. It's been the strangest day I ever went through. I'm all numb, I swear.

HAPPY: You mean he wouldn't see you?

BIFF: Well, I waited six hours for him, see? All day. Kept sending my name in. Even tried to date his secretary so she'd get me to him, but no soap.

HAPPY: Because you're not showin' the old confidence, Biff. He remembered you, didn't he?

BIFF: [*stopping* HAPPY *with a gesture*] Finally, about five o'clock, he comes out. Didn't remember who I was or anything. I felt like such an idiot, Hap.

HAPPY: Did you tell him my Florida idea?

BIFF: He walked away. I saw him for one minute. I got so mad I could've torn the walls down! How the hell did I ever get the idea I was a salesman there? I even believed myself that I'd been a salesman for him! And then he gave me one look and—I realized what a ridiculous lie my whole life has been! We've been talking in a dream for fifteen years. I was a shipping clerk.

HAPPY: What'd you do?

BIFF: [*with great tension and wonder*] Well, he left, see. And the secretary went out. I was all alone in the waiting-room. I don't now what came over me, Hap. The next thing I know I'm in his office—paneled walls, everything. I can't explain it. I—Hap, I took his fountain pen.

HAPPY: Geez, did he catch you?

BIFF: I ran out. I ran down all eleven flights. I ran and ran and ran.

HAPPY: That was an awful dumb—what'd you do that for?

BIFF: [*agonized*] I don't know, I just—wanted to take something, I don't know. You gotta help me, Hap, I'm gonna tell Pop.

HAPPY: You crazy? What for?

BIFF: Hap, he's got to understand that I'm not the man somebody lends that kind of money to. He thinks I've been spiting him all these years and it's eating him up.

HAPPY: That's just it. You tell him something nice.

BIFF: I can't.

HAPPY: Say you got a lunch date with Oliver tomorrow.

BIFF: So what do I do tomorrow?

HAPPY: You leave the house tomorrow and come back at night and say Oliver is thinking it over. And he thinks it over for a couple of weeks, and gradually it fades away and nobody's the worse.

BIFF: But it'll go on forever!

HAPPY: Dad is never so happy as when he's looking forward to something!
    [WILLY *enters.*]

HAPPY: Hello, scout!

WILLY: Gee, I haven't been here in years!
    [STANLEY *has followed* WILLY *in and sets a chair for him.* STANLEY *starts off but* HAPPY *stops him.*]

HAPPY: Stanley!
    [STANLEY *stands by, waiting for an order.*]

BIFF: [*going to* WILLY *with guilt, as to an invalid*] Sit down, Pop. You want a drink?

WILLY: Sure, I don't mind.

BIFF: Let's get a load on.

WILLY: You look worried.

BIFF: N-no. [*to* STANLEY] Scotch all around. Make it doubles.

STANLEY: Doubles, right. [*he goes*]

WILLY: You had a couple already, didn't you?

BIFF: Just a couple, yeah.

WILL: Well, what happened, boy? [*nodding affirmatively, with a smile*] Everything go all right?

BIFF: [*takes a breath, then reaches out and grasps* WILLY's *hand*] Pal . . . [*He is smiling bravely, and* WILLY *is smiling too.*] I had an experience today.

HAPPY: Terrific, Pop.

WILLY: That so? What happened?

BIFF: [*high, slightly alcoholic, above the earth*] I'm going to tell you everything from first to last. It's been a strange day. [*Silence. He looks around, composes himself as best he can, but his breath keeps breaking the rhythm of his voice.*] I had to wait quite a while for him, and—

WILLY: Oliver?

BIFF: Yeah, Oliver. All day, as a matter of cold fact. And a lot of—instances—facts, Pop, facts about my life came back to me. Who was it, Pop? Who ever said I was a salesman with Oliver?

WILLY: Well, you were.

BIFF: No, Dad, I was a shipping clerk.

WILLY: But you were practically—

BIFF: [*with determination*] Dad, I don't know who said it first, but I was never a salesman for Bill Oliver.

WILLY: What're you talking about?

BIFF: Let's hold on to the facts tonight, Pop. We're not going to get anywhere bullin' around. I was a shipping clerk.

WILLY: [*angrily*] All right, now listen to me—

BIFF: Why don't you let me finish?

WILLY: I'm not interested in stories about the past or any crap of that kind because the woods are burning, boys, you understand? There's a big blaze going on all around. I was fired today.

BIFF: [*shocked*] How could you be?

WILLY: I was fired, and I'm looking for a little good news to tell your mother, because the woman has waited and the woman has suffered. The gist of it is that I haven't got a story left in my head, Biff. So don't give me a lecture about facts and aspects. I am not interested. Now what've you got to say to me?

[STANLEY *enters with three drinks. They wait until he leaves.*]

WILLY: Did you see Oliver?

BIFF: Jesus, Dad!

WILLY: You mean you didn't go up there?

HAPPY: Sure he went up there.

BIFF: I did.—I saw him. How could they fire you?

WILLY: [*on the edge of his chair*] What kind of a welcome did he give you?

BIFF: He won't even let you work on commission?

WILLY: I'm out! [*driving*] So tell me, he gave you a warm welcome?

HAPPY: Sure, Pop, sure!

BIFF: [*driven*] Well, it was kind of—

WILLY: I was wondering if he'd remember you. [*to* HAPPY] Imagine, man doesn't see him for ten, twelve years and gives him that kind of a welcome!

HAPPY: Damn right!

BIFF: [*trying to return to the offensive*] Pop, look—

WILLY: You know why he remembered you, don't you? Because you impressed him in those days.

BIFF: Let's talk quietly and get this down to the facts, huh?

WILLY: [*as though Biff had been interrupting*] Well, what happened? It's great news, Biff. Did he take you into his office or'd you talk in the waiting-room?

BIFF: Well, he came in, see, and—

WILLY: [*with a big smile*] What'd he say? Betcha he threw his arm around you.

BIFF: Well, he kinda—

WILLY: He's a fine man. [*to* HAPPY] Very hard man to see, y'know.

HAPPY: [*agreeing*] Oh, I know.

WILLY: [*to* BIFF] Is that where you had the drinks?

BIFF: Yeah, he gave me a couple of—no, no!

HAPPY: [*cutting in*] He told him my Florida idea.

WILLY: Don't interrupt. [*to* BIFF] How'd he react to the Florida idea?

BIFF: Dad, will you give me a minute to explain?

WILLY: I've been waiting for you to explain since I sat down here! What happened? He took you into his office and what?

BIFF: Well—I talked. And—and he listened, see.

WILLY: Famous for the way he listens, y'know. What was his answer?

BIFF: His answer was—[*he breaks off, suddenly angry*] Dad, you're not letting me tell you what I want to tell you!

WILLY: [*accusing, angered*] You didn't see him, did you?

BIFF: I did see him!

WILLY: What'd you insult him or something? You insulted him, didn't you?

BIFF: Listen, will you let me out of it, will you just let me out of it!

HAPPY: What the hell!

WILLY: Tell me what happened!

BIFF: [*to* HAPPY] I can't talk to him!

[A *single trumpet note jars the ear. The light of green leaves stains the house, which holds the air of night and a dream.* YOUNG BERNARD *enters and knocks on the door of the house.*]

YOUNG BERNARD: [*frantically*] Mrs. Loman, Mrs. Loman!

HAPPY: Tell him what happened!

BIFF: [*to* HAPPY]Shut up and leave me alone!

WILLY: No, no! You had to go and flunk math!

BIFF: What math? What're you talking about?

YOUNG BERNARD: Mrs. Loman, Mrs. Loman!

[LINDA *appears in the house, as of old.*]

WILLY: [*wildly*] Math, math, math!

BIFF: Take it easy, Pop!

YOUNG BERNARD: Mrs. Loman!

WILLY: [*furiously*] If you hadn't flunked you'd've been set by now!

BIFF: Now, look, I'm gonna tell you what happened, and you're going to listen to me.

YOUNG BERNARD: Mrs. Loman!

BIFF: I waited six hours—

HAPPY: What the hell are you saying?

BIFF: I kept sending in my name but he wouldn't see me. So finally he . . .

[*He continues unheard as light fades low on the restaurant.*]

YOUNG BERNARD: Biff flunked math!

LINDA: No!

YOUNG BERNARD: Birnbaum flunked him! They won't graduate him!

LINDA: But they have to. He's gotta go to the university. Where is he? Biff! Biff!

YOUNG BERNARD: No, he left. He went to Grand Central.

LINDA: Grand—You mean he went to Boston!

YOUNG BERNARD: Is Uncle Willy in Boston?

LINDA: Oh, maybe Willy can talk to the teacher. Oh, the poor, poor boy!

[*Light on house area snaps out.*]

BIFF: [*at the table, now audible, holding up a gold fountain pen*] . . . so I'm washed up with Oliver, you understand? Are you listening to me?

WILLY: [*at a loss*] Yeah, sure. If you hadn't flunked—

BIFF: Flunked what? What're you talking about?

WILLY: Don't blame everything on me! I didn't flunk math—you did! What pen?

HAPPY: That was awful dumb, Biff, a pen like that is worth—

WILLY: [*seeing the pen for the first time*] You took Oliver's pen?

BIFF: [*weakening*] Dad, I just explained it to you.

WILLY: You stole Bill Oliver's fountain pen!

BIFF: I didn't exactly steal it! That's just what I've been explaining to you!

HAPPY: He had it in his hand and just then Oliver walked in, so he got nervous and stuck it in his pocket!

WILLY: My God, Biff!

BIFF: I never intended to do it, Dad!

OPERATOR'S VOICE: Standish Arms, good evening!

WILLY: [*shouting*] I'm not in my room!

BIFF: [*frightened*] Dad, what's the matter? [*He and* HAPPY *stand up.*]

OPERATOR: Ringing Mr. Loman for you!

WILLY: I'm not there, stop it!

BIFF: [*horrified, gets down on one knee before* WILLY] Dad, I'll make good, I'll make good. [WILLY *tries to get to his feet.* BIFF *holds him down.*] Sit down now.

WILLY: No, you're no good, you're no good for anything.

BIFF: I am, Dad, I'll find something else, you understand? Now don't worry about anything. [*He holds up* WILLY's *face*] Talk to me, Dad.

OPERATOR: Mr. Loman does not answer. Shall I page him?

WILLY: [*attempting to stand, as though to rush and silence the* OPERATOR] No, no, no!

HAPPY: He'll strike something, Pop.

WILLY: No, no . . .

BIFF: [*desperately, standing over* WILLY] Pop, listen! Listen to me! I'm telling you something good. Oliver talked to his partner about the Florida idea. You listening? He—he talked to his partner, and he came to me . . . I'm going to be all right, you hear? Dad, listen to me, he said it was just a question of the amount!

WILLY: Then you . . . got it?

HAPPY: He's gonna be terrific, Pop!

WILLY: [*trying to stand*] Then you got it, haven't you? You got it! You got it!

BIFF: [*agonized, holds* WILLY *down*] No, no. Look, Pop. I'm supposed to have lunch with them tomorrow. I'm just telling you this so you'll know that I can still make an impression, Pop. And I'll make good somewhere, but I can't go tomorrow, see?

WILLY: Why not? You simply—

BIFF: But the pen, Pop!

WILLY: You give it to him and tell him it was an oversight!

HAPPY: Sure, have lunch tomorrow!

BIFF: I can't say that—

WILLY: You were doing a crossword puzzle and accidentally used his pen!

BIFF: Listen, kid, I took those balls years ago, now I walk in with his fountain pen? That clinches it, don't you see? I can't face him like that! I'll try elsewhere.

PAGE'S VOICE: Paging Mr. Loman!

WILLY: Don't you want to be anything?

BIFF: Pop, how can I go back?

WILLY: You don't want to be anything, is that what's behind it?

BIFF: [*now angry at* WILLY *for not crediting his sympathy*] Don't take it that way! You think it was easy walking into that office after what I'd done to him? A team of horses couldn't have dragged me back to Bill Oliver!

WILLY: Then why'd you go?

BIFF: Why did I go? Why did I go! Look at you! Look at what's become of you!

[*Off left,* THE WOMAN *laughs.*]

WILLY: Biff, you're going to go to that lunch tomorrow, or—

BIFF: I can't go. I've got no appointment!

HAPPY: Biff, for . . . !

WILLY: Are you spiting me?

BIFF: Don't take it that way! Goddammit!

WILLY: [*strikes* BIFF *and falters away from the table*] You rotten little louse! Are you spiting me?

THE WOMAN: Someone's at the door, Willy!

BIFF: I'm no good, can't you see what I am?

HAPPY: [*separating them*] Hey, you're in a restaurant! Now cut it out, both of you! [*The girls enter.*] Hello, girls, sit down.

[THE WOMAN *laughs, off left.*]

MISS FORSYTHE: I guess we might as well. This is Letta.

THE WOMAN: Willy, are you going to wake up?

BIFF: [*ignoring* WILLY] How're ya, miss, sit down. What do you drink?

MISS FORSYTHE: Letta might not be able to stay long.

LETTA: I gotta get up very early tomorrow. I got jury duty. I'm so excited! Were you fellows ever on a jury?

BIFF: No, but I been in front of them! [*The girls laugh.*] This is my father.

LETTA: Isn't he cute? Sit down with us, Pop.

HAPPY: Sit him down, Biff!

BIFF: [*going to him*] Come on, slugger, drink us under the table. To hell with it! Come on, sit down, pal.

[*On* BIFF'*s last insistence,* WILLY *is about to sit.*]

THE WOMAN: [*now urgently*] Willy, are you going to answer the door!

[THE WOMAN'*s call pulls* WILLY *back. He starts right, befuddled.*]

BIFF: Hey, where are you going?

WILLY: Open the door.

BIFF: The door?

WILLY: The washroom . . . the door . . . where's the door?

BIFF: [*leading* WILLY *to the left*] Just go straight down.

[WILLY *moves left.*]

THE WOMAN: Willy, Willy, are you going to get up, get up, get up, get up?

[WILLY *exits left.*]

LETTA: I think it's sweet you bring your daddy along.

MISS FORSYTHE: Oh, he isn't really your father!

BIFF: [*at left, turning to her resentfully*] Miss Forsythe, you've just seen a prince walk by. A fine, troubled prince. A hard-working, unappreciated prince. A pal, you understand? A good companion. Always for his boys.

LETTA: That's so sweet.

HAPPY: Well, girls, what's the program? We're wasting time. Come on, Biff. Gather round. Where would you like to go?

BIFF: Why don't you do something for him?

HAPPY: Me!

BIFF: Don't you give a damn for him, Hap?

HAPPY: What're you talking about? I'm the one who—

BIFF: I sense it, you don't give a good goddam about him. [*He takes the rolled-up hose from his pocket and puts it on the table in front of* HAPPY] Look what I found in the cellar, for Christ's sake. How can you bear to let it go on?

HAPPY: Me? Who goes away? Who runs off and—

BIFF: Yeah, but he doesn't mean anything to you. You could help him—I can't! Don't you understand what I'm talking about? He's going to kill himself, don't you know that?

HAPPY: Don't I know it! Me!

BIFF: Hap, help him! Jesus . . . help him . . . Help me, help me, I can't bear to look at his face! [*Ready to weep, he hurries out, up right.*]

HAPPY: [*starting after him*] Where are you going?

MISS FORSYTHE: What's he so mad about?

HAPPY: Come on, girls, we'll catch up with him.

MISS FORSYTHE: [*as* HAPPY *pushes her out*] Say, I don't like that temper of his!

HAPPY: He's just a little overstrung, he'll be all right!

WILLY: [*off left, as* THE WOMAN *laughs*] Don't answer! Don't answer!

LETTA: Don't you want to tell your father—

HAPPY: No, that's not my father. He's just a guy. Come on, we'll catch Biff, and, honey, we're going to paint this town! Stanley, where's the check! Hey, Stanley!

    [*They exit.* STANLEY *looks toward left.*]

STANLEY: [*calling to* HAPPY *indignantly*] Mr. Loman! Mr. Loman!

    [STANLEY *picks up a chair and follows them off. Knocking is heard off left.* THE WOMAN *enters, laughing.* WILLY *follows her. She is in a black slip; he is buttoning his shirt. Raw, sensuous music accompanies their speech.*]

WILLY: Will you stop laughing? Will you stop?

THE WOMAN: Aren't you going to answer the door? He'll wake the whole hotel.

WILLY: I'm not expecting anybody.

THE WOMAN: Whyn't you have another drink, honey, and stop being so damn self-centered?

WILLY: I'm so lonely.

THE WOMAN: You know you ruined me, Willy? From now on, whenever you come to the office, I'll see that you go right through to the buyers. No waiting at my desk any more, Willy. You ruined me.

WILLY: That's nice of you to say that.

THE WOMAN: Gee, you are self-centered! Why so sad? You are the saddest, self-centeredest soul I ever did see-saw. [*She laughs.*] [*He kisses her.*] Come on inside, drummer boy. It's silly to be dressing in the middle of the night. [*as knocking is heard*] Aren't you going to answer the door?

WILLY: They're knocking on the wrong door.

THE WOMAN: But I felt the knocking. And he heard us talking in here. Maybe the hotel's on fire!

WILLY: [*his terror rising*] It's a mistake.

THE WOMAN: Then tell him to go away!

WILLY: There's nobody there.

THE WOMAN: It's getting on my nerves, Willy. There's somebody standing out there and it's getting on my nerves!

WILLY: [*pushing her away from him*] All right, stay in the bathroom here, and don't come out. I think there's a law in Massachusetts about it, so don't come out. It may be that new room clerk. He looked very mean. So don't come out. It's a mistake, there's no fire.

[*The knocking is heard again. He takes a few steps away from her, and she vanishes into the wing. The light follows him, and now he is facing* YOUNG BIFF, *who carries a suitcase.* BIFF *steps toward him. The music is gone.*]

BIFF: Why didn't you answer?

WILLY: Biff! What are you doing in Boston?

BIFF: Why didn't you answer? I've been knocking for five minutes, I called you on the phone—

WILLY: I just heard you. I was in the bathroom and had the door shut. Did anything happen home?

BIFF: Dad—I let you down.

WILLY: What do you mean?

BIFF: Dad . . .

WILLY: Biffo, what's this about? [*putting his arm around* BIFF] Come on, let's go downstairs and get you a malted.

BIFF: Dad, I flunked math.

WILLY: Not for the term?

BIFF: The term. I haven't got enough credits to graduate.

WILLY: You mean to say Bernard wouldn't give you the answers?

BIFF: He did, he tried, but I only got a sixty-one.

WILLY: And they wouldn't give you four points?

BIFF: Birnbaum refused absolutely. I begged him, Pop, but he won't give me those points. You gotta talk to him before they close the school. Because if he saw the kind of man you are, and you just talked to him in your way, I'm sure he'd come through for me. The class came right before practice, see, and I didn't go enough. Would you talk to him? He'd like you, Pop. You know the way you could talk.

WILLY: You're on. We'll drive right back.

BIFF: Oh, Dad, good work! I'm sure he'll change it for you!

WILLY: Go downstairs and tell the clerk I'm checkin' out. Go right down.

BIFF: Yes, sir! See, the reason he hates me, Pop—one day he was late for class so I got up at the blackboard and imitated him. I crossed my eyes and talked with a lithp.

WILLY: [*laughing*] You did? The kids like it?

BIFF: They nearly died laughing!

WILLY: Yeah? What'd you do?

BIFF: The thquare root of thixthy twee is . . . [WILLY *bursts out laughing;* BIFF *joins him.*] And in the middle of it he walked in!

[WILLY *laughs and* THE WOMAN *joins in offstage.*]

WILLY: [*without hesitation*] Hurry downstairs and—

BIFF: Somebody in there?

WILLY: No, that was next door.

BIFF: Somebody got in your bathroom!

[THE WOMAN *laughs offstage.*]

WILLY: No, it's the next room, there's a party—

THE WOMAN: [*enters, laughing. She lisps this*] Can I come in? There's something in the bathtub, Willy, and it's moving!

[WILLY *looks at* BIFF, *who is staring open-mouthed and horrified at* THE WOMAN.]

WILLY: Ah—you better go back to your room. They must be finished painting by now. They're painting her room so I let her take a shower here. Go back, go back . . . [*He pushes her.*]

THE WOMAN: [*resisting*] But I've got to get dressed, Willy, I can't—

WILLY: Get out of here! Go back, go back . . . [*suddenly striving for the ordinary*] This is Miss Francis, Biff, she's a buyer. They're painting her room. Go back, Miss Francis, go back . . .

THE WOMAN: But my clothes, I can't go out naked in the hall!

WILLY: [*pushing her offstage*] Get outa here! Go back, go back!

[BIFF *slowly sits down on his suitcase as the argument continues offstage.*]

THE WOMAN: Where's my stockings? You promised me stockings, Willy!

WILLY: I have no stockings here!

THE WOMAN: You had two boxes of size nine sheers for me, and I want them!

WILLY: Here, for God's sake, will you get outa here!

THE WOMAN: [*enters holding a box of stockings*] I just hope there's nobody in the hall. That's all I hope. [*to* BIFF] Are you football or baseball?

BIFF: Football.

THE WOMAN: [*angry, humiliated*] That's me too. G'night. [*She snatches her clothes from* WILLY, *and walks out.*]

WILLY: [*after a pause*] Well, better get going. I want to get to the school first thing in the morning. Get my suits out of the closet. I'll get my valise. [BIFF *doesn't move.*] What's the matter? [BIFF *remains motionless, tears falling.*] She's a buyer. Buys for J. H. Simmons. She lives down the hall—they're painting. You don't imagine—[*He breaks off. After a pause:*] Now listen, pal, she's just a buyer. She sees merchandise in her room and they have to keep it looking just so . . . [*Pause. Assuming command:*] All right, get my suits. [BIFF *doesn't move.*] Now stop crying and do as I say. I gave you an order. Biff, I gave you an order! Is that what you do when I give you an order? How dare you cry! [*putting his arm around* BIFF] Now look, Biff, when you grow up you'll understand about these things. You mustn't—you mustn't overemphasize a thing like this. I'll see Birnbaum first thing in the morning.

BIFF: Never mind.

WILLY: [*getting down beside* BIFF] Never mind! He's going to give you those points. I'll see to it.

BIFF: He wouldn't listen to you.

WILLY: He certainly will listen to me. You need those points for the U. of Virginia.

BIFF: I'm not going there.

WILLY: Heh? If I can't get him to change that mark you'll make it up in summer school. You've got all summer to—

BIFF: [*his weeping breaking from him*] Dad . . .

WILLY: [*infected by it*] Oh, my boy . . .

BIFF: Dad . . .

WILLY: She's nothing to me, Biff. I was lonely, I was terribly lonely.

BIFF: You—you gave her Mama's stockings! [*His tears break through and he rises to go.*]

WILLY: [*grabbing for* BIFF] I gave you an order!

BIFF: Don't touch me, you—liar!

WILLY: Apologize for that!

BIFF: You fake! You phony little fake! You fake! [*Overcome, he turns quickly and weeping fully goes out with his suitcase.* WILLY *is left on the floor on his knees.*]

WILLY: I gave you an order! Biff, come back here or I'll beat you! Come back here! I'll whip you!

[STANLEY *comes quickly in from the right and stands in front of* WILLY.]

WILLY: [*shouts at* STANLEY] I gave you an order . . .

STANLEY: Hey, let's pick it up, pick it up, Mr. Loman. [*He helps* WILLY *to his feet*] Your boys left with the chippies. They said they'll see you home.

[A SECOND WAITER *watches some distance away.*]

WILLY: But we were supposed to have dinner together.

[*Music is heard,* WILLY'*s theme.*]

STANLEY: Can you make it?

WILLY: I'll—sure, I can make it. [*suddenly concerned about his clothes*] Do I —I look all right?

STANLEY: Sure, you look all right. [*He flicks a speck off* WILLY'*s lapel.*]

WILLY: Here—here's a dollar.

STANLEY: Oh, your son paid me. It's all right.

WILLY: [*putting it in* STANLEY'*s hand*] No, take it. You're a good boy.

STANLEY: Oh, no, you don't have to . . .

WILLY: Here—here's some more, I don't need it any more. [*after a slight pause*] Tell me—is there a seed store in the neighborhood?

STANLEY: Seeds? You mean like to plant?

[*As* WILLY *turns,* STANLEY *slips the money back into his jacket pocket.*]

WILLY: Yes. Carrots, peas . . .

STANLEY: Well, there's hardware stores on Sixth Avenue, but it may be too late now.

WILLY: [*anxiously*] Oh, I'd better hurry. I've got to get some seeds. [*He starts off to the right.*] I've got to get some seeds, right away. Nothing's planted. I don't have a thing in the ground.

> [WILLY *hurries out as the light goes down.* STANLEY *moves over to the right after him, watches him off. The other waiter has been staring at* WILLY.]

STANLEY: [*to the* WAITER] Well, whatta you looking at?

> [*The* WAITER *picks up the chairs and moves off right.* STANLEY *takes the table and follows him. The light fades on this area. There is a long pause, the sound of the flute coming over. The light gradually rises on the kitchen, which is empty.* HAPPY *appears at the door of the house, followed by* BIFF. HAPPY *is carrying a large bunch of long-stemmed roses. He enters the kitchen, looks around for* LINDA. *Not seeing her, he turns to* BIFF, *who is just outside the house door, and makes a gesture with his hands, indicating "Not here, I guess." He looks into the living-room and freezes. Inside,* LINDA, *unseen, is seated,* WILLY's *coat on her lap. She rises ominously and quietly and moves toward* HAPPY, *who backs up into the kitchen, afraid.*]

HAPPY: Hey, what're you doing up? [LINDA *says nothing but moves toward him implacably*] Where's Pop? [*He keeps backing to the right, and now* LINDA *is in full view in the doorway to the living-room*] Is he sleeping?

LINDA: Where were you?

HAPPY: [*trying to laugh it off*] We met two girls, Mom, very fine types. Here, we brought you some flowers. [*offering them to her*] Put them in your room, Ma.

> [*She knocks them to the floor at* BIFF's *feet. He has now come inside and closed the door behind him. She stares at* BIFF, *silent.*]

HAPPY: Now what'd you do that for? Mom, I want you to have some flowers—

LINDA: [*cutting* HAPPY *off, violently to* BIFF] Don't you care whether he lives or dies?

HAPPY: [*going to the stairs*] Come upstairs, Biff.

BIFF: [*with a flare of disgust, to* HAPPY] Go away from me! [*to* LINDA] What do you mean, lives or dies? Nobody's dying around here, pal.

LINDA: Get out of my sight! Get out of here!

BIFF: I wanna see the boss.

LINDA: You're not going near him!

BIFF: Where is he? [*He moves into the living-room and* LINDA *follows.*]

LINDA: [*shouting after* BIFF] You invite him for dinner. He looks forward to it all day—[BIFF *appears in his parents' bedroom, looks around, and exits*]—and then you desert him there. There's no stranger you'd do that to!

HAPPY: Why? He had a swell time with us. Listen, when I—[LINDA *comes back into the kitchen*]—desert him I hope I don't outlive the day!

LINDA: Get out of here!

HAPPY: Now look, Mom . . .

LINDA: Did you have to go to women tonight? You and your lousy rotten whores!

> [BIFF *re-enters the kitchen.*]

HAPPY: Mom, all we did was follow Biff around trying to cheer him up! [*to* BIFF] Boy, what a night you gave me!

LINDA: Get out of here, both of you, and don't come back! I don't want you tormenting him any more. Go on now, get your things together! [*to* BIFF] You can sleep in his apartment. [*She starts to pick up the flowers and stops herself*] Pick up this stuff, I'm not your maid any more. Pick it up, you bum, you!

> [HAPPY *turns his back to her in refusal.* BIFF *slowly moves over and gets down on his knees, picking up the flowers.*]

LINDA: You're a pair of animals! Not one, not another living soul would have had the cruelty to walk out on that man in a restaurant!

BIFF: [*not looking at her*] Is that what he said?

LINDA: He didn't have to say anything. He was so humiliated he nearly limped when he came in.

HAPPY: But, Mom, he had a great time with us—

BIFF: [*cutting him off violently*] Shut up!

> [*Without another word,* HAPPY *goes upstairs.*]

LINDA: You! You didn't even go in to see if he was all right!

BIFF: [*still on the floor in front of* LINDA, *the flowers in his hand; with self-loathing*] No. Didn't. Didn't do a damned thing. How do you like that, heh? Left him babbling in a toilet.

LINDA: You louse. You . . .

BIFF: Now you hit it on the nose! [*He gets up, throws the flowers in the waste-basket*] The scum of the earth, and you're looking at him!

LINDA: Get out of here!

BIFF: I gotta talk to the boss, Mom. Where is he?

LINDA: You're not going near him. Get out of this house!

BIFF: [*with absolute assurance, determination*] No. We're gonna have an abrupt conversation, him and me.

LINDA: You're not talking to him!

> [*Hammering is heard from outside the house, off right.* BIFF *turns toward the noise.*]

LINDA: [*suddenly pleading*] Will you please leave him alone?

BIFF: What's he doing out there?

LINDA: He's planting the garden!

BIFF: [*quietly*] Now? Oh, my God!

> [BIFF *moves outside,* LINDA *following. The light dies down on them and comes up on the center of the apron as* WILLY *walks into it. He is carrying a flashlight, a hoe, and a handful of seed packets. He raps the top of the hoe sharply to fix it firmly, and then moves to the left, measuring off the distance with his foot. He holds the flashlight to look at the seed packets, reading off the instructions. He is in the blue of night.*]

WILLY: Carrots . . . quarter-inch apart. Rows . . . one-foot rows. [*he measures it off*] One foot. [*he puts down a package and measures off*] Beets. [*he puts down another package and measures again*] Lettuce. [*he reads the package, puts it down*] One foot—[*He breaks off as* BEN *appears at the right and moves slowly down to him.*] What a proposition, ts, ts. Terrific, terrific. 'Cause she's suffered, Ben, the woman has suffered. You understand me? A man can't go out the way he came in, Ben, a man has got to add up to something. You can't, you can't—[BEN *moves toward him as though to interrupt.*] You gotta consider, now. Don't answer so quick. Remember, it's a guaranteed twenty-thousand-dollar proposition. Now look, Ben, I want you to go through the ins and outs of this thing with me. I've got nobody to talk to, Ben, and the woman has suffered, you hear me?

BEN: [*standing still, considering*] What's the proposition?

WILLY: It's twenty thousand dollars on the barrelhead. Guaranteed, gilt-edged, you understand?

BEN: You don't want to make a fool of yourself. They might not honor the policy.

WILLY: How can they dare refuse? Didn't I work like a coolie to meet every premium on the nose? And now they don't pay off? Impossible!

BEN: It's called a cowardly thing, William.

WILLY: Why? Does it take more guts to stand here the rest of my life ringing up a zero?

BEN: [*yielding*] That's a point, William. [*He moves, thinking, turns.*] And twenty thousand—that *is* something one can feel with the hand, it is there.

WILLY: [*now assured, with rising power*] Oh, Ben, that's the whole beauty of it! I see it like a diamond, shining in the dark, hard and rough, that I can pick up and touch in my hand. Not like—like an appointment! This would not be another damned-fool appointment, Ben, and it changes all the aspects. Because he thinks I'm nothing, see, and so he spites me. But the funeral—[*straightening up*] Ben, that funeral will be massive! They'll come from Maine, Massachusetts, Vermont, New Hampshire! All the old-timers with the strange license plates—that boy will be thunder-struck, Ben, because he never realized—I am known! Rhode Island, New York, New Jersey—I am known, Ben, and he'll see it with his eyes once and for all. He'll see·what I am, Ben! He's in for a shock, that boy!

BEN: [*coming down to the edge of the garden*] He'll call you a coward.

WILLY: [*suddenly fearful*] No, that would be terrible.

BEN: Yes. And a damned fool.

WILLY: No, no, he mustn't, I won't have that! [*He is broken and desperate.*]

BEN: He'll hate you, William.

[*The gay music of the Boys is heard.*]

WILLY: Oh, Ben, how do we get back to all the great times? Used to be so full of light, and comradeship, the sleigh-riding in winter, and the ruddiness on his cheeks. And always some kind of good news coming up, always something nice coming up ahead. And never even let me carry the valises in the house, and simonizing, simonizing that little red car! Why, why can't I give him something and not have him hate me?

BEN: Let me think about it. [*He glances at his watch.*] I still have a little time. Remarkable proposition, but you've got to be sure you're not making a fool of yourself.

[BEN *drifts off upstage and goes out of sight.* BIFF *comes down from the left.*]

WILLY: [*suddenly conscious of* BIFF, *turns and looks up at him, then begins picking up the packages of seeds in confusion*] Where the hell is that seed? *Indignantly:* You can't see nothing out here! They boxed in the whole goddam neighborhood!

BIFF: There are people all around here. Don't you realize that?

WILLY: I'm busy. Don't bother me.

BIFF: [*taking the hoe from* WILLY] I'm saying good-by to you, Pop. [WILLY *looks at him, silent, unable to move.*] I'm not coming back any more.

WILLY: You're not going to see Oliver tomorrow?

BIFF: I've got no appointment, Dad.

WILLY: He put his arm around you, and you've got no appointment?

BIFF: Pop, get this now, will you? Everytime I've left it's been a fight that sent me out of here. Today I realized something about myself and I tried to explain it to you and I—I think I'm just not smart enough to make any sense out of it for you. To hell with whose fault it is or anything like that. [*he takes* WILLY's *arm*] Let's just wrap it up, heh? Come on in, we'll tell Mom. [*He gently tries to pull* WILLY *to left.*]

WILLY: [*frozen, immobile, with guilt in his voice*] No, I don't want to see her.

BIFF: Come on! [*He pulls again, and* WILLY *tries to pull away.*]

WILLY: [*highly nervous*] No, no, I don't want to see her.

BIFF: [*tries to look into* WILLY's *face, as if to find the answer there*] Why don't you want to see her?

WILLY: [*more harshly now*] Don't bother me, will you?

BIFF: What do you mean, you don't want to see her? You don't want them calling you yellow, do you? This isn't your fault; it's me, I'm a bum. Now come inside! [WILLY *strains to get away.*] Did you hear what I said to you?
[WILLY *pulls away and quickly goes by himself into the house.* BIFF *follows.*]

LINDA: [*to* WILLY] Did you plant, dear?

BIFF: [*at the door, to* LINDA] All right, we had it out. I'm going and I'm not writing any more.

LINDA: [*going to* WILLY *in the kitchen*] I think that's the best way, dear. 'Cause there's no use drawing it out, you'll just never get along.
[WILLY *doesn't respond.*]

BIFF: People ask where I am and what I'm doing, you don't know, and you don't care. That way it'll be off your mind and you can start brightening up again. All right? That clears it, doesn't it? [WILLY *is silent, and* BIFF *goes to him.*] You gonna wish me luck, scout? [*He extends his hand.*] What do you say?

LINDA: Shake his hand, Willy.

WILLY: [*turning to her, seething with hurt*] There's no necessity to mention the pen at all, y'know.

BIFF: [*gently*] I've got no appointment, Dad.

WILLY: [*erupting fiercely*] He put his arm around . . . ?

BIFF: Dad, you're never going to see what I am, so what's the use of arguing? If I strike oil I'll send you a check. Meantime forget I'm alive.

WILLY: [*to* LINDA] Spite, see?

BIFF: Shake hands, Dad.

WILLY: Not my hand.

BIFF: I was hoping not to go this way.

WILLY: Well, this is the way you're going. Good-by.

> [BIFF *looks at him a moment, then turns sharply and goes to the stairs.*]

WILLY: [*stops him with*] May you rot in hell if you leave this house!

BIFF: [*turning*] Exactly what is it that you want from me?

WILLY: I want you to know, on the train, in the mountains, in the valleys, wherever you go, that you cut down your life for spite!

BIFF: No, no.

WILLY: Spite, spite, is the word of your undoing! And when you're down and out, remember what did it. When you're rotting somewhere beside the railroad tracks, remember, and don't you dare blame it on me!

BIFF: I'm not blaming it on you!

WILLY: I won't take the rap for this, you hear?

> [HAPPY *comes down the stairs and stands on the bottom step, watching.*]

BIFF: That's just what I'm telling you!

WILLY: [*sinking into a chair at the table, with full accusation*] You're trying to put a knife in me—don't think I don't know what you're doing!

BIFF: All right, phony! Then let's lay it on the line. [*He whips the rubber tube out of his pocket and puts it on the table.*]

HAPPY: You crazy—

LINDA: Biff! [*She moves to grab the hose, but* BIFF *holds it down with his hand.*]

BIFF: Leave it there! Don't move it!

WILLY: [*not looking at it*] What is that?

BIFF: You know goddam well what that is.

WILLY: [*caged, wanting to escape*] I never saw that.

BIFF: You saw it. The mice didn't bring it into the cellar! What is this supposed to do, make a hero out of you? This supposed to make me sorry for you?

WILLY: Never heard of it.

BIFF: There'll be no pity for you, you hear it? No pity!

WILLY: [*to* LINDA] You hear the spite!

BIFF: No, you're going to hear the truth—what you are and what I am!

LINDA: Stop it!

WILLY: Spite!

HAPPY: [*coming down toward* BIFF] You cut it now!

BIFF: [*to* HAPPY] The man don't know who we are! The man is gonna know! [*to* WILLY] We never told the truth for ten minutes in this house!

HAPPY: We always told the truth!

BIFF: [*turning on him*] You big blow, are you the assistant buyer? You're one of the two assistants to the assistant, aren't you?

HAPPY: Well, I'm practically—

BIFF: You're practically full of it! We all are! And I'm through with it. [*to* WILLY] Now hear this, Willy, this is me.

WILLY: I know you!

BIFF: You know why I had no address for three months? I stole a suit in Kansas City and I was in jail. [*to* LINDA, *who is sobbing*] Stop crying. I'm through with it.

[LINDA *turns away from them, her hands covering her face.*]

WILLY: I suppose that's my fault!

BIFF: I stole myself out of every good job since high school!

WILLY: And whose fault is that?

BIFF: And I never got anywhere because you blew me so full of hot air I could never stand taking orders from anybody! That's whose fault it is!

WILLY: I hear that!

LINDA: Don't, Biff!

BIFF: It's goddam time you heard that! I had to be boss big shot in two weeks, and I'm through with it!

WILLY: Then hang yourself! For spite, hang yourself!

BIFF: No! Nobody's hanging himself, Willy! I ran down eleven flights with a pen in my hand today. And suddenly I stopped, you hear me? And in the middle of that office building, do you hear this? I stopped in the middle of that building and I saw—the sky. I saw the things that I love in this world. The work and the food and time to sit and smoke. And I looked at the pen and said to myself, what the hell am I grabbing this for? Why am I trying to become what I don't want to be? What am I doing in an office, making a contemptuous, begging fool of myself, when all I want is out there, waiting for me the minute I say I know who I am! Why can't I say that, Willy?

[*He tries to make* WILLY *face him, but* WILLY *pulls away and moves to the left.*]

WILLY: [*with hatred, threateningly*] The door of your life is wide open!

BIFF: Pop! I'm a dime a dozen, and so are you!

WILLY: [*turning on him now in an uncontrolled outburst*] I am not a dime a dozen! I am Willy Loman, and you are Biff Loman!

[BIFF *starts for* WILLY, *but is blocked by* HAPPY. *In his fury,* BIFF *seems on the verge of attacking his father.*]

BIFF: I am not a leader of men, Willy, and neither are you. You were never anything but a hard-working drummer who landed in the ash can like all the rest of them! I'm one dollar an hour, Willy! I tried seven states and couldn't raise it. A buck an hour! Do you gather my meaning? I'm not bringing home any prizes any more, and you're going to stop waiting for me to bring them home!

WILLY: [*directly to* BIFF] You vengeful, spiteful mut!

[BIFF *breaks from* HAPPY. WILLY, *in fright, starts up the stairs.* BIFF *grabs him.*]

BIFF: [*at the peak of his fury*] Pop, I'm nothing! I'm nothing, Pop. Can't you understand that? There's no spite in it any more. I'm just what I am, that's all.

[BIFF's *fury has spent itself, and he breaks down, sobbing, holding on to* WILLY, *who dumbly fumbles for* BIFF's *face.*]

WILLY: [*astonished*] What're you doing? What're you doing? [*to* LINDA] Why is he crying?

BIFF: [*crying, broken*] Will you let me go, for Christ's sake? Will you take that phony dream and burn it before something happens? [*struggling to contain himself, he pulls away and moves to the stairs*] I'll go in the morning. Put him—put him to bed. [*Exhausted,* BIFF *moves up the stairs to his room.*]

WILLY: [*after a long pause, astonished, elevated*] Isn't that—isn't that remarkable? Biff—he likes me!

LINDA: He loves you, Willy!

HAPPY: [*deeply moved*] Always did, Pop.

WILLY: Oh, Biff! [*staring wildly*] He cried! Cried to me. [*He is choking with his love, and now cries out his promise:*] That boy—that boy is going to be magnificent!

[BEN *appears in the light just outside the kitchen.*]

BEN: Yes, outstanding, with twenty thousand behind him.

LINDA: [*sensing the racing of his mind, fearfully, carefully*] Now come to bed, Willy. It's all settled now.

WILLY: [*finding it difficult not to rush out of the house*] Yes, we'll sleep. Come on. Go to sleep, Hap.

BEN: And it does take a great kind of a man to crack the jungle.

[*In accents of dread,* BEN's *idyllic music starts up.*]

HAPPY: [*his arm around* LINDA] I'm getting married, Pop, don't forget it. I'm changing everything. I'm gonna run that department before the year is up. You'll see, Mom. [*he kisses her*]

BEN: The jungle is dark but full of diamonds, Willy.

[WILLY *turns, moves, listening to* BEN.]

LINDA: Be good. You're both good boys, just act that way, that's all.

HAPPY: 'Night, Pop. [*He goes upstairs.*]

LINDA: [*to* WILLY] Come, dear.

BEN: [*with greater force*] One must go in to fetch a diamond out.

WILLY: [*to* LINDA, *as he moves slowly along the edge of the kitchen, toward the door*] I just want to get settled down, Linda. Let me sit alone for a little.

LINDA: [*almost uttering her fear*] I want you upstairs.

WILLY: [*taking her in his arms*] In a few minutes, Linda. I couldn't sleep right now. Go on, you look awful tired. [*He kisses her.*]

BEN: Not like an appointment at all. A diamond is rough and hard to the touch.

WILLY: Go on now. I'll be right up.

LINDA: I think this is the only way, Willy.

WILLY: Sure, it's the best thing.

BEN: Best thing!

WILLY: The only way. Everything is gonna be—go on, kid, get to bed. You look so tired.

LINDA: Come right up.

WILLY: Two minutes.

[LINDA *goes into the living-room, then reappears in her bedroom.* WILLY *moves just outside the kitchen door.*]

WILLY: Loves me. [*wonderingly*] Always loved me. Isn't that a remarkable thing? Ben, he'll worship me for it!

BEN: [*with promise*] It's dark there, but full of diamonds.

WILLY: Can you imagine that magnificence with twenty thousand dollars in his pocket?

LINDA: [*calling from her room*] Willy! Come up!

WILLY: [*calling into the kitchen*] Yes! Yes. Coming! It's very smart, you realize that, don't you, sweetheart? Even Ben sees it. I gotta go, baby. 'By! 'By! [*going over to* BEN, *almost dancing*] Imagine? When the mail comes he'll be ahead of Bernard again!

BEN: A perfect proposition all around.

WILLY: Did you see how he cried to me? Oh, if I could kiss him, Ben!

BEN: Time, William, time!

WILLY: Oh, Ben, I always knew one way or another we were gonna make it, Biff and I!

BEN: [*looking at his watch*] The boat. We'll be late. [*He moves slowly off into the darkness.*]

WILLY: [*elegiacally, turning to the house*] Now when you kick off, boy, I want a seventy-yard boot, and get right down the field under the ball, and when you hit, hit low and hit hard, because it's important, boy. [*he swings around and faces the audience*] There's all kinds of important people in the stands, and the first thing you know . . . [*suddenly realizing he is alone*] Ben! Ben, where do I . . . ? [*he makes a sudden movement of search*] Ben, how do I . . . ?

LINDA: [*calling*] Willy, you coming up?

WILLY: [*uttering a gasp of fear, whirling about as if to quiet her*] Sh! [*He turns around as if to find his way; sounds, faces, voices, seem to be swarming in upon him and he flicks at them, crying*] Sh! Sh! [*Suddenly music, faint and high, stops him. It rises in intensity, almost to an unbearable scream. He goes up and down on his toes, and rushes off around the house.*] Shhh!

LINDA: Willy?

[*There is no answer.* LINDA *waits.* BIFF *gets up off his bed. He is still in his clothes.* HAPPY *sits up.* BIFF *stands listening.*]

LINDA: [*with real fear*] Willy, answer me! Willy!

[*There is the sound of a car starting and moving away at full speed.*]

LINDA: No!

BIFF: [*rushing down the stairs*] Pop!

[*As the car speeds off, the music crashes down in a frenzy of sound, which becomes the soft pulsation of a single cello string.* BIFF *slowly returns to his bedroom. He and* HAPPY *gravely don their jackets.* LINDA *slowly walks out of her room. The music has developed into a dead march. The leaves of day are appearing over everything.*

CHARLEY *and* BERNARD, *somberly dressed, appear and knock on the kitchen door.* BIFF *and* HAPPY *slowly descend the stairs to the kitchen as* CHARLEY *and* BERNARD *enter. All stop a moment when* LINDA, *in clothes of mourning, bearing a little bunch of roses, comes through the draped doorway into the kitchen. She goes to* CHARLEY *and takes his arm. Now all move toward the audience, through the wall-line of the kitchen. At the limit of the apron,* LINDA *lays down the flowers, kneels, and sits back on her heels. All stare down at the grave.*]

REQUIEM

CHARLEY: It's getting dark, Linda.

[LINDA *doesn't react. She stares at the grave.*]

BIFF: How about it, Mom? Better get some rest, heh? They'll be closing the gate soon.

[LINDA *makes no move. Pause.*]

HAPPY: [*deeply angered*] He had no right to do that. There was no necessity for it. We would've helped him.

CHARLEY: [*grunting*] Hmmm.

BIFF: Come along, Mom.

LINDA: Why didn't anybody come?

CHARLEY: It was a very nice funeral.

LINDA: But where are all the people he knew? Maybe they blame him.

CHARLEY: Naa. It's a rough world, Linda. They wouldn't blame him.

LINDA: I can't understand it. At this time especially. First time in thirty-five years we were just about free and clear. He only needed a little salary. He was even finished with the dentist.

CHARLEY: No man only needs a little salary.

LINDA: I can't understand it.

BIFF: There were a lot of nice days. When he'd come home from a trip; or on Sundays, making the stoop; finishing the cellar; putting on the new porch; when he built the extra bathroom; and put up the garage. You know something, Charley, there's more of him in that front stoop than in all the sales he ever made.

CHARLEY: Yeah. He was a happy man with a batch of cement.

LINDA: He was so wonderful with his hands.

BIFF: He had all the wrong dreams. All, all, wrong.

HAPPY: [*almost ready to fight* BIFF] Don't say that!

BIFF: He never knew who he was.

CHARLEY: [*stopping* HAPPY'S *movement and reply. To* BIFF:] Nobody dast blame this man. You don't understand. Willy was a salesman. And for a salesman, there is no rock bottom to the life. He don't put a bolt to a nut, he don't tell you the law or give you medicine. He's a man way out there in the blue, riding on a smile and a shoeshine. And when they start not smiling back—that's an earthquake. And then you get yourself a couple of spots on your hat, and you're finished. Nobody dast blame this man. A salesman is got to dream, boy. It comes with the territory.

BIFF: Charley, the man didn't know who he was.

HAPPY: [*infuriated*] Don't say that!

BIFF: Why don't you come with me, Happy?

HAPPY: I'm not licked that easily. I'm staying right in this city, and I'm gonna beat this racket! [*He looks at* BIFF, *his chin set.*] The Loman Brothers!

BIFF: I know who I am, kid.

HAPPY: All right, boy. I'm gonna show you and everybody else that Willy Loman did not die in vain. He had a good dream. It's the only dream you can have—to come out number-one man. He fought it out here, and this is where I'm gonna win it for him.

BIFF: [*with a hopeless glance at* HAPPY, *bends toward his mother*] Let's go, Mom.

LINDA: I'll be with you in a minute. Go on, Charley. [*he hesitates*] I want to, just for a minute. I never had a chance to say good-by.

[CHARLEY *moves away, followed by* HAPPY. BIFF *remains a slight distance up and left of* LINDA. *She sits there, summoning herself. The flute begins, not far away, playing behind her speech.*]

LINDA: Forgive me, dear. I can't cry. I don't know what it is, but I can't cry. I don't understand it. Why did you ever do that? Help me, Willy, I can't cry. It seems to me that you're just on another trip. I keep expecting you. Willy, dear, I can't cry. Why did you do it? I search and search and I search, and I can't understand it, Willy. I made the last payment on the house today. Today, dear. And there'll be nobody home. [*a sob rises in her throat*] We're free and clear. [*sobbing more fully, released*] We're free. [BIFF *comes slowly toward her.*] We're free . . . We're free . . .

[BIFF *lifts her to her feet and moves out up right with her in his arms.* LINDA *sobs quietly.* BERNARD *and* CHARLEY *come together and follow them, followed by* HAPPY. *Only the music of the flute is left on the darkening stage as over the house the hard towers of the apartment buildings rise into sharp focus, and*]

THE CURTAIN FALLS

Samuel Beckett

Happy Days

CHARACTERS

WINNIE, *a woman about fifty*
WILLIE, *a man about sixty*

ACT I

Expanse of scorched grass rising centre to low mound. Gentle slopes down to front and either side of stage. Back an abrupter fall to stage level. Maximum of simplicity and symmetry.
Blazing light.
Very pompier trompe-l'oeil backcloth to represent unbroken plain and sky receding to meet in far distance.
Imbedded up to above her waist in exact centre of mound, WINNIE. *About fifty, well preserved, blond for preference, plump, arms and shoulders bare, low bodice, big bosom, pearl necklet. She is discovered sleeping, her arms on the ground before her, her head on her arms. Beside her on ground to her left a capacious black bag, shopping variety, and to her right a collapsible collapsed parasol, beak of handle emerging from sheath.*
To her right and rear, lying asleep on ground, hidden by mound, WILLIE.
Long pause. A bell rings piercingly, say ten seconds, stops. She does not move. Pause. Bell more piercingly, say five seconds. She wakes. Bell stops. She raises her head, gazes front. Long pause. She straightens up, lays her hands flat on ground, throws back her head and gazes at zenith. Long pause.

WINNIE: *[gazing at zenith]* Another heavenly day. *[Pause. Head back level, eyes front, pause. She clasps hands to breast, closes eyes. Lips move in inaudible prayer, say ten seconds. Lips still. Hands remain clasped. Low.]* For Jesus Christ sake Amen. *[Eyes open, hands unclasp, return to mound. Pause. She clasps hands to breast again, closes eyes, lips move again in inaudible addendum, say five seconds. Low.]* World without end Amen. *[Eyes open, hands unclasp, return to mound. Pause.]* Begin, Winnie. *[Pause.]* Begin your day, Winnie. *[Pause. She turns to bag, rummages in it without moving it from its place, brings out toothbrush, rummages again, brings out flat tube of toothpaste, turns back front, unscrews cap of tube, lays cap on ground, squeezes with difficulty small blob of paste on brush, holds tube in one hand and brushes teeth with other. She turns modestly aside and back to her right to*

spit out behind mound. In this position her eyes rest on WILLIE. *She spits out.
She cranes a little further back and down. Loud.*] Hoo-oo! [*Pause. Louder.*]
Hoo-oo! [*Pause. Tender smile as she turns back front, lays down brush.*] Poor
Willie— [*examines tube, smile off*]—running out —[*looks for cap*]—ah
well—[*finds cap*]—can't be helped—[*screws on cap*]—just one of those old
things—[*lays down tube*]—another of those old things—[*turns towards
bag*]—just can't be cured—[*rummages in bag*]—cannot be cured—[*brings
out small mirror, turns back front*]—ah yes—[*inspects teeth in mirror*]—
poor dear Willie—[*testing upper front teeth with thumb, indistinctly*]—
good Lord!—[*pulling back upper lip to inspect gums, do.*]—good God!—
[*pulling back corner of mouth, mouth open, do.*]—ah well—[*other corner,
do.*]—no worse—[*abandons inspection, normal speech*]—no better, no
worse—[*lays down mirror*]—no change—[*wipes fingers on grass*]—no
pain—[*looks for toothbrush*]—hardly any—[*takes up toothbrush*]—great
thing that—[*examines handle of brush*]—nothing like it—[*examines handle, reads*]—pure . . . what?—[*Pause.*]—what?—[*lays down brush*]—ah
yes—[*turns towards bag*]—poor Willie—[*rummages in bag*]—no zest—
[*rummages*]—for anything—[*brings out spectacles in case*]—no interest—
[*turns back front*]—in life—[*takes spectacles from case*]—poor dear
Willie—[*lays down case*]—sleep for ever—[*opens spectacles*]—marvellous
gift—[*puts on spectacles*]—nothing to touch it—[*looks for toothbrush*]—in
my opinion—[*takes up toothbrush*]—always said so—[*examines handle of
brush*]—wish I had it—[*examines handle, reads*]—genuine . . . pure . . .
what?—[*lays down brush*]—blind next—[*takes off spectacles*]—ah well—
[*lays down spectacles*]—seen enough—[*feels in bodice for handkerchief*]—I
suppose—[*takes out folded handkerchief*]—by now—[*shakes out handkerchief*]—what are those wonderful lines—[*wipes one eye*]—woe woe is
me—[*wipes the other*]—to see what I see—[*looks for spectacles*]—ah yes—
[*takes up spectacles*]—wouldn't miss it—[*starts polishing spectacles,
breathing on lenses*]—or would I?—[*polishes*]—holy light—[*polishes*]—bob
up out of dark—[*polishes*]—blaze of hellish light. [*Stops polishing, raises
face to sky, pause, head back level, resumes polishing, stops polishing, cranes
back to her right and down.*] Hoo-oo! [*Pause. Tender smile as she turns back
front and resumes polishing. Smile off.*] Marvellous gift—[*stops polishing,
lays down spectacles*]—wish I had it—[*folds handkerchief*]—ah well—[*puts
handkerchief back in bodice*]—can't complain—[*looks for spectacles*]—no
no—[*takes up spectacles*]—mustn't complain—[*holds up spectacles, looks
through lens*]—so much to be thankful for—[*looks through other lens*]—no
pain—[*puts on spectacles*]—hardly any—[*looks for toothbrush*]—wonderful
thing that—[*takes up toothbrush*]—nothing like it—[*examines handle of
brush*]—slight headache sometimes—[*examines handle, reads*]—guaranteed . . . genuine . . . pure . . . what?—[*looks closer*]—genuine pure . . .
—[*takes handkerchief from bodice*]—ah yes—[*shakes out handkerchief*]—

occasional mild migraine—[*starts wiping handle of brush*]—it comes—
[*wipes*]—then goes—[*wiping mechanically*]—ah yes—[*wiping*]—many
mercies—[*wiping*]—great mercies—[*stops wiping, fixed lost gaze, bro-
kenly*]—prayers perhaps not for naught—[*Pause, do.*]—first thing—[*Pause,
do.*]—last thing—[*head down, resumes wiping, stops wiping, head up,
calmed, wipes eyes, folds handkerchief, puts it back in bodice, examines
handle of brush, reads*]—fully guaranteed . . . genuine pure . . . —[*looks
closer*]—genuine pure . . . [*Takes off spectacles, lays them and brush down,
gazes before her.*] Old things. [*Pause.*] Old eyes. [*Long pause.*] On, Winnie.
[*She casts about her, sees parasol, considers it at length, takes it up and
develops from sheath a handle of surprising length. Holding butt of parasol in
right hand she cranes back and down to her right to hand over* WILLIE.] Hoo-
oo! [*Pause.*] Willie! [*Pause.*] Wonderful gift. [*She strikes down at him with
beak of parasol.*] Wish I had it. [*She strikes again. The parasol slips from her
grasp and falls behind mound. It is immediately restored to her by* WILLIE's
invisible hand.] Thank you, dear. [*She transfers parasol to left hand, turns
back front and examines right palm.*] Damp. [*Returns parasol to right hand,
examines left palm.*] Ah well, no worse. [*Head up, cheerfully.*] No better, no
worse, no change. [*Pause. Do.*] No pain. [*Cranes back to look down at*
WILLIE, *holding parasol by butt as before.*] Don't go off on me again now dear
will you please, I may need you. [*Pause.*] No hurry, no hurry, just don't curl
up on me again. [*Turns back front, lays down parasol, examines palms
together, wipes them on grass.*] Perhaps a shade off colour just the same.
[*Turns to bag, rummages in it, brings out revolver, holds it up, kisses it
rapidly, puts it back, rummages, brings out almost empty bottle of red
medicine, turns back front, looks for spectacles, puts them on, reads label.*]
Loss of spirits . . . lack of keenness . . . want of appetite . . . infants . . .
children . . . adults . . . six level . . . tablespoonfuls daily—[*head up,
smile*]—the old style!—[*smile off, head down, reads*]—daily . . . before and
after . . . meals . . . instantaneous . . . [*looks closer*]improvement.
[*Takes off spectacles, lays them down, holds up bottle at arm's length to see
level, unscrews cap, swigs it off head well back, tosses cap and bottle away in
WILLIE's direction. Sound of breaking glass.*] Ah that's better! [*Turns to bag,
rummages in it, brings out lipstick, turns back front, examines lipstick.*]
Running out. [*Looks for spectacles.*] Ah well. [*Puts on spectacles, looks for
mirror.*] Musn't complain. [*Takes up mirror, starts doing lips.*] What is that
wonderful line? [*Lips.*] Oh fleeting joys—[*lips*]—oh something lasting
woe. [*Lips. She is interrupted by disturbance from* WILLIE. *He is sitting up.
She lowers lipstick and mirror and cranes back and down to look at him.
Pause. Top back of* WILLIE's *bald head, trickling blood, rises to view above
slope, comes to rest.* WINNIE *pushes up her spectacles. Pause. His hand
appears with handkerchief, spreads it on skull, disappears. Pause. The hand
appears with boater, club ribbon, settles it on head, rakish angle, disappears.*

Pause. WINNIE *cranes a little further back and down.*] Slip on your drawers, dear, before you get singed. [*Pause.*] No? [*Pause.*] Oh I see, you still have some of that stuff left. [*Pause.*] Work it well in, dear. [*Pause.*] Now the other. [*Pause. She turns back front, gazes before her. Happy expression.*] Oh this is going to be another happy day! [*Pause. Happy expression off. She pulls down spectacles and resumes lips.* WILLIE *opens newspaper, hands invisible. Tops of yellow sheets appear on either side of his head.* WINNIE *finishes lips, inspects them in mirror held a little further away.*] Ensign crimson. [WILLIE *turns page.* WINNIE *lays down lipstick and mirror, turns towards bag.*] Pale flag.

[WILLIE *turns page.* WINNIE *rummages in bag, brings out small ornate brimless hat with crumpled feather, turns back front, straightens hat, smooths feather, raises it towards head, arrests gesture as* WILLIE *reads.*]

WILLIE: His Grace and Most Reverend Father in God Dr Carolus Hunter dead in tub.

[*Pause.*]

WINNIE: [*gazing front, hat in hand, tone of fervent reminiscence*] Charlie Hunter! [*Pause.*] I close my eyes—[*she takes off spectacles and does so, hat in one hand, spectacles in other,* WILLIE *turns page*]—and am sitting on his knees again, in the back garden at Borough Green, under the horse-beech. [*Pause. She opens eyes, puts on spectacles, fiddles with hat.*] Oh the happy memories!

[*Pause. She raises hat towards head, arrests gesture as* WILLIE *reads.*]

WILLIE: Opening for smart youth.

[*Pause. She raises hat towards head, arrests gesture, takes off spectacles, gazes front, hat in one hand, spectacles in other.*]

WINNIE: My first ball! [*Long pause.*] My second ball! [*Long pause. Closes eyes.*] My first kiss! [*Pause.* WILLIE *turns page.* WINNIE *opens eyes.*] A Mr Johnson, or Johnston, or perhaps I should say Johnstone. Very bushy moustache, very tawny. [*Reverently.*] Almost ginger! [*Pause.*] Within a toolshed, though whose I cannot conceive. We had no toolshed and he most certainly had no toolshed. [*Closes eyes.*] I see the piles of pots. [*Pause.*] The tangles of bast. [*Pause.*] The shadows deepening among the rafters.

[*Pause. She opens eyes, puts on spectacles, raises hat towards head, arrests gesture as* WILLIE *reads.*]

WILLIE: Wanted bright boy.

[*Pause.* WINNIE *puts on hat hurriedly, looks for mirror.* WILLIE *turns page.* WINNIE *takes up mirror, inspects hat, lays down mirror, turns towards bag. Paper disappears.* WINNIE *rummages in bag, brings out magnifying-glass, turns back front, looks for toothbrush. Paper reappears, folded, and begins to fan* WILLIE'S *face, hand invisible.* WINNIE *takes up toothbrush and examines handle through glass.*]

WINNIE: Fully guaranteed . . . [WILLIE *stops fanning*] . . . genuine pure . . .

[*Pause.* WILLIE *resumes fanning.* WINNIE *looks closer, reads.*] Fully guaranteed . . . [WILLIE *stops fanning*] . . . genuine pure . . . [*Pause.* WILLIE *resumes fanning.* WINNIE *lays down glass and brush, takes handkerchief from bodice, takes off and polishes spectacles, puts on spectacles, looks for glass, takes up and polishes glass, lays down glass, looks for brush, takes up brush and wipes handle, lays down brush, puts handkerchief back in bodice, looks for glass, takes up glass, looks for brush, takes up brush and examines handle through glass.*] Fully guaranteed . . . [WILLIE *stops fanning*] . . . genuine pure . . . [*pause,* WILLIE *resumes fanning*] . . . hog's [WILLIE *stops fanning, pause*] . . . setae. [*Pause.* WINNIE *lays down glass and brush, paper disappears,* WINNIE *takes off spectacles, lays them down, gazes front.*] Hog's setae. [*Pause.*] That is what I find so wonderful, that not a day goes by—[*smile*]—to speak in the old style—[*smile off*]—hardly a day, without some addition to one's knowledge however trifling, the addition I mean, provided one takes the pains. [WILLIE'*s hand reappears with a postcard which he examines close to eyes.*] And if for some strange reason no further pains are possible, why then just close the eyes—[*she does so*]—and wait for the day to come—[*opens eyes*]—the happy day to come when flesh melts at so many degrees and the night of the moon has so many hundred hours. [*Pause.*] That is what I find so comforting when I lose heart and envy the brute beast. [*Turning towards* WILLIE.] I hope you are taking in—[*She sees postcard, bends lower.*] What is that you have there, Willie, may I see? [*She reaches down with hand and* WILLIE *hands her card. The hairy forearm appears above slope, raised in gesture of giving, the hand open to take back, and remains in this position till card is returned.* WINNIE *turns back front and examines card.*] Heavens what are they up to! [*She looks for spectacles, puts them on and examines card.*] No but this is just genuine pure filth! [*Examines card.*] Make any nice-minded person want to vomit! [*Impatience of* WILLIE'*s fingers. She looks for glass, takes it up and examines card through glass. Long pause.*] What does the creature in the background think he's doing? [*Looks closer.*] Oh no really! [*Impatience of fingers. Last long look. She lays down glass, takes edge of card between right forefinger and thumb, averts head, takes nose between left forefinger and thumb.*] Pah! [*Drops card.*] Take it away! [WILLIE'*s arm disappears. His hand reappears immediately, holding card.* WINNIE *takes off spectacles, lays them down, gazes before her. During what follows* WILLIE *continues to relish card, varying angles and distance from his eyes.*] Hog's setae. [*Puzzled expression.*] What exactly is a hog? [*Pause. Do.*] A sow of course I know, but a hog . . . [*Puzzled expression off.*] Oh well what does it matter, that is what I always say, it will come back, that is what I find so wonderful, all comes back. [*Pause.*] All? [*Pause.*] No, not all. [*Smile.*] No no. [*Smile off.*] Not quite. [*Pause.*] A part. [*Pause.*] Floats up, one fine day, out of the blue. [*Pause.*] That is what I find so wonderful. [*Pause. She turns towards bag. Hand and card disappear. She makes to rummage in bag,*

arrests gesture.] No. [*She turns back front. Smile.*] No no. [*Smile off.*]
Gently Winnie. [*She gazes front.* WILLIE's *hand reappears, takes off hat,
disappears with hat.*] What then? [*Hand reappears, takes handkerchief from
skull, disappears with handkerchief. Sharply, as to one not paying attention.*] Winnie! [WILLIE *bows head out of sight.*] What *is* the alternative?
[*Pause.*] What *is* the al—[WILLIE *blows nose loud and long, head and hands
invisible. She turns to look at him. Pause. Head reappears. Pause. Hand
reappears with handkerchief, spreads it on skull, disappears. Pause. Hand
reappears with boater, settles it on head, rakish angle, disappears. Pause.*]
Would I had let you sleep on. [*She turns back front. Intermittent plucking at
grass, head up and down, to animate following.*] Ah yes, if only I could bear
to be alone, I mean prattle away with not a soul to hear. [*Pause.*] Not that I
flatter myself you hear much, no Willie, God forbid. [*Pause.*] Days perhaps
when you hear nothing. [*Pause.*] But days too when you answer. [*Pause.*] So
that I may say at all times, even when you do not answer and perhaps hear
nothing, something of this is being heard, I am not merely talking to myself,
that is in the wilderness, a thing I could never bear to do—for any length of
time. [*Pause.*] That is what enables me to go on, go on talking that is.
[*Pause.*] Whereas if you were to die—[*smile*]—to speak in the old style—
[*smile off*]—or go away and leave me, then what would I do, what *could* I do,
all day long, I mean between the bell for waking and the bell for sleep?
[*Pause.*] Simply gaze before me with compressed lips. [*Long pause while she
does so. No more plucking.*] Not another word as long as I drew breath,
nothing to break the silence of this place. [*Pause.*] Save possibly, now and
then, every now and then, a sigh into my looking-glass. [*Pause.*] Or a brief
. . . gale of laughter, should I happen to see the old joke again. [*Pause.
Smile appears, broadens and seems about to culminate in laugh when
suddenly replaced by expression of anxiety.*] My hair! [*Pause.*] Did I brush
and comb my hair? [*Pause.*] I may have done. [*Pause.*] Normally I do.
[*Pause.*] There is so little one *can* do. [*Pause.*] One does it all. [*Pause.*] All
one can. [*Pause.*]Tis only human. [*Pause.*] Human nature. [*She begins to
inspect mound, looks up.*] Human weakness. [*She resumes inspection of
mound, looks up.*] Natural weakness. [*She resumes inspection of mound.*] I
see no comb. [*Inspects.*] Nor any hairbrush. [*Looks up. Puzzled expression.
She turns to bag, rummages in it.*] The comb is here. [*Back front. Puzzled
expression.*] Perhaps I put them back, after use. [*Pause. Do.*] But normally I
do not put things back, after use, no, I leave them lying about and put them
back all together, at the end of the day. [*Smile.*] To speak in the old style.
[*Pause.*] The sweet old style. [*Smile off.*] And yet . . . I seem . . . to
remember . . . [*Suddenly careless.*] Oh well, what does it matter, that is
what I always say, I shall simply brush and comb them later on, purely and
simply, I have the whole—[*Pause. Puzzled.*] Them? [*Pause.*] Or it?
[*Pause.*] *Brush and comb it?* [*Pause.*] Sounds improper somehow. [*Pause.*

Turning a little towards WILLIE.] What would you say, Willie? [*Pause.
Turning a little further.*] What would you say, Willie, speaking of your hair,
them or it? [*Pause.*] The hair on your head, I mean. [*Pause. Turning a little
further.*] The hair on your head, Willie, what would you say speaking of the
hair on your head, them or it?

      [*Long pause.*]

WILLIE: It.

WINNIE: [*turning back front, joyfully*] Oh you are going to talk to me today, this is
going to be a happy day! [*Pause. Joy off.*] Another happy day. [*Pause.*] Ah
well, where was I, my hair, yes, later on, I shall be thankful for it later on.
[*Pause.*] I have my—[*raises hand to hat*]—yes, on, my hat on—[*lowers
hands*]—I cannot take it off now. [*Pause.*] To think there are times one
cannot take off one's hat, not if one's life were at stake. Times one cannot put
it on, times one cannot take it off. [*Pause.*] How often I have said, Put on
your hat now, Winnie, there is nothing else for it, take off your hat now,
Winnie, like a good girl, it will do you good, and did not. [*Pause.*] Could
not. [*Pause. She raises hand, frees a strand of hair from under hat, draws it
towards eye, squints at it, lets it go, hand down.*] Golden you called it, that
day, when the last guest was gone—[*hand up in gesture of raising a glass*]—
to your golden . . . may it never . . . [*voice breaks*] . . . may it never . . .
[*Hand down. Head down. Pause. Low.*] That day. [*Pause. Do.*] What day?
[*Pause. Head up. Normal voice.*] What now? [*Pause.*] Words fail, there are
times when even they fail. [*Turning a little towards* WILLIE.] Is that not so,
Willie? [*Pause. Turning a little further.*] Is not that so, Willie, that even
words fail, at times? [*Pause. Back front.*] What is one to do then, until they
come again? Brush and comb the hair, if it has not been done, or if there is
some doubt, trim the nails if they are in need of trimming, these things tide
one over. [*Pause.*] That is what I mean. [*Pause.*] That is all I mean. [*Pause.*]
That is what I find so wonderful, that not a day goes by—[*smile*]—to speak
in the old style—[*smile off*]—without some blessing—[WILLIE *collapses
behind slope, his head disappears,* WINNIE *turns towards event*]—in disguise.
[*She cranes back and down.*] Go back into your hole now, Willie, you've
exposed yourself enough. [*Pause.*] Do as I say, Willie, don't lie sprawling
there in this hellish sun, go back into your hole. [*Pause.*] Go on now,
Willie. [WILLIE *invisible starts crawling left towards hole.*] That's the man.
[*She follows his progress with her eyes.*] Not head first, stupid, how are you
going to turn? [*Pause.*] That's it . . . right round . . . now . . . back in.
[*Pause.*] Oh I know it is not easy, dear, crawling backwards, but it is
rewarding in the end. [*Pause.*] You have left your vaseline behind. [*She
watches as he crawls back for vaseline.*] The lid! [*She watches as he crawls
back towards hole. Irritated.*] Not head first, I tell you! [*Pause.*] More to the
right. [*Pause.*] The *right*, I said. [*Pause. Irritated.*] Keep your tail down,
can't you! [*Pause.*] Now. [*Pause.*] There! [*All these directions loud. Now in*

her normal voice, still turned towards him.] Can you hear me? [*Pause.*] I beseech you, Willie, just yes or no, can you hear me, just yes or nothing. [*Pause.*]

WILLIE: Yes.

WINNIE: [*turning front, same voice*] And now?

WILLIE: [*irritated*] Yes.

WINNIE: [*less loud*] And now?

WILLIE: [*more irritated*] Yes.

WINNIE: [*still less loud*] And now? [*A little louder.*] And now?

WILLIE: [*violently*] Yes!

WINNIE: [*same voice*] Fear no more the heat o' the sun. [*Pause.*] Did you hear that?

WILLIE: [*irritated*] Yes.

WINNIE: [*same voice*] What? [*Pause.*] What?

WILLIE: [*more irritated*] Fear no more.
       [*Pause.*]

WINNIE: [*same voice*] No more what? [*Pause.*] Fear no more what?

WILLIE: [*violently*] Fear no more!

WINNIE: [*normal voice, gabbled*] Bless you Willie I do appreciate your goodness I know what an effort it costs you, now you may relax I shall not trouble you again unless I am obliged to, by that I mean unless I come to the end of my own resources which is most unlikely, just to know that in theory you can hear me even though in fact you don't is all I need, just to feel you there within earshot and conceivably on the qui vive is all I ask, not to say anything I would not wish you to hear or liable to cause you pain, not to be just babbling away on trust as it is were not knowing and something gnawing at me. [*Pause for breath.*] Doubt. [*Places index and second finger on heart area, moves them about, brings them to rest.*] Here. [*Moves them slightly.*] Abouts. [*Hand away.*] Oh no doubt the time will come when before I can utter a word I must make sure you heard the one that went before and then no doubt another come another time when I must learn to talk to myself a thing I could never bear to do such wilderness. [*Pause.*] Or gaze before me with compressed lips. [*She does so.*] All day long. [*Gaze and lips again.*] No. [*Smile.*] No. no. [*Smile off.*] There is of course the bag. [*Turns towards it.*] There will always be the bag. [*Back front.*] Yes, I suppose so. [*Pause.*] Even when you are gone, Willie. [*She turns a little towards him.*] You *are* going, Willie, aren't you? [*Pause. Louder.*] You *will* be going soon, Willie, won't you? [*Pause. Louder.*] Willie! [*Pause. She cranes back and down to look at him.*] So you have taken off your straw, that is wise. [*Pause.*] You do look snug, I must say, with your chin on your hands and the old blue eyes like saucers in the shadows. [*Pause.*] Can you see me from there I wonder, I still wonder. [*Pause.*] No? [*Back front.*] Oh I know it does not follow when two are gathered together—[*faltering*]—in this way—[*normal*]—that because one sees the other the other sees the one, life has taught me that . . . too.

[*Pause.*] Yes, life I suppose, there is no other word. [*She turns a little towards him.*] Could you see me, Willie, do you think, from where you are, if you were to raise your eyes in my direction? [*Turns a little further.*] Lift up your eyes to me, Willie, and tell me can you see me, do that for me, I'll lean back as far as I can. [*Does so. Pause.*] No? [*Pause.*] Well never mind. [*Turns back painfully front.*] The earth is very tight today, can it be I have put on flesh, I trust not. [*Pause. Absently, eyes lowered.*] The great heat possibly. [*Starts to pat and stroke ground.*] All things expanding, some more than others. [*Pause. Patting and stroking.*] Some less. [*Pause. Do.*] Oh I can well imagine what is passing through your mind, it is not enough to have to listen to the woman, now I must look at her as well. [*Pause. Do.*] Well it is very understandable. [*Pause. Do.*] One does not appear to be asking a great deal, indeed at times it would seem hardly possible—[*voice breaks, falls to a murmur*]—to ask less—of a fellow-creature—to put it mildly—whereas actually—when you think about it—look into your heart—see the other— what he needs—peace—to be left in peace—then perhaps the moon—all this time—asking for the moon. [*Pause. Stroking hand suddenly still. Lively.*] Oh I say, what have we here? [*Bending head to ground, incredulous.*] Looks like life of some kind! [*Looks for spectacles, puts them on, bends closer. Pause.*] An emmet! [*Recoils. Shrill.*] Willie, an emmet, a live emmet! [*Seizes magnifying-glass, bends to ground again, inspects through glass.*] Where's it gone? [*Inspects.*] Ah! [*Follows its progress through grass.*] Has like a little white ball in its arms. [*Follows progress. Hand still. Pause.*] It's gone in. [*Continues a moment to gaze at spot through glass, then slowly straightens up, lays down glass, takes off spectacles and gazes before her, spectacles in hand. Finally.*] Like a little white ball.

[*Long pause. Gesture to lay down spectacles.*]

WILLIE: Eggs.
WINNIE: [*arresting gesture*] What?
[*Pause.*]
WILLIE: Eggs. [*Pause. Gesture to lay down glasses.*] Formication.
WINNIE: [*arresting gesture*] What!
[*Pause.*]
WILLIE Formication.

[*Pause. She lays down spectacles, gazes before her. Finally.*]
WINNIE: [*murmur*] God.[*Pause. WILLIE laughs quietly. After a moment she joins in. They laugh quietly together. WILLIE stops. She laughs on a moment alone. WILLIE joins in. They laugh together. She stops. WILLIE laughs on a moment alone. He stops. Pause. Normal voice.*] Ah well what a joy in any case to hear you laugh again, Willie, I was convinced I never would, you never would. [*Pause.*] I suppose some people might think us a trifle irreverent, but I doubt it. [*Pause.*] How can one better magnify the Almighty than by sniggering with him at his little jokes, particularly the poorer ones? [*Pause.*] I think you would back me up there, Willie. [*Pause.*] Or were we perhaps diverted by

two quite different things? [*Pause.*] Oh well, what does it matter, that is what I always say, so long as one . . . you know . . . what is that wonderful line . . . laughing wild . . . something something laughing wild amid severest woe. [*Pause.*] And now? [*Long pause.*] Was I lovable once, Willie? [*Pause.*] Was I ever lovable? [*Pause.*] Do not misunderstand my question, I am not asking you if you loved me, we know all about that, I am asking you if you found me lovable—at one stage. [*Pause.*] No? [*Pause.*] You can't? [*Pause.*] Well I admit it is a teaser. And you have done more than your bit already, for the time being, just lie back now and relax, I shall not trouble you again unless I am compelled to, just to know you are there within hearing and conceivably on the semi-alert is . . . er . . . paradise enow. [*Pause.*] The day is now well advanced. [*Smile.*] To speak in the old style. [*Smile off.*] And yet it is perhaps a little soon for my song. [*Pause.*] To sing too soon is a great mistake, I find. [*Turning towards bag.*] There is of course the bag. [*Looking at bag.*] The bag. [*Back front.*] Could I enumerate its contents? [*Pause.*] No. [*Pause.*] Could I, if some kind person were to come along and ask, What all have you got in that big black bag, Winnie? give an exhaustive answer? [*Pause.*]No. [*Pause.*] The depths in particular, who knows what treasures. [*Pause.*] What comforts. [*Turns to look at bag.*] Yes, there is the bag. [*Back front.*] But something tells me, Do not overdo the bag, Winnie, make use of it of course, let it help you . . . along, when stuck, by all means, but cast your mind forward, something tells me, cast your mind forward, Winnie, to the time when words must fail—[*she closes eyes, pause, opens eyes*]—and do not overdo the bag. [*Pause. She turns to look at bag.*] Perhaps just one quick dip. [*She turns back front, closes eyes, throws out left arm, plunges hand in bag and brings out revolver. Disgusted.*] You again! [*She opens eyes, brings revolver front and contemplates it. She weighs it in her palm.*] You'd think the weight of this thing would bring it down among the . . . last rounds. But no. It doesn't. Ever uppermost, like Browning. [*Pause.*] Brownie . . . [*Turning a little towards* WILLIE] Remember Brownie, Willie? [*Pause.*] Remember how you used to keep on at me to take it away from you? Take it away, Winnie, take it away, before I put myself out of my misery. [*Back front. Derisive.*] Your misery! [*To revolver.*] Oh I suppose it's a comfort to know you're there, but I'm tired of you. [*Pause.*] I'll leave you out, that's what I'll do. [*She lays revolver on ground to her right.*] There, that's your home from this day out. [*Smile.*] The old style! [*Smile off.*] And now? [*Long pause.*] Is gravity what it was, Willie, I fancy not. [*Pause.*] Yes, the feeling more and more that if I were not held—[*gesture*]—in this way, I would simply float up into the blue. [*Pause.*] And that perhaps some day the earth will yield and let me go, the pull is so great, yes, crack all round me and let me out. [*Pause.*] Don't you ever have that feeling, Willie, of being sucked up? [*Pause.*] Don't you have to cling on sometimes, Willie? [*Pause. She turns a little towards him.*] Willie.

[*Pause.*]

WILLIE: _Sucked_ up?

WINNIE: Yes love, up into the blue, like gossamer. [_Pause._] No? [_Pause._] You don't? [_Pause._] Ah well, natural laws, natural laws, I suppose it's like everything else, it all depends on the creature you happen to be. All I can say for my part is that for me they are not what they were when I was young and . . . foolish and . . . [_faltering, head down_] . . . beautiful . . . possibly . . . lovely . . . in a way . . . to look at. [_Pause. Head up._] Forgive me, Willie, sorrow keeps breaking in. [_Normal voice._] Ah well what a joy in any case to know you are there, as usual, and perhaps awake, and perhaps taking all this in, some of all this, what a happy day for me . . . it will have been. [_Pause._] So far. [_Pause._] What a blessing nothing grows, imagine if all this stuff were to start growing. [_Pause._] Imagine. [_Pause._] Ah yes, great mercies. [_Long pause._] I can say no more. [_Pause._] For the moment. [_Pause. Turns to look at bag. Back front. Smile._] No no. [_Smile off. Looks at parasol._] I suppose I might—[_takes up parasol_]—yes, I suppose I might . . . hoist this thing now. [_Begins to unfurl it. Following punctuated by mechanical difficulties overcome._] One keeps putting off—putting up—for fear of putting up—too soon—and the day goes by—quite by—without one's having put up—at all. [_Parasol now fully open. Turned to her right she twirls it idly this way and that._] Ah yes, so little to say, so little to do, and the fear so great, certain days, of finding oneself . . . left, with hours still to run, before the bell for sleep, and nothing more to say, nothing more to do, that the days go by, certain days go by, quite by, the bell goes, and little or nothing said, little or nothing done. [_Raising parasol._] That is the danger. [_Turning front._] To be guarded against. [_She gazes front, holding up parasol with right hand. Maximum pause._] I used to perspire freely. [_Pause._] Now hardly at all. [_Pause._] The heat is much greater. [_Pause._] The perspiration much less. [_Pause._] That is what I find so wonderful. [_Pause._] The way man adapts himself. [_Pause._] To changing conditions. [_She transfers parasol to left hand. Long pause._] Holding up wearies the arm. [_Pause._] Not if one is going along. [_Pause._] Only if one is at rest. [_Pause._] That is a curious observation. [_Pause._] I hope you heard that, Willie, I should be grieved to think you had not heard that. [_She takes parasol in both hands. Long pause._] I am weary, holding it up, and I cannot put it down. [_Pause._] I am worse off with it up than with it down, and I cannot put it down. [_Pause._] Reason says, Put it down, Winnie, it is not helping you, put the thing down and get on with something else. [_Pause._] I cannot. [_Pause._] I cannot move. [_Pause._] No, something must happen, in the world, take place, some change, I cannot, if I am to move again. [_Pause._] Willie. [_Mildly._] Help. [_Pause._] No? [_Pause._] Bid me put this thing down, Willie, I would obey you instantly, as I have always done, honoured and obeyed. [_Pause._] Please, Willie. [_Mildly._] For pity's sake. [_Pause._] No? [_Pause._] You can't? [_Pause._] Well I don't blame you, no, it would ill become me, who cannot move, to blame my Willie because he cannot speak. [*Pause.*] Fortunately I am in tongue again. [*Pause.*] That is what I find so wonderful, my two lamps, when one goes out the other burns brighter. [*Pause.*] Oh yes, great mercies. [*Maximum pause. The parasol goes on fire. Smoke, flames if feasible. She sniffs, looks up, throws parasol to her right behind mound, cranes back to watch it burning. Pause.*] Ah earth you old extinguisher. [*Back front.*] I presume this has occurred before, though I cannot recall it. [*Pause.*] Can you, Willie? [*Turns a little towards him.*] Can you recall this having occurred before? [*Pause. Cranes back to look at him.*] Do you know what has occurred, Willie? [*Pause.*] Have you gone off on me again? [*Pause.*] I do not ask if you are alive to all that is going on, I merely ask if you have not gone off on me again. [*Pause.*] Your eyes appear to be closed, but that has no particular significance we know. [*Pause.*] Raise a finger, dear, will you please, if you are not quite senseless. [*Pause.*] Do that for me, Willie, please, just the little finger, if you are still conscious. [*Pause. Joyful.*] Oh all five, you are a darling today, now I may continue with an easy mind. [*Back front.*] Yes, what ever occurred that did not occur before and yet . . . I wonder, yes, I confess I wonder. [*Pause.*] With the sun blazing so much fiercer down, and hourly fiercer, is it not natural things should go on fire never known to do so, in this way I mean, spontaneous like. [*Pause.*] Shall I myself not melt perhaps in the end, or burn, oh I do not mean necessarily burst into flames, no, just little by little be charred to a black cinder, all this—[*ample gesture of arms*]—visible flesh. [*Pause.*] On the other hand, did I ever know a temperate time? [*Pause.*] No. [*Pause.*] I speak of temperate times and torrid times, they are empty words. [*Pause.*] I speak of when I was not yet caught—in this way — and had my legs and had the use of my legs, and could seek out a shady place, like you, when I was tired of the sun, or a sunny place when I was tired of the shade, like you, and they are all empty words. [*Pause.*] It is no hotter today than yesterday, it will be no hotter tomorrow than today, how could it, and so on back into the far past, forward into the far future. [*Pause.*] And should one day the earth cover my breasts, then I shall never have seen my breasts, no one ever seen my breasts. [*Pause.*] I hope you caught something of that, Willie, I should be sorry to think you had caught nothing of all that, it is not every day I rise to such heights. [*Pause.*] Yes, something seems to have occurred, something has seemed to occur, and nothing has occurred, nothing at all, you are quite right, Willie. [*Pause.*] The sunshade will be there again tomorrow, beside me on this mound, to help me through the day. [*Pause. She takes up mirror.*] I take up this little glass, I shiver it on a stone—[*does so*]—I throw it away—[*does so far behind her*]—it will be in the bag again tomorrow, without a scratch, to help me through the day. [*Pause.*] No, one can do nothing. [*Pause.*] That is what I find so wonderful, the way things . . . [*voice breaks, head down*] . . . things . . . so wonderful. [*Long pause, head down. Finally turns, still bowed, to bag, brings out unidentifia-*

ble odds and ends, stuffs them back, fumbles deeper, brings out finally musical-box, winds it up, turns it on, listens for a moment holding it in both hands, huddled over it, turns back front, straightens up and listens to tune, holding box to breast with both hands. It plays the Waltz Duet "I love you so" from The Merry Widow. *Gradually happy expression. She sways to the rhythm. Music stops. Pause. Brief burst of hoarse song without words— musical-box tune–from* WILLIE. *Increase of happy expression. She lays down box.*] Oh this will have been a happy day! [*She claps hands.*] Again, Willie, again! [*Claps.*] Encore, Willie, please! [*Pause. Happy expression off.*] No? You won't do that for me? [*Pause.*] Well it is very understandable, very understandable. One cannot sing just to please someone, however much one loves them, no, song must come from the heart, that is what I always say, pour out from the inmost, like a thrush. [*Pause.*] How often I have said, in evil hours, Sing now, Winnie, sing your song, there is nothing else for it, and did not. [*Pause.*] Could not. [*Pause.*] No, like the thrush, or the bird of dawning, with no thought of benefit, to oneself or anyone else. [*Pause.*] And now? [*Long pause. Low.*] Strange feeling. [*Pause. Do.*] Strange feeling that someone is looking at me. I am clear, then dim, then gone, then dim again, then clear again, and so on, back and forth, in and out of someone's eye. [*Pause. Do.*] Strange? [*Pause. Do.*] No, here all is strange. [*Pause. Normal voice.*] Something says, Stop talking now, Winnie, for a minute, don't squander all your words for the day, stop talking and do something for a change, will you? [*She raises hands and holds them open before her eyes. Apostrophic.*] Do something! [*She closes hands.*] What claws! [*She turns to bag, rummages in it, brings out finally a nailfile, turns back front and begins to file nails. Files for a time in silence, then the following punctuated by filing.*] There floats up—into my thoughts—a Mr Shower—a Mr and perhaps a Mrs Shower—no—they are holding hands—his fiancée then more likely—or just some—loved one. [*Looks closer at nails.*] Very brittle today. [*Resumes filing.*] Shower—Shower—does the name mean any-thing—to you, Willie—evoke any reality, I mean—for you, Willie,—don't answer if you don't—feel up to it—you have done more—than your bit— already—Shower—Shower. [*Inspects filed nails.*] Bit more like it. [*Raises head, gazes front.*] Keep yourself nice, Winnie, that's what I always say, come what may, keep yourself nice. [*Pause. Resumes filing.*] Yes—Show-er—Shower—[*stops filing, raises head, gazes front, pause*]—or Cooker, perhaps I should say Cooker. [*Turning a little towards* WILLIE.] Cooker, Willie, does Cooker strike a chord? [*Pause. Turns a little further. Louder.*] Cooker, Willie, does Cooker ring a bell, the name Cooker? [*Pause. She cranes back to look at him. Pause.*] Oh really! [*Pause.*] Have you no handkerchief, darling? [*Pause.*] Have you no delicacy? [*Pause.*] Oh, Willie, you're not eating it! Spit it out, dear, spit it out! [*Pause. Back front.*] Ah well, I suppose it's only natural. [*Break in voice.*] Human. [*Pause. Do.*] What is one to do? [*Head down. Do.*] All day long. [*Pause. Do.*] Day after day. [*Pause. Head up. Smile. Calm.*] The old style! [*Smile off. Resumes nails.*] No, done him. [*Passes on to next.*] Should have put on my glasses. [*Pause.*] Too late now. [*Finishes left hand, inspects it.*] Bit more human. [*Starts right hand. Following punctuated as before.*] Well anyway—this man Shower—or Cooker—no matter—and the woman—hand in hand—in the other hands bags—kind of big brown grips—standing there gaping at me—and at last this man Shower—or Cooker—ends in er anyway—stake my life on that—What's she doing? he says—What's the idea? he says—stuck up to her diddies in the bleeding ground—coarse fellow—What does it mean? he says—What's it meant to mean?—and so on—lot more stuff like that—usual drivel—Do you hear me? he says—I do, she says, God help me—What do you mean, he says, God help you? [*Stops filing, raises head, gazes front.*] And you, she says, what's the idea of you, she says, what are you meant to mean? It is because you're still on your two flat feet, with your old ditty full of tinned muck and changes of underwear, draggng me up and down this fornicating wilderness, coarse creature, fit mate—[*with sudden violence*]—let go of my hand and drop for God's sake, she says, drop! [*Pause. Resumes filing.*] Why doesn't he dig her out? he says—referring to you, my dear—What good is she to him like that?—What good is he to her like that?—and so one—usual tosh—Good! she says, have a heart for God's sake—Dig her out, he says, dig her out, no sense in her like that—Dig her out with what? she says—I'd dig her out with my bare hands, he says—must have been man and—wife. [*Files in silence.*] Next thing they're away—hand in hand—and the bags—dim—then gone—last human kind—to stray this way. [*Finishes right hand, inspects it, lays down file, gazes front.*] Strange thing, time like this, drift up into the mind. [*Pause.*] Strange? [*Pause.*] No, here all is strange. [*Pause.*] Thankful for it in any case. [*Voice breaks.*] Most thankful. [*Head down. Pause. Head up. Calm.*] Bow and raise the head, bow and raise, always that. [*Pause.*] And now? [*Long pause. Starts putting things back in bag, toothbrush last. This operation, interrupted by pauses as indicated, punctuates following.*] It is perhaps a little soon—to make ready—for the night—[*stops tidying, head up, smile*]—the old style!—[*smile off, resumes tidying*]—and yet I do—make ready for the night—feeling it at hand—the bell for sleep—saying to myself—Winnie—it will not be long now, Winnie—until the bell for sleep. [*Stops tidying, head up.*] Sometimes I am wrong. [*Smile.*] But not often. [*Smile off.*] Sometimes all is over, for the day, all done, all said, all ready for the night, and the day not over, far from over, the night not ready, far, far from ready. [*Smile.*] But not often. [*Smile off.*] Yes, the bell for sleep, when I feel it at hand, and so make ready for the night—[*gesture*]—in this way, sometimes I am wrong—[*smile*]—but not often. [*Smile off. Resumes tidying.*] I used to think—I say I used to think—that all these things—put back into the bag—if too soon—

put back too soon—could be taken out again—if necessary—if needed—and so on—indefinitely—back into the bag—back out of the bag—until the bell—went. [*Stops tidying, head up, smile.*] But no. [*Smile broader.*] No no. [*Smile off. Resumes tidying.*] I suppose this—might seem strange—this—what shall I say—this what I have said—yes—[*she takes up revolver*]—strange—[*she turns to put revolver in bag*]—were it not—[*about to put revolver in bag she arrests gesture and turns back front*]—were it not—[*she lays down revolver to her right, stops tidying, head up*]—that all seems strange. [*Pause.*] Most strange. [*Pause.*] Never any change. [*Pause.*] And more and more strange. [*Pause. She bends to mound again, takes up last object, i.e. toothbrush, and turns to put it in bag when her attention is drawn to disturbance from* WILLIE. *She cranes back and to her right to see. Pause.*] Weary of your hole, dear? [*Pause.*] Well I can understand that. [*Pause.*] Don't forget your straw. [*Pause.*] Not the crawler you were, poor darling. [*Pause.*] No, not the crawler I gave my heart to. [*Pause.*] The hands and knees, love, try the hands and knees. [*Pause.*] The knees! The knees! [*Pause.*] What a curse, mobility! [*She follows with eyes his progress towards her behind mound, i.e. towards place he occupied at beginning of act.*] Another foot, Willie, and you're home. [*Pause as he observes last foot.*] Ah! [*Turns back front laboriously, rubs neck.*] Crick in my neck admiring you. [*Rubs neck.*] But it's worth it, well worth it. [*Turns slightly towards him.*] Do you know what I dream sometimes? [*Pause.*] What I dream sometimes, Willie. [*Pause.*] That you'll come round and live this side where I could see you. [*Pause. Back front.*] I'd be a different woman. [*Pause.*] Unrecognizable. [*Turning slightly toward him.*] Or just now and then, come round this side just every now and then and let me feast on you. [*Back front.*] But you can't, I know. [*Head down.*] I know. [*Pause. Head up.*] Well anyway—[*looks at toothbrush in her hand*]—can't be long now—[*looks at brush*]—until the bell. [*Top back of* WILLIE'S *head appears above slope.* WINNIE *looks closer at brush.*] Fully guaranteed. . . . [*head up*] . . . what's this it was? [WILLIE'S *hand appears with handkerchief, spreads it on skull, disappears.*] Genuine pure . . . fully guaranteed . . . [WILLIE'S *hand appears with boater, settles it on head, rakish angle, disappears*] . . . genuine pure . . . ah! hog's setae. [*Pause.*] What is a hog exactly? [*Pause. Turns slightly towards* WILLIE.] What exactly is a hog, Willie, do you know, I can't remember. [*Pause. Turning a little further, pleading.*] What is a hog, Willie, please! [*Pause.*]

WILLIE: Castrated male swine. [*Happy expression appears on* WINNIE'S *face.*] Reared for slaughter.

[*Happy expression increases.* WILLIE *opens newspaper, hands invisible. Tops of yellow sheets appear on either side of his head.* WINNIE *gazes before her with happy expression.*]

WINNIE: Oh this is a happy day! This will have been another happy day! [*Pause.*] After all. [*Pause.*] So far.

[*Pause. Happy expression off.* WILLIE *turns page. Pause He turns another page. Pause.*]

WILLIE: Opening for smart youth.

[*Pause.* WINNIE *takes off hat, turns to put it in bag, arrests gesture, turns back front. Smile.*]

WINNIE: No. [*Smile broader.*] No no. [*Smile off. Puts on hat again, gazes front, pause.*] And now? [*Pause.*] Sing. [*Pause.*] Sing your song, Winnie. [*Pause.*] No? [*Pause.*] Then pray. [*Pause.*] Pray your prayer, Winnie.

[*Pause.* WILLIE *turns page.*]

WILLIE: Wanted bright boy.

[*Pause.* WINNIE *gazes before her.* WILLIE *turns page. Pause. Newspaper disappears. Long pause.*]

WINNIE: Pray your old prayer, Winnie.

[*Long pause.*]

CURTAIN

ACT II

Scene as before.

WINNIE *imbedded up to neck, hat on head, eyes closed. Her head, which she can no longer turn, nor bow, nor raise, faces front motionless throughout act. Movements of eyes as indicated.*

Bag and parasol as before. Revolver conspicuous to her right on mound.

Long pause.

Bell rings loudly. She opens eyes at once. Bell stops. She gazes front. Long pause.

WINNIE: Hail, holy light. [*Long pause. She closes her eyes. Bell rings loudly. She opens eyes at once. Bell stops. She gazes front. Long smile. Smile off. Long pause.*] Someone is looking at me still. [*Pause.*] Caring for me still. [*Pause.*] That is what I find so wonderful. [*Pause.*] Eyes on my eyes. [*Pause.*] What is that unforgettable line? [*Pause. Eyes right.*] Willie. [*Pause. Louder.*] Willie. [*Pause. Eyes front.*] May one still speak of time? [*Pause.*] Say it is a long time now, Willie, since I saw you. [*Pause.*]Since I heard you. [*Pause.*] May one? [*Pause.*] One does. [*Smile.*] The old style! [*Smile off.*] There is so little one can speak of. [*Pause.*] One speaks of it all. [*Pause.*] All one can. [*Pause.*] I used to think . . . [*Pause.*] . . . I say I used to think that I would learn to talk alone. [*Pause.*] By that I mean to myself, the wilderness. [*Smile.*] But no. [*Smile broader.*] No no. [*Smile off.*] Ergo you are there. [*Pause.*] Oh no doubt you are dead, like the others, no doubt you have died, or gone away and left me, like the others, it doesn't matter, you are there. [*Pause. Eyes left.*] The bag too is there, the same as ever, I can see it. [*Pause. Eyes right. Louder.*] The bag is there, Willie, as good as ever, the one you gave me that day . . . to go to market. [*Pause. Eyes front.*] That day. [*Pause.*] What day?

[*Pause.*] I used to pray. [*Pause.*] I say I used to pray. [*Pause.*] Yes, I must confess I did. [*Smile.*] Not now. [*Smile broader.*] No no. [*Smile off. Pause.*] Then . . . now . . . what difficulties here, for the mind. [*Pause.*] To have been always what I am— and so changed from what I was. [*Pause.*] I am the one, I say the one, then the other. [*Pause.*] Now the one, then the other. [*Pause.*] Now the one, then the other. [*Pause.*] There is so little one can say, one says it all. [*Pause.*] All one can. [*Pause.*] And no truth in it anywhere. [*Pause.*] My arms. [*Pause.*] My breasts. [*Pause.*] What arms? [*Pause.*] What breasts? [*Pause.*] Willie. [*Pause.*] What Willie? [*Sudden vehement affirmation.*] My Willie! [*Eyes right, calling.*] Willie! [*Pause. Louder.*] Willie! [*Pause. Eyes front.*] Ah well, not to know, not to know for sure, great mercy, all I ask. [*Pause.*] Ah yes . . . then . . . now . . . beechen green . . . this . . . Charlie . . . kisses . . . this . . . all that . . . deep trouble for the mind. [*Pause.*] But it does not trouble mine. [*Smile.*] Not now. [*Smile broader.*] No no. [*Smile off. Long pause. She closes eyes. Bell rings loudly. She opens eyes. Pause.*] Eyes float up that seem to close in peace . . . to see . . . in peace. [*Pause.*] Not mine. [*Smile*] Not now. [*Smile broader.*] No no. [*Smile off. Long pause.*] Willie. [*Pause.*] Do you think the earth has lost its atmosphere, Willie? [*Pause.*] Do you, Willie? [*Pause.*] You have no opinion? [*Pause.*] Well that is like you, you never had any opinion about anything. [*Pause.*] It's understandable. [*Pause.*] Most. [*Pause.*] The earth-ball. [*Pause.*] I sometimes wonder. [*Pause.*] Perhaps not quite all. [*Pause.*] There always remains something. [*Pause.*] Of everything. [*Pause.*] Some remains. [*Pause.*] If the mind were to go. [*Pause.*] It won't of course. [*Pause.*] Not quite. [*Pause.*] Not mine. [*Smile*] Not now. [*Smile broader.*] No no. [*Smile off. Long pause.*] It might be the eternal cold. [*Pause.*] Everlasting perishing cold. [*Pause.*] Just chance, I take it, happy chance. [*Pause.*] Oh yes, great mercies, great mercies. [*Pause.*] And now? [*Long pause.*] The face. [*Pause.*] The nose. [*She squints down.*] I can see it . . . [*squinting down*] . . . the tip . . . the nostrils . . . breath of life . . . that curve you so admired . . . [*pouts*] . . . a hint of lip . . . [*pouts again*] . . . if I pout them out . . . [*sticks out tongue*] . . . the tongue of course . . . you so admired . . . if I stick it out . . . [*sticks it out again*] . . . the tip . . . [*eyes up*] . . . suspicion of brow . . . eyebrow . . . imagination possibly . . . [*eyes left*] . . . cheek . . . no . . . [*eyes right*] . . . no . . . [*distends cheeks*] . . . even if I puff them out . . . [*eyes left, distends cheeks again*] . . . no . . . no damask. [*Eyes front.*] That is all. [*Pause.*] The bag of course . . . [*eyes left*] . . . a little blurred perhaps . . . but the bag. [*Eyes front. Offhand.*] The earth of course and sky. [*Eyes right.*] The sunshade you gave me . . . that day . . . [*Pause.*] . . . that day . . . the lake . . . the reeds. [*Eyes front. Pause.*] What day? [*Pause.*] What reeds? [*Long pause. Eyes close. Bell rings loudly. Eyes open. Pause. Eyes right.*] Brownie of course. [*Pause.*] You remember Brownie, Willie, I can see him. [*Pause.*] Brownie is there,

Willie, beside me. [*Pause. Eyes front.*] That is all. [*Pause.*] What would I do
without them? [*Pause.*] What would I do without them, when words fail?
[*Pause.*] Gaze before me, with compressed lips. [*Long pause while she does
so.*] I cannot. [*Pause.*] Ah yes, great mercies, great mercies. [*Long pause.
Low.*] Sometimes I hear sounds. [*Listening expression. Normal voice.*] But
not often. [*Pause.*] They are a boon, sounds are a boon, they help me . . .
through the day. [*Smile*] The old style! [*Smile off.*] Yes, those are happy
days, when there are sounds. [*Pause.*] When I hear sounds. [*Pause.*] I used
to think . . . [*Pause.*] . . . I say I used to think they were in my head.
[*Smile.*] But no. [*Smile broader.*] No no. [*Smile off.*] That was just logic.
[*Pause.*] Reason. [*Pause.*] I have not lost my reason. [*Pause.*] Not yet.
[*Pause.*] Not all. [*Pause.*] Some remains. [*Pause.*] Sounds. [*Pause.*] Like
little . . . sunderings, little falls . . . apart. [*Pause. Low.*] It's things, Willie.
[*Pause. Normal voice.*] In the bag, outside the bag. [*Pause.*] Ah yes, things
have their life, that is what I always say, *things* have a life. [*Pause.*] Take my
looking-glass, it doesn't need me. [*Pause.*] The bell. [*Pause.*] It hurts like a
knife. [*Pause.*] A gouge. [*Pause.*] One cannot ignore it. [*Pause.*] How often
. . . [*Pause.*] . . . I say how often I have said, Ignore it, Winnie, ignore the
bell, pay no heed, just sleep and wake, sleep and wake, as you please, open
and close the eyes, as you please, or in the way you find most helpful.
[*Pause.*] Open and close the eyes, Winnie, open and close, always that.
[*Pause.*] But no. [*Smile.*] Not now. [*Smile broader.*] No no. [*Smile off.
Pause.*] What now? [*Pause.*] What now, Willie? [*Long Pause.*] There is my
story of course, when all else fails. [*Pause.*] A life. [*Smile*] A long life. [*Smile
off.*] Beginning in the womb, where life used to begin, Mildred has memories, she will have memories, of the womb, before she dies, the mother's
womb. [*Pause.*] She is now four or five already and has recently been given a
big waxen dolly. [*Pause.*] Fully clothed, complete outfit. [*Pause.*] Shoes,
socks, undies, complete set, frilly frock, gloves. [*Pause.*] White mesh.
[*Pause.*] A little white straw hat with a chin elastic. [*Pause.*] Pearly necklet.
[*Pause.*] A little picture-book with legends in real print to go under her arm
when she takes her walk. [*Pause.*] China blue eyes that open and shut.
[*Pause. Narrative.*] The sun was not well up when Milly rose, descended the
steep . . . [*Pause.*] . . . slipped on her nightgown, descended all along the
steep wooden stairs, backwards on all fours, though she had been forbidden
to do so, entered the . . . [*Pause.*] . . . tiptoed down the silent passage,
entered the nursery and began to undress Dolly. [*Pause.*] Crept under the
table and began to undress Dolly. [*Pause.*] Scolding her . . . the while.
[*Pause.*] Suddenly a mouse — [*Long pause.*] Gently, Winnie. [*Long pause.
Calling.*] Willie! [*Pause. Louder.*] Willie! [*Pause. Mild reproach.*] I sometimes find your attitude a little strange, Willie, all this time, it is not like you
to be wantonly cruel. [*Pause.*] Strange? [*Pause.*] No. [*Smile.*] Not here.
[*Smile broader.*] Not now. [*Smile off.*] And yet . . . [*Suddenly anxious.*] I do

hope nothing is amiss. [*Eyes right, loud.*] Is all well, dear? [*Pause. Eyes front. To herself.*] God grant he did not go in head foremost! [*Eyes right, loud.*] You're not stuck, Willie? [*Pause. Do.*] You're not jammed, Willie? [*Eyes front, distressed.*] Perhaps he is crying out for help all this time and I do not hear him! [*Pause.*] I do of course hear cries. [*Pause.*] But they are in my head surely. [*Pause.*] Is it possible that . . . [*Pause. With finality.*] No no, my head was always full of cries. [*Pause.*] Faint confused cries. [*Pause.*] They come. [*Pause.*] Then go. [*Pause.*] As on a wind. [*Pause.*] That is what I find so wonderful. [*Pause.*] They cease. [*Pause.*] Ah yes, great mercies, great mercies. [*Pause.*] The day is now well advanced. [*Smile. Smile off.*] And yet it is perhaps a little soon for my song. [*Pause.*] To sing too soon is fatal, I always find. [*Pause.*] On the other hand it is possible to leave it too late. [*Pause.*] The bell goes for sleep and one has not sung. [*Pause.*] The whole day has flown—[*smile, smile off*]—flown by, quite by, and no song of any class, kind or description. [*Pause.*] There is a problem here. [*Pause.*] One cannot sing . . . just like that, no. [*Pause.*] It bubbles up, for some unknown reason, the time is ill chosen, one chokes it back. [*Pause.*] One says, Now is the time, it is now or never, and one cannot. [*Pause.*] Simply cannot sing. [*Pause.*] Not a note. [*Pause.*] Another thing, Willie, while we are on this subject. [*Pause.*] The sadness after song. [*Pause.*] Have you run across that, Willie? [*Pause.*] In the course of your experience. [*Pause.*] No? [*Pause.*] Sadness after intimate sexual intercouse one is familiar with of course. [*Pause.*] You would concur with Aristotle there, Willie, I fancy. [*Pause.*] Yes, that one knows and is prepared to face. [*Pause.*] But after song . . . [*Pause.*] It does not last of course. [*Pause.*] That is what I find so wonderful. [*Pause.*] It wears away. [*Pause.*] What are those exquisite lines? [*Pause.*] Go forget me why should something o'er that something shadow fling . . . go forget me . . . why should sorrow . . . brightly smile . . . go forget me . . . never hear me . . . sweetly smile . . . brightly sing . . . [*Pause. With a sigh.*] One loses one's classics. [*Pause.*] Oh not all. [*Pause.*] A part. [*Pause.*] A part remains. [*Pause.*] That is what I find so wonderful, a part remains, of one's classics, to help one through the day. [*Pause.*] Oh yes, many mercies, many mercies. [*Pause.*] And now? [*Pause.*] And now, Willie? [*Long pause.*] I call to the eye of the mind . . . Mr. Shower—or Cooker. [*She closes her eyes. Bell rings loudly. She opens her eyes. Pause.*] Hand in hand, in the other hands bags. [*Pause.*] Getting on . . . in life. [*Pause.*] No longer young, not yet old. [*Pause.*] Standing there gaping at me. [*Pause.*] Can't have been a bad bosom, he says, in its day. [*Pause.*] Seen worse shoulders, he says, in my time. [*Pause.*] Does she feel her legs? he says. [*Pause.*] Is there any life in her legs? he says. [*Pause.*] Has she anything on underneath? he says. [*Pause.*] Ask her, he says, I'm shy. [*Pause.*] Ask her what? she says. [*Pause.*] Is there any life in her legs. [*Pause.*] Has she anything on underneath. [*Pause.*] Ask her yourself, she says. [*Pause. With*

sudden violence.] Let go of me for Christ sake and drop! [*Pause. Do.*] Drop
dead! [*Smile.*] But no. [*Smile broader.*] No no. [*Smile off.*] I watch them
recede. [*Pause.*] Hand in hand—and the bags. [*Pause.*] Dim. [*Pause.*]
Then gone. [*Pause.*] Last human kind—to stray this way. [*Pause.*] Up to
date. [*Pause.*] And now? [*Pause. Low.*] Help. [*Pause. Do.*] Help, Willie.
[*Pause. Do.*] No? [*Long pause. Narrative.*] Suddenly a mouse . . . [*Pause.*]
Suddenly a mouse ran up her little thigh and Mildred, dropping Dolly in her
fright, began to scream—[WINNIE *gives a sudden piercing scream*]—and
screamed and screamed—[WINNIE *screams twice*]—screamed and screamed
and screamed and screamed till all came running, in their night attire, papa,
mamma, Bibby and . . . old Annie, to see what was the matter . . . [*Pause.*]
. . . what on earth could possibly be the matter. [*Pause.*] Too late. [*Pause.*]
Too late. [*Long pause. Just audible.*] Willie. [*Pause. Normal voice.*] Ah
well, not long now, Winnie, can't be long now, until the bell for sleep.
[*Pause.*] Then you may close your eyes, then you must close your eyes—and
keep them closed. [*Pause.*] Why say that again? [*Pause.*] I used to think . . .
[*Pause.*] . . . I say I used to think there was no difference between one
fraction of a second and the next. [*Pause.*] I used to say . . . [*pause*] . . . I say
I used to say, Winnie, you are changeless, there is never any difference
between one fraction of a second and the next. [*Pause.*] Why bring that up
again? [*Pause.*] There is so little one can bring up, one brings up all.
[*Pause.*] All one can. [*Pause.*] My neck is hurting me! [*Pause.*] Ah that's
better. [*With mild irritation.*] Everything within reason. [*Long pause.*] I can
do no more. [*Pause.*] Say no more. [*Pause.*] But I must say more. [*Pause.*]
Problem here. [*Pause.*] No, something must move, in the world, I can't any
more. [*Pause.*] A zephyr. [*Pause.*] A breath. [*Pause.*] What are those
immortal lines? [*Pause.*] It might be the eternal dark. [*Pause.*] Black night
without end. [*Pause.*] Just chance, I take it, happy chance. [*Pause.*] Oh yes,
abounding mercies. [*Long pause.*] And now? [*Pause.*] And now, Willie?
[*Long pause.*] That day. [*Pause.*] The pink fizz. [*Pause.*] The flute glasses.
[*Pause.*] The last guest gone. [*Pause.*] The last bumper with the bodies
nearly touching. [*Pause.*] The look. [*Long pause.*] I hear cries. [*Pause.*]
Sing. [*Pause.*] Sing your old song, Winnie.

> [*Long pause. Suddenly alert expression. Eyes switch right.* WILLIE's *head
> appears to her right round corner of mound. He is on all fours, dressed to
> kill—top hat, morning coat, striped trousers, etc., white gloves in hand.
> Very long bushy white Battle of Britain moustache. He halts, gazes
> front, smooths moustache. He emerges completely from behind mound,
> turns to his left, halts, looks up at* WINNIE. *He advances on all fours
> towards centre, halts, turns head front, gazes front, strokes moustache,
> straightens tie, adjusts hat, advances a little further, halts, takes off hat
> and looks up at* WINNIE. *He is now not far from centre and within her field
> of vision. Unable to sustain effort of looking up he sinks head to ground.*]

WINNIE: [*mondaine*] Well this is an unexpected pleasure! [*Pause.*] Reminds me of the day you came whining for my hand. [*Pause.*] I worship you, Winnie, be mine. [*He looks up.*] Life a mockery without Win. [*She goes off into a giggle.*] What a get up, you do look a sight! [*Giggles.*] Where are the flowers? [*Pause.*] That smile today. [WILLIE *sinks head.*] What's that on your neck, an anthrax? [*Pause.*] Want to watch that, Willie, before it gets a hold on you. [*Pause.*] Where were you all this time? [*Pause.*] What were you doing all this time? [*Pause.*] Changing? [*Pause.*] Did you not hear me screaming for you? [*Pause.*] Did you get stuck in your hole? [*Pause. He looks up.*] That's right, Willie, look at me. [*Pause.*] Feast your old eyes, Willie. [*Pause.*] Does anything remain? [*Pause.*] Any remains? [*Pause.*] No? [*Pause.*] I haven't been able to look after it, you know. [*He sinks his head.*] You are still recognizable, in a way. [*Pause.*] Are you thinking of coming to live this side now . . . for a bit maybe? [*Pause.*] No? [*Pause.*] Just a brief call? [*Pause.*] Have you gone deaf, Willie? [*Pause.*] Dumb? [*Pause.*] Oh I know you were never one to talk, I worship you Winnie be mine and then nothing from that day forth only titbits from Reynolds' News. [*Eyes front. Pause.*] Ah well, what matter, that's what I always say, it will have been a happy day, after all, another happy day. [*Pause.*] Not long now, Winnie. [*Pause.*] I hear cries. [*Pause.*] Do you ever hear cries, Willie? [*Pause.*] No? [*Eyes back on* WILLIE.] [*Pause.*] Look at me again, Willie. [*Pause.*] Once more, Willie. [*He looks up. Happily.*] Ah! [*Pause. Shocked.*] What ails you, Willie, I never saw such an expression! [*Pause.*] Put on your hat, dear, it's the sun, don't stand on ceremony, I won't mind. [*He drops hat and gloves and starts to crawl up mound towards her. Gleeful.*] Oh I say, this is terrific! [*He halts, clinging to mound with one hand, reaching up with the other.*] Come on, dear, put a bit of jizz into it, I'll cheer you on. [*Pause.*] Is it me you're after, Willie . . . or is it something else? [*Pause.*] Do you want to touch my face . . . again? [*Pause.*] Is it a kiss you're after, Willie . . . or is it something else? [*Pause.*] There was a time when I could have given you a hand. [*Pause.*] And then a time before that again when I did give you a hand. [*Pause.*] You were always in dire need of a hand, Willie. [*He slithers back to foot of mound and lies with face to ground.*] Brrum! [*Pause. He rises to hands and knees, raises his face towards her.*] Have another go, Willie, I'll cheer you on. [*Pause.*] Don't look at me like that! [*Pause. Vehement.*] Don't look at me like that! [*Pause. Low.*] Have you gone off your head, Willie? [*Pause. Do.*] Out of your poor old wits, Willie?
      [*Pause.*]
WILLIE: [*just audible*] Win.
      [*Pause.* WINNIE's *eyes front. Happy expression appears, grows.*]
WINNIE: Win! [*Pause.*] Oh this *is* a happy day, this will have been another happy day! [*Pause.*] After all. [*Pause.*] So far.
      [*Pause. She hums tentatively beginning of song, then sings softly, musical-box tune.*]

Though I say not
What I may not
Let you hear,
Yet the swaying
Dance is saying,
Love me dear!
Every touch of fingers
Tells me what I know,
Says for you,
It's true, it's true,
You love me so!

> [*Pause. Happy expression off. She closes her eyes. Bell rings loudly. She opens her eyes. She smiles, gazing front. She turns her eyes, smiling, to* WILLIE, *still on his hands and knees looking up at her. Smile off. They look at each other. Long pause.*]

CURTAIN

Lorraine Hansberry

Raisin in the Sun

CHARACTERS

RUTH YOUNGER
TRAVIS YOUNGER
WALTER LEE YOUNGER, "BROTHER"
BENEATHA YOUNGER
LENA YOUNGER, "MAMA"
JOSEPH ASAGAI
GEORGE MURCHISON
KARL LINDNER
BOBO
MOVING MEN

The action of the play is set in Chicago's Southside, sometime between World War II and the present.

ACT ONE

SCENE 1. Friday morning.
SCENE 2. The following morning.

ACT TWO

SCENE 1. Later, the same day.
SCENE 2. Friday night, a few weeks later.
SCENE 3. Moving day, one week later.

ACT THREE

An hour later.

ACT I

SCENE I—— *The* YOUNGER *living room would be a comfortable and well-ordered room if it were not for a number of indestructible contradictions to this state of being. Its furnishings are typical and undistinguished and their primary feature now is that they have clearly had to accommodate the living of too many people for too many years—and they are tired. Still, we can see that at some time, a time probably no longer remembered by the family (except perhaps for* MAMA *)*

536

the furnishings of this room were actually selected with care and love and even hope—and brought to this apartment and arranged with taste and pride.

That was a long time ago. Now the once loved pattern of the couch upholstery has to fight to show itself from under acres of crocheted doilies and couch covers which have themselves finally come to be more important than the upholstery. And here a table or a chair has been moved to disguise the worn places in the carpet; but the carpet has fought back by showing its weariness, with depressing uniformity, elsewhere on its surface.

Weariness has, in fact, won in this room. Everything has been polished, washed, sat on, used, scrubbed too often. All pretenses but living itself have long since vanished from the very atmosphere of this room.

Moreover, a section of this room, for it is not really a room unto itself, though the landlord's lease would make it seem so, slopes backward to provide a small kitchen area, where the family prepares the meals that are eaten in the living room proper, which must also serve as dining room. The single window that has been provided for these "two" rooms is located in this kitchen area. The sole natural light the family may enjoy in the course of a day is only that which fights it way through this little window.

At left, a door leads to a bedroom which is shared by MAMA *and her daughter,* BENEATHA. *At right, opposite, is a second room (which in the beginning of the life of this apartment was probably a breakfast room) which serves as a bedroom for* WALTER *and his wife,* RUTH.

[*At Rise: It is morning dark in the living room.* TRAVIS *is asleep on the make-down bed at center. An alarm clock sounds from within the bedroom at right, and presently* RUTH *enters from that room and closes the door behind her. She crosses sleepily toward the window. As she passes her sleeping son she reaches down and shakes him a little. At the window she raises the shade and a dusky Southside morning light comes in feebly. She fills a pot with water and puts it on to boil. She calls to the boy, between yawns, in a slightly muffled voice.*

RUTH *is about thirty. We can see that she was a pretty girl, even exceptionally so, but now it is apparent that life has been little that she expected, and disappointment has already begun to hang in her face. In a few years, before thirty-five even, she will be known among her people as a "settled woman."*

She crosses to her son and gives him a good, final, rousing shake.]

RUTH: Come on now, boy, it's seven thirty! [*Her son sits up at last, in a stupor of sleepiness.*] I say hurry up, Travis! You ain't the only person in the world got to use a bathroom![*The child, a sturdy, handsome little boy of ten or eleven, drags himself out of the bed and almost blindly takes his towels and "today's clothes" from drawers and a closet and goes out to the bathroom, which is in an outside hall and which is shared by another family or families on the same floor.* RUTH *crosses to the bedroom door at right and opens it and calls in to her husband*] Walter Lee! . . . It's after seven thirty! Lemme see you do some waking up in there now! [*she waits*] You better get up from there, man! It's after seven thirty I tell you. [*She waits again.*] All right, you just go ahead and lay there and next thing you know Travis be finished and Mr.

Johnson'll be in there and you'll be fussing and cussing round here like a mad man! And be late too! [*she waits, at the end of patience.*] Walter Lee—it's time for you to get up!

[*She waits another second and then starts to go into the bedroom, but is apparently satisfied that her husband has begun to get up. She stops, pulls the door to, and returns to the kitchen area. She wipes her face with a moist cloth and runs her fingers through her sleep-disheveled hair in a vain effort and ties an apron around her housecoat. The bedroom door at right opens and her husband stands in the doorway in his pajamas, which are rumpled and mismated. He is a lean, intense young man in his middle thirties, inclined to quick nervous movements and erratic speech habits—and always in his voice there is a quality of indictment.*]

WALTER: Is he out yet?

RUTH: What you mean *out*? He ain't hardly got in there good yet.

WALTER: [*wandering in, still more oriented to sleep than to a new day*] Well, what was you doing all that yelling for if I can't even get in there yet? [*stopping and thinking*] Check coming today?

RUTH: They *said* Saturday and this is just Friday and I hopes to God you ain't going to get up here first thing this morning and start talking to me 'bout no money—'cause I 'bout don't want to hear it.

WALTER: Something the matter with you this morning?

RUTH: No—I'm just sleepy as the devil. What kind of eggs you want?

WALTER: Not scrambled. [RUTH *starts to scramble eggs.*] Paper come? [RUTH *points impatiently to the rolled up* Tribune *on the table, and he gets it and spreads it out and vaguely reads the front page.*] Set off another bomb yesterday.

RUTH: [*maximum indifference*] Did they?

WALTER: [*looking up*] What's the matter with you?

RUTH: Ain't nothing the matter with me. And don't keep asking me that this morning.

WALTER: Ain't nobody bothering you. [*reading the news of the day absently again*] Say Colonel McCormick is sick.

RUTH: [*affecting tea-party interest*] Is he now? Poor thing.

WALTER: [*sighing and looking at his watch*] Oh, me. [*He waits.*] Now what is that boy doing in that bathroom all this time? He just going to have to start getting up earlier. I can't be being late to work on account of him fooling around in here.

RUTH: [*turning on him*] Oh, no he ain't going to be getting up no earlier no such thing! It ain't his fault that he can't get to bed no earlier nights 'cause he got a bunch of crazy good-for-nothing clowns sitting up running their mouths in what is supposed to be his bedroom after ten o'clock at night . . .

WALTER: That's what you mad about, ain't it? The things I want to talk about with my friends just couldn't be important in your mind, could they?

[*He rises and finds a cigarette in her handbag on the table and crosses to the little window and looks out, smoking and deeply enjoying this first one.*]

RUTH: [*almost matter of factly, a complaint too automatic to deserve emphasis*] Why you always got to smoke before you eat in the morning?

WALTER: [*at the window*] Just look at 'em down there . . . Running and racing to work . . . [*he turns and faces his wife and watches her a moment at the stove, and then, suddenly*] You look young this morning, baby.

RUTH: [*indifferently*] Yeah?

WALTER: Just for a second—stirring them eggs. It's gone now—just for a second it was—you looked real young again. [*then, drily*] It's gone now—you look like yourself again.

RUTH: Man, if you don't shut up and leave me alone.

WALTER: [*looking out to the street again*] First thing a man ought to learn in life is not to make love to no colored woman first thing in the morning. You all some evil people at eight o'clock in the morning.

> [TRAVIS *appears in the hall doorway, almost fully dressed and quite wide awake now, his towels and pajanas across his shoulders. He opens the door and signals for his father to make the bathroom in a hurry.*]

TRAVIS: [*watching the bathroom*] Daddy, come on!

> [WALTER *gets his bathroom utensils and flies out to the bathroom.*]

RUTH: Sit down and have your breakfast, Travis.

TRAVIS: Mama, this is Friday. [*gleefully*] Check coming tomorrow, huh?

RUTH: You get your mind off money and eat your breakfast.

TRAVIS: [*eating*] This is the morning we supposed to bring the fifty cents to school.

RUTH: Well, I ain't got no fifty cents this morning.

TRAVIS: Teacher say we have to.

RUTH: I don't care what teacher say. I ain't got it. Eat your breakfast, Travis.

TRAVIS: I *am* eating.

RUTH: Hush up now and just eat!

> [*The boy gives her an exasperated look for her lack of understanding, and eats grudgingly.*]

TRAVIS: You think Grandmama would have it?

RUTH: No! And I want you to stop asking your grandmother for money, you hear me?

TRAVIS: [*outraged*] Gaaaleee! I don't ask her, she just gimme it sometimes!

RUTH: Travis Willard Younger—I got too much on me this morning to be—

TRAVIS: Maybe Daddy—

RUTH: *Travis!*

> [*The boy hushes abruptly. They are both quiet and tense for several seconds.*]

TRAVIS: [*presently*] Could I maybe go carry some groceries in front of the supermarket for a little while after school then?

RUTH: Just hush, I said. [*Travis jabs his spoon into his cereal bowl viciously, and rests his head in anger upon his fists.*] If you through eating, you can get over there and make up your bed.

> [*The boy obeys stiffly and crosses the room, almost mechanically, to the bed and more or less carefully folds the covering. He carries the bedding into his mother's room and returns with his books and cap.*]

TRAVIS: [*sulking and standing apart from her unnaturally*] I'm gone.

RUTH: [*looking up from the stove to inspect him automatically*] Come here. [*He crosses to her and she studies his head.*] If you don't take this comb and fix this here head, you better! [TRAVIS *puts down his books with a great sigh of oppression, and crosses to the mirror. His mother mutters under her breath about his "slubbornness."*] 'Bout to march out of here with that head looking just like chickens slept in it! I just don't know where you get your stubborn ways . . . And get your jacket, too. Looks chilly out this morning.

TRAVIS: [*with conspicuously brushed hair and jacket*] I'm gone.

RUTH: Get carfare and milk money—[*waving one finger*]—and not a single penny for no caps, you hear me?

TRAVIS: [*with sullen politeness*] Yes'm.

[*He turns in outrage to leave. His mother watches after him as in his frustration he approaches the door almost comically. When she speaks to him, her voice has become a very gentle tease.*]

RUTH: [*mocking; as she thinks he would say it*] Oh, Mama makes me so mad sometimes, I don't know what to do! [*She waits and continues to his back as he stands stock-still in front of the door.*] I wouldn't kiss that woman goodbye for nothing in this world this morning! [*The boy finally turns around and rolls his eyes at her, knowing the mood has changed and he is vindicated; he does not, however, move toward her yet.*] Not for nothing in this world! [*She finally laughs aloud at him and holds out her arms to him and we see that it is a way between them, very old and practiced. He crosses to her and allows her to embrace him warmly but keeps his face fixed with masculine rigidity. She holds him back from her presently and looks at him and runs her fingers over the features of his face. With utter gentleness—*] Now—whose little old angry man are you?

TRAVIS: [*The masculinity and gruffness start to fade at last.*] Aw gaalee—Mama . . .

RUTH: [*mimicking*] Aw—gaaaaalleeeee, Mama! [*She pushes him, with rough playfulness and finality, toward the door.*] Get on out of here or you going to be late.

TRAVIS: [*in the face of love, new aggressiveness*] Mama, could I *please* go carry groceries?

RUTH: Honey, it's starting to get so cold evenings.

WALTER: [*coming in from the bathroom and drawing a make-believe gun from a make-believe holster and shooting at his son.*] What is it he wants to do?

RUTH: Go carry groceries after school at the supermarket.

WALTER: Well, let him go . . .

TRAVIS: [*quickly, to the ally*] I *have* to—she won't gimme the fifty cents . . .

WALTER: [*to his wife only*] Why not?

RUTH: [*simply, and with flavor*] 'Cause we don't have it.

WALTER: [*to RUTH only*] What you tell the boy things like that for? [*Reaching down into his pants with a rather important gesture*] Here, son—

[*He hands the boy the coin, but his eyes are directed to his wife's.* TRAVIS *takes the money happily.*]

TRAVIS: Thanks, Daddy.

[*He starts out.* RUTH *watches both of them with murder in her eyes.*

WALTER *stands and stares back at her with defiance, and suddenly reaches into his pocket again on an afterthought.*]

WALTER: [*without even looking at his son, still staring hard at his wife*] In fact, here's another fifty cents . . . Buy yourself some fruit today—or take a taxicab to school or something!

TRAVIS: Whoopee—

[*He leaps up and clasps his father around the middle with his legs, and they face each other in mutual appreciation; slowly* WALTER LEE *peeks around the boy to catch the violent rays from his wife's eyes and draws his head back as if shot.*]

WALTER: You better get down now—and get to school, man.

TRAVIS: [*at the door*] O.K. Good-bye. [*He exits.*]

WALTER: [*after him, pointing with pride*] That's *my* boy. [*She looks at him in disgust and turns back to her work.*] You know what I was thinking 'bout in the bathroom this morning?

RUTH: No.

WALTER: How come you always try to be so pleasant!

RUTH: What is there to be pleasant 'bout!

WALTER: You want to know what I was thinking 'bout in the bathroom or not!

RUTH: I know what you thinking 'bout.

WALTER: [*ignoring her*] 'Bout what me and Willy Harris was talking about last night.

RUTH: [*immediately—a refrain*] Willy Harris is a good-for-nothing loud mouth.

WALTER: Anybody who talks to me has got to be a good-for-nothing loud mouth, ain't he? And what you know about who is just a good-for-nothing loud mouth? Charlie Atkins was just a "good-for-nothing loud mouth" too, wasn't he! When he wanted me to go in the dry-cleaning business with him. And now—he's grossing a hundred thousand a year. A hundred thousand dollars a year! You still call *him* a loud mouth!

RUTH: [*bitterly*] Oh, Walter Lee . . .

[*She folds her head on her arms over the table.*]

WALTER: [*rising and coming to her and standing over her*] You tired, ain't you? Tired of everything. Me, the boy, the way we live—this beat-up hole— everything. Ain't you? [*She doesn't look up, doesn't answer.*] So tired— moaning and groaning all the time, but you wouldn't do nothing to help, would you? You couldn't be on my side that long for nothing, could you?

RUTH: Walter, please leave me alone.

WALTER: A man needs for a woman to back him up . . .

RUTH: Walter—

WALTER: Mama would listen to you. You know she listen to you more than she do me and Bennie. She think more of you. All you have to do is just sit down with her when you drinking your coffee one morning and talking 'bout things like you do and—[*He sits down beside her and demonstrates graphically what he thinks her methods and tone should be.*]—you just sip your coffee, see, and say easy like that you been thinking 'bout that deal Walter Lee is so interested in, 'bout the store and all, and sip some more coffee, like what you saying ain't really that important to you—And the next thing you know, she be listening good and asking you questions and when I come home—I can tell her the details. This ain't no fly-by-night proposition, baby. I mean we figured it out, me and Willy and Bobo.

RUTH: [*with a frown*] Bobo?

WALTER: Yeah. You see, this little liquor store we got in mind cost seventy-five thousand and we figured the initial investment on the place be 'bout thirty thousand, see. That be ten thousand each. Course, there's a couple of hundred you got to pay so's you don't spend your life just waiting for them clowns to let your license get approved—

RUTH: You mean graft?

WALTER: [*frowning impatiently*] Don't call it that. See there, that just goes to show you what women understand about the world. Baby, don't *nothing* happen for you in this world 'less you pay *somebody* off!

RUTH: Walter, leave me alone! [*She raises her head and stares at him vigorously—then says, more quietly.*] Eat your eggs, they gonna be cold.

WALTER: [*straightening up from her and looking off*] That's it. There you are. Man say to his woman: I got me a dream. His woman say: Eat your eggs. [*sadly, but gaining in power*] Man say: I got to take hold of this here world, baby! And a woman will say: Eat your eggs and go to work. [*passionately now*] Man say: I got to change my life. I'm choking to death, baby! And his woman say—[*in utter anguish as he brings his fists down on his thighs*]— Your eggs is getting cold!

RUTH: [*softly*] Walter, that ain't none of our money.

WALTER: [*not listening at all or even looking at her*] This morning, I was lookin' in the mirror and thinking about it . . I'm thirty-five years old; I been married eleven years and I got a boy who sleeps in the living room—[*very, very quietly*]—and all I got to give him is stories about how rich white people live . . .

RUTH: Eat your eggs, Walter.

WALTER: *Damn my eggs . . . damn all the eggs that ever was!*

RUTH: Then go to work.

WALTER: [*looking up at her*] See—I'm trying to talk to you 'bout myself— [*shaking his head with the repetition*] —and all you can say is eat them eggs and go to work.

RUTH: [*wearily*] Honey, you never say nothing new. I listen to you every day, every night and every morning, and you never say nothing new. [*shrugging*] So you would rather *be* Mr. Arnold than be his chauffeur. So—I would *rather* be living in Buckingham Palace.

WALTER: That is just what is wrong with the colored woman in this world . . . Don't understand about building their men up and making 'em feel like they somebody. Like they can do something.

RUTH: [*drily, but to hurt*] There *are* colored men who do things.

WALTER: No thanks to the colored woman.

RUTH: Well, being a colored woman, I guess I can't help myself none.

[*She rises and gets the ironing board and sets it up and attacks a huge pile of rough-dried clothes, sprinkling them in preparation for the ironing and then rolling them into tight fat balls.*]

WALTER: [*mumbling*] We one group of men tied to a race of women with small minds.

[*His sister* BENEATHA *enters. She is about twenty, as slim and intense as her brother. She is not as pretty as her sister-in-law, but her lean, almost intellectual face has a handsomeness of its own. She wears a bright-red flannel nightie, and her thick hair stands wildly about her head. Her speech is a mixture of many things; it is different from the rest of the family's insofar as education has permeated her sense of English—and perhaps the Midwest rather than the South has finally—at last—won out in her inflection; but not altogether, because over all of it is a soft slurring and transformed use of vowels which is the decided influence of the Southside. She passes through the room without looking at either* RUTH *or* WALTER *and goes to the outside door and looks, a little blindly, out to the bathroom. She sees that it has been lost to the Johnsons. She closes the door with a sleepy vengeance and crosses to the table and sits down a little defeated.*]

WALTER: You should get up earlier.

BENEATHA: [*Her face in her hands. She is still fighting the urge to go back to bed.*] Really—would you suggest dawn? Where's the paper?

WALTER: [*pushing the paper across the table to her as he studies her almost clinically, as though he has never seen her before*] You a horrible-looking chick at this hour.

BENEATHA: [*drily*] Good morning, everybody.

WALTER: [*senselessly*] How is school coming?

BENEATHA: [*in the same spirit*] Lovely. Lovely. And you know, biology is the greatest. [*looking up at him*] I dissected something that looked like you yesterday.

WALTER: I just wondered if you've made up your mind and everything.

BENEATHA: [*gaining in sharpness and impatience*] And what did I answer yesterday morning—and the day before that?

RUTH: [*from the ironing board, like someone disinterested and old*] Don't be so nasty, Bennie.

BENEATHA: [*still to her brother*] And the day before that and the day before that!

WALTER: [*defensively*] I'm interested in you. Something wrong with that? Ain't many girls who decide—

WALTER: *and* BENEATHA: [*in unison*] —"to be a doctor."

[*silence*]

WALTER: Have we figured out yet just exactly how much medical school is going to cost?

RUTH: Walter Lee, why don't you leave that girl alone and get out of here to work?

BENEATHA: [*exits to the bathroom and bangs on the door*] Come on out of there, please!

[*She comes back into the room.*]

WALTER: [*looking at his sister intently*] You know the check is coming tomorrow.

BENEATHA: [*turning on him with a sharpness all her own*]. That money belongs to Mama, Walter, and it's for her to decide how she wants to use it. I don't care if she wants to buy a house or a rocket ship or just nail it up somewhere and look at it. It's hers. Not ours—*hers*.

WALTER: [*bitterly*] Now ain't that fine! You just got your mother's interest at heart, ain't you, girl? You such a nice girl—but if Mama got that money she can always take a few thousand and help you through school too—can't she?

BENEATHA: I have never asked anyone around here to do anything for me!

WALTER: No! And the line between asking and just accepting when the times comes is big and wide—ain't it!

BENEATHA: [*with fury*] What do you want from me, Brother—that I quit school or just drop dead, which!

WALTER: I don't want nothing but for you to stop acting holy 'round here. Me and Ruth done made some sacrifices for you—why can't you do something for the family?

RUTH: Walter, don't be dragging me in it.

WALTER: You are in it—Don't you get up and go work in somebody's kitchen for the last three years to help put clothes on her back?

RUTH: Oh, Walter—that's not fair . . .

WALTER: It ain't that nobody expects you to get on your knees and say thank you, Brother; thank you, Ruth; thank you, Mama—and thank you, Travis, for wearing the same pair of shoes for two semesters—

BENEATHA: [*dropping to her knees*] Well—I *do*—all right?—thank everybody . . . and forgive me for ever wanting to be anything at all . . . forgive me, forgive me!

RUTH: Please stop it! Your mama'll hear you.

WALTER: Who the hell told you you had to be a doctor? If you so crazy 'bout messing 'round with sick people—then go be a nurse like other women—or just get married and be quiet . . .

BENEATHA: Well—you finelly got it said . . . It took you three years but you finally got it said. Walter, give up; leave me alone—it's Mama's money.

WALTER: *He was my father, too!*

BENEATHA: So what? He was mine, too—and Travis' grandfather—but the insurance money belongs to Mama. Picking on me is not going to make her give it to you to invest in any liquor stores—[*underbreath, dropping into a chair*]—and I for one say, God bless Mama for that!

WALTER: [*to* RUTH] See—did you hear? Did you hear!

RUTH: Honey, please go to work.

WALTER: Nobody in this house is ever going to understand me.

BENEATHA: Because you're a nut.

WALTER: Who's a nut?

BENEATHA: You—you are a nut. Thee is mad, boy.

WALTER: [*looking at his wife and his sister from the door, very sadly*] The world's most backward race of people, and that's a fact.

BENEATHA: [*turning slowly in her chair*] And then there are all those prophets who would lead us out of the wilderness—[WALTER *slams out of the house*]—into the swamps!

RUTH: Bennie, why you always gotta be pickin' on your brother? Can't you be a little sweeter sometimes? [*Door opens.* WALTER *walks in.*]

WALTER: [*to* RUTH] I need some money for carfare.

RUTH: [*looks at him, then warms; teasing, but tenderly*] Fifty cents? [*She goes to her bag and gets money.*] Here, take a taxi.

[WALTER *exits.* MAMA *enters. She is a woman in her early sixties, full-bodied and strong. She is one of those women of a certain grace and beauty who wear it so unobstrusively that it takes a while to notice. Her dark-brown face is surrounded by the total whiteness of her hair, and, being a woman who has adjusted to many things in life and overcome many more, her face is full of strength. She has, we can see, wit and faith of a kind that keep her eyes lit and full of interest and expectancy. She is, in a word, a beautiful woman. Her bearing is perhaps most like the noble bearing of the women of the Hereros of Southwest Africa— rather as if she imagines that as she walks she still bears a basket or a vessel upon her head. Her speech, on the other hand, is as careless as her carriage is precise—she is inclined to slur everything—but her voice is perhaps not so much quiet as simply soft.*]

MAMA: Who that 'round here slamming doors at this hour?
[*She crosses through the room, goes to the window, opens it, and brings in a feeble little plant growing doggedly in a small pot on the window sill. She feels the dirt and puts it back out.*]

RUTH: That was Walter Lee. He and Bennie was at it again.

MAMA: My children and they tempers. Lord, if this little old plant don't get more sun than it's been getting it ain't never going to see spring again. [*She turns from the window.*] What's the matter with you this morning, Ruth? You looks right peaked. You aiming to iron all them things? Leave some for me. I'll get to 'em this afternoon. Bennie honey, it's too drafty for you to be sitting 'round half dressed. Where's your robe?

BENEATHA: In the cleaners.

MAMA: Well, go get mine and put it on.

BENEATHA: I'm not cold, Mama, honest.

MAMA: I know—but you so thin . . .

BENEATHA: [*irritably*] Mama, I'm not cold.

MAMA: [*seeing the make-down bed as* TRAVIS *has left it*] Lord have mercy, look at that poor bed. Bless his heart—he tries, don't he?
[*She moves to the bed* TRAVIS *has sloppily made up.*]

RUTH: No—he don't half try at all 'cause he knows you going to come along behind him and fix everything. That's just how come he don't know how to do nothing right now—you done spoiled that boy so.

MAMA: Well—he's a little boy. Ain't supposed to know 'bout housekeeping. My baby, that's what he is. What you fix for his breakfast this morning?

RUTH: [*angrily*] I feed my son, Lena!

MAMA: I ain't meddling—[*underbreath; busy-bodish*] I just noticed all last week he had cold cereal, and when it starts getting this chilly in the fall a child ought to have some hot grits or something when he goes out in the cold—

RUTH: [*furious*] I gave him hot oats—is that all right!

MAMA: I ain't meddling. [*pause*] Put a lot of nice butter on it? [RUTH *shoots her an angry look and does not reply.*] He likes lots of butter.

RUTH: [*exasperated*] Lena—

MAMA: [*to* BENEATHA . MAMA *is inclined to wander conversationally sometimes.*] What was you and your brother fussing 'bout this morning?

BENEATHA: It's not important, Mama.
> [*She gets up and goes to look out at the bathroom, which is apparently free, and she picks up her towels and rushes out.*]

MAMA: What was they fighting about?

RUTH: Now you know as well as I do.

MAMA: [*shaking her head*] Brother still worrying hisself sick about that money?

RUTH: You know he is.

MAMA: You had breakfast?

RUTH: Some coffee.

MAMA: Girl, you better start eating and looking after yourself better. You almost thin as Travis.

RUTH: Lena—

MAMA: Un-hunh?

RUTH: What are you going to do with it?

MAMA: Now don't you start, child. It's too early in the morning to be talking about money. It ain't Christian.

RUTH: It's just that he got his heart set on that store—

MAMA: You mean that liquor store that Willy Harris want him to invest in?

RUTH: Yes—

MAMA: We ain't no business people, Ruth. We just plain working folks.

RUTH: Ain't nobody business people till they go into business. Walter Lee say colored people ain't never going to start getting ahead till they start gambling on some different kinds of things in the world—investments and things.

MAMA: What done got into you, girl? Walter Lee done finally sold you on investing.

RUTH: No. Mama, something is happening between Walter and me. I don't know what it is—but he needs something—something I can't give him any more. He needs this chance, Lena.

MAMA: [*frowning deeply*] But liquor, honey—

RUTH: Well—like Walter say—I spec people going to always be drinking themselves some liquor.

MAMA: Well—whether they drinks it or not ain't none of my business. But whether I go into business selling it to 'em *is*, and I don't want that on my ledger this late in life. [*stopping suddenly and studying her daughter-in-law*] Ruth Younger, what's the matter with you today? You look like you could fall over right there.

RUTH: I'm tired.

MAMA: Then you better stay home from work today.

RUTH: I can't stay home. She'd be calling up the agency and screaming at them, "My girl didn't come in today—send me somebody! My girl didn't come in!" Oh, she just have a fit . . .

MAMA: Well, let her have it. I'll just call her up and say you got the flu—

RUTH: [*laughing*] Why the flu?

MAMA: 'Cause it sounds respectable to 'em. Something white people get, too. They know 'bout the flu. Otherwise they think you been cut up or something when you tell 'em you sick.

RUTH: I got to go in. We need the money.

MAMA: Somebody would of thought my children done all but starved to death the way they talk about money here late. Child, we got a great big old check coming tomorrow.

RUTH: [*sincerely, but also self-righteously*] Now that's your money. It ain't got nothing to do with me. We all feel like that—Walter and Bennie and me—even Travis.

MAMA: [*thoughtfully, and suddenly very far away*] Ten thousand dollars—

RUTH: Sure is wonderful.

MAMA: Ten thousand dollars.

RUTH: You know what you should do, Miss Lena? You should take yourself a trip somewhere. To Europe or South America or someplace—

MAMA: [*throwing up her hands at the thought*] Oh, child!

RUTH: I'm serious. Just pack up and leave! Go on away and enjoy yourself some. Forget about the family and have yourself a ball for once in your life—

MAMA: [*drily*] You sound like I'm just about ready to die. Who'd go with me? What I look like wandering 'round Europe by myself?

RUTH: Shoot—these here rich white women do it all the time. They don't think nothing of packing up they suitcases and piling on one of them big steamships and—swoosh!—they gone, child.

MAMA: Something always told me I wasn't no rich white woman.

RUTH: Well—what are you going to do with it then?

MAMA: I ain't rightly decided. [*Thinking. She speaks now with emphasis.*] Some of it got to be put away for Beneatha and her schoolin'—and ain't nothing going to touch that part of it. Nothing. [*She waits several seconds, trying to make up her mind about something, and looks at* RUTH *a little tentatively before going on.*] Been thinking that we maybe could meet the notes on a little old two-story somewhere, with a yard where Travis could play in the summertime, if we use part of the insurance for a downpayment and everybody kind of pitch in. I could maybe take on a little day work again, few days a week—

RUTH: [*studying her mother-in-law furtively and concentrating on her ironing, anxious to encourage without seeming to.*] Well, Lord knows, we've put enough rent into this here rat trap to pay for four houses by now . . .

MAMA: [*looking up at the words "rat trap" and then looking around and leaning back and sighing—in a suddenly reflective mood—*] "Rat trap"—yes, that's all it is. [*smiling*] I remember just as well the day me and Big Walter moved in here. Hadn't been married but two weeks and wasn't planning on living here no more than a year. [*She shakes her head at the dissolved dream.*] We was going to set away, little by little, don't you know, and buy a little place out in Morgan Park. We had even picked out the house. [*chuckling a little*] Looks right dumpy today. But Lord, child, you should know all the dreams I had 'bout buying that house and fixing it up and making me a little garden in the back—[*She waits and stops smiling.*] And didn't none of it happen. [*dropping her hands in a futile gesture*]

RUTH: [*keeps her head down, ironing*] Yes, life can be a barrel of disappointments, sometimes.

MAMA: Honey, Big Walter would come in here some nights back then and slump down on that couch there and just look at the rug, and look at me and look at the rug and then back at me—and I'd know he was down then . . . really down. [*after a second very long and thoughtful pause; she is seeing back to times that only she can see*] And then, Lord, when I lost that baby—little Claude—I almost thought I was going to lose Big Walter too. Oh, that man grieved hisself! He was one man to love his children.

RUTH: Ain't nothin' can tear at you like losin' your baby.

MAMA: I guess that's how come that man finally worked hisself to death like he done. Like he was fighting his own war with this here world that took his baby from him.

RUTH: He was sure a fine man, all right. I always liked Mr. Younger.

MAMA: Crazy 'bout his children! God knows there was plenty wrong with Walter Younger—hard-headed, mean, kind of wild with women—plenty wrong with him. But he sure loved his children. Always wanted them to have something—be something. That's where Brother gets all these notions, I reckon. Big Walter used to say, he'd get right wet in the eyes sometimes, lean his head back with the water standing in his eyes and say, "Seem like God didn't see fit to give the black man nothing but dreams—but He did give us children to make them dreams seem worth while." [*She smiles.*] He could talk like that, don't you know.

RUTH: Yes, he sure could. He was a good man, Mr. Younger.

MAMA: Yes, a fine man—just couldn't never catch up with his dreams, that's all.

[BENEATHA *comes in, brushing her hair and looking up to the ceiling, where the sound of a vacuum cleaner has started up.*]

BENEATHA: What could be so dirty on that woman's rugs that she has to vacuum them every single day?

RUTH: I wish certain young women 'round here who I could name would take inspiration about certain rugs in a certain apartment I could also mention.

BENEATHA: [*shrugging*] How much cleaning can a house need, for Christ's sakes.

MAMA: [*not liking the Lord's name used thus*] Bennie!

RUTH: Just listen to her—just listen!

BENEATHA: Oh, God!

MAMA: If you use the Lord's name just one more time—

BENEATHA: [*a bit of a whine*] Oh, Mama—

RUTH: Fresh—just fresh as salt, this girl!

BENEATHA: [*drily*] Well—if the salt loses its savor—

MAMA: Now that will do. I just ain't going to have you 'round here reciting the scriptures in vain—you hear me?

BENEATHA: How did I manage to get on everybody's wrong side by just walking into a room?

RUTH: If you weren't so fresh—

BENEATHA: Ruth, I'm twenty years old.

MAMA: What time you be home from school today?

BENEATHA: Kind of late. [*with enthusiasm*] Madeline is going to start my guitar lessons today.

[MAMA *and* RUTH *look up with the same expression.*]

MAMA: Your *what* kind of lessons?

BENEATHA: Guitar.

RUTH: Oh, Father!

MAMA: How come you done taken it in your mind to learn to play the guitar?

BENEATHA: I just want to, that's all.

MAMA: [*smiling*] Lord, child, don't you know what to do with yourself? How long it going to be before you get tired of this now—like you got tired of that little play-acting group you joined last year? [*looking at* RUTH] And what was it the year before that?

RUTH: The horseback-riding club for which she bought that fifty-five-dollar riding habit that's been hanging in the closet ever since!

MAMA: [*to* BENEATHA] Why you got to flit so from one thing to another, baby?

BENEATHA: [*sharply*] I just want to learn to play the guitar. Is there anything wrong with that?

MAMA: Ain't nobody trying to stop you. I just wonders sometimes why you has to flit so from one thing to another all the time. You ain't never done nothing with all that camera equipment you brought home—

BENEATHA: I don't flit! I—I experiment with different forms of expression—

RUTH: Like riding a horse?

BENEATHA: —People have to express themselves one way or another.

MAMA: What is it you want to express?

BENEATHA: [*angrily*] Me! [MAMA *and* RUTH *look at each other and burst into raucous laughter.*] Don't worry—I don't expect you to understand.

MAMA: [*to change the subject*] Who you going out with tomorrow night?

BENEATHA: [*with displeasure*] George Murchison again.

MAMA: [*pleased*] Oh—you getting a little sweet on him?

RUTH: You ask me, this child ain't sweet on nobody but herself—[*underbreath*] Express herself!

[*They laugh.*]

BENEATHA: Oh—I like George all right, Mama. I mean I like him enough to go out with him and stuff, but—

RUTH: [*for devilment*] What does *and stuff* mean?

BENEATHA: Mind your own business.

MAMA: Stop picking at her now, Ruth. [*a thoughtful pause, and then a suspicious sudden look at her daughter as she turns in her chair for emphasis*] What *does* it mean?

BENEATHA: [*wearily*] Oh, I just mean I couldn't ever really be serious about George. He's—he's so shallow.

RUTH: Shallow—what do you mean he's shallow? He's *Rich!*

MAMA: Hush, Ruth.

BENEATHA: I know he's rich. He knows he's rich, too.

RUTH: Well—what other qualities a man got to have to satisfy you, little girl?

BENEATHA: You wouldn't even begin to understand. Anybody who married Walter could not possibly understand.

MAMA: [*outraged*] What kind of way is that to talk about your brother?

BENEATHA: Brother is a flip—let's face it.

MAMA: [*to* RUTH , *helplessly*] What's a flip?

RUTH: [*glad to add kindling*] She's saying he's crazy.

BENEATHA: Not crazy. Brother isn't really crazy yet—he—he's an elaborate neurotic.

MAMA: Hush your mouth!

BENEATHA: As for George. Well. George looks good—he's got a beautiful car and he takes me to nice places and, as my sister-in-law says, he is probably the richest boy I will ever get to know and I even like him sometimes—but if the Youngers are sitting around waiting to see if their little Bennie is going to tie up the family with the Murchisons, they are wasting their time.

RUTH: You mean you wouldn't marry George Murchison if he asked you someday? That pretty, rich thing? Honey, I knew you was odd—

BENEATHA: No I would not marry him if all I felt for him was what I feel now. Besides, George's family wouldn't really like it.

MAMA: Why not?

BENEATHA: Oh, Mama—The Murchisons are honest-to-God-real-*live*-rich colored people, and the only people in the world who are more snobbish than rich white people are rich colored people. I thought everybody knew that. I've met Mrs. Murchison. She's a scene!

MAMA: You must not dislike people 'cause they well off, honey.

BENEATHA: Why not? It makes just as much sense as disliking people 'cause they are poor, and lots of people do that.

RUTH: [*a wisdom-of-the-ages manner. To* MAMA] Well, she'll get over some of this—

BENEATHA: Get over it? What are you talking about, Ruth? Listen, I'm going to be a doctor. I'm not worried about who I'm going to marry yet—if I ever get married.

MAMA *and* RUTH: *If!*

MAMA: Now, Bennie—

BENEATHA: Oh, I probably will . . . but first I'm going to be a doctor, and George, for one, still thinks that's pretty funny. I couldn't be bothered with that. I am going to be a doctor and everybody around here better understand that!

MAMA: [*kindly*] 'Course you going to be a doctor, honey, God willing.

BENEATHA: [*drily*] God hasn't got a thing to do with it.

MAMA: Beneatha—that just wasn't necessary

BENEATHA: Well—neither is God. I get sick of hearing about God.

MAMA: Beneatha!

BENEATHA: I mean it! I'm just tired of hearing about God all the time. What has He got to do with anything? Does he pay tuition?

MAMA: You 'bout to get your fresh little jaw slapped!

RUTH: That's just what she needs, all right!

BENEATHA: Why? Why can't I say what I want to around here, like everybody else?

MAMA: It don't sound nice for a young girl to say things like that—you wasn't brought up that way. Me and your father went to trouble to get you and Brother to church every Sunday.

BENEATHA: Mama, you don't understand. It's all a matter of ideas, and God is just one idea I don't accept. It's not important. I am not going out and be immoral or commit crimes because I don't believe in God. I don't even think about it. It's just that I get tired of Him getting credit for all the things

the human race achieves through its own stubborn effort. There simply is
no blasted God—there is only man and it is he who makes miracles!

> [MAMA *absorbs this speech, studies her daughter and rises slowly and
> crosses to* BENEATHA *and slaps her powerfully across the face. After,
> there is only silence and the daughter drops her eyes from her mother's
> face, and* MAMA *is very tall before her.*]

MAMA: Now—you say after me, in my mother's house there is still God. [*There is
a long pause and* BENEATHA *stares at the floor wordlessly.* MAMA *repeats the
phrase with precision and cool emotion.*] In my mother's house there is still
God.

BENEATHA: In my mother's house there is still God.

> [*a long pause*]

MAMA: [*walking away from* BENEATHA, *too disturbed for triumphant posture.
Stopping and turning back to her daughter*] There are some ideas we ain't
going to have in this house. Not long as I am at the head of this family.

BENEATHA: Yes, ma'am.

> [MAMA *walks out of the room.*]

RUTH: [*almost gently, with profound understanding*] You think you a woman,
Bennie—but you still a little girl. What you did was childish—so you got
treated like a child.

BENEATHA: I see. [*quietly*] I also see that everybody thinks it's all right for Mama
to be a tyrant. But all the tyranny in the world will never put a God in the
heavens!

> [*She picks up her books and goes out.*]

RUTH: [*goes to* MAMA'S *door*] She said she was sorry.

MAMA: [*coming out, going to her plant*] They frightens me, Ruth. My children.

RUTH: You got good children, Lena. They just a little off sometimes—but they're
good.

MAMA: No—there's something come down between me and them that don't let
us understand each other and I don't know what it is. One done almost lost
his mind thinking 'bout money all the time and the other done commence
to talk about things I can't seem to understand in no form or fashion. What
is it that's changing, Ruth?

RUTH: [*soothingly, older than her years*] Now . . . you taking it all too seriously.
You just got strong-willed children and it takes a strong woman like you to
keep 'em in hand.

MAMA: [*looking at her plant and sprinkling a little water on it*] They spirited all
right, my children. Got to admit they got spirit—Bennie and Walter. Like
this little old plant that ain't never had enough sunshine or nothing—and
look at it . . .

> [*She has her back to* RUTH, *who has had to stop ironing and lean
> against something and put the back of her hand to her forehead.*]

RUTH: [*trying to keep* MAMA *from noticing*] You . . . sure . . . loves that little old
thing, don't you? . . .

MAMA: Well, I always wanted me a garden like I used to see sometimes at the
back of the houses down home. This plant is close as I ever got to having
one. [*She looks out of the window as she replaces the plant.*] Lord, ain't

nothing as dreary as the view from this window on a dreary day, is there? Why ain't you singing this morning, Ruth? Sing that "No Ways Tired." That song always lifts me up so—[*She turns at last to see that* RUTH *has slipped quietly into a chair, in a state of semiconsciousness.*] Ruth! Ruth honey—what's the matter with you . . . Ruth!

SCENE II—— *It is the following morning; a Saturday morning, and house cleaning is in progress at the* YOUNGERS. *Furniture has been shoved hither and yon and* MAMA *is giving the kitchen-area walls a washing down.* BENEATHA, *in dungarees, with a handkerchief tied around her face, is spraying insecticide into the cracks in the walls. As they work, the radio is on and a Southside disk-jockey program is inappropriately filling the house with a rather exotic saxophone blues.* TRAVIS, *the sole idle one, is leaning on his arms, looking out of the window.*

TRAVIS: Grandmama, that stuff Bennie is using smells awful. Can I go downstairs, please?

MAMA: Did you get all them chores done already? I ain't seen you doing much.

TRAVIS: Yes'm—finished early. Where did Mama go this morning?

MAMA: [*looking at* BENEATHA] She had to go on a little errand.

TRAVIS: Where?

MAMA: To tend to her business.

TRAVIS: Can I go outside then?

MAMA: Oh, I guess so. You better stay right in front of the house, though . . . and keep a good lookout for the postman.

TRAVIS: Yes'm. [*He starts out and decides to give his* AUNT BENEATHA *a good swat on the legs as he passes her.*] Leave them poor little old cockroaches alone, they ain't bothering you none.

[*He runs as she swings the spray gun at him both viciously and playfully.* WALTER *enters from the bedroom and goes to the phone.*]

MAMA: Look out there, girl, before you be spilling some of that stuff on that child!

TRAVIS: [*teasing*] That's right—look out now!

[*He exits.*]

BENEATHA: [*drily*] I can't imagine that it would hurt him—it has never hurt the roaches.

MAMA: Well, little boys' hides ain't as tough as Southside roaches.

WALTER: [*into phone*] Hello—Let me talk to Willy Harris.

MAMA: You better get over there behind the bureau. I seen one marching out of there like Napoleon yesterday.

WALTER: Hello, Willy? It ain't come yet. It'll be here in a few minutes. Did the lawyer give you the papers?

BENEATHA: There's really only one way to get rid of them, Mama—

MAMA: How?

BENEATHA: Set fire to this building.

WALTER: Good. Good. I'll be right over.

BENEATHA: Where did Ruth go, Walter?

WALTER: I don't know.
    [*He exits abruptly.*]
BENEATHA: Mama, where did Ruth go?
MAMA: [*looking at her with meaning*] To the doctor, I think.
BENEATHA: The doctor? What's the matter? [*they exchange glances.*] You don't
    think—
MAMA: [*with her sense of drama*] Now I ain't saying what I think. But I ain't never
    been wrong 'bout a woman neither.
    [*The phone rings.*]
BENEATHA: [*at the phone*] Hay-lo . . . [*pause, and a moment of recognition*]
    Well—when did you get back! . . . And how was it? . . . Of course I've
    missed you—in my way . . . This morning? No . . . house cleaning and all
    that and Mama hates it if I let people come over when the house is like this
    . . . You *have?* Well, that's different . . . What is it—Oh, what the hell,
    come on over . . . Right, see you then.
    [*She hangs up.*]
MAMA: [*who has listened vigorously, as is her habit*] Who is that you inviting over
    here with this house looking like this? You ain't got the pride you was born
    with!
BENEATHA: Asagai doesn't care how houses look, Mama—he's an intellectual.
MAMA: *Who?*
BENEATHA: Asagai—Joseph Asagai. He's an African boy I met on campus. He's
    been studying in Canada all summer.
MAMA: What's his name?
BENEATHA: Asagai, Joseph. Ah-sah-guy . . . He's from Nigeria.
MAMA: Oh, that's the little country that was founded by slaves way back . . .
BENEATHA: No, Mama—that's Liberia.
MAMA: I don't think I never met no African before.
BENEATHA: Well, do me a favor and don't ask him a whole lot of ignorant
    questions about Africans. I mean, do they wear clothes and all that—
MAMA: Well, now, I guess if you think we so ignorant 'round here maybe you
    shouldn't bring your friends here—
BENEATHA: It's just that people ask such crazy things. All anyone seems to know
    about when it comes to Africa is Tarzan—
MAMA: [*indignantly*] Why should I know anything about Africa?
BENEATHA: Why do you give money at church for the missionary work?
MAMA: Well, that's to help save people.
BENEATHA: You mean save them from *heathenism*—
MAMA: [*innocently*] Yes.
BENEATHA: I'm afraid they need more salvation from the British and the French.
    [RUTH *comes in forlornly and pulls off her coat with dejection. They*
    both turn to look at her.]
RUTH: [*dispiritedly*] Well, I guess from all the happy faces—everybody knows.
BENEATHA: You pregnant?
MAMA: Lord have mercy, I sure hope it's a little old girl. Travis ought to have a
    sister.
    [BENEATHA *and* RUTH *give her a hopeless look for this grandmotherly*
    enthusiasm.]

BENEATHA: How far along are you?

RUTH: Two months.

BENEATHA: Did you mean to? I mean did you plan it or was it an accident?

MAMA: What do you know about planning or not planning?

BENEATHA: Oh, Mama.

RUTH: [*wearily*] She's twenty years old, Lena.

BENEATHA: Did you plan it, Ruth?

RUTH: Mind your own business.

BENEATHA: It is my business—where is he going to live, on the *roof?* [*There is silence following the remark as the three women react to the sense of it.*] Gee—I didn't mean that, Ruth, honest. Gee, I don't feel like that at all. I—I think it is wonderful.

RUTH: [*dully*] Wonderful.

BENEATHA: Yes—really.

MAMA: [*looking at* RUTH *worried*] Doctor say everything going to be all right?

RUTH: [*far away*] Yes—she says everything is going to be fine . . .

MAMA: [*immediately suspicious*] "She"—What doctor you went to?

[RUTH *folds over, near hysteria.*]

MAMA: [*worriedly hovering over* RUTH] Ruth honey—what's the matter with you—you sick?

[RUTH *has her fists clenched on her thighs and is fighting hard to suppress a scream that seems to be rising in her.*]

BENEATHA: What's the matter with her, Mama?

MAMA: [*working her fingers in* RUTH'S *shoulder to relax her*] She be all right. Women gets right depressed sometimes when they get her way. [*speaking softly, expertly, rapidly*] Now you just relax. That's right . . . just lean back, don't think 'bout nothing at all . . . nothing at all—

RUTH: I'm all right . . .

[*The glassy-eyed look melts and then she collapses into a fit of heavy sobbing. The bell rings.*]

BENEATHA: Oh, my God—that must be Asagai.

MAMA: [*to* RUTH] Come on now, honey. You need to lie down and rest awhile . . . then have some nice hot food.

[*They exit,* RUTH'S *weight on her mother-in-law.* BENEATHA, *herself profoundly disturbed, opens the door to admit a rather dramatic-looking young man with a large package.*)

ASAGAI: Hello, Alaiyo—

BENEATHA: [*holding the door open and regarding him with pleasure*] Hello . . . [*long pause*] Well—come in. And please excuse everything. My mother was very upset about my letting anyone come here with the place like this.

ASAGAI: [*coming into the room*] You look disturbed too . . . Is something wrong?

BENEATHA: [*still at the door, absently*] Yes . . . we've all got acute ghetto-itus. [*She smiles and comes toward him, finding a cigarette and sitting.*] So—sit down! How was Canada?

ASAGAI: [*a sophisticate*] Canadian.

BENEATHA: [*looking at him*] I'm very glad you are back.

ASAGAI: [*looking back at her in turn*] Are you really?

BENEATHA: Yes—very.

ASAGAI: Why—you were quite glad when I went away. What happened?

BENEATHA: You went away.

ASAGAI: Ahhhhhhhh.

BENEATHA: Before—you wanted to be so serious before there was time.

ASAGAI: How much time must there be before one knows what one feels?

BENEATHA: [*stalling this particular conversation. Her hands pressed together, in a deliberately childish gesture*] What did you bring me?

ASAGAI: [*handing her the package*] Open it and see.

BENEATHA: [*eagerly opening the package and drawing out some records and the colorful robes of a Nigerian woman*] Oh, Asagai! . . . You got them for me! . . . How beautiful . . . and the records too! [*She lifts out the robes and runs to the mirror with them and holds the drapery up in front of herself.*]

ASAGAI: [*coming to her at the mirror*] I shall have to teach you how to drape it properly. [*He flings the material about her for the moment and stands back to look at her.*] Ah—*Oh-pay-gay-day, oh-ghah-mu-shay.* [*a Yoruba exclamation for admiration*] You wear it well . . . very well . . . mutilated hair and all.

BENEATHA: [*turning suddenly*] My hair—what's wrong with my hair?

ASAGAI: [*shrugging*] Were you born with it like that?

BENEATHA: [*reaching up to touch it*] No . . . of course not.

[*She looks back to the mirror, disturbed.*]

ASAGAI: [*smiling*] How then?

BENEATHA: You know perfectly well how . . . as crinkly as yours . . . that's how.

ASAGAI: And it is ugly to you that way?

BENEATHA: [*quickly*] Oh, no—not ugly . . . [*more slowly, apologetically*] But it's so hard to manage when it's, well—raw.

ASAGAI: And so to accommodate that—you mutilate it every week?

BENEATHA: It's not mutilation!

ASAGAI: [*laughing aloud at her seriousness*] Oh . . . please! I am only teasing you because you are so very serious about these things. [*He stands back from her and folds his arms across his chest as he watches her pulling at her hair and frowning in the mirror.*] Do you remember the first time you met me at school? . . . [*He laughs.*] You came up to me and you said—and I thought you were the most serious little thing I had ever seen—you said: [*He imitates her.*] "Mr. Asagai—I want very much to talk with you. About Africa. You see, Mr. Asagai, I am looking for my *identity!*"

[*He laughs.*]

BENEATHA: [*turning to him, not laughing*] Yes—

[*Her face is quizzical, profoundly disturbed.*]

ASAGAI: [*still teasing and reaching out and taking her face in his hands and turning her profile to him*] Well . . . it is true that this is not so much a profile of a Hollywood queen as perhaps a queen of the Nile—[*a mock dismissal of the importance of the question*] But what does it matter? Assimilationism is so popular in your country.

BENEATHA: [*wheeling, passionately, sharply*] I am not an assimilationist!

ASAGAI: [*The protest hangs in the room for a moment and* ASAGAI *studies her, his laughter fading.*] Such a serious one. [*There is a pause.*] So—you like the robes? You must take excellent care of them—they are from my sister's personal wardrobe.

BENEATHA: [*with incredulity*] You—you sent all the way home—for me?

ASAGAI: [*with charm*] For you—I would do much more . . . Well, that is what I came for. I must go.

BENEATHA: Will you call me Monday?

ASAGAI: Yes . . . We have a great deal to talk about. I mean about identity and time and all that.

BENEATHA: Time?

ASAGAI: Yes. About how much time one needs to know what one feels.

BENEATHA: You never understood that there is more than one kind of feeling which can exist between a man and a woman—or, at least, there should be.

ASAGAI: [*shaking his head negatively but gently*] No. Between a man and a woman there need be only one kind of feeling. I have that for you . . . Now even . . . right this moment . . .

BENEATHA: I know—and by itself—it won't do. I can find that anywhere.

ASAGAI: For a woman it should be enough.

BENEATHA: I know—because that's what it says in all the novels that men write. But it isn't. Go ahead and laugh—but I'm not interested in being someone's little episode in America or—[*with feminine vengeance*]— one of them! (ASAGAI *has burst into laughter again.*) That's funny as hell, huh!

ASAGAI: It's just that every American girl I have known has said that to me. White—black—in this you are all the same. And the same speech, too!

BENEATHA: [*angrily*] Yuk, yuk, yuk!

ASAGAI: It's how you can be sure that the world's most liberated women are not liberated at all. You all talk about it too much!

[MAMA *enters and is immediately all social charm because of the presence of a guest.*]

BENEATHA: Oh—Mama—this is Mr. Asagai.

MAMA: How do you do?

ASAGAI: [*total politeness to an elder*] How do you do, Mrs. Younger. Please forgive me for coming at such an. outrageous hour on a Saturday.

MAMA: Well, you are quite welcome. I just hope you understand that our house don't always look like this. [*chatterish*] You must come again. I would love to hear all about—[*not sure of the name*]—your country. I think it's so sad the way our American Negroes don't know nothing about Africa 'cept Tarzan and all that. And all that money they pour into these churches when they ought to be helping you people over there drive out them French and Englishmen done taken away your land.

[*The mother flashes a slightly superior look at her daughter upon completion of the recitation.*]

ASAGAI: [*taken aback by this sudden and acutely unrelated expression of sympathy*] Yes . . . yes . . .

MAMA: [*smiling at him suddenly and relaxing and looking him over*] How many miles is it from here to where you come from?

ASAGAI: Many thousands.

MAMA: [*looking at him as she would* WALTER] I bet you don't half look after yourself, being away from your mama either. I spec you better come 'round here from time to time and get yourself some decent homecooked meals . . .

ASAGAI: [*moved*] Thank you. Thank you very much. [*They are all quiet, then—*] Well . . . I must go. I will call you Monday, Alaiyo.

MAMA: What's that he call you?

ASAGAI: Oh—"Alaiyo." I hope you don't mind. It is what you would call a nickname, I think. It is a Yoruba word. I am a Yoruba.

MAMA: [*looking at* BENEATHA] I—I thought he was from—

ASAGAI: [*understanding*] Nigeria is my country. Yoruba is my tribal origin—

BENEATHA: You didn't tell us what Alaiyo means . . . for all I know, you might be calling me Little Idiot or something . . .

ASAGAI: Well . . . let me see . . . I do not know how just to explain it . . . The sense of a thing can be so different when it changes languages.

BENEATHA: You're evading.

ASAGAI: No—really it is difficult . . . [*thinking*] It means . . . it means One for Whom Bread—Food—Is Not Enough. [*He looks at her.*] Is that all right?

BENEATHA: [*understanding, softly*] Thank you.

MAMA: [*looking from one to the other and not understanding part of it*] Well . . . that's nice . . . You must come see us again—Mr.—

ASAGAI: Ah-sah-guy . . .

MAMA: Yes . . . Do come again.

ASAGAI: Good-bye.

[*He exits.*]

MAMA: [*after him*] Lord, that's a pretty thing just went out here! [*insinuatingly, to her daughter*] Yes, I guess I see why we done commence to get so interested in Africa 'round here. Missionaries my aunt Jenny!

[*she exits.*]

BENEATHA: Oh, Mama! . . .

[*She picks up the Nigerian dress and holds it up to her in front of the mirror again. She sets the headdress on haphazardly and then notices her hair again and clutches at it and then replaces the headdress and frowns at herself. Then she starts to wriggle in front of the mirror as she thinks a Nigerian woman might.* TRAVIS *enters and regards her.*]

TRAVIS: You cracking up?

BENEATHA: Shut up.

[*She pulls the headdress off and looks at herself in the mirror and clutches at her hair again and squinches her eyes as if trying to imagine something. Then, suddenly, she gets her raincoat and kerchief and hurrieldy prepares for going out.*]

MAMA: [*coming back into the room*] She's resting now. Travis, baby, run next door and ask Miss Johnson to please let me have a little kitchen cleanser. This here can is empty as Jacob's kettle.

TRAVIS: I just came in.

MAMA: Do as you told. [*He exits and she looks at her daughter.*] Where you going?

BENEATHA: [*halting at the door*] To become a queen of the Nile!

[*She exits in a breathless blaze of glory.* RUTH *appears in the bedroom doorway.*]

MAMA: Who told you to get up?

RUTH: Ain't nothing wrong with me to be lying in no bed for. Where did Bennie go?

MAMA: [*drumming her fingers*] Far as I could make out—to Egypt. [RUTH *just looks at her.*] What time is it getting to?

RUTH: Ten twenty. And the mailman going to ring that bell this morning just like he done every morning for the last umpteen years.

[TRAVIS *comes in with the cleanser can.*]

TRAVIS: She say to tell you that she don't have much.

MAMA: [*angrily*] Lord, some people I could name sure is tight-fisted! [*directing her grandson*] Mark two cans of cleanser down on the list there. If she that hard up for kitchen cleanser, I sure don't want to forget to get her none!

RUTH: Lena—maybe the woman is just short on cleanser—

MAMA: [*not listening*] —Much baking powder as she done borrowed from me all these years, she could of done gone into the baking business!

[*The bell sounds suddenly and sharply and all three are stunned—serious and silent—mid-speech. In spite of all the other conversations and distractions of the morning, this is what they have been waiting for, even* TRAVIS, *who looks helplessly from his mother to his grandmother.* RUTH *is the first to come to life again.*]

RUTH: [*to* TRAVIS] Get down them steps, boy!

[TRAVIS *snaps to life and flies out to get the mail*]

MAMA: [*her eyes wide, her hand to her breast*] You mean it done really come?

RUTH: [*excited*] Oh, Miss Lena!

MAMA: [*collecting herself*] Well . . . I don't know what we all so excited about 'round here for. We known it was coming for months.

RUTH: That's a whole lot different from having it come and being able to hold it in your hands . . . a piece of paper worth ten thousand dollars . . . [TRAVIS *bursts back into the room. He holds the envelope high above his head, like a little dancer, his face is radiant and he is breathless. He moves to his grandmother with sudden slow ceremony and puts the envelope into her hands. She accepts it, and then merely holds it and looks at it.*] Come on! Open it . . . Lord have mercy, I wish Walter Lee was here!

TRAVIS: Open it, Grandmama!

MAMA: [*staring at it*] Now you all be quiet. It's just a check.

RUTH: Open it . . .

MAMA: [*still staring at it*] Now don't act silly . . . We ain't never been no people to act silly 'bout no money—

RUTH: [*swiftly*] We ain't never had none before—*open it!*

[MAMA *finally makes a good strong tear and pulls out the thin blue slice of paper and inspects it closely. The boy and his mother study it raptly over* MAMA'S *shoulders.*)

MAMA: Travis! [*She is counting off with doubt.*] Is that the right number of zeros.

TRAVIS: Yes'm . . . ten thousand dollars. Gaalee, Grandmama, you rich.

MAMA: [*She holds the check away from her, still looking at it. Slowly her face sobers into a mask of unhappiness.*] Ten thousand dollars. [*She hands it to* RUTH.] Put it away somewhere, Ruth. [*She does not look at* RUTH ; *her eyes seem to be seeing something somewhere very far off.*] Ten thousand dollars they give you. Ten thousand dollars.

TRAVIS: [*to his mother, sincerely*] What's the matter with Grandmama—don't she want to be rich?

RUTH: [*distractedly*] You go on out and play now, baby. [TRAVIS *exits.* MAMA *starts wiping dishes absently, humming intently to herself.* RUTH *turns to her, with kind exasperation.*] You've gone and got yourself upset.

MAMA: [*not looking at her*] I spec if it wasn't for you all . . . I would just put that money away or give it to the church or something.

RUTH: Now what kind of talk is that. Mr. Younger would just be plain mad if he could hear you talking foolish like that.

MAMA: [*stopping and staring off*] Yes . . . he sure would. [*sighing*] We got enough to do with that money, all right. [*She halts then, and turns and looks at her daughter-in-law hard; RUTH avoids her eyes and MAMA wipes her hands with finality and starts to speak firmly to RUTH.*] Where did you go today, girl?

RUTH: To the doctor.

MAMA: [*impatiently*] Now, Ruth . . . you know better than that. Old Doctor Jones is strange enough in his way but there ain't nothing 'bout him make somebody slip and call him "she"—like you done this morning.

RUTH: Well, that's what happened—my tongue slipped.

MAMA: You went to see that woman, didn't you?

RUTH: [*defensively, giving herself away*] What woman you talking about?

MAMA: [*angrily*] That woman who—

[*WALTER enters in great excitement.*]

WALTER: Did it come?

MAMA: [*quietly*] Can't you give people a Christian greeting before you start asking about money?

WALTER: [*to RUTH*] Did it come? [*RUTH unfolds the check and lays it quietly before him, watching him intently with thoughts of her own. WALTER sits down and grasps it close and counts off the zeros.*] Ten thousand dollars— [*He turns suddenly, frantically to his mother and draws some papers out of his breast pocket.*] Mama—look. Old Willy Harris put everything on paper—

MAMA: Son—I think you ought to talk to your wife . . . I'll go on out and leave you alone if you want—

WALTER: I can talk to her later—Mama, look—

MAMA: Son—

WALTER: WILL SOMEBODY PLEASE LISTEN TO ME TODAY!

MAMA: [*quietly*] I don't 'low no yellin' in this house, Walter Lee, and you know it—[*WALTER stares at them in frustration and starts to speak several times.*] And there ain't going to be no investing in no liquor stores. I don't aim to have to speak on that again.

[*a long pause*]

WALTER: Oh—so you don't aim to have to speak on that again? So *you* have decided . . . [*crumpling his papers*] Well, *you* tell that to my boy tonight when you put him to sleep on the living-room couch . . . [*turning to MAMA and speaking directly to her*] Yeah—and tell it to my wife, Mama, tomorrow when she has to go out of here to look after somebody else's kids. And tell it to *me*, Mama, every time we need a new pair of curtains and I have to watch *you* go out and work in somebody's kitchen. Yeah, you tell me then!

[*WALTER starts out.*]

RUTH: Where you going?

WALTER: I'm going out!

RUTH: Where?

WALTER: Just out of this house somewhere—

RUTH: [*getting her coat*] I'll come too.

WALTER: I don't want you to come!

RUTH: I got something to talk to you about, Walter.

WALTER: That's too bad.

MAMA: [*still quietly*] Walter Lee—[*She waits and he finally turns and looks at her.*] Sit down.

WALTER: I'm a grown man, Mama.

MAMA: Ain't nobody said you wasn't grown. But you still in my house and my presence. And as long as you are—you'll talk to your wife civil. Now sit down.

RUTH: [*suddenly*] Oh, let him go on out and drink himself to death! He makes me sick to my stomach! [*She flings her coat against him.*]

WALTER: [*violently*] And you turn mine too, baby! [RUTH *goes into their bedroom and slams the door behind her.*] That was my greatest mistake—

MAMA: [*still quietly*] Walter, what is the matter with you?

WALTER: Matter with me? Ain't nothing the matter with *me!*

MAMA: Yes there is. Something eating you up like a crazy man. Something more than me not giving you this money. The past few years I been watching it happen to you. You get all nervous acting and kind of wild in the eyes— [WALTER *jumps up impatiently at her words.*] I said sit there now, I'm talking to you!

WALTER: Mama—I don't need no nagging at me today.

MAMA: Seem like you getting to a place where you always tied up in some kind of knot about something. But if anybody ask you 'bout it you just tell at 'em and bust out the house and go out and drink somewheres. Walter Lee, people can't live like that. Ruth's a good, patient girl in her way—but you getting to be too much. Boy, don't make the mistake of driving that girl away from you.

WALTER: Why—what she do for me?

MAMA: She loves you.

WALTER: Mama—I'm going out. I want to go off somewhere and be by myself for a while.

MAMA: I'm sorry 'bout your liquor store, son. It just wasn't the thing for us to do. That's what I want to tell you about—

WALTER: I got to go out, Mama—
          [*He rises.*]

MAMA: It's dangerous, son.

WALTER: What's dangerous?

MAMA: When a man goes outside his home to look for peace.

WALTER: [*beseechingly*] Then why can't there never be no peace in this house then?

MAMA: You done found it in some other house?

WALTER: No—there ain't no woman! Why do women always think there's a woman somewhere when a man gets restless. [*coming to her*] Mama— Mama—I want so many things . . .

MAMA: Yes, son—

WALTER: I want so many things that they are driving me kind of crazy . . . Mama—look at me.

MAMA: I'm looking at you. You a good-looking boy. You got a job, a nice wife, a fine boy and—

WALTER: A job. [*looks at her*] Mama, a job? I open and close car doors all day long. I drive a man around in his limousine and I say, "Yes, sir; no sir; very good, sir; shall I take the Drive, sir?" Mama, that ain't no kind of job . . . that ain't nothing at all. [*very quietly*] Mama, I don't know if I can make you understand.

MAMA: Understand what, baby?

WALTER: [*quietly*] Sometimes it's like I can see the future stretched out in front of me—just plain as day. The future, Mama. Hanging over there at the edge of my days. Just waiting for me—a big, looming blank space—full of *nothing*. Just waiting for *me*. [*pause*] Mama—sometimes when I'm downtown and I pass them cool, quiet-looking restaurants where them white boys are sitting back and talking 'bout things . . . sitting there turning deals worth millions of dollars . . . sometimes I see guys don't look much older than me—

MAMA: Son—how come you talk so much 'bout money?

WALTER: [*with immense passion*] Because it is life, Mama!

MAMA: [*quietly*] Oh—[*very quietly*] So now it's life. Money is life. Once upon a time freedom used to be life—now it's money. I guess the world really do change . . .

WALTER: No—it was always money, Mama. We just didn't know about it.

MAMA: No . . . something has changed. [*She looks at him.*] You something new, boy. In my time we was worried about not being lynched and getting to the North if we could and how to stay alive and still have a pinch of dignity too . . . Now here come you and Beneatha—talking 'bout things we ain't never even thought about hardly, me and your daddy. You ain't satisfied or proud of nothing we done. I mean that you had a home; that we kept you out of trouble till you was grown; that you don't have to ride to work on the back of nobody's streetcar—You my children—but how different we done become.

WALTER: You just don't understand, Mama, you just don't understand.

MAMA: Son—do you know your wife is expecting another baby? [WALTER *stands, stunned, and absorbs what his mother has said.*] That's what she wanted to talk to you about. [WALTER *sinks down into a chair.*] This ain't for me to be telling—but you ought to know. [*She waits.*] I think Ruth is thinking 'bout getting rid of that child.

WALTER: [*slowly understanding*] No—no—Ruth wouldn't do that.

MAMA: When the world gets ugly enough—a woman will do anything for her family. *The part that's already living.*

WALTER: You don't know Ruth, Mama, if you think she would do that.

[RUTH *opens the bedroom door and stands there a little limp.*]

RUTH: [*beaten*] Yes I would too, Walter. [*pause*] I gave her a five-dollar down payment.

[*There is total silence as the man stares at his wife and the mother stares at her son.*]

MAMA: [*presently*]Well—[*tightly*] Well—son, I'm waiting to hear you say some-thing . . . I'm waiting to hear how you be your father's son. Be the man he was . . . [*pause*] Your wife say she going to destroy your child. And I'm waiting to hear you talk like him and say we a people who give children life, not who destroys them—[*She rises.*] I'm waiting to see you stand up and look like your daddy and say we done give up one baby to poverty and that we ain't going to give up nary another one . . . I'm waiting.

WALTER: Ruth—

MAMA: If you a son of mine, tell her! [WALTER *turns, looks at her and can say nothing. She continues, bitterly.*] You . . . you are a disgrace to your father's memory. Somebody get me my hat.

ACT II

SCENE I—— *Time: Later the same day.*

At rise: RUTH *is ironing again. She has the radio going. Presently* BENEATHA'S *bedroom door opens and* RUTH'S *mouth falls and she puts down the iron in fascination.*

RUTH: What have we got on tonight!

BENEATHA: [*emerging grandly from the doorway so that we can see her thoroughly robed in the costume Asagai brought.*] You are looking at what a well-dressed Nigerian woman wears—[*She parades for* RUTH, *her hair completely hidden by the headdress; she is coquettishly fanning herself with an ornate oriental fan, mistakenly more like Butterfly than any Nigerian that ever was.*] Isn't it beautiful? [*She promenades to the radio and, with an arrogant flourish, turns off the good loud blues that is playing.*] Enough of this assimilationist junk! [RUTH *follows her with her eyes as she goes to the photograph and puts on a record and turns and waits ceremoniously for the music to come up. Then, with a shout—*] O COMOGOSIAY!

[RUTH *jumps. The music comes up, a lovely Nigerian melody.* BE-NEATHA *listens, enraptured, her eyes far away—"back to the past." She begins to dance.* RUTH *is dumfounded.*]

RUTH: What kind of dance is that?

BENEATHA: A folk dance.

RUTH: [*Pearl Bailey*] What kind of folks do that, honey?

BENEATHA: It's from Nigeria. It's a dance of welcome.

RUTH: Who you welcoming?

BENEATHA: The men back to the village.

RUTH: Where they been?

BENEATHA: How should I know—out hunting or something. Anyway, they are coming back now . . .

RUTH: Well, that's good.

BENEATHA: [*with the record*]
Alundi, alundi
Alundi alunya
Jop pu a jeepua
Ang gu soooooooooo

Ai yai yae . . .
Ayehaye—alundi . . .

[WALTER *comes in during this performance; he has obviously been drinking. He leans against the door heavily and watches his sister, at first with distaste. Then his eyes look off—"back to the past"—as he lifts both his fists to the roof, screaming*]

WALTER: YEAH . . . AND ETHIOPIA STRETCH FORTH HER HANDS AGAIN! . . .

RUTH: [*drily, looking at him*] Yes—and Africa sure is claiming her own tonight. [*She gives them both up and starts ironing again.*]

WALTER: [*all in a drunken, dramatic shout*] Shut up! . . . I'm digging them drums . . . them drums move me! . . . [*He makes his weaving way to his wife's face and leans in close to her.*] In my *heart of hearts*—[*He thumps his chest.*]—I am much warrior!

RUTH: [*without even looking up*] In your heart of hearts you are much drunkard.

WALTER: [*coming away from her and starting to wander around the room, shouting*] Me and Jomo . . . [*Intently, in his sister's face. She has stopped dancing to watch him in this unknown mood*] That's my man, Kenyatta. [*shouting and thumping his chest*] FLAMING SPEAR! HOT DAMN! [*He is suddenly in possession of an imaginary spear and actively spearing enemies all over the room.*] OCOMOGOSIAY . . . THE LION IS WAKING . . . OWIMOWEH! [*He pulls his shirt open and leaps up on a table and gestures with his spear. The bell rings.* RUTH *goes to answer.*]

BENEATHA: [*to encourage* WALTER, *thoroughly caught up with this side of him*] OCOMOGOSIAY, FLAMING SPEAR!

WALTER: [*On the table, very far gone, his eyes pure glass sheets. He sees what we cannot, that he is a leader of his people, a great chief, a descendant of Chaka, and that the hour to march has come.*] Listen, my black brothers—

BENEATHA: OCOMOGOSIAY!

WALTER: —Do you hear the waters rushing against the shores of the coastlands—

BENEATHA: OCOMOGOSIAY!

WALTER: —Do you hear the screeching of the cocks in yonder hills beyond where the chiefs meet in council for the coming of the mighty war—

BENEATHA: OCOMOGOSIAY!

WALTER: —Do you hear the beating of the wings of the birds flying low over the mountains and the low places of our land—

[RUTH *opens the door.* GEORGE MURCHISON *enters.*]

BENEATHA: OCOMOGOSIAY!

WALTER: —Do you hear the singing of the women, singing the war songs of our fathers to the babies in the great houses . . . singing the sweet war songs? OH, DO YOU HEAR, MY BLACK BROTHERS!

BENEATHA: [*completely gone*] We hear you, Flaming Spear—

WALTER: Telling us to prepare for the greatness of the time—[*to* GEORGE] Black Brother!

[*He extends his hand for the fraternal clasp.*]

GEORGE: Black Brother, hell!

RUTH: [*having had enough, and embarrassed for the family*] Beneatha, you got company—what's the matter with you? Walter Lee Younger, get down off that table and stop acting like a fool . . .

[WALTER *comes down off the table suddenly and makes a quick exit to the bathroom.*]

RUTH: He's had a little to drink . . . I don't know what her excuse is.

GEORGE: [*to* BENEATHA] Look honey, we're going *to* the theatre—we're not going to be *in* it . . . so go change, huh?

RUTH: You expect this boy to go out with you looking like that?

BENEATHA: [*looking at* GEORGE] That's up to George. If he's ashamed of his heritage—

GEORGE: Oh, don't be so proud of yourself, Bennie—just because you look eccentric.

BENEATHA: How can something that's natural be eccentric?

GEORGE: That's what being eccentric means—being natural. Get dressed.

BENEATHA: I don't like that, George.

RUTH: Why must you and your brother make an argument out of everything people say?

BENEATHA: Because I hate assimilationist Negroes!

RUTH: Will somebody please tell me what assimila-whoever means!

GEORGE: Oh, it's just a college girl's way of calling people Uncle Toms—but that isn't what it means at all.

RUTH: Well, what does it mean?

BENEATHA: [*cutting* GEORGE *off and staring at him as she replies to* RUTH] It means someone who is willing to give up his own culture and submerge himself completely in the dominant, and in this case, *oppressive* culture!

GEORGE: Oh, dear, dear, dear! Here we go! A lecture on the African past! On our Great West African Heritage! In one second we will hear all about the great Ashanti empires; the great Songhay civilizations; and the great sculpture of Benin—and then some poetry in the Bantu—and the whole monologue will end with the word *heritage!* [*nastily*] Let's face it, baby, your heritage is nothing but a bunch of raggedy-assed spirituals and some grass huts!

BENEATHA: *Grass huts!* [RUTH *crosses to her and forcibly pushes her toward the bedroom.*] See there . . . you are standing there in your splendid ignorance talking about people who were the first to smelt iron on the face of the earth! [RUTH *is pushing her through the door.*] The Ashanti were performing surgical operations when the English—[RUTH *pulls the door to, with* BE- NEATHA *on the other side, and smiles graciously at* GEORGE. BENEATHA *opens the door and shouts the end of the sentence defiantly at* GEORGE]—were still tattooing themselves with blue dragons . . . [*She goes back inside.*]

RUTH: Have a seat, George. [*They both sit.* RUTH *folds her hands rather primly on her lap, determined to demonstrate the civilization of the family.*] Warm, ain't it? I mean for September. [*pause*] Just like they always say about Chicago weather: If it's too hot or cold for you, just wait a minute and it'll change. [*She smiles happily at this cliché of clichés.*] Everybody say it's got to do with them bombs and things they keep setting off. [*pause*] Would you like a nice cold beer?

GEORGE: No, thank you. I don't care for beer. [*He looks at his watch.*] I hope she hurries up.

RUTH: What time is the show?

GEORGE: It's an eight-thirty curtain. That's just Chicago, though. In New York standard curtain time is eight forty.

    [*He is rather proud of this knowledge.*]

RUTH: [*properly appreciating it*] You get to New York a lot?

GEORGE: [*offhand*] Few times a year.

RUTH: Oh—that's nice. I've never been to New York.

> [WALTER *enters. We feel he has relieved himself, but the edge of unreality is still with him.*]

WALTER: New York ain't got nothing Chicago ain't. Just a bunch of hustling people all squeezed up together—being "Eastern."

> [*He turns his face into a screw of displeasure.*]

GEORGE: Oh—you've been?

WALTER: *Plenty* of times.

RUTH: [*shocked at the lie*] Walter Lee Younger!

WALTER: [*sharing her down*] Plenty! [*pause*] What we got to drink in this house? Why don't you offer this man some refreshment. [*to* GEORGE] They don't know how to entertain people in this house, man.

GEORGE: Thank you—I don't really care for anything.

WALTER: [*feeling his head; sobriety coming*] Where's Mama?

RUTH: She ain't come back yet.

WALTER: [*Looking* MURCHISON *over from head to toe, scrutinizing his carefully casual tweed sports jacket over cashmere V-neck sweater over soft eyelet shirt and tie, and soft slacks, finished off with white buckskin shoes.*] Why all you college boys wear them fairyish-looking white shoes?

RUTH: Walter Lee!

> [GEORGE MURCHISON *ignores the remark.*]

WALTER: [*to* RUTH] Well, they look crazy as hell—white shoes, cold as it is.

RUTH: [*crushed*] You have to excuse him—

WALTER: No he don't! Excuse me for what? What you always excusing me for! I'll excuse myself when I needs to be excused! [*a pause*] They look as funny as them black knee socks Beneatha wears out of here all the time.

RUTH: It's the college *style*, Walter.

WALTER: Style, hell. She looks like she got burnt legs or something!

RUTH: Oh, Walter—

WALTER: [*an irritable mimic*] Oh, Walter! Oh, Walter! [*to* MURCHISON] How's your old man making out? I understand you all going to buy that big hotel on the Drive? [*He finds a beer in the refrigerator, wanders over to* MURCHISON, *sipping and wiping his lips with the back of his hand, and straddling a chair backwards to talk to the other man.*] Shrewd move. Your old man is all right, man. [*tapping his head and half winking for emphasis*] I mean he knows how to operate. I mean he thinks *big*, you know what I mean, I mean for a *home*, you know? But I think he's kind of running out of ideas now. I'd like to talk to him. Listen, man, I got some plans that could turn this city upside down. I mean I think like he does. *Big*. Invest big, gamble big, hell, lose *big* if you have to, you know what I mean. It's hard to find a man on this whole Southside who understands my kind of thinking—you dig? [*he scrutinizes* MURCHISON *again, drinks his beer, squints his eyes and leans in close, confidential, man to man.*] Me and you ought to sit down and talk sometimes, man. Man, I got me some ideas . . .

GEORGE: [*with boredom*] Yeah—sometimes we'll have to do that, Walter.

WALTER: [*understanding the indifference, and offended*] Yeah—well, when you get the time, man. I know you a busy little boy.

RUTH: Walter, please—

WALTER: [*bitterly, hurt*] I know ain't nothing in this world as busy as you colored college boys with your fraternity pins and white shoes . . .

RUTH: [*covering her face with humiliation*] Oh, Walter Lee—

WALTER: I see you all all the time—with the books tucked under your arms— going to your [*British A—a mimic*] "clahsses." And for what! What the hell you learning over there? Filling up your heads—[*counting off on his fingers*]—with the sociology and the psychology—but they teaching you how to be a man? How to take over and run the world? They teaching you how to run a rubber plantation or a steel mill? Naw—just to talk proper and read books and wear white shoes . . .

GEORGE: [*looking at him with distaste, a little above it all*] You're all wacked up with bitterness, man.

WALTER: [*intently, almost quietly, between the teeth, glaring at the boy*] And you—ain't you bitter, man? Ain't you just about had it yet? Don't you see no stars gleaming that you can't reach out and grab? You happy?—You contented son-of-a-bitch—you happy? You got it made? Bitter? Man, I'm a volcano. Bitter? Here I am a giant—surrounded by ants! Ants who can't even understand what it is the giant is talking about.

RUTH: [*passionately and suddenly*] Oh, Walter—ain't you with nobody!

WALTER: [*violently*] No! 'Cause ain't nobody with me! Not even my own mother!

RUTH: Walter, that's a terrible thing to say!

[BENEATHA *enters, dressed for the evening in a cocktail dress and earrings.*]

GEORGE: Well—hey, you look great.

BENEATHA: Let's go, George. See you all later.

RUTH: Have a nice time.

GEORGE: Thanks. Good night. [*to* WALTER, *sarcastically*] Good night, *Prometheus.*

[BENEATHA *and* GEORGE *exit.*]

WALTER: [*to* RUTH] Who is Prometheus?

RUTH: I don't know. Don't worry about it.

WALTER: [*in fury, pointing after* GEORGE] See there—they get to a point where they can't insult you man to man—they got to talk about something ain't nobody never heard of!

RUTH: How do you know it was an insult? [*to humor him*] Maybe Prometheus is a nice fellow.

WALTER: Prometheus! I bet there ain't even no such thing! I bet that simple-minded clown—

RUTH: Walter—

[*She stops what she is doing and looks at him.*]

WALTER: [*yelling*] Don't start!

RUTH: Start what?

WALTER: Your nagging! Where was I? Who was I with? How much money did I spend?

RUTH: [*plaintively*] Walter Lee—why don't we just try to talk about it . . .

WALTER: [*not listening*] I been out talking with people who understand me. People who care about the things I got on my mind.

RUTH: [*wearily*] I guess that means people like Willy Harris.

WALTER: Yes, people like Willy Harris.

RUTH: [*with a sudden flash of impatience*] Why don't you all just hurry up and go into the banking business and stop talking about it!

WALTER: Why? You want to know why? 'Cause we all tied up in a race of people that don't know how to do nothing but moan, pray and have babies!

[*The line is too bitter even for him and he looks at her and sits down.*]

RUTH: Oh, Walter . . . [*softly*] Honey, why can't you stop fighting me?

WALTER: [*without thinking*] Who's fighting you? Who even cares about you?

[*This line begins the retardation of his mood.*]

RUTH: Well—[*She waits a long time, and then with resignation starts to put away her things.*] I guess I might as well go on to bed . . . [*more or less to herself*] I don't know where we lost it . . . but we have . . . [*then, to him*] I—I'm sorry about this new baby, Walter. I guess maybe I better go on and do what I started . . . I guess I just didn't realize how bad things was with us . . . I guess I just didn't really realize—[*She starts out to the bedroom and stops.*] You want some hot milk?

WALTER: Hot milk?

RUTH: Yes—hot milk.

WALTER: Why hot milk?

RUTH: 'Cause after all that liquor you come home with you ought to have something hot in your stomach.

WALTER: I don't want no milk.

RUTH: You want some coffee then?

WALTER: No, I don't want no coffee. I don't want nothing hot to drink. [*almost plaintively*] Why you always trying to give me something to eat?

RUTH: [*standing and looking at him helplessly*] What else can I give you, Walter Lee Younger?

[*She stands and looks at him and presently turns to go out again. He lifts his head and watches her going away from him in a new mood which began to emerge when he asked her "Who cares about you?"*]

WALTER: It's been rough, ain't it, baby? [*She hears and stops but does not turn around and he continues to her back.*] I guess between two people there ain't never as much understood as folks generally thinks there is. I mean like between me and you—[*She turns to face him.*] How we gets to the place where we scared to talk softness to each other. [*He waits, thinking hard himself.*] Why you think it got to be like that? [*He is thoughtful, almost as a child would be.*] Ruth, what is it gets into people ought to be close?

RUTH: I don't know, honey. I think about it a lot.

WALTER: On account of you and me, you mean? The way things are with us. The way something done come down between us.

RUTH: There ain't so much between us, Walter . . . Not when you come to me and try to talk to me. Try to be with me . . . a little even.

WALTER: [*total honesty*] Sometimes . . . sometimes . . . I don't even know how to try.

RUTH: Walter—

WALTER: Yes?

RUTH: [*coming to him, gently and with misgiving, but coming to him*] Honey . . . life don't have to be like this. I mean sometimes people can do things so

that things are better . . . You remember how we used to talk when Travis
was born . . . about the way we were going to live . . . the kind of house
. . . [*She is stroking his head.*] Well, it's all starting to slip away from us . . .
    [MAMA *enters, and* WALTER *jumps up and shouts at her.*]

WALTER: Mama, where have you been?

MAMA: My—them steps is longer than they used to be. Whew! [*she sits down and
ignores him.*] How you feeling this evening, Ruth?
    [RUTH *shrugs, disturbed some at having been prematurely interrupted
    and watching her husband knowingly.*]

WALTER: Mama, where have you been all day?

MAMA: [*still ignoring him and leaning on the table and changing to more comfortable shoes*] Where's Travis?

RUTH: I let him go out earlier and he ain't come back yet. Boy, is he going to get
it!

WALTER: Mama!

MAMA: [*as if she has heard him for the first time*] Yes, son?

WALTER: Where did you go this afternoon?

MAMA: I went downtown to tend to some business that I had to tend to.

WALTER: What kind of business?

MAMA: You know better than to question me like a child, Brother.

WALTER: [*rising and bending over the table*] Where were you, Mama? [*bringing
his fists down and shouting*] Mama, you didn't go do something with that
insurance money, something crazy?
    [*The front door opens slowly, interrupting him, and* TRAVIS *peeks his
    head in, less than hopefully.*]

TRAVIS: [*to his mother*] Mama, I—

RUTH: "Mama I" nothing! You're going to get it boy! Get on in that bedroom and
get yourself ready!

TRAVIS: But I—

MAMA: Why don't you all never let the child explain hisself.

RUTH: Keep out if it now, Lena.
    [MAMA *clamps her lips together, and* RUTH *advances toward her son
    menacingly.*]

RUTH: A thousand times I have told you not to go off like that—

MAMA: [*holding out her arms to her grandson*] Well—at least let me tell him
something. I want him to be the first one to hear . . . Come here, Travis.
[*The boy obeys, gladly.*] Travis—[*She takes him by the shoulder and looks
into his face.*]—you know that money we got in the mail this morning?

TRAVIS: Yes'm—

MAMA: Well—what you think your grandmama gone and done with that money?

TRAVIS: I don't know, Grandmama.

MAMA: [*putting her finger on his nose for emphasis*] She went out and she bought
you a house! [*The explosion comes from* WALTER *at the end of the revelation
and he jumps up and turns away from all of them in a fury.* MAMA *continues, to* TRAVIS.] You glad about the house? It's going to be yours when
you get to be a man.

TRAVIS: Yeah—I always wanted to live in a house.

MAMA: All right, gimme some sugar then—[TRAVIS *puts his arms around her neck as she watches her son over the boy's shoulder. Then, to* TRAVIS, *after the embrace*] Now when you say your prayers tonight, you thank God and your grandfather—'cause it was him who give you the house—in his way.

RUTH: [*taking the boy from* MAMA *and pushing him toward the bedroom*] Now you get out of here and get ready for your beating.

TRAVIS: Aw, Mama—

RUTH: Get on in there—[*closing the door behind him and turning radiantly to her mother-in-law*] So you went and did it!

MAMA: [*quietly, looking at her son with pain*] Yes, I did.

RUTH: [*raising both arms classically*]

Praise God! [*Looks at* WALTER *a moment, who says nothing. She crosses rapidly to her husband.*] Please, honey—let me be glad . . . you be glad too. [*She has laid her hands on his shoulders, but he shakes himself free of her roughly, without turning to face her.*] Oh, Walter . . . a home . . . a home. [*She comes back to* MAMA.] Well—where is it? How big is it? How much it going to cost?

MAMA: Well—

RUTH: When we moving?

MAMA: [*smiling at her*] First of the month.

RUTH: [*throwing back her head with jubilance*] Praise God!

MAMA: [*tentatively, still looking at her son's back turned against her and* RUTH] It's—it's a nice house too . . . [*She cannot help speaking directly to him. An imploring quality in her voice, her manner, makes her almost like a girl now.*] Three bedrooms—nice big one for you and Ruth. . . . Me and Beneatha still have to share our room, but Travis have one of his own—and [*with difficulty*] I figure if the—new baby—is a boy, we could get one of them double-decker outfits . . . And there's a yard with a little patch of dirt where I could maybe get to grow me a few flowers . . . And a nice big basement . . .

RUTH: Walter honey, be glad—

MAMA: [*still to his back, fingering things on the table*] 'Course I don't want to make it sound fancier than it is . . . It's just a plain little old house—but it's made good and solid—and it will be *ours.* Walter Lee—it makes a difference in a man when he can walk on floors that belong to *him* . . .

RUTH: Where is it?

MAMA: [*frightened at this telling*] Well—well—it's out there in Clybourne Park—

[RUTH'S *radiance fades abruptly, and* WALTER *finally turns slowly to face his mother with incredulity and hostility.*]

RUTH: Where?

MAMA: [*matter-of-factly*] Four o six Clybourne Street, Clybourne Park.

RUTH: Clybourne Park? Mama, there ain't no colored people living in Clybourne Park.

MAMA: [*almost idiotically*] Well, I guess there's going to be some now.

WALTER: [*bitterly*] So that's the peace and comfort you went out and bought for us today!

MAMA: [*raising her eyes to meet his finally*] Son—I just tried to find the nicest place for the least amount of money for my family.

RUTH: [*trying to recover from the shock*] Well—well—'course I ain't one never been 'fraid of no crackers, mind you—but—well, wasn't there no other houses nowhere?

MAMA: Them houses they put up for colored in them areas way out all seem to cost twice as much as other houses. I did the best I could.

RUTH: [*Struck senseless with the news, in its various degrees of goodness and trouble, she sits a moment, her fists propping her chin in thought, and then she starts to rise, bring her fists down with vigor, the radiance spreading from cheek to cheek again.*] Well—well!—All I can say is—if this is my time in life—*my time*—to say good-bye [*and she builds with momentum as she starts to circle the room with an exuberant, almost tearfully happy release*]—to these Goddamned cracking walls!—[*She pounds the walls.*]— and these marching roaches!—[*She wipes at an imaginary army of marching roaches.*]—and this cramped little closet which ain't now or never was no kitchen!* . . . then I say it loud and good, *Hallelujah! and goodbye misery . . . I don't never want to see your ugly face again!* [*She laughs joyously, having practically destroyed the apartment, and flings her arms up and lets them come down happily, slowly, reflectively, over her abdomen, aware for the first time perhaps that the life therein pulses with happiness and not despair.*] Lena?

MAMA: [*moved, watching her happiness*] Yes, honey?

RUTH: [*looking off*] Is there—is there a whole lot of sunlight?

MAMA: [*understanding*] Yes, child, there's a whole lot of sunlight.
     [*long pause*]

RUTH: [*collecting herself and going to the door of the room* TRAVIS *is in*] Well—I guess I better see 'bout Travis. [*to* MAMA] Lord, I sure don't feel like whipping nobody today!
     [*She exits.*]

MAMA: [*The mother and son are left alone now and the mother waits a long time, considering deeply, before she speaks.*] Son—you—you understand what I done, don't you? [WALTER *is silent and sullen.*] I—I just seen my family falling apart today . . . just falling to pieces in front of my eyes . . . We couldn't of gone on like we was today. We was going backwards 'stead of forwards—talking 'bout killing babies and wishing each other was dead . . . When it gets like that in life—you just got to do something different, push on out and do something bigger . . . [*She waits.*] I wish you say something, son . . . I wish you'd say how deep inside you you think I done the right thing—

WALTER: [*crossing slowly to his bedroom door and finally turning there and speaking measuredly*] What you need me to say you done right for? *You* the head of this family. You run our lives like you want to. It was your money and you did what you wanted with it. So what you need for me to say it was all right for? [*bitterly, to hurt her as deeply as he knows is possible*] So you butchered up a dream of mine—you—who always talking 'bout your children's dreams . . .

MAMA: Walter Lee—
[*He just closes the door behind him.* MAMA *sits alone, thinking heavily*]

SCENE II—— *Time: Friday night. A few weeks later.*
At rise: Packing crates mark the intention of the family to move. BENEATHA *and*
GEORGE *come in, presumably from an evening out again.*

GEORGE: O.K. . . . O.K., whatever you say . . . [*They both sit on the couch. He
tries to kiss her. She moves away.*] Look, we've had a nice evening; let's not
spoil it, huh? . . .
　　　[*He again turns her head and tries to nuzzle in and she turns away
　　　from him, not with distaste but with momentary lack of interest; in a
　　　mood to pursue what they were talking about.*]
BENEATHA: I'm *trying* to talk to you.
GEORGE: We always talk.
BENEATHA: Yes—and I love to talk.
GEORGE: [*exasperated; rising*] I know it and I don't mind it sometimes . . . I want
you to cut it out, see—The moody stuff, I mean. I don't like it. You're a
nice-looking girl . . . all over. That's all you need, honey, forget the atmosphere. Guys aren't going to go for the atmosphere—they're going to go for
what they see. Be glad for that. Drop the Garbo routine. It doesn't go with
you. As for myself, I want a nice—[*groping*]—simple [*thoughtfully*]—
sophisticated girl . . . not a poet—O.K.?
　　　[*She rebuffs him again and he starts to leave.*]
BENEATHA: Why are you angry?
GEORGE: Because this is stupid! I don't go out with you to discuss the nature of
"quiet desperation" or to hear all about your thoughts—because the world
will go on thinking what it thinks regardless—
BENEATHA: Then why read books? Why go to school?
GEORGE: [*with artificial patience, counting on his fingers*] It's simple. You read
books—to learn facts—to get grades—to pass the course—to get a degree.
That's all—it has nothing to do with thoughts.
　　　[*a long pause*]
BENEATHA: I see. [*a longer pause as she looks at him*] Good night, George.
　　　[GEORGE *looks at her a little oddly, and starts to exit. He meets* MAMA
　　　coming in.]
GEORGE: Oh—hello, Mrs. Younger.
MAMA: Hello, George, how you feeling?
GEORGE: Fine—fine, how are you?
MAMA: Oh, a little tired. You know them steps can get you after a day's work.
You all have a nice time tonight?
GEORGE: Yes—a fine time. Well, good night.
MAMA: Good night. [*He exits.* MAMA *closes the door behind her.*] Hello, honey.
What you sitting like that for?
BENEATHA: I'm just sitting.
MAMA: Didn't you have a nice time?
BENEATHA: No.
MAMA: No? What's the matter?
BENEATHA: Mama, George is a fool—honest. [*She rises.*]

MAMA: [*Hustling around unloading the packages she has entered with. She stops.*] Is he, baby?

BENEATHA: Yes.

[BENEATHA *makes up* TRAVIS' *bed as she talks.*]

MAMA: You sure?

BENEATHA: Yes.

MAMA: Well—I guess you better not waste your time with no fools.

[BENEATHA *looks up at her mother, watching her put groceries in the refrigerator. Finally she gathers up her things and starts into the bedroom. At the door she stops and looks back at her mother.*]

BENEATHA: Mama—

MAMA: Yes, baby—

BENEATHA: Thank you.

MAMA: For what?

BENEATHA: For understanding me this time.

[*She exits quickly and the mother stands, smiling a little, looking at the place where* BENEATHA *just stood.* RUTH *enters.*]

RUTH: Now don't you fool with any of this stuff, Lena—

MAMA: Oh, I just thought I'd sort a few things out.

[*The phone rings.* RUTH *answers.*]

RUTH: [*at the phone*] Hello—Just a minute. [*goes to door*] Walter, it's Mrs. Arnold. [*Waits. Goes back to the phone. Tense*] Hello. Yes, this is his wife speaking . . . He's lying down now. Yes . . . well, he'll be in tomorrow. He's been very sick. Yes—I know we should have called, but we were so sure he'd be able to come in today. Yes—yes, I'm very sorry. Yes . . . Thank you very much. [*She hangs up.* WALTER *is standing in the doorway of the bedroom behind her.*] That was Mrs. Arnold.

WALTER: [*indifferently*] Was it?

RUTH: She said if you don't come in tomorrow that they are getting a new man . . .

WALTER: Ain't that sad—ain't that crying sad.

RUTH: She said Mr. Arnold has had to take a cab for three days . . . Walter, you ain't been to work for three days! [*This is a revelation to her.*] Where you been, Walter Lee Younger? [WALTER *looks at her and starts to laugh.*] You're going to lose your job.

WALTER: That's right . . .

RUTH: Oh, Walter, and with your mother working like a dog every day—

WALTER: That's sad too—Everything is sad.

MAMA: What you been doing for these three days, son?

WALTER: Mama—you don't know all the things a man what got leisure can find to do in this city . . . What's this—Friday night? Well—Wednesday I borrowed Willy Harris' car and I went for a drive . . . just me and myself and I drove and drove . . . Way out . . . way past South Chicago, and I parked the car and I sat and looked at the steel mills all day long. I just sat in the car and looked at them big black chimneys for hours. Then I drove back and I went to the Green Hat. [*pause*] And Thursday—Thursday I borrowed the car again and I got in it and I pointed it the other way and I drove the other way—for hours—way, way up to Wisconsin, and I looked at the farms, O just drove and looked at the farms. Then I drove back and I went to the Green Hat. [*pause*] And today—today I didn't get the car. Today I just walked. All over the Southside. And I looked at the Negroes and they looked at me and finally I just sat down on the curb at Thirty-ninth and South Parkway and I just sat there and watched the Negroes go by. And then I went to the Green Hat. You all sad? You all depressed? And you know where I am going right now—

[RUTH *goes out quietly.*]

MAMA: Oh, Big Walter, is this the harvest of our days?

WALTER: You know what I like about the Green Hat? [*He turns the radio on and a steamy, deep blues pours into the room.*] I like this little cat they got there who blows a sax . . . He blows. He talks to me. He ain't but 'bout five feet tall and he's got a conked head and his eyes is always closed and he's all music—

MAMA: [*rising and getting some papers out of her handbag*] Walter—

WALTER: And there's this other guy who plays the piano . . . and they got a sound. I mean they can work on some music . . . They got the best little combo in the world in the Green Hat . . . You can just sit there and drink and listen to them three men play and you realize that don't nothing matter worth a damn, but just being there—

MAMA: I've helped do it to you, haven't I, son? Walter, I been wrong.

WALTER: Naw—you ain't never been wrong about nothing, Mama.

MAMA: Listen to me, now. I say I been wrong, son. That I been doing to you what the rest of the world been doing to you. [*She stops and he looks up slowly at her and she meets his eyes pleadingly.*] Walter—what you ain't never understood is that I ain't got nothing, don't own nothing, ain't never really wanted nothing that wasn't for you. There ain't nothing as precious to me . . . There ain't nothing worth holding on to, money, dreams, nothing else—if it means—if it means it's going to destroy my boy. [*She puts her papers in front of him and he watches her without speaking or moving.*] I paid the man thirty-five hundred dollars down on the house. That leaves sixty-five hundred dollars. Monday morning I want you to take this money and take three thousand dollars and put it in a savings accout for Beneatha's medical schooling. The rest you put in a checking account—with your name on it. and from now on any penny that come out of it or that go in it is for you to look after. For you to decide. [*She drops her hands a little helplessly.*] It ain't much, but it's all I got in the world and I'm putting it in your hands. I'm telling you to be the head of this family from now on like you supposed to be.

WALTER: [*stares at the money*] You trust me like that, Mama?

MAMA: I ain't never stop trusting you. Like I ain't never stop loving you.

[*She goes out, and* WALTER *sits looking at the money on the table as the music continues in its idiom, he gets up, and, in mingled joy and desperation, picks up the money. At the same moment,* TRAVIS *enters for bed.*]

TRAVIS: What's the matter, Daddy? You drunk?

WALTER: [*sweetly, more sweetly than we have ever known him*] No, Daddy ain't drunk. Daddy ain't going to never be drunk again. . . .

TRAVIS: Well, good night, Daddy.

[*The* FATHER *has come from behind the couch and leans over, embracing his son.*]

WALTER: Son, I feel like talking to you tonight.

TRAVIS: About what?

WALTER: Oh, about a lot of things. About you and what kind of man you going to be when you grow up. . . . Son—son, what do you want to be when you grow up?

TRAVIS: A bus driver.

WALTER: [*laughing a little*] A what? Man, that ain't nothing to want to be!

TRAVIS: Why not?

WALTER: 'Cause, man—it ain't big enough—you know what I mean.

TRAVIS: I don't know then. I can't make up my mind. Sometimes Mama asks me that too. And sometimes when I tell her I just want to be like you—she says she don't want me to be like that and sometimes she says she does. . . .

WALTER: [*gathering him up in his arms*] You know what, Travis? In seven years you going to be seventeen years old. And things is going to be very different with us in seven years, Travis. . . . One day when you are seventeen I'll come home—home from my office downtown somewhere—

TRAVIS: You don't work in no office, Daddy.

WALTER: No—but after tonight. After what your daddy gonna do tonight, there's going to be offices—a whole lot of offices. . . .

TRAVIS: What you gonna do tonight, Daddy?

WALTER: You wouldn't understand yet, son, but your daddy's gonna make a transaction . . . a business transaction that's going to change our lives. . . . That's how come one day when you 'bout seventeen years old I'll come home and I'll be pretty tired, you know what I mean, after a day of conferences and secretaries getting things wrong the way they do . . . 'cause an executive's life is hell, man—[*The more he talks the farther away he gets.*] And I'll pull the car up on the driveway . . . just a plain black Chrysler, I think, with white walls—no—black tires. More elegant. Rich people don't have to be flashy . . . though I'll have to get something a little sportier for Ruth—maybe a Cadillac convertible to do her shopping in. . . . And I'll come up the steps to the house and the gardener will be clipping away at the hedges and he'll say, "Good evening, Mr. Younger." And I'll say, "Hello, Jefferson, how are you this evening?" And I'll go inside and Ruth will come downstairs and meet me at the door and we'll kiss each other and she'll take my arm and we'll go up to your room to see you sitting on the floor with the catalogues of all the great schools in America around you . . . All the great schools in the world! And—and I'll say, all right son—it's your seventeenth birthday, what is it you've decided? . . . Just tell me where you want to go to school and you'll go. Just tell me, what is it you want to be—and you'll *be* it. . . . Whatever you want to be—Yessir! [*He holds his arms open for* TRAVIS.] You just name it son . . . [TRAVIS *leaps into them.*] and I hand you the world!

[WALTER'S *voice has risen in pitch and hysterical promise and on the last line he lifts* TRAVIS *high.*]

SCENE III—— *Time: Saturday, moving day, one week later.*
Before the curtain rises. RUTH'S *voice, a strident, dramatic church alto, cuts through the silence.*

It is, in the darkness, a triumphant surge, a penetrating statement of expectation: "Oh, Lord, I don't feel no ways tired! Children, oh, glory hallelujah!"
As the curtain rises we see that RUTH *is alone in the living room, finishing up the family's packing. It is moving day. She is nailing crates and tying cartons.* BENEATHA *enters, carrying a guitar case, and watches her exuberant sister-in-law.*

RUTH: Hey!
BENEATHA: [*putting away the case*] Hi.
RUTH: [*pointing at a package*] Honey—look in that package there and see what I found on sale this morning at the South Center. [RUTH *gets up and moves to the package and draws out some curtains*] Lookahere—hand-turned hems!
BENEATHA: How do you know the window size out there?
RUTH: [*who hadn't thought of that*] Oh—Well, they bound to fit something in the whole house. Anyhow, they was too good a bargain to pass up. [RUTH *slaps her head, suddenly remembering something.*] Oh, Bennie—I meant to put a special note on that carton over there. That's your mama's good china and she wants 'em to be very careful with it.
BENEATHA: I'll do it.
[BENEATHA *finds a piece of paper and starts to draw large letters on it.*]
RUTH: You know what I'm going to do soon as I get in that new house?
BENEATHA: What?
RUTH: Honey—I'm going to run me a tub of water up to here . . . [*with her fingers practically up to her nostrils*] And I'm going to get in it—and I am going to sit . . . and sit . . . and sit in that hot water and the first person who knocks to tell *me* to hurry up and come out—
BENEATHA: Gets shot at sunrise.
RUTH: [*laughing happily*] You said it, sister! [*noticing how large* BENEATHA *is absent-mindedly making the note*] Honey, they ain't going to read that from no airplane.
BENEATHA: [*laughing herself*] I guess I always think things have more emphasis if they are big, somehow.
RUTH: [*looking up at her and smiling*] You and your brother seem to have that as a philosophy of life. Lord, that man—done changed so 'round here. You know—you know what we did last night? Me and Walter Lee?
BENEATHA: What?
RUTH: [*smiling to herself*] We went to the movies. [*looking at* BENEATHA *to see if she understands*] We went to the movies. You know the last time me and Walter went to the movies together?
BENEATHA: No.
RUTH: Me neither. That's how long it been. [*smiling again*] But we went last

night. The picture wasn't much good, but that didn't seem to matter. We
went—and we held hands.

BENEATHA: Oh, Lord!

RUTH: We held hands—and you know what.

BENEATHA: What?

RUTH: When we come out of the show it was late and dark and all the stores and
things was closed up . . . and it was kind of chilly and there wasn't many
people on the streets . . . and we was still holding hands, me and Walter.

BENEATHA: You're killing me.

[WALTER *enters with a large package. His happiness is deep in him; he
cannot keep still with his new-found exuberance. He is singing and
wiggling and snapping his fingers. He puts his package in a corner and
puts a phonograph record, which he has brought in with him, on the
record player. As the music comes up he dances over to* RUTH *and tries
to get her to dance with him. She gives in at last to his raunchiness and
in a fit of giggling allows herself to be drawn into his mood and together
they deliberately burlesque an old social dance of their youth.*]

BENEATHA: [*regarding them a long time as they dance, then drawing in her breath
for a deeply exaggerated comment which she does not particularly mean*]
Talk about—olddddddddddd-fashioneddddddd—Negroes!

WALTER: [*stopping momentarily*] What kind of Negroes?

[*He says this in fun. He is not angry with her today, nor with anyone.
He starts to dance with his wife again.*]

BENEATHA: Old-fashioned.

WALTER: [*as he dances with* RUTH] You know, when these New Negroes have
their convention—[*pointing at his sister*]—that is going to be the chairman
of the Committee on Unending Agitation. [*He goes on dancing, then
stops.*] Race, race, race! . . . Girl, I do believe you are the first person in the
history of the entire human race to successfully brainwash yourself.
[BENEATHA *breaks up and he goes on dancing. He stops again, enjoying his
tease.*] Damn, even the N double A C P takes a holiday sometimes!
[BENEATHA *and* RUTH *laugh. He dances with* RUTH *some more and starts to
laugh and stops and pantomimes someone over an operating table.*] I can
just see that chick someday looking down at some poor cat on an operating
table before she starts to slice him, saying . . . [*pulling his sleeves back
maliciously*] "By the way, what are your views on civil rights down there?
. . ."

[*He laughs at her again and starts to dance happily. The bell sounds.*]

BENEATHA: Sticks and stones may break my bones but . . . words will never hurt
me!

[BENEATHA *goes to the door and opens it as* WALTER *and* RUTH *go on
with the clowning.* BENEATHA *is somewhat surprised to see a quiet-
looking middle-aged white man in a business suit holding his hat and a
briefcase in his hand and consulting a small piece of paper.*]

MAN: Uh—how do you do, miss. I am looking for a Mrs.—[*he looks at the slip of
paper.*] Mrs. Lena Younger?

BENEATHA: [*smoothing her hair with slight embarrassment*] Oh—yes, that's my

mother. Excuse me [*She closes the door and turns to quiet the other two.*]
Ruth! Brother! Somebody's here. [*Then she opens the door. The man casts a
curious quick glance at all of them.*] Uh—come in please.

MAN: [*coming in*] Thank you.

BENEATHA: My mother isn't here now. Is it business?

MAN: Yes . . . well, of a sort.

WALTER: [*freely, the Man of the House*] Have a seat. I'm Mrs. Younger's son. I
look after most of her business matters.

       [RUTH *and* BENEATHA *exchange amused glances.*]

MAN: [*regarding* WALTER, *and sitting*] Well—My name is Karl Lindner . . .

WALTER: [*stretching out his hand*] Walter Younger. This is my wife—[RUTH
nods *politely.*]—and my sister.

LINDNER: How do you do.

WALTER: [*amiably, as he sits himself easily on a chair, leaning with interest
forward on his knees and looking expectantly into the newcomer's face*] What
can we do for you, Mr. Lindner!

LINDNER: [*some minor shuffling of the hat and briefcase on his knees*] Well—I am
a representative of the Clybourne Park Improvement Association—

WALTER: [*pointing*] Why don't you sit your things on the floor?

LINDNER: Oh—yes. Thank you. [*He slides the briefcase and hat under the chair.*]
And as I was saying—I am from the Clybourne Park Improvement Association and we have had it brought to our attention at the last meeting that you
people—or at least your mother—has bought a piece of residential property
at—[*He digs for the slip of paper again.*]—four o six Clybourne Street . . .

WALTER: That's right. Care for something to drink? Ruth, get Mr. Lindner a
beer.

LINDNER: [*upset for some reason*] Oh—no, really. I mean thank you very much,
but no thank you.

RUTH: [*innocently*] Some coffee?

LINDNER: Thank you, nothing at all.

      [BENEATHA *is watching the man carefully.*]

LINDNER: Well, I don't know how much you folks know about our organization.
[*He is a gentle man; thoughtful and somewhat labored in his manner.*] It is
one of these community organizations set up to look after—oh, you know,
things like block upkeep and special projects and we also have what we call
our New Neighbors Orientation Committee . . .

BENEATHA: [*drily*] Yes—and what do they do?

LINDNER: [*turning a little to her and then returning the main force to* WALTER]
Well—it's what you might call a sort of welcoming committee, I guess. I
mean they, we, I'm the chairman of the committee—go around and see the
new people who move into the neighborhood and sort of give them the
lowdown on the way we do things out in Clybourne Park.

BENEATHA: [*with appreciation of the two meanings, which escape* RUTH *and* WAL-
TER] Uh-huh.

LINDNER: And we also have the category of what the association calls—[*he looks
elsewhere.*]—uh—special community problems . . .

BENEATHA: Yes—and what are some of those?

WALTER: Girl, let the man talk.

LINDNER: [*with understated relief*] Thank you. I would sort of like to explain this thing in my own way. I mean I want to explain to you in a certain way.

WALTER: Go ahead.

LINDNER: Yes. Well. I'm going to try to get right to the point. I'm sure we'll all appreciate that in the long run.

BENEATHA: Yes.

WALTER: Be still now!

LINDNER: Well—

RUTH: [*still innocently*] Would you like another chair—you don't look comfortable.

LINDNER: [*more frustrated than annoyed*] No, thank you very much. Please. Well—to get right to the point I—[*a great breath, and he is off at last*] I am sure you people must be aware of some of the incidents which have happened in various parts of the city when colored people have moved into certain areas—[BENEATHA *exhales heavily and starts tossing a piece of fruit up and down in the air.*] Well—because we have what I think is going to be a unique type of organization in American community life—not only do we deplore that kind of thing—but we are trying to do something about it. [BENEATHA *stops tossing and turns with a new and quizzical interest to the man.*] We feel—[*gaining confidence in his mission because of the interest in the faces of the people he is talking to*]—we feel that most of the trouble in this world, when you come right down to it—[*He hits his knee for emphasis.*]—most of the trouble exists because people just don't sit down and talk to each other.

RUTH: [*nodding as she might in church, pleased with the remark*] You can say that again, mister.

LINDNER: [*more encouraged by such affirmation*] That we don't try hard enough in this world to understand the other fellow's problem. The other guy's point of view.

RUTH: Now that's right.

[BENEATHA *and* WALTER *merely watch and listen with genuine interest.*]

LINDNER: Yes—that's the way we feel out in Clybourne Park. And that's why I was elected to come here this afternoon and talk to you people. Friendly like, you know, the way people should talk to each other and see if we couldn't find some way to work this thing out. As I say, the whole business is a matter of *caring* about the other fellow. Anybody can see that you are a nice family of folks, hard working and honest I'm sure. [BENEATHA *frowns slightly, quizzically, her head tilted regarding him.*] Today everbody knows what it means to be on the outside of *something.* And of course, there is always somebody who is out to take advantage of people who don't always understand.

WALTER: What do you mean?

LINDNER: Well—you see our community is made up of people who've worked hard as the dickens for years to build up that little community. They're not rich and fancy people; just hard-working, honest people who don't really have much but those little homes and a dream of the kind of community they want to raise their children in. Now, I don't say we are perfect and there is a lot wrong in some of the things they want. But you've got to admit that a man, right or wrong, has the right to want to have the neighborhood he lives in a certain kind of way. And at the moment the overwhelming majority of our people out there feel that people get along better, take more of a common interest in the life of the community, when they share a common background. I want you to believe me when I tell you that race prejudice simply doesn't enter into it. It is a matter of the people of Clybourne Park believing, rightly or wrongly, as I say, that for the happiness of all concerned that our Negro families are happier when they live in their *own* communities.

BENEATHA: [*with a grand and bitter gesture*] This, friends, is the Welcoming Committee!

WALTER: [*dumfounded, looking at* LINDNER] Is this what you came marching all the way over here to tell us?

LINDNER: Well, now we've been having a fine conversation. I hope you'll hear me all the way through.

WALTER: [*tightly*] Go ahead, man.

LINDNER: You see—in the face of all things I have said, we are prepared to make your family a very generous offer . . .

BENEATHA: Thirty pieces and not a coin less!

WALTER: Yeah?

LINDNER: [*putting on his glasses and drawing a form out of the briefcase*] Our association is prepared, through the collective effort of our people, to buy the house from you at a financial gain to your family.

RUTH: Lord have mercy, ain't this the living gall!

WALTER: All right, you through?

LINDNER: Well, I want to give you the exact terms of the financial arrangement—

WALTER: We don't want to hear no exact terms of no arrangements. I want to know if you got any more to tell us 'bout getting together?

LINDNER: [*taking off his glasses*] Well—I don't suppose that you feel . . .

WALTER: Never mind how I feel—you got any more to say 'bout how people ought to sit down and talk to each other? . . . Get out of my house, man.
[*He turns his back and walks to the door.*]

LINDNER: [*looking around at the hostile faces and reaching and assembling his hat and briefcase*] Well—I don't understand why you people are reacting this way. What do you think you are going to gain by moving into a neighborhood where you just aren't wanted and where some elements—well—people can get awful worked up when they feel that their whole way of life and everything they've ever worked for is threatened.

WALTER: Get out.

LINDNER: [*at the door, holding a small card*] Well—I'm sorry it went like this.

WALTER: Get out.

LINDNER: [*almost sadly regarding* WALTER] You just can't force people to change their hearts, son.
[*He turns and put his card on a table and exits.* WALTER *pushes the*

door to with stinging hatred, and stands looking at it. RUTH *just sits and* BENEATHA *just stands. They say nothing.* MAMA *and* TRAVIS *enter.*]

MAMA: Well—this all the packing got done since I left out of here this morning. I testify before God that my children got all the energy of the dead. What time the moving men due?

BENEATHA: Four o'clock. You had a caller, Mama.
[*She is smiling, teasingly.*]

MAMA: Sure enough—who?

BENEATHA: [*Her arms folded saucily*] The Welcoming Committee.
[WALTER *and* RUTH *giggle.*]

MAMA: [*innocently*] Who?

BENEATHA: The Welcoming Committee. They said they're sure going to be glad to see you when you get there.

WALTER: [*devilishly*] Yeah, they said they can't hardly wait to see your face.
[*laughter*]

MAMA: [*sensing their facetiousness*] What's the matter with you all?

WALTER: Ain't nothing the matter with us. We just telling you 'bout the gentleman who came to see you this afternoon. From the Clybourne Park Improvement Association.

MAMA: What he want?

RUTH: [*in the same mood as* BENEATHA *and* WALTER] To welcome you, honey.

WALTER: He said they can't hardly wait. He said the one thing they don't have, that they just *dying* to have out there is a fine family of colored people! [*to* RUTH *and* BENEATH] Ain't that right!

RUTH *and* BENEATHA : [*mockingly*] Yeah! He left his card in case—
[*They indicate the card, and* MAMA *picks it up and throws it on the floor—understanding and looking off as she draws her chair up to the table on which she has put her plant and some sticks and some cord.*]

MAMA: Father, give us strength. [*knowingly—and without fun*] Did he threaten us?

BENEATHA: Oh—Mama—they don't do it like that any more. He talked Brotherhood. He said everybody ought to learn how to sit down and hate each other with good Christian fellowship.
[*She and* WALTER *shakes hands to ridicule the remark.*]

MAMA: [*sadly*] Lord, protect us . . .

RUTH: You should hear the money those folks raised to buy the house from us. All' we paid and then some.

BENEATHA: What they think we going to do—eat 'em?

RUTH: No, honey, marry 'em.

MAMA: [*shaking her head*] Lord, Lord, Lord . . .

RUTH: Well—that's the way the crackers crumble. Joke.

BENEATHA: [*laughingly noticing what her mother is doing*] Mama, what are you doing?

MAMA: Fixing my plant so it won't get hurt none on the way.

BENEATHA: Mama, you going to take *that* to the new house?

MAMA: Un-huh—

BENEATHA: That raggedy-looking old thing?

MAMA: [*stopping and looking at her*] It expresses me.

RUTH: [*with delight, to* BENEATHA] So there, Miss Thing!

> [WALTER *comes to* MAMA *suddenly and bends down behind her and squeezes her in his arms with all his strength. She is overwhelmed by the suddenness of it and, though delighted, her manner is like that of* RUTH *and* TRAVIS.]

MAMA: Look out now, boy! You make me mess up my thing here!

WALTER: [*His face lit, he slips down on his knees beside her, his arms still about her.*] Mama . . . you know what it means to climb up in the chariot?

MAMA: [*gruffly, very happy*] Get on away from me now . . .

RUTH: [*near the gift-wrapped package, trying to catch* WALTER'S *eye*] Psst—

WALTER: What the old song say, Mama . . .

RUTH: Walter—Now?

> [*She is pointing at the package.*]

WALTER: [*Speaking the lines, sweetly, playfully, in his mother's face*]
> I got wings . . . you got wings . . .
> All God's Children got wings . . .

MAMA: Boy—get out of my face and do some work . . .

WALTER: When I get to heaven gonna put on my wings,
> Gonna fly all over God's heaven . . .

BENEATHA: [*teasingly, from across the room*] Everybody talking 'bout heaven ain't going there!

WALTER: [*to* RUTH, *who is carrying the box across to them*] I don't know, you think we ought to give her that . . . Seems to me she ain't been very appreciative around here.

MAMA: [*eyeing the box, which is obviously a gift*] What is that?

WALTER: [*taking it from* RUTH *and putting it on the table in front of* MAMA] Well—what do you think? Should we give it to her?

RUTH: Oh—she was pretty good today.

MAMA: I'll good you—

> [*She turns her eyes to the box again.*]

BENEATHA: Open it, Mama.

> [*She stands up, looks at it, turns and looks at all of them, and then presses her hands together and does not open the package.*]

WALTER: [*sweetly*] Open it, Mama. It's for you. [MAMA *looks in his eyes. It is the first present in her life without its being Christmas. Slowly she opens her package and lifts out, one by one, a brand-new sparkling set of gardening tools.* WALTER *continues, prodding.*] Ruth made up the note—read it . . .

MAMA: [*picking up the card and adjusting her glasses*] "To our own Mrs. Miniver—Love from Brother, Ruth and Beneatha." Ain't that lovely . . .

TRAVIS: [*tugging at his father's sleeve*] Daddy, can I give her mine now?

WALTER: All right son. [TRAVIS *flies to get his gift.*] Travis didn't want to go in with the rest of us, Mama. He got his own. [*somewhat amused*] We don't know what it is . . .

TRAVIS: [*racing back in the room with a large hatbox and putting it in front of his grandmother*] Here!

MAMA: Lord have mercy, baby. You done gone and bought your grandmother a hat?

TRAVIS: [*very proud*] Open it!

> [*She does and lifts out an elaborate, but very elaborate, wide garden-*
> *ing hat, and all the adults break up at the sight of it.*]

RUTH: Travis, honey, what is that?

TRAVIS: [*who thinks it is beautiful and appropriate*] It's a gardening hat! Like the
ladies always have on in the magazines when they work in their gardens.

BENEATHA: [*giggling fiercely*] Travis—we were trying to make Mama Mrs.
Miniver—not Scarlett O'Hara!

MAMA: [*indignantly*] What's the matter with you all! This here is a beautiful hat!
[*absurdly*] I always wanted me one just like it!

> [*She pops it on her head to prove it to her grandson, and the hat is*
> *ludicrous and considerably oversized.*]

RUTH: Hot dog! Go, Mama!

WALTER: [*doubled over with laughter*] I'm sorry, Mama—but you look like you
ready to go out and chop you some cotton sure enough!

> [*They all laugh except* MAMA, *out of deference to* TRAVIS' *feelings.*]

MAMA: [*gathering the boy up to her*] Bless your heart—this is the prettiest hat I
ever owned— [WALTER, RUTH *and* BENEATHA *chime in—noisily, festively and*
insincerely congratulating TRAVIS *on his gift.*] What are we all standing here
for? We ain't finished packin' yet. Bennie, you ain't packed one book.

> [*The bell rings.*]

BENEATHA: That couldn't be the movers . . . it's not hardly two good yet—

> [BENEATHA *goes into her room,* MAMA *starts for door.*]

WALTER: [*turning, stiffening*] Wait—wait—I'll get it.

> [*He stands and looks at the door.*]

MAMA: You expecting company, son?

WALTER: [*just looking at the door*] Yeah—yeah . . .

> [MAMA *looks at* RUTH, *and they exchange innocent and unfrightened*
> *glances.*]

MAMA: [*not understanding*] Well, let them in, son.

BENEATHA: [*from her room*] We need some more string.

MAMA: Travis—you run to the hardware and get me some string cord.

> [MAMA *goes out and* WALTER *turns and looks at* RUTH. TRAVIS *goes to a*
> *dish for money.*]

RUTH: Why don't you answer the door, man?

WALTER: [*suddenly bounding across the floor to her*] 'Cause sometimes it hard to
let the future begin! [*stooping down in her face*]

> I got wings! You got wings!
> All God's children got wings!

> [*He crosses to the door and throws it open. Standing there is a very*
> *slight little man in a not too prosperous business suit and with haunted*
> *frightened eyes and a hat pulled down tightly, brim up, around his*
> *forehead.*
> TRAVIS *passes between the men and exits.* WALTER *leans deep in the*
> *man's face, still in his jubilance*]

> When I get to heaven gonna put on my wings,
> Gonna fly all over God's heaven . . .

> [*The little man just stares at him*]

> Heaven—

[*Suddenly he stops and looks past the little man into the empty hall-way.*] Where's Willy, man?

BOBO: He ain't with me.

WALTER: [*not disturbed*] Oh—come on in. You know my wife.

BOBO: [*dumbly, taking off his hat*] Yes—h'you, Miss Ruth.

RUTH: [*quietly, a mood apart from her husband already, seeing* BOBO] Hello, Bobo.

WALTER: You right on time today . . . Right on time. That's the way! [*He slaps* BOBO *on his back.*] Sit down . . . lemme hear.

[RUTH *stands stiffly and quietly in back of them, as though somehow she senses death, her eyes fixed on her husband.*]

BOBO: [*his frightened eyes on the floor, his hat in his hands*] Could I please get a drink of water, before I tell you about it, Walter Lee?

[WALTER *does not take his eyes off the man.* RUTH *goes blindly to the tap and gets a glass of water and brings it to* BOBO.]

WALTER: There ain't nothing wrong, is there?

BOBO: Lemme tell you—

WALTER: Man—didn't nothing go wrong?

BOBO: Lemme tell you—Walter Lee. [*looking at* RUTH *and talking to her more than to* WALTER] You know how it was. I got to tell you how it was. I mean first I got to tell you how it was all the way . . . I mean about the money I put in, Walter Lee . . .

WALTER: [*with taut agitation now*] What about the money you put in?

BOBO: Well—it wasn't much as we told you—me and Willy—[*He stops.*] I'm sorry, Walter. I got a bad feeling about it. I got a real bad feeling about it . . .

WALTER: Man, what you telling me about all this for? . . . Tell me what happened in Springfield . . .

BOBO: Springfield.

RUTH: [*like a dead woman*] What was supposed to happen in Springfield?

BOBO: [*to her*] This deal that me and Walter went into with Willy—Me and Willy was going to go down to Springfield and spread some money 'round so's we wouldn't have to wait so long for the liquor license . . . That's what we were going to do. Everybody said that was the way you had to do, you understand, Miss Ruth?

WALTER: Man—what happened down there?

BOBO: [*a pitiful man, near tears*] I'm trying to tell you, Walter.

WALTER: [*screaming at him suddenly*] THEN TELL ME, GODDAMMIT . . . WHAT'S THE MATTER WITH YOU?

BOBO: Man . . . I didn't go to no Springfield, yesterday.

WALTER: [*halted, life hanging in the moment*] Why not?

BOBO: [*the long way, the hard way to tell*] 'Cause I didn't have no reasons to . . .

WALTER: Man, what are you talking about!

BOBO: I'm talking about the fact that when I got to the train station yesterday morning—eight o'clock like we planned . . . Man—*Willy didn't never show up.*

WALTER: Why . . . where was he . . . where is he?

BOBO: That's what I'm trying to tell you . . . I don't know . . . I waited six hours . . . I called his house . . . and I waited . . . six hours . . . I waited in that train station six hours . . . [*breaking into tears*] That was all the extra money I had in the world . . . [*looking up at* WALTER *with the tears running down his face*] Man, Willy is gone.

WALTER: Gone, what you mean Willy is gone? Gone where? You mean he went by himself. You mean he went off to Springfield by himself—to take care of getting the license—[*turns and looks anxiously at* RUTH] You mean maybe he didn't want too many people in on the business down there? [*looks to* RUTH *again, as before*] You know Willy got his own ways. [*looks back to* BOBO] Maybe you was late yesterday and he just went on down there without you. Maybe—maybe—he's been callin' you at home tryin' to tell you what happened or something. Maybe—maybe—he just got sick. He's somewhere—he's got to be somewhere. We just got to find him—me and you got to find him. [*grabs* BOBO *senselessly by the collar and starts to shake him*] We got to!

BOBO: [*in sudden angry, frightened agony*] What's the matter with you, Walter! When a cat take off with your money he don't leave you no maps!

WALTER: [*turning madly, as though he is looking for* WILLY *in the very room*] Willy! . . . Willy . . . don't do it . . . Please don't do it . . . Man, not with that money . . . Man, please, not with that money . . . Oh, God . . . Don't let it be true . . . [*He is wandering around, crying out for* WILLY *and looking for him or perhaps for help from God.*] Man . . . I trusted you . . . Man, I put my life in your hands . . . [*He starts to crumple down on the floor as* RUTH *just covers her face in horror.* MAMA *opens the door and comes into the room, with* BENEATHA *behind her.*] Man . . . [*He starts to pound the floor with his fists, sobbing wildly.*] That money is made out of my father's flesh . . .

BOBO: [*standing over him helplessly*] I'm sorry, Walter . . . [*Only* WALTER'S *sobs reply.* BOBO *puts on his hat.*] I had my life staked on this deal, too . . . [*He exits.*]

MAMA: [*to* WALTER] Son—[*She goes to him, bends down to him, talks to his bent head.*] Son . . . Is it gone? Son, I gave you sixty-five hundred dollars. Is it gone? All of it? Beneatha's money too?

WALTER: [*lifting his head slowly*] Mama . . . I never . . . went to the bank at all . . .

MAMA: [*not wanting to believe him*] You mean . . . your sister's school money . . . you used that too . . . Walter? . . .

WALTER: Yessss! . . . All of it . . . It's all gone . . .

[*There is total silence.* RUTH *stands with her face covered with her hands;* BENEATHA *leans forlornly against a wall, fingering a piece of red ribbon from the mother's gift.* MAMA *stops and looks at her son without recognition and then, quite without thinking about it, starts to beat him senselessly in the face.* BENEATHA *goes to them and stops it.*]

BENEATHA: Mama!

[MAMA *stops and looks at both of her children and rises slowly and wanders vaguely, aimlessly away from them.*]

MAMA: I seen . . . him . . . night after night . . . come in . . . and look at that rug . . . and then look at me . . . the red showing in his eyes . . . the veins moving in his head . . . I seen him grow thin and old before he was forty

. . . working and working and working like somebody's old horse . . .
killing himself . . . and you—you give it all away in a day . . .

BENEATHA: Mama—

MAMA: Oh, God . . . [*She looks up to Him.*] Look down here—and show me the
strength.

BENEATHA: Mama—

MAMA: [*folding over*] Strength . . .

BENEATHA: [*plaintively*] Mama . . .

MAMA: Strength!

ACT III

An hour later.
At curtain, there is a sullen light of gloom in the living room, gray light not
unlike that which began the first scene of Act One. At left we can see WALTER
within his room, alone with himself. He is stretched out on the bed, his shirt
out and open, his arms under his head. He does not smoke, he does not cry out,
he merely lies there, looking up at the ceiling, much as if he were alone in the
world.
In the living room BENEATHA *sits at the table, still surrounded by the now*
almost ominous packing crates. She sits looking off. We feel that this is a mood
struck perhaps an hour before, and it lingers now, full of the empty sound of
profound disappointment. We see on a line from her brother's bedroom the
sameness of their attitudes. Presently the bell rings and BENEATHA *rises without*
ambition or interest in answering. It is ASAGAI, *smiling broadly, striding into*
the room with energy and happy expectation and conversation.

ASAGAI: I came over . . . I had some free time. I thought I might help with the
packing. Ah, I like the look of packing crates! A household in preparation
for a journey! It depresses some people , . . but for me . . . it is another
feeling. Something full of the flow of life, do you understand? Movement,
progress . . . It makes me think of Africa.

BENEATHA: Africa!

ASAGAI: What kind of a mood is this? Have I told you how deeply you move me?

BENEATHA: He gave away the money, Asagai . . .

ASAGAI: Who gave away what money?

BENEATHA: The insurance money. My brother gave it away.

ASAGAI: Gave it away?

BENEATHA: He made an investment! With a man even Travis wouldn't have
trusted.

ASAGAI: And it's gone?

BENEATHA: Gone!

ASAGAI: I'm very sorry . . . And you, now?

BENEATHA: Me? . . . Me? . . . Me I'm nothing . . . Me. When I was very small
. . . we used to take our sleds out in the wintertime and the only hills we
had were the ice-covered stone steps of some houses down the street. And

we used to fill them in with snow and make them smooth and slide down them all day . . . and it was very dangerous you know . . . far too steep . . . and sure enough one day a kid named Rufus came down too fast and hit the sidewalk . . . and we saw his face just split open right there in front of us . . . And I remember standing there looking at his bloody open face thinking that was the end of Rufus. But the ambulance came and they took him to the hospital and they fixed the broken bones and they sewed it all up . . . and the next time I saw Rufus he just had a little line down the middle of his face . . . I never got over that . . .

> [WALTER *sits up, listening on the bed. Throughout this scene it is important that we feel his reaction at all times, that he visibly respond to the words of his sister and* ASAGAI.]

ASAGAI: What?

BENEATHA: That that was what one person could do for another, fix him up—sew up the problem, make him all right again. That was the most marvelous thing in the world . . . I wanted to do that. I always thought it was the one concrete thing in the world that a human being could do. Fix up the sick, you know—and make them whole again. This was truly being God . . .

ASAGAI: You wanted to be God?

BENEATHA: No—I wanted to cure. It used to be so important to me. I wanted to cure. It used to matter. I used to care. I mean about people and how their bodies hurt . . .

ASAGAI: And you've stopped caring?

BENEATHA: Yes—I think so.

ASAGAI: Why?

> [WALTER *rises, goes to the door of his room and is about to open it, then stops and stands listening, leaning on the door jamb.*]

BENEATHA: Because it doesn't seem deep enough, close enough to what ails mankind—I mean this thing of sewing up bodies or administering drugs. Don't you understand? It was a child's reaction to the world. I thought that doctors had the secret to all the hurts. . . . That's the way a child sees things—or an idealist.

ASAGAI: Children see things very well sometimes—and idealists even better.

BENEATHA: I know that's what you think. Because you are still where I left off—you still care. This is what you see for the world, for Africa. You with the dreams of the future will patch up all Africa—you are going to cure the Great Sore of colonialism with Independence——

ASAGAI: Yes!

BENEATHA: Yes—and you think that one word is the pencillin of the human spirit: "Independence!" But then what?

ASAGAI: That will be the problem for another time. First we must get there.

BENEATHA: And where does it end?

ASAGAI: End? Who even spoke of an end? To life? To living?

BENEATHA: An end to misery!

ASAGAI: [*smiling*] You sound like a French intellectual.

BENEATHA: No! I sound like a human being who just had her future taken right out of her hands! While I was sleeping in my bed in there, things were happening in this world that directly concerned me—and nobody asked me, consulted me—they just went out and did things—and changed my life. Don't you see there isn't any real progress, Asagai, there is only one large circle that we march in, around and around, each of us with our own little picture—in front of us—our own little mirage that we think is the future.

ASAGAI: That is the mistake.

BENEATHA: What?

ASAGAI: What you just said—about the circle. It isn't a circle—it is simply a long line—as in geometry, you know, one that reaches into infinity. And because we cannot see the end—we also cannot see how it changes. And it is very odd but those who see the changes are called "idealists"—and those who cannot, or refuse to think, they are the "realists." It is very strange, and amusing too, I think.

BENEATHA: You—you are almost religious.

ASAGAI: Yes . . . I think I have the religion of doing what is necessary in the world—and of worshipping man—because he is so marvelous, you see.

BENEATHA: Man is foul! And the human race deserves its misery!

ASAGAI: You see: *you* have become the religious one in the old sense. Already, and after such a small defeat, your are worshipping despair.

BENEATHA: From now on, I worship the truth—and the truth is that people are puny, small and selfish. . . .

ASAGAI: Truth? Why is it that you despairing ones always think that only you have the truth? I never thought to see *you* like that. You! Your brother made a stupid, childish mistake—and you are grateful to him. So that now you can give up the ailing human race on account of it. You talk about what good is struggle; what good is anything? Where are we all going? And why are we bothering?

BENEATHA: *And you cannot answer it!* All your talk and dreams about Africa and Independence. Independence and then what? What about all the crooks and petty thieves and just plain idiots who will come into power to steal and plunder the same as before—only now they will be black and do it in the name of the new Independence—You cannot answer that.

ASAGAI: [*shouting over her*] I *live the answer!* [*pause*] In my village at home it is the exceptional man who can even read a newspaper . . . or who ever *sees* a book at all. I will go home and much of what I will have to say will seem strange to the people of my village . . . But I will teach and work and things will happen, slowly and swiftly. At times it will seem that nothing changes at all . . . and then again . . . the sudden dramatic events which make history leap into the future. And then quiet again. Retrogression even. Guns, murder, revolution. And I even will have moments when I wonder if the quiet was not better than all that death and hatred. But I will look about my village at the illiteracy and disease and ignorance and I will not wonder long. And perhaps . . . perhaps I will be a great man . . . I mean perhaps I will hold on to the substance of truth and find my way always with the right course . . . and perhaps for it I will be butchered in my bed some night by the servants of empire . . .

BENEATHA: *The martyr!*

ASAGAI: . . . or perhaps I shall live to be a very old man, respected and esteemed in my new nation . . . And perhaps I shall hold office and this is what I'm trying to tell you, Alaiyo; perhaps the things I believe now for my country will be wrong and outmoded, and I will not understand and do terrible things to have things my way or merely to keep my power. Don't you see that there will be young men and women, not British soldiers then, but my own black countrymen . . . to step out of the shadows some evening and slit my then useless throat? Don't you see they have always been there . . . that they always will be. And that such a thing as my own death will be an advance? They who might kill me even . . . actually replenish me!

BENEATHA: Oh, Asagai, I know all that.

ASAGAI: Good! Then stop moaning and groaning and tell me what you plan to do.

BENEATHA: Do?

ASAGAI: I have a bit of a suggestion.

BENEATHA: What?

ASAGAI: [*rather quietly for him*] That when it is all over—that you come home with me—

BENEATHA: [*slapping herself on the forehead with exasperation born of misunderstanding*] Oh—Asagai—at this moment you decide to be romantic!

ASAGAI: [*quickly understanding the misunderstanding*] My dear, young creature of the New World—I do not mean across the city—I mean across the ocean; home—to Africa.

BENEATHA: [*slowly understanding and turning to him with murmured amazement*] To—to Nigeria?

ASAGAI: Yes! . . . [*smiling and lifting his arms playfully*] Three hundred years later the African Prince rose up out of the seas and swept the maiden back across the middle passage over which her ancestors had come—

BENEATHA: [*unable to play*] Nigeria?

ASAGAI: Nigeria. Home. [*coming to her with genuine romantic flippancy*] I will show you our mountains and our stars; and give you cool drinks from gourds and teach you the old songs and the ways of our people—and, in time, we will pretend that—[*very softly*]—you have only been away for a day—

[*She turns her back to him, thinking. He swings her around and takes her full in his arms in a long embrace which proceeds to passion.*)

BENEATHA: [*pulling away*] You're getting me all mixed up—

ASAGAI: Why?

BENEATHA: Too many things—too many things have happened today. I must sit down and think. I don't know what I feel about anything right this minute.

[*She promptly sits down and props her chin on her fist.*]

ASAGAI: [*charmed*] All right, I shall leave you. No—don't get up. [*touching her, gently, sweetly*] Just sit awhile and think . . . Never be afraid to sit awhile and think. [*He goes to door and looks at her.*] How often I have looked at you and said, "Ah—so this is what the New World hath finally wrought
. . ."

[*He exits. BENEATHA sits on alone. Presently WALTER enters from his room and starts to rummage through things, feverishly looking for something. She looks up and turns in her seat.*]

BENEATHA: [*hissingly*] Yes—just look at what the New World hath wrought! . . . Just look! [*She gestures with bitter disgust.*] There he is! *Monsieur le petit bourgeois noir*—himself! There he is—Symbol of a Rising Class! Entrepreneur! Titan of the system! [WALTER *ignores her completely and continues frantically and destructively looking for something and hurling things to floor and tearing things out of their place in his search.* BENEATHA *ignores the eccentricity of his actions and goes on with the monologue of insult.*] Did you dream of yachts on Lake Michigan, Brother? Did you see yourself on that Great Day sitting down at the Conference Table, surrounded by all the mighty bald-headed men in America? All halted, waiting, breathless, waiting for your pronouncements on industry? Waiting for you—Chairman of the Board? [WALTER *finds what he is looking for—a small piece of white paper—and pushes it in his pocket and puts on his coat and rushes out without ever having looked at her. She shouts after him.*] I look at you and I see the final triumph of stupidity in the world!

> [*The door slams and she returns to just sitting again.* RUTH *comes quickly out of* MAMA'S *room.*]

RUTH: Who was that?

BENEATHA: Your husband.

RUTH: Where did he go?

BENEATHA: Who knows—maybe he has an appointment at U.S. Steel.

RUTH: [*anxiously, with frightened eyes*] You didn't say nothing bad to him, did you?

BENEATHA: Bad? Say anything bad to him? No—I told him he was a sweet boy and full of dreams and everything is strictly peachy keen, as the ofay kids say!

> [MAMA *enters from her bedroom. She is lost, vague, trying to catch hold, to make some sense of her former command of the world, but it still eludes her. A sense of waste overwhelms her gait; a measure of apology rides on her shoulders. She goes to her plant, which has remained on the table, looks at it, picks it up and takes it to the window sill and sits it outside, and she stands and looks at it a long moment. Then she closes the window, straightens her body with effort and turns around to her children.*]

MAMA: Well—ain't it a mess in here, though? [*a false cheerfulness, a beginning of something*] I guess we all better stop moping around and get some work done. All this unpacking and everything we got to do. [RUTH *raises her head slowly in response to the sense of the line; and* BENEATHA *in similar manner turns very slowly to look at her mother.*] One of you all better call the moving people and tell 'em not to come.

RUTH: Tell 'em not to come?

MAMA: Of course, baby. Ain't no need in 'em coming all the way here and having to go back. They charges for that too. [*She sits down, fingers to her brow, thinking.*] Lord, ever since I was a little girl, I always remembers people saying, "Lena—Lena Eggleston, you aims too high all the time. You needs to slow down and see life a little more like it is. Just slow down some." That's what they always used to say down home—"Lord, that Lena Eggleston is a high-minded thing. She'll get her due one day!"

RUTH: No, Lena . . .

MAMA: Me and Big Walter just didn't never learn right.

RUTH: Lena, no! We gotta go. Bennie—tell her . . . [*She rises and crosses to* BENEATHA *with her arms outstretched.* BENEATHA *doesn't respond.*] Tell her we can still move . . . the notes ain't but a hundred and twenty-five a month. We got four grown people in this house—we can work . . .

MAMA: [*to herself*] Just aimed too high all the time—

RUTH: [*turning and going to* MAMA *fast—the words pouring out with urgency and desperation*] Lena—I'll work . . . I'll work twenty hours a day in all the kitchens in Chicago . . . I'll strap my baby on my back if I have to and scrub all the floors in America and wash all the sheets in America if I have to—but we got to move . . . We got to get out of here . . .

[MAMA *reaches out absently and pats* RUTH'S *hand.*]

MAMA: No—I see things differently now. Been thinking 'bout some of the things we could do to fix this place up some. I seen a second-hand bureau over on Maxwell Street just the other day that could fit right here. [*She points to where the new furniture might go.* RUTH *wanders away from her.*] Would need some new handles on it and then a little varnish and then it look like something brand-new. And—we can put up them new curtains in the kitchen . . . Why this place be looking fine. Cheer us all up so that we forget trouble ever came . . . [*to* RUTH] And you could get some nice screens to put up in your room round the baby's bassinet . . . [*She looks at both of them, pleadingly.*] Sometimes you just got to know when to give up some things . . . and hold on to what you got.

[WALTER *enters from the outside, looking spent and leaning against the door, his coat hanging from him.*]

MAMA: Where you been, son?

WALTER: [*breathing hard*] Made a call.

MAMA: To who, son?

WALTER: To The Man.

MAMA: What man, baby?

WALTER: The Man, Mama, Don't you know who The Man is?

RUTH: Walter Lee?

WALTER: *The Man.* Like the guys in the streets say—The Man. Captain Boss—Mistuh Charley . . . Old Captain Please Mr. Bossman . . .

BENEATHA: [*suddenly*] Lindner!

WALTER: That's right! That's good. I told him to come right over.

BENEATHA: [*fiercely, understanding*] For what? What do you want to see him for!

WALTER: [*looking at his sister*] We going to do business with him.

MAMA: What you talking 'bout, son?

WALTER: Talking 'bout life, Mama. You all always telling me to see life like it is. Well—I laid in there on my back today . . . and I figured it out. Life just like it is. Who gets and who don't get. [*He sits down with his coat on and laughs.*] Mama, you know it's all divided up. Life is. Sure enough. Between the takers and the "tooken." [*He laughs.*] I've figured it out finally. [*He looks around at them.*] Yeah. Some of us always getting "tooken." [*He laughs.*] People like Willy Harris, they don't never get "tooken." And you know why the rest of us do? 'Cause we all mixed up. Mixed up bad. We get to looking 'round for the right and the wrong; and we worry about it and cry about it and stay up nights trying to figure out 'bout the wrong and the right of things all the time . . . And all the time, man, them takers is out there operating, just taking and taking. Willy Harris? Shoot—Willy Harris don't even count. He don't even count in the big scheme of things. But I'll say one thing for old Willy Harris . . . he's taught me something. He's taught me to keep my eye on what counts in this world. Yeah—[*shouting out a little*] Thanks, Willy!

RUTH: What did you call that man for, Walter Lee?

WALTER: Called him to tell him to come over to the show. Gonna put on a show for the man. Just what he wants to see. You see, Mama, the man came here today and he told us that them people out there where you want us to move—well they so upset they willing to pay us not to move out there. [*He laughs again.*] And—and oh, Mama—you would of been proud of the way me and Ruth and Bennie acted. We told him to get out . . . Lord have mercy! We told the man to get out. Oh, we was some proud folks this afternoon, yeah. [*He lights a cigarette.*] We were still full of that old-time stuff . . .

RUTH: [*coming toward him slowly*] You talking 'bout taking them people's money to keep us from moving in that house?

WALTER: I ain't just talking 'bout it, baby—I'm telling you that's what's going to happen.

BENEATHA: Oh, God! Where is the bottom! Where is the real honest-to-God bottom so he can't go any further!

WALTER: See—that's the old stuff. You and that boy that was here today. You all want everybody to carry a flag and a spear and sing some marching songs, huh? You wanna spend your life looking into things and trying to find the right and the wrong part, huh? Yeah. You know what's going to happen to that boy someday—he'll find himself sitting in a dungeon, locked in forever—and the takers will have the key! Forget it, baby! There ain't no causes—there ain't nothing but taking in this world, and he who takes most is smartest—and it don't make a damn bit of difference *how*.

MAMA: You making something inside me cry, son. Some awful pain inside me.

WALTER: Don't cry, Mama. Understand. That white man is going to walk in that door able to write checks for more money than we ever had. It's important to him and I'm going to help him . . . I'm going to put on the show, Mama.

MAMA: Son—I come from five generations of people who was slaves and sharecroppers—but ain't nobody in my family never let nobody pay 'em no money that was a way of telling us we wasn't fit to walk the earth. We ain't never been that poor. [*raising her eyes and looking at him*] We ain't never been that dead inside.

BENEATHA: Well—we are dead now. All the talk about dreams and sunlight that goes on in this house. All dead.

WALTER: What's the matter with you all! I didn't make this world! It was give to me this way! Hell, yes, I want me some yachts someday! Yes, I want to hang some real pearls 'round my wife's neck. Ain't she supposed to wear no pearls? Somebody tell me—tell me, who decides which women is suppose to wear pearls in this world. I tell you I am a *man*—and I think my wife should wear some pearls in this world!

[*This last line hangs a good while and* WALTER *begins to move about*

*the room. The word "Man" has penetrated his consciousness; he mum-
bles it to himself repeatedly between strange agitated pauses as he
moves about.*]

MAMA: Baby, how you going to feel on the inside?

WALTER: Fine! . . . Going to feel fine . . . a man . . .

MAMA: You won't have nothing left then, Walter Lee.

WALTER: [*coming to her*] I'm going to feel fine, Mama. I'm going to look that
son-of-a-bitch in the eyes and say—[*He falters.*]—and say, "All right, Mr.
Lindner—[*He falters even more.*]—that's your neighborhood out there.
You got the right to keep it like you want. You got the right to have it like
you want. Just write the check and—the house is yours." And, and I am
going to say—[*His voice almost breaks.*] And you—you people just put the
money in my hand and you won't have to live next to this bunch of stinking
niggers! . . . [*He straightens up and moves away from his mother, walking
around the room.*] Maybe—maybe I'll just get down on my black knees
. . . [*He does so; RUTH and BENNIE and MAMA watch him in frozen horror.*]
Captain, Mistuh, Bossman. [*He starts crying.*] A-hee-hee-hee! [*wringing
his hands in profoundly anguished imitation*] Yasssssuh! Great White
Father, just gi' ussen de money, fo' God's sake, and we's ain't gwine come
out deh and dirty up yo' white folks neighborhood . . .

[*He breaks down completely, then gets up and goes into the bedroom.*]

BENEATHA: That is not a man. That is nothing but a toothless rat.

MAMA: Yes—death done come in this here house. [*She is nodding, slowly,
reflectively.*] Done come walking in my house. On the lips of my children.
You what supposed to be my beginning again. You—what supposed to be
my harvest. [*to BENEATHA*] You—you mourning your brother?

BENEATHA: He's no brother of mine.

MAMA: What you say?

BENEATHA: I said that individual in that room is no brother of mine.

MAMA: That's what I thought you said. You feeling like you better than he is
today? [BENEATHA *does not answer.*] Yes? What you tell him a minute ago?
That he wasn't a man? Yes? You give him up for me? You done wrote his
epitaph too—like the rest of the world? Well, who give you the privilege?

BENEATHA: Be on my side for once! You saw what he just did, Mama! You saw
him—down on his knees. Wasn't it you who taught me—to despise any
man who would do that. Do what he's going to do.

MAMA: Yes—I taught you that. Me and your daddy. But I thought I taught you
something else too . . . I thought I taught you to love him.

BENEATHA: Love him? There is nothing left to love.

MAMA: There is always something left to love. And if you ain't learned that, you
ain't learned nothing. [*looking at her*] Have you cried for that boy today? I
don't mean for yourself and for the family 'cause we lost the money. I mean
for him; what he been through and what it done to him. Child, when do
you think is the time to love somebody the most; when they done good and
made things easy for everybody? Well then, you ain't through learning—
because that ain't the time at all. It's when he's at his lowest and can't
believe in hisself 'cause the world done whipped him so. When you starts
measuring somebody, measure him right, child, measure him right. Make

sure you done taken into account what hills and valleys he come through before he got to wherever he is.

[TRAVIS *bursts into the room at the end of the speech, leaving the door open.*]

TRAVIS: Grandmama—the moving men are downstairs! The truck just pulled up.

MAMA: [*turning and looking at him*] Are they, baby? They downstairs?

[*she sighs and sits.* LINDNER *appears in the doorway. He peers in and knocks lightly, to gain attention, and comes in. All turn to look at him.*]

LINDNER: [*hat and briefcase in hand*] Uh—hello . . . [RUTH *crosses mechanically to the bedroom door and opens it and lets it swing open freely and slowly as the lights come up on* WALTER *within, still in his coat, sitting at the far corner of the room. He looks up and out through the room to* LINDNER.]

RUTH: He's here.

[A *long minute passes and* WALTER *slowly gets up.*]

LINDNER: [*coming to the table with efficiency, putting his briefcase on the table and starting to unfold papers and unscrew fountain pens*] Well, I certainly was glad to hear from you people. [WALTER *has begun the trek out of the room, slowly and awkwardly, rather like a small boy, passing the back of his sleeve across his mouth from time to time.*] Life can really be so much simpler than people let it be most of the time. Well—with whom do I negotiate? You, Mrs. Younger, or your son here? [MAMA *sits with her hands folded on her lap and her eyes closed as* WALTER *advances.* TRAVIS *goes close to* LINDNER *and looks at the papers curiously.*] Just some official papers, sonny.

RUTH: Travis, you go downstairs.

MAMA: [*opening her eyes and looking into* WALTER'S] No. Travis, you stay right here. And you make him understand what you doing, Walter Lee. You teach him good. Like Willy Harris taught you. You show where our five generations done come to. Go ahead, son—

WALTER: [*looks down into his boy's eyes.* TRAVIS *grins at him merrily and* WALTER *draws him beside him with his arm lightly around his shoulders.*] Well, Mr. Lindner. [BENEATHA *turns away.*] We called you—[*There is a profound, simple groping quality in his speech.*]—because, well, me and my family [*He looks around and shifts from one foot to the other.*] Well—we are very plain people . . .

LINDNER: Yes—

WALTER: I mean—I have worked as a chauffeur most of my life—and my wife here, she does domestic work in people's kitchens. So does my mother. I mean—we are plain people . . .

LINDNER: Yes, Mr. Younger—

WALTER: [*really like a small boy, looking down at his shoes and then up at the man*] And—uh—well, my father, well, he was a laborer most of his life.

LINDNER: [*absolutely confused*] Uh, yes—

WALTER: [*looking down at his toes once again*] My father almost beat a man to death once because this man called him a bad name or something, you know what I mean?

LINDNER: No, I'm afraid I don't.

WALTER: [*finally straightening up*] Well, what I mean is that we come from people who had a lot of pride. I mean—we are very proud people. And that's my sister over there and she's going to be a doctor—and we are very proud—

LINDNER: Well—I am sure that is very nice, but—

WALTER: [*starting to cry and facing the man eye to eye*] What I am telling you is that we called you over here to tell you that we are very proud and that this is—this is my son, who makes the sixth generation of our family in this country, and that we have all thought about your offer and we have decided to move into our house because my father—my father—he earned it. [MAMA *has her eyes closed and is rocking back and forth as though she were in church, with her head nodding the amen yes.*] We don't want to make no trouble for nobody or fight no causes—but we will try to be good neighbors. That's all we got to say. [*He looks the man absolutely in the eyes.*] We don't want your money.

[*He turns and walks away from the man.*]

LINDNER: [*looking around at all of them*] I take it then that you have decided to occupy.

BENEATHA: That's what the man said.

LINDNER: [*to* MAMA *in her reverie*] Then I would like to appeal to you, Mrs. Younger. You are older and wiser and understand things better I am sure . . .

MAMA: [*rising*] I am afraid you don't understand, My son said we was going to move and there ain't nothing left for me to say. [*shaking her head with double meaning*] You know how these young folks is nowadays, mister. Can't do a thing with 'em. Good-bye.

LINDNER: [*folding up his materials*] Well—if you are that final about it . . . There is nothing left for me to say. [*He finishes. He is almost ignored by the family, who are concentrating on* WALTER LEE. *At the door* LINDNER *halts and looks around.*] I sure hope you people know what you're doing.

[*He shakes his head and exits.*]

RUTH: [*looking around and coming to life*] Well, for God's sake—if the moving men are here—LET'S GET THE HELL OUT OF HERE!

MAMA: [*into action*] Ain't it the truth! Look at all this here mess. Ruth, put Travis' good jacket on him . . . Walter Lee, fix your tie and tuck your shirt in, you look just like somebody's hoodlum. Lord have mercy, where is my plant? [*She flies to get it amid the general bustling of the family, who are deliberately trying to ignore the nobility of the past moment.*] You all start on down . . . Travis child, don't go empty-handed . . . Ruth, where did I put that box with my skillets in it? I want to be in charge of it myself . . . I'm going to make us the biggest dinner we ever ate tonight . . . Beneatha, what's the matter with them stockings? Pull them things up, girl . . .

[*The family stars to file out as two moving men appear and begin to carry out the heavier pieces of furniture, bumping into the family as they move about.*]

BENEATHA: Mama, Asagai—asked me to marry him today and go to Africa—

MAMA: [*in the middle of her getting-ready activity*] He did? You ain't old enough to marry nobody—[*seeing the moving men lifting one of her chairs pre-*

cariously] Darling, that ain't no bale of cotton, please handle it so we can sit
in it again. I had that chair twenty-five years . . .
    [*The movers sigh with exasperation and go on with their work.*]
BENEATHA: [*girlishly and unreasonably trying to pursue the conversation*] To go
to Africa, Mama—be a doctor in Africa . . .
MAMA: [*distracted*] Yes, baby—
WALTER: Africa! What he want you to go to Africa for?
BENEATHA: To practice there . . .
WALTER: Girl, if you don't get all them silly ideas out your head! You better
marry yourself a man with some loot . . .
BENEATHA: [*angrily, precisely as in the first scene of the play*] What have you got
to do with who I marry!
WALTER: Plenty. Now I think George Murchison—
    [*He and* BENEATHA *go out yelling at each other vigorously;* BENEATHA
    is heard saying that she would not marry GEORGE MURCHISON *if he were
    Adam and she were Eve, etc. The anger is loud and real till their voices
    diminish.* RUTH *stands at the door and turns to* MAMA *and smiles
    knowingly.*]
MAMA: [*fixing her hat at last*] Yeah—they something all right, my children . . .
RUTH: Yeah—they're something. Let's go, Lena.
MAMA: [*stalling, starting to look around at the house*] Yes—I'm coming. Ruth—
RUTH: Yes?
MAMA: [*quietly, woman to woman*] He finally come into his manhood today,
didn't he? Kind of like a rainbow after the rain . . .
RUTH: [*biting her lip lest her own pride explode in front of* MAMA] Yes, Lena.
    [WALTER'S *voice calls for them raucously.*]
MAMA: [*waving* RUTH *out vaguely*] All right, honey—go on down. I be down
directly.
    [RUTH *hesitates, then exits.* MAMA *stands, at last alone in the living
    room, her plant on the table before her as the lights start to come down.
    She looks around at all the walls and ceilings and suddenly, despite
    herself, while the children call below, a great heaving thing rises in her
    and she puts her fist to her mouth, takes a final desperate look, pulls her
    coat about her, pats her hat and goes out. The lights dim down. The
    door opens and she comes back in, grabs her plant, and goes out for the
    last time.*]

David Rabe

Streamers

CHARACTERS

MARTIN
RICHIE
CARLYLE
BILLY
ROGER
COKES
ROONEY
M. P. LIEUTENANT
PFC HINSON, M.P.
PFC CLARK, M.P.
FOURTH M. P.

ACT I

The set is a large cadre room thrusting angularly toward the audience. The floor is wooden and brown. Brightly waxed in places, it is worn and dull in other sections. The back wall is brown and angled. There are two lights at the center of the ceiling, They hang covered by green metal shades. Against the back wall and to the stage right side are three wall lockers, side by side. Stage center in the back wall is the door, the only entrance to the room. It opens onto a hallway that runs off to the latrines, showers, other cadre rooms and larger barracks rooms. There are three bunks. BILLY'S *bunk is parallel to* ROGER'S *bunk. They are upstage and on either side of the room, and face downstage.* RICHIE'S *bunk is downstage and at a right angle to* BILLY'S *bunk. At the foot of each bunk is a green wooden footlocker. There is a floor outlet near* ROGER'S *bunk. He uses it for his radio. A reading lamp is clamped on to the metal piping at the head of* RICHIE'S *bunk. A wooden chair stands beside the wall lockers. Two mops hang in the stage left corner near a trash can.*

It is dusk as the lights rise on the room. RICHIE *is seated and bowed forward wearily on his bunk. He wears his long-sleeved khaki summer dress uniform. Upstage behind him is* MARTIN, *a thin, dark young man, pacing, worried. A white towel stained red with blood is wrapped around his wrist. He paces several steps and falters, stops. He stands there.*

RICHIE: Honest to god, Martin, I don't know what to say anymore. I don't know what to tell you.

MARTIN: [*beginning to pace again*] I mean it. I just can't stand it. Look at me.

RICHIE: I know.

MARTIN: I hate it.

RICHIE: We've got to make up a story. They'll ask you a hundred questions.

MARTIN: Do you know how I hate it?

RICHIE: Everybody does. Don't you think I hate it, too?

MARTIN: I enlisted, though. I enlisted and I hate it.

RICHIE: I enlisted, too.

MARTIN: I vomit every morning. I get the dry heaves. In the middle of every night.

> [*He flops down on the corner of* BILLY'S *bed and sits there, slumped forward, shaking his head.*]

RICHIE: You can stop that. You can.

MARTIN: No.

RICHIE: You're just scared. It's just fear.

MARTIN: They're all so mean, they're all so awful. I've got two years to go. Just thinking about it is going to make me sick. I thought it would be different from the way it is.

RICHIE: But you could have died, for God's sake.

> [RICHIE *has turned now; he is facing* MARTIN.]

MARTIN: I just wanted out.

RICHIE: I might not have found you, though. I might not have come up here.

MARTIN: I don't care. I'd be out.

> [*The door opens and a black man in filthy fatigues—they are grease-stained and dark with sweat—stands there. He is* CARLYLE, *looking about.* RICHIE, *seeing him, rises and moves toward him.*]

RICHIE: No. Roger isn't here right now.

CARLYLE: Who isn't?

RICHIE: He isn't here.

CARLYLE: They tole me a black boy livin' in here. I don't see him.

> [*He looks suspiciously about the room.*]

RICHIE: That's what I'm saying. He isn't here. He'll be back later. You can come back later. His name is Roger.

MARTIN: I slit my wrist.

> [*Thrusting out the bloody, towel-wrapped wrist toward* CARLYLE.]

RICHIE: Martin! Jesus!

MARTIN: I did.

RICHIE: He's kidding. He's kidding.

CARLYLE: What was his name? Martin?

> [CARLYLE *is confused and the confusion has made him angry. He moves toward* MARTIN.]

You Martin?

MARTIN: Yes.

> [*As* BILLY, *a white in his mid-twenties, blond and trim, appears in the door, whistling, carrying a slice of pie on a paper napkin. Sensing something, he falters, looks at* CARLYLE, *then* RICHIE.]

RICHIE: Hey, what's goin' on?

CARLYLE: [*turning, leaving*] Nothin', man. Not a thing.
> [BILLY *looks questioningly at* RICHIE. *Then, after placing the piece of pie on the chair beside the door, he crosses to his footlocker.*]

RICHIE: He came in looking for Roger, but he didn't even know his name.

BILLY: [*sitting on his footlocker, he starts taking off his shoes.*] How come you weren't at dinner, Rich? I brought you a piece of pie. Hey, Martin.
> [MARTIN *thrusts out his towel-wrapped wrist.*]

RICHIE: Oh, for God's sake, Martin!
> [*He whirls away.*]

BILLY: Huh?

MARTIN: I did.

RICHIE: You are disgusting, Martin.

MARTIN: No. It's the truth. I did. I am not disgusting.

RICHIE: Well, maybe it isn't disgusting, but it certainly is disappointing.

BILLY: What are you guys talking about?
> [*Sitting there, he really doesn't know what is going on.*]

MARTIN: I cut my wrists. I slashed them, and Richie is pretending I didn't.

RICHIE: I am not. And you only cut one wrist and you didn't slash it.

MARTIN: I can't stand the army anymore, Billy.
> [*He is moving now to petition* BILLY, *and* RICHIE *steps between them.*]

RICHIE: Billy, listen to me. This is between Martin and me.

MARTIN: It's between me and the army, Richie.

RICHIE: [*taking* MARTIN *by the shoulders as* BILLY *is now trying to get near* MARTIN] Let's just go outside and talk, Martin. You don't know what you're saying.

BILLY: Can I see? I mean, did he really do it?

RICHIE: No!

MARTIN: I did.

BILLY: That's awful. Jesus. Maybe you should go to the infirmary.

RICHIE: I washed it with peroxide. It's not deep. Just let us be. Please. He just needs to straighten out his thinking a little, that's all.

BILLY: Well, maybe I could help him?

MARTIN: Maybe he could.

RICHIE: [*Suddenly pushing at* MARTIN, RICHIE *is angry and exasperated. He wants* MARTIN *out of the room.*] Get out of here, Martin. Billy, you do some push-ups or something.
> [*Having been pushed toward the door,* MARTIN *wanders out.*]

BILLY: No.

RICHIE: I know what Martin needs.
> [RICHIE *whirls and rushes into the hall after* MARTIN, *leaving* BILLY *scrambling to get his shoes on.*]

BILLY: You're no doctor, are you? I just want to make sure he doesn't have to go to the infirmary, then I'll leave you alone.
> [*One shoe on, he grabs up the second and runs out the door into the hall after them.*]

Martin! Martin, wait up!
> [*Silence. The door has been left open. Fifteen or twenty seconds pass. Then someone is heard coming down the hall. He is singing "Get a Job"*

and trying to do the voices and harmonies of a vocal group. ROGER, *a tall, well-built black in long-sleeved khakis, comes in the door. He has a laundry bag over his shoulder, a pair of clean civilian trousers and a shirt on a hanger in his other hand. After dropping the bag on his bed, he goes to his wall locker, where he carefully hangs up the civilian clothes. Returning to the bed, he picks up the laundry and then, as if struck, he throws the bag down on the bed, tears off his tie and sits down angrily on the bed. For a moment, with his head in his hands, he sits there. Then, resolutely, he rises, takes up the position of attention, and simply topples forward, his hands leaping out to break his fall at the last instant and put him into the push-up position. Counting in a hissing, whispering voice, he does ten pushups before giving up and flopping onto his belly. He simply doesn't have the will to do any more. Lying there, he counts rapidly on.*]

ROGER: Fourteen, fifteen. Twenty. Twenty-five.

[BILLY, *shuffling dejectedly back in, sees* ROGER *lying there.* ROGER *springs to his feet, heads toward his footlocker, out of which he takes an ashtray and a pack of cigarettes.*]

You come in this area, you come in here marchin', boy: standin' tall.

[BILLY, *having gone to his wall locker, is tossing a* Playboy *magazine onto his bunk. He will also remove a towel, a Dopp kit and a can of foot powder.*]

BILLY: I was marchin'.

ROGER: You call that marchin'?

BILLY: I was as tall as I am; I was marchin'—what do you want?

ROGER: Outa here, man; outa this goddamn typin'-terrors outfit and into some kinda real army. Or else out and free.

BILLY: So go; who's stoppin' you; get out. Go on.

ROGER: Ain't you a bitch.

BILLY: You and me more regular army than the goddamn sergeants around this place, you know that?

ROGER: I was you, Billy boy, I wouldn't be talkin' so sacrilegious so loud, or they be doin' you like they did the ole sarge.

BILLY: He'll get off.

ROGER: Sheee-it, he'll get off.

[*Sitting down on the side of his bed and facing* BILLY, ROGER *lights up a cigarette.* BILLY *has arranged the towel, Dopp kit and foot powder on his own bed.*]

Don't you think L.B.J. want to have some sergeants in that Vietnam, man? In Disneyland, baby? Lord have mercy on the ole sarge. He goin' over there to be Mickey Mouse.

BILLY: Do him a lot of good. Make a man outa him.

ROGER: That's right, that's right. He said the same damn thing about himself and you, too, I do believe. You know what's the ole boy's MOS? His Military Occupation Specialty? Demolitions, baby. Expert is his name.

BILLY: [*Taking off his shoes and beginning to work on a sore toe,* BILLY *hardly looks up.*] You're kiddin' me.

ROGER: Do I jive?

BILLY: You mean that poor ole bastard who cannot light his own cigar for shakin' is supposed to go over there blowin' up bridges and shit? Do they wanna win this war or not, man?

ROGER: Ole sarge was over in Europe in the big one, Billy. Did all kinds a bad things.

BILLY: [*Swinging his feet up onto the bed,* BILLY *sits, cutting the cuticles on his toes, powdering his feet.*] Was he drinkin' since he got the word?

ROGER: Was he breathin', Billy? Was he breathin'?

BILLY: Well, at least he ain't cuttin' his fuckin' wrists.

> [*Silence.* ROGER *looks at* BILLY, *who keeps on working.*]

Man, that's the real damn army over there, ain't it? That ain't shinin' your belt buckle and standin' tall. And we might end up in it, man.

> [*Silence.* ROGER, *rising, begins to sort his laundry.*]

Roger . . . you ever ask yourself if you'd rather fight in a war where it was freezin' cold or one where there was awful snakes? You ever ask that question?

ROGER: Can't say I ever did.

BILLY: We used to ask it all the time. All the time. I mean, us kids sittin' out on the back porch tellin' ghost stories at night. 'Cause it was Korea time and the newspapers were fulla pictures of soldiers in snow with white frozen beards; they got these rags tied around their feet. And snakes. We hated snakes. Hated 'em. I mean, it's bad enough to be in the jungle duckin' bullets, but then you crawl right into a goddamn snake. That's awful. That's awful.

ROGER: I don't sound none too good.

BILLY: I got my draft notice, goddamn Vietnam didn't even exist. I mean, it existed, but not as in a war we might be in. I started crawlin' around the floor a this house where I was stayin' 'cause I'd dropped outa school, and I was goin' "Bang, bang," pretendin'. Jesus.

ROGER: [*Continuing with his laundry, he tries to joke.*] My first goddamn formation in basic, Billy, this NCO's up there jammin' away about how some a us are goin' to be dyin' in the war. I'm sayin', "What war? What that crazy man talkin' about?"

BILLY: Us, too. I couldn't believe it. I couldn't believe it. And now we got three people goin' from here.

ROGER: Five.

> [*They look at each other, and then turn away, each returning to his task.*]

BILLY: It don't seem possible. I mean, people shootin' at you. Shootin' at you to kill you.

> [*Slight pause.*]

It's somethin'.

ROGER: What did you decide you preferred?

BILLY: Huh?·

ROGER: Did you decide you would prefer the snakes or would you prefer the snow? 'Cause it look like it is going to be the snakes.

BILLY: I think I had pretty much made my mind up on the snow.

ROGER: Well, you just let 'em know that, Billy. Maybe they get one goin' special just for you up in Alaska. You can go to the Klondike. Fightin' some snowmen.

[RICHIE *bounds into the room and shuts the door as if to keep out something dreadful. He looks at* ROGER *and* BILLY *and crosses to his wall locker, pulling off his tie as he moves. Tossing the tie into the locker, he begins unbuttoning the cuffs of his shirt.*]

RICHIE: Hi, hi, hi, everybody. Billy, hello.

BILLY: Hey.

ROGER: What's happenin', Rich?

[*Moving to the chair beside the door,* RICHIE *picks up the pie* BILLY *left there. He will place the pie atop the locker, and then, sitting, he will remove his shoes and socks.*]

RICHIE: I simply did this rather wonderful thing for a friend of mine, helped him see himself in a clearer, more hopeful light—little room in his life for hope? And I feel very good. Didn't Billy tell you?

ROGER: About what?

RICHIE: About Martin.

ROGER: No.

BILLY: [*looking up and speaking pointedly*] No.

[RICHIE *looks at* BILLY *and then at* ROGER. RICHIE *is truly confused.*]

RICHIE: No? No?

BILLY: What do I wanna gossip about Martin for?

RICHIE: [*He really can't figure out what is going on with* BILLY. *Shoes and socks in hand, he heads for his wall locker.*] Who was planning to gossip? I mean, it did happen. We could talk about it. I mean, I wasn't hearing his goddamn confession. Oh, my sister told me Catholics were boring.

BILLY: Good thing I ain't one anymore.

RICHIE: [*Taking off his shirt, he moves toward* ROGER.] It really wasn't anything, Roger, except Martin made this rather desperate, pathetic gesture for attention that seems to have brought to the surface Billy's more humane and protective side.

[*Reaching out, he tousles* BILLY'S *hair.*]

BILLY: Man, I am gonna have to obliterate you.

RICHIE: [*Tossing his shirt into his locker.*] I don't know what you're so embarrassed about.

BILLY: I just think Martin's got enough trouble without me yappin' to everybody.

[RICHIE *has moved nearer* BILLY, *his manner playful and teasing.*]

RICHIE: "Obliterate"? "Obliterate," did you say? Oh, Billy, you better say "shit," "ain't" and "motherfucker" real quick now or we'll all know just how far beyond the fourth grade you went.

ROGER: [*Having moved to his locker, in which he is placing his folded clothes*] You hear about the ole sarge, Richard?

BILLY: [*Grinning*] You ain't . . . shit . . . motherfucker.

ROGER: [*Laughing*] All right.

RICHIE: [*Moving center and beginning to remove his trousers*] Billy, no, no. Wit is my domain. You're in charge of sweat and running around the block.

ROGER: You hear about the ole sarge?

RICHIE: What about the ole sarge? Oh, who cares? Let's go to a movie. Billy, wanna? Let's go. C'mon.

[*Trousers off, he hurries to his locker.*]

BILLY: Sure. What's playin'?

RICHIE: I don't know. Can't remember. Something good, though.

[*With a* Playboy *magazine he has taken from his locker,* ROGER *is setting down on his bunk, his back toward both* BILLY *and* RICHIE.]

BILLY: You wanna go, Rog?

RICHIE: [*In mock irritation*] Don't ask Roger! How are we going to kiss and hug and stuff if he's there?

BILLY: That ain't funny, man.

[*He is stretched out on his bunk, and* RICHIE *comes bounding over to flop down and lie beside him.*]

RICHIE: And what time will you pick me up?

BILLY: [*He pushes at* RICHIE, *knocking him off the bed and onto the floor.*] Well, you just fall down and wait, all right?

RICHIE: Can I help it if I love you?

[*leaping to his feet, he will head to his locker, remove his shorts, put on a robe.*]

ROGER: You gonna take a shower, Richard?

RICHIE: Cleanliness is nakedness, Roger.

ROGER: Is that right? I didn't know that. Not too many people know that. You may be the only person in the world who knows that.

RICHIE: And godliness is in there somewhere, of course.

[*Putting a towel around his neck, he is gathering toiletries to carry to the shower.*]

ROGER: You got your own way a lookin' at things, man. You cute.

RICHIE: That's right.

ROGER: You g'wan, have a good time in that shower.

RICHIE: Oh, I will.

BILLY: [*Without looking up from his feet, which he is powdering*] And don't drop your soap.

RICHIE: I will if I want to.

[*Already out the door, he slams it shut with a flourish.*]

BILLY: Can you imagine bein' in combat with Richie—people blastin' away at you—he'd probably want to hold your hand.

ROGER: Ain't he somethin'?

BILLY: Who's zat?

ROGER: He's all right.

BILLY: [*Rising, he heads toward his wall locker, where he will put the powder and Dopp kit.*] Sure he is, except he's livin' under water.

[*Looking at* BILLY, ROGER *senses something unnerving; it makes* ROGER *rise, and return his magazine to his footlocker.*]

ROGER: I think we oughta do this area, man. I think we oughta do our area. Mop and buff this floor.

BILLY: You really don't think he means that shit he talks, do you?

ROGER: Huh? Awwww, man . . . Billy, no.

BILLY: I'd put money on it, Roger, and I ain't got much money.

[BILLY *is trying to face* ROGER *with this, but* ROGER, *seated on his bed, has turned away. He is unbuttoning his shirt.*]

ROGER: Man, no, no. I'm tellin' you, lad, you listen to the ole Rog. You seen that picture a that little dolly he's got in his locker? He ain't swish, man, believe me—he's cool.

BILLY: It's just that ever since we been in this room, he's been different somehow. Somethin'.

ROGER: No, he ain't.

[BILLY *turns to his bed, where he carefully starts folding the towel. Then he looks at* ROGER.]

BILLY: You ever talk to any a these guys—queers, I mean? You ever sit down, just rap with one of 'em?

ROGER: Hell, no; what I wanna do that for? Shit, no.

BILLY: [*Crossing to the trash can in the corner, where he will shake the towel empty*] I mean, some of 'em are okay guys, just way up this bad alley, and you say to 'em, "I'm straight, be cool," they go their own way. But then there's these other ones, these bitches, man, and they're so crazy they think anybody can be had. Because they been had themselves. So you tell 'em you're straight and they just nod and smile. You ain't real to 'em. They can't see nothin' but themselves and these goddamn games they're always playin'.

[*Having returned to his bunk, he is putting on his shoes.*]

I mean, you can be decent about anything, Roger, you see what I'm sayin'? We're all just people, man, and some of us are hardly that. That's all I'm sayin'.

[*There is a slight pause as he sits there thinking. Then he gets to his feet.*]

I'll go get some buckets and stuff so we can clean up, okay? This area's a mess. This area ain't standin' tall.

ROGER: That's good talk, lad; this area a midget you put it next to an area standin' tall.

BILLY: Got to be good fuckin' troopers.

ROGER: That's right, that's right. I know the meanin' of the words.

BILLY: I mean, I just think we all got to be honest with each other—you understand me?

ROGER: No, I don't understand you; one stupid fuckin' nigger like me—how's that gonna be?

BILLY: That's right; mock me, man. That's what I need. I'll go get the wax.

[*Out he goes, talking to himself and leaving the door open. For a moment* ROGER *sits, thinking, and then he looks at* RICHIE'S *locker and gets to his feet and walks to the locker which he opens and looks at the pinup hanging on the inside of the door. He takes a step backward, looking.*]

ROGER: Sheee-it.

[*Through the open door comes* CARLYLE. ROGER *doesn't see him. And* CARLYLE *stands there looking at* ROGER *and the picture in the locker.*]

CARLYLE: Boy . . . whose locker you lookin' into?

ROGER: [*He is startled, but recovers.*] Hey, baby, what's happenin'?

CARLYLE: That ain't your locker, is what I'm askin', nigger. I mean, you ain't got no white goddamn woman hangin' on your wall.

ROGER: Oh, no—no, no.

CARLYLE: You don't wanna be lyin' to me, 'cause I got to turn you in you lyin' and you do got the body a some white goddamn woman hangin' there for you to peek at nobody around but you—you can be thinkin' about that sweet wet pussy an' maybe it hot an' maybe it cool.

ROGER: I could be thinkin' all that, except I know the penalty for lyin'.

CARLYLE: Thank God for that.

> [*Extending his hand, palm up*]

ROGER: That's right. This here the locker of a faggot.

> [*And* ROGER *slaps* CARLYLE'S *hand, palm to palm.*]

CARLYLE: Course it is; I see that; any damn body know that.

> [ROGER *crosses toward his bunk and* CARLYLE *swaggers about, pulling a pint of whiskey from his hip pocket.*]

You want a shot? Have you a little taste, my man.

ROGER: Naw.

CARLYLE: C'mon. C'mon. I think you a Tom you don't drink outa my bottle.

> [*He thrusts the bottle towrad* ROGER *and wipes a sweat- and grease-stained sleeve across his mouth.*]

ROGER: [*Taking the bottle*] Shit.

CARLYLE: That right. How do I know? I just got in. New boy in town. Somewhere over there; I dunno. They dump me in amongst a whole bunch a pale, boring motherfuckers.

> [CARLYLE *is exploring the room. Finding* BILLY'S *Playboy, he edges onto* BILLY'S *bed and leafs nervously through the pages.*]

I just come in from P Company, man, and I been all over this place, don't see too damn many of us. This outfit look like it a little short on soul. I been walkin' all around, I tell you, and the number is small. Like one hand you can tabulate the lot of 'em. We got few brothers I been able to see, is what I'm sayin'. You and me and two cats down in the small bay. That's all I found.

> [*As* ROGER *is about to hand the bottle back,* CARLYLE, *almost angrily, waves him off.*]

No, no, you take another; take you a real taste.

ROGER: It ain't so bad here. We do all right.

CARLYLE: [*He moves, shutting the door. Suspiciously, he approaches* ROGER.] How about the white guys? They give you any sweat? What's the situation? No jive. I like to know what is goin' on within the situation before that situation get a chance to be closin' in on me.

ROGER: [*Putting the bottle on the footlocker, he sits down.*] Man, I'm tellin' you, it ain't bad. They're just pale, most of 'em, you know. They can't help it; how they gonna help it? Some of 'em got little bit a soul, couple real good boys around this way. Get 'em little bit of Coppertone, they be straight, man.

CARLYLE: How about the NCOs? We got any brother NCO watchin' out for us or they all white, like I goddamn well KNOW all the officers are? Fuckin' officers always white, man; fuckin' snow cones and bars everywhere you look.

> [CARLYLE *cannot stay still. He moves to his right, his left; he sits, he stands.*]

ROGER: First sergeant's a black man.

CARLYLE: All right; good news. Hey, hey, you wanna go over the club with me, or maybe downtown? I got wheels. Let's be free.

> [*Now he rushes at* ROGER.]

Let's be free.

ROGER: Naw . . .

CARLYLE: Ohhh, baby . . . !

> [*He is wildly pulling at* ROGER *to get him to the door.*]

ROGER: Some other time. I gotta get the area straight. Me and the guy sleeps in here too are gonna shape the place up a little.

> [ROGER *has pulled free, and* CARLYLE *cannot understand. It hurts him, depresses him.*]

CARLYLE: You got a sweet deal here an' you wanna keep it, that right?

> [*He paces about the room, opens a footlocker, looks inside.*]

How you rate you get a room like this for yourself—you and a couple guys?

ROGER: Spec. 4. The three of us in here Spec 4.

CARLYLE: You get a room then, huh?

> [*And suddenly, without warning or transition, he is angry.*]

Oh, man, I hate this goddamn army. I hate this bastard army. I mean, I just got outa basic—off leave—you know? Back on the block for two weeks—and now here. They don't pull any a that petty shit, now, do they—that goddamn petty basic training bullshit? They do and I'm gonna be bustin' some head—my hand is gonna be upside all kinds a heads, 'cause I ain't gonna be able to endure it, man, not that kinda crap—understand?

> [*And again, he is rushing at* ROGER.]

Hey, hey, oh, c'mon, let's get my wheels and make it, man, do me the favor.

ROGER: How'm I gonna? I got my obligations.

> [*And* CARLYLE *spins away in anger.*]

CARLYLE: Jesus, baby, can't you remember the outside? How long it been since you been on leave? It is so sweet out there, nigger; you got it all forgot. I had such a sweet, sweet time. They doin' dances, baby, make you wanna cry. I hate this damn army.

> [*The anger overwhelms him.*]

All these mother-actin' jack givin' you jive about what you gotta do and what you can't do. I had a bad scene in basic—up the hill and down the hill; it ain't somethin' I enjoyed even a little. So they do me wrong here, Jim, they gonna be sorry. Some-damn-body! And this whole Vietnam THING—I do not dig it.

> [*He falls on his knees before* ROGER. *It is a gesture that begins as a joke, a mockery. And then a real fear pulses through him to nearly fill the pose he has taken.*]

Lord, Lord, don't let 'em touch me. Christ, what will I do, they DO! Whooooooooooooooo! And they pullin' guys outa here, too, ain't they? Pullin' 'em like weeds, man; throwin' 'em into the fire. It's shit, man.

ROGER: They got this ole sarge sleeps down the hall—just today they got him.

CARLYLE: Which ole sarge?

ROGER: He sleeps just down the hall. Little guy.

CARLYLE: Wino, right?

ROGER: Booze hound.

CARLYLE: Yeh; I seen him. They got him, huh?

ROGER: He's goin'; gotta be packing his bags. And three other guys two days ago. And two guys last week.

CARLYLE: [*Leaping up from* BILLY'S *bed*] Ohhh, them bastards. And everybody just takes it. It ain't our war, brother. I'm tellin' you. that's what gets me, nigger. It ain't our war nohow because it ain't our country, and that's what burns my ass—that and everybody just sittin' and takin' it. They gonna be bustin' balls, man—kickin' and stompin'. Everybody here maybe one week from shippin' out to get blown clean away and, man, whata they doin'? They doin' what they told. That what they doin'. Like you? Shit! You gonna straighten up your goddamn area! Well, that ain't for me; I'm getting hat, and makin' it out where it's sweet and the people's livin'. I can't cut this jive here, man. I'm tellin' you. I can't cut it.

> [*He has moved toward* ROGER, *and behind him now* RICHIE *enters, running, his hair wet, traces of shaving cream on his face. Toweling his hair, he falters, seeing* CARLYLE. *Then he crosses to his locker.* CARLYLE *grins at* ROGER, *looks at* RICHIE, *steps toward him and gives a little bow.*]

My name is Carlyle; what is yours?

RICHIE: Richie.

CARLYLE: [*He turns toward* ROGER *to share his joke.*] Hello. Where is Martin? That cute little Martin.

> [*And* RICHIE *has just taken off his robe as* CARLYLE *turns back.*]

You cute, too, Richie.

RICHIE: Martin doesn't live here.

> [*Hurriedly putting on underpants to cover his nakedness*]

CARLYLE: [*Watching* RICHIE, *he slowly turns toward* ROGER.] You ain't gonna make it with me, man?

ROGER: Naw . . . like I tole you. I'll catch you later.

CARLYLE: That's sad, man; make me cry in my heart.

ROGER: You g'wan get your head smokin'. Stop on back.

CARLYLE: Okay, okay. Got to be one man one more time.

> [*On the move for the door, his hand extended palm up behind him, demanding the appropriate response*]

Baby! Gimme! Gimme!

> [*lunging,* ROGER *slaps the hand.*]

ROGER: G'wan home! G'wan home.

CARLYLE: You gonna hear from me.

> [*And he is gone out the door and down the hallway.*]

ROGER: I can . . . and do . . . believe . . . that.

> [RICHIE, *putting on his T-shirt, watches* ROGER, *who stubs out his cigarette, then crosses to the trash can to empty the ashtray.*]

RICHIE: Who was that?

ROGER: Man's new, Rich. Dunno his name more than that "Carlyle" he said. He's new—just outa basic.

RICHIE: [*Powdering his thighs and under his arms*] Oh, my God . . .

> [As BILLY *enters, pushing a mop bucket with a wringer attached and carrying a container of wax*]

ROGER: Me and Billy's gonna straighten up the area. You wanna help?

RICHIE: Sure, sure; help, help.

BILLY: [*Talking to* ROGER, *but turning to look at* RICHIE, *who is still putting powder under his arms*] I hadda steal the wax from Third Platoon.

ROGER: Good man.

BILLY: [*Moving to* RICHIE, *joking, yet really irritated in some strange way*] What? Whata you doin', singin'? Look at that, Rog. He's got enough jazz there for an entire beauty parlor. [*Grabbing the can from* RICHIE'S *hand*] What is this? Baby Powder! BABY POWDER!

RICHIE: I get rashes.

BILLY: Okay, okay, you get rashes, so what? They got powder for rashes that isn't baby powder.

RICHIE: It doesn't work as good; I've tried it. Have you tried it?

> [*Grabbing* BILLY'S *waist,* RICHIE *pulls him close.* BILLY *knocks* RICHIE'S *hands away.*]

BILLY: Man, I wish you could get yourself straight. I'll mop, too, Roger—okay? Then I'll put down the wax and you can spread it?

> [*He has walked away from* RICHIE.]

RICHIE: What about buffing?

ROGER: In the morning.

> [*He is already busy mopping up near the door.*]

RICHIE: What do you want me to do?

BILLY: [*Grabbing up a mop, he heads downstage to work.*] Get inside your locker and shut the door and don't holler for help. Nobody'll know you're there; you'll stay there.

RICHIE: But I'm so pretty.

BILLY: NOW! [*Pointing to* ROGER. *He wants to get this clear.*] Tell that man you mean what you're sayin', Richie.

RICHIE: Mean what?

BILLY: That you really think you're pretty.

RICHIE: Of course I do; I am. Don't you think I am? Don't you think I am, Roger?

ROGER: I tole you—you fulla shit and you cute, man. Carlyle just tole you you cute, too.

RICHIE: Don't you think it's true, Billy?

BILLY: It's like I tole you, Rog.

RICHIE: What did you tell him?

BILLY: That you go down; that you go up and down like a Yo-Yo and you go blowin' all the trees like the wind.

> [RICHIE *is stunned. He looks at* ROGER, *and then he turns and stares into his own locker. The others keep mopping.* RICHIE *takes out a towel, and putting it around his neck, he walks to where* BILLY *is working. He stands there, hurt, looking at* BILLY.]

RICHIE: What the hell made you tell him I been down, Billy?

BILLY: [*Still mopping*] It's in your eyes; I seen it.

RICHIE: What?

BILLY: You.

RICHIE: What is it, Billy, you think you're trying to say? You and all your wit and intelligence—your *humanity*.

BILLY: I said it, Rich; I said what I was tryin' to say.

RICHIE: *Did* you?

BILLY: I think I did.

RICHIE: *Do* you?

BILLY: Loud and clear, baby.

> [*Still mopping*]

ROGER: They got to put me in with the weirdos. Why is that, huh? How come the army *hate* me, do this shit to me—*know* what to do.

[*Whimsical and then suddenly loud, angered, violent*]

Now you guys put socks in your mouths, right now—get shut up—or I am gonna beat you to death with each other. Roger got work to do. To be doin' it!

RICHIE: [*Turning to his bed, he kneels upon it.*] Roger, I think you're so innocent sometimes. Honestly, it's not such a terrible thing. Is it, Billy?

BILLY: How would I know?

[*He slams his mop into the bucket.*]

Oh, go fuck yourself.

RICHIE: Well, I can give it a try, if that's what you want. Can I think of you as I do?

BILLY: [*throwing down his mop*] GODDAMMIT! That's it! IT!

[*He exits, rushing into the hall and slamming the door behind him. ROGER looks at RICHIE. Neither quite knows what is going on. Suddenly the door bursts open and BILLY storms straight over to RICHIE, who still kneels on the bed.*]

Now I am gonna level with you. Are you gonna listen? You gonna hear what I say, Rich, and not what you think I'm sayin'?

[*RICHIE turns away as if to rise, his manner flippant, disdainful.*]

No! Don't get cute; don't turn away cute. I wanna say somethin' straight out to you and I want you to hear it!

RICHIE: I'm all ears, goddamit! For what, however, I do not know, except some boring evasion.

BILLY: At least wait the hell till you hear me!

RICHIE: [*in irritation*] Okay, okay! What?

BILLY: Now this is level, Rich; this is straight talk.

[*He is quiet, intense. This is difficult for him. He seeks the exactly appropriate words of explanation.*]

No b.s. No tricks. What you do on the side, that's your business and I don't care about it. But if you don't cut the cute shit with me, I'm gonna turn you off. Completely. You ain't gonna get a good mornin' outa me, you understand, because it's gettin' bad around here. I mean, I know how you think—how you keep lookin' out and seein' yourself, and that's what I'm tryin' to tell you because that's all that's happenin', Rich. That's all there is to it when you look out at me and think there's some kind of approval or whatever you see in my eyes—you're just seein' yourself. And I'm talkin' the simple quiet truth to you, Rich. I swear I am.

[*BILLY looks away from RICHIE now and tries to go back to the mopping. It is embarrassing for them all. ROGER has watched, has tried to keep working. RICHIE has flopped back on his bunk. There is a silence.*]

RICHIE: How . . . do . . . you want me to be? I don't know how else to be.

BILLY: Ohhh, man, that ain't any part of it.

[*The mop is clenched in his hands.*]

RICHIE: Well, I don't come from the same kind of world as you do.

BILLY: Damn, Richie, you think Roger and I come off the same street?

ROGER: Shit . . .

RICHIE: All right. Okay. But I've just done what I wanted all of my life. If I wanted to do something, I just did it. Honestly. I've never had to work or anything like that and I've always had nice clothing and money for cab fare. Money for whatever I wanted. Always. I'm not like you are.

ROGER: You ain't sayin' you really done that stuff, though, Rich.

RICHIE: What?

ROGER: That fag stuff.

RICHIE: [*He continues looking at* ROGER *and then he looks away.*] Yes.

ROGER: Do you even know what you're sayin', Richie? Do you even know what it means to be a fag?

RICHIE: Roger, of course I know what it is. I just told you I've done it. I thought you black people were· supposed to understand all about suffering and human strangeness. I thought you had depth and vision from all your suffering. Has someone been misleading me? I just told you I did it. I know all about it. Everything. All the various positions.

ROGER: Yeh, so maybe you think you've tried it, but that don't make you it. I mean, we used to . . . in the old neighborhood, man, we had a couple dudes swung that way. But they was weird, man. There was one little fella, he was a screamin' goddamn faggot . . . uh . . .

[*He considers* RICHIE, *wondering if perhaps he has offended him.*]
Ohh, ohhh, you ain't no screamin' goddamn faggot, Richie, no matter what you say. And the baddest man on the block was my boy Jerry Lemon. So one day Jerry's got the faggot in one a them ole deserted stairways and he's bouncin' him off the walls. I'm just a little fella, see, and I'm watchin' the baddest man on the block do his thing. So he come bouncin' back into me instead of Jerry, and just when he hit, he gave his ass this little twitch, man, like he thought he was gonna turn me on. I'd never a thought that was possible, man, for a man to be twitchin' his ass on me, just like he thought he was a broad. Scared me to death. I took off runnin'. Oh, oh, that ole neighborhood put me into all kinds a crap. I did some sufferin', just like Richie says. Like this once, I'm swingin' on up the street after school, and outa this phone booth comes this man with a goddamned knife stickin' outa his gut. So he sees me and starts tryin' to pull his motherfuckin' coat out over the handle, like he's worried about how he looks, man. "I didn't know this was gonna happen," he says. And then he falls over. He was just all of a sudden dead, man; just all of a sudden dead. You ever seen anything like that, Billy? Any crap like that?

[BILLY, *sitting on* ROGER'S *bunk, is staring at* ROGER.]

BILLY: You really seen that?

ROGER: Richie's a big-city boy.

RICHIE: Oh, no; never anything like that.

ROGER: "Momma, help me," I am screamin'. "Jesus, Momma, help me." Little fella, he don't know how to act, he sees somethin' like that.

[*For a moment they are still, each thinking.*]

BILLY: How long you think we got?

ROGER: What do you mean?

[ROGER *is handing up the mops;* BILLY *is now kneeling on* ROGER'S *bunk.*]

BILLY: Till they pack us up, man, ship us out.

ROGER: To the war, you mean? To Disneyland? Man, I dunno; that up to them IBM's. Them machines is figurin' that. Maybe tomorrow, maybe next week, maybe never.

[*The war—the threat of it—is the one thing they share.*]

RICHIE: I was reading they're planning to build it all up to more than five hundred thousand men over there. Americans. And they're going to keep it that way until they win.

BILLY: Be a great place to come back from, man, you know? I keep thinkin' about that. To have gone there, to have been there, to have seen it and lived.

ROGER: [*Settling onto* BILLY'S *bunk, he lights a cigarette.*] Well, what we got right here is a fool, gonna probably be one a them five hundred thousand, too. Do you know I cry at the goddamn anthem yet sometimes? The flag is flying at a ball game, the ole Roger gets all wet in the eye. After all the shit been done to his black ass. But I don't know what I think about this war. I do not know.

BILLY: I'm tellin' you, Rog—I've been doin' a lot a readin' and I think it's right we go. I mean, it's just like when North Korea invaded South Korea or when Hitler invaded Poland and all those other countries. He just kept testin' everybody and when nobody said no to him, he got so committed he couldn't back out even if he wanted. And that's what this Ho Chi Minh is doin'. And all these other Communists. If we let 'em know somebody is gonna stand up against 'em, they'll back off, just like Hitler would have.

ROGER: There is folks, you know, who are sayin' L.B.J. is the Hitler, and not ole Ho Chi Minh at all.

RICHIE: [*Talking as if this is the best news he's heard in years*] Well, I don't know anything at all about all that, but I am certain I don't want to go—whatever is going on. I mean, those Vietcong don't just shoot you and blow you up, you know. My God, they've got these other awful things they do: putting elephant shit on these stakes in the ground and then you step on 'em and you got elephant shit in a wound in your foot. The infection is horrendous. And then there's these caves they hide in and when you go in after 'em, they've got these snakes that they've tied by their tails to the ceiling. So it's dark and the snake is furious from having been hung by its tail and you crawl right into them—your face. My God.

BILLY: They do not.

[BILLY *knows he has been caught; they all know it.*]

RICHIE: I read it, Billy. They do.

BILLY: [*Completely facetious, yet the fear is real*] That's bullshit, Richie.

ROGER: That's right, Richie. They maybe do that stuff with the elephant shit, but nobody's gonna tie a snake by its fail, let ole Billy walk into it.

BILLY: That's disgusting, man.

ROGER: Guess you better get ready for the Klondike, my man.

BILLY: That is probably the most disgusting thing I ever heard. I DO NOT WANT TO GO! NOT TO NOWHERE WHERE THAT KINDA SHIT IS GOIN' ON! L.B.J. is Hitler; suddenly I see it all very clearly.

ROGER: Billy got him a hatred for snakes.

RICHIE: I hate them, too. They're hideous.

BILLY: [*And now, as a kind of apology to* RICHIE, BILLY *continues his self-ridicule far into the extreme.*] I mean, that is one of the most awful things I ever heard of any person doing. I mean, any person who would hang a snake by its tail in the dark of a cave in the hope that some other person might crawl into it and get bitten to death, that first person is somebody who oughta be shot. And I hope the five hundred thousand other guys that get sent over there kill 'em all—all them gooks—get 'em all driven back into Germany, where they belong. And in the meantime, I'll be holding the northern border against the snowmen.

ROGER: [*Rising from* BILLY'S *bed*] And in the meantime before that, we better be gettin' at the ole area here. Got to be strike troopers.

BILLY: Right.

RICHIE: Can I help?

ROGER: Sure. Be good.

    [*And* ROGER *crosses to his footlocker and takes out a radio.*]

Think maybe I put on a little music, though it's gettin' late. We got time. Billy. you think?

BILLY: Sure.

    [*Getting nervously to his feet*]

ROGER: Sure. All right. We can be doin' it to the music.

    [*He plugs the radio into the floor outlet as* BILLY *bolts for the door.*]

BILLY: I gotta go pee.

ROGER: You watch out for the snakes.

BILLY: It's the snowmen, man; the snowmen.

    [BILLY *is gone and "Ruby," sung by Ray Charles, comes from the radio. For a moment, as the music plays,* ROGER *watches* RICHIE *wander about the room, pouring little splashes of wax onto the floor. Then* RICHIE *moves to his bed and lies down, and* ROGER, *shaking his head, starts leisurely to spread the wax, with* RICHIE *watching.*]

RICHIE: How come you and Billy take all this so seriously—you know.

ROGER: What?

RICHIE: This army nonsense. You're always shining your brass and keeping your footlocker neat and your locker so neat. There's no point to any of it.

ROGER: We here, ain't we, Richie? We in the army.

    [*Still working the wax*]

RICHIE: There's no point to any of it. And doing those pushups, the two of you.

ROGER: We just see a lot a things the same way is all. Army ought to be a serious business, even if sometimes it ain't.

RICHIE: You're lucky, you know, the two of you. Having each other for friends the way you do. I never had that kind of friend ever. Not even when I was little.

ROGER: [*After a pause during which* ROGER, *working, sort of peeks at* RICHIE *every now and then*] You ain't really inta that stuff, are you, Richie?

    [*It is a question that is a statement.*]

RICHIE: [*Coyly he looks at* ROGER.] What stuff is that, Roger?

ROGER: That fag stuff, man. You know. You ain't really into it, are you? You maybe messed in it a little in all—am I right?

RICHIE: I'm very weak, Roger. And by that I simply mean that if I have an impulse to do something, I don't know how to deny myself. If I feel like doing something, I just do it. I . . . will . . . admit to sometimes wishin' I . . . was a little more like you . . . and Billy, even, but not to any severe extent.

ROGER: But that's such a bad scene, Rich. You don't want that. Nobody wants that. Nobody wants to be a punk. Not nobody. You wanna know what I think it is? You just got in with the wrong bunch. Am I right? You just got in with a bad bunch. That can happen. And that's what I think happened to you. I bet you never had a chance to really run with the boys before. I mean, regular normal guys like Billy and me. How'd you come in the army, huh, Richie? You get drafted?

RICHIE: No.

ROGER: That's my point, see.

> [*He has stopped working. He stands, leaning on the mop, looking at* RICHIE.]

RICHIE: About four years ago, I went to this party. I was very young, and I went to this party with a friend who was older and . . . this "fag stuff," as you call it, was going on . . . so I did it.

ROGER: And then you come in the army to get away from it, right? Huh?

RICHIE: I don't know.

ROGER: Sure.

RICHIE: I don't know, Roger.

ROGER: Sure; sure. And now you're gettin' a chance to run with the boys for a little, you'll get yourself straightened around. I know it for a fact; I know that thing.

> [*From off there is the sudden loud bellowing sound of Sergeant* ROONEY.]

ROONEY: THERE AIN'T BEEN NO SOLDIERS IN THIS CAMP BUT ME. I BEEN THE ONLY ONE—I BEEN THE ONLY ME!

> [*And* BILLY *comes dashing into the room.*]

BILLY: Oh, boy.

ROGER: Guess who?

ROONEY: FOR SO LONG I BEEN THE ONLY GODDAMN ONE!

BILLY: [*leaping onto his bed and covering his face with a* Playboy *magazine as* RICHIE *is trying to disappear under his sheets and blankets and* ROGER *is trying to get the wax put away so he can get into his own bunk*] Hut who hee whor—he's got some Yo-Yo with him, Rog!

ROGER: Huh?

> [*As* COKES *and* ROONEY *enter. Both are in fatigues and drunk and big-bellied. They are in their fifties, their hair whitish and cut short. Both men carry whiskey bottles, beer bottles.* COKES *is a little neater than* ROONEY, *his fatigue jacket tucked in and not so rumpled, and he wears canvas-sided jungle boots.* ROONEY, *very disheveled, chomps on the stub of a big cigar. They swagger in, looking for fun, and stand there side by side.*]

ROONEY: What kinda platoon I got here? You buncha shit sacks. Everybody look sharp.

> [*The three boys lie there, unmoving.*]

Off and on!

COKES: OFF AND ON!
> [*He seems barely conscious, wavering as he stands.*]

ROGER: What's happenin', Sergeant?

ROONEY: [*shoving his bottle of whiskey at* ROGER, *who is sitting up*] Shut up, Moore! You want a belt?
> [*splashing whiskey on* ROGER'S *chest*]

ROGER: How can I say no?

COKES: My name is Cokes!

BILLY: [*rising to sit on the side of his bed*] How about me, too?

COKES: You wait your turn.

ROONEY: [*He looks at the three of them as if they are fools. Indicates* COKES *with a gesture.*] Don't you see what I got here?

BILLY: Who do I follow for my turn?

ROONEY: [*suddenly, crazily petulant*] Don't you see what I got here? Everybody on their feet and at attention!
> [BILLY *and* ROGER *climb from their bunks and stand at attention. They don't know what* ROONEY *is mad at.*]

I mean it!
> [RICHIE *bounds to the position of attention.*]

This here is my friend, who in addition just come back from the war! The goddamn war! He been to it and he come back.
> [ROONEY *is patting* COKES *gently, proudly.*]

The man's a fuckin' hero!
> [ROONEY *hugs* COKES, *almost kissing him on the cheek.*]

He's always been a fuckin' hero.
> [COKES, *embarrassed in his stupor, kind of wobbles a little from side to side.*]

COKES: No-o-o-o-o-o . . .
> [*And* ROONEY *grabs him, starts pushing him toward* BILLY's *footlocker.*]

ROONEY: Show 'em your boots, Cokes. Show 'em your jungle boots.
> [*With a long, clumsy step,* COKES *climbs onto the footlocker,* ROONEY *supporting him from behind and then bending to lift one of* COKES' *booted feet and display it for the boys.*]

Lookee that boot. That ain't no everyday goddamn army boot. That is a goddamn jungle boot! That green canvas is a jungle boot 'cause a the heat, and them little holes in the bottom are so the water can run out when you been walkin' in a lotta water like in a jungle swamp.
> [*He is extremely proud of all this; he looks at them.*]

The army ain't no goddamn fool. You see a man wearin' boots like that, you might as well see he's got a chestful a medals, 'cause he been to the war. He don't have no boots like that unless he been to the war! Which is where I'm goin' and all you slaphappy motherfuckers, too. Got to go kill some gooks.
> [*He is nodding at them, smiling.*]

That's right.

COKES: [*Bursting loudly from his stupor*] Gonna piss on 'em. Old booze. 'At's what I did. Piss in the rivers. Goddamn GI's secret weapon is old booze and he's pissin' it in all their runnin' water. Makes 'em yellow. Ahhhha ha, ha, ha!

[*He laughs and laughs, and* ROONEY *laughs, too, hugging* COKES.]
ROONEY: Me and Cokesy been in so much shit together we oughta be brown.
[*And then he catches himself, looks at* ROGER.]
Don't take no offense at that, Moore. We been swimmin' in it. One
Hundred and First Airborne, together. One-oh-one. Screamin' goddamn
Eagles!
[*Looking at each other, face to face, eyes glinting, they make sudden
loud screaming-eagle sounds.*]
This ain't the army; you punks ain't in the army. You ain't ever seen the
army. The army is Airborne! Airborne!
COKES: [*beginning to stomp his feet*] Airborne, Airborne! ALL THE WAY!
[*As* RICHIE, *amused and hoping for a drink, too, reaches out toward*
ROONEY]
RICHIE: Sergeant, Sergeant, I can have a little drink, too.
[ROONEY *looks at him and clutches the bottle.*]
ROONEY: Are you kiddin' me? You gotta be kiddin' me.
[*He looks to* ROGER.]
He's kiddin' me, ain't he, Moore?
[*and then to* BILLY *and then to* COKES]
Ain't he, Cokesy?
[COKES *steps forward and down with a thump, taking charge for his
bewildered friend.*]
COKES: Don't you know you are tryin' to take the booze from the hand a the
future goddamn Congressional Honor winner . . . Medal . . . ?
[*And he looks lovingly at* ROONEY. *He beams.*]
Ole Rooney, Ole Rooney.
[*He hugs* ROONEY'S *head.*]
He almost done it already.
[*And* ROONEY, *overwhelmed, starts screaming "Aggggghhhhhhhhhh,"
a screaming-eagle sound, and making clawing eagle gestures at the air.
He jumps up and down, stomping his feet.* COKES *instantly joins in,
stomping and jumping and yelling.*]
ROONEY: Let's show these shit sacks how men are men jumpin' outa planes.
Aggggghhhhhhhhhh.
[*Stomping and yelling, they move in a circle,* ROONEY *followed by*
COKES.]
A plane fulla yellin' stompin' men!
COKES: All yellin' stompin' men!
[*They yell and stomp, making eagle sounds, and then* ROONEY *leaps
up on* BILLY'S *bed and runs the length of it until he is on the footlocker,*
COKES *still on the floor, stomping.* ROONEY *makes a gesture of hooking
his rip cord to the line inside the plane. They yell louder and louder and*
ROONEY *leaps high into the air, yelling, "GERONIMO-O-O-O!" as*
COKES *leaps onto the locker and then high into the air, bellowing,
"GERONIMO-O-O-O!" They stand side by side, their arms held up in
the air as if grasping the shroud lines of open chutes. They seem to float
there in silence.*]
What a feelin' . . .

ROONEY: Beautiful feelin' . . .

> [*For a moment more they float there, adrift in the room, the sky, their memory.* COKES *smiles at* ROONEY.]

COKES: Remember that one guy, O'Flannigan . . . ?

ROONEY: [*nodding, smiling, remembering*] O'Flannigan . . .

COKES: He was this one guy . . . O'Flannigan . . .

> [*He moves now toward the boys,* BILLY, ROGER *and* RICHIE, *who have gathered on* ROGER'S *bed and footlocker.* ROONEY *follows several steps, then drifts backward onto* BILLY'S *bed, where he sits and then lies back, listening to* COKES.]

We was testing chutes where you could just pull a lever by your ribs here when you hit the ground—see—and the chute would come off you, because it was just after a whole bunch of guys had been dragged to death in an unexpected and terrible wind at Fort Bragg. So they wanted you to be able to release the chute when you hit if there was a bad wind when you hit. So O'Flannigan was this kinda joker who had the goddamn sense a humor of a clown and nerves, I tell you, of steel, and he says he's gonna release the lever midair, then reach up, grab the lines and float on down, hanging.

> [*His hand paws at the air, seeking a rope that isn't there.*]

I see him pull the lever at five hundred feet and he reaches up to two fistfuls a air, the chute's twenty feet above him, and he went into the ground like a knife.

> [*The bottle, held high over his head, falls through the air to the bed, all watching it.*]

BILLY: Geezus.

ROONEY: [*Nodding gently*] Didn't get to sing the song, I bet.

COKES: [*Standing, staring at the fallen bottle*] No way.

RICHIE: What song?

ROONEY: [*he rises up, mysteriously angry.*] Shit sack! Shit sack!

RICHIE: What song, Sergeant Rooney?

ROONEY: "Beautiful Streamer," shit sack.

> [COKES, *gone into another reverie, is staring skyward.*]

COKES: I saw this one guy—never forget it. Never.

BILLY: That's Richie, Sergeant Rooney. He's a beautiful screamer.

RICHIE: He said "streamer," not "screamer," asshole.

> [COKES *is still in his reverie.*]

COKES: This guy with his chute goin' straight up above him in a streamer, like a
> tulip, only white, you know. All twisted and never gonna open. Like a big
> icicle sticking straight up above him. He went right by me. We met eyes,
> sort of. He was lookin' real puzzled. He looks right at me. Then he looks up
> in the air at the chute, then down at the ground.

ROONEY: Did *he* sing it?

COKES: He didn't sing it. He started going like this.

> [COKES *reaches desperately upward with hands and begins to claw at the sky while his legs pump up and down.*]

Like he was gonna climb right up the air.

RICHIE: Ohhhhh, Geezus.

BILLY: God.

[ROONEY *has collapsed backward on* BILLY'S *bed and he lies there and then he rises.*]

ROONEY: Cokes got the Silver Star for rollin' a barrel a oil down a hill in Korea into forty-seven chinky Chinese gooks who were climbin' up the hill and when he shot into it with his machine gun, it blew them all to grape jelly.

[COKES, *rocking a little on his feet, begins to hum and then sing "Beautiful Streamer," to the tune of Stephen Foster's "Beautiful Dreamer."*]

COKES: "Beautiful streamer, open for me . . . The sky is above me . . ."

[*And then the singing stops.*]

But the one I remember is this little guy in his spider hole, which is a hole in the ground with a lid over it.

[*And he is using* RICHIE'S *footlocker before him as the spider hole. He has fixed on it, is moving toward it.*]

And he shot me in the ass as I was runnin' by, but the bullet hit me so hard—

[*His body kind of jerks and he runs several steps.*]

—it knocked me into this ditch where he couldn't see me. I got behind him.

[*Now at the head of* RICHIE'S *bed, he begins to creep along the side of the bed as if sneaking up on the footlocker.*]

Crawlin'. And I dropped a grenade into his hole.

[*He jams a whiskey bottle into the footlocker, then slams down the lid.*]

Then sat on the lid, him bouncin' and yellin' under me. Bouncin' and yellin' under the lid. I could hear him. Feel him. I just sat there.

[*Silence.* ROONEY *waits, thinking, then leans forward.*]

ROONEY: He was probably singin' it.

COKES: [*Sitting there*] I think so.

ROONEY: You think we should let 'em hear it?

BILLY: We're good boys. We're good ole boys.

COKES: [*Jerking himself to his feet, he staggers sideways to join* ROONEY *on* BILLY'S *bed.*] I don't care who hears it, I just wanna be singin' it.

[ROONEY *rises; he goes to the boys on* ROGER'S *bed and speaks to them carefully, as if lecturing people on something of great importance.*]

ROONEY: You listen up; you just be listenin' up, 'cause if you hear it right you can maybe stop bein' shit sacks. This is what a man sings, he's goin' down through the air, his chute don't open.

[*Flopping back down on the bunk beside* COKES, ROONEY *looks at* COKES *and then at the boys. The two older men put their arms around each other and they begin to sing.*]

ROONEY AND COKES: [*singing*]

Beautiful streamer,
 Open for me,
The sky is above me,
But no canopy.

BILLY: [*Murmuring*] I don't believe it.

ROONEY AND COKES

 Counted ten thousand,
 Pulled on the cord.

My chute didn't open,
I shouted, "Dear Lord."

Beautiful streamer,
This looks like the end,
The earth is below me,
My body won't bend.

Just like a mother
Watching o'er me,
Beautiful streamer,
Ohhhhh, open for me.

ROGER: Un-fuckin'-believable.
ROONEY: [*Beaming with pride*] Ain't that a beauty.
   [*And then* COKES *topples forward onto his face and flops limply to his
   side. The three boys leap to their feet.* ROONEY *lunges toward* COKES.]
RICHIE: Sergeant!
ROONEY: Cokie! Cokie!
BILLY: Jesus.
ROGER: Hey!
COKES: Huh? Huh?
   [COKES *sits up.* ROONEY *is kneeling beside him.*]
ROONEY: Jesus, Cokie.
COKES: I been doin' that; I been doin' that. It don't mean nothin'.
ROONEY: No, no.
COKES: [*Pushing at* ROONEY, *who is trying to help him get back to the bed.*
   ROONEY *agrees with everything* COKES *is now saying and the noises he makes
   are little animal noises.*] I told 'em when they wanted to send me back I ain't
   got no leukemia; they wanna check it. They think I got it. I don't think I got
   it. Rooney? Whata you think?
ROONEY: No.
COKES: My mother had it. She had it. Just 'cause she did and I been fallin' down.
ROONEY: It don't mean nothin'.
COKES: [*He lunges back and up onto the bed.*] I tole 'em I fall down 'cause I'm
   drunk. I'm drunk all the time.
ROONEY: You'll be goin' back over there with me, is what I know, Cokie.
   [*He is patting* COKES, *nodding, dusting him off.*]
   That's what I know.
   [*As* BILLY *comes up to them, almost seeming to want to be a part of the
   intimacy they are sharing*]
BILLY: That was somethin', Sergeant Cokes. Jesus.
   [ROONEY *whirls on him, ferocious, pushing him.*]
ROONEY: Get the fuck away, Wilson! Whata you know? Get the fuck
   away. You don't know shit. Get away! You don't know shit.
   [*And he turns to* COKES, *who is standing up from the bed.*]
   Me and Cokes are goin' to the war zone like we oughta. Gonna blow it to
   shit.
   [*He is grabbing at* COKES, *who is laughing. They are both laughing.*
   ROONEY *whirls on the boys.*]

Ohhh, I'm gonna be so happy to be away from you assholes; you pussies. Not one regular army people among you possible. I swear it to my mother who is holy. You just be watchin' the papers for doin' darin' brave deeds. 'Cause we're old hands at it. Makin' shit disappear. Goddamn whooosh!

COKES: Whooosh!

ROONEY: Demnalitions. Me and . . .

> [*And then he knows he hasn't said it right.*]

Me and Cokie . . . Demnal . . . Demnali . . .

RICHIE: [*Still sitting on* ROGER'S *bed*] You can do it, Sergeant.

BILLY: Get it.

> [*He stands by the lockers and* ROONEY *glares at him.*]

ROGER: 'Cause you're cool with dynamite, is what you're tryin' to say.

ROONEY: [*Charging at* ROGER, *bellowing*] Shut the fuck up, that's what you can do; and go to goddamn sleep. You buncha shit . . . sacks. Buncha mothers—know-it-all motherin' shit sacks—that's what you are.

COKES: [*Shoulders back, he is taking charge.*] Just goin' to sleep is what you can do, 'cause Rooney and me fought it through two wars already and we can make it through this one more and leukemia that comes or doesn't come—who gives a shit? Not guys like us. We're goin' just pretty as pie. And it's lights-out time, ain't it, Rooney?

ROONEY: Past it, goddammit. So the lights are goin' out.

> [*There is fear in the room, and the three boys rush to their wall lockers, where they start to strip to their underwear, preparing for bed.* ROONEY *paces the room, watching them, glaring.*]

Somebody's gotta teach you soldierin'. You hear me? Or you wanna go outside and march around awhile, huh? We can do that if you wanna. Huh? You tell me? Marchin' or sleepin'? What's it gonna be?

RICHIE: [*Rushing to get into bed*] Flick out the ole lights, Sergeant; that's what we say.

BILLY: [*Climbing into bed*] Put out the ole lights.

ROGER: [*In bed and pulling up the covers*] Do it.

COKES: Shut up.

> [*He rocks forward and back, trying to stand at attention. He is saying good night.*]

And that's an order. Just shut up. I got grenades down the hall. I got a pistol. I know where to get nitro. You don't shut up, I'll blow . . . you . . . to . . . fuck.

> [*Making a military left face. he stalks to the wall switch and turns the lights out.* ROONEY *is watching proudly, as* COKES *faces the boys again. He looks at them.*]

That's right.

> [*In the dark, there is only a spill of light from the hall coming in the open door.* COKES *and* ROONEY *put their arms around each other and go out the door, leaving it partly open.* RICHIE, ROGER *and* BILLY *lie in their bunks, staring. They do not move. They lie there. The sergeants seem to have vanished soundlessly once they went out the door. Light touches each of the boys as they lie there.*]

ROGER: [*He does not move.*] Lord have mercy, if that ain't a pair. If that ain't one pair a beauties.

BILLY: Oh, hey.
> [*He does not move.*]

ROGER: Too much, man—too, too much.

RICHIE: They made me sad; but I loved them, sort of. Better than movies.

ROGER: Too much. Too, too much.
> [*Silence*]

BILLY: What time is it?

ROGER: Sleep time, men, Sleep time.
> [*Silence*]

BILLY: Right.

ROGER: They were somethin'. Too much.

BILLY: Too much.

RICHIE: Night.

ROGER: Night.
> [*Silence*]
> Night, Billy.

BILLY: Night.
> [RICHIE *stirs in his bed.* ROGER *turns onto his side.* BILLY *is motionless.*]

BILLY: I . . . had a buddy, Rog—and this is the whole thing, this is the whole point—a kid I grew up with, played ball with in high school, and he was a tough little cat, a real bad man sometimes. Used to have gangster pictures up in his room. Anyway, we got into this deal where we'd drive on down to the big city, man, you know, hit the bad spots, let some queer pick us up . . . sort of . . . long enough to buy us some good stuff. It was kinda the thing to do for a while, and we all did it, the whole gang of us. So we'd let these cats pick us up, most of 'em old guys, and they were hurtin' and happy as hell to have us, and we'd get a lot of free booze, maybe a meal, and we'd turn 'em on. Then pretty soon they'd ask us did we want to go over to their place. Sure, we'd say, and order one more drink, and then when we hit the street, we'd tell 'em to kiss off. We'd call 'em fag and queer and jazz like that and tell 'em to kiss off. And Frankie, the kid I'm tellin' you about, he had a mean streak in him and if they gave us a bad time at all, he'd put 'em down. That's the way he was. So that kinda jazz went on and on for sort of a long time and it was a good deal if we were low on cash or needed a laugh and it went on for a while. And then Frankie—one day he come up to me—and he says he was goin' home with the guy he was with. He said, what the hell, what did it matter? And he's sayin'—Frankie's sayin'—why don't I tag along? What the hell, he's sayin', what does it matter who does it to you, some broad or some old guy, you close your eyes, a mouth's a mouth, it don't matter—that's what he's sayin'. I tried to talk him out of it, but he wasn't hearin' anything I was sayin'. So the next day, see, he calls me up to tell me about it. Okay, okay, he says, it was a cool scene, he says; they played poker, a buck minimum, and he made a fortune. Frankie was eatin' it up, man. It was a pretty way to live, he says. So he stayed at it, and he had this nice little girl he was goin' with at the time. You know the way a real bad cat can sometimes do that—have a good little girl who's crazy about him and he is for her, too, and he's a different cat when he's with her?

ROGER: Uh-huh.

[*The hall light slants across* BILLY'S *face.*]

BILLY: Well, that was him and Linda, and then one day he dropped her, he cut her loose. He was hooked, man. He was into it, with no way he knew out—you understand what I'm sayin'? He had got his ass hooked. He had never thought he would and then one day he woke up and he was on it. He just hadn't been told, that's the way I figure it; somebody didn't tell him somethin' he shoulda been told and he come to me wailin' one day, man, all broke up and wailin', my boy Frankie, my main man, and he was a fag. He was a faggot, black Roger, and I'm not lyin'. I am not lyin' to you.

ROGER: Damn.

BILLY: So that's the whole thing, man; that's the whole thing.

[*Silence. They lie there.*]

ROGER: Holy . . . Christ. Richie . . . you hear him? You hear what he said?

RICHIE: He's a storyteller.

ROGER: What you mean?

RICHIE: I mean, he's a storyteller, all right; he tells stories, all right.

ROGER: What are we into now? You wanna end up like that friend a his, or you don't believe what he said? Which are you sayin'?

[*The door bursts open. The sounds of machine guns and cannon are being made by someone, and* CARLYLE, *drunk and playing, comes crawling in.* ROGER, RICHIE *and* BILLY *all pop up, startled, to look at him.*]

Hey, hey, what's happenin'?

BILLY: Who's happenin'?

ROGER: You attackin' or you retreatin', man?

CARLYLE: [*looking up; big grin*] Hey, baby . . . ?

[*continues shooting, crawling. The three boys look at each other.*]

ROGER: What's happenin', man? Whatcha doin'?

CARLYLE: I dunno, soul; I dunno. Practicin' my duties, my new abilities.

[*Half sitting, he flops onto his side, starts to crawl.*]

The low crawl, man; like I was taught in basic, that's what I'm doin'. You gotta know your shit, man, else you get your ass blown so far away you don't ever see it again. Oh, sure, you guys don't care. I know it. You got it made. You got it made. I don't got it made. You got a little home here, got friends, people to talk to. I got nothin'. You got jobs they probably ain't ever gonna ship you out, you got so important jobs. I got no job. They don't even wanna give me a job. I know it. They are gonna kill me. They are gonna send me over there to get killed, goddammit. WHAT'S A MATTER WITH ALL YOU PEOPLE?

[*The anger explodes out of the grieving and* ROGER *rushes to kneel beside* CARLYLE. *He speaks gently, firmly.*]

ROGER: Hey, man, get cool, get some cool, purchase some cool, man.

CARLYLE: Awwwww . . .

[*Clumsily, he turns away.*]

ROGER: Just hang in there.

CARLYLE: I don't wanna be no DEAD man. I don't wanna be the one they all thinkin' is so stupid he's the only one'll go, they tell him; they don't even have to give him a job. I got thoughts, man, in my head; alla time, burnin', burnin' thoughts a understandin'.

ROGER: Don't you think we know that, man? It ain't the way you're sayin' it.

CARLYLE: It is.

ROGER: No. I mean, we all probably gonna go. We all probably gonna have to go.

CARLYLE: No-o-o-o-.

ROGER: I mean it.

CARLYLE: [*Suddenly he nearly topples over.*] I am very drunk.
[*And he looks up at* ROGER.]
You think so?

ROGER: I'm sayin' so. And I am sayin', "No sweat." No point.
[CARLYLE *angrily pushes at* ROGER, *knocking him backward.*]

CARLYLE: Awwwww, dammit, dammit, mother . . . shit . . . it . . . ohhhhhh.
[*Sliding to the floor, the rage and anguish softening into only breathing*]
I mean it. I mean it.
[*Silence. He lies there.*]

ROGER: What . . . a you doin' . . . ?

CARLYLE: Huh?

ROGER: I don't know what you're up to on our freshly mopped floor.

CARLYLE: Gonna go sleep—okay? No sweat . . .
[*Suddenly very polite, he is looking up.*]
Can I, soul? Izzit all right?

ROGER: Sure, man, sure, if you wanna, but why don't you go where you got a bed? Don't you like beds?

CARLYLE: Dunno where's zat. My bed. I can' fin' it. I can' fin' my own bed. I looked all over, but I can' fin' it anywhere. GONE!
[*Slipping back down now, he squirms to make a nest. He hugs his bottle.*]

ROGER: [*Moving to his bunk, where he grabs a blanket*] Okay, okay, man. But get on top a this, man.
[*He is spreading the blanket on the floor, trying to help* CARLYLE *get on it.*]
Make it softer, C'mon, c'mon . . . get on this.
[BILLY *has risen with his own blanket, and is moving now to hand it to* ROGER.]

BILLY: Cat's hurtin', Rog.

ROGER: Ohhhhh, yeh.

CARLYLE: Ohhhhh . . . it was so sweet at home . . . it was so sweet, baby; so-o-o good. They doin' dances make you wanna cry. . . .
[*Hugging the blankets, he drifts in a kind of dream.*]

ROGER: I know, man.

CARLYLE: So sweet . . . !
[BILLY *is moving back to his own bed, where, quietly, he sits.*]

ROGER: I know, man.

CARLYLE: So sweet . . . !

ROGER: Yeh.

CARLYLE: How come I gotta be here?

> [*On his way to the door to close it,* ROGERS *falters, looks at* CARLYLE *then moves on toward the door.*]

ROGER: I dunno, Jim.

> [BILLY *is sitting and watching, as* ROGER *goes on to the door, gently closes it and returns to his bed.*]

BILLY: I know why he's gotta be here, Roger. You wanna know? Why don't you ask me?

ROGER: Okay. How come he gotta be here?

BILLY: [*smiling*] Freedom's frontier, man. That's why.

ROGER: [*Settled on the edge of his bed and about to lie back*] Oh . . . yeh . . .

> [*As a distant bugle begins to play taps and* RICHIE, *carrying a blanket, is approaching* CARLYLE, ROGER *settles back;* BILLY *is staring at* RICHIE; CARLYLE *does not stir; the bugle plays.*]

Bet that ole sarge don't live a year, Billy. Fuckin' blow his own ass sky high.

> [RICHIE *has covered* CARLYLE. *He pats* CARLYLE'S *arm, and then straightens in order to return to his bed.*]

BILLY: Richie . . . !

> [BILLY'S *hissing voice freezes* RICHIE. *He stands, and then he starts again to move, and* BILLY'S *voice comes again and* RICHIE *cannot move.*]

Richie . . . how come you gotta keep doin' that stuff?

> [ROGER *looks at* BILLY, *staring at* RICHIE, *who stands still as a stone over the sleeping* CARLYLE.]

How come?

ROGER: He dunno, man. Do you? You dunno, do you, Rich?

RICHIE: No.

CARLYLE: [*From deep in his sleep and grieving*] It . . . was . . . so . . . pretty . . . !

RICHIE: No.

> [*The lights are fading with the last soft notes of taps.*]

ACT II

SCENE I—— *Lights come up on the cadre room. It is late afternoon and* BILLY *is lying on his stomach, his head at the foot of the bed, his chin resting on his hands. He wears gym shorts and sweat socks; his T-shirt lies on the bed and his sneakers are on the floor.* ROGER *is at his footlocker, taking out a pair of sweat socks. His sneakers and his basketball are on his bed. He is wearing his khakis.*

A silence passes, and then ROGER *closes his footlocker and sits on his bed, where he starts lacing his sneakers, holding them on his lap.*

BILLY: Rog . . . you think I'm a busybody? In any way?

> [*Silence.* ROGER *laces his sneakers.*]

Roger?

ROGER: Huh? Uh-uh.

BILLY: Some people do. I mean, back home;

[*He rolls slightly to look at* ROGER.]

Or that I didn't know how to behave. Sort of.

ROGER: It's time we maybe get changed, don't you think?

[ROGER *rises and goes to his locker. He takes off his trousers, shoes and socks.*]

BILLY: Yeh. I guess. I don't feel like it, though. I don't feel good, don't know why.

ROGER: Be good for you, man; be good for you.

[*Pulling on his gym shorts,* ROGER *returns to his bed, carrying his shoes and socks.*]

BILLY: Yeh.

[BILLY *sits up on the edge of his bed.* ROGER, *sitting, is bowed over, putting on his socks.*]

I mean, a lot a people thought like I didn't know how to behave in a simple way. You know? That I overcomplicated everything. I didn't think so. Don't think so, I just thought I was seein' complications that were there but nobody else saw.

[*He is struggling now to put on his T-shirt. He seems weary, almost weak.*]

I mean, Wisconsin's a funny place. All those clear-eyed people sayin' "Hello" and lookin' you straight in the eye. Everybody's good, you think, and happy and honest. And then there's all of a sudden a neighbor who goes mad as a hatter. I had a neighbor who came out of his house one morning with axes in both hands. He started then attackin' the cars that were driving up and down in front of his house. An' we all knew why he did it, sorta.

[*He pauses; he thinks.*]

It made me wanna be a priest then. I wanted to be a priest then. I was sixteen. Priests could help people. Could take away what hurt 'em. I wanted that, I thought. Somethin', huh?

ROGER: [*He has the basketball in his hands.*] Yeh. But everybody's got feelin's like that sometimes.

BILLY: I don't know.

ROGER: You know, you oughta work on a little jump shot, my man. Get you some kinda fall-away jumper to go with that beauty of a hook. Make you tough out there.

BILLY: Can't fuckin' do it. Not my game. I mean, like that bar we go to. You think I could get a job there bartendin', maybe? I could learn the ropes.

[*He is watching* ROGER, *who has risen to walk to his locker.*]

You think I could get a job there off-duty hours?

ROGER: [*Pulling his locker open to display the pinup on the inside of the door.*] You don't want no job. It's that little black-haired waitress you wantin' to know.

BILLY: No, man. Not really.

ROGER: It's okay. She tough, man.

[*He begins to remove his uniform shirt. He will put on an O.D. T-shirt to go to the gym.*]

BILLY: I mean, not the way you're sayin' it, is all. Sure, there's somethin' about her. I don't know what. I ain't even spoke to her yet. But somethin'. I mean, what's she doin' there? When she's dancin', it's like she knows somethin'. She's degradin' herself, I sometimes feel. You think she is?

ROGER: Man, you don't even know the girl. She's workin'.

BILLY: I'd like to talk to her. Tell her stuff. Find out about her. Sometimes I'm thinkin' about her and it and I got a job there, I get to know her and she and I get to be real right, man—close, you know. Maybe we screw, maybe we don't. It's nice . . . whatever.

ROGER: Sure. She a fine-lookin' chippy, Billy. Got nice cakes. Nice little titties.

BILLY: I think she's smart, too.

[ROGER *starts laughing so hard he almost falls into his locker.*]

Oh, all I do is talk. "Yabba-yabba." I mean, my mom and dad are really terrific people. How'd they ever end up with somebody so weird as me?

[ROGER *moves to him, jostles him.*]

ROGER: I'm tellin' you, the gym and a little ball is what you need. Little exercise. Little bumpin' into people. The soul is tellin' you.

[BILLY *rises and goes to his locker, where he starts putting on his sweat clothes.*]

BILLY: I mean, Roger, you remember how we met in P Company? Both of us brand-new. You started talkin' to me. You just started talkin' to me and you didn't stop.

ROGER: [*Hardly looking up*] Yeh.

BILLY: Did you see somethin' in me made you pick me?

ROGER: I was talkin' to everybody, man. For that whole day. Two whole days. You was just the first one to talk back friendly. Though you didn't say much, as I recall.

BILLY: The first white person, you mean.

[*Wearing his sweat pants,* BILLY *is now at his bed, putting on his sneakers.*]

ROGER: Yeh. I was tryin' to come outa myself a little. Do like the fuckin' head shrinker been tellin' me to stop them fuckin' headaches I was havin', you know. Now let us do fifteen or twenty push-ups and get over to that gymnasium, like I been sayin'. Then we can take our civvies with us—we can shower and change at the gym.

[ROGER *crosses to* BILLY, *who flops down on his belly on the bed.*]

BILLY: I don't know . . . I don't know what it is I'm feelin'. Sick like.

[ROGER *forces* BILLY *up onto his feet and shoves him playfully downstage, where they both fall forward into the push-up position, side by side.*]

ROGER: Do 'em, trooper. Do 'em. Get it.

[ROGER *starts.* BILLY *joins in. After five,* ROGER *realizes that* BILLY *has his knees on the floor. They start again. This time,* BILLY *counts in double time. They start again. At about "seven,"* RICHIE *enters. Neither* BILLY *nor* ROGER *sees him. They keep going.*]

ROGER AND BILLY: . . . seven, eight, nine, ten . . .

RICHIE: No, no; no, no; no, no. no. That's not it; that's not it.

[*They keep going, yelling the numbers louder and louder.*]

ROGER AND BILLY: . . . *eleven, twelve, thirteen* . . .

> [RICHIE *crosses to his locker and gets his bottle of cologne, and then returning to the center of the room to stare at them, he stands there dabbing cologne on his face.*]

ROGER AND BILLY: . . . *fourteen, fifteen.*

RICHIE: You'll never get it like that. You're so far apart and you're both humping at the same time. And all that counting. It's so unromantic.

ROGER: [*Rising and moving to his bed to pick up the basketball*] We was exercisin', Richard. You heard a that?

RICHIE: Call it what you will, Roger.

> [*With a flick of his wrist,* ROGER *tosses the basketball to* BILLY.]

Everybody has their own cute little pet names for it.

BILLY: Hey!

> [*And he tosses the ball at* RICHIE, *hitting him in the chest, sending the cologne bottle flying.* RICHIE *yelps, as* BILLY *retrieves the ball and, grabbing up his sweat jacket from the bed, heads for the door.* ROGER, *at his own locker, has taken out his suit bag of civilian clothes.*]

You missed.

RICHIE: Billy, Billy, Billy, please, please, the ruffian approach will not work with me. It impresses me not even one tiny little bit. All you've done is spill my cologne.

> [*He bends to pick up the cologne from the floor.*]

BILLY: That was my aim.

ROGER: See you.

> [BILLY *is passing* RICHIE. *Suddenly* RICHIE *sprays* BILLY *with cologne, some of it getting on* ROGER, *as* ROGER *and* BILLY, *groaning and cursing at* RICHIE, *rush out the door.*]

RICHIE: Try the more delicate approach next time, Bill.

> [*Having crossed to the door, he stands a moment, leaning against the frame. Then he bounces to* BILLY'S *bed, sings "He's just my Bill," and squirts cologne on the pillow. At his locker, he deposits the cologne, takes off his shirt, shoes and socks. Removing a hard-cover copy of Pauline Kael's* I Lost It at the Movies *from the top shelf of the locker, he bounds to the center of the room and tosses the book the rest of the way to the bed. Quite pleased with himself, he fidgets, pats his stomch, then lowers himself into the push-up position, goes to his knees and stands up.*]

Am I out of my fuckin mind? Those two are crazy. I'm not crazy.

> [RICHIE *pivots and strides to his locker. With an ashtray, a pack of matches and a pack of cigarettes, he hurries to his bed and makes himself comfortable to read, his head propped up on a pillow. Settling himself, he opens the book, finds his place, thinks a little, starts to read. For a moment he lies there. And then* CARLYLE *steps into the room. He comes through the doorway looking to his left and right. He comes several steps into the room and looks at* RICHIE. RICHIE *sees him. They look at each other.*]

CARLYLE: Ain't nobody here, man?

RICHIE: Hello, Carlyle. How are you today?

CARLYLE: Ain't nobody here?

[*He is nervous and angrily disappointed.*]

RICHIE: Who do you want?

CARLYLE: Where's the black boy?

RICHIE: Roger? My God, why do you keep calling him that? Don't you know his name yet? Roger. Roger.

[*He thickens his voice at this, imitating someone very stupid.* CARLYLE *stares at him.*]

CARLYLE: Yeh. Where is he?

RICHIE: I am not his keeper, you know. I am not his private secretary, you know.

CARLYLE: I do not know. I do not know. That is why I am asking. I come to see him. You are here. I ask you. I don't know. I mean, Carlyle made a fool outa himself comin' in here the other night, talkin' on and on like how he did. Lay on the floor. He remember. You remember? It all one hype, man; that all one hype. You know what I mean. That ain't the real Carlyle was in here. This one here and now the real Carlyle. Who the real Richie?

RICHIE: Well . . . the real Richie . . . has gone home. To Manhattan. I, however, am about to read this book.

[*Which he again starts to try to do*]

CARLYLE: Oh. Shit. Jus' you the only one here, then, huh?

RICHIE: So it would seen.

[*He looks at the air and then under the bed as if to find someone.*]

So it would seem. Did you hear about Martin?

CARLYLE: What happened to Martin? I ain't seen him.

RICHIE: They are shipping him home. Someone told about what he did to himself. I don't know who.

CARLYLE: Wasn't me. Not me. I keep that secret.

RICHIE: I'm sure you did.

[*Rising, walking toward* CARLYLE *and the door, cigarette pack in hand*]

You want a cigarette? Or don't you smoke? Or do you have to go right away?

[*closing the door*]

There's a chill sometimes coming down the hall, I don't know from where.

[*Crossing back to his bed and climbing in*]

And I think I've got the start of a little cold. Did you want the cigarette?

[CARLYLE *is staring at him. Then he examines the door and looks again at* RICHIE. *He stares at* RICHIE, *thinking, and then he walks toward him.*]

CARLYLE: You know what I bet? I been lookin' at you real close. It just a way I got about me. And I bet if I was to hang my boy out in front of you, my big boy, man, you'd start wantin' to touch him. Be beggin' and talkin' sweet to ole Carlyle. Am I right or wong?

[*He leans over* RICHIE.]

What do you say?

RICHIE: Pardon?

CARLYLE: You heard me. Ohhh. I am so restless, I don't even understand it. My

big black boy is what I was talkin' about. My thing, man; my rope, Jim.
HEY, RICHIE!

[*And he lunges, then moves his fingers through* RICHIE'S *hair.*]

How long you been a punk? Can you hear me? Am I clear? Do I talk funny?

[*He is leaning close.*]

Can you smell the gin on my mouth?

RICHIE: I mean, if you really came looking for Roger, he and Billy are gone
to the gymnasium. They were—

CARLYLE: No.

[*He slides down on the bed, his arm placed over* RICHIE'S *legs.*]

I got no athletic abilities. I got none. No moves. I don't know. HEY,
RICHIE!

[*leaning close again*]

I just got this question I asked. I got no answer.

RICHIE: I don't know . . . what . . . you mean.

CARLYLE: I heard me. I understood me. "How long you been a punk?" is the
question I asked. Have you got a reply?

RICHIE: [*confused, irritated, but fascinated*] Not to that question.

CARLYLE: Who do if you don't? I don't. How'm I gonna?

[*Suddenly there is whistling in the hall, as if someone might enter,
footsteps approaching, and* RICHIE *leaps to his feet and scurries away
toward the door, tucking in his undershirt as he goes.*]

Man, don't you wanna talk to me? Don't you wanna talk to ole Carlyle?

RICHIE: Not at the moment.

CARLYLE: [*He is rising, starting after* RICHIE, *who stands nervously near* ROGER'S
bed.] I want to talk to you, man; why don't you want to talk to me? We can
be friends. Talkin' back and forth, sharin' thoughts and bein' happy.

RICHIE: I don't think that's what you want.

CARLYLE: [*He is very near to* RICHIE.] What do I want?

RICHIE: I mean, to talk to me.

[RICHIE, *as if repulsed, crosses away. But it is hard to tell if the move is
genuine or coy.*]

CARLYLE: What am I doin'? I am talkin'. DON'T YOU TELL ME I AIN'T
TALKIN' WHEN I AM TALKIN'! COURSE I AM. Bendin' over backwards.

[*And pressing his hands against himself in his anger, he has touched
the grease on his shirt, the filth of his clothing, and this ignites the
anger.*]

Do you know they still got me in that goddamn P Company? That goddamn
transient company. It like they think I ain't got no notion what a home is.
No nose for no home—like I ain't never had no home. I had a home. IT
LIKE THEY THINK THERE AIN'T NO PLACE FOR ME IN THIS
MOTHER ARMY BUT K.P. ALL SUDSY AND WRINKLED AND
SWEATIN'. EVERY DAY SINCE I GOT TO THIS SHIT HOUSE,
MISTER! HOW MANY TIMES YOU BEEN ON K.P.? WHEN'S THE
LAST TIME YOU PULLED K.P.?

[*He has roared down to where* RICHIE *had moved, the rage possessing
him.*]

RICHIE: I'm E.D.

CARLYLE: You E.D.? You E.D.? You Edie, are you? I didn't ask you what you friends call you, I asked you when's the last time you had K.P.?

RICHIE: [*Edging toward his bed. He will go there, get and light a cigarette.*] E.D. is "Exempt from Duty."

CARLYLE: [*Moving after* RICHIE] You ain't got no duties? What shit you talkin' about? Everybody in this fuckin' army got duties. That what the fuckin' army all about. You ain't got no duties, who got 'em?

RICHIE: Because of my job, Carlyle. I have a very special job. And my friends don't call me Edie.

[*Big smile*]

They call me Irene.

CARLYLE: That mean what you sayin' is you kiss ass for somebody, don't it? Good for you.

[*Seemingly relaxed and gentle, he settles down on* RICHIE'S *bed. He seems playful and charming.*]

You know the other night I was sleepin' there. You know.

RICHIE: Yes.

CARLYLE: [*Gleefully, enormously pleased*] You remember that? How come you remember that? You sweet.

RICHIE: We don't have people sleeping on our floor that often, Carlyle.

CARLYLE: But the way you crawl over in the night, gimme a big kiss on my joint. That nice.

RICHIE: [*Shocked, he blinks.*] What?

CARLYLE: Or did I dream that?

RICHIE: [*laughing in spite of himself*] My God, you're outrageous!

CARLYLE: Maybe you dreamed it.

RICHIE: What . . . ? No. I don't know.

CARLYLE: Maybe you did, then; you didn't dream it.

RICHIE: How come you talk so much?

CARLYLE: I don't talk, man, who's gonna talk? YOU?

[*He is laughing and amused, but there is an anger near the surface now, an ugliness.*]

That bore me to death. I don't like nobody's voice but my own. I am so pretty. Don't like nobody else face.

[*And then viciously, he spits out at* RICHIE.]

You goddamn face ugly fuckin' queer punk!

[*and* RICHIE *jumps in confusion.*]

RICHIE: What's the matter with you?

CARLYLE: You goddamn ugly punk face. YOU UGLY!

RICHIE: Nice mouth.

CARLYLE: That's right. That's right. And you got a weird mouth. Like to suck joints.

[*As* RICHIE *storms to his locker, throwing the book inside. He pivots, grabbing a towel, marching toward the door.*]

Hey, you gonna jus' walk out on me? Where you goin'? You c'mon back. Hear?

RICHIE: That's my bed, for chrissake.

[*He lunges into the hall.*]

CARLYLE: You'd best.

[*Lying there, he makes himself comfortable. He takes a pint bottle from his back pocket.*]

You come back, Richie, I tell you a good joke. Make you laugh, make you cry.

[*He takes a big drink.*]

That's right. Ole Frank and Jesse, they got the stagecoach stopped, all the peoples lined up—Frank say, "All right, peoples, we gonna rape all the men and rob all the women." Jesse say, "Frank, no, no—that ain't it—we gonna—" And this one little man yell real loud, "You shut up, Jesse; Frank knows what he's doin'."

[*Loudly, he laughs and laughs.* BILLY *enters. Startled at the sight of* CARLYLE *there in* RICHIE'S *bed,* BILLY *falters, as* CARLYLE *gestures toward him.*]

Hey, man . . . ! Hey, you know, they send me over to that Vietnam, I be cool, 'cause I been dodgin' bullets and shit since I been old enough to get on pussy make it happy to know me. I can get on, I can do my job.

[BILLY *looks weary and depressed. Languidly he crosses to his bed. He still wears his sweat clothes.* CARLYLE *studies him, then stares at the ceiling.*]

Yeh. I was just layin' here thinkin' that and you come in and out it come, words to say my feelin'. That my problem. That the black man's problem altogether. You ever considered that? Too much feelin'. He too close to everthing. He is, man; too close to his blood, to his body. It ain't that he don't have no good mind, but he BELIEVE in his body. Is . . . that Richie the only punk in this room, or is there more?

BILLY: What?

CARLYLE: The punk; is he the only punk?

[*Carefully he takes one of* RICHIE'S *cigarettes and lights it.*]

BILLY: He's all right.

CARLYLE: I ain't askin' about the quality of his talent, but is he the only one, is my question?

BILLY: [*He does not want to deal with this. He sits there.*] You get your orders yet?

CARLYLE: Orders for what?

BILLY: To tell you where you work.

CARLYLE: I'm P Company, man. I work in P Company. I do K.P. That all. Don't deserve no more. Do you know I been in this army three months and ten days and everybody still doin' the same shit and sayin' the same shit and wearin' the same green shitty clothes? I ain't been happy one day, and that a lotta goddamn misery back to back in this ole boy. Is that Richie a good punk? Huh? Is he? He takes care of you and Roger—that how come you in this room, the three of you?

BILLY: What?

CARLYLE: [*Emphatically*] You and Roger are hittin' on Richie, right?

BILLY: He's not queer, if that's what you're sayin'. A little effeminate, but that's all, no more; if that's what you're sayin'.

CARLYLE: I'd like to get some of him myself if he a good punk, is what I'm sayin'.

That's what I'm sayin'! You don't got no understandin' how a man can maybe be a little diplomatic about what he's sayin' sorta sideways, do you? Jesus.

BILLY: He don't do that stuff.

CARLYLE: [*Lying there*] What stuff?

BILLY: Listen, man. I don't feel too good, you don't mind.

CARLYLE: What stuff?

BILLY: What you're thinkin'.

CARLYLE: What . . . am I thinkin'?

BILLY: You . . . know.

CARLYLE: Yes, I do. It in my head, that how come I know. But how do you know? I can see your heart, Billy boy, but you cannot see mine. I am unknown. You . . . are known.

BILLY: [*As if he is about to vomit, and fighting it*] You just . . . talk fast and keep movin', don't you? Don't ever stay still.

CARLYLE: Words to say my feelin', Billy boy.

[RICHIE *steps into the room. He sees* BILLY *and* CARLYLE, *and freezes.*] There he is. There he be.

[RICHIE *moves to his locker to put away the towel.*]

RICHIE: He's one of them who hasn't come down far out of the trees yet, Billy; believe me.

CARLYLE: You got rudeness in your voice, Richie—you got meanness I can hear about ole Carlyle. You tellin' me I oughta leave—is that what you think you're doin'? You don't want me here?

RICHIE: You come to see Roger, who isn't here, right? Man like you must have important matters to take care of all over the quad; I can't imagine a man like you not having extremely important things to do all over the world, as a matter of fact, Carlyle.

CARLYLE: [*He rises. He begins to smooth the sheets and straighten the pillow. He will put the pint bottle in his back pocket and cross near to* RICHIE.] Ohhhh, listen—don't mind all the shit I say. I just talk bad, is all I do; I don't do bad. I got to have friends just like anybody else. I'm just bored and restless, that all; takin' it out on you two. I mean, I know Richie here ain't really no punk, not really. I was just talkin', just jivin' and entertainin' my own self. Don't take me serious, not ever. I get on out and see you all later.

[*He moves for the door,* RICHIE *right behind him, almost ushering him.*]

You be cool, hear? Man don't do the jivin', he the one gettin' jived. That what my little brother Henry tell me and tell me.

[*Moving leisurely, he backs out the door and is gone.* RICHIE *shuts the door. There is a silence as* RICHIE *stands by the door.* BILLY *looks at him and then looks away.*]

BILLY: I am gonna have to move myself outa here, Roger decides to adopt that sonofabitch.

RICHIE: He's an animal.

BILLY: Yeh, and on top a that, he's a rotten person.

RICHIE: [*He laughs nervously, crossing nearer to* BILLY.] I think you're probably right.

[*Still laughing a little, he pats* BILLY'S *shoulder and* BILLY *freezes at the touch. Awkwardly* RICHIE *removes his hand and crosses to his bed. When he has lain down,* BILLY *bends to take off his sneakers, then lies back on his pillow, staring, thinking, and there is a silence.* RICHIE *does not move. He lies there, struggling to prepare himself for something.*]

Hey . . . Billy?

[*very slight pause*]

Billy?

BILLY: Yeh.

RICHIE: You know that story you told the other night?

BILLY: Yeh . . . ?

RICHIE: You know . . .

BILLY: What . . . about it?

RICHIE: Well, was it . . . about you?

[*pause*]

I mean, was it . . . ABOUT YOU? Were you Frankie?

[*This is difficult for him.*]

Are . . . you Frankie? Billy?

[BILLY *is slowly sitting up.*]

BILLY: You sonofabitch . . . !

RICHIE: Or was it really about somebody you knew . . . ?

BILLY: [*Sitting, outraged and glaring*] You didn't hear me at all!

RICHIE: I'm just asking a simple question, Billy, that's all I'm doing.

BILLY: You are really sick. You know that? Your brain is really, truly rancid! Do you know there's a theory now it's genetic? That it's all a matter of genes and shit like that?

RICHIE: Everything is not so ungodly cryptic, Billy.

BILLY: You. You, man, and the rot it's makin' outa your feeble fuckin' brain.

[ROGER, *dressed in civilian clothes, bursts in and* BILLY *leaps to his feet.*]

ROGER: Hey, hey, anyone got a couple bucks he can loan me?

BILLY: Rog, where you been?

ROGER: [*Throwing the basketball and his sweat clothes into his locker*] I need five. C'mon.

BILLY: Where you been? That asshole friend a yours was here.

ROGER: I know, I know. Can you gimme five?

RICHIE: [*He jumps to the floor and heads for his locker.*] You want five. I got it. You want ten or more, even?

[BILLY, *watching* RICHIE, *turns, and nervously paces down right, where he moves about, worried.*]

BILLY: I mean, we gotta talk about him, man; we gotta talk about him.

ROGER: [*as* RICHIE *is handing him two fives*] 'Cause we goin' to town together. I jus' run into him out on the quad, man, and he was feelin' real bad 'bout the way he acted, how you guys done him, he was fallin' down apologizin' all over the place.

BILLY: [As RICHIE *marches back to his bed and sits down*] I mean, he's got a lotta weird ideas about us; I'm tellin' you.

ROGER: He's just a little fucked up in his head is all, but he ain't trouble.

[*He takes a pair of sunglasses from the locker and puts them on.*]
BILLY: Who needs him? I mean, we don't need him.
ROGER: You gettin' too nervous, man. Nobody said anything about anybody needin' anybody. I been on the street all my life; he brings back home. I played me a little ball, Billy; took me a shower. I'm feelin' good!
[*He has moved down to* BILLY.]
BILLY: I'm tellin' you there's something wrong with him, though.
ROGER: [*Face to face with* BILLY, ROGER *is a little irritated.*] Every black man in the world ain't like me, man; you get used to that idea. You get to know him, and you gonna like him. I'm tellin' you. You get to be laughin' just like me to hear him talk his shit. But you gotta relax.
RICHIE: I agree with Billy, Roger.
ROGER: Well, you guys got it all worked out and that's good, but I am goin' to town with him. Man's got wheels. Got a good head. You got any sense, you'll come with us.
BILLY: What are you talkin' about—come with you? I just tole you he's crazy.
ROGER: And I tole you you're wrong.
RICHIE: We weren't invited.
ROGER: I'm invitin' you.
RICHIE: No, I don't wanna.
ROGER: [*He moves to* RICHIE; *it seems he really wants* RICHIE *to go.*] You sure, Richie? C'mon.
RICHIE: No.
ROGER: Billy? He got wheels, we goin' in drinkin', see if gettin' our heads real bad don't just make us feel real good. You know what I mean. I got him right, you got him wrong.
BILLY: But what if I'm right?
ROGER: Billy, Billy, the man is waitin' on me. You know you wanna. Jesus. Bad cat like that gotta know the way. He been to D.C. before. Got cousins here. Got wheels for the weekend. You always talkin' how you don't do nothin'—you just talk it. Let's do it tonight—stop talkin'. Be cruisin' up and down the strip, leanin' out the window, bad as we wanna be. True cool is a car. We can flip a cigarette out the window—we can watch it bounce. Get us some chippies. You know we can. And if we don't, he knows a cathouse, it fulla cats.
BILLY: You serious?
RICHIE: You mean you're going to a whorehouse? That's disgusting.
BILLY: Listen who's talkin'. What do you want me to do? Stay here with you?
RICHIE: We could go to a movie or something.
ROGER: I am done with this talkin'. You goin', you stayin'?
[*He crosses to his locker, pulls into view a wide-brimmed black and shiny hat, and puts it on, cocking it at a sharp angle.*]
BILLY: I don't know.
ROGER: [*Stepping for the door*] I am goin'.
BILLY: [*Turning,* BILLY *sees the hat.*] I'm going. Okay! I'm going! Going, going, going!
[*And he runs to his locker.*]
RICHIE: Oh, Billy, you'll be scared to death in a cathouse and you know it.

BILLY: BULLSHIT!

[*He is removing his sweat pants and putting on a pair of gray corduroy trousers.*]

ROGER: Billy got him a lion-tamer 'tween his legs!

[*The door bangs open and* CARLYLE *is there, still clad in his filthy fatigues, but wearing a going-to-town black knit cap on his head and carrying a bottle.*]

CARLYLE: Man, what's goin' on? I been waitin' like throughout my fuckin' life.

ROGER: Billy's goin', too. He's gotta change.

CARLYLE: He goin', too! Hey! Beautiful! That beautiful!

[*His grin is large, his laugh is loud.*]

ROGER: Didn't I tell you, Billy?

CARLYLE: That beautiful, man; we all goin' to be friends!

RICHIE: [*sitting on his bed*] What about me, Carlyle?

[CARLYLE *looks at* RICHIE, *and then at* ROGER *and then he and* ROGER *begin to laugh.* CARLYLE *pokes* ROGER *and they laugh as they are leaving.* BILLY, *grabbing up his sneakers to follow, stops at the door, looking only briefly at* RICHIE. *Then* BILLY *goes and shuts the door. The lights are fading to black.*]

SCENE II—— *In the dark, taps begins to play. And then slowly the lights rise, but the room remains dim. Only the lamp attached to* RICHIE'S *bed burns and there is the glow and spill of the hallway coming through the transom.* BILLY, CARLYLE, ROGER *and* RICHIE *are sprawled about the room.* BILLY, *lying on his stomach, has his head at the foot of his bed, a half-empty bottle of beer dangling in his hand. He wears a blue oxford-cloth shirt and his sneakers lie beside his bed.* ROGER, *collapsed in his own bed, lies upon his back, his head also at the foot, a Playboy magazine covering his face and a half-empty bottle of beer in his hands, folded on his belly. Having removed his civilian shirt, he wears a white T-shirt.* CARLYLE *is lying on his belly on* RICHIE'S *bed, his head at the foot, and he is facing out.*

RICHIE *is sitting on the floor, resting against* ROGER'S *footlocker. He is wrapped in a blanket. Beside him is an unopened bottle of beer and a bottle opener.*

They are all dreamy in the dimness as taps plays sadly on and then fades into silence. No one moves.

RICHIE: I don't know where it was, but it wasn't here. And we were all in it—it felt like—but we all had different faces. After you guys left, I only dozed for a few minutes, so it couldn't have been long. Roger laughed a lot and Billy was taller. I don't remember all the details exactly, and even though we were the ones in it, I know it was about my father. He was a big man. I was six. He was a very big man when I was six and he went away, but I remember him. He started drinking and staying home making model airplanes and boats and paintings by the numbers. We had money from mom's family, so he was just home all the time. And then one day I was coming home from kindergarten, and as I was starting up the front walk he came out the door and he had these suitcases in his hands. He was leaving, see, sneaking out, and I'd caught him. We looked at each other and I just knew and I started crying. He yelled at me, "Don't you cry; don't you start crying." I tried to grab him and he pushed me down in the grass. And then he was gone. G-O-N-E.

BILLY: And that was it? That was it?

RICHIE: I remember hiding my eyes. I lay in the grass and hid my eyes and waited.

BILLY: He never came back?

RICHIE: No.

CARLYLE: Ain't that some shit. Now, I'm a jive-time street nigger. I knew where my daddy was all the while. He workin' in this butcher shop two blocks up the street. Ole Mom used to point him out. "There he go. That him—that your daddy." We'd see him on the street, "There he go."

ROGER: Man couldn't see his way to livin' with you—that what you're sayin'?

CARLYLE: Never saw the day.

ROGER: And still couldn't get his ass outa the neighborhood?

[RICHIE *begins trying to open his bottle of beer.*]

CARLYLE: Ain't that a bitch. Poor ole bastard just duck his head—Mom pointin' at him—he git this real goddamn hangdog look like he don't know who we talkin' about and he walk a little faster. Why the hell he never move away I don't know, unless he was crazy. But I don't think so. He come up to me once—I was playin'. "Boy," he says, "I ain't your daddy. I ain't. Your momma's crazy." "Don't you be callin' my momma crazy, Daddy," I tole him. Poor ole thing didn't know what to do.

RICHIE: [*Giving up; he can't get the beer open.*] Somebody open this for me? I can't get this open.

[BILLY *seems about to move to help, but* CARLYLE *is quicker, rising a little on the bunk and reaching.*]

CARLYLE: Ole Carlyle get it.

[RICHIE *slides along the floor until he can place the bottle in* CARLYLE'S *outstretched hand.*]

RICHIE: Then there was this once—there was this TV documentary about these bums in San Francisco, this TV guy interviewing all these bums, and just for maybe ten seconds while he was talkin' . . .

[*Smiling,* CARLYLE *hands* RICHIE *the opened bottle.*]

. . . to this one bum, there was this other one in the background jumpin' around like he thought he was dancin' and wavin' his hat, and even though there wasn't anything about him like my father and I didn't really ever see his face at all, I just kept thinkin': That's him. My dad. He thinks he's dancin'.

[*They lie there in silence and suddenly, softly,* BILLY *giggles, and then he giggles a little more and louder.*]

BILLY: Jesus!

RICHIE: What?

BILLY: That's ridiculous, Richie; sayin' that, thinkin' that. If it didn't look like him, it wasn't him, but you gotta be makin' up a story.

CARLYLE: [*Shifting now for a more comfortable position, he moves his head to the pillow at the top of the bed.*] Richie first saw me, he didn't like me much nohow, but he thought it over now, he changed his way a thinkin'. I can see that clear. We gonna be one big happy family.

RICHIE: Carlyle likes me, Billy; he thinks I'm pretty.

CARLYLE: [*Sitting up a little to make his point clear*] No, I don't think you pretty. A broad is pretty. Punks ain't pretty. Punk—if he good-lookin'—is cute. You cute.

RICHIE: He's gonna steal me right away, little Billy. You're so slow, Bill. I prefer a man who's decisive.

[*He is lying down now on the floor at the foot of his bed.*]

BILLY: You just keep at it, you're gonna have us all believin' you are just what you say you are.

RICHIE: Which is more than we can say for you.

[*Now* ROGER *rises on his elbow to light a cigarette.*]

BILLY: Jive, jive.

RICHIE: You're arrogant, Billy. So arrogant.

BILLY: What are you—on the rag?

RICHIE: Wouldn't it just bang your little balls if I were!

ROGER: [*to* RICHIE]. Hey, man. What's with you?

RICHIE: Stupidity offends me; lies and ignorance offend me.

BILLY: You know where we was? The three of us? All three of us, earlier on? To the wrong side of the tracks, Richard. One good black upside-down whorehouse where you get what you buy, no jive along with it—so if it's a lay you want and need, you go! Or don't they have faggot whorehouses?

ROGER: IF YOU GUYS DON'T CUT THIS SHIT OUT I'M GONNA BUST SOMEBODY'S HEAD!

[*Angrily he flops back on his bed. There is a silence as they all lie there.*]

RICHIE: "Where we *was*," he says. Listen to him. "Where we *was*." And he's got more school, Carlyle, than you have fingers and . . .

[*He has lifted his foot onto the bed; it touches, presses,* CARLYLE'S *foot.*]

. . . It's this pseudo-earthy quality he feigns—but inside he's all cashmere.

BILLY: That's a lie.

[*Giggling, he is staring at the floor.*]

I'm polyester, worsted and mohair.

RICHIE: You have a lot of school, Billy; don't say you don't.

BILLY: You said "fingers and toes"; you didn't say "a lot."

CARLYLE: I think people get dumber the more they put their butts into some schoolhouse door.

BILLY: It depends on what the hell you're talkin' about.

[*Now he looks at* CARLYLE, *and sees the feet touching.*]

CARLYLE: I seen cats on the block, they knew what was shakin'—then they got into all this school jive and, man, every year they went, they come back they didn't know nothin'.

[BILLY *is staring at* RICHIE'S *foot pressed and rubbing* CARLYLE'S *foot.*

RICHIE *sees* BILLY *looking.* BILLY *cannot believe what he is seeing. It fills him with fear. The silence goes on and on.*]

RICHIE: Billy, why don't you and Roger go for a walk?

BILLY: What?

[*He bolts to his knees. He is frozen on his knees on the bed.*]

RICHIE: Roger asked you to go downtown, you went, you had fun.

ROGER: [*Having turned, he knows almost instantly what is going on.*] I asked you, too.

RICHIE: You asked me; you *begged* Billy. I said no. Billy said no. You took my ten dollars. You begged Billy. I'm asking you a favor now—go for a walk. Let Carlyle and me have some time.

[*Silence*]

CARLYLE: [*He sits up, uneasy and wary.*] That how you work it?

ROGER: Work what?

CARLYLE: Whosever turn it be.

BILLY: No, no, that ain't the way we work it, because we don't work it.

CARLYLE: See? See? There it is—that goddamn education showin' through. All them years in school. Man, didn't we have a good time tonight? You rode in my car. I showed you a good cathouse, all that sweet black pussy. Ain't we friends? Richie likes me. How come you don't like me?

BILLY: 'Cause if you really are doin' what I think you're doin', you're a fuckin' animal!

[CARLYLE *leaps to his feet, hand snaking to his pocket to draw a weapon.*]

ROGER: Billy, no.

BILLY: NO, WHAT?!

ROGER: Relax, man; no need.

[*He turns to* CARLYLE; *patiently, wearily, he speaks.*]

Man, I tole you it ain't goin' on here. We both tole you it ain't goin' on here.

CARLYLE: Don't you jive me, nigger. You goin' for a walk like I'm askin', or not? I wanna get this clear.

ROGER: Man, we live here.

RICHIE: It's my house, too, Roger; I live here, too.

[RICHIE *bounds to his feet, flinging the blanket that has been covering him so it flies and lands on the floor near* ROGER'S *footlocker.*]

ROGER: Don't I know that? Did I say somethin' to make you think I didn't know that?

[*Standing,* RICHIE *is removing his trousers and throwing them down on his footlocker.*]

RICHIE: Carlyle is my guest.

[*Sitting down on the side of his bed and facing out, he puts his arms around* CARLYLE'S *thigh.* ROGER *jumps to his feet and grabs the blanket from the foot of his bed. Shaking it open, he drops onto the bed, his head at the foot of the bed and facing off as he covers himself.*]

ROGER: Fine. He your friend. This your home. So that mean he can stay. It don't mean I gotta leave. I'll catch you all in the mornin'.

BILLY: Roger, what the hell are you doin'?

ROGER: What you better do, Billy. It's gettin' late. I'm goin' to sleep.

BILLY: What?

ROGER: Go to fucking bed, Billy. Get up in the rack, turn your back and look at the wall.

BILLY: You gotta be kiddin'.

ROGER: DO IT!

BILLY: Man . . . !

ROGER: Yeah . . . !

BILLY: You mean just . . .

ROGER: It been goin' on a long damn time, man. You ain't gonna put no stop to it.

CARLYLE: You . . . ain't . . . serious.

RICHIE: [*Both he and* CARLYLE *are staring at* ROGER *and then* BILLY, *who is staring at* ROGER.] Well, I don't believe it. Of all the childish . . . infantile
. . .

CARLYLE: Hey!

[*silence*]

HEY! Even I got to say this is a little weird, but if this the way you do it . . .

[*And he turns toward* RICHIE *below him.*]

. . . it the way I do it. I don't know.

RICHIE: With them right here? Are you kidding? My God, Carlyle, that'd be obscene.

[*Pulling slightly away from* CARLYLE]

CARLYLE: Ohhh, man . . . they backs turned.

RICHIE: No.

CARLYLE: What I'm gonna do?

[*Silence. He looks at them, all three of them.*]

Don't you got no feelin' for how a man feel? I don't understand you two boys. Unless'n you a pair of motherfuckers. That what you are, you a pair of motherfuckers? You slits, man. DON'T YOU HEAR ME!? I DON'T UNDERSTAND THIS SITUATION HERE. I THOUGHT WE MADE A DEAL!

[RICHIE *rises, starts to pull on his trousers.* CARLYLE *grabs him.*]

YOU GET ON YOUR KNEES, YOU PUNK, I MEAN NOW, AND YOU GONNA BE ON MY JOINT FAST OR YOU GONNA BE ONE BUSTED PUNK, AM I UNDERSTOOD?

[*He hurls* RICHIE *down to the floor.*]

BILLY: I ain't gonna have this going on here; Roger, I can't.

ROGER: I been turnin' my back on one thing or another all my life.

RICHIE: Jealous, Billy?

BILLY: [*getting to his feet*] Just go out that door, the two of you. Go. Go on out in the bushes or out in some field. See if I follow you. See if I care. I'll be right here and I'll be sleepin', but it ain't gonna be done in my house. I don't have much in this goddamn army, but *here* is mine.

[*He stands beside his bed.*]

CARLYLE: I WANT MY FUCKIN' NUT! HOW COME YOU SO UPTIGHT? HE WANTS ME! THIS BOY HERE WANTS ME! WHO YOU TO STOP IT?

ROGER: [*spinning to face* CARLYLE *and* RICHIE] That's right, Billy. Richie one a those people want to get fucked by niggers, man. It what he know was gonna happen all his life—can be his dream come true. Ain't that right, Richie!

[*Jumping to his feet,* RICHIE *starts putting on his trousers.*]

Want to make it real in the world, how a nigger is an animal. Give 'em an inch, gonna take a mile. Ain't you some kinda fool, Richie? Hear me, Carlyle.

CARLYLE: Man, don't make me no nevermind what he think he's provin' an' shit, long as I get my nut. I KNOW I ain't no animal, don't have to prove it.

RICHIE: [*Pulling at* CARLYLE'S *arm, wanting to move him toward the door.*] Let's go. Let's go outside. The hell with it.

[*But* CARLYLE *tears himself free; he squats furiously down on the bunk, his hands seizing it, his back to all of them.*]

CARLYLE: Bull shit. Bullshit! I ain't goin' no-fuckin'-where—this jive ass ain't runnin' me. Is this you house or not?

[*He doesn't know what is going on; he can hardly look at any of them.*]

ROGER: [*Bounding out of bed, hurling his pillow across the room*] I'm goin' to the fuckin' john, Billy. Hang it up, man; let 'em be.

BILLY: No.

ROGER: I'm smarter than you—do like I'm sayin'.

BILLY: It ain't right.

ROGER: Who gives a big rat's ass!

CARLYLE: Right on, bro! That boy know; he do.

[*He circles the bed toward them.*]

Hear him. Look into his eyes.

BILLY: This fuckin' army takin' everything else away from me, they ain't takin' more than they got. I see what I see—I don't run, don't hide.

ROGER: [*Turning away from* BILLY, *he stomps out the door, slamming it.*] You fuckin' well better learn.

CARLYLE: That right. Time for more schoolin'. Less number one.

[*Stealthily he steps and snaps out the only light, the lamp clamped to* RICHIE'S *bed.*]

You don't see what you see so well in the dark. It dark in the night. Black man got a black body—he disappear.

[*The darkness is so total they are all no more than shadows.*]

RICHIE: Not to the hands; not to the fingers.

[*Moving from across the room toward* CARLYLE]

CARLYLE: You do like you talk, boy, you gonna make me happy.

[*As* BILLY, *nervously clutching his sneaker, is moving backward.*]

BILLY: Who says the lights go out? Nobody goddamn asked me if the lights go out.

[BILLY, *lunging to the wall switch, throws it. The overhead lights flash on, flooding the room with light.* CARLYLE *is seated on the edge of* RICHIE'S *bed,* RICHIE *kneeling before him.*]

CARLYLE: I DO, MOTHERFUCKER, I SAY!

[*and the switchblade seems to leap from his pocket to his hand.*]

I SAY! CAN'T YOU LET PEOPLE BE?

[BILLY *hurls his sneaker at the floor at* CARLYLE'S *feet. Instantly* CARLYLE *is across the room, blocking* BILLY'S *escape out the door.*]

Goddamn you, boy! I'm gonna cut your ass, just to show you how it feel—and cuttin' can happen. This knife true.

RICHIE: Carlyle, now c'mon.

CARLYLE: Shut up, pussy.

RICHIE: Don't hurt him, for chrissake.

CARLYLE: Goddamn man throw a shoe at me, he don't walk around clean in the world thinkin' he can throw another. He get some shit come back at him.

> [BILLY *doesn't know which way to go, and then* CARLYLE, *jabbing the knife at the air before* BILLY'S *chest, has* BILLY *running backward, his eyes fixed on the moving blade. He stumbles, having run into* RICHIE'S *bed. He sprawls backward and* CARLYLE *is over him.*]

No, no; no, no. Put you hand out there. Put it out.

> [*Slight pause;* BILLY *is terrified.*]

DO THE THING I'M TELLIN'!

> [BILLY *lets his hand rise in the air and* CARLYLE *grabs it, holds it.*]

That's it. That's good. See? See?

> [*The knife flashes across* BILLY'S *palm; the blood flows.* BILLY *winces, recoils, but* CARLYLE'S *hand still clenches and holds.*]

BILLY: Motherfucker.

> [*Again the knife darts, cutting, and* BILLY *yelps.* RICHIE, *on his knees beside them, turns away.*]

RICHIE: Oh, my God, what are you—

CARLYLE: [*In his own sudden distress,* CARLYLE *flings the hand away.*] That you blood. The blood inside you, you don't ever see it there. Take a look how easy it come out—and enough of it come out, you in the middle of the worst goddamn trouble you ever gonna see. And know I'm the man can deal that kinda trouble, easy as I smile. And I smile . . . easy. Yeah.

> [BILLY *is curled in upon himself, holding the hand to his stomach as* RICHIE *now reaches tentatively and shyly out as if to console* BILLY, *who repulses the gesture.* CARLYLE *is angry and strangely depressed. Forlornly he slumps onto* BILLY'S *footlocker as* BILLY *staggers up to his wall locker and takes out a towel.*]

Bastard ruin my mood, Richie. He ruin my mood. Fightin' and lovin' real different in the feelin's I got. I see blood come outa somebody like that, it don't make me feel good—hurt me—hurt on somebody. I thought was my friend. But I ain't supposed to see. One dumb nigger. No mind, he thinks, no heart, no feelings a gentleness. You see how that ain't true, Richie. Goddamn man threw a shoe at me. A lotta people woulda cut his heart out. I gotta make him know he throw shit, he get shit. But I don't hurt him bad, you see what I mean?

> [BILLY'S *back is to them, as he stands hunched at his locker, and suddenly his voice, hissing, erupts.*]

BILLY: Jesus . . . H . . . Christ . . . ! Do you know what I'm doin'? Do you know what I'm standin' here doin'?

> [*He whirls now; he holds a straight razor in his hand. A bloody towel is wrapped around the hurt hand.* CARLYLE *tenses, rises, seeing the razor.*]

I'm a twenty-four-year-old goddamn college graduate—intellectual goddamn scholar type—and I got a razor in my hand. I'm thinkin' about comin' up behind one black human being and I'm thinkin' nigger this and nigger that—I wanna cut his throat. THAT IS RIDICULOUS. I NEVER FACED ANYBODY IN MY LIFE WITH ANYTHING TO KILL THEM. YOU UNDERSTAND ME? I DON'T HAVE A GODDAMN THING ON THE LINE HERE!

[*The door opens and* ROGER *rushes in, having heard the yelling.* BILLY *flings the razor into his locker.*]

Look at me, Roger, look at me. I got a cut palm—I don't know what happened. Jesus Christ, I got sweat all over me when I think a what I was near to doin'. I swear it. I mean, do I think I need a reputation as a killer, a bad man with a knife?

[*He is wild with the energy of feeling free and with the anger at what these others almost made him do.* CARLYLE *slumps down on the footlocker; he sits there.*]

Bullshit! I need shit! I got sweat all over me. I got the mile record in my hometown. I did four forty-two in high school and that's the goddamn record in Windsor County. I don't need approval from either one of the pair of you.

[*And he rushes at* RICHIE.]

You wanna be a goddamn swish—a goddamn faggot-queer—GO! Suckin' cocks and takin' it in the ass, the thing of which you dream—GO! AND YOU—

[*Whirling on* CARLYLE]

You wanna be a bad-assed animal, man get it on—go—but I wash my hands. I am not human as you are. I put you down, I put you down—

[*He almost hurls himself at* RICHIE.]

—you gay little piece a shit cake—SHIT CAKE. AND YOU—

[*Hurt, confused,* RICHIE *turns away, nearly pressing his face into the bed beside which he kneels, as* BILLY *has spun back to tower over the pulsing, weary* CARLYLE.]

—you are your own goddamn fault, SAMBO! SAMBO!

[*And the knife flashes up in* CARLYLE'S *hand into* BILLY'S *stomach, and* BILLY *yelps.*]

Ahhhhhhhhh.

[*And pushes at the hand.* RICHIE *is till turned away.*]

RICHIE: Well, fuck you, Billy.

BILLY: [*He backs off the knife.*] Get away, get away.

RICHIE: [*As* ROGER, *who could not see because* BILLY'S *back is to him, is approaching* CARLYLE *and* BILLY *goes walking up toward the lockers as if he knows where he is going, as if he is going to go out the door and to a movie, his hands holding his belly*] You're so-o messed up.

ROGER: [*To* CARLYLE] Man, what's the matter with you?

CARLYLE: Don't nobody talk that weird shit to me, you understand?

ROGER: You jive, man. That's all you do—jive!

[BILLY, *striding swiftly, walks flat into the wall lockers; he bounces, turns, They are all looking at him.*]

RICHIE: Billy! Oh, Billy!

[ROGER *looks at* RICHIE.]

BILLY: Ahhhhhhh. Ahhhhhhh.

> [ROGER *looks at* CARLYLE *as if he is about to scream, and beyond him,* BILLY *turns from the lockers, starts to walk again, now staggering and moving toward them.*]

RICHIE: I think . . . he stabbed him. I think Carlyle stabbed Billy. Roger!

> [ROGER *whirls to go to* BILLY, *who is staggering downstage and angled away, hands clenched over his belly.*]

BILLY: Shut up! It's just a cut, it's just a cut. He cut my hand, he cut gut.

> [*He collapses onto his knees just beyond* ROGER'S *footlocker.*]

It took the wind out of me, scared me, that's all.

> [*Fiercely he tries to hide the wound and remain calm.*]

ROGER: Man, are you all right?

> [*He moves to* BILLY, *who turns to hide the wound. Till now no one is sure what happened.* RICHIE *only "thinks"* BILLY *has been stabbed.* BILLY *is pretending he isn't hurt. As* BILLY *turns from* ROGER, *he turns toward* RICHIE *and* RICHIE *sees the blood.* RICHIE *yelps and they all begin talking and yelling simultaneously.*]

CARLYLE: You know what I was learnin', he was learnin' to talk all that weird shit, cuttin', baby, cuttin', the ways and means a shit, man, razors.

ROGER: You all right? Or what? He slit you?

BILLY: Just took the wind outa me, scared me.

RICHIE: Carlyle, you stabbed him, you stabbed him.

CARLYLE: Ohhhh, pussy, pussy, pussy, Carlyle know what he do.

ROGER: [*Trying to lift* BILLY] Get up, okay? Get up on the bed.

BILLY: [*Irritated, pulling free*] I am on the bed.

ROGER: What?

RICHIE: No, Billy, no, you're not.

BILLY: Shut up!

RICHIE: You're on the floor.

BILLY: I'm on the bed. I'm on the bed.

> [*Emphatically. And then he looks at the floor.*]

What?

ROGER: Let me see what he did.

> [BILLY'S *hands are clenched on the wound.*]

Billy, let me see where he got you.

BILLY: [*Recoiling*] NO-O-O-O-O-O, you nigger!

ROGER: [*He leaps at* CARLYLE.] What did you do?

CARLYLE: [*Hunching his shoulders, ducking his head*] Shut up.

ROGER: What did you do, nigger—you slit him or stick him?

> [*And then he tries to get back to* BILLY.]

Billy, let me see.

BILLY: [*Doubling over till his head hits the floor*] NO-O-O-O-O-O! Shit, shit, shit.

RICHIE: [*Suddenly sobbing and yelling*] Oh, my God, my God, ohhhh, ohhhh, ohhhh.

> [*Bouncing on his knees on the bed*]

CARLYLE: FUCK IT, FUCK IT, I STUCK HIM. I TURNED IT. This mother army break my heart. I can't be out there where it pretty, don't wanna live! Wash me clean, shit face!

RICHIE: Ohhhh, ohhhhh, ohhhhhhhh. Carlyle stabbed Billy, oh, ohhhh, I never saw such a thing in my life. Ohhhhhh.

[As ROGER *is trying gently, fearfully to straighten* BILLY *up*]
Don't die, Billy; don't die.

ROGER: Shut up and go find somebody to help. Richie, go!

RICHIE: Who? I'll go, I'll go.

[*Scrambling off the bed*]

ROGER: I don't know. JESUS CHRIST! DO IT!

RICHIE: Okay. Okay. Billy, don't die. Don't die.

[*Backing for the door, he turns and runs.*]

ROGER: The sarge, or C.Q.

BILLY: [*Suddenly doubling over, vomiting blood.* RICHIE *is gone.*] Ohhhhhhhh. Blood. Blood.

ROGER: Be still, be still.

BILLY: [*Pulling at a blanket on the floor beside him*] I want to stand up. I'm————vomiting————
[*Making no move to stand, only to cover himself*]
————blood. What does that mean?

ROGER: [*Slowly standing*] I don't know.

BILLY: Yes, yes, I want to stand up. Give me blanket, blanket.

[*He rolls back and forth, fighting to get the blanket over him.*]

ROGER: RIICCHHHIIIEEEE!

[*As* BILLY *is furiously grappling with the blanket*]
No, no.
[*He looks at* CARLYLE, *who is slumped over, muttering to himself.* ROGER *runs for the door.*]
Wait on, be tight, be cool.

BILLY: Cover me. Cover me.

[*At last he gets the blanket over his face. The dark makes him grow still. He lies there beneath his blanket. Silence. No one moves. And then* CARLYLE *senses the quiet; he turns, looks. Slowly, wearily, he rises and walks to where* BILLY *lies. He stands over him, the knife hanging loosely from his left hand as he reaches with his right to gently take the blanket and lift it slowly fromm* BILLY'S *face. They look at each other.* BILLY *reaches up and pats* CARLYLE'S *hand holding the blanket.*]
I don't want to talk to you right now, Carlyle. All right? Where's Roger? Do you know where he is?
[*Slight pause*]
Don't stab me anymore, Carlyle, okay? I was dead wrong doin' what I did. I know that now. Carlyle, promise me you won't stab me anymore. I couldn't take it. Okay? I'm cold . . . my blood . . . is . . .
[*From off comes a voice.*]

ROONEY: Cokesy? Cokesy wokesy?

[*And* ROONEY *staggers into the doorway, very drunk, a beer bottle in his hand.*]

Ollie-ollie oxen-freeee.

[*He looks at them.* CARLYLE *quickly, secretly, slips the knife into his pocket.*]

How you all doin'? Everbody drunk, huh? I los' my friend.

[*He is staggering sideways toward* BILLY'S *bunk, where he finally drops down, sitting.*]

Who are you, soldier?

[CARLYLE *has straightened, his head ducked down as he is edging for the door.*]

Who are you, soldier?

[*And* RICHIE, *running, comes roaring into the room. He looks at* ROONEY *and cannot understand what is going on.* CARLYLE *is standing.* ROONEY *is just sitting there. What is going on?* RICHIE *moves along the lockers, trying to get behind* ROONEY, *his eyes never off* CARLYLE.]

RICHIE: Ohhhhhh, Sergeant Rooney, I've been looking for you everywhere— where have you been? Carlyle stabbed Billy, he stabbed him.

ROONEY: [*Sitting there*] What?

RICHIE: Carlyle stabbed Billy.

ROONEY: Who's Carlyle?

RICHIE: He's Carlyle.

[*As* CARLYLE *seems about to advance, the knife again showing in his hand*]

Carlyle, don't hurt anybody more!

ROONEY: [*On his feet, he is staggering toward the door.*] You got a knife there? What's with the knife? What's goin' on here?

[CARLYLE *steps as if to bolt for the door, but* ROONEY *is in the way, having inserted himself between* CARLYLE *and* RICHIE, *who has backed into the doorway.*]

Wait! Now wait!

RICHIE: [*As* CARLYLE *raises the knife*] Carlyle, don't!

[RICHIE *runs from the room.*]

ROONEY: You watch your step, you understand. You see what I got here?

[*He lifts the beer bottle, waves it threateningly.*]

You watch your step, motherfucker. Relax. I mean, we can straighten all this out. We—

[CARLYLE *lunges at* ROONEY, *who tenses.*]

I'm just askin' what' goin' on, that all I'm doin'. No need to get all—

[*And* CARLYLE *swipes at the air again;* ROONEY *recoils.*]

Motherfucker. Motherfucker.

[*He seems to be tensing, his body gathering itself for some mighty effort. And he throws his head back and gives the eagle yell.*]

Eeeeeeeeeeaaaaaaaaahhhhh! Eeeeeaaaaaaaaahhhhhhhhhhh!

[CARLYLE *jumps; he looks left and right.*]

Goddamit, I'll cut you good.

[*He lunges to break the bottle on the edge of the wall lockers. The bottle shatters and he yelps, dropping everything.*]

Ohhhhhh! Ohhhhhhhhh!

[CARLYLE *bolts, running from the room.*]

I hurt myself, I cut myself. I hurt my hand.

[*Holding the wounded hand, he scurries to* BILLY'S *bed, where he sis on the edge, trying to wipe the blood away so he can see the wound.*]

I cut—

[*Hearing a noise, he whirls, looks;* CARLYLE *is plummeting in the door and toward him.* ROONEY *stands.*]

I hurt my hand, goddammit!

[*The knife goes into* ROONEY'S *belly. He flails at* CARLYLE.]

I HURT MY HAND! WHAT ARE YOU DOING? WHAT ARE YOU DOING? WAIT! WAIT!

[*He turns away, falling to his knees, and the knife goes into him again and again.*]

No fair. No fair!

[ROGER, *running, skids into the room, headed for* BILLY, *and then he sees* CARLYLE *on* ROONEY, *the leaping knife.* ROGER *lunges, grabbing* CARLYLE, *pulling him to get him off* ROONEY. CARLYLE *leaps free of* ROGER, *sending* ROGER *flying backward. And then* CARLYLE *begins to circle* ROGER'S *bed. He is whimpering, wiping at the blood on his shirt as if to wipe it away.* ROGER *backs away as* CARLYLE *keeps waving the knife at him.* ROONEY *is crawling along the floor under* BILLY'S *bed and then he stops crawling, lies there.*]

CARLYLE: You don't tell nobody on me you saw me do this, I let you go, okay? Ohhhhhhh.

[*Rubbing, rubbing at the shirt*]

Ohhhhh, how'm I gonna get back to the world now, I got all this mess to—

ROGER: What happened? That you—I don't understand that you did this! That you did—

CARLYLE: YOU SHUT UP! Don't be talkin' all that weird shit to me—don't you go talkin' all that weird shit!

ROGER: Nooooooooooo!

CARLYLE: I'm Carlyle, man. You know me. You know me.

[*He turns, he flees out the door.* ROGER, *alone, looks about the room.* BILLY *is there.* ROGER *moves toward* BILLY, *who is shifting, undulating on his back.*]

BILLY: Carlyle, no; oh, Christ, don't stab me anymore. I'll die. I will—I'll die. Don't make me die. I'll get my dog after you. I'LL GET MY DOG AFTER YOU!

[ROGER *is saying, "Oh, Billy, man, Billy." He is trying to hold* BILLY. *Now he lifts* BILLY *into his arms.*]

ROGER: Oh, Billy; oh, man. GODDAMMIT, BILLY!

[*As a* MILITARY POLICE LIEUTENANT *comes running in the door, his .45 automatic drawn, and he levels it at* ROGER]

LIEUTENANT: Freeze, soldier! Not a quick move out of you. Just real slow, straighten your ass up.

[ROGER *has gone rigid; the* LIEUTENANT *is advancing on him. Tentatively* ROGER *turns, looks.*]

ROGER: Huh? No.

LIEUTENANT: Get your ass against the lockers.

ROGER: Sir, no. I—

LIEUTENANT: [*Hurling* ROGER *away toward the wall lockers*] MOVE!

 [*As another M.P., Pfc* HINSON, *comes in, followed by* RICHIE, *flushed and breathless*]

 Hinson, cover this bastard.

HINSON: [*Drawing his .45 automatic, moving on* ROGER] Yes, sir.

 [*The* LIEUTENANT *frisks* ROGER, *who is spread-eagled at the lockers.*]

RICHIE: What? Oh, sir, no, no. Roger, What's going on?

LIEUTENANT: I'll straighten this shit out.

ROGER: Tell 'em to get the gun off me, Richie.

LIEUTENANT: SHUT UP!

RICHIE: But sir, sir, he didn't do it. Not him.

LIEUTENANT: [*Fiercely he shoves* RICHIE *out of the way.*] I told you, all of you, to shut up.

 [*He moves to* ROONEY'S *body.*]

 Jesus, God, This Sfc is cut to shit. He's cut to shit.

 [*He hurries to* BILLY'S *body.*]

 This man is cut to shit.

 [*As* CARLYLE *appears in the doorway, his hands cuffed behind him, a third M.P., Pfc* CLARK, *shoving him forward.* CARLYLE *seems shocked and cunning, his mind whirring.*]

CLARK: Sir, I got this guy on the street, runnin' like a streak a shit.

 [*He hurls the struggling* CARLYLE *forward and* CARLYLE *stumbles toward the head of* RICHIE'S *bed as* RICHIE, *seeing him coming, hurries away along* BILLY'S *bed and toward the wall lockers.*]

RICHIE: He did it! Him, him!

CARLYLE: What is going on here? I don't know what is going on here!

CLARK: [*Club at the ready, he stations himself beside* CARLYLE.] He's got blood all over him, sir. All over him.

LIEUTENANT: What about the knife?

CLARK: No, sir. He must have thrown it away.

 [*As a fourth M.P. has entered to stand in the doorway, and* HINSON, *leaving* ROGER, *bends to examine* ROONEY. *He will also kneel and look for life in* BILLY.]

LIEUTENANT: You throw it away, soldier?

CARLYLE: Oh, you thinkin' about how my sister got happened, too. Oh, you ain't so smart as you think you are! No way!

ROGER: Jesus God almighty.

LIEUTENANT: What happened here? I want to know what happened here.

HINSON: [*Rising from* BILLY'S *body*] They're both dead, sir. Both of them.

LIEUTENANT: [*Confidential, almost whispering*] I know they're both dead. That's what I'm talkin' about.

CARLYLE: Chicken blood, sir. Chicken blood and chicken hearts is what all over me. I was goin' on my way, these people jump out the bushes be pourin' it all over me. Chicken blood and chicken hearts.

 [*Thrusting his hands out at* CLARK]

You goin' take these cuffs off me, boy?

LIEUTENANT: Sit him down, Clark. Sit him down and shut him up.

CARLYLE: This my house, sir. This my goddamn house.

[CLARK *grabs him, begins to move him.*]

LIEUTENANT: I said to shut him up.

CLARK: Move it; move!

[*Struggling to get* CARLYLE *over to* ROGER'S *footlocker as* HINSON *and the other M.P. exit*]

CARLYLE: I want these cuffs taken off my hands.

CLARK: You better do like you been told. You better sit and shut up!

CARLYLE: I'm gonna be thinkin' over here. I'm gonna be thinkin' it all over. I got plannin' to do. I'm gonna be thinkin' in my quietness; don't you be makin' no mistake.

[*He slumps over, muttering to himself.* HINSON *and the other M.P. return, carrying a stretcher. They cross to* BILLY, *chattering with each other about how to go about the lift. They will lift him; they will carry him out.*]

LIEUTENANT: [*To* RICHIE] You're Wilson?

RICHIE: No, sir.

[*Indicating* BILLY]

That's Wilson, I'm Douglas.

LIEUTENANT: [*To* ROGER] And you're Moore. And you sleep here.

ROGER: Yes, sir.

RICHIE: Yes, sir. And Billy slept here and Sergeant Rooney was our platoon sergeant and Carlyle was a transient, sir. He was a transient from P Company.

LIEUTENANT: [*Scrutinizing* ROGER] And you had nothing to do with this?

[*To* RICHIE]

He had nothing to do with this?

ROGER: No, sir, I didn't.

RICHIE: No, sir, he didn't. I didn't either. Carlyle went crazy and he got into a fight and it was awful. I didn't even know what it was about exactly.

LIEUTENANT: How'd the Sfc get involved?

RICHIE: Well, he came in, sir.

ROGER: I had to run off to call you, sir. I wasn't here.

RICHIE: Sergeant Rooney just came in—I don't know why—he heard all the yelling, I guess—and Carlyle went after him. Billy was already stabbed.

CARLYLE: [*Rising, his manner that of a man who is taking charge*] All right now, you gotta be gettin' the fuck outa here. All of you. I have decided enough of the shit has been goin' on around here and I am tellin' you to be gettin' these motherfuckin' cuffs off me and you gettin' me a bus ticket home. I am quittin' this jive-time army.

LIEUTENANT: You are doin' what?

CARLYLE: No, I ain't gonna be quiet. No way. I am quittin' this goddamn—

LIEUTENANT: You shut the hell up, soldier. I am ordering you.

CARLYLE: I don't understand you people! Don't you people understand when a man be talkin' English at you to say his mind? I have quit the army!

[*as* HINSON *returns*]

LIEUTENANT: Get him outa here!

RICHIE: What's the matter with him?

LIEUTENANT: Hinson! Clark!

[*They move, grabbing* CARLYLE, *and they drag him, struggling, toward the door.*]

CARLYLE: Oh, no. Oh, no. You ain't gonna be doin' me no more. I been tellin'you. To get away from me. I am stayin' here. This my place, not your place. You take these cuffs off me like I been tellin' you! My poor little sister Lin Sue understood what was goin' on here! She tole me! She knew!

[*He is howling in the hallway now.*]

You better be gettin' these cuffs off me!

[*Silence.* ROGER, RICHIE *and the* LIEUTENANT *are all staring at the door. The* LIEUTENANT *turns, crosses to the foot of* ROGER'S *bed.*]

LIEUTENANT: All right now. I will be getting to the bottom of this. You know I will be getting to the bottom of this.

[*He is taking two forms from his clipboard.*]

RICHIE: Yes, sir.

[HINSON *and the fourth M.P. return with another stretcher. They walk to* ROONEY, *talking to one another about how to lift him. They drag him from under the bed. They will roll him onto the stretcher, lift him and walk out.* ROGER *moves, watching them, down along the edge of* BILLY'S *bed.*]

LIEUTENANT: Fill out these forms. I want your serial number, rank, your MOS, the NCOIC of your work. Any leave coming up will be canceled. Tomorrow at 0800 you will report to my office at the provost marshal's headquarters. You know where that is?

ROGER: [*As the two M.P.'s are leaving with the stretcher and* ROONEY'S *body*] Yes, sir.

RICHIE: Yes, sir.

LIEUTENANT: [*Crossing to* ROGER, *he hands him two cards.*] Be prepared to do some talking. Two perfectly trained and primed strong pieces of U.S. Army property got cut to shit up here. We are going to find out how and why. Is that clear?

RICHIE: Yes, sir.

ROGER: Yes, sir.

[*The* LIEUTENANT *looks at each of them. He surveys the room. He marches out.*]

RICHIE: Oh, my God. Oh. Oh.

[*He runs to his bed and collapses, sitting hunched down at the foot. He holds himself and rocks as if very cold.* ROGER, *quietly, is weeping. He stands and then walks to his bed. He puts down the two cards. He moves purposefully up to the mops hanging on the wall in the corner. He takes one down. He moves with the mop and the bucket to* BILLY'S *bed, where* ROONEY'S *blood stains the floor. He mops.* RICHIE, *in horror, is watching.*]

RICHIE: What . . . are you doing?

ROGER: This area a mess, man.

[*Dragging the bucket, carrying the mop, he moves to the spot where* BILLY *had lain. He begins to mop.*]

RICHIE: That's Billy's blood, Roger. His blood.

ROGER: Is it?

RICHIE: I feel awful.

ROGER: [*He keeps mopping.*] How come you made me waste all that time talkin'
shit to you, Richie? All my time talkin' shit, and all the time you was a
faggot, man; you really was. You shoulda jus' tole ole Roger. He don't care.
All you gotta do is tell me.

RICHIE: I've been telling you. I did.

ROGER: Jive, man, jive!

RICHIE: No!

ROGER: You did bullshit all over us! ALL OVER US!

RICHIE: I just wanted to hold his hand, Billy's hand, to talk to him, go to the
movies hand in hand like he would with a girl or I would with someone
back home.

ROGER: But he didn't wanna; *he* didn't wanna.

> [*Finished now,* ROGER *drags the mop and bucket back toward the
> corner.* RICHIE *is sobbing; he is at the edge of hysteria.*]

RICHIE: He did.

ROGER: No, man.

RICHIE: He did. He did. It's not my fault.

> [ROGER *slams the bucket into the corner and rams the mop into the
> bucket. Furious, he marches down to* RICHIE. *Behind him* SERGEANT
> COKES, *grinning and lifting a wine bottle, appears in the doorway.*]

COKES: Hey!

> [RICHIE, *in despair, rolls onto his belly.* COKES *is very, very happy.*]

Hey! What a day, gen'l'men. How you all doin'?

ROGER: [*Crossing up near the head of his own bed*] Hello, Sergeant Cokes.

COKES: [*Affectionate and casual, he moves near to* ROGER.] How you all doin'?
Where's ole Rooney? I lost him.

ROGER: What?

COKES: We had a hell of a day, ole Rooney and me, lemme tell you. We been
playin' hide-and-go-seek, and I was hidin', and now I think maybe he
started hidin' without tellin' me he was gonna and I can't find him and I
thought maybe he was hidin' up here.

RICHIE: Sergeant, he—

ROGER: No. No, we ain't see him.

COKES: I gotta find him. He knows how to react in a tough situation. He didn't
come up here looking for me?

> [ROGER *moves around to the far side of his bed, turning his back to*
> COKES. *Sitting,* ROGER *takes out a cigarette, but he does not light it.*]

ROGER: We was goin' to sleep, Sarge. Got to get up early. You know the way this
mother army is.

COKES: [*Nodding, drifting backward, he sits down on* BILLY'S *bed.*] You don't
mind I sit here a little. Wait on him. Got a little wine. You can have some.

> [*Tilting his head way back, he takes a big drink and then, looking
> straight ahead, corks the bottle with a whack of his hand.*]

We got back into the area—we had been downtown—he wanted to play
hide-and-go-seek. I tole him okay, I was ready for that. He hid his eyes. So I
run and hid in the bushes and then under this Jeep. 'Cause I thought it was

better. I hid and I hid and I hid. He never did come. So finally, I got tired—I figured I'd give up, come lookin' for him. I was way over by the movie theater. I don't know how I got there. Anyway, I got back here and I figured maybe he come up here lookin' for me, figurin' I was hidin' up with you guys. You ain't seen him, huh?

ROGER: No, we ain't seen him. I tole you that, Sarge.

COKES: Oh.

RICHIE: Roger!

ROGER: He's drunk, Richie! He's blasted drunk. Got a brain turned to mush!

COKES: [*in deep agreement*] That ain't no lie.

ROGER: Let it be for the night, Richie. Let him be for the night.

COKES: I still know what's goin' on, though. Never no worry about that. I always know what's goin' on. I always know. Don't matter what I drink or how much I drink. I always still know what's goin' on. But . . . I'll be goin' maybe and look for Rooney.

[*But rising, he wanders down center.*]

But . . . I mean, we could be doin' that forever. Him and me. Me under the Jeep. He wants to find me, he goes to the Jeep. I'm over here. He comes here. I'm gone. You know, maybe I'll just wait a little while more I'm here. He'll find me then if he comes here. You guys want another drink.

[*Turning, he goes to* BILLY'S *footlocker, where he sits and takes another enormous guzzle of wine.*]

Jesus, what a goddamn day we had. Me and Rooney started drivin' and we was comin' to this intersection and out comes this goddamn Chevy. I try to get around her, but no dice. BINGO! I hit her in the left rear. She was furious. I didn't care. I gave her my name and number. My car had a headlight out, the fender bashed in. Rooney wouldn't stop laughin'. I didn't know what to do. So we went to D.C. to this private club I know. Had ten or more snorts and decided to get back here after playin' some snooker. That was fun. On the way, we picked up this kid from the engineering unit, hitchhiking. I'm starting to feel real clear-headed now. So I'm comin' around this corner and all of a sudden there's this car stopped dead in front of me. He's not blinkin' to turn or anything. I slam on the brakes, but it's like puddin' the way I slide into him. There's a big noise and we yell. Rooney starts laughin' like crazy and the kid jumps outa the back and says he's gonna take a fuckin' bus. The guy from the other car is swearin' at me. My car's still workin' fine, so I move it off to the side and tell him to do the same, while we wait for the cops. He says he wants his car right where it is and he had the right of way 'cause he was makin' a legal turn. So we're waitin' for the cops. Some cars go by. The guy's car is this big fuckin' Buick. Around the corner comes this little red Triumph. The driver's this blond kid got this blond girl next to him. You can see what's gonna happen. There's this fuckin' car sittin' there, nobody in it. So the Triumph goes crashin' into the back of the Buick with nobody in it. BIFF-BANG-BOOM. And everything stops. We're staring. It's all still. And then that fuckin' Buick kinda shudders and starts to move. With nobody in it. It starts to roll from the impact. And it rolls just far enough to get where the road starts a downgrade. It's driftin' to the right. It's driftin' to the shoulder and over it and onto this hill, where it's pickin' up speed 'cause the hill is steep and then it disappears over the side, and into the dark, just rollin' real quiet. Rooney fall over, he's laughin', so hard. I don't know what to do. In a minute the cops come and in another minute some guy comes runnin' up over the hill to tell us some other guy had got run over by this car with nobody in it. We didn't know what to think. This was fuckin' unbelievable to us. But we found out later from the cops that this wasn't true and some guy had got hit over the head with a bottle in a bar and when he staggered out the door it was just at the instant that this fuckin' Buick with nobody in it went by. Seein' this, the guy stops cold and turns around and just goes back into the bar. Rooney is screamin' at me how we been in four goddamn accidents and fights and how we have got out clean. So then we got everything all straightened out and we come back here to play hide-and-seek 'cause that's what ole Rooney wanted.

[*He is taking another drink, but finding the bottle empty.*]

Only now I can't find him.

[*Near* RICHIE'S *footlocker stands a beer bottle and* COKES *begins to move toward it. Slowly he bends and grasps the bottle; he straightens, looking at it. He drinks. And settles down on* RICHIE'S *footlocker.*]

I'll just sit a little.

[RICHIE, *lying on his belly, shudders. The sobs burst out of him. He is shaking.* COKES, *blinking, turns to study* RICHIE.]

What's up? Hey, what're you cryin' about, soldier? Hey?

[RICHIE *cannot help himself.*]

What's he cryin' about?

ROGER: [*Disgustedly, he sits there*] He's cryin' 'cause he's a queer.

COKES: Oh. You a queer, boy?

RICHIE: Yes, Sergeant.

COKES: Oh.

   [*Pause*]

How long you been a queer?

ROGER: All his fuckin' life.

RICHIE: I don't know.

COKES: [*Turning to scold* ROGER] Don't be yellin' mean at him. Boy, I tell you it's a real strange thing the way havin' leukemia gives you a lotta funny thoughts about things. Two months ago—or maybe even yesterday—I'da called a boy who was a queer a lotta awful names. But now I just wanna be figurin' things out. I mean, you ain't kiddin' me out about ole Rooney, are you, boys, 'cause of how I'm a sergeant and you're enlisted men, so you got some idea a vengeance on me? You ain't doin' that, are you, boys?

ROGER: No.

RICHIE: Ohhhh. Jesus. Ohhhh. I don't know what's hurtin' in me.

COKES: No, no, boy. You listen to me. You gonna be okay. There's a lotta worse things in this world than bein' a queer. I seen a lot of 'em, too. I mean, you could have leukemia. That's worse. That can kill you. I mean, it's okay. You listen to the ole sarge. I mean, maybe I was a queer, I wouldn't have leukemia. Who's to say? Lived a whole different life. Who's to say? I keep thinkin' there was maybe somethin' I coulda done different. Maybe not drunk so much. Or if I'd killed more gooks, or more Krauts or more dinks. I was kind-hearted sometimes. Or if I'd had a wife and I had some kids. Never had any. But my mother did and she died of it anyway. Gives you a whole funny different way a lookin' at things, I'll tell you. Ohhhhh, Rooney, Rooney.

[*Slight pause*]

Or if I'd let that little gook outa that spider hole he was in, I was sittin' on it. I'd let him out now, he was in there.

[*He rattles the footlocker lid under him.*]

Oh, how'm I ever gonna forget it? That funny little guy. I'm runnin' along, he pops up outa that hole. I'm never gonna forget him—how'm I ever gonna forget him? I see him and dive, goddamn bullet hits me in the side, I'm midair, everything's turnin' around. I go over the edge of this ditch and I'm crawlin' real fast. I lost my rifle. Can't find it. Then I come up behind him. He's half out of the hole. I bang him on top of his head, stuff him back into the hole with a grenade for company. Then I'm sittin' on the lid and it's made outa steel. I can feel him in there, though, bangin' and yellin' under me, and his yelling I can hear is begging for me to let him out. It was like a goddamn Charlie Chaplin movie, everybody fallin' down and clumsy, and him in there yellin' and bangin' away, and I'm just sittin' there lookin' around. And he was Charlie Chaplin. I don't know who I was. And then he blew up.

[*Pause*]

Maybe I'll just get a little shut-eye right sittin' here while I'm waitin' for ole Rooney. We figure it out. All of it. You don't mind I just doze a little here, you boys?

ROGER: No.

RICHIE: No.

[ROGER *rises and walks to the door. He switches off the light and gently closes the door. The transom glows.* COKES *sits in a flower of light.* ROGER *crosses back to his bunk and settles in, sitting.*]

COKES: Night, boys.

RICHIE: Night, Sergeant.

[COKES *sits there, fingers entwined, trying to sleep.*]

COKES: I mean, he was like Charlie Chaplin. And then he blew up.

ROGER: [*Suddenly feeling very sad for this old man*] Sergeant . . . maybe you was Charlie Chaplin, too.

COKES: No. No.

[*Pause*]

No. I don't know who I was. Night.

ROGER: You think he was singin' it?

COKES: What?

ROGER: You think he was singin' it?

COKES: Oh, yeah. Oh, yeah; he was singin' it.

[*Slight pause.* COKES, *sitting on the footlocker, begins to sing a makeshift language imitating Korean, to the tune of "Beautiful Streamer." He begins with an angry, mocking energy that slowly becomes a dream, a lullaby, a farewell, a lament.*]

yo no som lo no

Ung toe lo knee
Ra so me la lo
La see see oh doe.
Doe no tee ta ta
Too low see see
Ra mae me lo lo
Ah boo boo boo eee.
Boo boo eee booo eeee
La so lee lem
Lem lo lee da ung
Uhhh so ba booooo ohhhh.
Boo booo eee ung ba
Eee eee la looo
Lem lo lala la
Eeee oohhh ohhh ohhh ohhhhh.

> [*In the silence, he makes the soft, whispering sound of a child imitating
> an explosion, and his entwined fingers come apart. The dark figures of*
> RICHIE *and* ROGER *are near. The lingering light fades.*]